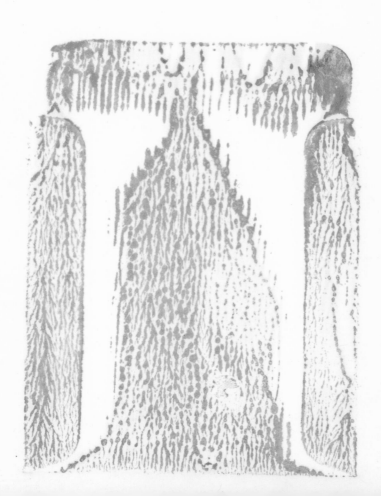

# A
# LITERARY
# HISTORY
# OF
# FRANCE

# A LITERARY HISTORY OF FRANCE

General Editor: P. E. CHARVET
*Fellow of Corpus Christi College, Cambridge*

Volume I
## THE MIDDLE AGES AND THE RENAISSANCE
*by* J. P. COLLAS
*Professor of French at Queen Mary College, University of London*

Volume II
## THE SEVENTEENTH CENTURY 1600–1715
*by* P. J. YARROW
*Professor of French at the University of Newcastle upon Tyne*

Volume III
## THE EIGHTEENTH CENTURY 1715–1789
*by* ROBERT NIKLAUS
*Professor of French at the University of Exeter*

Volume IV
## THE NINETEENTH CENTURY 1789–1870
*by* P. E. CHARVET

Volume V
## THE NINETEENTH AND TWENTIETH CENTURIES 1870–1940
*by* P. E. CHARVET

# A LITERARY HISTORY OF FRANCE

## Volume II
# THE SEVENTEENTH CENTURY
1600–1715

# A LITERARY
# HISTORY OF FRANCE

## VOLUME II
## The Seventeenth Century

1600–1715

### P. J. YARROW

*Professor of French at
the University of Newcastle upon Tyne*

LONDON · ERNEST BENN LIMITED

NEW YORK · BARNES & NOBLE INC

First published 1967 by Ernest Benn Limited
Bouverie House · Fleet Street · London · EC4
and Barnes & Noble Inc. · 105 Fifth Avenue · New York 10003

Distributed in Canada by
The General Publishing Company Limited · Toronto

Printed in Great Britain

# FOREWORD BY THE GENERAL EDITOR

IN HIS QUEST for the past, the historian proper deals with a variety of evidence, documentary and other, which is of value to him only for the light it sheds on events and on the men who played a part in them. The historian of literature has before him documents in manuscript or print that exist in their own right, books and ever more books, as the centuries unfold. Within the space allotted to him, his first task must be to give the maximum amount of relevant information about them, but, if he is to avoid producing a mere compilation of unrelated and therefore meaningless facts, he is bound to organize his matter into some sort of pattern.

Time itself does this for him to some extent by keeping alive the memory of those writers and books that retain their relevance, and, often enough, setting one school of writers against another, as successive generations seek to establish their own originality by revolt against their immediate predecessors.

At whatever point in time the historian of literature may stand, he is bound to adopt as a basis of his work the patterns time gives him, although he knows well enough that, just as the tide and the waves may alter the patterns they themselves are for ever imprinting on the sands of the sea shore, time, bringing with it changing tastes and values, will alter these patterns, at least in detail or emphasis.

Within these broad natural patterns come problems of arrangement. Here inevitably a degree of arbitrariness creeps in. Some writers are dubbed precursors, as though they themselves had consciously played the role of prophet in a wilderness, others are marked down as 'epigoni'—poor fellows! Had they but known!—others again are lumped together because they are seen to have in common the characteristics of an age, though

ix

they may have had no relations with each other; chronology must often be sacrificed to the need of tidiness. Thus does the historian of literature try to create from the vigorous and confused growth he is faced with, at least on the surface, an ordered garden, where the reader may wander and get an impression to store away in his memory, of neatness and controlled change, an impression helpful, indeed indispensable, as a preliminary to the study of the subject, but not to be confused with the reality.

Nor is this all. Should the historian of literature, need he, smother his personal responses? And if he should (which we doubt and indeed have not tried to do), is this really possible? Within the kindly Doctor Jekyll, recording in detached tones his literary history, seeking to give an objective picture of an age, explaining, elucidating, lurks Mr. Hyde, the critic, ready to leap out at the reader on the slightest provocation and wreak his mischief. As in all of us, the levels of his personality that may respond to stimuli are numerous: intellectual, emotional, moral, spiritual; more numerous still the sources of interest whence the stimuli may come: historical and social, psychological, linguistic and stylistic, aesthetic. Literature is a vast catchment area all these streams flow into; a book, a great book is like a burning glass that concentrates the rays of human experience into one bright point; it burns itself into our memories and may even sear the soul.

If he be wise, Mr. Hyde the critic will use as his criterium of judgment only the degree to which he feels his own experience has been enriched, his own perceptiveness extended. Thus will he avoid being too rigid or narrow in his attitudes and avoid the temptation of for ever seeking some underlying principle that controls the whole mechanism. Since the corpus of a writer's work is the expression of his experience, since the writer belongs to a given age, a given people, the works may easily become the pretext for an exercise in individual or national psychology. Conversely, the idea of race, the age, the accumulated legacy of history—its momentum, in a word—may be invoked as cause and explanation of the works. Or again, since the works have their place in one or more given art-forms, they may be seen as no more than moments in the evolution of these.

Such ideas and unifying theories have their value no doubt; the people, the society, the age, the art-forms all bear on the question, but who is to assess their impact? They leave the mystery of individual genius and of artistic creation intact; to emphasize them at the expense of the latter is really using the history of literature for other ends. Admittedly books do not spring from nothing, but whether we consider them historically or critically, in the last resort they stand, as we observed at the outset of this foreword, in their own right, and their value depends upon their impact on the individual; every book has three aspects: what the author meant to express, what the book contains, and the image the reader carries away with him; this latter changes with every reader of the book and depends as much upon himself as upon the book and the author.

From its early beginnings in the ninth century down to the present day, French literature can claim a continued existence of 1100 years. What country, beside our own, can boast such literary wealth, such resource, such powers of renewal? The authors of this history, the first of its kind in English, have been only too well aware of the difficulties attendant upon so vast an enterprise. Their hope is that it may give to all readers of French literature a coherent background against which particular periods or writers may be studied and enjoyed in greater depth.

P.E.C.

# PREFACE

THE PRESENT VOLUME deals mainly with those seventeenth-century writers who may be deemed to have survived—i.e. whose works are accessible in nineteenth- or twentieth-century editions. Even so, I am uncomfortably aware both of the gaps in the following pages and of their inadequacy.

The spelling of the quotations has been modernized; the punctuation is that of the edition used. The date given for plays is normally that of the first performance.

The pages on *Timocrate* in Chapter 6 are reproduced, with modifications, from *Orpheus*, 1956, by kind permission of the editor, Professor E. Rapisarda.

I am grateful to those who have been kind enough to read the whole or part of this volume in draft—particularly Professor J. Lough, of the University of Durham; the General Editor, Mr. P. E. Charvet; my colleague, Mrs. E. T. Dubois, of the University of Newcastle upon Tyne; Dr. J. D. Biard, of the University of Exeter; and my wife. They have all saved me from some slips and blunders. I am also grateful to my daughter for the note on p. 387, and to my colleague, Miss N. E. Ratcliff, and my wife for reading the galley- and the page-proofs respectively.

P.J.Y.

# CONTENTS

xv

# General Survey

## Chapter 1

# GENERAL SURVEY

THE SEVENTEENTH CENTURY, already so modern and yet in some ways still medieval, is a period of contrasts, and derives much of its richness and vitality from its dual nature. Three pairs of contradictory tendencies help to explain the period.

The first is the conflict between royal authority and feudalism, between centralization and anarchy, between the forces of order and the forces of disorder, which helps to account for the vigorous, independent, individual, passionate nature of the people of the age. If the seventeenth century is *le grand siècle* it is largely because it felt itself to be great, because it more or less consciously aimed at greatness.

Je ne le quitte [i.e. le monde], [wrote the dying Richelieu to Mazarin,] qu'avec regret de n'avoir pas achevé les grandes choses que j'avais entreprises pour la gloire de mon roi et de ma patrie [ ... ] je vous remets mon ouvrage entre les mains, sous l'aveu de notre bon maître, pour le conduire à sa perfection.

'Oubliez les choses basses et vous portez à choses grandes, dignes de votre naissance,' Bérulle admonished Louis XIII. Louis XIV, in his turn, noted:

Les projets ordinaires et communs sont faits pour les âmes communes; mais ceux qui prétendent s'élever au-dessus de leurs pareils doivent concevoir de grandes et illustres pensées, qui puissent effectivement mériter cette immortalité que l'on se promet quelquefois trop légèrement.

His minister, Colbert, told Clerville: 'Nous ne sommes pas en un règne de petites choses, et il est impossible d'imaginer rien de trop grand.' For Colbert, indeed, 'aucun homme n'a de mérite, de satisfaction et de gloire, qu'autant qu'il entreprend des choses difficiles, et qu'il en vient à bout.' King, nobles, ministers, soldiers, poets and men of letters were eager for glory. 'Il faut aussi,' wrote abbé Tallemant, 'que tous vos sujets, dans leurs emplois différents, surpassent les autres hommes, et qu'ainsi notre siècle devienne en quelque sorte digne du prince qui en est tout l'ornement.'[1]

[1] This quotation and the preceding ones are taken from J.-E. Fidao-Justiniani, *Qu'est-ce qu'un classique? Essai d'histoire et de critique positive. Le Héros ou du Génie*, Paris, 1930.

3

The spirit of the age is admirably illustrated in the project of the French Academy, drawn up by Faret in 1634, and submitted to Richelieu. Faret stated boldly

que notre langue plus parfaite déjà que pas une des autres vivantes, pourrait bien enfin succéder à la Latine, comme la Latine à la Grecque, si on prenait plus de soin qu'on n'avait fait jusqu'ici de l'élocution[2] . . .

Some thirty-five years later, Faret's prophecy has come to pass: Bouhours is confident that the French language has now reached perfection and that France has achieved pre-eminence:

Les changements qui se sont faits depuis trente ans ont servi de dernières dispositions à cette perfection où la langue française devait parvenir sous le règne du plus grand monarque de la terre.

Le siècle présent est pour la France ce que le siècle passé était pour l'Italie. On dirait que tout l'esprit et toute la science du monde soit maintenant parmi nous et que tous les autres peuples soient barbares en comparaison des Français.

Although the establishment of more settled conditions led to the development of social life, to a growing refinement and more polished manners, much coarseness and crudity remained. When, in the Louvre, one admires Lebrun's magnificent painting of the chancellor, Séguier, proudly seated on his horse, clad in splendid robes of cloth of gold, and surrounded by attendants, two of whom are holding parasols over his head, Tallemant's description of him should be borne in mind: 'Le Chancelier est l'homme du monde qui mange le plus mal proprement et qui a les mains les plus sales.' On the one hand, splendour and magnificence, formal politeness and a very elaborate etiquette, gallantry and a taste for romantic love, which creeps even into such unlikely places as Corneille's *Œdipe* and Racine's *Thébaïde*. On the other, Gaston d'Orléans declared roundly, 'Je ne suis guères propre à la galanterie qui règne encore, de faire le malade, d'être pâle et de s'évanouir,' and Bussy-Rabutin observed:

Depuis ce temps-là, je n'ai point douté que la hardiesse en amour n'avançât fort les affaires; je sais bien qu'il faut aimer avec respect pour être aimé; mais assurément pour être récompensé, il faut entreprendre, et l'on voit plus d'effrontés réussir sans amour, que de respectueux avec la plus grande passion du monde.

These two trends are reflected in the long romances and in the burlesque and realist trend. Just as in *L'Astrée*, the fickle Hylas is contrasted with Céladon, the ideal lover, so, in seventeenth-century literature as a whole, Régnier, Sorel, Scarron, and Furetière have a place beside Malherbe, d'Urfé, Racine, and Bossuet.

*    •    •

[2] I.e. style.

The second conflict is between reason and faith. The seventeenth century was an age, not only of religious reform and of good works, but of saintliness, asceticism, and mysticism. Gentlemen like M. de Renty and M. de Bernières divided their time between pious exercises and active charity; devoted their fortunes to the Church and the poor; wore hairshirts and spiked belts or crosses with nails which dug into their flesh; ate sparingly and slept uncomfortably; and tried to subordinate their will completely to that of God, with whom they felt themselves able to commune directly through prayer. Their piety did not exclude violence, and their asceticism took exaggerated forms – the seventeenth-century touch. One day, when a coach and six drove past the holy sacrament without stopping or without the passengers' doffing their hats, M. de Renty sprang to the horses' heads, stopped the vehicle, and compelled those within to bow respectfully. Mme de Boisdavid, visiting a girl dying of a repulsive disease, gave her her own shift, and herself donned the girl's pus-saturated garment. M. de Laval, later Bishop of Quebec, when visiting hospitals, would take between his lips, and suck, bandages soaked with pus.

The missionaries who went to evangelize Canada were eager for martyrdom, notwithstanding the cruel tortures inflicted by the Indians on their victims. In 1659, M. de Laval, in danger of being captured by the Iroquois, wrote: 'Je ne puis vous exprimer la paix et la consolation de mon cœur, de me voir dans un lieu où je suis en l'attente du moment précieux de sacrifier ma vie à Notre-Seigneur.' The same spirit animated Port-Royal in times of persecution. When an attempt was made to reconcile the Jansenists with their enemies, Arnauld's niece, Sœur Angélique de Saint-Jean, wrote to him:

Port-Royal des Champs n'est qu'un avec nous; hasardez-nous. Peut-être que nous serons les valets de pied des princes de l'armée d'Achab, qui devaient entrer les premiers dans le combat et gagner la bataille. A tout hasard on n'expose pas grand'chose, et quand nous y péririons, l'Eglise n'y perdra point ceux qui pourront davantage la défendre. Quel autre intérêt avons-nous en ce monde que d'acquérir le royaume des Cieux?

If faith was strong, the human mind was at the same time rapidly becoming emancipated. The waning influence of religion and the growth of rationalism manifest themselves in three ways in the seventeenth century: in the tendency to look for moral guidance, not to the Church, but to the ancient philosophers, either to the stoics or to the epicureans; in the growing scepticism about traditional beliefs, about miracles and the supernatural, even religion itself; and in the interest in science, which led to a new conception of the universe. To the first two of these manifestations we shall return later. Here, it may not be out of place to recall that the seventeenth century was a great scientific age, and that the people of seventeenth-century France took a considerable interest and played a considerable part in the scientific revolution which was taking place.

Broadly speaking, in the course of the period, the Aristotelian conception of the world and of the universe was replaced by the modern one. Two things should be remembered about Aristotelian science. It left plenty of room for divine intervention:

A universe constructed on the mechanics of Aristotle had the door half-way open for spirits already; it was a universe in which unseen hands had to be in constant operation, and sublime Intelligences had to roll the planetary spheres around. Alternatively, bodies had to be endowed with souls and aspirations, with a 'disposition' to certain kinds of motion, so that matter itself seemed to possess mystical qualities.[3]

Moreover, since St. Thomas Aquinas, the Aristotelian doctrine had become part of Christian theology, so that an attack on it was regarded as an attack on the Church itself. In the course of the seventeenth century, Aristotle was routed; science was freed from metaphysics and from mysticism; interest passed from substance and qualities to matter and motion; modern scientific method was established – Galileo is often regarded as the first great scientist in the modern sense; a mechanistic universe was substituted for one requiring constant intervention by the spirit world; and the modern cosmology came into being.[4]

The most spectacular developments came in physics and in astronomy, came indeed as the result of a man of genius's perception that the same laws were at work in both. As early as 1543, Copernicus had suggested that the earth revolved round the sun, but his theory was not generally accepted, and long remained indeed a hypothesis rather than a proven fact. Progress was made by Kepler, who discovered the laws of planetary motion, and Galileo, who, through his newly-invented telescope, discovered the satellites of Jupiter and sunspots. The first of these discoveries showed that, if the earth with its moon revolved round the sun, as Copernicus had suggested, it would by no means be unique; the second destroyed the Aristotelian view that the heavenly bodies were immaculate and unchanging, since not only had the sun spots, but these showed the sun to be rotating. But satisfactory answers had not yet been given to the main objections to the Copernican theory: what kept the heavenly bodies moving in their courses, and why, if the earth was moving, did it not keep leaving loose objects behind it? Descartes's theory of vortices was an attempt to explain

---

[3] H. Butterfield, *The Origins of Modern Science*, 1949, p. 7.
[4] Boileau ridicules the Aristotelian philosophy in his *Arrêt burlesque* (1671).

the movement of the heavenly bodies; but it was Newton who, in his *Principia* (1687), finally solved the problem. Galileo had shown that the speed of a falling object was proportional to the time of fall and that a moving body did not require a force to keep it moving but would continue to move unless something stopped it. Newton discovered the law of gravity, suggested that the courses of the heavenly bodies were the result of this force acting on bodies already in motion, and demonstrated mathematically that this theory alone satisfactorily explained the observed facts.

Great progress was made in other fields at the same time. Harvey's discovery of the circulation of the blood was published in 1628 in his *Exercitatio Anatomica de Motu Cordis et Sanguinis*. Torricelli, with his famous vacuum, demonstrated at once the existence of atmospheric pressure and the fact that nature does not abhor a vacuum. Descartes invented co-ordinate geometry, Pascal the mathematical theory of probability, and Newton and Leibnitz the infinitesimal calculus; Gassendi revived the atomic theory. The practical application of the new discoveries was not overlooked, and instruments and machines were invented to facilitate man's labours. The telescope and the microscope were invented early in the century; the thermometer, the pendulum clock, the barometer (1643), and the air-pump followed. Pascal invented a calculating machine, and another Frenchman, Denys Papin, devised a pressure-cooker and constructed the first paddle-steamer. In the theatre, more and more elaborate effects were produced by machines.

The scientific movement did not leave France untouched. Two of the great writers of the seventeenth century, Descartes and Pascal, were men of science. Scientists corresponded with each other and met in unofficial gatherings, such as the academy of the brothers Dupuy in Paris. The government encouraged the movement: a botanical garden, the Jardin du Roi, was established, and the Académie des Sciences founded in 1666. The interest in scientific matters began to spread among the general public. For ten years, from 1632, regular lectures were given at Renaudot's establishment;[5] from 1665 until 1667, Jean de Soudier, sieur de Richesource, held a series of 'conférences académiques et oratoires'; in 1666, M. de Fontenay began a course of lectures on physics and chemistry. Other courses in science and philosophy (not yet two separate things) were given by Louis de Lesclache, M. de Launay, Jacques Rohault, Régis, the chemist Lémery, and Du Verney. At Régis's lectures, according to Fontenelle, the concourse of

---

[5] Théophraste Renaudot, a doctor with a resourceful turn of mind, set up a pawn-shop and a *bureau d'adresses* (a labour exchange and information bureau), and founded the *Gazette*.

people was such that a private house could not conveniently contain them, and that people had to arrive early to secure seats.

Amongst the society of the day, there was considerable interest in science. Men of letters, such as Chapelain, d'Aubignac, and Cotin, and noblemen, such as Condé, Conti, and the duc de Bourbon, were interested in science. The chemist, Lémery, was admitted to the salon of the prince de Condé. Scientists began to write in French, and the *Journal des Savants* (founded 1665) was published in French. Even women were interested in the new scientific theories. At Rohault's lectures, the front row was reserved for ladies; the anatomist Du Verney, Lémery, and Régis also attracted a feminine public. Jean de la Forge in his *Cercle des Femmes savantes* (1663) enumerates no fewer than sixty-seven *femmes savantes*, and some of the *précieuses* mentioned in Somaize's *Dictionnaire des Précieuses* are described as being interested in mathematics, science, and philosophy. Of Mme de Chataignères, for example, he writes: 'Sa bibliothèque n'est composée que de livres de chimie qu'elle a perpétuellement dans les mains.' The most conspicuous of the hostesses devoted to science and philosophy was Mme de la Sablière. Books were written for the purpose of bringing the new philosophy within reach of women – such as René Bary's *Fine Philosophie accommodée à l'intelligence des dames* (1660) and Poulain de la Barre's *Education des Dames* (1674). It is no accident that Molière wrote a play about *Les Femmes savantes* at this period, or that Boileau included a *savante* in his tenth satire.

Science and *libertinage* (i.e. free thought or scepticism), of course, sometimes overlapped. *Libertins*, such as Gassendi, Naudé, and La Mothe le Vayer, were interested in science; and scientists were sometimes sceptics – Christian Huygens, for example, was doubtful about personal immortality. Experiment was proving more reliable than traditional beliefs; the supernatural was becoming more and more superfluous as an aid to the understanding of the universe; and the Church had very largely identified itself with Aristotle, whose views were becoming more and more untenable – Galileo was condemned in 1616 and 1633 for maintaining that the earth went round the sun. Père Rapin in his *Comparaison de Platon et d'Aristote* (1678) attacked the new science precisely for its anti-Aristotelian, anti-religious tendency:

Ce sont toutefois ces nouveaux philosophes et ces demi-savants, qui paraissent les plus déchaînés contre la philosophie ancienne, qu'ils entreprennent de décrier, pour en établir une moderne, préjudiciable aux bonnes mœurs, et dangereuse à la Religion. Ce qui doit obliger ceux qui ont du zèle à s'affectionner à l'ancienne philosophie, que saint Thomas[6] a tant louée, dont il s'est servi si utilement pour expliquer nos

[6] Aquinas.

mystères: et qui ne s'est trouvée fausse, que par le faux usage qu'on en
a fait.

This passage reminds us that, closely related to the conflict
between reason and science, on the one hand, and faith, on the
other, is a further one – between humanism and modernism,
between respect and disrespect for the ancients. Boys were brought
up on Latin and Greek; Aristotle's *Poetics* was regarded as
authoritative; writers treated classical subjects and adapted classical models. But this is only one side of the picture. There was at
the same time a strong movement of revolt againt the tyranny of
the ancients, which, indeed, had begun in the previous century.
Descartes, in the *Discours de la Méthode*, recognized that it is
good to know something of past ages, but added, 'lorsqu'on est
trop curieux des choses qui se pratiquaient aux siècles passés, on
demeure fort ignorant de celles qui se pratiquent en celui-ci'. He
begins the *Traité des Passions* by pouring scorn on what the
ancients had said on that subject. Pascal rejected the authority of
the ancients in science, which he regarded as progressing indefi-
nitely:

Ceux que nous appelons anciens étaient véritablement nouveaux en
toutes choses, et formaient l'enfance des hommes proprement; et comme
nous avons joint à leurs connaissances l'expérience des siècles qui les
ont suivis, c'est en nous que l'on peut trouver cette antiquité que nous
révérons dans les autres.                 (*Fragment d'un Traité du Vide*)

The feeling that the ancients had not said the last word was not
confined to scientists and philosophers. Malherbe, says Racan,
'n'estimait point du tout les Grecs'. Théophile wrote, scathingly:

> La sotte antiquité nous a laissé des fables
> Qu'un homme de bon sens ne croit pas recevables . . .

and insisted:

Il faut écrire à la moderne; Démosthène et Virgile n'ont point écrit en
notre temps, et nous ne saurions écrire en leur siècle; leurs livres, quand
ils les firent, étaient nouveaux, et nous en faisons tous les jours de vieux.

Ogier, in his preface to Schelandre's *Tyr et Sidon* (1628), similarly
argued that, taste having changed since Greek times, the ancients
cannot be imitated blindly:

nous les imiterons bien mieux si nous donnons quelque chose au génie de
notre pays et au goût de notre langue, que non pas en nous obligeant de
suivre pas à pas et leur intention et leur élocution . . .

D'Urfé, in the preface to *Sylvanire* (1627), had said much the same.
Saint-Amant, in 1629, insisted that the study of the classics was

not essential to a writer. The same independence is found in a
greater than these – Corneille.

Je me donne ici quelque sorte de liberté de choquer les anciens [...]
Puisque les sciences et les arts ne sont jamais à leur période, il m'est
permis de croire qu'ils n'ont pas tout su, et que de leurs instructions on
peut tirer des lumières qu'ils n'ont pas eues. Je leur porte du respect
comme à des gens qui nous ont frayé le chemin, et qui après avoir
défriché un pays fort rude, nous ont laissé à le cultiver.

(Preface to *Clitandre*)

In the preface to *La Veuve*, he remarks irreverently, 'on épouse
malaisément des beautés si vieilles'.

The last pair of conflicting trends, baroque and classicism, will
be dealt with in Chapters 2 and 6.

The presence of all these tendencies in the life and literature of
the time gave the seventeenth-century writer considerable latitude,
and seventeenth-century literature great diversity. Perhaps the
principal achievement of the greatest writers of the age was to
strike a balance between opposing forces – to combine dignity
with realism, respect for antiquity with independence ('Mon
imitation n'est point un esclavage', as La Fontaine wrote), religious
faith with independence of thought, above all strong individuality
and strong passions with self-discipline. Curbed exuberance,
disciplined vigour: there lies the secret of the greatness of the
*grand siècle*.

Le dix-septième siècle était—à le considérer dans sa volonté affirmée,
et même, en gros, dans sa conduite—généreux ensemble et réglé,
héroïque et prudent. Et c'est là le miracle, qu'on n'a jamais revu depuis.[7]

[7] J.-E. Fidao-Justiniani, *Discours sur la raison classique*, 1937, p. 113.

# Part I

1600–1630

*Chapter 2*

# INTRODUCTION

THE ALTERNATION of order and disorder, the weakness of the central government and the strength of the forces opposed to it, are evident in this period. During the civil wars of the second half of the sixteenth century, a weak monarchy had attempted to assert itself in the face of two hostile parties — the Catholic League, which aimed not merely at suppressing Protestantism, but at increasing the powers of the nobles, and turning France into a loose federation of provinces with a puppet king; and the Huguenots, who aimed at establishing an independent state of their own. Henry IV, who succeeded to the throne in 1589, was able, by his military skill, his conversion to Catholicism, his tolerance and his leniency to his enemies, to extend his authority over the whole of France. The Edict of Nantes (1598) established the principle of religious toleration, but contained the seeds of future trouble, since it allowed the Huguenots to retain about a hundred fortresses in the South-West of France, and to hold an assembly every three years.

From 1598 until 1610, when he was assassinated by Ravaillac, Henry IV, seconded by his great minister, the Huguenot, Sully, strove to restore prosperity and order to France. Brigandage was suppressed; the budget was balanced, and taxation reduced; agriculture and trade were encouraged, and new industries established. Communications were improved: new roads were built; the canal de Briare was dug between the Seine and the Loire; and a system of public coaches was set up. Sully installed a large pump by the Seine, La Samaritaine, to improve the water supply of Paris, and the capital was embellished by the construction of the Pont-Neuf, the Place Dauphine, parts of the Tuileries, and the Place Royale (now the Place des Vosges).

Peace and prosperity were short-lived, however. On Henry IV's death, he was succeeded by his son, Louis XIII, a boy of nine. The effective ruler of the kingdom, consequently, was Henry's widow, Maria de' Medici, who dismissed Sully, ruled with the aid of an Italian favourite, Concini, the maréchal d'Ancre, and squandered her resources. The nobles took advantage of her weakness and revolted under Condé in 1614; a second revolt, the following year, was joined by the Huguenots. In 1616, Louis XIII, now of age,[1] had Concini arrested (the officer sent to arrest him killed him) and replaced him by his own equally incompetent favourite, Albert de Luynes. Maria de' Medici joined forces with the nobles against her son, and renewed risings took place in 1619 and 1620.

The Huguenots were a further cause of anxiety. Disquieted by Maria de' Medici's alliance with Spain, they had, at the Assembly of Saumur, in 1611, given themselves an almost republican constitution; they had risen in revolt in 1615; and they had never observed the Edict of Nantes to the extent of tolerating Catholicism in Béarn, or restored Church property seized during the civil wars. In 1620, Louis XIII gathered an army and attacked them. Three years later, the Treaty of Montpellier stripped the Huguenots of all their fortresses except two, Montpellier itself and La Rochelle. In 1624, Louis XIII, after having tried to govern without a principal minister since Luynes's death in 1621, found himself compelled to call to power a former protégé of his mother's, Cardinal Armand-Jean du Plessis de Richelieu, Bishop of Luçon.

This was a period of intense religious activity, the period when the Counter-Reformation reached France – for, in 1615, an assembly of Bishops resolved to promulgate the decrees of the Council of Trent in France. Many religious orders entered France from Italy or Spain. In 1603, the Jesuits, who had been expelled, were allowed to return, and by 1610 had thirty-five colleges in France. In 1604, Mme Acarie founded a branch of the Carmelites of the Reform in Paris; in 1611, the Carmelite friars were introduced into France; houses of the Celestial Annunciades were founded at Nancy (1616) and in Paris (1621); the Discalced Augustinians (1620) and the Feuillantines (1622) were established in Paris. A much-needed movement of reform spread through the existing religious orders. It began in the Benedictine houses in Lorraine, which formed themselves into the Congrégation de Sainte-Vanne; the Benedictine monasteries of France followed their example, and banded together in the Congrégation de Saint-Maur (1621). The Order of Cluny, a branch of the Benedictine Order, was reformed in 1621. Of the many other monasteries and convents which were reformed, one, Port-Royal, deserves particular mention.

In 1599, the abbess of Port-Royal accepted Jacqueline Arnauld, then seven and a half years old, as her coadjutress and successor. For the time being, Jacqueline was placed in the convent of Maubuisson. At Port-Royal, there was an ignorant confessor who

---

[1] French kings attained their majority on entering their fourteenth year.

did not understand the *Pater*, did not know the Catechism, and
spent his time hunting; virtually no sermons had been preached
for thirty years; communion was taken but once a month and on
the great feast days; and the nuns, thirteen in number, wore gloves
and masks, and got up masquerades at carnival time. The state
of Maubuisson was even worse. Its abbess, Angélique d'Estrées,
was the sister of Henry IV's mistress, Gabrielle d'Estrées, and
is said to have had fourteen children, four of them with her in the
convent. The nuns used to go and dance with the monks of Saint-
Martin of Pontoise and did not know how to confess.[2] In 1602,
when the abbess of Port-Royal died, Jacqueline Arnauld, henceforth better known as Mère Angélique, took her place as abbess.
She at first felt no vocation for her new way of life, but was converted by a sermon delivered by a Capuchin monk in 1608. She
began to reform her convent and called in her sister, Jeanne,
Mère Agnès, to assist. The nuns took a vow of poverty and gave
up their private possessions to the convent. Contact with the outside world was replaced by such rigid seclusion that, in 1609,
Mère Angélique refused admittance to her own father — the famous
'journée du guichet'. So effective was the reform that Port-Royal
was invited to reform other convents: sometimes it was asked
to send nuns to help with advice, sometimes prioresses or abbesses
visited Port-Royal to study the reform that had been carried out
there.

Much was done, too, to improve the secular clergy. In 1611,
Bérulle founded the French Oratory for secular priests, members
of which were sent to help Bishops reform their dioceses. The
Oratory set up seminaries for priests and colleges for the education
of boys, and, by the end of the century, it owned seventy-five
houses, including some fifteen seminaries. In 1612, Adrien Bour-
doise founded the Communauté de Saint-Nicolas du Chardonnet,
a house where parish priests could live together, with the object
of increasing their fervour and aptitude. In 1625, Saint Vincent de
Paul founded the Congrégation de la Mission, for the purpose of
training priests to carry out missions in country districts. Can-
didates for the priesthood could go into retreat there, too, before
ordination, and regular lectures were held every Tuesday for the
priests of Paris. Eventually, the Congrégation de la Mission
founded seminaries.

The wretchedness of the poor was alleviated. In 1610, Saint
François de Sales, Bishop of Geneva, together with Mme de

---

[2] In 1617, the abbot of Cîteaux sent a representative to inquire into
Maubuisson. Mme d'Estrées locked the monk and his followers in a
tower, kept them without food for four days, and had him whipped every
morning. It took a regular siege to dislodge her. Subsequently, Mère Angélique was called in to reform the convent.

Chantal (Mme de Sévigné's grandmother), founded the Visitandines, an order for the relief of the poor and the sick. In 1617, Saint Vincent de Paul started a Confrérie de Dames de la Charité at Châtillon-les-Dombes, a lay society with the same object.

The Jesuits – and later the Oratory – looked after the education of boys, but girls had hitherto been neglected. In 1598, Alix le Clerc, with Saint Pierre Fourrier, founded the Congrégation de Notre-Dame at Mattaincourt for the education of girls; by 1640, it owned forty-seven houses. In 1608, Jeanne de Lestonnac, a niece of Montaigne, founded the Compagnie de Notre-Dame for the same purpose: when she died, in 1640, it had thirty houses. The Ursulines, established in Paris by Bérulle and Mme de Sainte-Beuve in 1612, and the Dominican nuns, established in Paris by Anne de Caumont in 1626, also kept schools for girls.

If this was a period of religious reform and active charity, it was also an age of marked rationalistic or even anti-religious tendencies. The stoical philosophy, borrowed from the ancients – the attempt to rise superior to the blows of fortune and the ills of life by the exercise of the reason – , was no doubt given a new impetus by the civil wars:

En un temps ordinaire et tranquille, on se prépare [wrote Montaigne] à des accidents modérés et communs; mais en cette confusion où nous sommes depuis trente ans, tout homme français, soit en particulier, soit en général, se voit à chaque heure sur le point de l'entier renversement de sa fortune. D'autant faut-il tenir son courage fourni de provisions plus fortes et vigoureuses.                              (*Essais*, III, 12)

Expressed in some of Montaigne's essays, but formulated particularly in the works of Guillaume du Vair (*De la constance ès calamités publiques*, 1590; *De la philosophie morale des stoïques*, 1603), stoicism was widely practised by the men and women of the seventeenth century.[3]

Another prevalent attitude was scepticism based on mistrust of reason. To combat the argument of the Reformers, that the basis of knowledge in religious matters is the Scriptures, Catholic theologians had retorted that, since there is no certainty about any point of doctrine and no agreement upon the interpretation of the scriptures, we can only fall back upon the traditions of the Church. The scepticism implicit in this attitude was reinforced – after the discovery and publication in 1562 and 1569 of the works of Sextus Empiricus – by Pyrrhonism or universal doubt. Since on any question a multiplicity of opinions exist, since human senses are untrustworthy and our reason fallible, there are no grounds for believing

[3] An affinity has been traced between stoicism, with its stress on reason and will and its mistrust of passion, and classicism, with its stress on technique and its mistrust of inspiration and imagination. Certainly, Malherbe was a stoic, and translated Seneca's *De Beneficiis* and Epistles.

that we can have any knowledge of anything at all, and therefore all we can do is to suspend belief. It was possible to use this attitude in the service of religion by concluding that, in the lack of certain knowledge, we must accept the truth of revealed religion – this is the system known as 'fideism', most forcefully expressed by Montaigne in his *Apologie de Raymond Sebond*.

The difficulty about fideism is that it is not always easy to tell whether a writer is genuinely religious or merely masking universal scepticism behind a simulacrum of religious faith. The difficulty is particularly acute in the case of the *De la Sagesse* (1601) of Pierre Charron (1541–1603), a work written by a dignitary of the Church and adopted by the free-thinkers or *libertins* as their Bible. Charron's book is a treatise on human wisdom, a comprehensive study of man and a guide to human conduct in which he ranges from statecraft to the upbringing of children. The *sage*, says Charron, lives according to nature and reason, which, it is true, he identifies, not only with each other, but with the moral law within each of us and with God. Knowledge is impossible: the senses are unreliable, and the human mind not only creates a multiplicity of contradictory opinions – 'ce qui est impie, injuste, abominable en un lieu, est piété, justice, et honneur ailleurs; et ne sçauroit nommer une loi, coutume, créance reçue ou rejetée généralement partout' – but we are constantly changing our minds. Most widely-held opinions are mistaken; credulity is a common fault:

Combien de bourdes, faux et supposés miracles, visions et révélations reçues au monde, qui ne furent jamais! (les vrais miracles autorisés par l'église, sont à part, l'on ne touche point à cela).

The *sage*, while observing the laws and customs of the country in which he lives, rejects popular opinions, and preserves his freedom of judgment. The best minds are the most sceptical:

Au troisième et plus haut étage sont les hommes doués d'un esprit vif et clair, jugement fort, ferme et solide, qui ne se contentent d'un ouï-dire, ne s'arrêtent aux opinions communes et reçues, ne se laissent gagner et préoccuper à la créance publique, de laquelle ils ne s'étonnent point, sachant qu'il y a plusieurs bourdes, faussetés et impostures reçues au monde avec approbation et révérence publique: mais examinent toutes choses qui se proposent, sondent mûrement, et cherchent sans passion les causes, motifs et ressorts, jusques à la racine, aimant mieux douter et tenir en suspens leur créance, que par une trop molle et lâche facilité, ou légèreté, ou précipitation de jugement, se paître de fausseté, et affirmer ou se tenir assurés de chose de laquelle ils ne peuvent avoir raison certaine.

Occasional passages of *De la Sagesse* might be construed as unfavourable to religion. Charron casts doubts on the value of the sacraments and affirms that penance is bad; he asserts that it is

more noble to live in the world than to be a hermit or a monk; and
he points out that all religions are alike, that they all offer
miracles and prophecies in evidence of their truth, that they all
think that God takes delight in the spectacle of suffering, inflicted on oneself or on others, that they are all 'étranges et
horribles au sens commun'. Virtue, he says, has little to do with
religion, since, on the one hand, it is possible to be virtuous without
it, and, on the other, few people believe sufficiently for their
religion to affect their lives – in any case, a man who is virtuous
only because he hopes to go to Heaven or dreads going to Hell is
not truly virtuous. Moreover, one's religion is a matter of chance –
'la nation, le pays, le lieu donne la religion'.

One can understand why the freethinker or *libertin* read
Charron. On the other hand, whether Charron himself was a
*libertin* or not, must remain in doubt. He continually excepts
Christianity from his scepticism and insists that it must be accepted
without question and that truth is known only to God; he had
previously written a book, *Les Trois Vérités* (1594), asserting the
necessity for religion, the superiority of the Christian religion over
all others, and the superiority, within Christianity, of Catholicism
over Protestantism; and he was not only a dignitary of the Church,
but enjoyed the confidence of his fellow-clergy. The very restricted
place of religion in the life of the *sage* and the remarks quoted
above may not be evidence of irreligion. But one can understand
why the Sorbonne disapproved of the work.

Be that as it may, there is little doubt that, in the seventeenth
century, there were those whose scepticism extended even to
religion itself – here again, no doubt, the religious wars had had
some effect. The poet, Malherbe, according to Tallemant des
Réaux,

n'était pas autrement persuadé de l'autre vie, et disait quand on lui
parlait de l'enfer ou du paradis: 'J'ai vécu comme les autres, je veux
mourir comme les autres, et aller où vont les autres.'

Cosmo Ruggieri, who died in Paris in 1615, is reported to have
said on his deathbed: 'Fols que vous êtes, allez, il n'y a point
d'autres diables que les ennemis qui nous tourmentent en ce monde,
ni d'autre Dieu que les rois et princes qui seuls nous peuvent avancer et faire du bien.' The anonymous author of a poem, the
*Quatrains du Déiste* (1623 or earlier), attacks the Christian conception of God as a capricious and tyrannical being, subject to
human passions, cruel and vindictive, and delighting in the infliction
of eternal punishments. He claims that religions were invented by
men to discipline the populace; rejects the doctrine of the Fall as incompatible with the omniscience and omnipotence of the Supreme

Being, and the doctrine of Hell as inconsistent with his goodness; and denounces self-inflicted torments as an encroachment on God's prerogative, and austerity as a rejection of his gifts. *Libertins* were sufficiently numerous about 1620 to be denounced by two priests – Père Garasse in his *Recherches des recherches et autres œuvres de M. Etienne Pasquier* (1622) and his *Doctrine curieuse des beaux esprits de ce temps* (1623), and Père Mersenne in his *Impiété des déistes, athées et libertins de ce temps* (1624). In the second of his books, Garasse summarizes the tenets of the *libertins* as contempt for the mass of mankind and its beliefs, denial of God and scepticism about the Scriptures, belief in fate, belief in nature and the satisfaction of the senses, and doubt whether spirit can exist apart from matter and hence whether the human soul can be immortal.

Such heterodox doctrines, of course, exposed their exponents to severe penalties. Vanini was burnt at Toulouse in 1619 for his book, *De admirandis Naturae reginae deaeque mortalium arcanis*. Two years later, Jean Fontanier was strangled and burnt at the stake for his *Trésor inestimable ou Mausérisme*. In 1624, the Parlement of Paris dispersed a meeting arranged by a group of alchemists, at which Antoine Villon was to have presided, Jean Bitault was to have defended anti-Aristotelian theses, and Etienne de Claves to have performed experiments; the Sorbonne condemned the theses, and Bitault and Villon were banished from Paris. The following year, the poet, Théophile, against whom Garasse's *Doctrine curieuse* was directed, was condemned to banishment.

Religion, stoicism, and scepticism were not mutually exclusive. From scepticism, as we have seen, the conclusion could be drawn that the only certainty lies in divine revelation. Charron's *sage* is not only sceptical about everything (except Christianity); he is also a stoic – esteeming himself only for his will-power, subduing his passions, cultivating detachment, and practising moderation and self-control. Many other Christians, both laymen and theologians, were influenced by stoicism.

The age of the Counter-Reformation was also the age of baroque art and literature, and there is clearly an affinity between the two movements, though the exact relationship between them is a matter for dispute.

The word baroque, first used in art history, conjures up majestic façades, twisted outlines, spiral columns, oval courtyards, and swirling draperies. We think of Bernini's statues – Daphne being transformed into a laurel tree, Louis XIV on a prancing horse, St. Theresa in ecstasy with spectators watching from balconies. We recall baroque paintings: strong contrasts of light and shade;

objects seen from unusual angles, foreshortened or viewed obliquely, with the distinction between foreground and background blurred; Caravaggio's Fall of St. Paul at Damascus, in which the most prominent object is the rump of the saint's horse; portraits of Mary Magdalen, repentant, with uplifted, tearful eyes; ceilings showing the heavens opening and angels descending or carrying mortals aloft; Rubens's series of scenes from the life of Maria de' Medici in the Louvre, representing her and her spouse in all the majesty of kingship; paintings of skulls and skeletons. We think of the restless movement of baroque fountains, of sumptuous churches like S. Maria della Vittoria in Rome,[4] all gold and marble and precious stones. Baroque art is a magnificent, ostentatious art; an art expressing movement and addicted to *trompe-l'œil*; the art of a world shaken by the Reformation and the division of Christendom, by the discovery of the New World and the new cosmology, but confident that the tide had turned, fundamentally unstable perhaps, but exuberant.

If baroque art has been known and appreciated for a comparatively long time, only in the last generation or so have scholars detected features akin to those of baroque art, sculpture, and architecture in the European literature of the late sixteenth and the seventeenth centuries – in Tasso and Marino in Italy, in Cervantes and Góngora in Spain, in Shakespeare and Ben Jonson in England, as well as in many French writers of the period. Consequently, the literature of the first half of the seventeenth century has come to be appreciated in its own right, instead of being dismissed as irregular, or considered as interesting only in so far as it prepared what came later. The fundamental characteristics of baroque literature, as of baroque art and architecture, are the sense of instability and the desire to assert.

Baroque literature, like baroque art, is a literature of movement. It is dynamic, full of energy and exuberance. It stresses the fluidity of things, the mutability of the world, the inconstancy of fortune. The vicissitudes through which the baroque hero passes leave him bewildered, make him wonder whether he is waking or dreaming. The world and man are seen as ever-changing and paradoxical. The themes of fickleness and inconstancy, false appearances and illusion occur and recur. Disguises, confusion of identity, doubles or characters playing two parts abound in drama; so do hypocrites, madmen (who see the world differently from others), magicians and enchanters (who create illusions), plays within plays, and plays showing the stage on the stage. Visions of a topsy-turvy world

---

[4] French examples are the Sorbonne church and the Val de Grâce. French baroque has been called a 'baroque dompté'; this is as true in art as in literature.

or a world gone mad are evoked; these lines from Garnier's
*Bradamante* (1582) are typical of a host of others:

> Plutôt l'eau de Dordone encontre-mont ira,
> Le terroir quercinois plutôt s'aplatira,
> Le jour deviendra nuit et la nuit ténébreuse
> Comme un jour de soleil deviendra lumineuse,
> Que Roger, ce Roger que j'abhorre sur tous,
> Soit tant que je vivrai de Bradamante époux.

Baroque literature appeals to the emotions; the reason is
mistrusted. It is fond of strong contrasts, and delights in showing the
contradictory nature of man. It aims at giving sensuous pleasure,
at embellishing and making pleasurable the things it depicts —
nature is described in terms of precious stones, and the sensuous
associations of religion are stressed. It is often grandiloquent, and
depicts characters who are larger than life, whether they are heroic
or extravagant caricatures. It likes to portray strong emotions, to
show violent deeds and atrocities, to shock or arouse surprise. Extreme states of mind and mixed emotions are favourite subjects;
and some writers dwell on the unpleasant, gruesome aspects of life
or death.

To these themes correspond a certain number of stylistic devices
— a fondness for hyperbole, for paradoxical antitheses, and for
oxymoron; a fondness for such symbols of evanescence as water,
wind, and the rainbow; a fondness for double-entendre, puns,
word-play and word echoes,

> O mer amère, mère à la mère d'amours . . .
>                          (Schelandre, *Tyr et Sidon*, 1608)

There is a fondness, too, for forced and enigmatical metaphors,[5]
and for conceits, in which the literal and the figurative meanings
merge and are confused:

> Je baignerai mes mains folâtres
> Dans les ondes de tes cheveux.
>                          (Théophile)

The chiaroscuro of baroque painters sometimes occurs in baroque
poetry, and the shifting point of view of the baroque artist appears
as a love for piling up images — as in this speech from Rotrou's
*Captifs*, full, too, of paradox and oxymoron:

> Vous l'entendez, la douleur qui me presse
> Se peut dire un plaisir où manque l'allégresse,
> Un agréable écueil, un redoutable port;
> Un penser qu'on nourrit et qui donne la mort;

---

[5] Obtained by transposing the ideas contained in the epithet and the
noun—e.g. for Saint-Amant, a darting fish is a 'sagette vivante', and a
glow-worm a 'belle escarboucle qui chemines'; Tristan calls a peacock
'cet Avril animé, ce firmament volage'.

Un pénible travail qu'au séjour où nous sommes
Les dieux ont envoyé pour le repos des hommes;
Une captivité qui s'aime en ses liens;
Un bien source de maux, un mal source de biens;
Un principe de vie, et sa fin tout ensemble;
Une fièvre qui fait et qu'on brûle et qu'on tremble;
Une manne funeste, un fiel délicieux;
Un savoureux poison qui se boit par ses yeux;
Une douce amertume, une douceur amère;
Une charge à la fois et pesante et légère;
Une mourante vie, un renaissant trépas;
Une flamme qui brûle et ne consume pas;
Un ciel où l'on se plaint, un enfer où l'on s'aime;
Une belle prison qu'on se bâtit soi-même.

A good example of literary baroque is an early poem of Malherbe, *Les Larmes de Saint Pierre* (1587), an imitation of an Italian poem by Tansillo. The theme, a religious one, the remorse of St. Peter, betrays the baroque love of extreme emotional states. St. Peter's remorse at having betrayed Christ is great and expressed in extreme terms:

Mon regret est si grand, et ma faute si grande,
Qu'*une mer éternelle à mes yeux je demande*
Pour pleurer à jamais le péché que j'ai fait,

he says, and his actions suit his language:

. . . le chétif en ce point se lamente,
S'arrache les cheveux, se bat et se tourmente . . .
. . . . . . . . . .
C'est alors[6] que ses cris *en tonnerres* éclatent,
Ses soupirs se font *vents, qui les chênes combattent,*
Et ses pleurs, qui tantôt descendaient mollement,
*Ressemblent un torrent* qui des hautes montagnes,
Ravageant et noyant les voisines campagnes,
Veut que tout l'univers ne soit qu'un élément.

The theme of martyrdom is introduced, in the description of the massacre of the Innocents. Religion is here given pleasurable associations, and the massacre is described without any crude details. The Innocents were, in fact, lucky to die so young:

Ce furent de beaux lis, qui mieux que la nature,
*Mêlants à leur blancheur l'incarnate peinture,*[7]
Que tira de leur sein le couteau criminel,
Devant que d'un hiver la tempête et l'orage
A leur teint délicat pussent faire dommage,
S'en allèrent fleurir au printemps éternel.

In similar vein, Christ's footsteps are described as having 'une odeur de parfums d'Assyrie'.

[6] On seeing Christ's footsteps.
[7] Cf.                          Here lay Duncan,
    His silver skin lac'd with his golden blood . . .

The theme of the mutability of fortune occurs:

> Que d'hommes fortunés en leur âge première,
> Trompés de l'inconstance à nos ans coutumière,
> Du depuis se sont vus en étrange langueur,
> Qui fussent morts contents, si le Ciel amiable,
> Ne les abusant pas en ton sein variable,
> Au temps de leur repos eût coupé ta longueur.

There is, too, the sense of movement. St. Peter's state of mind is thus described:

> La mer a dans le sein moins de vagues courantes
> Qu'il n'a dans le cerveau de formes différentes,
> Et n'a rien toutefois qui le mette en repos,
> Car aux flots de la peur sa navire qui tremble
> Ne trouve point de port . . .

Above all, we are shown his gestures, his movements. He is seen in perpetual motion — 's'arrache les cheveux, se bat et se tourmente [ . . . ] chemine toujours [ . . . ]'. He shouts and sighs and weeps, he adores Christ's footsteps:

> Il y fiche les yeux, il les baigne, il les baise,
> Il se couche dessus . . .

So, too, the arrival of the Innocents in Heaven is vividly described — the excitement, the celebrations:

> Que d'applaudissements, de rumeur et de presse!
> Que de feux, que de jeux, que de traits de caresse . . .

Each of these nouns conjures up a movement or a series of movements.

The sense of paradox pervades the poem. It is paradoxical that Peter the faithful — 'De vaillant fait couard, de fidèle fait traître', — should have betrayed his master, and that the short life of the Innocents should be more profitable than St. Peter's long one:

> Le peu qu'ils ont vécu leur fut grand avantage,
> Et le trop que je vis ne me fait que dommage,
> Cruelle occasion du souci qui me nuit:
> Quand j'avais de ma foi l'innocence première,
> *Si la nuit de ma mort m'eût privé de lumière,*
> *Je n'aurais pas la peur d'une immortelle nuit.*

The last two lines give paradoxical expression to a paradoxical idea. Life itself is a paradox: the happy die soon, the miserable are long-lived:

> Ceux qui te veulent mal sont ceux que tu conserves,

– this idea is developed at length in four stanzas. Paradoxical lines abound:

D'acquérir par ma perte un triomphe à ma foi ...

Ils se virent sous l'onde et se virent au port ...

The metaphors are baroque — for example:

se mettre au visage
*Sur le feu de sa honte une cendre d'ennui.*

It is a little far-fetched to talk of the fire of his shame; but to carry the metaphor further, to make the fire concrete and talk of covering it up with the ashes of grief, is characteristic of the period. In another stanza, Christ is seen as an archer shooting arrows at St. Peter:

Les yeux furent les arcs, les œillades les flèches
Qui percèrent son âme, et remplirent de brèches
Le rempart qu'il avait si lâchement gardé.

Cet assaut, comparable à l'éclat d'une foudre,
Pousse et jette d'un coup ses défenses en poudre ...

Here again, a metaphor is worked out in elaborate detail. Not only is Christ an archer, but the eyes are the bows, the glances the arrows, and St. Peter's breast the defence work: this metaphor occupies three stanzas. Similarly, the Innocents are likened to a fleet putting out to sea, and Herod to a pirate. There is, too, a detailed personification of Aurora and the Sun on the day of the crucifixion: Aurora with a vase of dead flowers in one hand and a pitcher of tears in the other, wearing a veil of mist and storm clouds, the Sun moving slowly, 'comme un criminel qui chemine au trépas'.

If *Les Larmes de Saint Pierre* has been chosen to illustrate certain aspects of baroque, it is because its author is the chief representative of the movement towards order and discipline in literature, towards 'classicism', in this period.[8] Boileau's lines about Malherbe are well known:

Enfin Malherbe vint, et, le premier en France,
Fit sentir dans les vers une juste cadence,
D'un mot mis à sa place enseigna le pouvoir,
Et réduisit la muse aux règles du devoir.
Par ce sage écrivain la langue réparée
N'offrit plus rien de rude à l'oreille épurée.
Les stances avec grâce apprirent à tomber,
Et le vers sur le vers n'osa plus enjamber.
Tout reconnut ses lois; et ce guide fidèle
Aux auteurs de ce temps sert encore de modèle.

[8] Baroque features persist in Malherbe to the end—the themes of transience and mutability, the occasional baroque metaphor, humanized and idealized nature, the love of pomp and magnificence, the grandiloquence, and the love of paradox.

Reacting against the Pléiade, Malherbe crossed out more than half his copy of Ronsard, writing comments in the margin; and when Racan asked if he approved of the rest, he crossed out what was left. Chapelain once found him lying on a couch, singing

> D'où venez-vous, Jeanne?
> Jeanne, d'où venez ... ?

'J'aimerais mieux,' he said, 'avoir fait cela que toutes les œuvres de Ronsard.'[9] He wrote very severe comments in his copy of Desportes, whom indeed he once told, when he was dining with him, that his soup was better than his translation of the Psalms.

Malherbe was a purist in matters of language. Even on his deathbed he corrected his nurse, who had used a word which he did not consider good French; and when his confessor reprimanded him, he said that 'il voulait jusques à la mort maintenir la pureté de la langue française'. He opposed borrowings from the Greek and compound epithets; he objected to Latinisms, archaisms, dialect and technical words, and the abuse of diminutives; and he insisted that poetry should obey the normal rules of grammar. For him, the standard to be observed was the speech of the 'crocheteurs du Port-au-Foin', of whom he said that they were his 'maîtres pour le langage'. This, no doubt, was an exaggeration, but it is clear that he wanted poetry to be written in the language of every-day speech (but with the exclusion of *mots bas*), not in a special, artificial, poetic language. He also wanted it to be clear, precise, and logical, and not to offend common sense. He objected to vague, exaggerated statements such as 'mille' or 'cent tourments', and would observe that perhaps there were only ninety-nine. He disliked poetic fictions (though not conventional mythology): when Régnier (the nephew of Desportes), in his *Discours au Roi*, described France as a nymph rising in the air, Malherbe asked him when it happened, observing that he had lived in France for fifty years without noticing any such phenomenon.

For Malherbe, poetry was a matter of hard work. He objected to hiatus, enjambement, and padding (*chevilles*); he insisted on the strict use of the caesura, and in elegies he wanted each group of four lines, and preferably each couplet, to be complete in itself. He was hard to please where rhyme was concerned. He disliked false and inexact rhymes, such as *âme* and *flamme*, or *innocence* and *puissance*, or *grand* and *prend* (*en* and *an* were then, it seems, slightly differently pronounced). Above all, he disliked easy rhymes: he condemned the rhyming of words formed from the same root (*admettre, commettre, promettre*), the rhyming of a word with its compound (*temps, printemps*), and the rhyming of

---

[9] One is reminded of Molière's Alceste and M. Jourdain.

words associated in meaning (*montagne, campagne; père, mère; défense, offense*). His reason was that difficult rhymes were more likely than obvious ones to lead to interesting ideas:

> La raison qu'il disait pourquoi il fallait plutôt rimer des mots éloignés que ceux qui avaient de la convenance est que l'on trouvait de plus beaux vers en les rapprochant qu'en rimant ceux qui avaient presque une même signification; et s'étudiait fort à chercher des rimes rares et stériles, sur la créance qu'il avait qu'elles lui faisaient produire quelques nouvelles pensées, outre qu'il disait que cela sentait son grand poète de tenter les rimes difficiles qui n'avaient point encore été rimées.          (Racan)

Malherbe was a powerful influence, if less of an innovator, perhaps, than Boileau imagined. French poets towards the end of the sixteenth century had been moving towards greater clarity and a more rigorous technique; though Malherbe went further than his predecessors, formulated a coherent and comprehensive doctrine, and asserted it in an intransigent and peremptory way. Nor is it true that 'tout reconnut ses lois'. Régnier bitterly attacked him in his ninth satire, written after Malherbe's insult to Desportes. He criticizes Malherbe for cavalierly dismissing all his predecessors as worthless, for his concentration on technical details, and his lack of real poetry – indeed, he suggests that the interest in technique springs from a desire to cover up the lack of real poetic feeling:

> Nul aiguillon divin n'élève leur[10] courage,
> Ils rampent bassement, faibles d'inventions,
> Et n'osent, peu hardis, tenter les fictions,
> Froids à l'imaginer, car s'ils font quelque chose,
> C'est proser de la rime et rimer de la prose,
> Que l'art lime et relime et polit de façon
> Qu'elle rend à l'oreille un agréable son;
> Et voyant qu'un beau feu leur cervelle n'embrase,
> Ils attifent leurs mots, ajolivent leur phrase,
> Affectent leur discours, tout si relevé d'art,
> Et peignent leurs défauts de couleurs et de fard...

Théophile, without attacking Malherbe like Régnier, claimed the right to go his own way:

> Imiter qui voudra les merveilles d'autrui.
> Malherbe a très bien fait, mais il a fait pour lui...
> ...........
> J'approuve que chacun écrive à sa façon:
> J'aime sa renommée, et non pas sa leçon.
> *(Elégie à une dame)*

Even his disciples, Maynard and Racan, did not rigorously observe all his precepts; still less such later poets as Corneille and La Fontaine.

[10] That of Malherbe and his disciples.

## Chapter 3

# POETS

### I. MALHERBE

FRANÇOIS DE MALHERBE (1555–1628), a forthright Norman with (from 1605 onwards) a position at court, did not share the lofty conception of poetry of the Pléiade or the Romantics later. For him, technique was of greater importance than inspiration, and the poet was not the unacknowledged legislator of mankind. 'Voyez-vous, Monsieur,' he told Racan, 'si nos vers vivent après nous, toute la gloire que nous en pouvons espérer est qu'on dira que nous avons été deux excellents arrangeurs de syllabes.' He remarked to a friend that 'un bon poète n'était pas plus utile à l'Etat qu'un bon joueur de quilles'; and, when the conversation turned on politics, he would observe that 'il ne fallait point se mêler de la conduite d'un vaisseau où l'on n'était que simple passager'. On the other hand, poetry for Malherbe, if it was not a means of conveying social or political truth, could confer immortality:

> Par les Muses seulement
> L'homme est exempt de la Parque,
> Et ce qui porte leur marque
> Demeure éternellement.

Nor did he doubt that he possessed this gift:

> Tous vous savent louer, mais non également;
> Les ouvrages communs vivent quelques années:
> Ce que Malherbe écrit dure éternellement.

Malherbe, as one would expect, has not the variety of subjects or the range of thought of Ronsard. His poems fall into four main groups, official poems, religious poems, consolations, and love poems.

The official poems, written for particular occasions and to flatter the great (Henry IV, Maria de' Medici, Louis XIII, Gaston d'Orléans, Richelieu, etc.) are full of hyperbolical praise of the beauty and virtue of the queens and princesses and of the valour and wisdom of the kings and their counsellors, of the prosperity

27

they give France in time of peace and their victories in war. His heroes, superhuman and godlike, move in a world of gods. Maria de' Medici's beauty —

> Telle n'est point la Cythérée,
> Quand, d'un nouveau feu s'allumant,
> Elle sort pompeuse et parée
> Pour la conquête d'un amant:
> Telle ne luit en sa carrière
> Des mois l'inégale courrière;
> Et telle dessus l'horizon
> L'Aurore au matin ne s'étale,
> Quand les yeux mêmes de Céphale
> En feraient la comparaison.

— has, we are told, caused Neptune to fall in love with her, with the result that he delayed her ten days on her way from Italy to France.[1] Henry IV in war is likened successively to a torrent and to Mars, and the flash of his eyes to lightning. The lamentations of Alcandre (Henry IV) on the enforced absence of his mistress move the river-god and the nymphs; and when an attempt was made on the King's life, the river-god, who, we are told, had come out to watch the alterations to the Louvre,

> ... se resserra tout à l'heure
> Au plus bas lieu de sa demeure,
> Et ses nymphes dessous les eaux,
> Toutes sans voix et sans haleine,
> Pour se cacher furent en peine
> De trouver assez de roseaux.

M. de Bellegarde, on his way to Florence to fetch Maria de' Medici, is accompanied by Hymen in person, and is no less godlike. It would seem that Malherbe was severer on poetic fictions in other people's verse than in his own.

Another characteristic feature is the *pointe*. What need has the princesse de la Trimouille to seek warmer climes,

> Vous de qui chaque pas fait naître mille fleurs?

Why did the attempted assassination of Henry IV not cause the sun to plunge France into eternal darkness? Because the assassin waited until the sun had gone down. The death of Mlle de Conti is justified on the grounds that

> ... la terre était brûlée
> S'ils [les Destins] n'eussent tué ce flambeau.

Similarly, the Queen Mother is consoled for the death of one of her three sons, on the grounds that:

> N'a-t-il [le Ciel] pas moins failli d'en ôter un du nombre
> Que d'en partager trois en un seul univers?

[1] Maria de' Medici is similarly surrounded by gods in the scenes from her life painted by Rubens.

At times one is tempted to think that genuine feeling raises Malherbe above the level of a court poet, and turns him into a national poet, celebrating civil concord and royal authority. In the *Prière pour le roi allant en Limousin*, for example, the poet and the theme are well suited to each other. Henry IV is worthy of Malherbe's praise, and there is no reason to doubt the genuineness of Malherbe's sense of France's good fortune in having him as its King. The gratitude for the cessation of civil strife and for the merits of Henry, contrasted with the *rois fainéants* who delegate their responsibilities to flatterers, and the sense of the dangers lying in wait for France and averted only by the presence of the King, are not misplaced; nor is the indignation over the renewal of civil war in the *Ode pour le Roi allant châtier la rébellion des Rochelois et chasser les Anglais*. One is, however, beset with doubts when one finds the regency of Maria de' Medici being praised with equal enthusiasm.

The love poems, whether written on Malherbe's own account or for his patrons, Henry IV and M. de Bellegarde, are conventional and artificial, but often not without charm. Malherbe sings of the beauty of his (or another's) mistress, laments her absence, complains of her cruelty, and asserts his fidelity; but there is little evidence of sincerity or genuine feeling. The praise of the woman's beauty is exaggerated – her complexion is composed of roses and lilies, or like ivory or snow; her eyes are like suns or stars, her voice is musical, and her breath perfumed.[2] If nature puts in an appearance, it is pleasing, but artificial and personified:

> Sus debout la merveille des belles,
> Allons voir sur les herbes nouvelles
> Luire un émail dont la vive peinture
> Défend à l'art d'imiter la nature.

> L'air est plein d'une haleine de roses,
> Tous les vents tiennent leurs bouches closes,
> Et le Soleil semble sortir de l'onde
> Pour quelque amour plus que pour luire au monde.

> On dirait, à lui voir sur la tête
> Ses rayons comme un chapeau de fête,
> Qu'il s'en va suivre en si belle journée
> Encore un coup la fille de Pénée.

The impression of artificiality given by the love poems is enhanced by the *pointes*. Theologians may dispute where Hell is:

> Amour en soit loué, je n'en suis point en peine:
> Où Caliste n'est point, c'est là qu'est mon enfer.

[2] Cf. Shakespeare's condemnation of this convention in Sonnet No. 130:
My mistress's eyes are nothing like the sun . . .

It is useless for Caliste to pray for God's mercy when she is herself so merciless. Nevertheless, Malherbe's love poems can be very
attractive, as the following noble sonnet:

> Beaux et grands bâtiments d'éternelle structure,
> Superbes de matière et d'ouvrages divers,
> Où le plus digne Roi qui soit en l'univers
> Aux miracles de l'art fait céder la nature;
>
> Beau parc et beaux jardins, qui dans votre clôture
> Avez toujours des fleurs et des ombrages verts,
> Non sans quelque démon qui défend aux hivers
> D'en effacer jamais l'agréable peinture;
>
> Lieux qui donnez aux cœurs tant d'aimables désirs,
> Bois, fontaines, canaux, si parmi vos plaisirs
> Mon humeur est chagrine et mon visage triste,
>
> Ce n'est point qu'en effet vous n'ayez des appas;
> Mais quoi que vous ayez, vous n'avez point Caliste,
> Et moi je ne vois rien, quand je ne la vois pas.

Both in his love poetry and in his official verse, Malherbe sometimes treats general themes—the two stanzas *A Monseigneur le
Cardinal de Richelieu,* for instance, are a reflection on human life.
He is, perhaps, at his best when he can do this freely, as in the
quatrain written for a fountain in the Hôtel de Rambouillet:

> Vois-tu, passant, couler cette onde,
> Et s'écouler incontinent?
> Ainsi fuit la gloire du monde,
> Et rien que Dieu n'est permanent.

And it is because he is free to treat general themes in the paraphrases of the psalms and in the *Consolations* that these are of
more interest to us than his official verse or his love poems. To
considerations on the rôle of fortune in human life, the alternation
of happiness and misery, the transience of worldly things, the
implacability of death, eternal preoccupations of mankind, Malherbe gives noble and dignified expression.

It is interesting to see how the psalms in Malherbe's paraphrases
are modified to suit the taste of the time. The version of Psalm
cxlvi, for example, not only stresses the transience of life more
than the original, but is less simple; Malherbe, it is evident, is
striving after nobility and dignity. Where the original says: 'Put
not your trust in princes, nor in the son of man, in whom there is
no help,' Malherbe ignores the son of man, and develops only the
idea of princes:

> En vain, pour satisfaire à nos lâches envies,
> Nous passons près des rois tout le temps de nos vies,

A souffrir des mépris et ployer les genoux;
Ce qu'ils peuvent n'est rien; ils sont comme nous sommes,
    Véritablement hommes,
    Et meurent comme nous.

Similarly, in Psalm viii, where the original says that God has
given man dominion over all things, 'all sheep and oxen, yea, and
the beasts of the field; the fowl of the air, and the fish of the sea,'
Malherbe suppresses the *mots bas* and renders the passage thus:

Sitôt que le besoin excite son désir,
Qu'est-ce qu'en ta largesse il ne trouve à choisir?
Et par ton règlement l'air, la mer et la terre
        N'entretiennent-ils pas
Une secrète loi de se faire la guerre,
A qui de plus de mets fournira ses repas?

The *Consolations* express the stoical philosophy. It is useless to
give way to grief, since death spares no one:

Le pauvre en sa cabane, où le chaume le couvre,
        Est sujet à ses lois,
Et la garde qui veille aux barrières du Louvre
        N'en défend point nos rois.

De murmurer contr'elle et perdre patience,
        Il est mal à propos:
Vouloir ce que Dieu veut est la seule science
        Qui nous met en repos.

Such is the conclusion of the best-known and the finest of
Malherbe's poems, the *Consolation à M. du Périer*. This, incidentally, is one of the few poems in which Malherbe tells us
something of himself:

De moi, déjà deux fois d'une pareille foudre[3]
        Je me suis vu perclus,
Et deux fois la raison m'a si bien fait résoudre
        Qu'il ne m'en souvient plus.

Non qu'il ne me soit grief que la tombe possède
        Ce qui me fut si cher;
Mais en un accident qui n'a point de remède,
        Il n'en faut point chercher.

In stressing the need for rigorous technique, in giving the
example of a style that is at once clear, concise, and vigorous,
Malherbe was a salutary and necessary influence – how necessary,
the style of Alexandre Hardy or of Régnier shows. But Malherbe
was more than a master of technique. If it is difficult for us
nowadays completely to share the enthusiasm of La Fontaine for

[3] Malherbe had lost two children.

Malherbe,[4] Malherbe will always be read for the forceful, poetic expression he gives to general truths:

> Tout le plaisir des jours est en leurs matinées,
> La nuit est déjà proche à qui passe midi.
>
> *(Sur le mariage du Roi et de la Reine)*

> Et rose elle a vécu ce que vivent les roses,
> L'espace d'un matin.[5]
>
> *(Consolation à M. du Périer)*

## II. TWO INDEPENDENTS: RÉGNIER
## AND THÉOPHILE

Mathurin Régnier (1573–1613), the nephew of Desportes, was an admirer of the Pléiade. He praises Ronsard, Jodelle, and his uncle in his poems; his fourth satire is an imitation of Ronsard's *Discours à Pierre L'Escot*; and there are many echoes of Ronsard in his verse. In opposition to Malherbe and his school, he remains faithful to the Pléiade:

> Je vais le grand chemin que mon oncle m'apprit,
> Laissant là ces docteurs que les Muses instruisent
> En des arts tout nouveaux . . .
>
> (Satire IX)

For him, poetry is a matter of enthusiasm or fire, of being carried away, not of technique (Satire V). The reader of Régnier is sometimes inclined to regret this attachment to the old ways, for his verse is often rambling and diffuse. It is difficult not to feel, for example, that the long sentence with which the ninth satire opens would have gained in clarity without losing force if it had been condensed and broken up. Nor is the progress of the thought in some of Régnier's longer poems – Satire V or Satire X, for example – always as clear as it might be.

These defects, however, do not make Régnier a negligible poet. The most distinctive feature of his verse, perhaps, is its realism. Here, for example, is a description of a seventeenth-century doctor from Satire IV:

> si j'eusse étudié,
> Jeune, laborieux, sur un banc à l'école,
> Galien, Hippocrate, ou Jason, ou Barthole,

---

[4] La Fontaine is said to have been so excited by his first introduction to Malherbe's verse that he spent his nights learning Malherbe's poems by heart, and his days walking in the woods of Château-Thierry, declaiming them aloud. In *Daphné*, Malherbe is classed as one of the nine great poets of the world, along with Homer, Anacreon, Pindar, Virgil, Horace, Ovid, Ariosto, and Tasso.

[5] According to an anecdote, this line—originally 'Et Rosette a vécu . . .' —is due to a printer's error.

Une cornette au col, debout dans un parquet,
A tort et à travers je vendrais mon caquet,
Ou bien tâtant le pouls, le ventre et la poitrine,
J'aurais un beau teston pour juger d'une urine,
Et me prenant au nez loucher dans un bassin
Des ragoûts qu'un malade offre à son médecin,
En dire mon avis, former une ordonnance
D'un réchappe-s'il peut, puis d'une révérence
Contrefaire l'honnête et, quand viendrait au point,
Dire en serrant la main: 'Dame! il n'en fallait point.'[6]

In Satire V, the corrupt manners of the age are described; in
Satire XVII, typical scenes and characters of Paris are evoked;
in the second elegy, Régnier's flirtatious mistress speaks and moves
before our eyes. Some of the satires are devoted entirely to
humorous and realistic descriptions of scenes from everyday life.
Satire VIII describes a meeting with a bore, who is not altogether
unlike the Oronte of Molière's *Misanthrope*; Satire XI describes
a dinner party, from which Régnier escapes only to stumble into
a brothel (Satire XII). In these two satires, the realism is rather
crude; and, in the manner of the later burlesque writers, Régnier
dwells excessively on unpleasant details, as in the lengthy description of a pedant whom he meets at the dinner party:

Sa bouche est grosse et torte et semble en son porfil
Celle-là d'Alizon qui retordant du fil
Fait la moue aux passants, et féconde en grimace,
Bave comme au printemps une vieille limace.
Un rateau mal rangé pour ses dents paraissait,
Où le chancre et la rouille en monceaux s'amassait,
Dont pour lors je connus, grondant quelques paroles,
Qu'expert il en savait crever ses éverolles,
Qui me fit bien juger qu'aux veilles des bons jours
Il en soulait rogner ses ongles de velours.
Sa barbe sur sa joue éparse à l'aventure,
Où l'art est en colère avecque la nature,
En bosquets s'élevait, où certains animaux,
Qui des pieds, qui des mains, lui faisaient mille maux.

This rather distasteful burlesque realism is absent from the
famous Satire XIII. This shows us Macette, a former prostitute,
who, in her old age, has assumed a mask of religion, trying to
corrupt Régnier's mistress — not knowing that she is overheard:
a deliciously comic scene.

With realism — in Régnier, as so often in literature — is associated
criticism of society. Justice has become a matter of self-interest,

---

[6] Cf. Villon:

Hé! Dieu, se j'eusse estudié
Ou temps de ma jeunesse folle
Et a bonnes meurs dedié,
J'eusse maison et couche molle.

something to be bought and sold. Learning is despised, and merit unrewarded:

> Pourvu qu'on soit morguant, qu'on bride sa moustache,
> Qu'on frise ses cheveux, qu'on porte un grand panache,
> Qu'on parle baragouin et qu'on suive le vent,
> En ce temps du jourd'hui l'on n'est que trop savant.

(Satire III)

Poetry similarly goes unrewarded, and, in any case, true poetry is extinct, Malherbe and his school having corrupted taste. The way to get on in the world is to fawn on the great; and the corruption of the court and the hypocrisy essential to the successful courtier are attacked in Satire III. It is, in fact, an age without virtue, an age of hypocrisy, a topsy-turvy age – which is why, in reaction, Régnier has become a satirist (Satire XV).

In his criticism of the age, Régnier does not overlook literature. He describes poor, ill-dressed poets in Satire II, and shows them paying court to the great for sustenance in Satire IV, in which, too, he castigates *libertin* poets and Malherbe and his school. Malherbe and his disciples are anathema to Régnier, who returns to the attack in his ninth,[7] tenth, and eleventh satires.

Unlike Malherbe, Régnier puts a good deal of himself directly into his verse. In Satire II, he tells of his visit to Italy as a boy in the service of Cardinal de Joyeuse, and describes himself visiting his uncle Desportes's house at Vanves; and he evokes his father in Satires IV and X. There are self-portraits in Satires III, XIII, and XV. He tells us how poetic inspiration comes to him against his will and at inconvenient moments (Satire XV); and he confesses his pleasure-loving, amorous disposition in Satires VII ('Toute femme m'agrée') and XVI – in which he shows that age has not diminished his amorousness, but has changed his taste ('J'aime un amour facile et de peu de défense'). We see him in love and jealous in his first three elegies.

His philosophy of life changes as his mood changes, or as he grows old. His desire for a comfortable church living and a life of studious tranquillity are expressed in Satire III. A similar epicurean philosophy is expressed in Satire VI, an attack on honour for preventing us from enjoying life:

> Ha! que c'est chose belle et fort bien ordonnée,
> Dormir dans un lit la grasse matinée,
> En dame de Paris, s'habiller chaudement,
> A la table s'asseoir, manger humainement,
> Se reposer un peu, puis monter en carrosse,
> Aller à Gentilly caresser une rosse,
> Pour escroquer sa fille . . .

----

[7] See above, p. 26.

By Satire XVII, however, his attitude has changed: one should curb one's desires and ambitions, he now says, and pursue virtue. In his *Poésies spirituelles*, we find him growing old, repenting of his wasted and ill-spent youth, and turning to God. There is something of François Villon in Mathurin Régnier.

Régnier's poems are fascinating for the picture of an age and of a man that emerges from them. In them, much of the later seventeenth century is contained in germ. His comic realism is continued by the burlesque writers, and later by Molière and Boileau. In using satire as a means of attacking his literary antipathies, he anticipates Boileau. His epicurean philosophy and his love of tranquillity remind us of La Fontaine. His criticisms of his age are taken up again later by Boileau and La Bruyère.

Théophile de Viau (1590–1626) is in many ways the antithesis of Malherbe. As one might expect of a *libertin*, a disciple of nature, he prefers nature to artifice:

> La nature est inimitable,
> Et dans sa beauté véritable
> Elle éclate si vivement
> Que l'art gâte tous ses ouvrages
> Et lui fait plutôt mille outrages
> Qu'il ne lui donne un ornement.

Naturalness is his ideal in poetry, too. In the *Elégie à une Dame*, which is virtually his *art poétique*, he rejects Malherbe and confesses:

> Je ne veux point unir le fil de mon sujet:
> Diversement je laisse et reprends mon objet,
> Mon âme, imaginant, n'a point la patience
> De bien polir les vers et ranger la science.
> La règle me déplaît, j'écris confusément:
> Jamais un bon esprit ne fait rien qu'aisément.
> . . . . . . . . . . .
> Je veux faire des vers qui ne soient pas contraints,
> Promener mon esprit par des petits desseins,
> Chercher des lieux secrets où rien ne me déplaise,
> Méditer à loisir, rêver tout à mon aise,
> Employer toute une heure à me mirer dans l'eau,
> Ouïr, comme en songeant, la course d'un ruisseau,
> Ecrire dans le bois, m'interrompre, me taire,
> Composer un quatrain sans songer à le faire.

Spontaneous, personal, and sincere, except in a few poems written as tasks, he writes freely of himself — his opinions, his loves, his life. He describes his father's estates and his own birthplace. His exiles and his imprisonment bulk large in his poetry: he tells us how he spends his time in exile or in prison, what his emotions are, protests his innocence, complains of the defection of his friends, or pleads for mercy.

Théophile rebels against the conventional love poetry of the age (though he occasionally conforms to convention):

> Je n'entends point les lois ni les façons d'aimer,
> Ni comme Cupidon se mêle de charmer.
>
> (*A Monsieur du Fargis*)

The mistresses he addresses are real ladies:

> Amaranthe, Philis, Caliste, Pasithée
> Je hais cette mollesse à vos yeux affectée;
> Ces titres recherchés avecques tant d'appas
> Témoignent qu'en effet vos yeux n'en avaient pas.
> Au sentiment divin de ma douce furie,
> Le plus beau nom du monde est le nom de Marie.

And the emotions he expresses – whether he is affirming his devotion, pleading for forgiveness, asking for favours, rejoicing that he is cured of his love, lamenting a separation, complaining that he is ill-treated by his mistress or resolving to break with her, narrating his loves or analysing his emotions – give an impression of sincerity and truth, enhanced by an occasional, sometimes charming, sometimes refreshing, dash of sensuality.

Théophile's verse reflects the independence of his mind.[8] He is, no doubt, one of the rare spirits of whom he speaks:

> Parmi tant de fuseaux la Parque en sait retordre
> Où la contagion du vice n'a su mordre,
> Et le ciel en fait naître encore infinité
> Qui retiennent beaucoup de la divinité,
> Des bons entendements qui sans cesse travaillent
> Contre l'erreur du peuple, et jamais ne défaillent,
> Et qui, d'un sentiment hardi, grave et profond,
> Vivent tout autrement que les autres ne font.
> Mais leur divin génie est forcé de se feindre,
> Et les rend malheureux s'il ne se peut contraindre . . .
>
> (*Elégie à une Dame*)

Although pious sentiments appear in some of the poems written in prison, he is usually irreverent. He tells his mistress that

---

[8] Two interesting passages give an impression of an inquiring mind. In a poem to Monsieur du Fargis, refusing to write love poetry for another, Théophile says that every lover would require a different kind of verse.

> . . . pour lui satisfaire et bien peindre sa flamme
> Je voudrais par avant avoir connu son âme.

In another, we see him curious to know M. de Candale's experiences in detail:

> Tu me dois accorder deux heures de loisir
> Pour contenter ici mon curieux désir,
> Me faire un long récit de toutes les traverses
> Que t'ont fait tant de mers et de terres diverses.

... si le Ciel d'une pareille flamme
Nous inspirait sa volonté dans l'âme,
Tous les mortels, d'une invincible foi,
Obéiraient à ta divine loi.

He does not believe in Providence or divine intervention in the world. He denounces stoicism and defends the natural expression of grief and sorrow:

L'effort de la raison, et ce combat farouche
Contre nos sentiments quand la douleur nous touche,
Importune la vie, et son fâcheux secours
Nuit plus que si le mal prenait son juste cours.[9]

For him, nature is the guide to conduct:

J'approuve qu'un chacun suive en tout la nature:
Son empire est plaisant et sa loi n'est pas dure;
Ne suivant que son train jusqu'au dernier moment,
Même dans ses malheurs on passe heureusement.

(*Satire première*)[10]

He is – usually, at least – independent towards the great. He refuses, for instance, to flatter M. de Candale, who is but a man:

N'attends point qu'en ton nom honteusement j'écrive
Ce qui ne fut jamais sur la troyenne rive,
Que je t'appelle Achille, et que tu sois vanté
Par tant de faux exploits qu'on a jadis chanté.

(*Elégie à M. de C ...*)

Similarly, he expresses his distaste for the hypocrisy to which court life constrains one, and for the haughty insolence of the great: for him what matters is not wealth but ability. As we have seen,[11] he is independent in literature and disrespectful towards the ancients: he is sceptical of the exploits of ancient heroes, and criticizes the inconsistencies of Virgil's Aeneas.

Théophile is also a lover of external nature:

J'aime un beau jour, des fontaines claires, l'aspect des montagnes, l'étendue d'une grande plaine, de belles forêts; l'Océan, ses vagues, son calme, ses rivages ...

(*Fragments d'une Histoire comique*)

[9] Cf. 'Je ne résiste point par philosophie aux atteintes du malheur: car c'est accroître son injure, et tout le combat que le discours fait contre la tristesse la rengrège sans doute et la prolonge' (*Fragments d'une Histoire comique*). Cf., too, Théophile's letter to Des Barreaux on the death of the latter's father: 'Lorsque les douleurs sont justes, c'est une tyrannie que de les détourner, et une résolution soudaine en des accidents outrageux est une constance qui tient beaucoup de la bête et fort peu de la nature de l'homme.'
[10] Cf.

Heureux, tandis qu'il est vivant,
Celui qui va toujours suivant
Le grand maître de la nature,
Dont il se croit la créature.

[11] See pp. 9 and 26.

Although, in the manner of his age, he sees nature as peopled by pagan divinities and as animated by human emotions – e.g. he tells a friend that when his letter reached him (Théophile), the neighbouring river was so overjoyed that it overflowed its banks –, nevertheless, his nature poetry is pleasing and often evocative. Such poems as *Le Matin* and *L'Hiver* are, in the baroque manner, a succession of vignettes illustrating different aspects of the subject. Some of his best nature poetry is contained in *La Maison de Sylvie*, a series of odes written at Chantilly towards the end of his career. One example must suffice:

> Les rayons du jour, égarés
> Parmi des ombres incertaines,
> Eparpillent leurs feux dorés
> Dessus l'azur de ces fontaines;
> Son or, dedans l'eau confondu,
> Avecques ce cristal fondu
> Mêle son teint et sa nature,
> Et sème son éclat mouvant,
> Comme la branche, au gré du vent,
> Efface et marque sa peinture.
>
> (Ode VI)

Here, Théophile depicts the rays of the sun stealing into the half light of the wood (an example of chiaroscuro); and the reflection of the light in the water, and the perpetual play of light and shadow on its surface as the branches move about incessantly, are vividly and delightfully portrayed.

Sincere and independent, and at his best a poet of great charm, Théophile is an interesting, rather than a great, poet. Whereas Malherbe is flawless, but not always of interest, Théophile is almost always interesting, but does not always give memorable expression to his ideas and his emotions. A Théophile with the technique of Malherbe, a Malherbe with the personality and outlook of Théophile, would have been a really great poet.


### III. LA CEPPÈDE, A BAROQUE RELIGIOUS POET

The Provençal poet, Jean de la Ceppède (1548–1623), published his *Imitation des psaumes de la pénitence de David* in 1594, and his *Théorèmes spirituels* in two parts, in 1613 and 1622. The *Théorèmes*, his main work, is a sequence of over five hundred sonnets on the life and death of Christ (Part I) and on the events following the crucifixion (the four books of Part II deal with Hell, the appearances of Christ on earth, the ascension, and the coming of the Holy Ghost). Not all these sonnets are of equal interest, and they perhaps gain by being detached in anthologies

rather than read through in sequence; but at his best La Ceppède
has remarkable intensity of feeling.

One characteristic feature is his symbolism. He is fond of detect-
ing symbolical significance in the actions of Christ, of showing how
the New Testament is prefigured by the Old, or of drawing elaborate parallels between the life of Christ and natural phenomena.
Here, for example, is a comparison of Christ's life to the sun passing
through four of the signs of the zodiac:

> Ce grand Soleil, de qui l'autre n'est qu'une flamme
> Par quatre des maisons du grand Cercle a passé.
> Par celle de la Vierge, où neuf mois sa belle âme
> A de son corps égal l'organe compassé.
>
> Par celle du Verseau, quand son œil a tracé
> Sa douleur par son pleur, en maint acte sans blâme,
> Par celle du Taureau, quand son corps terrassé
> S'est pour victime offert sur le gibet infâme.
>
> Or à ce jour il entre en celle du Lion
> Perruqué de lumière, il darde un million
> De rayons flamboyants sur les deux Hémisphères,
>
> Et sa voix rugissante, et son frémissement
> Au sortir de la tombe épouvantent les fères,
> Et les rangent au joug de leur amendement.

Here is the same kind of subtlety with which other poets of the
period invent elaborate and detailed metaphors; but intellectualism
in La Ceppède by no means excludes emotion or poetry, as the
sextet with its magnificent description of Christ on High ('perruqué
de lumière') calling sinners to repentance, shows.

In the following poem, instead of a comparison, there is an
elaborate antithesis between the tree with the forbidden fruit and
the cross:

> Satan par le bois vert notre aïeule ravit,
> Jésus par le bois sec à Satan l'a ravie;
> Le bois vert à l'Enfer notre aïeule asservit.
> Le bois sec a d'Enfer la puissance asservie;
>
> Satan sur le bois vert vit sa rage assouvie,
> Jésus sur le bois sec son amour assouvit.
> Le bois vert donna mort à toute âme qui vit,
> Le bois sec, ô merveille! à tous morts donne vie.
>
> Le bois sec aujourd'hui triomphe du bois vert,
> Le vert ferma le Ciel, le sec l'a réouvert
> Et nous y reconduit par voies fort aisées.
>
> Il a tout satisfait, il a tout mérité,
> Sur ce bois sec la Grâce atteint la Vérité,
> La Justice et la Paix s'y sont entrebaisées.

This sonnet illustrates another feature of La Ceppède's verse, his forceful use of repetition. He is not a poet of understatement, but drives his point home with repeated blows of the hammer: 'Satan ... Jésus ... Le bois vert ... Le bois sec ...' The first ten lines consist of five pairs of antithetical lines, the second line in each pair almost exactly reproducing the first. Similarly, the first nine lines of another sonnet ('L'amour l'a de l'Olympe ici bas fait descendre') begin with the word *amour*, and in another ('un Ange avait prédit le temps de sa venue'), the important part played by angels in Christ's life is emphasized by the eight-fold repetition of the word *ange*.

Repetition is one means by which La Ceppède achieves emotional intensity. At other times, he brings out, by his vivid portrayal of Christ's humiliation and sufferings, of the contrast between his divinity and his treatment at the hands of men, the greatness of his sacrifice and love·

> O Royauté tragique! ô vêtement infâme!
> O poignant Diadème! ô Sceptre rigoureux!
> O belle, et chère tête! ô l'amour de mon âme!
> O mon Christ seul fidèle, et parfait amoureux.
>
> On vous frappe, ô saint chef, et ces coups douloureux
> Font que votre Couronne en cent lieux vous rentame.
> Bourreaux assenez-le d'une tranchante lame,
> Et versez tout à coup ce pourpre généreux.
>
> Faut-il pour une mort qu'il en souffre dix mille?
> Hé! voyez que le sang, qui de son chef distille
> Ses prunelles détrempe, et rend leur jour affreux.
>
> Ce pur sang, ce Nectar, prophané se mélange
> A vos sales crachats, dont la sanglante fange
> Change ce beau visage en celui d'un lépreux.

Christ's plight is emphasized by words such as *crachats*, *fange*, and *lépreux*; his divinity by the first quatrain, consisting entirely of exclamations, and by such words as *pourpre* and *nectar* to describe his blood.[12]

Finally, La Ceppède, in some of his sonnets, shows himself to be an imaginative narrative poet, vividly describing the scene with a wealth of picturesque detail; for example, Christ is thus taken to the place of crucifixion:

> Le Tribun prend la tête, et conduit sa Cohorte.
> Maint fifre, maint tambour anime le Soudard.
> Parmi les bataillons vole maint étendard
> Et cent armés à cru font la seconde escorte.

[12] In the penitential psalms, La Ceppède elaborates the original text and intensifies the emotion.

De cent chevau-légers l'une, et l'autre aile est forte.
Au mitan les bourreaux mènent Christ par la hart.
Tout autour les Sergeants font un double rempart.
Tout marche en ordonnance. On arrive à la porte.

## IV. TWO DISCIPLES OF MALHERBE: RACAN AND MAYNARD

The main disciples of Malherbe were Racan and Maynard. Racan (1589–1670) wrote much the same kinds of verse as his master – eulogistic odes, a *consolation*, a good deal of love poetry, and (later in life) translations of the Psalms. His verse is attractive but conventional, though two of his poems stand apart from the rest – an ode ('Vous qui riez de mes douleurs'), humorously describing an inn in which he was billeted, and the famous *stances* ('Tirsis, il faut penser à la retraite'), his best as well as his best-known poem, in which he sings the joys of a modest country life.[13]

François Maynard (1582 or 1583–1646) also cultivated the same genres as Malherbe – love poetry of a conventional kind; poems in praise of the royal family, ministers of state, or patrons; denunciations of the enemies of the state; court ballets; assertions of his own undying fame; and a little religious verse. These are diversified by complaints of the court, where virtue is not prized, and which has left him unrewarded, praise of country life, nostalgia for Paris, admonitions to enjoy the present, and drinking songs. One of his best poems is the ode, 'Alcippe, reviens dans nos bois'. Spurned by the court, Alcippe is urged to go into retirement and prepare for death, and the poem develops into a noble meditation on the inexorability of death and the impermanence of all things, not unworthy to stand beside Villon's famous *ballade*.

There is another side to Maynard's talent, too. He is a satirist, and a considerable part of his work consists of satirical epigrams and odes. He attacks society for its injustice – a *savetier* can make a fortune, whereas men of letters starve (unless they are playwrights) – and contrasts society ladies, with their false complexions and their airs, unfavourably with country girls. The ode, 'Puissant protecteur de mes vers', contains a general attack on the society of his age. Some of his best poems in this satirical vein contain a humorous description of such characters as a *nouvelliste*, a provincial magistrate, a coward, an ignorant theologian, or a braggadocio, with a grotesque realism which recalls Régnier or the later burlesque writers.

[13] For his pastoral play, *Les Bergeries*, see below, Chapter 5.

## Chapter 4

# PROSE-WRITERS

### I. THE NOVEL

L'*ASTRÉE* of Honoré d'Urfé (1567–1625) was composed over a long period of years: begun when its author was twenty, the first three parts were published in 1607, 1610, and 1619 respectively, and the last two in 1627 by his secretary, Baro.[1] The success of the work was immediate and enduring. La Rochefoucauld used to shut himself up every year and read it right through, and La Fontaine confessed:

> Etant petit garçon je lisais son roman,
> Et je le lis encore ayant la barbe grise.

L'*Astrée* is a work of great charm, and the modern reader who is not repelled by its length may derive considerable pleasure from it; especially if he reads it as d'Urfé's contemporaries first read it—a volume every few years.

The action takes place in ancient Gaul, on the banks of the Lignon, in d'Urfé's beloved Forez, and is concerned with the loves of shepherds and shepherdesses, of 'nymphs' (i.e. noble ladies) and knights. But there is no attempt to depict the manners and the mentality of the dark ages or the lives of humble peasants. Indeed, d'Urfé's shepherds are not real shepherds; they belong to 'bonnes et anciennes familles' which resolved to live as shepherds in order to escape the aggression of Rome. This, no doubt, explains their extreme civility. The nymph, Léonide, for example, going to spend a day with Astrée and her companions, is thus greeted by Diane:

'Grande nymphe, il serait peut-être meilleur pour nous que vous eussiez seulement notre connaissance par le rapport de la renommée, puisqu'elle nous est tant avantageuse; toutefois, puisqu'il vous plaît de nous faire cet honneur, nous le recevrons, comme nous sommes obligées de recevoir avec révérence les grâces qu'il plaît au Ciel de nous faire.' A ces dernières paroles [d'Urfé continues], elles la mirent entre elles, et la

---

[1] It is uncertain how far the Fifth Part is the work of d'Urfé and how far it is Baro's.

menèrent au hameau de Diane, où elle fut reçue d'un si bon visage, et avec tant de civilité, qu'elle s'étonnait comme il était possible qu'entre les bois et les pâturages, des personnes tant accomplies fussent élevées.

At the opening of the book, Céladon, being greeted coldly by Astrée, who believes him to be faithless, throws himself into the Lignon and is borne away by the stream. He is rescued and tended by the princess Galathée, who falls in love with him and tries to keep him with her. He escapes, lives (disguised as a woman) on intimate terms with Astrée, and, after various adventures, is eventually united with her. Such is the framework of the novel; but Astrée and Céladon are merely two characters in a world almost as complex as that of Balzac's *Comédie humaine*, and the narrative of their adventures is constantly interrupted and diversified by that of those about them, whose adventures, indeed, sometimes influence and impinge on theirs. D'Urfé anticipates Balzac, not only in the multiplicity of his characters and episodes, but even in the technique of the *personnages reparaissants*. Characters of whom we hear in an intercalated story, recur in another episode or the main plot, so that we have the impression of a complex society. D'Urfé's technique is highly developed in other respects, too. He is fond, for example, of interrupting a story and continuing it later. Another favourite device of his is to mention or describe an event, and reserve until later the precise circumstances or the explanation. Thus, at the opening of *L'Astrée*, we read that Astrée thinks Céladon unfaithful; it is not until the fourth book that we learn the full story of the loves of Astrée and Céladon and by what trick Astrée was led to mistrust her lover. Similarly, although, early in the volume, Galathée rescues Céladon, it is not till the Fifth Book that we learn how and why. In Book I, Laonice and Tyrcis appear; their story is not related until Book VII. We learn that there is a story to the loves of Célion and Bellinde long before the story is told; a hint of the mutual love of Léonide and Polémas arouses the reader's interest long before the details are given in Book X. There is, too, a comic element, not only in the adventures and arguments of the fickle Hylas, but in such an episode as that of Mélandre who, disguised as a knight, takes part in a single combat but cannot manage her horse or her arms.

The great affair of the lives of d'Urfé's characters is love, the essential quality of the *honnête homme*, for, as Sylvie says,

parce que l'amant ne désire rien davantage, que d'être aimé, pour être aimé, il faut qu'il se rende aimable, et ce qui rend aimable, est cela même qui rend honnête l'homme.

The love which the book holds up as an example is primarily spiritual; the lover must submit to the absolute dominion of his mistress. Astrée, for example, in a letter to Céladon, complains of his ill-humour:

vous me faites tort, de disposer sans que je le sache, de ce qui est à moi; car par la donation que vous m'avez faite, et que j'ai reçue, et vous et tout ce qui est de vous m'appartient.

What is love? asks Silvandre.

C'est mourir en soi, pour revivre en autrui, c'est ne se point aimer que d'autant que l'on est agréable à la chose aimée, et bref, c'est une volonté de se transformer, s'il se peut entièrement en elle.

The essence of this conception of love is expressed in Céladon's *Douze Tables des Lois d'amour* in the second volume. Love in a noble heart is undying—'amour ne meurt jamais en un cœur généreux,' says d'Urfé, 'que la racine n'en soit entièrement arrachée'; lovers die of unrequited love. Céladon's state of mind, when he is banished from Astrée, is pitiable:

Déjà par deux fois le jour avait fait place à la nuit avant que ce berger se ressouvînt de manger, car ses tristes pensers l'occupaient de sorte, et la mélancolie lui remplissait si bien l'estomac qu'il n'avait point d'appétit d'autre viande, que de celle que le ressouvenir de ses ennuis pouvait lui préparer, détrempée avec tant de larmes que ses yeux semblaient deux sources de fontaine.

But love, in *L'Astrée*, is not always spiritual or ideal. D'Urfé's lovers and ladies are all different, and all love in different ways. Lycidas is less constant than his brother, Céladon. 'Lycidas qui n'avait point de patience, fit dessein plusieurs fois de ne l'aimer plus,' we are told; and, although he loves Philis, he succumbs to the pursuit of Olimpe and gets her with child. Hylas represents sensuality and inconstancy, and has his female counterpart in Stelle, whom he eventually marries. Even Céladon assumes feminine dress in order to be admitted to the temple and see Astrée naked.

Love is the main interest of the characters, and they and their creator thoroughly understand it. They are close observers of each other and—already in 1607—can analyse love and comment on its progress with the subtlety typical of the seventeenth century. Callirée, curious about her brother's feelings for Diane, tells him that, had she been a man, she would have loved Diane.

'Je pense, répliqua-t-il, que si cela était, vous ne seriez pas sans affaire: car à ce que j'ai pu juger, elle est d'une humeur, qui ne serait pas aisée à fléchir, outre que Filidas en meurt de jalousie, et Amidor la veille de sorte, que jamais elle n'est sans l'un des deux.'

Callirée is quick to see the implications of this reply: 'O mon frère, s'écria-t-elle, tu es pris, puisque tu as remarqué ces particularités!' She then gives him some shrewd advice about wooing. Hylas, too, is a keen observer:

Car ressouvenez-vous, gentil Paris, que quoi que feigne une femme, elle ne peut s'empêcher de ressentir la perte d'un amant, d'autant qu'il semble que ce soit un outrage à sa beauté, et la beauté étant ce que ce sexe a de plus cher, est la partie la plus sensible qui soit en elles.

In addition to its narrative technique, its diversity, its skilful characterization, and its psychological subtlety, *L'Astrée* owes much of its charm to the style of its author. Clear and unhurried, well-knit and harmonious, his sentences are a delight to read. To take one specimen at random:

Cela fut cause que Galathée se résolut de parler le moins souvent qu'il lui serait possible à Lindamor, et de trouver quelque invention pour lui envoyer de ses lettres, et en recevoir secrètement. Et pour cet effet, elle fit dessein sur Fleurial, neveu de la nourrice d'Amasis, et frère de la sienne, duquel elle avait souvent reconnu la bonne volonté, parce qu'étant jardinier en ses beaux jardins de Montbrison, ainsi que son père toute sa vie l'avait été, lorsqu'on y menait promener Galathée, il la prenait bien souvent entre ses bras, et lui allait amassant les fleurs qu'elle voulait. Et vous savez que ces amitiés d'enfance, étant comme sucées avec le lait, se tournent presque en nature, outre qu'elle savait bien que tous vieillards étant avares, faisant du bien à cestuy-ci, elle se l'acquerrait entièrement.

Although this paragraph consists of three sentences, they are so closely linked, the second and third both beginning with 'Et', as almost to form one. One notices, too, how careful d'Urfé is to make everything clear, to explain all the circumstances and analyse the reasons for Galathée's choice of a messenger. It is interesting to see the psychological realism, the absence of sentimentality: Fleurial is devoted to Galathée, but he is also fond of money, and Galathée relies on his greed to reinforce his loyalty. D'Urfé, for all his idealism, never loses sight of human nature.

D'Urfé's prose, like his story, is diversified: narrative, discussion and argument, conversation, subtle reasoning, letters, poems and songs, all play their part. Indeed, one reason for the appeal of the book in its own day was probably that it served, not only to entertain, but also as a manual of letter-writing, of polite conversation, of etiquette, and social behaviour. Leisurely in its style and the progress of its narrative, transporting us into a world of shepherds, nymphs, and druids, and yet at the same time creating convincing characters and shrewdly analysing human nature, uniting subtlety with charm, *L'Astrée* appeals both to the escapist and to the psychologist in us all.

The first and the best of the long historical romances of the seventeenth century, *L'Astrée* had many successors, though in most the pastoral setting was discarded. Gomberville (1600–74)[2] was d'Urfé's immediate successor; a later generation was delighted by the novels of La Calprenède (1601 or 1610–63),[3] and recognized itself in Mlle de Scudéry (1607–1701), the authoress of the *Grand Cyrus* (ten volumes, 1649–53) and of *Clélie* (ten volumes, 1654–1660), with its famous *Carte de Tendre*.

If psychological realism characterizes *L'Astrée*, a more earthy kind of realism is found in a number of other works of the same period: the *Moyen de Parvenir* of Béroalde de Verville (1556–1629?), the *Aventures du Baron de Fæneste* of Agrippa d'Aubigné (1551–1630), the anonymous *Caquets de l'Accouchée*, and the *Francion* of Charles Sorel (c. 1602–74).

The *Moyen de Parvenir* (1610?) describes an imaginary feast at which the guests argue and exchange anecdotes; amusing, though bawdy, the book continues the French 'gaulois' tradition and is clearly influenced by Rabelais. The *Baron de Fæneste* (1617–30), by the author of *Les Tragiques*,[4] is a series of conversations, mainly between the cowardly, swashbuckling braggart, the Catholic baron de Fæneste, the exponent of *paraître*, and the Protestant Enay, who represents *être*. In the course of the conversations, Fæneste relates his life and adventures, his experience at court and in the field, and narrates various anecdotes and exploits. The dress, the manners, and the fashionable speech of the day are described, religious controversies are touched on, and the book ends with an allegorical description of the age as the triumph of impiety, ignorance, cowardice, and greed. Here, too, the influence of Rabelais is visible. The *Caquets de l'Accouchée* (1623)[5] is a series of conversations amongst women visiting, according to the custom, a friend in childbed. These lively dialogues, particularly the first three,[6] castigate the age, of which they afford some vivid glimpses – the extravagance and immorality of the middle classes who have taken to aping their betters, the rapacity and dishonesty of officials, the corruption of justice, the cost of living and the prevalence of mendicity – , and form a valuable social document.

The most notable work in this vein of comic realism, however, is the *Histoire comique de Francion* (1623–33), the chief work of the novelist Charles Sorel. *Francion* is a somewhat formless work. In Book I, which, like Goldsmith's comedy, might bear the

---

[2] *Carithée* (1621); *Polexandre* (1629–37).
[3] *Cassandre* (1642–5); *Cléopâtre* (1647–58).
[4] *Les Tragiques*, though not published until 1616, were begun in 1575 and clearly belong to the sixteenth century; they are, therefore, discussed in Volume I of this *History*.
[5] The various parts had appeared separately in the previous year.
[6] The others are by different hands.

subtitle, *The Mistakes of a Night*, the hero, Francion, attempting
to keep an assignation with his mistress, is involved in a series of
comic episodes. In Book II, the story of his mistress's life is related.
In Books III to VI, Francion relates his own life. He falls in love
with an Italian widow, Naïs, whose portrait he sees, and sets out to
go and see her in Book VII;[7] his adventures on the way and his
marriage with Naïs fill the remaining four books. But the story
is not the main interest of the novel. *Francion* is a highly entertaining work, interesting above all for the picture it gives of seventeenth-century life and society; it has been called 'le premier en
date des romans de mœurs français' – in this connection, the
first seven books, those published in 1623, are the best. In reaction
to Honoré d'Urfé – indeed, Sorel parodied *L'Astrée* in a later
novel, *Le Berger extravagant* (1627) – , Sorel deliberately aimed at
the realism of everyday life.

J'ai représenté aussi naïvement qu'il se pouvait faire, les humeurs, les
actions, et les propos ordinaires de toutes les personnes que j'ai mises
sur les rangs,

he says in the preface to the 1623 edition, and claims with some
justice in a later preface

que dans mon livre on peut trouver la langue française tout entière, et
que je n'ai point oublié les mots dont use le vulgaire, ce qui ne se voit
pas partout, car dans les livres sérieux l'on n'a pas la liberté de se
plaire à cela et cependant ces choses basses sont souvent plus agréables
que les plus relevées.

*Francion* contains comic episodes, accounts of pranks and practical jokes, not dissimilar to some of those in Béroalde de Verville,
but the realism of Sorel goes deeper than this. Many aspects of
seventeenth-century French life are vividly described. Francion
visits the court, with its turbulent pages, and its ignorant, extravagant, and debauched courtiers, addicted to *galimatias*, and witnesses a court ballet. The palais de justice is described, and various
features of the legal profession criticized – the sale of magistracies
to incompetent young men of wealth, the practice among these
same young magistrates of dressing as noblemen, the rapacity and
the venality of lawyers. At the other end of the social scale, we see
the Paris underworld, with its prostitutes and bawds, and its bands
of thieves and cardsharpers in league with the officers of justice.
A village wedding is amusingly described at length. Francion,
dressed as a charlatan, vaunts his wares, and an extractor of teeth
exercises his trade on the Pont-Neuf. Nor is the world of letters
absent. Francion goes to a bookshop, makes the acquaintance of

[7] These books were redivided in subsequent editions into eight.

the bookseller, and is introduced to literary circles in the capital; he alludes unkindly to Malherbe.

The most unforgettable pages, however, are those dealing with the education of Francion at the collège de Lisieux in Paris. The hard life of the boys, starved by a parsimonious housemaster, shivering with cold in unheated rooms in winter, and brutally punished for any offence – their habits, their dress, and their pranks; their teachers, dirty and pedantic – exemplified by Hortensius; their lessons and their performance of a tragedy – all pass before us. Schoolboys, the following glimpse of Francion suggests, do not change much over the centuries:

Figurez-vous donc de voir entrer Francion en classe, le caleçon sortant de son haut de chausse jusques à ses souliers, la robe mise tout de travers, et le porte-feuille dessous le bras, tâchant de donner un pourri[8] à l'un et une nasarde à l'autre: toujours j'avais un roman caché dessus moi, que je lisais en mettant mes autres livres au devant, de peur que le Régent ne l'aperçût . . .

*Francion* has another side to it: the hero is proposed as an ideal character, in whom Sorel clearly embodies some of his own views – Sorel's own works are attributed to Francion in Book XI. Francion is a kind of knight-errant: 'Il me semblait que comme Hercule, je ne fusse né que pour chasser les monstres de la terre,' he says; and he is described as 'notre Marquis qui veut tout savoir, et qui veut punir tous les forfaits qu'il voit commettre.' He unites all the most admirable personal qualities:

Il avait bonne façon: il chantait bien: il jouait de plusieurs instruments de musique: il était d'une humeur la plus douce et la plus complaisante du monde: il était grandement savant, parlait extrêmement bien, et écrivait encore mieux, et ce n'était point sur un seul sujet, mais sur tous. Il composait en vers et en prose, et réussissait à tous les deux. Quand il parlait d'une chose sérieuse, il ne disait que des merveilles; et s'il tombait en des railleries, il eût fait rire un Stoïque. L'on en voit assez qui ont quelqu'une de ces perfections mais où sont ceux qui les ont toutes, et encore en un degré éminent, comme il les avait?

Since Francion is an idealized Sorel, his views are not without interest. He is a disciple of the stoics, able to control his desires and preserving undismayed his fortitude, his serenity, and his good humour in the most disheartening circumstances. He is something of a philosopher: in prison, he reflects,

qu'il valait bien autant être enfermé comme il était, que d'être en franchise parmi le monde, où c'est une folie que d'espérer quelque vrai repos. Pour le moins il était là délivré de la vue des débordements du siècle, et avait tout loisir de nourrir son esprit de diverses pensées, et de philosopher profondément.

[8] A kind of blow.

Free from the superstitions of the vulgar, convinced that the belief in spirits and in magic is based on 'des accidents ordinaires et naturels, mais dont la cause est inconnue à leurs esprits simples et grossiers,' he is something of a *libertin* in both senses of the word, addicted to sensual pleasures and free from prejudice. '[Je] m'étudiai à savoir la raison naturelle de toutes choses,' he says, 'et avoir de bons sentiments en toutes occasions, sans m'arrêter aux opinions vulgaires.' He disseminates his 'nouvelle philosophie' at court, which has led M. Adam to suggest that Francion may be a portrait of Théophile. He attacks the institution of marriage and upholds free love; one advantage of which would be that

l'on serait contraint d'abolir toute prééminence et toute noblesse, chacun serait égal, et les fruits de la terre seraient communs. Les lois naturelles seraient alors révérées toutes seules.

Despite this, Francion is not free from a bias in favour of noble birth. He is proud of his own noble birth, and wants nobles to be noble, to realize that true nobility does not reside in external qualities or endowments:

ce n'est pas savoir bien piquer un cheval, ni manier une épée, ni se pannader avec de riches accoutrements [...] c'est avoir une âme qui résiste à tous les assauts que lui peut livrer la fortune, et qui ne mêle rien de bas parmi ses actions.

One of the 'principaux ornements de la noblesse' is also liberality. He despises the baseness and vulgarity of the lower orders, insists that bourgeois should not dress above their station, and has a particular hatred for lawyers, tax farmers, and merchants, against whom he forms a band of young men.

But if Sorel's ideas give a certain added interest to *Francion*, its perennial appeal lies in its amusing, though sometimes coarse, comic episodes, and in its portrayal of seventeenth-century types and scenes.

## II. SAINT FRANÇOIS DE SALES

The *Introduction à la vie dévote* (1609, revised edition 1619), the best-known work of Saint François de Sales (1567–1622), is deeply imbued with the spirit of the Counter-Reformation or what Brémond has called 'l'humanisme dévot'. The teaching of its author has none of the forbidding austerity of the Jansenists later in the century; he has, indeed, far more in common with their rivals, the Jesuits. He is well aware of the limitations of human nature, and never demands the impossible or runs the risk of repelling the neophyte; he is perfectly content to allow the hope of Heaven or the fear of Hell to play their part in the meditations

of his charge, and he is chary of forbidding over-frequent communion. The main concern of Saint François de Sales is to make
religion attractive and to bring the devout life within reach of the
layman – the *Introduction*, in fact, is based on his letters to Mme
de Charmoisy, the wife of a kinsman, whose spiritual director he
was. He points out, for instance, not without humour, that the
devout life is less exacting than the social round:

Nous avons vu des gentils hommes et des dames passer la nuit entière,
ains plusieurs nuits de suite, à jouer aux échecs et aux cartes. Y a-t-il
une attention plus chagrine, plus mélancolique et plus sombre que celle-
là? les mondains néanmoins ne disaient mot, les amis ne se mettaient
point en peine; et pour la méditation d'une heure, ou pour nous voir
lever un peu plus matin qu'à l'ordinaire pour nous préparer à la communion, chacun court au médecin, pour nous faire guérir de l'humeur
hypocondriaque et de la jaunisse. On passera trente nuits à danser: nul
ne s'en plaint; et pour la veille seule de la nuit de Noël, chacun tousse et
crie au ventre le jour suivant.

He excels at making the devout life seem delicious, as when he
describes the various satisfactions it gives, or the Heavenly host
inviting the sinner to change his ways, or the delights of prayer:

L'oraison faite en l'union de ce divin sacrifice [the mass] a une force
indicible, de sorte, Philothée, que par icelui, l'âme abonde en célestes
faveurs, comme appuyée sur son bien-aimé, qui la rend si pleine d'odeurs
et suavités spirituelles, qu'elle ressemble à une colonne de fumée de
bois aromatique, de la myrrhe, de l'encens et de toutes les poudres du
parfumeur, comme il est dit ès Cantiques.

The devout life, insists Saint François, is not the preserve of
the monk or the nun; worldly life is equally compatible with
religion:

Je veux dire, un avocat doit savoir passer de l'oraison à la plaidoirie; le
marchand, au trafic; la femme mariée, au devoir de son mariage et au
tracas de son ménage, avec tant de douceur et de tranquillité que pour
cela son esprit n'en soit point troublé; car, puisque l'un et l'autre est
selon la volonté de Dieu, il faut faire le passage de l'un à l'autre en esprit
d'humilité et dévotion.

The pious person should be contented with his profession, since
God can be served by the performance of one's daily tasks, and
since there is time, even in the busiest life, for worship and prayer.
But, if one lives in the world, one cannot imitate the saints exactly;
and Saint François is always ready to temper the demands of
religion in the interests of life in society. Every profession requires
different virtues, and one should cultivate particularly those of
one's own profession. It is right to keep one's proper rank in
society, to care about one's reputation, to amass wealth; there is
no obligation to be poor. Chastity does not preclude marriage;
and though Saint François deprecates second marriages, he does

not completely condemn them. Civility need not be sacrificed to truthfulness – Saint François is no Alceste. It is wrong to shun society, and if one mixes in society, one should behave like an *honnête homme*. Saint François does not use the expression, but his advice to the *dévot* on the best way to behave in society would not be out of place in a treatise on *honnêteté*: he must allow a 'joie modérée' to predominate in his conversation, and he should dress well:

Pour moi, je voudrais que mon dévot et ma dévote fussent toujours les mieux habillés de la troupe, mais les moins pompeux et affétés, et, comme il est dit au proverbe, qu'ils fussent parés de grâce, bienséance et dignité.

Even one's religious duties may be modified if they conflict with one's duties to one's superiors – e.g. if, by going frequently to communion, we offend those in authority over us, we need not go above once a fortnight. As for the religious austerities to which the seventeenth-century convert was prone, Saint François counsels moderation. Fasting and the use of the hairshirt and the lash should not be carried too far; there is nothing wrong in having particular friendships; and he lays stress on the need for recreation. If he disapproves of gambling and dancing, he does not condemn even these absolutely.

He is indulgent towards the weaknesses of human nature. He knows that the *dévot* is liable to be assailed by temptation and that he will traverse periods of spiritual aridity; and he is ready to counsel means of resisting the one and combating the other. But, wise and understanding as he is, he is never lax; on occasion, in condemning love affairs, for example, he can be intransigent: 'J'écrie tout haut à quiconque est tombé dans ces pièges d'amourettes: "Taillez, tranchez, rompez" '. . .

Saint François seems to be conscious that, if his book is to make religion attractive, it must be itself attractive. The style is clear and harmonious, and the work is diversified by anecdotes, quotations, and illustrations, drawn mainly from the lives of the Saints or the Scriptures. The most striking feature, however, is the proliferation of similes, one of the chief attractions of the *Introduction* and reminiscent of the baroque architect's love of ornament. Saint François's similes, though, are more than mere ornaments; they serve a functional purpose, enabling him to make his points clearly and vividly:

Le scorpion qui nous a piqués est vénéneux en nous piquant, mais étant réduit en huile c'est un grand médicament contre sa propre piqûre: le péché n'est honteux que quand nous le faisons, mais étant converti en confession et pénitence, il est honorable et salutaire.

Whatever the point to be made, an apt and striking comparison
wells up in Saint François's mind. His similes are very varied.
Sometimes they are brief, sometimes long and elaborate, consisting
sometimes of a whole anecdote. There is one on almost every page;
at times we find a whole cluster of them:

Et je leur montre que comme les mères perles vivent emmi la mer sans
prendre aucune goutte d'eau marine, et que vers les îles Chélidoines il
y a des fontaines d'eau bien douce au milieu de la mer, et que les
piraustes volent dedans les flammes sans brûler leurs ailes, ainsi peut
une âme vigoureuse et constante vivre au monde sans recevoir aucune
humeur mondaine, trouver des sources d'une douce piété au milieu des ondes
amères de ce siècle, et voler entre les flammes des convoitises terrestres sans
brûler les ailes des sacrés désirs de la vie dévote.            (Préface)

A passage such as this reminds us of the contemporary baroque
poets; so does the occasional elaborate and far-fetched comparison:

... comme une femme enceinte prépare le berceau, les linges et bandelettes, et même une nourrice pour l'enfant qu'elle espère faire, encore
qu'il ne soit pas au monde, ainsi Notre Seigneur ayant sa bonté grosse et
enceinte de vous, prétendant de vous enfanter au salut et vous rendre
sa fille, prépara sur l'arbre de la Croix tout ce qu'il fallait pour vous: votre
berceau spirituel, vos linges et bandelettes, votre nourrice et tout ce qui
était convenable pour votre bonheur.

Saint François draws his similes from a wide range of sources –
the Bible, Church history and the lives of Saints, and classical
antiquity, but also, and chiefly, from agriculture and natural history
(he has an especial fondness for bees and honey), the various
activities of society, and everyday life. The best, perhaps, are the
familiar, homely ones which show that Saint François, the mystic,
was also a close observer of the humble reality around him:

Un enfant pleurera tendrement, s'il voit donner un coup de lancette à sa
mère qu'on saigne; mais si à même temps sa mère, pour laquelle il
pleurait, lui demande une pomme ou un cornet de dragées qu'il tient en
sa main, il ne le voudra nullement lâcher.

The *Introduction à la vie dévote* is an attractive compound of
mysticism, practical advice, psychological penetration, and shrewd
observation. It is a delight to read, for the qualities of the style
and the poetry of the similes, if for no other reason; but even the
Protestant and the non-believer may derive profit, as well as
pleasure, from contact with the tolerance and the tranquil wisdom
of this kindly 'Gentleman Saint'.


### III. BALZAC

Though the works of Guez de Balzac (1597–1654) can still
give pleasure, it is unlikely that his reputation will ever again stand

as high as it did in his own time, when he was regarded as the restorer of the eloquence of antiquity, the '*unico eloquente*'. 'L'Eloquence,' says the *Avertissement* to the third edition of his letters, 's'y voit mise au plus haut degré de gloire et d'admiration où les Romains et les Grecs l'aient jamais élevée'; and Tallemant des Réaux, à propos of the first appearance of these letters in 1624, writes:

Il est certain que nous n'avions rien vu d'approchant en France, et que tous ceux qui ont bien écrit en prose depuis, et qui écriront bien à l'avenir en notre langue, lui en auront l'obligation.

Balzac, indeed, did for prose what Malherbe had done for verse — 'nous devons à ce grand homme le bel arrangement de nos mots et la belle cadence de nos périodes,' says Bouhours; and there are several points of similarity between the two. Like Malherbe, Balzac wrote slowly:

Mais véritablement un homme qui s'est proposé l'idée de la perfection, et qui travaille pour l'Eternité, ne peut rien laisser sortir de son esprit qu'après s'être longtemps consulté soi-même.

He prized above all — as he says of his Socrate chrétien — 'la douceur et la netteté', and, like Malherbe, he is often more interesting for the nobility and harmony of his style than for the intrinsic interest of the matter.

This is not, however, to say that the subject-matter of his works is devoid of interest. Balzac protested against the view that style was everything:

Il est vrai que je donne beaucoup à l'élocution, et je sais que les grandes choses ont besoin de l'aide des paroles, et qu'après avoir été bien conçues, elles doivent être heureusement exprimées. Il me fâche seulement que de la moindre partie de la Rhétorique des anciens on en veuille faire toute la nôtre, et que pour contenter les petits esprits, il faille que nos ouvrages ressemblent à ces victimes, à qui on ôtait le cœur, et on laissait seulement la langue de reste.

*Le Prince* (1631), if it takes the form of an extravagant panegyric of Louis XIII and a justification of his policy, is also an expression of a political doctrine, a portrait of the ideal sovereign. *Le Prince* was completed by *Aristippe ou de la Cour* (1658), in which Balzac insists on the importance of the wise choice of ministers by the sovereign, lists the different types to be avoided, and gives an account of the good minister. A passage from a letter of 1621 may serve as a summary of these works:

Pour moi, comme je trouve bon que la puissance souveraine soit modérée par le conseil des gens de bien, je n'ai jamais approuvé qu'elle fût affaiblie par la désobéissance des rebelles. La liberté ne doit pas être plus éloignée de la servitude que de la licence, et pour rendre un Etat heureux il faut qu'un Prince aime ses sujets qui le redoutent.

If, in some of the early letters, it is possible to detect leanings towards *libertinage* (not least in their somewhat lax morality), Balzac, particularly after the condemnation of Théophile, an old associate of his, returned to the Catholic fold, and in his *Socrate chrétien* (1652) he gives his profession of faith, and discusses various religious matters. In his letters, on which his reputation mainly rests, he touches on many subjects. In some, on the death of a friend or patron, he eulogizes the dead and exhorts the living to be comforted (we are reminded of the *Consolations* of Malherbe). In others, he treats general themes or gives general advice – discusses the transience of beauty, recommends patience in misfortune, counsels chastity (but considers that it should be coupled with leniency towards the frailty of others), gives advice about life at court or in society, and expounds the principles of *honnêteté*. Sometimes he touches on literary topics, describing his own aims in writing, or giving his views on *Le Cid* or *Cinna*. Sometimes he discusses politics or current affairs. Most interesting, perhaps, are those letters in which he strikes a personal note – those in which he describes Rome or his life there or his sufferings from sciatica, those in which he describes his country estate and his daily life, or expresses his tastes, his preference for seclusion, and his love of nature.

Nevertheless, it is as a stylist that he was most influential. Balzac's style is clear and harmonious:

La diction en [of his letters] est pure, les paroles autant choisies qu'elles le peuvent être, pour n'avoir rien d'affecté, le sens clair et net, et les périodes accomplies de tous leurs nombres,

wrote Richelieu. There is nothing rambling or formless about Balzac's sentences; the sixteenth century gives way in his prose to the symmetry and the balance of the seventeenth. He particularly excelled in the long, artistically-constructed period – the following paragraph from *Le Prince* may, perhaps, remind the English reader of Gibbon:

Lorsque les Goths, les Vandales, les Gépides, les Alains, les Huns, les Quades, les Hérules et ces autres ennemis du genre humain, quittèrent leur misérable patrie et coururent diverses contrées de l'univers pour chercher de plus heureuses demeures et un ciel moins fâcheux que celui de leur naissance, Lorsqu'avec des visages extraordinaires, une parole non articulée et des peaux de bêtes sauvages, qui les cachaient jusques aux yeux, ils portèrent de tous côtés la mort et la servitude, et qu'il se fit un changement presque universel de lois, de coutumes, de gouvernement et de langage: Si Dieu eût suscité un prince comme le nôtre, qui eût pu fermer à ces gens du Nord l'entrée des Gaules et de l'Italie, et les eût renvoyés habiter leurs forêts et souffrir les rigueurs de leur Hiver éternel; S'il y eût eu un Louis le Juste pour opposer aux Gensérics et aux Alarics, pour châtier Attila et Totila, et semblables usurpateurs qu'on ne saurait nommer sans se faire mal à la bouche et blesser les oreilles françaises; la vertu de ce généreux défenseur de la liberté serait aujourd'hui en vénération partout où il s'assemble des hommes et où l'on observe quelque forme de police. Il ne nous resterait rien de lui que la piété publique ne consacrât et ne mît au nombre des choses saintes: Son triomphe durerait encore et se continuerait par l'équitable postérité dans la succession de tous les âges.

The danger of this kind of writing is that it may sometimes seem strained, as Balzac himself admitted in a letter to Boisrobert:

J'avoue que j'écris de la même sorte qu'on bâtit les temples et les palais, et que je tire quelquefois les choses de loin, comme il faut faire deux milles lieues pour amener en Espagne les trésors de l'Amérique.

And too many of his letters are filled with extravagant or over-elaborate compliments, which explain why Balzac's style should have lent itself to parody (by Sorel in the person of Hortensius in the eleventh book of his *Francion*), how a comedy could be made by piecing together passages of Balzac (*La Comédie des Comédies*, 1628?), and why Boileau should later complain of his 'affectation' and his 'enflure' — 'les deux vices les plus opposés au genre épistolaire'. But if Balzac's grandiloquence sometimes degenerates into empty word-spinning, at his best, when the matter is worthy of the style, he is a master of French prose.

*Chapter 5*

# DRAMA

## I. TRAGEDY

IF THE undramatic tragedy of the sixteenth century, with its interminable speeches and its lack of action and dramatic interest, survived into the early years of the seventeenth century – in some of the plays of Montchrétien, for instance –, a more theatrical kind of play was being evolved.

The chief – though not the only – playwright of the period was Alexandre Hardy (c. 1572–1632). Employed by a company of actors and probably the first professional dramatist, Hardy was extraordinarily prolific. Only a small proportion of his enormous output of between six and seven hundred plays has, however, survived. He published *Théagène et Chariclée* in eight *journées* in 1623 and a selection of his other plays in five volumes (1624–1628): this contains thirty-three plays in all – presumably the best: twelve tragedies, sixteen tragi-comedies, and five pastorals. The bulk of his work is lost, and one cannot regret it.

Whereas the tragedies of the great seventeenth-century dramatists, Corneille and Racine, show a given situation working itself out, those of Hardy show the successive episodes of a story. A typical play is *Coriolan* (probably written before 1610), thus constructed:

*Act I.*
*Scene 1.* Coriolan complains of the ingratitude of the populace and vows to be revenged. Volomnie, his mother, beseeches him, in vain, to submit.
*Scene 2.* He is summoned before the tribunes and tried in the presence of the Senate and a chorus of Roman citizens. He is accused of tyranny and condemned to perpetual banishment.
*Act II.*
*Scene 1.* Consumed by hatred, Coriolan determines to join the chief enemies of Rome, the Volsci.
*Scene 2.* The leader of the Volsci, Amfidie, bewails the invincibility of Rome. The arrival of a stranger is reported.
*Scene 3.* Coriolan is brought in, reveals himself, and offers his services. Amfidie welcomes him and undertakes to serve under him.
*Act III.*
*Scene 1.* [Coriolan, having inflicted severe defeats on Rome is besieging

56

the city.] The Senate hears his peace terms and instructs its ambassadors to return and appeal to him again.
*Scene 2.* Monologue of Coriolan: his thirst for revenge.
*Scene 3.* Coriolan receives the ambassadors once more: he refuses to relent.
*Act IV.*
*Scene 1.* Valérie resolves to ask Coriolan's mother to intercede.
*Scene 2.* Monologue of Amfidie: jealous and mistrustful of Coriolan, he is resolved to destroy him.
*Scene 3.* Valérie persuades Coriolan's mother, Volomnie, to appeal to her son.
*Scene 4.* Volomnie and Valérie appear before Coriolan and the council of the Volsci. Coriolan agrees to withdraw his army from Rome, knowing that this means his death.
*Act V.*
*Scene 1.* Dreams and omens fill Coriolan, who has raised the siege, with forebodings. He is summoned before the council of the Volsci.
*Scene 2.* Coriolan appears before the council. Amfidie calls on him to justify himself. Coriolan is found guilty of treachery and murdered.
*Scene 3.* Monologue of Volomnie: her forebodings. A messenger arrives and relates the death of Coriolan to her. Her laments.

It is apparent from this summary both that there is much more action than in Renaissance tragedy, and that, unlike both his Renaissance predecessors and his later seventeenth-century successors, Hardy knows nothing of the unities or of the *bienséances*. The action of the play obviously requires several months at least, and the scene shifts between several different localities – the *décor simultané*[1] was clearly used in the staging of the play. In some of his plays, the unity of action is disregarded: the first three acts of *Panthée* deal with Araspe's attempt to seduce Panthée, the last two with the death of her husband in Cyrus's service. The first three acts and a half of *Timoclée* describe the revolt of Athens and Thebes against Alexander; the last one and a half show the rape of Timoclée after the storming of Thebes. Action is shown on the stage – the death of Coriolan, for example. In *Méléagre*, the audience sees Méléagre's uncles taking from Atalante the boar's head she has won, and being killed later by Méléagre. In *Achille*, a battle is shown; and in *Timoclée*, we see the Macedonians storming Thebes, and Timoclée being raped and later drowning her assailant. This last example shows that Hardy is not only not averse from violent action, but does not attach importance to propriety in the narrower sense. In *Scédase*, two young men rape and murder two girls on the stage; *Lucrèce* is a play about an adulteress.

In most, not all, of Hardy's tragedies there is a chorus. Sometimes the chorus recites odes commenting on the action in the Greek manner. In some plays, there are no choric odes, but groups of people play a part in the action, one of them acting as spokes-

[1] See below, p. 115.

man for the rest.[2] In *Coriolan*, there are a chorus of Roman citizens, the Roman senate, the council of the Volsci, and a chorus of Roman ladies: the first scene of the third act, in fact, is entirely between three such groups, the Senate, the chorus of Romans, and the ambassadors of the Senate.

With the possible exception of *Timoclée*, in which the heroine, who has murdered her ravisher, is pardoned and reinstated in her possessions by Alexander, all Hardy's tragedies have an unhappy ending. There is usually no suspense, no doubt about the eventual outcome – often unambiguously foretold by dreams, omens and ghosts –, though, in *Panthée* and *Lucrèce*, the outcome is not known from the outset and might have been different. The tragic principle varies. Love brings about the downfall of Didon and Achille. In other plays, the hero or heroine suffers from the criminal nature of his fellow-men: Daire is betrayed by his own followers; Scédase's daughters are the victims of the lust of two young men, and their father kills himself in protest against the injustice of the world. Alexander (in *La Mort d'Alexandre*) and Lucrèce (in *Lucrèce*) are punished for their own crimes. *Alcméon* – which is in spirit not unlike Corneille's *Médée* later – is a play of violence and horror, of passion and revenge. Alcméon has killed his mother, but at his father's behest, and he is the helpless victim of an adulterous passion. His wife administers a poison to him which drives him mad, and in his madness he murders his children. His wife's brothers fight with him, and all three are killed.

Hardy is not easy reading. His language is archaic, he has a fondness for long sentences which it is not always easy to disentangle, and he is often bombastic. On the other hand, his style is more concrete than that of his successors, and abounds in touches of natural description and elaborate similes. His lovers can dwell in detail on the charms of their ladies; and one may regret that such a passage as this could find no place in Corneille or Racine:

> Elle [la commune] use de ses chefs ainsi que du platane,
> Que par un temps serein le voyageur profane,
> Ebranche ses rameaux, regrettables alors
> Qu'un nuage vengeur lui mouille tout le corps:
> De même nous voyons à sec sur le rivage
> Un vaisseau dépecé par l'injure de l'âge,
> Où le marchand ingrat a dépouillé cent fois
> Les avares trésors de l'un et l'autre Indois,
> Qui bâtit sa fortune, et préserva sa vie,
> Tels, tels sont les effets journaliers de l'envie . . .
> (*Coriolan*)

[2] As is shown by *Alcée*:
> Au nom de tous un porte le suffrage.

The absence of any preoccupation with *bienséance* gives his verse a picturesqueness which disappeared from later seventeenth-century drama:

> Encor si je portais de toi dans mes entrailles,
> Par la fuite absenté quelque gage d'amour:
> Et qu'un petit Aenée apparût en ma Cour,
> Folâtre en jeux d'enfants du tout abandonnée;
> Je ne réputerais ma couche infortunée!
>
> *(Didon se sacrifiant)*

Hardy's tragedies represent a transitional stage in French drama. They at once continue the Renaissance and anticipate Corneille and Racine. They contain more action than those of Jodelle or Garnier, but there is little suspense, surprise, or psychological interest. Some of the stylistic features which Hardy inherited from his predecessors he passed on to Corneille—the fondness for *sentences* and stychomythia, for verbal repetition and parallelism between lines (though Hardy lacks Corneille's skill):

> { Je ne puis, je ne puis d'espoir me rassurer,
> { Je ne puis rien de bon pour mon fils augurer;
> Développé d'un banc, un gouffre le menace.
> { Sujet ainsi qu'il fut à une populace,
> { Sujet à rendre compte à un peuple étranger,
> En quoi plus périlleux je prévois son danger,
> { De ce qui s'est omis en sa charge passée,
> { D'une paix à quoi l'a ma prière forcée,
> Aux Volsques dommageable, aux Volsques qui pouvaient
> Mieux user contre nous des armes qu'ils avaient ...
>
> *(Coriolan)*

Like Corneille, Hardy is fond of council scenes, though again without Corneille's mastery. The first two acts of *Timoclée* are council scenes: in the first, Alexander and his councillors debate how to treat the rebels; in the second, the Athenians debate whether to help Thebes or not. Moreover, if Hardy's tragedies are irregular, they are quite simple, and in the main observe the unity of tone—there is little or no admixture of comedy, and none of the mixture of prose and verse we find in Shakespeare. In fact, if *Coriolan* has been discussed in some detail, it is partly to show how different it is from Shakespeare's tragedy on the same subject. Hardy's play is very much less complex—he gives us none of those conversations amongst groups of citizens, those impressions of different aspects of Coriolanus himself, which build up a comprehensive picture of the hero. In Hardy's play, which begins with the exile of Coriolanus from Rome, we do not really know why the people turn against him. No doubt the chief difference between Shakespeare and Hardy is that the former is a far more gifted poet and dramatist than the latter; but it is clear, too, that Hardy is not aiming at the same kind of play as Shakespeare.

Much more readable than the plays of Alexandre Hardy are the six tragedies published by Antoine de Montchrétien (1575?–1621),[3] whose verse is always clearer and more mellifluous than the crabbed and obscure style of Hardy. In the sixteenth-century tradition, some of his plays contain little action and lengthy monologues – *Sophonisbe* and *David*, for instance. *La Reine d'Ecosse* is broken-backed into the bargain, since Elizabeth is the centre of interest for two acts and Mary Queen of Scots for the last three. His other three tragedies, however, contain more action and are much more interesting. They seem to show some progression in dramatic technique. In *Les Lacènes*, a stirring play of heroic despair, the downfall of the hero is foretold at the outset. In *Aman*, it is not, and the humiliation of Aman in the fifth act, at the moment when his self-satisfaction is at its peak, is effective and dramatic. Indeed, it is by no means difficult to find this play nearer in spirit to the Bible than, and prefer it to, Racine's tragedy on the same subject. In *Hector*, though the dénouement is forecast at the beginning, there is an element of suspense. Andromaque, alarmed by a dream, tries to keep Hector at home. She fails but subsequently appeals to Priam and Hecuba, and, in reply to their entreaties, Hector agrees to remain away from the battle. A messenger announces that the Greeks have routed the Trojans, and this news is too much for Hector, who departs. Andromaque appeals once more to Priam, who consents to recall Hector. Then we learn that Hector has defeated Achilles. Not till Act V are we sure of Hector's fate. Here we have something of the dramatic technique of the later seventeenth century: unity of time, place, and action, continual suggestions that catastrophe may be avoided, and tragedy springing from the character of the hero.

Only one other tragedy of the period deserves to be mentioned. Théophile's *Amours tragiques de Pyrame et Thisbé* (c. 1621). Whereas Hardy's plays have little more than historical interest, *Pyrame* is a pleasure to read. Although written for the *décor multiple*, the play observes the unity of time: indeed, like a play of Corneille or Racine, it does not show the various episodes of a story, but begins near the crisis. When the play opens, Pyrame and Thisbé are in love; the enmity of the King, who is Pyrame's rival, causes them to elope together, with the unfortunate outcome familiar to us from the *Midsummer Night's Dream*. The action is simple – perhaps over-simple, since not all the scenes are strictly necessary to the development of the plot, and the fifth act consists

---

[3] *Sophonisbe* was published in 1596; his collected tragedies in 1601 (The second edition, 1604, contained *Hector* for the first time.)

of two lengthy monologues (the laments first of Pyrame, then of Thisbé). Moreover, the dénouement, brought about by the fortuitous appearance of a lion, would not have satisfied the requirements of the later seventeenth century.

*Pyrame*, a tragedy based on the invincibility of passion, expresses the philosophy of nature of Théophile, the *libertin*:

> On ne saurait dompter la passion humaine;
> Contre amour la raison est importune et vaine...          (I, 2)

> Laissez faire à Nature...                                 (II, 1)

It contains, too, an interesting attack on tyranny, on the doctrine that the sovereign is superior to the moral law. Above all, it is the work of Théophile, the poet. Not only has the style a limpidity which is lacking in Hardy, but there are some passages of memorable poetry – fine natural descriptions, and lines in which the two lovers give touching expression to their mutual love.


## II. TRAGI-COMEDY

Tragi-comedy seems to have enjoyed at least as much popularity as tragedy: Hardy's published work contains rather more tragi-comedies than tragedies, and, at the end of the period, tragi-comedy came to be the most popular genre. The most obvious difference between Hardy's tragedies and his tragi-comedies is that the latter end happily (*Aristoclée* is an exception); but there are others. The play still tells a story, but it is usually much more eventful, and the issue is in doubt, so that the reader or spectator is often left wondering what will happen next or how the happy ending will be brought about. Time and place are treated with even greater freedom than in the tragedies. In *La Force du Sang*, for example, the heroine, who has been raped in the interval between Acts I and II, tells her mother in Act III, scene 1, that nine months have elapsed since this misfortune, and that she is about to give birth to a child. In Act III, scene 4, the child, already six years old, appears on the stage. The action of *Félismène* passes from Spain to Germany; that of *Phraarte* takes place partly in Thrace, partly in Macedon; that of *Elmire* alternates between Egypt and Germany, with some scenes set in Italy as well. The first three acts of *Gésippe* are set in Athens; the last two in Rome; and, since the two parts of the play deal with separate episodes with a considerable lapse of time in between, the play is broken-backed. The action of the tragi-comedies is more complex and there are sometimes subplots – the love of the marquis de Bade for Elmire in the play of that name, and that of Don Sancho for Précieuse in *La Belle Egyptienne,* are inessential to the main plot. Nor are the *bienséances* respected: there is plenty of action on the stage, and a good deal of impropriety in the ordinary sense. The heroine of *La Force du Sang,* as we have said, is raped. In *Gésippe,* the hero, finding that his friend loves his bride to be, sends him to sleep with her on his wedding night. The heroine of *Phraarte* succumbs to her lover and appears on the stage with her child before marrying him at the end. In *Elmire ou l'heureuse bigamie,* a married Christian knight escapes from an Egyptian prison with the aid of a princess to whom he promises marriage; the Pope consents to this bigamous marriage, and the play ends with the knight promising to sleep with his two wives alternately.

The subjects are highly diversified. Some are on mythological subjects, *Procris, Alceste, Ariadne ravie, Le Ravissement de Proserpine,* and *La Gigantomachie* (which is, strictly speaking, described as a 'poème dramatique'). There is a strong vein of fancy in some of these. *Procris* deals with the love of the goddess, Aurora, for the mortal, Cephalis. In *Alceste,* Pluto, sitting in council, hears how Hercules has invaded his domains and captured Cerberus. *Ariadne ravie* ends with Bacchus coming to marry the deserted Ariadne. In *Le Ravissement de Proserpine* and *La Gigantomachie* (which relates the war between the Titans and the gods), the principal characters are all superhuman or divine. The other tragicomedies, whether the setting is classical or modern, are usually highly *romanesque,* and many are, in fact, taken from prose fiction – *Cornélie, La Force du Sang,* and *La Belle Egyptienne* from stories of Cervantes, *Félismène* from Montemayor's *Diana.* In all, there is plenty of scope for spectacle. In *La Gigantomachie,* the Titans fight the gods; Félismène dressed as a man kills her lover's assailants; and Pluto, one of the main characters in *Le Ravissement de Proserpine,* is thus described:

> Plus noir que son Enfer une paupière épaisse,
> Dont le poil hérissé comme d'un ours se dresse,
> Ses regards de travers feraient peur à la mort . . .

*Aristoclée* and *Dorise* stand somewhat apart from the other tragicomedies. *Aristoclée,* indeed, with its classical subject and its unhappy ending, might be considered as one of Hardy's tragedies – and one of the best, a tragedy of character. The dénouement is well motivated by the nature of the protagonists – the violence of the rejected suitor, the indecision of the father, and the fatalism of the bridegroom. *Dorise,* on the other hand, with its badinage and its love-plot, anticipates the kind of comedy that Corneille was to write in *Mélite.*

Apart from choric odes in *Arsacome* (III, 1) and *Aristoclée* (V, 3), the chorus has disappeared from Hardy's tragi-comedies; although in several plays a band of relatives, shepherds, children, villagers, soldiers, or the like puts in an appearance and speaks through the mouth of one of its number.

The term 'tragi-comedy' does not mean that the play is half a comedy. Comedy is entirely lacking in some of Hardy's tragi-comedies, though in others there are occasional comic scenes or an element of comedy. In the mythological plays, this is often provided by the mockery of one of the gods – e.g. Pan and Silenus at the end of *Ariadne ravie*, Momus in *Le Ravissement de Proserpine* and *La Gigantomachie*. In Act II of *Alceste*, Admetus's father and mother, after saying that they would gladly die to save their son, are given the opportunity of exchanging their lives for his – and find pretexts for refusing. In Act II of *Procris*, Cephalis assumes a disguise and makes love to his wife to test her fidelity; she is susceptible to his blandishments. In *Le Ravissement de Proserpine*, Pluto, with his amorous desires, and Venus, with her hypocrisy, are comic figures; so is Vulcan in *La Gigantomachie*, disgruntled, taunted by Mercury and Pallas, and bullied by Mars. A pert page provides a moment of comic relief in *Félismène* (II, 3). In *Gésippe*, the tone of the conversation between the heroine and the nurse (II, 2) and of the badinage between the lovers (II, 4) is that of comedy.

Hardy's tragi-comedies are too varied in character for any one of them to be typical; but an analysis of one may help to give some impression of the genre. Here is a brief summary of *La Belle Egyptienne:*

*Act I.*
*Scene 1.* Don Jean de Carcame declares his love to the gipsy-girl, Précieuse. Finding her virtuous, he asks her to marry him. She tells him that, according to the custom of the gipsies, he must live for two years as a gipsy first. He agrees.
*Scene 2.* Monologue by Don Sancho, who plans to seduce Précieuse by his verses and gifts of money.
*Act II.*
*Scene 1.* Don Sancho, disguised as Clément, presents Précieuse with some verses.
*Scene 2.* Don Jean, after a conflict between honour and love, sends word to Précieuse that he will join the gipsies the next day.
*Scene 3.* Don Ferdinand, seneschal of Seville, exhorts his wife, Guiomar, to control her grief: she has been inconsolable since the disappearance of their daughter in infancy ten years previously. Guiomar thinks that the child was stolen by gipsies.
*Scene 4.* The captain of the gipsies receives Don Jean into the band and gives him the name Andres. Précieuse shows him Clément's verses.
*Act III.*
*Scene 1.* Clément is attacked by the gipsies' dogs. Two gipsies take him into the encampment for treatment.

*Scene 2.* Clément is brought to Précieuse's grandmother to be healed of his wounds. Précieuse tells Andres that this is her poet. A little jealous, Andres tries to sound Clément, who denies that he is in love with Précieuse.
*Act IV.*
*Scene 1.* Carduche, a wealthy village girl, soliloquizes: she has fallen in love with Andres.
*Scene 2.* Andres undertakes to help Clément—who has killed two men—to escape to Italy. Carduche asks Andres to marry her; he tells her that he loves another, and she departs in dudgeon.
*Scene 3.* Précieuse soliloquizes: she has had a dream portending misfortune to Andres, followed by their happy marriage.
*Scene 4.* Carduche complains to the Alcade that a gipsy has stolen her jewels. The Alcade orders the gipsies to be pursued.
*Scene 5.* The Alcade and the villagers come to the gipsies' camp. Carduche accuses Andres of the theft, and the jewels are found in his valise (where Carduche had concealed them). He is arrested; a soldier strikes Andres, and Andres kills him.
*Act V.*
*Scene 1.* Don Ferdinand and Guiomar converse. The gipsies have been brought to Seville, where Don Ferdinand is to try Andres. Guiomar has seen Précieuse, who reminded her of her own lost daughter, and has sent for her.
*Scene 2.* Précieuse appeals to Guiomar to help Andres.
*Scene 3.* Précieuse's so-called grandmother decides to restore Précieuse to her real parents as the best means of saving Andres.
*Scene 4.* Andres in prison. The gaoler comes to take him before the judge.
*Scene 5.* Guiomar, overjoyed to have her daughter again, undertakes that the old gipsywoman shall not be punished. She sends for her husband and tells him the whole story of their daughter and Don Jean de Carcame. Since Don Jean's father is an old friend of Don Ferdinand's, Don Ferdinand is delighted that his daughter should want to marry him. Don Ferdinand sends for Don Jean (Andres) and resolves to play a trick on him. When Don Jean is brought in, Don Ferdinand tells him that he must die but that he must first marry Précieuse. Then he tells him who Précieuse is, and welcomes him as his son-in-law.

A romantic love story, a lover disguised as a gipsy, a long-lost daughter found again, action on the stage, changes of scene, a subplot (the Clément episode), an admixture of comedy (the avarice of Précieuse's grandmother), scenes from low life and from high life—such are the ingredients of an early seventeenth-century tragi-comedy

The distinction between tragedy and tragi-comedy is not always clear-cut. Four of Hardy's plays, for example—*Procris, Alceste, Ariadne, Aristoclée*—, are described as tragi-comedies on the title page and as tragedies in the *arguments* prefixed; the first three are also described as tragedies in the page headings, and the fourth has an unhappy ending. A contemporary of Hardy's, Jean de Schelandre (c. 1585–1635), wrote a play, *Tyr et Sidon*, which was published as a tragedy (dedicated to James I of England) in 1608 and, in 1628, in a revised and augmented form, as a tragi-comedy.

Based on a novel, *Fantaisies amoureuses* (1601), *Tyr et Sidon,* romantic and unhistorical, is more akin, even in the 1608 version, despite its unhappy ending, its choruses, and its lengthy mono- logues, to Hardy's tragi-comedies than to his tragedies. The 1628 version, which is in two parts or *journées*, is even more interesting. The tragedy of 1608, with a new happy ending sub- stituted for the earlier dénouement, forms the second *journée* of the later version, though one or two scenes have passed into the first *journée* and some new ones been added. Whereas the 1608 version is relatively regular, the 1628 play is not – indeed, it was published with a preface by Ogier that is a powerful plea for irregularity and the mixture of comedy and tragedy. There are no choruses; the action moves freely from place to place and be- tween Tyre and Sidon, and is nearly all shown on the stage instead of being merely narrated; and, above all, the jealous husband, Zorote, provides a good deal of bawdy comedy. If *Tyr et Sidon* displays essentially the same characteristics as the tragi-comedies of Hardy (though the comic element is more pronounced than in any of his), its author was a much better poet and his play is far more readable. It is with justice that it has been described as the seventeenth-century French play 'qui offre le plus de ressemblances avec le théâtre élisabéthain'.[4]

### III. THE PASTORAL

A passage from *Tyr et Sidon* may perhaps help to explain the appeal of the pastoral. Aristarque, King of Sidon, contrasts his lot with that of humble shepherds:

> O cent fois plus heureux ceux qui passent leurs âges
> A guider un troupeau sur l'émail des herbages!
> Si leur sceptre est, non d'or mais de frêne ébranché
> Si leur corps n'est de soie ains de toile caché,
> S'ils ont leurs mets friands au fonds d'une mallette
> Sils n'ont pour leur palais qu'une basse logette,
> Pour leur suite un mâtin, si leur nom n'est connu
> Qu'en un coin du hameau dont leur tige est venu:[5]
> Aussi sont-ils exempts à jamais de l'envie,
> Leur âme en cet état de gloire est assouvie,
> Ils dorment en repos sans crainte du boucon,[6]
> Ils n'ont de leurs flatteurs un pénible soupçon,
> Ils n'ont à contenter tant d'avides sangsues
> Qui briguent en la cour récompenses non dues,
> Surtout ils sont à eux et ne sont obligés
> De venger envers tous le droit des affligés,

---

[4] J. D. Hubert, 'Les Funestes Amours de Belcar et Méliane', *Revue d'Histoire littéraire*, vol. 58, 1958, p. 16.
[5] Sometimes masculine in the sixteenth and early seventeenth centuries.
[6] = poison.

Le faix d'un grand état sur leur dos ne repose,
Ils n'ont soin des méfaits dont ils ne sont pas cause,
Ils ne sont appelés par blâmes différents
Pour paisibles, couards, pour justiciers, tyrans.

(1608 version, IV, 1)

If the pastoral play in France can be traced as far back as 1566, the real vogue of the genre began about 1590, and lasted until the 1630's; in the 1620's it was for a time the leading genre. Strongly influenced by a number of Italian and Spanish works — Montemayor's *Diana* (1559), Tasso's *Aminta* (1573), Groto's *Pentimento amoroso* (1576), Guarini's *Pastor Fido* (1589), Bonarelli's *Filli di Sciro* (1607) — and, after 1607, by *L'Astrée*, the pastoral is a highly conventional genre, but an attractive one, with its Arcadian setting of forests and pastures, its preoccupation with love, and the naïveté of some of its characters. Honoré d'Urfé tells us in *L'Astrée* that the actors did not wear

des habits de bureau, des sabots ni des accoutrements malfaits, comme les gens de village les portent ordinairement. Au contraire, s'ils leur donnent une houlette en la main, elle est peinte et dorée, leurs jupes sont de taffetas, leur panetière bien troussée et quelquefois faite de toile d'or ou d'argent.

The pastoral deals with love. The love of a shepherd and a shepherdess is usually thwarted by parental opposition; though sometimes a rival may, by a trick, sow the seeds of jealousy in the mind of one of the lovers, and sometimes the obstacle to their marriage is the devotion of one to celibacy — in *L'Amour victorieux* of Hardy, two shepherds love two girls, who, however, resolve to take vows to Diana. There is often a whole chain of lovers: in Hardy's *Alphée*, Mélanie loves Euriale, who loves a dryad, who loves a satyr, who loves Corine, who loves Daphnis, who loves and is loved by Alphée, but who cannot marry her because her father withholds his consent. When there is a chain of lovers, the first pair is united at the end of the play, and the rejected suitor transfers his affections to the girl who loves him, and so on. A suitor who is rejected by the girl's parents for his poverty is usually found at the end to be, not a penniless orphan, but the long-lost child of wealthy parents. Sometimes an unhappy lover attempts to kill himself — always unsuccessfully. A stock character in the pastoral is the magician or sibyl, whose enchantments retard or accelerate the happy dénouement: in Hardy's *Alphée*, the enchantress turns Daphnis into a rock, Alphée into a fountain, and Isandre into a tree — all on the stage. In some of Hardy's plays, the gods — Pan, Cupid, or Venus — appear and bring about the dénouement. Another stock character is the satyr, who usually attempts to rape one of the shepherdesses. There is often an echo scene, in which the hero or heroine, soliloquizing, receives encouraging advice from an echo:

ALPHÉE

Hélas! ton sort ore me désespère. ECHO. Espère.
O douce voix! ô agréable son,
Qui te retient vif en quelque façon,
Présumes-tu qu'après la destinée
Je puisse, Echo, vivre qu'infortunée? ECHO. Fortunée.
Moi fortunée? ha! ne me déçois pas,
Tout mon bonheur ne pend que du trépas. ECHO. Pas.

etc. etc.

(*Alphée*, IV, 5)

There is a comic element in some pastorals. The satyr is a figure of fun, hideous to behold, scorned by the shepherdesses, mocked by all, and beaten mercilessly. When, in *Alphée*, the dryad, who loves the satyr, places a garland on his head, we recall Bottom and Titania in *A Midsummer Night's Dream*. In Hardy's *Corine*, Caliste eludes the attempts of the two girls who love him to make him choose between them; finally he promises to marry whichever can remain silent longest, with comic results.

Although the pastoral tended to disappear after 1630, it was not without influence on the subsequent drama of France. The origins of Corneille's comedies are to be sought in the pastoral rather than in comedy proper; and it left its mark on the serious drama, too. Whereas both the tragedy and the tragi-comedy of the first thirty years of the century tell a story, the pastoral – like the later tragedy of the century – deals with a situation, sometimes simple, sometimes complex, but always a situation. Moreover, the situations of the pastoral recur in later seventeenth-century tragedy. In Hardy's *Alcée*, for example, at the opening of the play, Alcée has two suitors, Démocle and Dorilas; she prefers Démocle, whereas her father favours Dorilas, the richer of the two. Dorilas is loved by Cydippe.

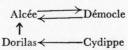

In the course of the play, Alcée's father is brought to consent to the marriage of his daughter with Démocle, and Dorilas transfers his affections to Cydippe. This is essentially the same situation as that of Corneille's *Tite et Bérénice*.

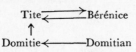

Even the chains of lovers passed into subsequent seventeenth-century tragedy – Corneille's *Pertharite* and Racine's *Andromaque*

are two notable examples. Dealing as it did with a situation, the pastoral required less time and a more restricted locality; it therefore fitted easily into the framework of the unities, and it is not surprising that it was in a pastoral play – Mairet's *Silvanire* (1630) – that the unities were first consciously applied, and that they were defended in the prefaces to pastorals.[7]

Of the many pastoral plays of this period, only a few can be mentioned here. Montchrétien published a *Bergerie* with his tragedies (1601); five pastorals, in decasyllabic verse, figure in the published works of Alexandre Hardy; and Honoré d'Urfé, the author of *L'Astrée*, published a play, *Sylvanire*, in 1627. But the most famous and most readable example of the genre is Racan's *Bergeries*, published in 1625, but written some five years earlier. This play observes the unity of time and the *bienséances*. Composed of the stock ingredients of the pastoral, it is worth reading for its clear and easy-flowing verse, its attractive descriptions of nature, and some realistic dialogue – e.g. I, 3, between Silène, the practical, sensible shepherd, and his daughter, Arténice.

Si l'histoire littéraire [says A. Adam] attachait moins de prix aux questions de forme et de technique, elle ferait des *Bergeries* la première en date de nos comédies de mœurs, la plus certain origine des comédies de Corneille.

In the first part of the seventeenth century, the genres combine easily. There is a pastoral scene in the fifth act of Hardy's tragicomedy, *Félismène*, and his *Dorise*, another tragi-comedy, resembles a pastoral in its plot. Similarly, some pastorals include elements of tragi-comedy. The chief of these is Mairet's *tragicomédie pastorale, Sylvie* (1626), which deals with the love of two princes, one for a shepherdess and the other for the sister of the first, so that characters of royal degree and shepherds appear side by side. As in *Les Bergeries*, there are in *Sylvie* some pleasing descriptive passages.

### IV. COMEDY

It is certain that the comic tradition did not die out between 1600 and 1630. The company of the Comédiens du Roi, which in 1630 established itself permanently in Paris at the Hôtel de Bourgogne, included three great comic actors, Turlupin, Gros-Guillaume, and Gautier-Garguille; full-length comedies were certainly performed, and it is likely that theatrical performances

---

[7] 1631, Isnard's preface to Pichou's *Filis de Scire*; 1631, preface to Mairet's *Silvanire*; 1631, preface to Gombauld's *Amaranthe*; 1632, preface to Rayssiguier's *Aminte*; 1632, preface to Dalibray's *Aminte*; 1634, preface to Dalibray's *Pompe Funèbre*.

concluded with a farce; and the popularity of comedy is further attested by the success of the mountebank, Tabarin, who performed short comic sketches and farces on the Pont-Neuf, to draw the crowds and sell quack medicines. But very few of the comedies and farces of the period have survived — a few farces of Tabarin and others, and one or two comedies, notably Troterel's *Corrivaux* (1612) in verse, and an anonymous play in prose, *Les Ramoneurs* (c. 1624), which has been attributed to Hardy.[8]

Sometimes lively and amusing, these plays are usually indecent and bawdy; and the influence of Italian comedy is evident in the stock characters — the pedant, the braggadocio, the wily valet — who keep appearing. *Les Ramoneurs*, the best of the surviving full-length comedies is an intrigue play, describing how a lover triumphs over obstacles and wins his mistress. There are one or two touches of realism, such as a scene in a fruitshop and a description of a chimney sweep.

[8] In addition, the dramatist, Larivey, who, in 1579, had published a collection of six comedies, translated or adapted from the Italian, published three more in 1611 — probably written much earlier.

# Part II

1630–1660

*Chapter 6*

# INTRODUCTION

RICHELIEU found royal authority weak, the nobles rebellious and independent, the Huguenots disaffected; outside France, the Thirty Years' War had begun, and the Catholic powers were winning easy victories over the Protestant states of Germany. Richelieu's policy, as he says in his *Testament politique*, was to 'ruiner le parti huguenot, rabaisser l'orgueil des grands, réduire tous ses[1] sujets en leur devoir, et relever son nom dans les nations étrangères au point où il devait être'.

All this he accomplished. He ordered the feudal fortresses of the nobles to be dismantled, and tried to curb their independent spirit by forbidding duelling (1626); he allowed them no share in the government of France, and made more and more use of *intendants* to enforce the royal will in the provinces. He also strengthened royal power by reducing the privileges of the provincial *états* and the *parlements*, and by founding a navy. The Huguenots he attacked in 1625 and 1626; in 1627, he laid siege to their stronghold, La Rochelle, which capitulated the following year. In 1629, the peace of Alais or *Edit de Grâce* stripped the Huguenots of all their fortified towns and political rights, and transformed them into peaceable and industrious citizens.

The last point of his programme involved France in foreign wars. It was Richelieu's policy to weaken the power of the Catholic Habsburgs, who occupied the thrones of Spain and the Holy Roman Empire, by espousing the cause of the Protestants abroad; though a Cardinal, he placed the interests of France before those of his Church. In 1624, he drove the Spaniards out of the Valtelline Pass, which was the only direct means of communication between their domains in Italy and the Austrian possessions on the other side of the Alps. Then, by a series of campaigns between 1629 and 1631, he installed a Frenchman, the duc de Nevers, in the disputed duchy of Mantua and Monferrato, which, lying as it did between the Milanese and Savoy, provided a useful means of bringing pressure to bear on the independent and vacillating Duke of Savoy. In 1629, Richelieu entered into an alliance with Gustavus

[1] Louis XIII's.

73

Adolphus of Sweden, though without intervening directly in the
Thirty Years' War. A number of German principalities sought, and
were granted, French protection against Swedes or Spaniards; and
in 1635, seeing the Protestants coming off decidedly the worst,
Richelieu decided to intervene directly in the war. The following
year, the Spaniards invaded France from the North and seized
Corbie, but were driven back.

Though it was a period of growing centralization and autocracy,
the age of Richelieu was far from being a settled period. Besides
the wars against the Huguenots and the Thirty Years' War, there
were numerous conspiracies or risings, mostly aiming at getting
rid of Richelieu by making Gaston d'Orléans King in place of
his brother, Louis XIII, who remained childless until 1638: the
conspiracy of Chalais (1626); the *Journée des Dupes* – an attempt
by Maria de' Medici to browbeat her son, Louis XIII, into dismissing Richelieu, which very nearly succeeded (1630); the rebellion of
Montmorency (1632); revolts of peasants in protest against the
heavy taxation necessitated by the wars – the *Croquants* in the
South-West (1636), and the *Va-nu-pieds* in Normandy (1639); the
rebellion of the comte de Soissons (1641); and the conspiracy of
Cinq-Mars, the King's favourite (1642).

Richelieu died in 1642 and Louis XIII the following year. The
first part of the reign of Louis XIV (1643–61) was an even more
unsettled and disturbed period than the preceding ones. Louis
XIV being a child, his mother, Anne of Austria, governed as regent
with the help of her favourite (and possibly husband), Cardinal
Mazarin. Once the strong hand of Richelieu was removed, a reaction set in. At court, a clique was formed against Mazarin,
the *cabale des Importants*; but its chief members were imprisoned
or banished from court. Meanwhile, the war continued. In 1643,
the duc d'Enghien (later prince de Condé) defeated the Spaniards
at Rocroy, and news of the victory was received with great exultation in France. But military glory meant heavy taxation, and there
were further revolts of peasants in 1643 and 1644. Mazarin's new
taxes and his unscrupulous, even dishonest, manipulation of the
finances irritated all classes of society and met with increasing
opposition from the parlement of Paris. Moreover, the growing
power of the government under Richelieu and the usurpation by
the intendants of powers hitherto exercised by governors, *lieu-
tenants généraux*, and *bureaux de finance*, had irritated both
nobles and officials. The result of all this discontent was the civil
war of the Fronde (1648–53), which ended in victory for Mazarin
and the royal power. Condé left France and fought for the Spaniards; the parlement was forbidden to interfere any more in politics.

Though the Thirty Years' War had come to an end in 1648 with the Treaty of Westphalia, the war between France and Spain dragged on until 1659, when the Treaty of the Pyrenees was signed. Both these treaties extended French territory; in addition, the Treaty of the Pyrenees provided for the marriage of the young Louis XIV with Maria Theresa of Spain.

During this period, social life flourished in Paris. The great nobles, impoverished by inflation and more and more dependent on the King for financial support, were tending to settle in Paris and live at court. Hostesses began to hold salons, the most famous of which is that of Mme de Rambouillet.

Catherine de Vivonne, marquise de Rambouillet (1588?–1665) gave up going to court, according to Tallemant des Réaux, at the age of twenty:

Elle disait qu'elle n'y trouvait rien de plaisant, que de voir comme on se pressait pour y entrer, et que quelquefois il lui est arrivé de se mettre en une chambre pour se divertir du méchant ordre qu'il y a pour ces choses-là en France. Ce n'est pas qu'elle n'aimât le divertissement, mais c'était en particulier.

She herself designed the Hôtel de Rambouillet according to her own ideas and introduced several new features. She was the first to place the staircase at the side of the building instead of in the middle, so that a large number of rooms could open out into one another; other novel features, according to Tallemant, were the lofty ceilings and the large doors and windows situated opposite one another. Tallemant adds that, when the Queen Mother built the Luxembourg, she sent her architects to see the Hôtel de Rambouillet. Another innovation of Mme de Rambouillet was to have her chief room painted blue:

C'est la première qui s'est avisée de faire peindre une chambre d'une autre couleur que de rouge ou de tanné; et c'est ce qui a donné à sa grand chambre le nom de la *Chambre bleue*. (Tallemant)

Here, and in summer at Rambouillet, she gathered round her 'ce qu'il y avait de plus galant à la Cour, et de plus poli parmi les beaux-esprits du siècle'. At the age of thirty-five or so (i.e. c. 1623), she became the victim of a strange affliction: she could not tolerate heat, whether from a fire or from the sun. She was thus virtually confined to the house, and in the house could not bear a fire near her; hence she imported from Spain the idea of alcoves:

La compagnie se va chauffer dans l'antichambre; quand il gèle, elle se tient sur son lit, les jambes dans un sac de peau d'ours, et elle dit plaisammant, à cause de la grande quantité de coiffes qu'elle met l'hiver, qu'elle devient sourde à la Saint-Martin, et qu'elle recouvre l'ouïe à Pâques. (Tallemant)

In running her salon, Mme de Rambouillet was seconded by her eldest daughter, Julie d'Angennes (1607–71), beautiful, graceful, and witty, who eventually married M. de Montausier after a court-ship of thirteen years.[2]

Mme de Rambouillet received a very varied company – great nobles, such as Bassompierre and the maréchal de Schomberg, Condé and his family, the duchesses de Rohan and de Chevreuse; Mlle Paulet the daughter of the inventor of the tax known as La Paulette;[3] prelates, such as Cardinal de la Valette and Godeau, Bishop of Grasse, nicknamed the 'nain de la princesse Julie'; men of letters, such as Malherbe, Racan, Gombauld, Chapelain, Benserade, Conrart (Godeau's cousin), des Yveteaux, Scudéry and his sister, and Voiture. There was talk – about all manner of things, but very often about literature and questions of language. The novelist, Gomberville, for example, having boasted that he had not used the conjunction *car* once in his novel, *Polexandre*, Mme de Rambouillet and her guests discussed whether or not it should be replaced by *pour ce que*: Voiture wrote a delightful letter on the subject. On another occasion, after a discussion at the Academy, Chapelain propounded a problem to the Hôtel de Rambouillet: whether the correct form of the word was *muscadin* or *muscardin* – again Voiture wrote an amusing little poem on the subject. Sometimes Mme de Rambouillet hired the actors of the Marais theatre to perform at the Hôtel. Some-times authors read their plays there, as Corneille is said to have read *Polyeucte*. Sometimes the habitués of the Hôtel acted them-selves: shortly after the siege of Corbie, when the two Arnaulds returned on leave, a performance of *Sophonisbe* was improvised at short notice, each part being shared between two or three actors.

They wrote and read and discussed poems, *rondeaux*, *énigmes*, *métamorphoses*,[4] each having their period of favour. Sometimes

[2] The long delay was not due to her romantic notions. It appears from Tallemant that she did not care for Montausier and consented to marry him to please her mother. The day before she gave her consent, 'elle était aussi éloignée de mariage que jamais'. Tallemant adds that, in his opinion, she married also to prolong her social life. 'Je pense pourtant qu'elle considéra aussi que d'une vieille fille elle devenait une nouvelle mariée, et telle jeune femme qui ne lui eût pas cédée et ne l'eût pas crue, la regarda aussitôt comme une personne de qui elle pouvait appren-dre à bien vivre; et puis, comme j'ai déjà remarqué, cela la remettait tout de nouveau dans le monde, et elle aime fort les divertissements.'

[3] The Government raised money by selling magistrates the right to pass on to their heirs their offices, which, in consequence, became virtu-ally hereditary.
Mlle Paulet, says Tallemant, 'chantait mieux que personne de son temps'. He adds in a note: 'On trouva deux rossignols crevés sur le bord d'une fontaine où elle avait chanté tout le soir.'

[4] Compositions imagining what precious stone, bird, flower, etc., it would be appropriate for a person to be turned into.

the group would be split by a friendly controversy, such as the *querelle de la belle Matineuse*: Voiture having translated a sonnet by Annibal Caro, Malleville wrote three versions of it, and the relative merits of Voiture's and Malleville's poems became a subject of debate. In 1641, M. de Montausier presented Julie d'Angennes with the *Guirlande de Julie*, a magnificent volume of madrigals composed by the circle in her honour – each containing the compliments of a different flower. The rose, for example, says:

> Alors que je me vois si belle et si brillante,
> Dans ce teint dont l'éclat fait naître tant de vœux,
> L'excès de ma beauté moi-même me tourmente:
> Je languis pour moi-même et brûle de mes feux,
> Et je crains qu'aujourd'hui la ROSE ne finisse
> Par ce qui fit jadis commencer le Narcisse.
>
> (M. Habert de Cerisy)

Mme de Rambouillet's concern was to amuse her guests. Sometimes, the party would visit the country houses of friends near Paris – that of the Arnaulds at Pomponne, that of Mme du Vigean near Montmorency, or that of Mme de Combalet (Richelieu's niece) at Rueil. Mme de Rambouillet was fond of surprising her friends. When the Bishop of Lisieux visited her at Rambouillet, she invited him to take a walk in a meadow in which was a circle of rocks:

Quand il fut assez près de ces roches pour entrevoir à travers les feuilles des arbres, il aperçut en divers endroits je ne sais quoi de brillant. Etant plus proche, il lui sembla qu'il discernait des femmes, et qu'elles étaient vêtues en nymphes. La Marquise, au commencement, ne faisait pas semblant de rien voir de ce qu'il voyait. Enfin, étant parvenus jusques aux roches, ils trouvèrent Mlle de Rambouillet et toutes les demoiselles de la maison, vêtues effectivement en nymphes, qui, assises sur les roches, faisaient le plus agréable spectacle du monde. Le bonhomme en fut si charmé, que depuis il ne voyait jamais la Marquise sans lui parler des roches de Rambouillet.

(Tallemant)

One day, when the company was assembled at the Hôtel de Rambouillet, they heard a noise behind the tapestry covering the outside wall; a door opened, and Julie d'Angennes was revealed, 'vêtue superbement', in a 'grand cabinet tout à fait magnifique, et merveilleusement bien éclairé', which Mme de Rambouillet had had built secretly. To surprise Montausier, she had a series of cascades and ornamental ponds constructed in the grounds of Rambouillet. On another occasion, the Hôtel de Rambouillet paid a surprise visit to the Arnaulds at Pomponne. Two or three of the men dressed up as billeting officers and called on M. Arnauld d'Andilly with an order to billet a number of men. As he was arguing, a trumpet sounded, Godeau thrust a straw lance at him, and the rest of the party arrived in coaches or on horseback.[5]

The Hôtel de Rambouillet, with its neat wit, its brilliancy and high spirits, its concern with purity of language, its love of light verse, helped to refine French society. But we must not over-estimate the refinement of the Hôtel de Rambouillet, or we shall get the seventeenth century out of perspective. A remark of Talle-mant about the excessive delicacy of Mme de Rambouillet is illuminating: 'Elle est un peu trop délicate [ . . . ] On n'oserait prononcer le mot de cul; cela va dans l'excès, surtout quand on est en liberté.' When a young lady, Mlle de Marolle, was thrown out of her carriage, we find Voiture writing some *Stances sur une dame dont la jupe fut retroussée en versant en un carrosse à la campagne*:

> Philis, je suis dessous vos lois:
> Et sans remède à cette fois
> Mon âme est votre prisonnière.
> Mais sans justice et sans raison,
> Vous m'avez pris par le derrière:
> N'est-ce pas une trahison?

Again, some of the practical jokes played at the Hôtel de Ram-bouillet strike one as unkind – the comte de Guiche, for example, was invited to supper and all the dishes he most disliked were placed before him; true, a magnificent meal was served afterwards. One night, they took in his clothes, to make him think that he had swollen overnight from eating too many mushrooms. Once, Mme de Rambouillet was reading with her back to the screens: hearing a noise, she looked round and saw two bears looking over – Voiture had introduced them to play a trick on her. In retaliation, she had a sonnet of his printed and bound up in an old volume, to make him think that he had been guilty of plagiary. Mlle de Rambouillet threw a jugful of water over the head of Voiture, who had a horror of getting wet.

The Hôtel de Rambouillet lost its lustre at the outbreak of the Fronde,[6] but, though it was the most famous of the seventeenth-century salons, it was not the only one or the last. Many other hostesses formed groups – Mme des Loges (whose salon closed in 1629, when she returned to her province); the pedantic Mme d'Auchy; the courtezans, Marion de Lorme and Ninon de Lenclos. After the Fronde, there were the salons of Foucquet, the *surin-*

---

[5] Similarly, when the Hôtel visited Mme du Vigean, they were taken through her grounds, suddenly came upon an orchestra of twenty-four lutes and violins, and saw Mlle de Bourbon and Mlle d'Aubry, dressed as Diana and a nymph, standing on a pedestal in a niche.

[6] Julie d'Angennes was married in 1645; Voiture died, and the Fronde broke out, in 1648; Mlle Paulet died in 1650.

*tendant des finances*, of Mme de Sablé, of the Grande Mademoiselle, and the famous *Samedis* of Mlle de Scudéry. It was after
the Fronde that the salons began to be ridiculed[7] and that the
word *précieuse* was used to describe the type of lady, with a fondness for theorizing about love (Ninon de Lenclos called the
*précieuses* 'les jansénistes de l'amour') and an affected way of
speaking, who frequented them.

The influence of the salons on life and on literature in the
seventeenth century was considerable. They were undoubtedly a
civilizing influence, encouraging men and women to aim at distinction in manners, dress, and speech. They helped to formulate
and spread the seventeenth-century ideal of the *honnête homme*,
the gentleman and the man of taste, as opposed to the boor and
the pedant. They helped to establish the principle of *bienséance*
in language and in literature. They helped to purify the French
language and make French style light and witty. Some of the
expressions they created have lasted (*style châtié, tour d'esprit,
faire figure dans le monde, laisser mourir la conversation*), though
the *précieuses* ridiculed by Molière and Somaize seem to have
been guilty of affectation.[8]

They encouraged an interest in literature, though their influence
was not, perhaps, entirely good: each circle favoured its own pet
author; they cultivated the kind of poetry which could serve as a
social amusement, the minor genres, neat, ingenious, witty poems
with an effective final conceit, love poems from which genuine

---

[7] D'Aubignac, *Nouvelle histoire du temps ou Relation véritable du
Royaume de Coquetterie* (1655); Saint-Evremond, *Le Cercle* (1656); abbé
de Pure, *La Prétieuse* (a farce played by the Italians) (1656) and *La Prétieuse ou le Mystère des Ruelles*, 4 vols. (1656–8); Molière, *Les Précieuses
ridicules* (1659); *La Déroute des Précieuses* (a ballet performed in 1659);
Scarron, *Epître chagrine au maréchal d'Albret* (1659 or 1660); Gilbert,
*La vraie et la fausse précieuse* (a comedy acted by Molière's company,
1660); Chappuzeau, *L'Académie des Femmes* (a comedy, 1661); Somaize,
*Les Véritables Précieuses* and *Le Procès des Précieuses* (two comedies,
1660), and *Le Grand Dictionnaire des Précieuses* (1660–1).

[8] The characteristics of the language of the *précieuses* are: (1) Vague,
stock expressions, such as *un je ne sais quoi, air* (*un bel air*). They liked
to interlard their speech with such phrases as *ma chère, car enfin, à n'en
point mentir*. (2) Exaggeration—*furieusement, du dernier bourgeois, j'ai un
furieux tendre pour les gens d'esprit*, etc. (3) Abstract words—*ôtez le super-
flu de cet ardent* (snuff the candle). (4) Novelty. Sometimes they would use
old words in a new way: *des cheveux bien plantés, travestir sa pensée*.
Sometimes they would replace ordinary words by far-fetched synonyms:
*un zéphyr* (a fan), *le sublime* (the brain), *apportez-moi une dédale* (comb)
*que je délabyrinthe mes cheveux*. And they were fond of—sometimes witty
—periphrases: *l'instrument de la propreté* (a broom), *le cher nécessaire*
(drink), *le conseiller des grâces* (a looking-glass), *le siège* or *l'empire de
Vulcan* (the fireplace), *visiter les Naïades* (to swim), *les commodités de
la conversation* (chairs), *les chers souffrants* (feet), *le bouillon des deux
sœurs* (an enema), *contentez l'envie que ce siège a de vous embrasser* (sit
down), *attachez un peu la réflexion de votre odorat sur ces gants-là* (smell
those gloves).

passion is carefully excluded; and seventeenth-century writers blame the feminine influence of the salons for the prevailing love of affectation and *galanterie*:

C'est ce qui oblige nos poètes à privilégier si fort la galanterie sur le théâtre, et à tourner tous leurs sujets sur des tendresses outrées, pour plaire davantage aux femmes, qui se sont érigées en arbitres de ces divertissements, et qui ont usurpé le droit d'en décider.

(Rapin, *Réflexions sur la poétique*)

On the other hand, they encouraged the love of subtle psychological analysis, which is such an important feature of the literature of the *grand siècle*. They were interested in the analysis of love and fond of discussing *questions d'amour*. The salon of Mme de Sablé, for example, was invited to consider whether love and affection are incompatible emotions, and which is the greater crime – to boast of the genuine favours one has been vouchsafed by a lady or to boast falsely of favours one has not received. Other such questions were, whether it is harder to pass from friendship to love or from love to friendship, whether we should hate someone of whom we are over-fond and who does not return our affection, and what we should do if our affections point one way and our reason another.[9] Mlle de la Martinière wrote a letter to M. Amat, distinguishing between nine different kinds of *estime*, and M. Amat replied with an analysis of twelve ways of sighing. It was in the salon of Mlle de Scudéry that the famous *Carte de Tendre*, later incorporated in *Clélie*, was elaborated. The Grande Mademoiselle launched the vogue of *portraits* (analyses of character).

Finally, the salons helped on the cause of emancipation of women and of feminine education. In the salons, men and women met on equal terms, or if there was inequality, it was the men who had to regard the women as superior deities and obey their behests; and in some, an interest was taken in theology, moral questions, philosophy and science. The *précieuses* who appear in the novel, *La Prétieuse* (1656–8), by abbé de Pure (1620–80), are bitterly opposed to girls being married to husbands of their parents' choosing and to the institution of marriage. According to one of them, *préciosité* is a deliberate attempt on the part of women to assert their intellectual equality.

Besides the salons, groups of men were formed to share some common interest. One such still exists.

Environ l'année 1629 [writes Pellisson], quelques particuliers, logés en divers endroits de Paris, ne trouvant rien de plus incommode dans cette

[9] In abbé de Pure's novel, *La Prétieuse*, the following questions are discussed: whether it is better to love an unmarried girl or a married woman; whether it is possible to love too well; and which kind of women love best—*laides, coquettes, prudes*, or *bigotes*.

grande ville, que d'aller fort souvent se chercher les uns les autres sans se trouver, résolurent de se voir un jour de la semaine chez l'un d'eux.[10]

They were all men of letters – Godeau, Conrart, Gombauld, Chapelain, and five others. They would talk, read and discuss their writings, and then take a walk or a meal together. Although they had agreed to keep their meetings secret, the secret was not kept. One of the group, Malleville, brought along Faret, the author of a treatise on *L'Honnête Homme,* and he in his turn mentioned the circle to Desmarets de Saint-Sorlin and Boisrobert, both of whom attended meetings. Boisrobert, who acted as a kind of literary secretary and jester to Richelieu, told his master of the meetings. Richelieu commissioned Boisrobert to invite the group to become a public body under his protection; and, though they were reluctant, especially those who were in the service of enemies of Richelieu, they felt bound to accept. Chapelain, indeed, pointed out that they had no choice, that Richelieu 'ne voulait pas médiocrement ce qu'il voulait' and would not brook opposition, that he would be offended by a refusal and might make them suffer for it, and that he could certainly put a stop to their meetings. His advice prevailed. This was in 1634.

The number of members of the new body was fixed at forty, and additional members were chosen, including Boisrobert and Desmarets de Saint-Sorlin. A *directeur* and a *chancelier* (both to be changed every two months) were chosen by lot, and a perpetual secretary chosen by vote – the first was Conrart. The new body took the title of the Académie française, and drew up its statutes. One article stated that:

La principale fonction de l'Académie sera de travailler avec tout le soin et toute la diligence possible à donner des règles certaines à notre langue et à la rendre pure, éloquente et capable de traiter les arts et les sciences.
(§ 24)

Another specified how this general aim was to be achieved:

Il sera composé un Dictionnaire, une Grammaire, une Rhétorique et une Poétique sur les observations de l'Académie. (§ 26)

Other statutes stated that the Academy should examine the style of the best French authors, and that every meeting should begin with a talk by a member of the Academy, which should later be scrutinized.

The parlement of Paris was reluctant to register the letters patent bringing the Academy into existence. Apparently, there were wild rumours about the purpose of the new body, and the

[10] Chapelain, in the preface to the translation of the second part of *Guzman d'Alfarache* (1620) speaks of a 'vertueuse assemblée de gens doctes, faisant profession particulière d'examiner et s'indiquer les livres, pour le langage notamment.' Was this the same group or a forerunner?

parlement, or a section of it, was mistrustful. The letters patent
were not registered until 10 July 1637, and then only on the
express condition that the Academy should not be concerned with
anything but language and literature:

A la charge que ceux de ladite Assemblée et Académie, ne connaîtront que
de l'ornement, embellissement et augmentation de la langue française, et
des livres qui seront par eux faits, et par autres personnes qui le désire-
ront et voudront.

It was on 13 June 1637 that the Academy had agreed to examine
*Le Cid*; and it seems likely that one reason, at least, why Richelieu
wanted it to undertake that task was to remove the suspicions of
the parlement by showing that the purpose of the new institution
was genuinely literary and linguistic. After Richelieu's death, the
chancellor, Séguier, was chosen to be *protecteur* of the Academy,
and from 1643 onwards, it met regularly at his house, having
previously had no fixed abode.

At first, in accordance with the statutes and *règlements*, at
each meeting, an Academician would deliver a discourse or read
a paper on some topic chosen by himself, which was subsequently
examined by a committee. The Academy also examined works
by Academicians and the standard French writers – it spent three
months examining Malherbe's *Stances sur le roi allant en
Limousin*, and even then the last four stanzas were left untouched.[11] In its scrutiny, the Academy was concerned with purity,
clarity, and accuracy; and it is interesting to see that only one
stanza of Malherbe's poem (the sixteenth) was considered flawless.
It objected, for example, to the line,

> O Dieu! dont *les bontés*, de nos larmes touchées,

on the grounds that *la bonté* would be better, and thought the
line,

> . . . à rien d'imparfait ta louange n'aspire,

was not good French. Much of Scudéry's *Observations sur le Cid*
and of the *Sentiments de l'Académie sur le Cid*, indeed of seventeenth-century criticism in general, are concerned with such questions.

In 1637, came the *querelle du Cid*, and the following year the
Academy set to work on its Dictionary, which eventually appeared
in 1694. The *Rhétorique* and the *Poétique* were never composed,
and France had to wait until the twentieth century for the
grammar of the Academy. One of its members, however, Vaugelas
(1595–1650), published a volume of *Remarques sur la langue*

---

[11] In 1700, we find the Academy examining Balzac's *Aristippe*.

*française* in 1647, which to some extent filled the gap. This is not a grammar, but a French seventeenth-century equivalent of Fowler's *Modern English Usage*, discussing controversial points of language, correcting common errors, laying down the distinction between pairs of synonyms (*créance* and *croyance*, for example), and establishing the gender of doubtful words – Vaugelas insists that *rencontre* should always be feminine, and that *le voile* and *la voile* mean quite separate things. Other points that he discusses are the rule for the agreement of past participles, when one should say *on* and when *l'on*, and whether one should write *submission* or *soumission*, *je peux* or *je puis*.

It is interesting to see how Vaugelas resolves these questions. In the lengthy preface and in the body of the work, he insists that one must obey usage, 'le maître et le souverain des langues vivantes'. By usage, he means good usage, 'la façon de parler de la plus saine partie de la Cour, conformément à la façon d'écrire de la plus saine partie des auteurs du temps'. We are far here from Malherbe's 'crocheteurs'; for Vaugelas, 'le peuple n'est le maître que du mauvais usage'. We are equally far from pedantry. Language, he maintains, is a matter neither of reason nor of scholarship, and he declares roundly that, if he wanted to clear up a doubtful point, he would rather consult a man or a woman with no Latin or Greek, since these languages have no bearing on French. Usage being the deciding factor, one must not stand out against it; nor must one follow the example of tradespeople, even where their trade is concerned. Sailors use the verb *naviguer*; but the court says *naviger*, which is therefore correct. Similarly, although the expression *voire même* is good French, it has fallen from favour at court and is best avoided. Vaugelas regrets that the word *face* should have gone out of fashion as a synonym for *visage* and sees no sound reasons for it; but the fact must be accepted. Nay, further, the expression *sur le minuit* is obviously wrong, since *minuit* is feminine; nevertheless, at court, people say *sur le minuit*, and that, therefore, is the correct form. Some people object to the use of *songer* as a synonym for *penser*: they are wrong to 'disputer avec l'usage par la raison'.

The court is the final authority for the spoken language. For questions affecting the written language, such as unusual words and unsounded agreements, one consults the best writers. Only if the court and the best writers fail to solve a problem, does one consult grammarians and linguistic specialists. Finally, if they cannot resolve a difficulty, one must fall back, as a last resort, on analogy. Should one write *prendre à témoin* or *prendre à témoins*? Vaugelas decides, on the analogy of *prendre à partie*, which is invariable, that the former is correct in all circumstances.

Though he is aware that languages change, Vaugelas is convinced that the principles he has laid down are permanently valid:

Car il sera toujours vrai qu'il y aura un bon et un mauvais usage, que le mauvais sera composé de la pluralité des voix, et le bon de la plus saine partie de la Cour, et des écrivains du temps; qu'il faudra toujours parler et écrire selon l'usage qui se forme de la cour et des auteurs, et que lorsqu'il sera douteux ou inconnu, il en faudra croire les maîtres de la langue, et les meilleurs écrivains.

Malherbe, Balzac, the salons, the Academy, and Vaugelas, all helped to spread the conviction that language is a serious matter, that to write correctly and clearly is difficult but important. We have, too, in Vaugelas, the sense that French, after a period of evolution, has reached such a pitch of perfection that it is a fit vehicle for the expression of all thought, and worthy to stand beside the classical tongues:

Il n'y a jamais eu de langue, où l'on ait écrit plus purement et plus nettement qu'en la nôtre, qui soit plus ennemie des équivoques et de toute sorte d'obscurité, plus grave et plus douce tout ensemble, plus propre pour toutes sortes de styles, plus chaste en ses locutions, plus judicieuse en ses figures, qui aime plus l'élégance et l'ornement, mais qui craigne plus l'affectation. [ ... ] Elle sait tempérer ses hardiesses avec la pudeur et la retenue qu'il faut avoir, pour ne pas donner dans ces figures monstrueuses, où donnent aujourd'hui nos voisins dégénérant de l'éloquence de leurs pères. [ ... ] Il n'y en a point qui observe plus le nombre et la cadence dans ses périodes, que la nôtre; en quoi consiste la véritable marque de la perfection des langues.

One of the first tasks of the Academy was to express its opinion of *Le Cid* and of Scudéry's hostile *Observations sur le Cid*, which it did in the *Sentiments de l'Académie Française sur le Cid* (1637), largely the work of Chapelain. The Academy thus played a considerable part in establishing the classical doctrine; and, since the main tenets of this doctrine were already in existence in 1637, this seems an appropriate moment to summarize them. The so-called 'classical' doctrine – the word was not, of course, used in the seventeenth century, any more than the term 'baroque' –, common both to the theorists and to the great writers of the period, was derived from the Italian and German commentators of Aristotle's *Poetics*, and from Horace.

In the first place, it was generally accepted that art must have a moral purpose:

Il est vrai que c'est le but que se propose la poésie, que de plaire: mais ce n'est pas le principal, comme prétendent les autres. En effet, la poésie étant un art, doit être utile par la qualité de sa nature, et par la subordination essentielle que tout art doit avoir à la politique, dont la fin générale est le bien public.                    (Rapin, *Réflexions sur la poétique*)

The moral aim can be achieved in many ways – by the use of
*sentences* and *maximes*, by portraying virtuous characters and the
pernicious effects of vice, by the reward of virtue and the punishment of vice, and by the use of allegory. Scudéry criticized *Le Cid*
because Chimène is an immoral heroine, who allows her love for
Rodrigue to take precedence over her duty to avenge her father,
and marries the man who killed her father; and the Academy upheld his criticism. Molière, Racine, La Fontaine, all agree that art
must instruct and please; Corneille argues that the theatre must
please first and foremost, but he admits that it will not achieve this
aim unless it instructs as well. The moral aim, however, was not to
be crudely pursued:

Il faut sentir l'instruction; mais il ne faut pas la voir; il faut qu'elle soit
dans toutes les parties du poème; mais il ne faut pas qu'elle s'y montre;
il ne faut pas qu'elle die elle-même: J'y suis.          (Balzac, *VIᵉ Discours*)

And, of course, we may wonder whether the writer always had a
moral aim in view – La Fontaine in writing the *Contes*, for
instance.

It was held that human nature was unchanging, that what
pleased one age would please another, and that there were
standards of taste and beauty, standards which were the same at
all times and in different spheres. 'Toutes les bonnes choses se
ressemblent par une conformité de perfection,' writes Méré, who
is fond of illustrating bad or good taste in style by imagining the
equivalent in dress.[12] One can attain this perfection in a work of
art by following rules. Poets need genius; but they also need to
know the rules, and to be acquainted with the works of their predecessors: the importance of technique and craftsmanship is
emphasized. D'Aubignac, for example, in his *Pratique du Théâtre*
(1657) says that one must study not only Aristotle and Horace and
their commentators, Castelvetro, Vida, Heinsius, Vossius, La
Mesnardière, Scaliger, and so forth, but all the works of the Greek
and Latin poets as well. Rapin, in an interesting passage which
anticipates Diderot's *Paradoxe sur le Comédien*,[13] insists that
poetry is not written in a frenzy:

Car quoiqu'en effet le discours du poète doive en quelque façon ressem-
bler au discours d'un homme inspiré: il est bon toutefois d'avoir l'esprit
fort serein, pour savoir s'emporter, quand il le faut, et pour régler ses
emportements: et cette sérénité d'esprit, qui fait le sangfroid, et le jugement, est une des parties des plus essentielles du génie de la poésie.

(*Réflexions*)

[12] Cf. Pascal, *Pensées*, No. 32 (in the Brunschvicg edition).
[13] Méré anticipates Diderot more exactly: he argues that an actor does
not feel the passion he is representing, and that if he did, it would be a
blunder (*Sixième Discours*).

Indeed, the greater the genius of the poet, he goes on to say, the greater the need for it to be held in check by discipline and rules: 'Car la raison doit être encore plus forte que le génie, pour savoir jusques où l'emportement doit aller.'

The theorists insist that the rules must be obeyed. The Academy in its *Sentiments* states categorically that an irregular play will give pleasure only in so far as it is regular, and that, if a regular play does not succeed, it is the fault of the author, not of the rules. D'Aubignac and Rapin agree: 'On ne va à la perfection que par ces règles, et on s'égare dès qu'on ne les suit pas,' says the latter. Molière, it is true, pleased the public by irregular plays:

Mais je prétends que ni lui, ni les autres ne plaisent jamais, que par les règles: ils ont des traits naturels par où ils réussissent, et ces traits sont des coups de l'art: car l'art n'est autre chose, comme j'ai dit, que le bon sens réduit en méthode. Ce ne sont que ces traits qui plaisent dans les pièces irrégulières, où ce qui est irrégulier ne plaît jamais, parce qu'il n'est jamais naturel.                                        (*Réflexions*)

The rules, it will be noticed, are, for Rapin, 'le bon sens réduit en méthode'. They are not to be obeyed because of the *authority* of Aristotle or anyone else, but because they are sensible. 'Les règles du théâtre ne sont pas fondées en autorité, mais en raison,' says d'Aubignac; and if the ancients did not follow them, they were wrong. Aristotle cannot be accepted uncritically, because the theatre has changed considerably since his day. On this point, Corneille is at one with d'Aubignac. The avowed object of his commentary on Aristotle is to 'accorder les règles anciennes avec les agréments modernes'; but, though he pays lip service to Aristotle, he never hesitates to disagree with him. It is clear that, for Corneille, if the ancient rules are incompatible with the *agréments modernes*, they must go.

The first of the rules is the imitation of nature: in other words, the writer must understand human nature, must study the passions. Imitation must not be servile; not everything is to be imitated, nor must nature be imitated exactly – selection, stylization and idealization, all have a part to play. If the poet wishes to describe external nature, it is only the 'beaux endroits' which he must describe, according to Rapin.

The second rule is the imitation of the ancients, because they have stood the test of time. Racine, for example, in the preface to *Iphigénie*, writes:

J'ai reconnu avec plaisir, par l'effet qu'a produit sur notre théâtre tout ce que j'ai imité d'Homère ou d'Euripide, que le bon sens et la raison étaient les mêmes dans tous les siècles. Le goût de Paris s'est trouvé conforme à celui d'Athènes. Mes spectateurs ont été émus des mêmes choses qui ont mis autrefois en larmes le plus savant peuple de la Grèce . . .

But what is meant by imitation? This is a crucial question for the understanding of seventeenth-century literature. In the first place, imitation of the ancients means studying their works so as to acquire their qualities.

Il faut poser pour une maxime indubitable, que jamais personne ne sera savant dans la poésie dramatique, que par le secours des anciens, et l'intelligence de leurs ouvrages.                                   (D'Aubignac)

For Rapin, the study of the ancients is the means of acquiring impeccable taste:

Car personne ne doute que les ouvrages des anciens ne soient les sources les plus pures, d'où l'on peut tirer ces richesses et ces trésors, d'où se forme le bon sens, et d'où naît ce discernement admirable, par lequel on distingue le vrai d'avec le faux dans les beautés de la nature, auxquelles il faut s'attacher pour bien sentir celles de l'art [...] Et tout bien considéré, on ne trouve rien de sain ni rien de solide, que dans le commerce qu'on peut avoir avec eux. Il n'y a rien de faux dans leur esprit, rien d'égaré dans leurs manières, rien d'affecté dans leur caractère: tout y va au bon sens, pour lequel ils avaient un goût si sûr, que ces expressions brillantes, qui éblouissent les gens du commun, et tout cet attirail de beaux sentiments, et de belles pensées leur étaient entièrement inconnues. Ainsi dès qu'on s'écarte de ces sources si pures, on est sujet à prendre des détours, et à ne pas marcher sûrement dans la voie des belles lettres: qu'on ne peut bien apprendre que par eux. (*Les Comparaisons des grands hommes de l'antiquité, qui ont le plus excellé dans les belles lettres.*)

Imitation does not mean direct imitation, which is deprecated from the early years of the seventeenth century onwards. Chapelain, in the preface to the first twelve books of his epic, *La Pucelle*, specifies that he has imitated his models 'dans le général, sans emprunter ou copier leurs pensées ni leurs paroles'.[14]

It is true that seventeenth-century writers do sometimes adapt works of the ancients – Corneille in his *Médée* and his *Œdipe*, for example, Molière in *L'Avare*, Racine in *Andromaque*, *Iphigénie*, and *Phèdre*, La Fontaine in his fables and in *Psyché*. But they

---

[14] He goes on to say this kind is allowed only 'dans les endroits où l'on prétend le renvier [= renchérir] sur leurs efforts, non comme traducteur, mais comme émulateur, non avec les mêmes mots, mais avec d'autres ou équivalents, ou frappés à un coin plus digne.' For Bouhours, similarly, verbal imitation is plagiary, unless the original is improved: 'Je veux bien qu'il [le bel esprit] imite les grands modèles de l'antiquité, pourvu qu'il tâche de les surpasser en les imitant [...] Je veux bien aussi qu'il se serve dans les rencontres des pensées des bons auteurs, pourvu qu'il y ajoute des beautés nouvelles et qu'à l'exemple des abeilles, qui changent en miel ce qu'elles prennent sur les fleurs, non seulement il choisisse ce qu'il y a de bon dans les livres, mais encore qu'il se fasse propre ce qu'il choisit et qu'il le rende meilleur par l'usage qu'il en fait.' Méré says much the same: 'Mais il se faut bien garder de prendre leurs inventions, ni leurs pensées, si ce n'est qu'on enchérisse par-dessus les inventeurs, comme Virgile a pris quelques vers d'Homère, pour les mieux tourner, et le Tasse à même dessein en a traduit de l'un et de l'autre.' (*De l'Esprit*)

treat their models freely, even cavalierly, and the result is always a modern, original work. There is a great difference between the sixteenth century and the seventeenth century in this respect. Garnier, for example, to write his *Antigone*, translated Seneca's *Phoenissae* literally in his first two acts and Sophocles's *Antigone* in his last two; the third act alone has some claim to originality, and follows Statius closely. This servility is far removed from the independence of the seventeenth-century writers, who, when they do adapt a classical model, transform it into something quite different. Saint-Amant admits that he has treated the same subject as Ovid:

> Je le confesse; mais je n'ai pris de lui que le sujet tout simple, lequel j'ai conduit et manié selon ma fantaisie; que, s'il s'y rencontre en quelque endroit des choses qu'il ait dites, c'est que je les y ai trouvées si convenables et si nécessaires que la matière me les eût fournies d'elle-même, quand il ne m'en aurait pas ouvert le chemin, et que je ne les en pouvais ôter sans faire une faute ...

La Fontaine, in the preface to the *Contes*, says that

> il retranche, il amplifie, il change les incidents et les circonstances, quelquefois le principal événement et la suite: enfin, ce n'est plus la même chose, c'est proprement une nouvelle nouvelle; et celui qui l'a inventée aurait bien de la peine à reconnaître son propre ouvrage.

Molière, Corneille, and Racine might say the same. It should not be overlooked, either, that the seventeenth-century writers adapt modern writers at least as frequently, probably rather more frequently, than they adapt classical models. *Le Cid* was taken from Guillen de Castro's *Mocedades del Cid*; *Le Menteur* and *La Suite du Menteur* are based on Spanish originals; so are many of the comedies of Thomas Corneille and of Scarron. Rotrou used Italian sources; so sometimes did Molière.

Another rule is unity of tone. Boileau criticizes Ariosto in the *Dissertation sur Joconde* for mixing different tones, and says in the *Art poétique*:

> Il faut que chaque chose y soit mise en son lieu;
> Que le début, la fin répondent au milieu;
> Que d'un art délicat les pièces assorties
> N'y forment qu'un seul tout de diverses parties ...

'Il ne faut point [ ... ] faire rire et pleurer dans une même nouvelle,' writes La Fontaine in the preface to the *Contes*, and, in the preface to *Psyché*, 'l'uniformité de style est la règle la plus étroite que nous ayons'. In the theatre, this involved the separation of the genres. But the genres were less separate than one might think. In the first half of the century, mixed genres flourished: the pastoral contained comic elements, tragi-comedy combined tragedy and comedy, comedy was not uniformly comic. In the second half of the century, new mixed genres take their place: the *comédie-ballet,* the machine play, the opera, all combining several arts. Even the distinction between comedy and tragedy is not absolute. There are comic elements in the tragedies of Corneille and Racine, and Molière comes close to tragedy at times. There is, of course, no equivalent in Racine or Corneille of the porter scene in *Macbeth* or the graveyard scene in *Hamlet,* but it has been said, with some truth:

Molière avait fait entrer dans la comédie tout ce qu'elle pouvait comporter de tragédie; Racine a fait entrer dans la tragédie tout ce qu'elle pouvait comporter de comédie.                                        (Rigal)

The rules of *vraisemblance* and *bienséance* are of the first importance. Poetry, says Chapelain in his *Lettre sur la règle des 24 heures,* will only achieve its effect if it is convincing. Its object is to 'proposer à l'esprit, pour le purger de ses passions déréglées, les objets comme vrais et comme présents'. Verisimilitude and imitation of nature are, in fact, the same thing: 'l'imitation en tous poèmes doit être si parfaite qu'il ne paraisse aucune différence entre la chose imitée et celle qui imite...' (Chapelain). It was in the name of *vraisemblance* that the rules of the unities were introduced into the theatre; and much seventeenth-century criticism is preoccupied with it, and appears to us somewhat niggling in consequence. Scudéry, for instance, argues that Don Diègue, in *Le Cid,* is discourteous to leave five hundred gentlemen at his house while he goes and looks for his son, that there could not have been so many gentlemen at a small court like that of Seville, that there should have been a chain across the harbour to stop the Moors coming up the river, and that it is improbable that a girl should marry the man who killed her father. Valincour thinks that it is unlikely that M. de Clèves in Mme de Lafayette's novel should have first seen his future wife in a jeweller's shop – 'on n'a jamais laissé à une fille de seize ans le soin d'assortir des pierreries'.

A consequence of the principle of *vraisemblance* is that historical fact, even if true, should not necessarily be reproduced. Scudéry went so far as to suggest that historical subjects should be eschewed; the Academy disagreed, but stated firmly that historical fact should be altered in the interests of *vraisemblance.* In *Le Cid,* it suggested, another ending should have been provided – the Count should have turned out not to be Chimène's father, or should not have died from his wound, or the marriage should have been shown to be essential to the welfare of the state; though it would have been better if Corneille had chosen a different subject altogether. D'Aubignac, too, considers that the poet can alter history 'non seulement aux circonstances, mais encore en la principale action, pourvu qu'il fasse un beau poème', and thinks that

Camille in *Horace* ought to have rushed on to Horace's sword, and that Massinisse should have died at the end of Corneille's *Sophonisbe*. The principle of *vraisemblance*, by excluding the abnormal and the unusual, by eliminating chance, thus tends towards universality, an ideal which is expressed by Chapelain in the *Lettre sur l'Adonis* and the *Sentiments de l'Academie*. Art, says the Academy, 'se proposant l'idée universelle des choses, les épure des défauts et des irrégularités particulières que l'histoire par la séverité de ses lois est contrainte d'y souffrir'. For Rapin, *vraisemblance* is the means by which the poet recovers the archetypal idea:

> Car la vérité ne fait les choses que comme elles sont; et la vraisemblance les fait comme elles doivent être. La vérité est presque toujours défectueuse, par le mélange des conditions singulières, qui la composent. Il ne naît rien au monde, qui ne s'éloigne de la perfection de son idée en naissant. Il faut chercher des originaux et des modèles dans la vraisemblance, et dans les principes universels des choses: où il n'entre rien de matériel et de singulier, qui les corrompe. C'est par là que les portraits de l'histoire sont moins parfaits que les portraits de la poésie...
> *(Réflexions sur la poétique)*

This by no means implies that all *invraisemblance* is excluded from seventeenth-century literature, however. Corneille stated in his *Discours* that 'les grand sujets [ ... ] doivent toujours aller au delà du vraisemblable' – i.e. that the humdrum events of everyday life are not sufficient for tragedy. Thomas Corneille, in the preface to his *Timocrate* (1656), says that 'tout ce qui peut arriver sans violenter beaucoup l'ordre commun de la nature, doit être réputé vraisemblable' – and it is only in this sense that his play is probable. Somaize similarly, in the preface to *Le Procès des Précieuses* (1660), defines *vraisemblance* as:

> tout ce qui, bien qu'extraordinaire par sa nouveauté, tombe néanmoins assez dessous les sens pour persuader à l'esprit que cela peut arriver sans renverser l'ordre établi dans le cours des choses, ce qui dépend souvent bien plus de l'arrangement des actions que des actions mêmes.[15]

The rule of the unities itself necessitated a number of improbabilities in stage plays, as we shall see; and the convention that characters on the stage should speak in verse is improbable, as Chapelain pointed out:

> Et en cela notre langue se peut dire plus malheureuse qu'aucune autre, étant obligée, outre le vers, à la tyrannie de la rime, laquelle ôte toute la vraisemblance au théâtre et toute la créance à ceux qui y portent quelque étincelle de jugement.      *(Lettre sur la règle des vingt-quatre heures)*

[15] The point of view of Thomas Corneille and Somaize is not far removed from that of Mr. Puff in Sheridan's *Critic*: 'What the plague! a play is not to show occurrences that happen every day, but things just so strange, that though they never did, they might happen.'

Finally, the principle of *vraisemblance* did not exclude the supernatural.

Le merveilleux est tout ce qui est contre le cours ordinaire de la nature. Le vraisemblable est tout ce qui est conforme à l'opinion du public. Le changement de Niobé en rocher est une aventure, qui tient du merveilleux: mais elle devient vraisemblable, dès qu'une divinité à qui ce changement n'est pas impossible, s'en mêle.                        (Rapin, *Réflexions*)

In Corneille, there is the *merveilleux chrétien* of *Polyeucte*, and the magic spells of Médee; in Molière, the divine punishment of the chief character of *Dom Juan*; and in Racine's *Phèdre*, Hippolyte is killed by a sea monster sent by Neptune.[16]

*Bienséance* is a far-reaching principle. At times, it is almost indistinguishable from *vraisemblance*. D'Aubignac, for instance, criticizes Corneille's *Œdipe* because in it Œdipe, a king's son, travels alone: this is at once contrary to *bienséance* and to *vraisemblance*. Rapin, in one place, uses it in the sense of 'ordonnance', arrangement; in an interesting passage in the *Réflexions sur la poétique*, he attributes almost every defect to an infraction of the rule of *bienséance*:

Sans elle les autres règles de la poésie sont fausses: parce qu'elle est le fondement le plus solide de cette vraisemblance, qui est si essentielle à cet art. Car ce n'est que par la bienséance que la vraisemblance a son effet: tout devient vraisemblable, dès que la bienséance garde son caractère dans toutes les circonstances. On pèche d'ordinaire contre cette règle, ou parce que l'on confond le sérieux avec le plaisant, comme a fait le Pulci dans son poème du Morgante; ou qu'on donne des mœurs disproportionnées à la qualité des personnes, comme le Guarini a fait à ses bergères, qui sont trop polies, de même que celles de Ronsard sont trop grossières; ou parce qu'on ne pense pas à rendre vraisemblables les aventures merveilleuses, comme fait Arioste dans son Roland; ou qu'on ne prépare pas assez les grands événements par une conduite naturelle, comme Bernardo Tasso dans son poème des Amadis et dans son Floridante; ou qu'on n'a pas soin de soutenir les caractères des personnes, comme Théophile dans sa tragédie de Pyrame et Thisbé; ou qu'on suit plutôt son génie que la nature, comme Lopé de Vega, qui s'abandonne trop à son esprit, et qui fourre ses imaginations partout; ou qu'on n'a pas de modestie, comme Dante, qui invoque son propre esprit pour sa divinité, et comme Boccace, qui parle sans cesse de lui-même; ou qu'on dit tout indifféremment sans pudeur, comme le chevalier Marin dans son Adonis. Enfin tout ce qui est contre les règles du temps, des mœurs, des sentiments, de l'expression, est contraire à la bienséance, qui est la plus universelle de toutes les règles.                        (*Réflexions sur la poétique*)

[16] In the preface to the first twelve books of *La Pucelle*, Chapelain defends the miraculous, but adds that 'lorsque je dressai mon plan et que je donnai la forme poétique à ce véritable événement j'eus un soin particulier de le conduire de telle sorte que tout ce que j'y fais faire par la puissance divine, s'y pût croire fait par la seule force humaine élevée au plus haut point où la nature soit capable de monter.'

In other words, *bienséance* is virtually the sum of all the other rules. Nevertheless, the rule of *bienséance* chiefly implies two things.

First, characters must be true to themselves, must, as Chapelain puts it, 'parler chacun selon sa condition, son âge, son sexe', a valet should speak like a valet, and a king like a king: Scudéry attacked Don Fernand in *Le Cid* because he does not act like a king. Furthermore, characters must have their accustomed characters (i.e. be historically true):

Au moins il faut tâcher de parler des mœurs conformément à l'opinion publique: on doit faire Ajax farouche comme l'a fait Sophocle; Polyxène et Iphigénie généreuses, comme les a faites Euripide. Il faut enfin que les mœurs soient proportionnées à l'âge, au sexe, à la qualité, aux emplois, et à la fortune des personnes...                          (Rapin, *Réflexions*)

Boileau in the *Art poétique* agrees:

> Qu'Agamemnon soit fier, superbe, intéressé,
> Que pour ses Dieux Enée ait un respect austère.
> Conservez à chacun son propre caractère.
> Des siècles, des pays étudiez les mœurs...

Characters must also be consistent:

> D'un nouveau personnage inventez-vous l'idée?
> Qu'en tout avec soi-même il se montre d'accord,
> Et qu'il soit jusqu'au bout tel qu'on l'a vu d'abord.
>                                                   (*Art poétique*)

Second, a work should suit the public for which it was written – 'Si le sujet n'est conforme aux mœurs et aux sentiments des spectateurs, il ne réussira jamais,' says d'Aubignac. This has three consequences:

(1) History must be changed, not only in the interests of *vraisemblance*, but in those of *bienséance* as well; it must be made to suit contemporary taste. Corneille's Rodogune is not married to the father before she marries the son; his Nicomède does not kill his father, as his historical prototype had done. Racine's Andromaque is not the concubine of Pyrrhus, as the equivalent character in Euripides is that of Neoptolemus; and Racine explains in his preface:

Andromaque ne connaît point d'autre mari qu'Hector, ni d'autre fils qu'Astyanax. J'ai cru en cela me conformer à l'idée que nous avons maintenant de cette princesse.

The reason for these changes is that characters who offended against the *bienséances* would forfeit the sympathy of the audience. Racine goes on to say:

Et je doute que les larmes d'Andromaque eussent fait sur l'esprit de mes spectateurs l'impression qu'elles y ont faite, si elles avaient coulé pour un autre fils que celui qu'elle avait d'Hector.

The great dramatists did not, however, always observe this principle: Corneille allows his Sophonisbe to marry Massinisse while her first husband, Syphax, is still alive; his Attila dies of a haemorrhage, as in history (though not actually of nose-bleeding); and Racine, unlike some of his predecessors who turned Phèdre into Thésée's betrothed, keeps the situation of a stepmother in love with her stepson.

(2) The crude, the obscene, and the improper – according to contemporary ideas – must be avoided:

> ... le lecteur français veut être respecté;
> Du moindre sens impur la liberté l'outrage,
> Si la pudeur des mots n'en adoucit l'image.
>
> (Boileau, *Art poétique*)

D'Aubignac criticizes Corneille's *Sophonisbe* because it shows two queens conversing with their *suivantes*; Corneille's defenders retorted that they were not *suivantes* but *dames d'honneur*. D'Aubignac similarly objects to Viriate's suggesting that Sertorius should marry her, to Pompée's explaining to his ex-wife that his new wife is a wife in name only, to the way in which Corneille's characters interrupt each other. Subligny criticizes *Andromaque*, because Oreste addresses Pylade as *tu*, though Pylade is a king like himself, because Pyrrhus ought not to go in search of Oreste who is a mere ambassador, and because Oreste, a king, should not be an ambassador. Another critic says that Théramène ought not to encourage the love of Hippolyte for Aricie in *Phèdre* and that Aricie admits too easily that she loves Hippolyte. Valincour suggests that Mme de Chartres in *La Princesse de Clèves* should have accompanied her daughter to the jeweller's.

The style should be noble; words considered *bas* must be avoided. Boileau points out how capricious language is:

En effet, les langues ont chacune leur bizarrerie: mais la française est principalement capricieuse sur les mots; et bien qu'elle soit riche en beaux termes sur de certains sujets, il y en a beaucoup où elle est fort pauvre; et il y a un très grand nombre de petites choses qu'elle ne saurait dire noblement. Ainsi, par exemple, bien que dans les endroits les plus sublimes elle nomme sans s'avilir un mouton, une chèvre, une brebis, elle ne saurait, sans se diffamer, dans un style un peu élevé, nommer un veau, une truie, un cochon. Le mot de génisse en français est fort beau, surtout dans une églogue; *vache* ne s'y peut pas souffrir. *Pasteur* et *berger* y sont du plus bel usage; *gardeur de pourceaux* ou *gardeur de bœufs* y seraient horribles.  (*IXᵉ Réflexion sur Longin*)

In the second half of the century it became impossible, in noble language, to refer to parts of the body, except by such vague words as *sein*, *flanc*, or *estomac*. Boileau considered that the art of poetry was to name trivial objects 'sans s'avilir', and told Maucroix in a letter that the two lines of his which La Fontaine most admired

were those in which (in his first *Epître*) he referred to the establishment of the lace industry in France:

> Et nos voisins frustrés de ces tributs serviles
> Que payait à leur art le luxe de nos villes.

(3) In tragedy, nothing must be shown on the stage which might
'ensanglanter la scène' or shock the public, nothing violent or low
or base. Fights, battles, duels and violent death cease to be shown.
Suicides are allowed, but only in the last scene, and the convention
required that a suicide should not both make a last speech on the
stage and kill himself there as well – he may kill himself and die
immediately, or he may make a speech but commit suicide or at
least expire offstage: Phèdre, for example, takes poison before
coming on to the stage to speak and die.

As regards style, clarity and purity are required: on this point
the seventeenth century is one.

Finally, there were particular rules for the various genres – the
epic (which included the novel), tragedy and comedy, and the
various kinds of verse composition (the idyll, the ode, and so forth
– but not the fable). Those affecting the theatre will be considered
in Chapter 8.[17]

Such, then, is French classicism, a compromise between several
different influences – admiration for antiquity inherited from the
Renaissance; the growing authority of reason and common sense
(*vraisemblance*); and the influence of the salons (*bienséance*). The
rules, as we have just attempted to summarize them, were far
from absolute – they were guiding principles rather than rules,
not always observed, susceptible of divergent interpretations (as the
literary controversies of the period show), and sometimes contradictory (e.g. the principles of imitation of nature and historical
accuracy conflicted with the principles both of *vraisemblance* and
of *bienséance*), thus allowing the writer a great deal of latitude.
Moreover, they were mitigated by the need to please. The salons
disliked pedantry, and as a whole the seventeenth century regarded
it as less important to be correct than to give pleasure. During the
*querelle du Cid*, Balzac wrote to Scudéry:

> Or s'il est vrai que la satisfaction des spectateurs soit la fin que se pro-
> posent les spectacles, et que les maîtres mêmes du métier aient quelque-
> fois appelé de César au peuple, le Cid du peuple français ayant plu aussi

[17] The main works mentioned in the foregoing pages are: Chapelain,
*Lettre sur le poème d'Adonis du Chevalier Marino* (1623), *Lettre sur la
règle des vingt-quatre heures*, *Discours de la poésie représentative*, and
the preface to the first twelve books of *La Pucelle* (1656); Scudéry,
*Observations sur le Cid* (1637); the *Sentiments de l'Académie sur le Cid*
(1637); d'Aubignac, *La Pratique du Théâtre* (1657); Corneille, *Discours*
(1660); Bouhours, *Entretiens d'Ariste et d'Eugène* (1671); Boileau, *Art
poétique* (1674); Rapin, *Réflexions sur la poétique* (1674).

bien que la fleur du poète grec, ne serait-il point vrai qu'il a obtenu la fin de la représentation, et qu'il est arrivé à son but, encore que ce ne soit pas par le chemin d'Aristote, ni par les adresses de sa poétique.

There is nothing frigid or anaemic about seventeenth-century classicism. The perplexed, tormented characters of Corneille and Racine have little in common with the 'edle Einfalt und stille Grösse' of Winckelmann or the serenity of Goethe's *Iphigenie*. The great seventeenth-century writers lived in no ivory tower; if they achieved the universal, it was not at the expense of the contemporary, the topical, or the personal. Seventeenth-century classicism was a discipline imposed on people of robust individuality who were in need of discipline. It was imposed, too, on a baroque sensibility. Baroque characteristics abound all through the period we are considering, but perhaps the best way to illustrate the combination of classicism and baroque is to consider Thomas Corneille's *Timocrate* (1656). This play, after all, was the greatest dramatic success of the century. A French play in the seventeenth century was more than usually successful if it ran for twenty or twenty-five performances; few had over thirty. *Timocrate* is said not only to have run for eighty performances, but even to have been played for a time in both the theatres of Paris. In other words, it must have hit the taste of its public unerringly.

Now *Timocrate* is a classical play. It obeys the rule of the unities; the stage is never left empty; the *bienséances* are observed, and no physical action takes place on the stage. On the other hand, one can hardly claim that Thomas Corneille was trying to analyse the basic, timeless passions of humanity, or that his tragedy is primarily a psychological study; and his play can be considered *vraisemblable* only if we accept his own claim,[18] that virtually anything possible is probable.

If the technique is classical, the theme, the confusion of identities, is baroque. *Timocrate* is *Amphitryon* or the *Comedy of Errors* in reverse: instead of two men with but one appearance, we have one man with two appearances. The basic situation is paralleled by the constant use of double-entendre throughout the play. And underlying the tragedy is the sense that the world is an illusion, that reality is elusive. In the first four acts, the hero, Cléomène, is not one man, but two or even more: there is Cléomène talking and acting, usually in an unexpected way; there is Cléomène explaining – sometimes giving more than one explanation – why he should talk and act so; and there is the reality under these façades, concealed from us until the end of Act IV. In Act I, scene 3, for example, Cléomène advises the Queen to accept Timocrate's offer

[18] See above, p. 90.

of peace in exchange for the hand of the princess. His advice is unexpected and surprising. The reason he gives for it at the time is
that peace is a good thing. To Nicandre later, he explains that
really his motive was a selfish one: since he cannot himself marry
Eriphile, he would rather she married someone she cannot love than
someone she might love. Still later, he tells Eriphile that he advised
the Queen to accept Timocrate's offer because Timocrate is the
most worthy of all her suitors. But, of course, the true explanation
– which we do not know till the end of Act IV – is that he himself
is Timocrate. No wonder that the brain reels, or that the Queen
should explain in a typical, baroque phrase: 'Je me perds, je
m'égare.' Nicandre is similarly enigmatic; in fact, he takes up and
continues the theme of the deceptiveness of appearances in Act V
when the identity of Timocrate is no longer in doubt. His actions
in that act belie his words; or rather, they would belie his words,
were it not that in the light of his subsequent actions it becomes
clear that his words were capable of a different construction
from the one we at first put upon them.

The play is designed to surprise and stupefy the spectator.
It consists of a series of surprises, culminating in the discovery
that Cléomène is Timocrate; and a similar straining after
dramatic effect and abnormal situations is seen in the Queen's
dilemma. She has vowed that Cléomène shall marry her daughter
and that Timocrate shall die: what is she to do when it is
discovered that Timocrate and Cléomène are one and the same?
The baroque love of the grandiose is reflected in the extreme
magnanimity of the characters. We find, too, the sense of the
mutability of life, of man as the plaything of fate:

> Tel est l'injuste effet des caprices du sort.
> Son ordre aveuglément contre nous se déploie.
> Il me chassa d'Argos, c'est lui qui me renvoie;
> Forcé par ses décrets je reviens en ces lieux.

And the inherent topsy-turviness and paradoxicality of the world
are evident all through the play in the abundance of oxymoron
and paradoxical antithesis:

> Et j'ai pu m'attirer un traitement semblable
> Par le plus bel effet dont l'amour soit capable?

> Afin de mieux aimer j'ai voulu me haïr
> Et je me suis trahi de peur de vous trahir.
> . . . . . . . . . . .
> . . . j'eusse été perfide à le paraître moins.

> . . . je te fais une injustice
> Par un principe de vertu.

J'aime ce que je perds, et je perds ce que j'aime.

J'ai cru que vous trahir c'était être fidèle.

The work of religious reform and of active assistance to the poor and needy continued apace. Provision was at last made for the education of the clergy by Olier, who founded the seminary of Saint-Sulpice in Paris in 1642, and Père Eudes, who founded the Société des prêtres du séminaire de Jésus et Marie at Caen in 1643. Both Olier and Eudes founded other seminaries elsewhere subsequently. In 1633, Saint Vincent de Paul, together with Louise de Marillac, founded a secular society of Filles de la Charité to tend the sick and the old, and to look after foundlings. In 1638, he opened a home for these last, and in 1653 the Hospice du Saint Nom de Jésus for old men. Henry Buch, a shoemaker and a friend of M. de Renty, in order to combat impiety amongst working men, formed communities where, without taking vows, they could live together in poverty, chastity, and piety — the frères cordonniers (1645) and the frères tailleurs (1647).

The work of individuals was seconded or even inspired by the Compagnie du Saint-Sacrement, known to its enemies as the Cabale des Dévots. This was a secret society, the idea of which was first conceived by the duc de Ventadour in 1627, and which, with the help of his director, Philippe d'Angoumois, a Capuchin friar, abbé de Grignan, and Henri de Pichery, maître d'hôtel du Roi, he eventually founded in 1629. Carefully chosen collaborators, drawn from all ranks of society, were enlisted, and branches were founded all over France. Statutes were drawn up; the society was approved by Louis XIII in 1631, and enjoyed the support of Anne of Austria. There was a Superior, a Director (always a priest), a Secretary, and six councillors, elected every three months. Meetings were held every Thursday. The society was kept strictly secret; not even the Bishop of a diocese was allowed to know of its work or membership unless he happened to belong to it. Among its members one finds ecclesiastics, such as Saint Vincent de Paul, abbé Olier, Père Suffren (a Jesuit and confessor to the King and the Queen Mother), and Bossuet; magistrates, like Chrétien de Lamoignon and his son Guillaume, d'Argenson, and d'Ormesson; great nobles, like maréchal de Schomberg, the comte de Noailles, the duc de Liancourt, and the prince de Conti; and humbler folk, such as M. de Renty (who joined in 1638 and was Superior eleven times) and his friend, the shoemaker, Henry Buch.

The purpose of the society was to do good and combat evil —

i.e. what it regarded as such. Members of the society visited the sick and the poor, and gave alms. They visited prisons and alleviated the lot of the inmates. They founded hospitals and poor-houses, notably the Hôpital Général of Paris. During the Fronde, *magasins charitables* were set up, and missions sent to devastated parishes. A successful campaign against duelling was carried out: in 1651, a number of gentlemen were persuaded to undertake publicly not to fight duels.

D'abord [writes Mademoiselle], cette proposition fut tournée en ridicule, parce qu'elle avait été faite par certains dévots qui étaient assez ridicules eux-mêmes, et qu'il n'y avait eu que des estropiés qui avaient signé. On disait, c'est qu'ils ne sont pas en état de marcher, quand on leur a donné sur les oreilles; c'est pourquoi ils ont trouvé cet expédient. Néanmoins la proposition était bonne en soi, elle trouva des partisans, elle fut autorisée, et elle a très bien réussi, on se bat fort peu.

The Compagnie, through the influence of its members, reformed various abuses (e.g. in the administration of prisons), and suppressed various unseemly customs (e.g. at carnival time). It had prostitutes imprisoned and gaming houses closed, and was solicitous for the welfare of girls coming to seek employment in Paris. It gave money for the repair of churches, and tried to ensure that priests resided in their parishes and performed their duties properly, and that Church fasts and Lent were strictly observed — butchers who sold meat on fast days, and innkeepers who sold wine during the hours of church services, were prosecuted. It supported missions at home and overseas, and in 1663 founded the séminaire des Missions étrangères. 'On peut dire enfin,' says Rapin, 'que la plupart des bonnes œuvres les plus célèbres de ce siècle et les plus glorieuses à la religion ont été le fruit de cette sainte compagnie.'

Some of its activities were — to our ideas, at least — more questionable. Husbands were informed of the misconduct of their wives; blasphemers were severely punished; attempts were made to persuade doctors not to visit patients who did not call in their confessors. The Compagnie opposed Jansenism, and brought pressure to bear on Louis XIV to ban Molière's *Tartuffe*. It suppressed Protestant books, schools, churches, and hospitals, excluded Protestants from official positions and guilds, and tried to prevent mixed marriages. It attempted to have Jews banished from the country. Such intolerance, however, was that of the age, and it is only fair to quote d'Argenson's impression of the first meeting he attended:

Le 17ᵉ de novembre [1656], j'eus l'honneur d'entrer pour la première fois dans la Compagnie, et j'y remarquai d'abord tant de vertu et un si grand fonds de l'esprit de l'Evangile que j'en fus charmé; j'y trouvais tant de zèle pour la religion catholique, tant de charité pour les misérables, tant de sagesse pour la conduite des bonnes œuvres, et tant de simplicité, de sincérité, de soumission à rendre compte de ses actions au Supérieur, que je crus voir une assemblée de premiers chrétiens, qui n'avaient qu'une même volonté pour le service de leur Maître et pour le secours de leurs frères.

In 1660, the members of a branch of the Company, the Ermitage of Caen, founded by M. de Bernières, carried out some noisy demonstrations against the Jansenists, not only at Caen, but also at Falaise, Argentan, and Séez. A Jansenist, Charles du Four, published a pamphlet against them, *Mémoire pour faire connaître l'esprit et la conduite de la Compagnie établie en la ville de Caen et appelée 'L'Ermitage'*, giving details about the company at large. The Archbishop of Rouen denounced them to Mazarin, who had his own reasons for disliking the Compagnie du Saint-Sacrement:

Le cardinal fut d'autant plus susceptible de ces impressions qu'il avait déjà en quelque façon expérimenté le zèle de quelques dévots qui voulurent lui donner des avis sur sa conduite, et il avait été choqué de certains billets qu'il trouvait, ou sous son couvert quand il se mettait à table, ou dans sa poche quand il changeait d'habits, ou sur la table de son cabinet quand il s'enfermait pour travailler.                    (Rapin, *Mémoires*)

Mazarin ordered an inquiry, and on 13 December 1660 the parlement of Paris, presided over by Lamoignon, himself a member, forbade all secret assemblies. The Company, though not directly named, was illegal; and it resolved to obey, though its officers continued to meet until 1665. Branches in the provinces survived even longer.

The work of evangelization of Canada was particularly active in this period. Mme de Peltrie and Mme Martin sailed thither in 1639; Montreal was founded in 1642. Père Isaac Jogues was martyred in 1644, Père Antoine Daniel in 1648, and Père Jean de Brébeuf with three others in 1649. Mgr de Laval was chosen to be the first bishop of Canada in 1659. Missionaries were active elsewhere, too – in China and Africa, for example.

In the religious history of this period, an important part is played by Port-Royal, which became the headquarters of a movement known as Jansenism. In 1626, the situation of Port-Royal being unhealthy and the house too small for the vastly increased number of nuns, the convent was transferred to Paris: henceforth, the original convent, which was reopened in 1648, is known as Port-Royal des Champs, and the new one – which still stands – as Port-Royal de Paris. In 1636, Saint-Cyran (1581–1643) became director to Port-Royal; he had known Cornelius Jansen or Jansenius, Bishop of Ypres, in his youth and they studied the fathers of the Church together for many years; and it is through him that Port-Royal became Jansenist. Another important development took place in 1638, when two nephews of Mère Angélique, Antoine Lemaître and his brother, M. de Séricourt, were converted, and went into retreat in a building adjoining Port-Royal. They were the first of the *solitaires*. Others soon joined them, and they began to teach boys – this is the origin of the *petites écoles*, regularly established in Paris in 1646 and transferred to Port-Royal des Champs in 1650.

In 1640, Jansenius's book, the *Augustinus*, was published posthumously at Louvain; it was reprinted at Paris in 1641 and at Rouen in 1643. As Voltaire neatly points out:

Pendant que les jésuites établissaient leur science moyenne et leur congruisme, Cornélius Jansénius, évêque d'Ypres, renouvelait quelques idées de Baïus, dans un gros livre sur Saint Augustin, qui ne fut imprimé qu'après sa mort; de sorte qu'il devint chef de secte, sans jamais s'en douter. Presque personne ne lut ce livre, qui a causé tant de troubles; mais Duvergier de Hauranne, abbé de Saint-Cyran, ami de Jansénius, homme aussi ardent qu'écrivain diffus et obscur, vint à Paris, et persuada de jeunes docteurs et quelques vieilles femmes.

The book was denounced by Habert, the theologal of Notre-Dame, in three sermons preached in Paris in 1642 and 1643, which gave rise to a controversy; and, in 1643, the book was condemned by the Pope. The same year, Mère Angélique's youngest brother, 'le grand Arnauld', published a book called *La Fréquente Communion*.

Broadly speaking, the Jesuits had a fundamental faith in human nature, stressed the mercy of God and human free will, and tried to appeal to as wide a public as possible. Wishing to make it easy and pleasant for people to practise religion, they were inclined to be lenient with their penitents. In contrast, Jansenism stands for purity and austerity. The Jansenists, reacting against the moral laxity of the age and against the Jesuits, wanted a return to the primitive Church, and believed that salvation must be preceded by the experience of conversion. They were convinced that the sacraments should be respected, that only those who were truly contrite and had sincerely done penance for their sins should be admitted to communion, and that the sacraments are useless unless one genuinely loves God: Saint Vincent de Paul complained that after the publication of Arnauld's book, the number of people taking communion dropped alarmingly. Their religion stressed the omniscience and the omnipotence of God at the expense of human free will. For the Jansenists, the essential doctrine is that of the Fall and the Redemption. Since the Fall, man has been debased, incapable of doing good, capable only of sin. Grace alone can save man, and

Grace is all-powerful and cannot be resisted.[19] Grace is not given
to all; from all eternity, God has ordained who shall be saved – this
is the doctrine of predestination, which goes back to St. Augustine. In fact, however, God only rewards merit. Since no man knows
whether he is one of the elect or not, he must lead as strict a
Christian life as he can; the life of a Christian is a perpetual
penance.

In 1649, a former Jesuit, Nicolas Cornet, *syndic* of the Faculty
of Theology, submitted to the faculty five propositions that
represented, he claimed, the doctrine of Jansenius. The parlement
of Paris, a Gallican and anti-Jesuit body, forbade the Faculty
of Theology to debate the propositions. The Jesuits obtained the
signature of eighty-five bishops to a letter urging the Pope to
examine the propositions. In 1652, the Pope appointed a special
congregation for the purpose, and, in 1653, the propositions were
condemned – though, to complicate matters, the Pope said that
he did not mean to condemn St. Augustine and the doctrine
of efficient grace. The following year, the Pope declared that in
condemning the propositions he had condemned the doctrine
of Jansenius as expressed in the *Augustinus*.

The controversy flared up again in 1655, when the duc de
Liancourt, a friend of Port-Royal, was refused absolution by his
confessor on account of his Jansenist sympathies. Arnauld in
protest wrote a *Première Lettre à une Personne de Condition*,
which brought forth a number of replies. He followed it up in
October, 1655, with a *Seconde Lettre à un Duc et Pair*, in which
he denied that the propositions were in Jansenius (the *question
de fait*) and quoted St. Peter as an example of a just man who
had lacked the necessary grace to act aright (the *question de
droit*).[20] The book was denounced to the *syndic* of the Faculty
of Theology, a Molinist,[21] who appointed a commission of Molinist
sympathies to examine it. Arnauld was condemned on the *question
de fait* on 14 January 1656, and, on 29 January, on all points.
The Jesuits persuaded the government to close the *petites écoles*
and disperse the *solitaires*. A serious persecution, however, was
averted by the *miracle de la Sainte Épine* (24 March): Pascal's

[19] According to Pascal (Letter 18 of the *Provinciales*), the Jansenists
held that grace could be resisted—if they had not, they would have been
Calvinists. But the distinction is a nice one: for the Jansenists, though
man can resist grace, grace deprives him of the will to resist. In any case,
Calvin made the same distinction.
[20] The dogma of Papal infallibility was not declared until the nineteenth century. The Jansenists maintained that the Pope had the right to
decide whether a doctrine was orthodox or not (*question de droit*), but
was as liable to be wrong in matters of fact as anyone else. But Arnauld
disagreed with the Pope even over the *question de droit*.
[21] I.e. a follower of the Jesuit theologian and casuist, Molina.

niece was cured of a lachrymal ulcer by the application of a holy relic.

> Des personnes qui ont longtemps vécu avec elle [writes Voltaire] m'ont assuré que sa guérison avait été fort longue, et c'est ce qui est bien vraisemblable; mais ce qui ne l'est guère, c'est que Dieu, qui ne fait point de miracles pour amener à notre religion les dix-neuf vingtièmes de la terre, à qui cette religion est ou inconnue ou en horreur, eût en effet inter- rompu l'ordre de la nature en faveur d'une petite fille, pour justifier une douzaine de religieuses qui prétendaient que Cornélius Jansénius n'avait point écrit une douzaine de lignes qu'on lui attribue, ou qu'il les avait écrites dans une autre intention que celle qui lui est imputée.[22]

Be that as it may, everyone – the court and all Paris, save the Jesuits – thought that a miracle had been worked to show that God was on the side of Port-Royal. Eighty other miracles followed. The *solitaires* were allowed to return, though the schools were not reopened.

In 1656, a new Pope, Alexander VII, declared that his pre- decessor had condemned the *Augustinus* in the sense intended by Jansenius, and the Assembly of the clergy of France drew up a formulary to be signed by churchmen:

> Je me soumets sincèrement à la Constitution de N.S.P. le Pape Innocent X . . ., et je condamne de cœur et de bouche la doctrine des cinq Propo- sitions de Cornélius Jansénius, contenues dans son livre intitulé *Augustinus*, que le Pape et les Evêques ont condamnée; laquelle doctrine n'est point celle de saint Augustin, que Jansénius a mal expliquée contre le vrai sens de ce saint Docteur.

But the parlement of Paris refused to register the Pope's Bull, and nothing further was done for the moment.

At the same time, *libertins* abounded; in 1640, La Mothe le Vayer remarked, 'Jamais le nombre des athées n'a été si grand qu'aujourd'hui'. Gaston d'Orléans, the brother of Louis XIII, was of their number; so were the notorious Des Barreaux and the writer, Cyrano de Bergerac, to whom we shall return. The salons of Ninon de Lenclos and of Habert de Montmor, a councillor of the parlement of Paris and a disciple of Gassendi, were two of their meeting grounds.

It was in this period that a group of scholarly *libertins* – Gabriel Naudé (1600–53), François de La Mothe le Vayer (1588–1672), and Pierre Gassendi (1592–1655) – published their works. All three were sceptical of the supernatural. Naudé, in particular, critically examined popular superstitions – alchemy,

---

[22] Sainte-Beuve points out that several days elapsed before the girl was examined by a doctor. He suggests that the cause of the trouble may have been a blocked tear duct, which could easily have been cured but for the ignorance of seventeenth-century doctors, and which the pressure of the thorn, applied with fervour, would be enough to clear.

magic, prophecies, miracles, witchcraft, diabolic possession, the influence of comets — and historical legends and fables, and found them to be baseless, the product of imposture or of credulity. He gave a rationalistic interpretation of history, from which he eliminated Providence, and he regarded virtue and religion as two distinct things. Like Naudé, La Mothe le Vayer was sceptical of supernatural phenomena and, like him, by implication, even of Christian miracles. In his *Dialogues* (1630–1), he continued the Pyrrhonism of Montaigne, showing that reason is powerless to attain truth; that there has never been universal agreement about anything — moral standards, the immortality of the soul, or the existence and nature of God; and that, for every belief, the contrary opinion exists. Whether La Mothe le Vayer was sincere in the fideism he professed, or whether his scepticism extended as far as the Christian religion, is a moot point. Since Gassendi, the chief member of the group, was a priest, there is no reason to doubt his faith. He attacked Aristotle in his *Exercitationes paradoxicae adversus Aristoteleos* (1624); and, in his life of Epicurus (1647) and subsequent works, he rehabilitated Epicurus and expounded his philosophy — not only his deterministic atomic theory, but also his ethical system. For Gassendi, the aim of life is happiness, to be achieved by virtue and wisdom, a philosophy which is pagan rather than Christian in its inspiration. In opposition to Descartes, he held that animals have a material kind of soul, and that innate ideas do not exist.

However audacious the ideas of these three *libertins érudits*, their influence was restricted. They were not always consistent, and tended to express contradictory ideas in different works; they were obliged to be circumspect; and they were not anxious to proselytize. Many of their works were written in Latin and not accessible to the general public; and, whatever their private beliefs may have been, they professed Catholicism.[23]

If their scepticism was still based on mistrust of, rather than faith in, reason, this period witnessed the appearance of a philosopher who, in the face of the Pyrrhonists, asserted the possibility of knowledge and the pre-eminence of reason: René Descartes.

[23] For Cyrano de Bergerac, see below, chapter 10. One other *libertin* work should be mentioned, the anonymous *Theophrastus redivivus* (1659). This put forward the view that all religions were false and man-made; it maintained that man was an animal, not a superior being; and it proposed an ethical code based on nature and society (one must aim at self-preservation and not do to others what one would not that they should do to oneself).

## Chapter 7

# DESCARTES

CONVINCED by three dreams he dreamt on the night of 10–11 November 1619 that he was destined to found a universal science, René Descartes (1596–1650) set out to achieve certain knowledge by the use of his reason. The story of his quest – somewhat arranged – is related in his intellectual autobiography, the *Discours de la Méthode*.[1]

This first appeared in 1637 in a volume, the full title of which is: *Discours de la Méthode pour bien conduire sa raison, et chercher la vérité dans les sciences. Plus La Dioptrique. Les Météores. Et La Géométrie. Qui sont des essais de cette Méthode.* It was, in fact, intended to serve as a preface to three scientific works, these last illustrating the value of the principles expounded in the first. Descartes was not primarily a philosopher in the modern sense of the word; he was rather a scientist, interested in philosophy only in so far as it was necessary to provide a basis for scientific knowledge. In the preface to a later work, the *Principes de la Philosophie*, he defines philosophy as the study of wisdom (*sagesse*), and adds that, by *sagesse*,

on n'entend pas seulement la prudence dans les affaires, mais une parfaite connaissance de toutes les choses que l'homme peut savoir, tant pour la conduite de sa vie, que pour la conservation de sa santé et l'invention de tous les arts . . .

He goes on to say:

Ainsi toute la philosophie est comme un arbre, dont les racines sont la métaphysique, le tronc est la physique, et les branches qui sortent de ce tronc sont toutes les autres sciences, qui se réduisent à trois principales, à savoir la médecine, la mécanique et la morale [ . . . ]

Or comme ce n'est pas des racines, ni du tronc des arbres, qu'on cueille les fruits, mais seulement des extrémités de leurs branches, ainsi la principale utilité dépend de celles de ses parties qu'on ne peut apprendre que les dernières.

---

[1] A reaction against Pyrrhonism was setting in. Mersenne, in his *Vérité des Sciences* (1625), asserted that at least the appearances of things, phenomena, can be studied, so that scientific knowledge is possible.

In the *Discours* itself, he explains that, if he has resolved to publish his work, it is because his discoveries are conducive to 'le bien général de tous les hommes':

Car elles m'ont fait voir qu'il est possible de parvenir à des connaissances qui soient fort utiles à la vie, et qu'au lieu de cette philosophie spécula-tive, qu'on enseigne dans les écoles, on en peut trouver une pratique, par laquelle, connaissant la force et les actions du feu, de l'eau, de l'air, des astres, des cieux et de tous les autres corps qui nous environnent, aussi distinctement que nous connaissons les divers métiers de nos artisans, nous les pourrions employer en même façon à tous les usages auxquels ils sont propres, et ainsi nous rendre comme maîtres et possesseurs de la nature. Ce qui n'est pas seulement à désirer pour l'invention d'une infinité d'artifices, qui feraient qu'on jouirait, sans aucune peine, des fruits de la terre et de toutes les commodités qui s'y trouvent, mais principalement aussi pour la conservation de la santé, laquelle est sans doute le premier bien et le fondement de tous les autres biens de cette vie; car même l'esprit dépend si fort du tempérament, et de la disposition des organes du corps que, s'il est possible de trouver quelque moyen qui rende com-munément les hommes plus sages et plus habiles qu'ils n'ont eté jusques ici, je crois que c'est dans la médecine qu'on doit le chercher.

He adds that the progress of medicine will not only banish disease, but old age – Descartes was convinced at this time that he was on the verge of discovering the secret of longevity.[2]

The *Discours* is not a dogmatic treatise – Descartes specifically says that his purpose is not to teach 'la méthode que chacun doit suivre pour bien conduire sa raison, mais seulement de faire voir en quelle sorte j'ai tâché de conduire la mienne'. Hence the autobiographical form in which the work is cast. Moreover, it is written in French, not in Latin, because Descartes hopes that 'ceux qui ne se servent que de leur raison naturelle toute pure jugeront mieux de mes opinions que ceux qui ne croient qu'aux livres anciens'. He is thus one of the first to popularize philosophy and science, to appeal to the public at large: he stated in a letter that he wanted even women to understand the *Discours*.

The first three parts of the *Discours* are preparatory to the fourth, in which he relates how he found a basis for knowledge; the fifth outlines some of his discoveries; and in the sixth he explains why he decided to publish his work.

The first part opens with a statement of the importance of method. All men have an equal share of *bon sens* or reason, defined as the 'puissance de bien juger, et distinguer le vrai d'avec le faux'; and yet they do not think alike, because they do not all apply their reason equally well.

---

[2] 'Je n'ai jamais eu plus de soin de me conserver que maintenant,' he wrote to Huygens on 4 December 1637, 'et au lieu que je pensais autrefois que la mort ne me pût ôter que trente ou quarante ans tout au plus, elle ne saurait désormais me surprendre qu'elle ne m'ôte l'espérance de plus d'un siècle.'

Car ce n'est pas assez d'avoir l'esprit bon, mais le principal est de l'appli-
quer bien [...] Ceux qui ne marchent que fort lentement peuvent avancer
beaucoup davantage, s'ils suivent toujours le droit chemin, que ne font
ceux qui courent, et qui s'en éloignent.

Descartes explains that he believes he has found the right method
to search for truth, but, since he may be wrong, he proposes
to set it out in a personal way, to tell the story of his life, of his
quest and its results, to 'représenter ma vie comme en un tableau'.

After this preamble, he describes his education and his dissatisfaction with it. He surveys the various branches of knowledge
and shows that there is no certainty in any. The study of antiquity, without being valueless, has little relevance to modern
life. There is little to be learned from the classics: the fables of
antiquity are fictitious; their histories do not accurately represent
events; and their moral philosophy is unsound. Eloquence and
poetry cannot be learned. Theology is useless, since those who
have not studied it are as able to be virtuous and achieve Heaven
as those who have. Philosophy is vain, since philosophers disagree
among themselves about everything. Mathematics alone finds
favour in Descartes's eyes, but he regrets that, though it provides
a firm basis, nothing has so far been constructed on it.

Descartes has no doubt that the fault is in the sciences, not in
himself. Educated in a distinguished college, he was in no way
inferior to his fellow-students; and he had no reason to suppose
his own age to be in any way inferior to those which had preceded
it. Like Faust, though in a somewhat different spirit – 'j'avais
toujours un extrême désir d'apprendre à distinguer le vrai d'avec
le faux, pour voir clair en mes actions, et marcher avec assurance
en cette vie' –, he quitted the study for the world, and travelled,
observing the disparity of customs and opinions in different
countries. The first part ends – like an act of a classical tragedy –
with the resolution he came to after some years of this life: 'je
pris un jour résolution d'étudier aussi en moi-même, et d'employer toutes les forces de mon esprit à choisir les chemins que je
devais suivre'.

Part II tells us what came of that resolution, during the winter
that Descartes spent in a *poêle* (a room heated by a stove) in
Germany in 1619. This part opens with the statement that a
work composed by one man is likely to be more perfect than
one composed piecemeal by many. Just as, if one wants a handsome house, it is better to pull down the old one and rebuild than
to tinker with it, so he resolves to doubt everything he has learned
and start afresh. He doubts because he knows, from his studies
and his travels, that all opinions, however contradictory, have
their supporters, that fashions change, and that a Frenchman and

a foreigner will think differently, simply because they are used to different ways of life – in other words, that opinions are largely a matter of custom. Here, we are reminded of Montaigne and the Pyrrhonists; but Descartes is at pains to stress the difference:

Non que j'imitasse pour cela les sceptiques, qui ne doutent que pour douter, et affectent d'être toujours irrésolus: car, au contraire, tout mon dessein ne tendait qu'à m'assurer, et à rejeter la terre mouvante et le sable, pour trouver le roc ou l'argile.

In order to achieve certainty, as Descartes has already stated, a method is required; and, in this Second Part, he outlines his method, based on the best principles of logic, geometry, and algebra. It consists of four principles. The first is that clarity is a test of truth; Descartes resolves

de ne recevoir jamais aucune chose pour vraie, que je ne la connusse évidemment être telle: c'est-à-dire, d'éviter soigneusement la précipitation et la prévention; et de ne comprendre rien de plus en mes jugements, que ce qui se présenterait si clairement et si distinctement à mon esprit, que je n'eusse aucune occasion de le mettre en doute.

The other three are to break up difficulties into as many parts as possible, in order to tackle them separately; to think systematically, passing from the simple to the complex; and to make periodical comprehensive reviews so as to be sure of not having overlooked anything. With this method, Descartes affirms, one is bound to reach truth:

Ces longues chaînes de raisons, toutes simples et faciles, dont les géomètres ont coutume de se servir, pour parvenir à leurs plus difficiles démonstrations, m'avaient donné occasion de m'imaginer que toutes les choses, qui peuvent tomber sous la connaissance des hommes, s'entresuivent en même façon et que, pourvu seulement qu'on s'abstienne d'en recevoir aucune pour vraie qui ne le soit, et qu'on garde toujours l'ordre qu'il faut pour les déduire les unes des autres, il n'y en peut avoir de si éloignées auxquelles enfin on ne parvienne, ni de si cachées qu'on ne découvre.

Descartes then describes how he trained himself to apply this method to the solution of difficulties in mathematics, and how, not being mature enough for his main task at twenty-three, he prepared himself for it by practising his method and by eradicating prejudices and preconceived ideas from his mind.

In the Third Part, Descartes deals with a different matter. He was not ready for his main task, but he had to live in society. He therefore drew up a provisional code of behaviour – to obey the laws and customs of his own country and, in cases of doubt, to favour moderate, rather than extreme, opinions; to be resolute and, having once taken a decision, to adhere to it without wavering; to cultivate stoical detachment – 'de tâcher toujours plutôt à me vaincre que la fortune, et à changer mes désirs que l'ordre du monde'; and to persevere in his search for knowledge. The first three of these principles, as we shall see, passed into his *Traité des Passions*. Descartes then relates how, having also resolved to exempt religious truths from his systematic doubt, he travelled for nine years, preparing himself for his task, until (in 1628) he finally settled in Holland, where he could live a peaceful and secluded life, 'aussi solitaire et retiré que dans les déserts les plus écartés'.

In the Fourth Part, Descartes tells how he finally embarked upon his task. Since the senses are unreliable and the reason fallible, he rejected all the ideas that had ever entered his mind. One thing, however, he could not doubt – that, as he thought, he must exist. 'Je pense, donc je suis.' Not only is this statement indubitably true, he claims, but it provides a test for truth:

> Et ayant remarqué qu'il n'y a rien du tout en ceci: *je pense, donc je suis*, qui m'assure que je dis la vérité, sinon que je vois très clairement que, pour penser, il faut être: je jugeai que je pouvais prendre, pour règle générale, que les choses que nous concevons fort clairement et fort distinctement sont toutes vraies . . .

Descartes now noted that, since he doubted, he was imperfect; in other words, he had in his mind the idea of a perfect being, infinite, eternal, omniscient. But the idea of such a being cannot come from nothing or from an imperfect being: it could not, therefore, have originated in Descartes's own mind. It could only have come from the perfect being itself; therefore the perfect being, i.e. God, exists. A further proof is that perfection implies existence – a being that did not exist would lack one of the qualities of perfection.

The existence of God provides a guarantee that clear and distinct ideas are true, and that the reason is a check on the aberrations of the senses: 'Car enfin, soit que nous veillions, soit que nous dormions, nous ne nous devons jamais laisser persuader qu'à l'évidence de notre raison.'

In the Fifth Part, Descartes outlines the further conclusions he derived from these truths by the application of his method:

> . . . j'ose dire que, non seulement j'ai trouvé moyen de me satisfaire en peu de temps, touchant toutes les principales difficultés dont on a coutume de traiter en la philosophie, mais aussi que j'ai remarqué certaines lois, que Dieu a tellement établies en la nature, et dont il a imprimé de telles notions en nos âmes, qu'après y avoir fait assez de réflexion, nous ne saurions douter qu'elles ne soient exactement observées, en tout ce qui est ou qui se fait dans le monde. Puis, en considérant la suite de ces lois, il me semble avoir découvert plusieurs vérités plus utiles et plus importantes que tout ce que j'avais appris auparavant, ou même espéré d'apprendre.

He illustrates this by summarizing an earlier, unpublished, treatise of his on *Le Monde* and *L'Homme*. Had God, he asserts, created matter in a state of chaos and left it to behave according to natural laws, the universe as we know it would have resulted. This, he is careful to say, is not necessarily how the universe originated, 'car il est bien plus vraisemblable que, dès le commencement, Dieu l'a rendu tel qu'il devait être'; nevertheless it could have originated in this way, without the intervention of God. Then, turning to man, he gives his conclusions about the relationship of the body and soul, and the way the body works. Man, for Descartes, is a machine, except that he has the power of reason and speech, and therefore a soul. Animals lack the power of reason and have no souls. The human soul is 'd'une nature entièrement indépendante du corps' and therefore 'elle n'est point sujette à mourir avec lui'.

Finally, in the Sixth Part, Descartes explains why he decided to publish his work and why he wrote it in French.

The *Méditations métaphysiques*, published in Latin in 1641, develop the metaphysical speculations contained in the Fourth Part of the *Discours*; the *Principes de la Philosophie*, published – also in Latin – in 1644, expound Descartes's views about the universe and the earth (i.e. cosmology and physics). His moral philosophy is contained in the *Traité des Passions*, published in French in 1649.

This work, with its analysis of the passions and the fine distinctions between such emotions as *admiration* and *étonnement*, or *affection*, *amitié*, and *dévotion*, bears the hallmark of its period. It is divided into three parts, in the first of which Descartes explains the mechanism of the body and the interaction of the body and the soul through the pineal gland. The passions are emotions of the soul, caused by sensations in the body which propel animal spirits into the soul by way of the nerves and the pineal gland.

In the second and third parts, Descartes analyses the passions in turn, first the six basic passions (admiration, love, hatred, desire, joy, and sorrow), and then those derived from them. He explains how they are caused, and discusses their physical effects – why some cause laughter and tears, why envy turns one a leaden colour and anger some red and some white, why hatred takes away the appetite, and so forth. Love, for example – *l'amour*, not love between men and women, which he classifies under the heading of *désir* –, produces these effects:

... je remarque en l'amour, quand elle est seule, c'est-à-dire quand elle n'est accompagnée d'aucune forte joie ou désir, ou tristesse, que le battement du pouls est égal et beaucoup plus grand et plus fort que de

coutume; qu'on sent une douce chaleur dans la poitrine, et que la digestion des viandes se fait fort promptement dans l'estomac, en sorte que
cette passion est utile pour la santé.

For Descartes, the passions are useful. They predispose the
soul in favour of those actions which are necessary for the preservation or well-being of the body – fear, sorrow, and hatred, to
avoid what is noxious; admiration, love, and desire, to seek what
is good. At the same time they automatically prepare the body
to act in fulfilment of the impulse to which they give rise – 'la
même agitation des esprits qui a coutume de les causer dispose
le corps aux mouvements qui servent à l'exécution de ces choses'.
They are moreover a source of happiness. Although Descartes
considers that the consciousness of virtue can give a purely
spiritual joy which makes a man immune to his passions, he
nevertheless begins his closing chapter with the words:

Au reste, l'âme peut avoir ses plaisirs à part; mais pour ceux qui lui
sont communs avec le corps, ils dépendent entièrement des passions: en
sorte que les hommes qu'elles peuvent le plus émouvoir sont capables de
goûter le plus de douceur en cette vie.

The passions, then, are 'toutes bonnes de leur nature'. On
the other hand, they must not be heeded uncritically. They are
dangerous in excess – admiration, for example, leads to a desire
for knowledge, but uncritical admiration leads to the indiscrimi-
nate dissipation of our interests. They may mislead us, by making
us shun what is good for us or desire what is bad for us; they
may exaggerate the good and bad qualities of the objects of our
desire or abhorrence; they may perpetuate a state of mind after
it has ceased to be necessary. They must therefore be controlled.
Now, the soul is indivisible, so that there can be no conflict within
it, only a conflict between body and soul; and the will is always
free. It is true that, just as the will cannot be directly affected
by the body, so it cannot influence the passions directly, since
the origin of the passions is outside us and they are often associated with reflex actions over which we have no control. We
cannot, for example, stop ourselves from being afraid or from
turning pale. But the will can control the actions of the body, and
it can influence the passions by means of the reason. If we are
afraid, for example, instead of running away, we should consider
that the danger may be less great than we imagine, and that
resistance is safer and more honourable than flight. If immediate
action is necessary, we should think of all the reasons for not
acting in accordance with the passion of the moment – for not
running away, if we are afraid; and, if immediate action is not
necessary, we must refrain from taking any decision until time
and repose have cooled our blood.

Mastery of the passions and the use of the free will are, for Descartes, the only things worthy of esteem in man:

Je ne remarque en nous qu'une seule chose qui nous puisse donner juste raison de nous estimer, à savoir l'usage de notre libre arbitre, et l'empire que nous avons sur nos volontés; car il n'y a que les seules actions qui dépendent de ce libre arbitre pour lesquelles nous puissions avec raison être loués ou blâmés; et il nous rend en quelque façon semblables à Dieu en nous faisant maîtres de nous-mêmes, pourvu que nous ne perdions point par lâcheté les droits qu'il nous donne.

To esteem oneself for anything else is mere *orgueil*. Such self-mastery is within the power of all men – just as a dog can be trained not to run after a partridge, so men can be trained to control their passions. *Génerosité* – the name which Descartes gives to this self-mastery – is 'comme la clef de toutes les autres vertus et un remède général contre tous les dérèglements des passions'. The *généreux* never lacks will power 'pour entreprendre et exécuter toutes les choses qu'il jugera être les meilleures; ce qui est suivre parfaitement la vertu'. He prizes 'bonne volonté' alone, not wealth or ability; he regards himself as inferior to none, but since 'bonne volonté' is common to all men, he is humble and despises none. He is compassionate. He is detached, desiring only those things which are in our power (such as virtue), not those which do not depend on us and which are preordained by Providence.

Ceux qui sont généreux en cette façon [says Descartes] sont naturellement portés à faire de grandes choses, et toutefois à ne rien entreprendre dont ils ne se sentent capables; et pour ce qu'ils n'estiment rien de plus grand que de faire du bien aux autres hommes et de mépriser son propre intérêt, pour ce sujet ils sont toujours parfaitement courtois, affables et officieux envers un chacun. Et avec cela ils sont entièrement maîtres de leurs passions, particulièrement des désirs, de la jalousie et de l'envie, à cause qu'il n'y a aucune chose dont l'acquisition ne dépende pas d'eux qu'ils pensent valoir assez pour mériter d'être beaucoup souhaitée; et de la haine envers les hommes, à cause qu'ils les estiment tous; et de la peur, à cause que la confiance qu'ils ont en leur vertu les assure; et enfin de la colère, à cause que, n'estimant que fort peu toutes les choses qui dépendent d'autrui, jamais ils ne donnent tant d'avantage à leurs ennemis que de reconnaître qu'ils en sont offensés.

The antithesis of the *généreux* is the *âmes faibles*, who are the victims of their warring passions, or whose decisions are not based on right judgments; who are dependent on things outside themselves, capable of all vices, servile to those from whom they have something to gain and insolent to the rest, puffed up with pride in prosperity and humble in adversity; who often repent of what they have done and are ungrateful, vindictive, and irresolute.

The *généreux* – like the Descartes of the *morale provisoire* –

is resolute, and cultivates stoical detachment; he also conforms to society. The passions of *gloire* and *honte* are necessary, says Descartes,

... car, encore que le peuple juge très mal, toutefois, à cause que nous ne pouvons vivre sans lui, et qu'il nous importe d'en être estimés, nous devons souvent suivre ses opinions plutôt que les nôtres, touchant l'extérieur de nos actions.

But if he recommends detachment, Descartes is poles apart from the stoics in other ways. The passions, he affirms, are in themselves good and necessary to a happy life; they are not to be subjugated or extirpated, but merely to be controlled or held in check. His ideal is not a passive sage, but an active hero – 'ceux qui sont généreux en cette façon sont naturellement portés à faire de grandes choses'.

In Descartes – whose influence was slight before 1670, but considerable thereafter – are united many of the main aspects of seventeenth-century thought – religious faith, stoicism, rationalism, contempt for the ancients and faith in scientific progress. He combated Pyrrhonism and provided a basis for scientific knowledge. He rejected authority in any but religious matters; he contributed to the discredit of Aristotelianism; and he attempted a new synthesis of religion and reason.

Religious faith is fundamental to Descartes's philosophy. Not only does he expressly exclude religion from his systematic doubt, but the conclusions he reaches are based on it. It is the belief in God, in a God who does not deceive us, which enables him to construct his philosophy. The clear and distinct ideas, of which alone we can be certain, come from God; and we can be sure that the senses are trustworthy, only because they, too, come from God. As Descartes says in his *Méditations*:

Et ainsi je reconnais très clairement que la certitude et la vérité de toute science dépend de la seule connaissance du vrai Dieu: en sorte qu'avant que je le connusse je ne pouvais savoir parfaitement aucune autre chose. Et à présent que je le connais, j'ai le moyen d'acquérir une science parfaite touchant une infinité de choses ...

If his philosophy was based on religion, it was also intended to support it and to provide rational arguments in favour of the existence of God and the immortality of the soul.

But the fusion of reason and religion was less successful than Descartes imagined. Not everyone found his proofs of the existence of God convincing. A contemporary critic, Pierre Petit, for example, pointed out that the presence of the idea of God in Descartes's mind really proved nothing:

Et ainsi, sans chercher davantage d'où elle peut venir en nous, si c'est des dépendances de notre être ou si c'est du dehors, et si ce dehors est un Etre tout plein de perfections, c'est-à-dire Dieu même, il semble qu'on peut s'en tenir à quelqu'une de ces raisons: ou des perfections particulières que nous reconnaissons en chaque chose du monde et que nous ramassons toutes ensemble, ou de la vertu formatrice qui opère en nous de bien plus grands miracles et qui nous fait presque semblables à nos prédecesseurs, ou de la préoccupation d'esprit qui nous vient de l'éducation, ou des violentes impressions que nous ont données ceux qui nous ont élevés, ou même de la politique et société des hommes qui en interdit la négative.[3]

Arnauld pointed out that Descartes argues in a circle — the only reason we have for believing what we perceive clearly and distinctly is that God exists; but our only reason for believing in the existence of God is that we clearly and evidently perceive it. And not everyone found that Descartes's philosophy confirmed his religion.

Qu'a fait Descartes [asks Saint-Evremond] par sa démonstration prétendue d'une substance purement spirituelle, d'une substance qui doit penser éternellement? Qu'a-t-il fait par des spéculations si épurées? Il a fait croire que la religion ne le persuadait pas, sans pouvoir persuader ni lui, ni les autres par ses raisons.

In the long run, Descartes probably did more to strengthen scepticism than religious faith. In proving the existence of God and the immortality of the soul, he provided at best a basis for a religion of the head rather than of the heart, for deism rather than for Christianity. His insistence that one should accept as truth only what was clearly true was more conducive to a sceptical attitude than to faith. Moreover, his mechanistic conception of man and the universe left little place for the soul or for God. It is true that he distinguished between man with the power of thought and a soul, and the brute creation without either; but, since not everyone accepted this distinction between man and animals, the way was open for the conclusion that man, too, might be a mere machine. As for his conception of the universe, Pascal protested:

Je ne puis pardonner à Descartes; il aurait bien voulu, dans toute sa philosophie, se pouvoir passer de Dieu; mais il n'a pu s'empêcher de lui faire donner une chiquenaude, pour mettre le monde en mouvement; après cela, il n'a plus que faire de Dieu.         (Pensées, No. 77)

The comment is not altogether fair to Descartes, who believed that the continuous intervention of God was necessary to maintain the universe in being; but it illustrates the impression his philosophy made on others.

[3] Quoted by R. Pintard, Le Libertinage érudit dans la première moitié du XVIIe siècle (1943), p. 357.

## Chapter 8

# THE THEATRE

GREAT changes came over the Parisian theatre in the 1630's:
Paris acquired two resident companies of actors; the theatre
gained in prestige and became fashionable and respectable;
the classical doctrine was introduced into stage plays; and a great
dramatist emerged — Pierre Corneille.

Since 1548, the Confrérie de la Passion — a guild for the
performance of passion plays — had held a monopoly of dramatic
representation in the French capital and owned the only theatre,
the Hôtel de Bourgogne. It had, however, long since ceased to
perform plays itself and had taken to renting its theatre to
various itinerant companies. In 1629, a company known as the
Comédiens du Roi took a three years' lease of the Hôtel de
Bourgogne, which they subsequently kept renewing, with the
result that they occupied the theatre continuously until 1680.[1]
This was the first permanently resident company in the capital.
It had three famous comic actors, Gros-Guillaume, Gautier-
Garguille, and Turlupin, and specialized in farce; but by 1637
all three had died, and Bellerose had become the chief actor of
the company, which concentrated more and more on serious
plays.

At the end of 1629, a second company, that of Montdory and
Le Noir, settled in Paris. They rented a *jeu de paume* (an enclosed
tennis court, which could easily be transformed into a theatre)
and opened their season in December 1629 with Corneille's
*Mélite*. In addition to having to pay the rent of the *jeu de
paume*, they had to pay the Confrérie de la Passion an écu for
each performance. After three moves, they found a permanent
home in 1634 in the *jeu de paume des Marais* in the rue Vieille-
du-Temple. This company, too, had its comic actor, Jodelet, who,
however, was transferred to the Hôtel de Bourgogne by order
of the King at the end of 1634, together with his brother, L'Espy,
Le Noir and his wife, and two others — Jodelet and L'Espy
returned to the Marais in 1641. They also had the great tragic
actor, Montdory, who created the part of Rodrigue in *Le Cid*,

---

[1] The Confrérie de la Passion was abolished in 1677.

but who, shortly afterwards, in August 1637, had an apoplectic fit while playing in Tristan's *Mariane*, and had to retire from the stage. In his stead, they recruited Floridor, who eventually became *directeur*. The Marais theatre was burnt down on 15 January 1644, and the reconstructed theatre, which reopened in October, was much improved.

For several years until 1647, the Marais theatre was the principal theatre in Paris: it was there that Corneille's plays were performed. In 1647, Floridor was transferred to the Hôtel de Bourgogne by royal decree and the Confrérie de la Passion ordered to modernize their theatre. Moreover, it seems that the loss of Floridor meant the loss of his friend, Corneille, and that Corneille's plays, from *Héraclius* onwards, were performed at the Hôtel de Bourgogne. Henceforth the Marais theatre took second place, but specialized in machine plays to draw the public.

Besides these two companies, there were occasionally others. In 1635, a third company was performing in the faubourg Saint-Germain. In 1644, a company which called itself the Illustre Théâtre – of which Molière was a member – attempted to establish itself in Paris, but it came to grief the following year. An Italian company settled in Paris, too, that same year, 1645, but more successfully.

Plays were usually performed three times a week, in the afternoons: according to an edict of 1609,[2] they were to begin in winter at 2.0 p.m. and end at 4.30. The theatres were long and narrow – roughly three times as long as wide –, a shape which had its disadvantages: d'Aubignac complained that most of the boxes were too far away and ill-situated. The main floor space, which was flat, constituted the *parterre*, where most of the spectators had to stand, though benches along the side walls allowed some eighty spectators to be seated. There were two rows of boxes along the side walls, with a gallery or *paradis* above, and, at the back, a single row of boxes and a balcony or *amphithéâtre* above. The hall was ill-lit (from economy), both it and the stage being lit by candles: it has been surmised that the length of acts was conditioned by the necessity of snuffing the candles every half-hour or so. Violins played between the acts. In the early seventeenth century, the stage setting used was the *décor multiple* or *simultané*, handed down from the Middle Ages. Several different scenes were shown at once – the main one represented by a back-cloth, the others by two or three boxes or compartments (*mansions*) at each side. It was understood that the stage in any scene was an extension of the box in which the actors first appeared. There was sometimes a curtain in front of

[2] Or 1619—there is some doubt about the date.

each box, but there was no front curtain covering the whole
stage before 1647, and even then it was not used as the front
curtain is nowadays; it went up before the play began, and the
stage remained visible until the whole performance was concluded (except perhaps in machine plays). In the 1630's, the
compartments were reduced in number, and, in the next decade,
the *décor multiple* gave way more and more to the *décor unique*,
a single stage set, a consequence of the introduction of the unity
of place. In tragedy, the stage would represent a room in a palace,
in comedy a house or a square. An upper stage over the main
stage was useful for machines and supernatural appearances.
Actors and actresses wore contemporary seventeenth-century
dress, their costumes (which they provided themselves) being
more sumptuous in tragedy than in comedy.

So successful was *Le Cid* that spectators were allowed to sit on
the stage, a practice which, later in the century, became permanent. Tallemant des Réaux wrote (c. 1657):

Il y a à cette heure une incommodité épouvantable à la comédie, c'est
que les deux côtés du théâtre sont tout pleins de jeunes gens assis sur
des chaises de paille; cela vient de ce qu'ils ne veulent pas aller au
parterre, quoiqu'il y ait souvent des soldats à la porte, et que les pages ni
les laquais ne portent plus d'épées. Les loges sont fort chères, et il y
faut songer de bonne heure: pour un écu, ou pour un demi-louis, on est
sur le théâtre; mais cela gâte tout, et il ne faut quelquefois qu'un insolent pour tout troubler.

Molière describes just such an *insolent* in *Les Fâcheux*.

The theatrical companies were democratically organized. There
was a director, but he was elected by his colleagues, and decisions
were made collectively: new colleagues were admitted, and plays
accepted or rejected, by vote. Profits were shared, each actor
receiving a whole, a half, or a quarter share, according to his
status. In Corneille's *Illusion comique*, we see a company sharing
out the profits after a performance. Besides the actors, there were
a number of other employees, such as the door-keeper and the
decorator, on a fixed wage and with no say in the affairs of the
company. Authors got either a share of the profits from the
performances of their plays until they were published (when they
became public property – hence plays were not usually published
until at least six months after first performance), or, sometimes,
a fixed sum instead.

The flourishing state of the theatre after 1630 was celebrated
by Corneille in his *Illusion comique* (1635 or 1636):

A présent le théâtre
Est en un point si haut que chacun l'idolâtre,
Et ce que votre temps voyait avec mépris

Est aujourd'hui l'amour de tous les bons esprits,
L'entretien de Paris, le souhait des provinces,
Le divertissement le plus doux de nos princes,
Les délices du peuple, et le plaisir des grands . . .

Contemporaries agree in attributing this change to Richelieu.

. . . ce fut par ses libéralités qu'elle [la scène] reçut de nouvelles forces,
et qu'elle commença de rentrer dans ses anciens droits, sa première
beauté, sa noblesse et sa splendeur,

wrote abbé d'Aubignac; and Tallemant des Réaux said:

La Comédie pourtant n'a été en honneur que depuis que le cardinal de
Richelieu en a pris soin, et avant cela, les honnêtes femmes n'y allaient
point.[3]

Richelieu was keenly interested in the theatre.

Tous ceux qui se sentaient quelque génie ne manquaient pas de travailler
pour le théâtre: c'était le moyen d'approcher des grands, et d'être favo-
risé du premier ministre, qui, de tous les divertissements de la Cour, ne
goûtait presque que celui-là,

writes Pellisson in his *Histoire de l'Académie française*. Pellisson
proceeds to explain how Richelieu used his influence:

Non seulement il assistait avec plaisir à toutes les comédies nouvelles;
mais encore il était bien aise d'en conférer avec les poètes, de voir leur
dessein en sa naissance, et de leur fournir lui-même des sujets. Que s'il
connaissait un bel esprit qui ne se portât pas par sa propre inclination à
travailler en ce genre, il l'y engageait insensiblement par toutes sortes de
soins et de caresses.

Richelieu even employed a group of five poets to write plays to
his direction, each one composing a different act. Rotrou, Bois-
robert, Claude de L'Estoile, Guillaume Colletet, and (for a time)
Corneille, were the members of this team, which produced the
*Comédie des Tuileries* (1635), *La Grande Pastorale* (1637), and
*L'Aveugle de Smyrne* (1637). Subsequently, Desmarets de Saint-
Sorlin wrote three plays on Richelieu's behalf, *Roxane* (1639),
*Mirame* (1641), and *Europe* (1642). *Mirame* inaugurated the new,
large theatre which formed part of Richelieu's magnificent palace,
the Palais Cardinal. Richelieu gave pensions to Mairet, Rotrou,
and Corneille, and financial assistance to the Marais theatre:
Montdory was in receipt of a pension from him from 1634
onwards. He gave private performances of plays — another source
of remuneration for the actors. Other noblemen followed his
example. The duc de Montmorency and the comte de Belin were
other benefactors of the Marais; so was Mme de Rambouillet —
according to Tallemant, Montdory's renown began with a performance of Mairet's *Virginie* at her house in 1633. Royalty,

[3] Doubts have been cast on the accuracy of the last remark.

too, took an interest in the theatre. Actors were redistributed between the theatres by the King's orders in 1634, 1642, and 1647. In 1641, the Hôtel de Bourgogne and the Marais were in receipt of royal pensions of 12,000*l.* and 6,000*l.* respectively.

Besides encouraging actors and playwrights, Richelieu attempted to suppress indecency on the stage. Abbé d'Aubignac tells us that impurity was 'absolument bannie' from his own private theatre; and, in 1641, a royal edict forbade actors to show any 'actions malhonnêtes' on the stage or to use indecent words or equivocal language. Richelieu was, no doubt, helped in this aim by the growing influence of Mme de Rambouillet and her salon. Drama, says Scarron in *Le Roman comique*, 'est aujourd'hui purgée, au moins à Paris, de tout ce qu'elle avait de licencieux'.

Even the establishment of the classical doctrine was due to some extent to Richelieu: it was he who imposed on the Academy the task of examining *Le Cid*; and it was for him that La Mesnardière's *Poétique* and d'Aubignac's *Pratique du Théâtre* were written.

The rules for the theatre were elaborate. The subject of a tragedy – since the pastoral and tragi-comedy disappeared about this time, only tragedy and comedy need be considered – must be historical, because tragedy normally deals with the actions of kings, and these are known to the audience:

les grands accidents des couronnes sont ordinairement connus aux hommes, et [...] si le jugement sur cette réflexion vient à se douter qu'ils soient inventés, la créance lui manque soudain et ensuite l'effet que la seule créance eût produit.

(Chapelain, *Lettre sur la règle des vingt-quatre heures*)

Lip service was paid to the Aristotelian doctrine of catharsis by means of pity and terror, but with little conviction. Pity was stressed more than terror. Corneille, who is very sceptical about this part of Aristotle's teaching, thinks that it is enough if *either* pity *or* terror is aroused, and is quite prepared to substitute admiration for both. In practice, love was regarded as the chief of the tragic passions, though there were some protests. Corneille considered that love was not a fit subject for tragedy and should take second place only, and abbé de Villiers in his *Entretien sur les tragédies de ce temps* (1675) expressed the wish that Racine would give up 'les sujets tendres et passionnés'.

The Aristotelian precept, that the hero should be neither wholly virtuous nor wholly bad, was accepted in theory – except by Corneille who maintained that the hero might be either wholly virtuous (Polyeucte) or wholly wicked (Cléopâtre in *Rodogune*):

but, in practice, other dramatists frequently portray handsome, valiant, gallant, young heroes.

A tragedy consists of an *exposition*, a *nœud*, and a *dénouement*. The exposition should contain all the elements of the action — important new characters must not appear without warning later, as the Moors do in the third act of *Le Cid*; and the action should follow logically and necessarily from the opening situation. The *nœud* is formed by obstacles to the hero's happiness, and the situation is modified from time to time by external events or *péripéties*, which should be prepared, but not foreseen, says d'Aubignac. These *péripéties* or changes of fortune bring about alternations of hopes and fears, create suspense, and make the play dramatic. Although Scudéry in his *Observations sur le Cid* considers that suspense is necessary to tragi-comedy, not tragedy, most seventeenth-century theorists consider it an essential ingredient of all drama:

Le plaisir exquis est dans la suspension d'esprit, quand le poète dispose de telle sorte son action que le spectateur est en peine du moyen par où il en sortira.                    (Chapelain, *Discours de la poésie représentative*)

cette attente ou suspension qui doit toujours régner au Théâtre [...] tous les agréments d'une pièce, qui consiste presque toujours en la surprise et en la nouveauté.                    (D'Aubignac, *Pratique du Théâtre*)

les préparations des incidents y [i.e. in tragedy] doivent être ménagées de telle sorte, qu'elles ne servent pas à rendre les événements froids, en leur ôtant ce qu'ils peuvent avoir de grâce par la surprise. Car il est important de remarquer, que préparer un incident, ce n'est pas tout à fait dire les choses, qui le puissent découvrir: mais c'est dire seulement ce qui peut donner lieu à l'auditeur de le deviner. Ce qui doit même être ménagé. Car le plaisir des spectateurs est d'attendre toujours quelque chose de surprenant, et de contraire à leurs préjugés. Et rien ne doit tant régner au théâtre que la suspension: parce que le principal plaisir, qu'on y prend, est la surprise.                    (Rapin, *Réflexions sur la poétique*)

> Que le trouble, toujours croissant de scène en scène,
> A son comble arrivé se débrouille sans peine.
> L'esprit ne se sent point plus vivement frappé
> Que lorsqu'en un sujet d'intrigue enveloppé
> D'un secret tout à coup la vérité connue
> Change tout, donne à tout une face imprévue.
>                    (Boileau, *Art poétique*)

The dénouement should be necessary, rapid, and complete. A tragedy may end with the death of the main characters, but happy endings are not uncommon. The seventeenth century did not regard an unhappy ending as essential. For d'Aubignac, a tragedy is 'une chose magnifique, sérieuse, grave et convenable aux agitations et aux grands revers de la fortune des Princes',

and a play bears the title 'seulement en considération des incidents et des personnes dont elle représente la vie, et non pas à
raison de la catastrophe'. For Corneille, a play is a tragedy if it
deals with persons of exalted rank who are in danger of losing
their lives or their states, or of banishment; if they are of lower
rank or if, being of exalted rank, they are exposed to lesser risks,
it is a comedy.

The unities of time, place, and action must be obeyed.[4] The
most important, the unity of action, which applied to all poetry,
not merely to dramatic poetry, meant that it must be impossible
to suppress any part of the play without making the rest unintel-
ligible; that all the elements of the play must be continuously
present from first to last and must follow logically from one
another, not be the result of chance; and that subplots must have
a bearing on the main plot. The action should not be too
complex:

... je nie que le meilleur poème dramatique soit celui qui embrasse le
plus d'actions, et dis au contraire qu'il n'en doit contenir qu'une et qu'il ne
la faut encore de bien médiocre longueur; que d'autre sorte elle embarrasserait la scène et travaillerait extrêmement la mémoire.

(Chapelain, *Lettre sur la règle des vingt-quatre heures*)

For d'Aubignac, the essential in a play is *discours*, not incidents,
and if there are too many incidents there will be no room for
*discours*.

The unity of time was a consequence of the principle of
*vraisemblance*. Nothing could be less *vraisemblable* than to show
the events of ten years in two hours and a half; what the spectator sees on the stage should occupy the time it is supposed to
take – i.e. if an act lasts for half an hour, it should show the
events of half an hour. This does not mean that the action of a
play must take only two hours and a half. Aristotle allows a day,
though Chapelain and d'Aubignac would reduce this to twelve
hours (i.e. a day or a night), while Corneille would allow up to
thirty hours. But the extra time allowed must elapse between the
acts. The unity of time requires the dramatist to 'ouvrir le
théâtre le plus près qu'il est possible de la catastrophe'
(d'Aubignac) – i.e. French tragedy is, as Napoleon was to say
later, a 'crise'. Unity of place is a consequence of *vraisemblance*

---

[4] The unities were first introduced into the theatre in a pastoral play,
Mairet's *Silvanire* (1630), published with a preface in 1631. They made
their way into comedy the same year. Corneille was the first to apply
them in tragi-comedy, in *Clitandre* (1631). They were introduced into
tragedy in 1634. There were some protests—Ogier's preface to Schelandre's *Tyr et Sidon* (1628), the preface to Mareschal's *Généreuse Alle-
mande* (1630), the preface to Scudéry's *Ligdamon et Lidias* (1631), etc.—
but they were firmly established in the theatre by the *querelle du Cid*.

and the unity of time. It is necessary, says Chapelain, because the
eye is less flexible than the mind:

l'œil est aussi bien juge que l'esprit des actions de la scène, et [...]
l'œil ne peut être persuadé que ce qu'il voit en trois heures et sur un même
lieu se soit passé en trois mois plus ou moins et en des lieux différents,
au contraire de l'esprit qui conçoit en un moment et se porte facilement
à croire les choses arrivées en plusieurs temps et en plusieurs provinces.

(*Discours de la poésie représentative*)

The unities, however, were introduced gradually and not
applied strictly. It has been calculated that, of fifty-one tragedies
written between 1652 and 1672, only twelve observe the unity of
action strictly. As for the unity of time, acts did not always show
the events of half an hour. Scudéry pointed out that in the fifth
act of *Le Cid*, in the time it takes to recite 140 lines, Rodrigue
goes off, arms himself, arrives at the place where he is to fight
Don Sanche, and defeats his adversary, who returns to Chimène.
But the same criticism could be made of *Phèdre*. In the fifth act,
Hippolyte departs and a few minutes later we hear not only of
his death but also of the arrival on the scene of Aricie, who left
after him. Corneille in his *Discours* points out similar defects
in the fifth acts of *Héraclius* and *Nicomède*. As for the unity of
place, it was at first interpreted as a wide area, a town or a forest,
and then reduced to a room in a palace. But M. Scherer observes
that in most seventeenth-century plays, the place is either left
indeterminate or involves *invraisemblance* – it is improbable that
all the characters should meet there; or, since they all do, that a
character should so often say that he has been searching all over
for another whom he finds at last on the stage. In *Britannicus*,
the Emperor and his prisoners are equally free to use the same
room. Critics are fond of pointing out the failings of dramatists
in this respect. Corneille, in his *Discours*, considers that only
*Horace*, *Polyeucte*, and *Pompée* satisfactorily observe the unity
of place; d'Aubignac says that 'hors *les Horaces* de M. Corneille,
je doute que nous en ayons un seul [poème], où l'unité du lieu
soit rigoureusement gardée'; and M. Scherer thinks that the
only seventeenth-century plays that observe the rule strictly and
without absurdity are Corneille's *Suivante* and Racine's *Iphigénie*
and *Phèdre*.

A tragedy consists of between 1650 and 1900 lines and is
divided into five acts, of which the first contains the exposition, the
next three the *nœud*, and the fifth act the dénouement.

Dans le premier acte les fondements de l'histoire se jettent; dans le
second les difficultés commencent à naître; dans le troisième le trouble
se renforce; dans le quatrième les choses sont désespérées; dans le

cinquième, le désespoir continuant, le nœud se démêle par des voies inespérées et produit la merveille.

(Chapelain, *Discours de la poésie représentative*)

The opening of the play, thinks d'Aubignac, should be 'éclatante',

ce qui se fait ou par le nombre ou par la majesté des acteurs, ou par un spectacle magnifique, ou par une narration extraordinaire, ou par quelque autre subtile invention du Poète.

Similarly, the last acts should be superior to the earlier ones, 'soit par la nécessité des événements, ou par la grandeur des passions, soit pour la rareté des spectacles'. The acts should be approximately equal in length and divided into scenes, not less than three and not more than seven or eight, according to d'Aubignac – though, in fact, some have more (there are eleven scenes in the fourth act of Racine's *Iphigénie*). The last acts tend to have more scenes, i.e. more movement, than the earlier ones. In principle, every entrance or exit begins a new scene (though sometimes the entrance or departure of a minor character is ignored, and sometimes the hero may be left alone on the stage to pronounce a short monologue without a new scene beginning). Scenes are linked (*liaison des scènes*), and though in theory several different methods of linking them existed, in practice these can be reduced to two – *liaison de présence* (when a character or characters already on stage are joined or left by a companion or companions) and *liaison de fuite* (when one or more characters leave the stage to avoid someone who is approaching).

Every entrance or exit should be clearly motivated:

Ce qui est absolument nécessaire, comme fondé sur la vraisemblance, est que nulle entrée de personnage sur la scène et nulle sortie ne soit sans nécessité, et qu'il paraisse toujours pourquoi ils arrivent et partent.

(Chapelain, *Discours de la poésie représentative*)

Moreover, the same character should not be on the stage at the end of one act and the beginning of the next – lest, says d'Aubignac, the audience should realize that he has not had enough time to go and do what he had to do and return. Within the scene, one finds one of a number of stock features – e.g. maxims and *sentences*, stichomythia, and, above all, *récits*. These last, it was held, should be addressed by someone who knew what had happened and had reason to tell it, to someone who had a genuine interest in it – i.e. they, too, should be *vraisemblable* and dramatic.

Comedy differs from tragedy in several ways: it may treat an invented subject; it deals with characters of lower rank in a more familiar style; the dénouement is usually a marriage or several marriages; and a farce may be in three acts or one act instead of five. Otherwise it must obey the same general rules as tragedy. This, for example, is how La Fontaine praises Terence's *Eunuch*:

Le sujet en est simple, comme le prescrivent nos maîtres; il n'est point embarrassé d'incidents confus; il n'est point chargé d'ornements inutiles et détachés; tous les ressorts y remuent la machine, et tous les moyens y acheminent à la fin. Quant au nœud, c'est un des plus beaux et des moins communs de l'antiquité. Cependant il se fait avec une facilité merveilleuse, et n'a pas une seule de ces contraintes que nous voyons ailleurs. La bienséance et la médiocrité, que Plaute ignorait, s'y rencontrent partout: le parasite n'y est point goulu par-delà la vraisemblance; le soldat n'y est point fanfaron jusqu'à la folie, les expressions y sont pures, les pensées délicates; et pour comble de louange, la nature y instruit tous les personnages, et ne manque jamais de leur suggérer ce qu'ils ont à faire et à dire.

Hence, as the result both of the theory of scholars and the practice of dramatists, there arose this unique form of drama. A historical play, dealing with kings and queens or classical heroes and their loves, in which the main characters are attended by confidants, in which the characters do not eat and drink and scarcely have bodies, in which the interest is mainly psychological and the ending may be happy; a highly dramatic form of play, dealing with a crisis, in which such action as there is takes place off stage and is recounted in *récits*, in which a constant succession of *péripéties* causes hope and fear to alternate and creates suspense, from which everything irrelevant and undramatic has been eliminated; a five-act play in alexandrines, using *style noble* and avoiding *mots bas*, obeying the rules of *vraisemblance*, *bienséance*, and the unities, in which the characters address one another scrupulously as *Seigneur* and *Madame*, and Junie (as Lady Morgan complained in 1816) 'with that politeness which never forgets itself on any occasion asks pardon of Agrippina for leaving her abruptly to seek her lover, who is expiring under the hands of his assassins':[5] such is seventeenth-century tragedy. It was a highly conventional and sophisticated form. But it was in this mould that some of the supreme creations of the human mind were cast.

It is sometimes suggested that seventeenth-century drama springs from the conflict between the authors, with their love of form, and the demands of their popular public.[6] Professor Carrington Lancaster thinks that 'there is no reason to suppose that the

[5] Similarly, Philoctète in Rotrou's *Hercule mourant* apologizes to Iole for having orders to kill her lover:

    Madame, avec regret je suis son homicide;
    Mais tous respects sont vains contre la loi d'Alcide.

[6] E.g. J. Scherer, *La Dramaturgie classique en France*, p. 433.

audience differed materially from those of Spain and England of the same period.'[7] In fact, however, the French theatre public seems to have been more restricted, to have formed a much smaller proportion of the population, than Shakespeare's. With a population probably not more than half the size of that of Paris, Shakespeare's London had more and larger theatres than Molière's Paris. Plays were regularly performed at five or six theatres, and the capacity of the public theatres has been estimated at about two thousand. Paris, in contrast, from 1629 to 1659, had two theatres, or three if we count the Italians, who played in their own language. It is true that the number then increased: Molière's company arrived in Paris in 1658, and a Spanish company, patronized by the Queen, the following year – this last seems to have played chiefly at court and not to have enjoyed much success. In 1673, after the death of Molière, his company and that of the Marais were combined; and in the same year the Spaniards recrossed the Pyrenees. In 1680, the two remaining French companies were combined to form the Comédie-Française.

Moreover, the French theatres gave only three performances a week, and then not all the year round. They were closed for about a fortnight before Easter, on public and religious holidays, when the illness of an actor or actress prevented performance, and when a rival spectacle threatened to draw away their audience – on 17 July 1676, 'l'on ne joua point à cause de l'exécution de Mme de Brinvilliers', notes La Grange.[8] Nor is the size of the French audiences comparable with those of Elizabethan London. According to Carrington Lancaster, five or six hundred persons filled the Hôtel de Bourgogne fairly well, and the audience of the Théâtre Guénégaud, where Molière's company played after his death, averaged 400 and never reached 1,200. It seems unlikely that Molière's own public ever exceeded 1,000. The Comédie-Française seems to have contained a maximum of about 1,400 spectators. The first thirty-four performances of the newly opened theatre in 1680 drew 15,610 spectators, an average of 459, and the Registers of the Comédie-Française show that audiences were often 300 or less, sometimes below 200, occasionally under one hundred. Professor Lough has examined attendances at the Comédie-Française in the year 1682–3, a good year for the theatre, then the only French theatre in Paris. In that year, 150,000 tickets were sold, an average of 500 a day. He shows that comparatively few regular spectators would account for this figure and that Voltaire could not

---

[7] *History of French Dramatic Literature in the Seventeenth Century*, Part I, vol. II, p. 713.

[8] According to Boursault, the first performance of *Britannicus* was ill-attended, because the potential audience had been drawn away by the execution of the marquis de Courboyer.

be far out when, in the following century, he estimated that not more than four thousand people attended the theatre regularly. A successful play, which might run for between fifteen and twenty-five performances, might draw a total audience of between ten and seventeen thousand. Only an unusually successful play could run for longer and draw a larger public. It seems unlikely that more than three or four thousand people went to the theatre in a week: this is probably less than one per cent of the population.

Admission to the French theatres seems to have been much more expensive than to the Jacobean theatre. Shakespeare's groundling could see a play for one penny, in an age when the working man earned a shilling a day, and eggs cost a halfpenny each. In Paris, on the other hand, from 1652 to 1699,[9] a place in the *parterre* cost fifteen sous, a shilling in the English money of the time. This was very nearly a full day's wage: a workman in Paris would earn between fifteen and twenty sous a day, though certain favoured trades seem to have been better paid.[10] A private soldier got five sous a day, out of which he had to feed and clothe himself; in 1678, in Paris, John Locke engaged a servant for twenty-eight écus (i.e. eighty-four livres – less than five sous a day)[11] and a livery coat a year. It seems unlikely that the Parisian lower classes can have been able to go to the theatre.

It is possible to be a little more precise about the nature of the seventeenth-century public. It was certainly rowdy. D'Aubignac complains of the disorders caused

... par la licence que plusieurs mal-vivants ont de porter l'épée dans les lieux destinés aux divertissements publics, et d'y attaquer insolemment des gens d'honneur, qui n'ont point d'autres armes pour leur défense que l'autorité des lois. [ ... ] Les représentations sont incessamment troublées par de jeunes débauchés, qui n'y vont que pour signaler leur insolence, qui mettent l'effroi partout, et qui souvent commettent des meurtres.

(*Pratique du Théâtre*)

Furetière in his Dictionary writes:

Le *parterre* serait le plus beau lieu pour entendre la comédie, sans les incommodes qui s'y trouvent, sans les querelles qui y arrivent.          (1690)

The porters at the door were often wounded and sometimes killed – it is said that four porters were killed on the day of the

[9] Prices had been lower earlier—they were fixed at five sous for the *parterre* and ten for the *loges* in 1609 (or 1619), and, by 1634, had risen to nine or ten for the *parterre* and nineteen or twenty for the *loges*. But the cost of living had gone up.
[10] John Locke notes that, in 1678, the silk weavers of Tours were earning thirty or thirty-five sous a day (formerly, they had earned considerably more).
[11] The livre consisted of twenty sous, subdivided into twelve deniers (cf. our pounds, shillings, and pence). An écu was worth three livres.

first performance of La Serre's *Thomas Morus*, and five on that of Scudéry's *Amour tyrannique*. The tastes of the theatre public were not over-refined – as mentioned above, the theatres thought it advisable to close on the day of the execution of Mme de Brinvilliers, and the first performance of *Britannicus* was poorly attended because it clashed with a public execution. But we must not conclude, therefore, that the audience was a popular one: Mme de Sévigné, too, went to see the last of Mme de Brinvilliers.

The audience was heterogeneous, too. The *loges* and the seats on the stage were occupied by nobles, whereas the *parterre* was more mixed. It contained no doubt representatives of the various classes who claimed the right of free entry – musketeers and members of the *maison du Roi*, as well as pages and lackeys in attendance upon their masters. There were also pickpockets (or *filous*),[12] and more respectable members of the public, such as lawyer's clerks,[13] the dramatic poets,[14] and 'gens de collège, de palais ou de commerce'.[15] These last, the *gens de commerce*, seem to have been particularly important, for there are many references in the seventeenth century to the 'marchands de la rue Saint-Denis'.

Le Marquis de Courboyer [ . . . ] ayant attiré à son spectacle tout ce que la rue S. Denis a de marchands, qui se rendent régulièrement à l'Hôtel de Bourgogne, pour avoir la principale vue de tous les ouvrages qu'on y représente, je me trouvai si à mon aise [ . . . ]

writes Boursault in his *Artémise et Poliante* (1670) of the first performance of *Britannicus*; and Donneau de Visé, in his comedy, *Zélinde* (1663), makes Argimont, a lace merchant of the rue Saint-Denis, say:

La plupart des marchands de la rue Saint Denis aiment fort la comédie, et nous sommes quarante ou cinquante, qui allons ordinairement aux premières représentations de toutes les pièces nouvelles; et quand elles

---

[12] Scarron, in the *Roman comique*, complains of the presence 'des filous, des pages et des laquais, et autres ordures du genre humain, que la facilité de prendre des manteaux y attire encore plus que ne faisaient autrefois les mauvaises plaisanteries des farceurs' . . .

[13]
>    Un clerc, pour quinze sous, sans craindre le holà,
>    Peut aller au parterre attaquer *Attila*.
>                                              (Boileau, *Satire IX*)

[14] In 1642, Sorel writes of the *parterre* that 'l'on y trouve quelquefois de fort honnêtes gens, et même la plupart de nos poètes, qui sont les plus capables de juger des pièces ne vont point ailleurs' (*Maison des Jeux*). Boursault tells us: 'Les auteurs [ . . . ] ont la malice de s'attrouper pour décider souverainement des pièces de théâtre, et [ . . . ] s'arrangent d'ordinaire sur un banc de l'Hôtel de Bourgogne qu'on appelle le banc formidable, à cause des injustices qu'on y rend' . . .          (*Artémise et Poliante*)

[15] D'Argenson, à propos of a performance of 15 March 1700, refers to 'la foule des spectateurs, la plupart gens de collège, de palais ou de commerce'.

ont quelque chose de particulier, et qu'elles font grand bruit, nous nous mettons quatre ou cinq ensemble, et louons une loge, pour nos femmes; car pour nous, nous nous contentons d'aller au parterre. Nous y menons dimanche, quatre ou cinq marchandes, de cette rue, avec la femme d'un notaire, et celle d'un procureur.

The rue Saint-Denis was the fashionable shopping centre of Paris; these were wealthy merchants, in contact with their aristocratic customers.

The *parterre*, then, consisted of two main constituent parts, a turbulent element and a bourgeois element. The turbulent element no doubt consisted mainly of those who got in without paying, and who were thus probably a minority and scarcely typical of the audience as a whole. This is supported by a passage in Sorel's *Maison des Jeux* (1642):

Le parterre est fort incommode pour la presse qui s'y trouve de mille marauds mêlés parmi les honnêtes gens, auxquels ils veulent quelquefois faire des affronts, et, ayant fait des querelles pour un rien, mettent la main à l'épée, et interrompent toute la comédie. Dans leur plus parfait repos ils ne cessent aussi de parler, de siffler et de crier, et pour ce qu'ils n'ont rien payé à l'entrée, et qu'ils ne viennent là qu'à faute d'autre occupation, ils ne se soucient guère d'entendre ce que disent les comédiens.

The *marauds* are here contrasted with the *honnêtes gens*. In the interests of the latter, attempts were made all through the century to eliminate the rowdy elements. A second speaker in the *Maison des Jeux* says that such disorders are less frequent now than formerly; and a poster of the Hôtel de Bourgogne of 1658 has at the bottom the words: 'Défenses aux soldats d'y entrer sur peine de la vie.' But one of Molière's porters was killed later by soldiers indignant at being refused free entry. A further edict of 1673 led Chappuzeau to write: 'C'est ainsi que tous les désordres ont été bannis, et que le bourgeois peut venir avec plus de plaisir à la comédie.' Nevertheless, a disturbance caused by musketeers led to yet a further edict of the King forbidding the 'officiers de sa maison, ses gardes, gens-d'armes, chevau-légers, mousquetaires et tous autres' to enter without paying. Further incidents and further edicts continued to succeed one another.

A fair summary of the seventeenth-century public is that of Doneau, who, speaking of the success of Molière's *Sganarelle*, writes:

il s'y [i.e. in Paris] est néanmoins trouvé assez de personnes de condition pour remplir plus de quarante fois les loges, et le théâtre du Petit-Bourbon, et assez de bourgeois pour remplir autant de fois le parterre.[16]

[16] Le Vert, in the *Avis au Lecteur* of *Le Docteur amoureux* (published in 1638), says that 'les comédiens [...] ont toujours convié les honnêtes gens et attiré le Bourgeois sous le nom de Fabrice.'

Nobles, mainly in the boxes and on the stage, then, and bourgeois in the *parterre*. It seems likely, moreover, that it was the taste of the upper classes and the court which predominated, in the choice, if not in the success, of plays. Both actors and authors depended to a considerable extent on the nobles for their livelihood. Authors looked to the nobles for financial support and received sums of money in return for dedicatory notices; and actors derived a considerable part of their income from *visites* — private performances in the houses of noblemen. Between 16 April 1659 and 11 August 1672, the register of La Grange records 115 *visites*. Moreover, the actors must have counted on the nobility for the greater part of the takings at their ordinary performances. In fact, Chappuzeau tells us that new plays were performed between November and Easter, when the court was in Paris or at Saint-Germain. Even if the *parterre* made up half or more of the audience, it was not the more lucrative part. In Molière's theatre, a place in the *parterre* cost fifteen sous; the *3mes loges* cost twenty sous, the *2mes loges* thirty sous, the amphitheatre three livres, the *loges basses* five livres ten sous, and a seat on the stage itself six livres. At the first performance of *Le Malade imaginaire*, there were 682 spectators, of whom 394 were in the *parterre*; but whereas these last paid but 591 livres, the minority of 288 paid 1,401. At a performance of *Psyché* on Sunday, 20 November 1672, there were 925 paying spectators, 514 in the *parterre*; the total receipts were 1,316 livres ten sous. But whereas the majority in the *parterre* paid only 385 livres ten sous, the 411 others paid 931 livres. One cannot help feeling that the actors must have been particularly sensitive to the reactions of that part of the audience which sat on the stage.

According to Donneau de Visé, the success of a play depended on the first performance, and on the *salons*:

Le bruit qui se répand après sa première représentation est toujours ce qui décide de son sort, et ce bruit ne lui peut jamais être avantageux, quand même elle serait bonne, lorsqu'elle a été mal reçue dans les lectures qu'on en a faites.                    (*Nouvelles Nouvelles*)

Since prices were doubled at first performances, there seems little likelihood of a popular audience on that important occasion. The practice of reading plays in *salons* shows that the authors at least thought that the taste of the *salons* was influential. Mascarille, in *Les Précieuses ridicules*, no doubt exaggerates when he says:

C'est la coutume ici qu'à nous autres gens de condition les auteurs viennent lire leurs pièces nouvelles, pour nous engager à les trouver belles, et leur donner de la réputation; et je vous laisse à penser, si, quand nous disons quelque chose, le parterre ose nous contredire.

And one of the speakers in Donneau de Visé's *Nouvelles Nouvelles* argues that such readings are useless. But the authors – including Molière – thought they were worth trying.

Nor must the court be forgotten. Royal patronage was important to both actors and authors. Authors looked to the King for pensions and gratuities, and the theatres received large subsidies from Louis XIV (the Italians 15,000 livres a year, the Hôtel de Bourgogne 12,000, the Marais and Molière's company 6,000 each).[17] Moreover, according to Chappuzeau, companies which played at court were richly rewarded. 'C'est son goût [the court's] qu'il faut étudier pour trouver l'art de réussir,' says Dorante in Molière's *Critique de l'Ecole des Femmes*. On at least one occasion, the taste of the King and the court was able to influence the reception of a play. Racine's *Plaideurs* failed in Paris, but made Louis XIV laugh heartily. 'Le lendemain,' says Louis Racine, '[ ... ] il [Racine] se félicitait de l'approbation que la cour avait donnée à sa pièce, dont le mérite fut enfin reconnu à Paris.'[18]

In conclusion, then, a restricted public, consisting mainly of the upper and middle classes, with the taste of the former predominating. This was already the position in the 'thirties:

Nous ne sommes pas dans ces républiques, où le peuple donnait les gouvernements et les charges; et où les poètes étaient contraints de composer, ou des tragédies horribles, pour plaire à leur goût bizarre, ou des comédies basses, pour s'accommoder à la portée de leurs esprits. Ceux qui ne composent des ouvrages que par un honnête divertissement, ne doivent avoir pour but que l'estime des honnêtes gens, et c'est à leur jugement qu'ils adressent toutes leurs inventions et leurs pensées.

(Desmarets de Saint-Sorlin, *Argument* of *Les Visionnaires*)

But we must not distinguish too sharply between the taste of the different classes. Molière first won Louis XIV's favour with one of the farces which had been successful in the provinces, and all classes could enjoy a public execution.

If seventeenth-century drama is the result of a compromise between regularity and vigour, we must not, then, conclude that it was played to a popular audience. Vigour and independence were not in the seventeenth century the apanage of the populace, for whom, indeed, it is difficult to feel that seventeenth-century drama was really adapted. Mercier in the following century provides some confirmation of this, when he complains:

Shakespear est pour les Anglais un poète bien plus national que Corneille ne l'est pour nous. [ ... ] Que signifie donc cette salle de spectacle vide,

[17] Molière's subsidy was later increased to 7,000l.
[18] Another example is *Le Grondeur* of Palaprat and Brueys.

cet amphithéâtre solitaire? La voix des acteurs le plus souvent ne frappe
que les murailles; tout l'intérêt, toute la vie du drame est étouffé.
[...] Il serait d'un bon gouvernement de veiller aux plaisirs du petit
peuple: il a tant de fardeaux à supporter, qu'il faut être barbare pour lui
refuser des fêtes et des amusements [...]                    (*Du Théâtre*)

## Chapter 9

# DRAMA

A NEW generation of dramatists arose in the last year or so of
the third decade of the century. Mairet, whose first play was
performed as early as 1625, was soon joined by Rotrou,
Scudéry, Corneille, and Du Ryer, to name only the most important. The new generation revived comedy, a genre which — except
in the form of short farces — had not hitherto thrived in seventeenth-century France; and it introduced the rule of the unities
into the pastoral, comedy, and tragedy successively. Tragedy, the
most important genre of the new age, after having been neglected
for some years in favour of tragi-comedy, was revived in 1634 by
Mairet with his *Sophonisbe* and by Rotrou with his *Hercule mourant*, and subsequently transformed by the greatest dramatist of the
period, Pierre Corneille.

## I. CORNEILLE

Pierre Corneille (1606–84) began his career as a writer of
comedies. His first play, *Mélite* (1629), gave a fresh lease of life
to the genre. It was followed by a tragi-comedy, *Clitandre* (1630–
1631), four comedies (*La Veuve*, 1631–2; *La Galerie du Palais*,
1632–3; *La Suivante*, 1632–3; and *La Place Royale*, 1633–4), a
tragedy (*Médée*, 1635), and another comedy of a somewhat different character, *L'Illusion comique* (1635–6). Finally, early in 1637,
there was performed the work by which he eclipsed his rivals and
established himself as incontestably the greatest dramatist of the
period — *Le Cid*. This play, though in later editions described as a
tragedy, was originally called a tragi-comedy, an appellation fully
justified by its colourful, Spanish setting, its romantic, adventurous
plot, and its happy ending. It gave rise to a heated controversy,
and was, on the whole, condemned by the Academy at the end of
the year. Thereafter, except for two more comedies (*Le Menteur*,
1643–4, and *La Suite du Menteur*, 1644–5) and three plays desig-
nated *comédies héroïques* (*Dom Sanche*, 1649–50; *Tite et Bérénice*, 1670; and *Pulchérie*, 1672), Corneille wrote nothing for the
stage save tragedies.

Tragedy, however, as conceived by Corneille, was something rather different from what it had been in the hands of his predecessors and contemporaries. Hitherto, tragedy had usually depicted the downfall and death of a historical or mythical character from classical antiquity, such as Dido, Coriolanus, or Alexander. Moreover, the downfall of the hero or heroine was usually announced at the outset by forebodings or a dream, which were progressively realized in the course of the play; suspense and reversals of fortune played little or no part. Rotrou's *Hercule mourant*, in which Hercule's death begins early in the play, is of this type; so, on the whole, is Mairet's *Sophonisbe*;[1] and though, in Tristan's *Mariane*, there is a conflict in Herod's breast between love and jealousy, the issue is not in doubt. Tragicomedy, on the other hand, was more exciting and dramatic: it treated a subject taken from a novel or invented; it contained a succession of adventures and *péripéties*; and, if the ending was happy, the manner by which it would be brought about was in doubt until the end, so that there was plenty of opportunity for surprise and suspense.

Corneille's tragedy is a fusion of tragedy and tragi-comedy. This is true already of his first essay in the genre, *Médée* (1635): Médée wreaks vengeance on her faithless husband, Jason, but it is not certain until late in the play that she will not be appeased or foiled, and she escapes at the end of the fifth act. In his subsequent plays, he retains the historical subject of tragedy, together with the political interest and the council scenes that we find in Hardy, for example. On the other hand, he makes use of reversals of fortune to arouse suspense and surprise; he gives love a more prominent place than it had normally had in tragedy, and often introduces a pair of young lovers; and he frequently has a happy ending. There is even, in Cornelian tragedy, a certain admixture of comedy – the characters of Félix in *Polyeucte* or of Prusias in *Nicomède*, for instance, the irony of Nicomède and many other characters, or the quarrels between two jealous women that we find in some plays.

There is usually a conflict in a tragedy of Corneille. It may take various forms. It may, for example, be an internal conflict, a conflict between love and honour or duty or *raison d'Etat*, as in *Le Cid*, *Horace* (1640), *Tite et Bérénice* (1670), or *Pulchérie* (1672), for example. It may also be a conflict between different points of view or attitudes to the same problem. A good example of this is *Horace*, in which the main characters reach different solutions to the problem of reconciling the demands of the state with their personal affections – Horace suppresses human emo-

---

[1] See below, pp. 140–1.

tions, Camille rejects the claims of her country, and the other characters adopt intermediary attitudes. *Polyeucte* depicts the clash between paganism and Christianity. In *La Mort de Pompée* (1643–4), Ptolomée and his advisers are governed by *raison d'Etat* and Machiavellian principles, whereas César and Cléopâtre do not separate the maxims of government and those of honour and virtue. In *Sertorius* (1662), Sertorius and Pompée conceive of their duty to their country in diametrically opposed ways. And it may also be a conflict between different characters or groups – between Cléopâtre on the one hand, and her sons and Rodogune on the other in *Rodogune* (1644–5), between Marcelle and Placide in *Théodore* (1645–6), between the usurper, Martian, and the supporters of the legitimate heir in *Héraclius* (1646–7), between Rome and Nicomède in *Nicomède* (1651), between Attila and his captive kings and princesses in *Attila* (1667), and so forth. These three kinds of conflict, of course, are not always separate: if *Nicomède*, for example, shows the conflict between Nicomède and Rome, it also shows the different attitudes that can be adopted towards the supremacy of Rome – Nicomède and Laodice are prepared to resist Rome to the end, Prusias and Arsinoé seek the alliance of Rome, and Attale changes sides in the course of the play.

Corneille's first play was performed in 1629, and his last in 1674. His career thus spans a long period, and one which saw a number of changes of taste. In a very general way, one can distinguish four main periods in his work. The first is from *Mélite* to 1636. The second is that of *Le Cid, Horace, Cinna* 1640–1), and *Polyeucte* (1642–3), four plays which deal with a conflict within the breast of the character or characters. In the third, from *La Mort de Pompée* to *Pertharite* (1651–2), the conflicts become external rather than internal – conflicts between individuals or groups, rather than conflicts within the individual. After the failure of *Pertharite* in 1651 or 1652, Corneille abandoned the theatre for a number of years. The last period of his activity opens in 1659 with *Œdipe* and lasted until *Suréna* (1674). In this period, he tends to write a type of tragedy which has been described as 'matrimonial' – i.e. in which the interests of the characters and of the party or state are bound up with a ruler's choice of a wife. It should be remembered that in this last period, Corneille and Racine were contemporaries and rivals.

Since Corneille wrote thirty-two plays during a career which lasted for forty-five years, and since he was constantly experimenting and seeking novelty, it is impossible in a few pages either to discuss all his plays or to single out any one as typical. Perhaps the best thing to do is to examine two, one from the earlier part of his career and one from the end.

*Cinna* (1640–1) is the first tragedy of Corneille which observes the rules. *Le Cid* was a tragi-comedy, and *Horace* does not obey the unity of action, strictly interpreted. *Cinna*, however, deals with a single unified action, and opens at the moment of crisis, so that a time span of a few hours is adequate for the events of the play.[2] The play is interesting as a psychological study and for the problems it raises (Machiavellianism in government v. honour and magnanimity) – problems which have not ceased to concern the modern world; but it is also very skilfully and dramatically constructed, so that suspense is maintained and surprise achieved right up to the dénouement: we are far, not only from the elegiac tragedy of the Renaissance, but from that of Alexandre Hardy. The situation at the beginning of the play is that Emilie, the adopted daughter of the Emperor, Auguste, wishes to be revenged on Auguste, who put her father to death. She has persuaded her lover, Cinna, a favourite of Auguste, to organize a conspiracy against his royal master.

*Act I.*
*Scene 1.* Emilie soliloquizes: she is torn between love of Cinna (whose life will be in danger if the conspiracy is discovered) and hatred of Auguste.
*Scene 2.* Her confidante, Fulvie, tries to persuade her to renounce her vengeance. They debate the arguments in favour of the two possible courses of action. It is too late, Emilie decides, however, to put an end to the conspiracy.
*Scene 3.* Cinna enters and describes the meeting of the conspirators and the plan of action.
*Scene 4.* A messenger summons Cinna to the palace. Emilie and Cinna think that the conspiracy has been discovered; Emilie urges Cinna to flee.

In the first two scenes, Emilie vacillates, and we do not know whether the assassination will take place or not. Then comes a scene in which Cinna expresses his confidence of success, followed by one of consternation. The act is composed of different types of scene – a monologue, a debate, narrative – and shows a variety of different moods. It ends on a note of suspense: why is Cinna called to the palace?

*Act II.*
*Scene 1.* This magnificent scene contains at least three surprises. Not only has Auguste not discovered the conspiracy, he has summoned Cinna and his fellow-conspirator, Maxime, to advise him whether he should abdicate or not. Moreover, instead of advising him to abdicate, as we should expect, we find Cinna, in the magnificent political debate which follows, urging Auguste to remain on the throne. Suspense is maintained until the end, as

[2] The unity of place is not strictly observed. The scene changes between the apartment or house of Emilie and that of Auguste, and the scenes are not linked in the fourth act.

the powerful arguments of Cinna and Maxime succeed one another. Auguste finally resolves to keep his throne, and to reward his advisers—Cinna's reward is the hand of Emilie.

*Scene 2.* The explanation of Cinna's unexpected advice is now given. By abdication, Auguste would have escaped assassination—Cinna wants him to remain Emperor so that he shall not escape his fate. This gives rise to a further debate between Maxime and Cinna, whether it would be better for Auguste to abdicate or to be assassinated. The scene ends with Maxime asking Cinna whether he thinks Emilie (of whose hatred for Auguste he is unaware) will obey the Emperor and marry him. The two conspirators depart to continue their conversation elsewhere.

*Act III.*
*Scene 1.* Maxime has just learnt from Cinna that Emilie loves him. He, too, we learn, loves Emilie. His confidant, the freedman, Euphorbe, advises him to betray Cinna.
*Scene 2.* Cinna tells Maxime that he no longer wishes to kill Auguste; he is torn between gratitude for Auguste's favours and love of Emilie.
*Scene 3.* He expresses his hesitation in a soliloquy, at the end of which he resolves to appeal to Emilie.
*Scene 4.* A debate between Cinna and Emilie: Emilie is determined not to relent towards Auguste. Cinna, with an ill grace, agrees to carry out his undertaking to murder Auguste, but threatens to kill himself afterwards.
*Scene 5.* Left alone with Fulvie, Emilie hesitates, but finally adheres to her decision.

Throughout this act, then, the future course of events has been in doubt. Until the end, Cinna's vacillation has made it seem doubtful whether the assassination of Auguste will take place. At the end, it seems that Cinna will kill Auguste, but kill himself afterwards.

*Act IV.*
*Scene 1.* Euphorbe betrays the conspiracy to Auguste and says that Maxime has jumped into the Tiber.
*Scene 2.* Auguste soliloquizes: he does not know whether to punish or forgive the conspirators; he reaches no conclusion.
*Scene 3.* His wife, Livie, urges him to forgive. He combats her arguments, and departs, saying:

Le ciel m'inspirera ce qu'ici je dois faire.

*Scene 4.* Although Cinna has again been sent for, Emilie feels an irrational tranquillity.
*Scene 5.* The audience is surprised to see Maxime enter. He tries to persuade Emilie to flee with him and offers her his love. She rejects it.
*Scene 6.* Left alone, Maxime is filled with shame. He decides to punish Euphorbe and kill himself.

The conspiracy has been discovered, but we do not know what will happen to the conspirators. The fifth act is needed to satisfy our curiosity.

*Act V.*
*Scene 1.* Auguste makes Cinna see that he is not the heroic figure he had imagined, and tells him to choose his punishment.

*Scene 2.* We are surprised to see Emilie enter and confess her part in the plot. The scene ends with Auguste threatening Emilie and Cinna:

> Oui, je vous unirai, couple ingrat et perfide . . .

*Scene 3.* Maxime—to our surprise—enters and reveals his villainy—his betrayal of Cinna was due, not to remorse, but to jealousy. This final blow puts an end to Auguste's vacillation. He—and this is the last surprise—forgives the culprits, and by this act wins their friendship, even that of Emilie.

Uncertainty and suspense are maintained, and surprise succeeds surprise right up to the end of the play. But there is nothing melodramatic about *Cinna*. The suspense is largely created by natural conflicts within the breast of the characters and their consequent vacillation. Everything is adequately motivated and carefully prepared — Emilie's final capitulation, by her doubts at the beginning of the play; Cinna's, by the advice he gives Auguste in the second act, by the gratitude he feels for Auguste's favours, and by his vacillation in the third; Auguste's clemency, by his hesitations throughout the play, by Livie's advice, by his confidence that heaven will inspire him, and by the irrational tranquillity of Emilie at the end of Act IV. A psychologically convincing, highly dramatic play, then, treating a universal theme: such is *Cinna*.

*Suréna* (1674) is rather different. Here again, there is a political theme, that of *raison d'Etat* versus personal inclinations, and that of the relations between a king and an over-powerful subject; but *Suréna* does not, on the whole, arouse suspense or surprise. The main characters are in a hopeless situation, from which, their nature being what it is, there is no escape, and the action moves relentlessly to the final catastrophe, the assassination of Suréna by his royal master, Orode. The play — and this again makes it, not unique, but something of an exception in Corneille's work — has an unhappy ending, and is a true tragedy in the narrowest sense of the word, and a strangely moving one. Suréna, the Parthian general, and Eurydice, the daughter of the King of Armenia whom he has vanquished, are secretly in love but, for political reasons, condemned to marry other partners — Eurydice is to marry Pacorus, the son of Orode, King of the Parthians, in order to cement a durable alliance between the two countries, and Orode is determined to ensure Suréna's loyalty by marrying him to his own daughter, Mandane. Neither Eurydice nor Suréna can bring themselves to accept these marriages, thereby encompassing their own destruction.

A feature of the structure of *Suréna* — characteristic of Corneille, though not so evident in *Cinna* — is a fondness for symmetry, for similar, though sometimes contrasting, scenes. There is symmetry in the situation of *Suréna*: leaving aside the

King, the main protagonists are two pairs of brothers and sisters, with, in each case, the sister loving, or destined to marry, the opposite brother;[3] both brothers are rivals for the hand of Eurydice.[4] In Act I, we learn in successive scenes that Eurydice loves Suréna and that Suréna loves Eurydice, and then see them together. Act II shows three attempts by Pacorus to find out — from Suréna, from Eurydice, and from Suréna's sister, Palmis — the name of Eurydice's lover; Act III shows Orode's attempts to find out whom Suréna loves. Act IV shows attempts to make Eurydice marry Pacorus, followed by an attempt to make Suréna marry Mandane. The form of a play of Corneille is aesthetically satisfying.

Since La Bruyère's famous, though not altogether accurate, remark, that Corneille 'peint les hommes comme ils devraient être', the idea has gained currency that Corneille's heroes and heroines are people of strong will power, who obey their reason, and sacrifice their inclinations to their duty. There is no space to discuss this notion in detail, but it may have become clear from the brief analyses above that neither *Cinna* nor *Suréna* provide evidence in its favour.

In *Cinna*, Emilie, in the very first scene of the play, makes it clear that

> J'aime encor plus Cinna que je ne hais Auguste . . .

— a line which forecasts the dénouement of the play. Maxime betrays Cinna from jealousy. Cinna sees himself as a brave and resolute character, and is gradually stripped of his illusions as the play advances. His description of the nobility and zeal of the conspirators he has enlisted (I, 3) contrasts with that of Auguste in Act V:

> Le reste ne vaut pas l'honneur d'être nommé:
> Un tas d'hommes perdus de dettes et de crimes,
> Que pressent de mes lois les ordres légitimes,
> Et qui, désespérant de les plus éviter,
> Si tout n'est renversé, ne sauraient subsister.
>                                         (V, 1)

He has concealed from his fellow-conspirators his love for Emilie and her interest in the plot; his advice to Auguste not to abdicate is motivated by his fear of losing Emilie if he does not kill Auguste; he vacillates as the moment for action approaches, and realizes that he 'ne forme qu'en lâche un dessein généreux'; and though, in the first act, thinking that he had been betrayed, he had said,

> S'il est pour me trahir des esprits assez bas,
> Ma vertu pour le moins ne me trahira pas;

[3] Cf. *Horace*.
[4] To a lesser degree, symmetry is present in the situation of *Cinna*: Emilie has two lovers, Cinna and Maxime.

> Vous la verrez, brillante au bord des précipices,
> Se couronner de gloire en bravant les supplices,
> Rendre Auguste jaloux du sang qu'il répandra,
> Et le faire trembler alors qu'il me perdra.
>
>                                         (I, 4)

— when Auguste accuses him of having conspired against him, he immediately denies it:

> Moi, Seigneur! moi, que j'eusse une âme si traîtresse!
> Qu'un si lâche dessein . . .                    (V, 1)

Auguste makes him see himself as he really is:

> Apprends à te connaître, et descends en toi-même:
> On t'honore dans Rome, on te courtise, on t'aime,
> Chacun tremble sous toi, chacun t'offre des vœux:
> Ta fortune est bien haut, tu peux ce que tu veux;
> Mais tu ferais pitié même à ceux qu'elle irrite,
> Si je t'abandonnais à ton peu de mérite.
> Ose me démentir, dis-moi ce que tu vaux,
> Conte-moi tes vertus, tes glorieux travaux,
> Les rares qualités par où tu m'as dû plaire,
> Et tout ce qui t'élève au-dessus du vulgaire.
> Ma faveur fait ta gloire, et ton pouvoir en vient:
> Elle seule t'élève, et seule te soutient;
> C'est elle qu'on adore, et non pas ta personne:
> Tu n'as crédit ni rang qu'autant qu'elle t'en donne,
> Et pour te faire choir je n'aurais aujourd'hui
> Qu'à retirer la main qui seule est ton appui.
>
>                                         (V, 1)

As for Auguste, at the opening of the play, he is tired and dis-illusioned, and afraid of being assassinated like Julius Caesar (II, 1). Throughout the play, he wavers between a policy of rigour and one of leniency; and, if he finally decides in favour of clemency, the decision is not so much his as that of the gods.

In *Suréna*, Pacorus, jealous, tries to find out whom Eurydice loves, to pry into her heart, to worm her secret out of Palmis by a promise of marriage. Neither Suréna nor Eurydice will re-nounce their love. Eurydice — like Sabine in *Horace* — makes it clear that her fortitude is purely external:

> Mon intrépidité n'est qu'un effort de gloire,
> Que, tout fier qu'il paraît, mon cœur n'en veut pas croire.
> Il est tendre, et ne rend ce tribut qu'à regret
> Au juste et dur orgueil qu'il dément en secret.
>
>                                         (IV, 2)

Palmis acknowledges her lack of power over her emotions:

> Je voudrais le pouvoir;
> Mais pour ne plus aimer que sert de le vouloir?
>
>                                         (II, 3)

There is an interesting passage in which she tells Orode that she
wishes to remain at court in order to see her faithless lover suffer
from the knowledge that his wife loves another man:

> ... il est des plaisirs qu'une amante trahie
> Goûte au milieu des maux qui lui coûtent la vie:
> Je verrai l'infidèle, inquiet, alarmé
> D'un rival inconnu, mais ardemment aimé,
> Rencontrer à mes yeux sa peine dans son crime,
> Par les mains de l'hymen devenir ma victime,
> Et ne me regarder, dans ce chagrin profond,
> Que le remords en l'âme, et la rougeur au front.
>
> (III, 3)

The characters in *Cinna* and *Suréna* are interesting; none can be
called 'Cornelian'.

The brief analyses given above do no justice, either to the
variety of scenes in Corneille, or to his psychological subtlety
and penetration. Two passages in *Suréna* may perhaps help to
illustrate this last point. Sillace tells Orode that Suréna is perhaps
less indifferent to Eurydice than he seems:

> Il m'a paru, Seigneur, si froid, si retenu ...
> Mais vous en jugerez quand il sera venu.
> Cependant je dirai que cette retenue
> Sent une âme de trouble et d'ennuis prévenue;
> Que ce calme paraît assez prémédité
> Pour ne répondre pas de sa tranquillité;
> Que cette indifférence a de l'inquiétude,
> Et que cette froideur marque un peu trop d'étude.
>
> (III, 1)

Pacorus tells Suréna that he has guessed his secret:

> L'amour dans sa prudence est toujours indiscret;
> A force de se taire il trahit son secret:
> Le soin de le cacher découvre ce qu'il cache,
> Et son silence dit tout ce qu'il craint qu'on sache.
> Ne cachez plus le vôtre, il est connu de tous,
> Et toute votre adresse a parlé contre vous.
>
> (IV, 4)

Nor should it be forgotten that, if Corneille is remembered as a
great dramatist, it is because he was also a great poet, capable
of great variety, of what Mme de Sévigné calls 'ces tirades qui
font frissonner' (they are not lacking in *Cinna*), of scenes of discussion, of argument, of debate, of scenes in which politeness
veils hostility, of irony, of passion, and of tenderness. *Suréna*,
though it does not lack irony, is particularly rich in passages of
melancholy resignation and moving tenderness. Eurydice tells
Suréna:

> Je veux qu'un noir chagrin à pas lents me consume,
> Qu'il me fasse à longs traits goûter son amertume;

> Je vieux, sans que la morte ose me secourir,
> Toujours aimer, toujours souffrir, toujours mourir.
>
> (I, 3)

— lines in which the pathos is enhanced by the music of the verse, with its alliteration and assonance. Another short speech of Eurydice illustrates this clearly. Pacorus asks her what it avails to marry her if her heart is unwilling ('si le cœur en murmure'), to which she replies, movingly — and alliteratively,

> Quel mal pourrait causer le murmure du mien,
> S'il murmurait si bas, qu'aucun n'en apprît rien?
>
> (II, 2)

## II. THE CONTEMPORARIES OF CORNEILLE:
### TRAGEDY AND TRAGI-COMEDY

Jean Mairet (1604–86), probably the leading dramatist before *Le Cid*, wrote a dozen plays, tragi-comedies, pastorals, tragedies, and a comedy,[5] but he is chiefly remembered nowadays for his *Sophonisbe*, performed in 1634 and usually regarded as the first seventeenth-century French classical tragedy. This reputation it deserves on many counts: the action is simple and the interest is centred on the feelings of the main characters; there is no chorus; the unities are observed; and history is changed in the interests of *bienséance* and *vraisemblance* — Syphax dies in battle (so that Sophonisbe can marry Massinisse without committing bigamy), and Massinisse kills himself after the death of Sophonisbe. Although a dream, a prophecy, forebodings, and omens leave no doubt of the eventual tragic outcome, the play is not devoid of dramatic interest; in discarding the dramatic system of Alexandre Hardy, Mairet has not returned to the elegiac tragedy of the Renaissance. In Act I, scene 1, for instance, Syphax, having intercepted a letter from Sophonisbe to Massinisse, calls on her to defend herself, which, unsuccessfully, she attempts to do. In Act II, scene 1, we see Sophonisbe torn between her love for the enemy of her country and a feeling of shame. The account of the battle between Syphax and the Romans is in two parts, like the more famous one in *Horace* later, and the first report suggests that Syphax may be victorious, whereas the second tells of his defeat. In Act III, Sophonisbe's women urge her to save herself by winning Massinisse's love, and the interview between her and Massinisse, in which the inflammable Numidian is duly vamped, is intensely dramatic. In

---

[5] For Mairet's *Sylvie*, see Chapter 5; his comedy, *Les Galanteries du duc d'Ossone*, is mentioned later in the present chapter.

Act IV, scene 1, a love scene between Massinisse and Sophonisbe
is dramatically interrupted by the arrival of the Roman messenger.
The two plays of Du Ryer (c. 1600–58) which are available
in modern editions are both simply constructed, and in both the
situation leads logically and inevitably to an unhappy dénouement. *Alcionée* (1637), derived from Ariosto's *Orlando furioso*
and influenced no doubt by *Le Cid*, deals with a princess who
loves, and is loved by, an adventurer who has made war on her
country because her father would not let him marry his daughter.
Torn between love of Alcionée and hatred of the enemy of her
country coupled with a sense of his inferior birth, she finally, in
obedience to her father's wishes, rejects his suit, and he kills
himself. 'Il n'y eut jamais de tragédie moins intriguée,' wrote
abbé d'Aubignac in his *Pratique du Théâtre*, 'et pourtant en
avons-nous vu peu qui aient eu un plus favorable succès.' *Saül*
(1640) is equally simple and moving. The old King, abandoned
by God for his disobedience, refuses to recall David and consults
the witch of Endor. The spirit of Samuel, whom she conjures up,
foretells that he will be defeated and die in battle along with his
sons and be succeeded by David; and this prophecy fills him with
despair. After a vain attempt to save Jonathan's life by sending
him away, he accepts his destiny, witnesses the death of his sons
in battle and kills himself.

The most prolific of the contemporaries of Corneille was Jean
de Rotrou (1609–50). Like Hardy, Rotrou was employed as
the *poète à gages* of a company of actors, and in a score of years
he wrote nearly forty plays – tragi-comedies, tragedies, and comedies – often adapted from Latin, Spanish, or Italian originals. In
his tragedies and tragi-comedies – the distinction is not always
clear – he is primarily interested in telling a story, and the
favourite features of the age abound – disguises, prison scenes,
children lost or exchanged in infancy and recognized at the end
of the play, double-entendre and talking at cross-purposes. The
best of them are *Saint Genest* (published in 1647), *Venceslas*
(1647), and *Cosroès* (published in 1649), though *Laure persécutée*
(1637) deserves to be read, particularly for its somewhat Shake-
spearean fourth act. *Saint Genest*, a tragedy influenced by Corneille's *Polyeucte*, deals with a Roman actor who, playing the
part of a Christian martyr on the stage, throws himself into his
part with such fervour that he becomes a Christian and accepts
martyrdom himself. *Venceslas*, a tragi-comedy, later called a
tragedy, is interesting for the character of the hero, Ladislas,
a vicious prince who, in the course of the play, reveals his
essential nobility, and for the struggle in the mind of his father,
Venceslas, between the desire to punish Ladislas (who has un-

wittingly killed his brother) and love for him. *Cosroès* is a political play, in which the rightful heir, dispossessed in favour of his younger stepbrother, places himself at the head of a revolt and seizes power. The play is interesting for the struggle for power, for the conflict in the mind of the hero between filial obedience and the maintenance of his rights, between family affection and *raison d'Etat*, for the conflict in the stepbrother between loyalty to his brother and ambition, and for the discussions of political principles.

Rotrou's influence on his contemporaries and successors was not inconsiderable. His *Hypocondriaque* (1628) offers some points of similarity with Corneille's *Mélite* (the hero, believing his mistress unfaithful, goes mad); and *Cosroès* provided the starting-point of *Nicomède*. Racine made use of his *Antigone* (1637) and his *Iphigénie en Aulide* (1640?) in writing *La Thébaïde* and *Iphigénie* respectively. The sitution of Iole in *Hercule mourant*, compelled to choose between marrying Hercule and seeing him put her lover to death, may have suggested the not dissimilar blackmail of Andromaque by Pyrrhus in Racine's *Andromaque*; and Racine borrowed from Rotrou's *Bélissaire* (published in 1644) the scene in *Britannicus* in which Junie receives Britannicus coldly, because Néron, a concealed witness of the interview, has threatened to put him to death if she does not. In *Les Sosies*, Rotrou adapted Plautus's *Amphitruo* to the French stage before Molière, and the Turkish scenes in *Le Bourgeois gentilhomme* owe something to *La Sœur*. But Rotrou is of more than merely historical interest; some, at least, of his plays still deserve to be read for their intrinsic merits.

Tristan l'Hermite wrote five tragedies, a tragi-comedy (*La Folie du Sage*), and a pastoral.[6] *La Mariane* (1636), one of the most successful tragedies of the period, treats a subject already exploited by Hardy, that of the wife of Herod. The insane jealousy of Herod which makes him an easy prey to false accusations against his wife, the madness to which grief brings him after he has caused her to be put to death, and the noble disdain of Mariane are admirably and movingly portrayed. Long before Racine's *Andromaque*, this play of Tristan ends with one of the main characters mad from grief and remorse on the stage. *La Folie du Sage* (1642?), a tragi-comedy, is particularly noteworthy for the scenes in which the *sage*, Ariste, his wits unhinged by the supposed death of his daughter, condemns philosophers, throws his books on the floor in a frenzy (III, 4), and – in a vein reminiscent of Hamlet – meditates on man and on medicine (IV, 1).[7]

---

[6] Besides a comedy, which will be mentioned below.

[7] The soliloquy in which he debates whether to commit suicide or not (I, 2) is reminiscent of Hamlet's famous speech.

*La Mort de Sénèque* (1644) is perhaps the best of his plays. A dramatization of portions of Tacitus, it deals less with Seneca than with a conspiracy against Nero, a false accusation of complicity with which brings about Seneca's death. The blandishments of Poppée, the courage and steadfastness of the freedwoman, Epicaris, under torture and her defiance of Néron and Poppée, and the noble resignation of Sénèque, in contrast to the cowardice of the other conspirators, are admirably portrayed. Showing as it does the meeting of the conspirators, followed by their arrest, interrogation, torture, and execution, the play is highly dramatic.

One of the best of the tragedies of Corneille's contemporaries is certainly Cyrano de Bergerac's *Mort d'Agrippine* (1653?), a powerful and powerfully written play of vengeance, hatred, and jealousy. One or two passages are particularly noteworthy and may reveal the unorthodox opinions of the poet. Whereas, in the drama of the period, the divinity of kings is a commonplace, Séjanus in this play emphasizes their kinship with their subjects:

> Mon sang n'est point Royal, mais l'héritier d'un Roi
> Porte-t-il un visage autrement fait que moi?
> Encor qu'un toit de chaume eût couvert ma naissance,
> Et qu'un Palais de marbre eût logé son enfance,
> Qu'il fût né d'un grand Roi, moi d'un simple Pasteur,
> Son sang auprès du mien est-il d'autre couleur?
> Mon nom serait au rang des héros qu'on renomme,
> Si mes prédécesseurs avaient saccagé Rome;
> Mais je suis regardé comme un homme de rien,
> Car mes prédécesseurs se nommaient gens de bien.
>
> (II, 4)

And he denounces the gods with remarkable vehemence:

> Ces enfants de l'effroi,
> Ces beaux riens qu'on adore, et sans savoir pourquoi,
> Ces altérés du sang des bêtes qu'on assomme,
> Ces Dieux que l'homme a faits, et qui n'ont point fait l'homme,
> Des plus fermes états ce fantasque soutien,
> Va, va, Térentius, qui les craint ne craint rien.
>
> (II, 4)

Finally, it was in this period that the long career of Corneille's brother, Thomas, began. His career is strangely similar to that of his brother, with a time-lag of twenty years. Born in Rouen in 1625, and like his brother educated for the bar, he, too, began by writing comedies and subsequently turned to tragedy. From 1649 to 1656, he wrote eight comedies, one of which, however, *Les Illustres Ennemis*, despite the appellation, comedy, is in fact what would earlier have been called a tragi-comedy, or what

Pierre Corneille might have termed a 'comédie héroïque'. Then, in 1656, he wrote his first tragedy, *Timocrate*, which ran for six months at the Marais theatre, an unparalleled success for the seventeenth century: indeed, according to Donneau de Visé, for a time it was on at both theatres simultaneously. Something has been said of *Timocrate* above;[8] here we may add that the success of the play was well deserved and is not hard to explain. It has many of the favourite ingredients of the seventeenth century – magnanimous and generous characters, an adventurer in whom valour compensates for lowly origins (like Corneille's Don Sanche, he turns out to be a king), a council scene and a political interest, love and gallantry, with, in addition, and this is its novelty, an element of mystery, something of the appeal of a detective novel. *Timocrate* is an exciting, enjoyable, well-constructed, dramatic play, with a good deal of charm, one that is still capable of being read with pleasure. It is full of innuendo and double-entendre, and every scene brings some reversal of the situation, some new factor which leaves the action in doubt, so that suspense is maintained, and surprise follows surprise, until the last scene of the play. In *Timocrate* and in other plays of this period (*Bérénice*, 1657; *Darius*, 1659), Thomas Corneille combines imitation of his brother (*Timocrate* is full of reminiscences of *Le Cid* and *Dom Sanche*) with a love of romanesque imbroglio, disguise, confusion of identity, and heroes and heroines of unknown parentage and incredible magnanimity, ready to sacrifice anything to their love.[9]

## III. CORNEILLE AND HIS CONTEMPORARIES: COMEDY

It is scarcely an exaggeration to say that seventeenth-century comedy was the creation of Pierre Corneille with his first play, *Mélite* (1629), in the preface to which he prides himself on having written a comedy without stock characters and one which portrayed the 'conversation des honnêtes gens'. It is true that in the first respect Baro had anticipated him (so Carrington Lancaster affirms) in his 'poème héroïque', *Célinde* (1628), and that realistic dialogue and badinage between lovers can be found in the pastoral and in one or two scenes in Hardy's tragi-comedies.[10] It is true, too, that the plot of *Mélite* – two lovers separated by the trick

8 See pp. 95–7.
9 *Les Illustres Ennemis*, in which the heroine is prepared to make incredible sacrifices to her *gloire*, is an exception; so is *Commode* (1657), a simple, straightforward play with a happy ending.
10 E.g. *Gésippe*, I, 2 and 4; *Dorise*, III, 2 and IV, 2.

of a jealous rival – is that of the pastoral or of such tragi-comedies as Hardy's *Dorise* or Rotrou's *Hypocondriaque* (1628). Nevertheless, these debts, or possible debts, must not blind us to the originality of Corneille, which consists in developing the realism found here and there in some previous plays, freeing it from the extraordinary events and the unreal or fantastic setting of the tragicomedy or pastoral, and placing it in its natural setting, that of the upper classes of a French city. With Corneille, realism – which had already entered the novel and verse – enters the theatre. 'La comédie,' wrote Corneille in the preface to his second comedy, *La Veuve*, 'n'est qu'un portrait de nos actions, et de nos discours, et la perfection des portraits consiste en la ressemblance.'

*La Veuve* and the three comedies that followed it – *La Galerie du Palais*, *La Suivante*, and *La Place Royale* – deal, like *Mélite* and like the pastoral, with lovers separated by the trick of a rival or some obstacle; they are set in Paris; and they contain a good deal of realism – natural dialogue, social criticism (in the form of a protest against the practice of parents of marrying their daughters to the highest bidder), and allusions to contemporary literary tastes, to fashions and to manners. *La Galerie* and *La Place Royale* are set in real parts of Paris, and in the former we see shop-keepers receiving their customers, discussing their wares, and quarrelling with each other.

Other writers continued the realism of Corneille. Du Ryer's *Vendanges de Suresne* (1633), like *La Galerie*, is set in a real locality – 'Le théâtre représente Suresne' – and contains several references to contemporary manners – what attentions win the love of girls (I, 1), how girls may attract men (I, 6), the vain politeness of the age (I, 2); there are discussions whether bourgeois parents should marry their daughter to a nobleman or not; and in one scene (III, 2), Polidor shows some verses to Tirsis, and Philémon describes the rival poets criticizing a play in the theatre. In Gougenot's *Comédie des Comédiens* (1631-2), three acts in prose show the actor, Bellerose, forming a new company, the members of which quarrel about their parts and recruit new actors, after which they perform a three-act play in verse.[11]

A particularly delightful play is Discret's *Alizon* (1636), which gives an attractive glimpse of middle-class Parisian life:

une dame de mes amies m'ayant fait le récit des grotesques et véritables amours de la veuve d'un pauvre bourgeois de Paris, j'en ai traité l'histoire en rime sous le nom d'Alizon Fleurie, avec des paroles les plus approchantes de la sorte de parler des personnages qui y sont introduits, et chacun selon sa condition pour rendre le sujet plus risible,

[11] Scudéry's rival *Comédie des Comédiens* was performed in 1632. These plays anticipate Molière's *Impromptu de Versailles*.

writes the author in his *Avertissement au lecteur*. Alizon is an
elderly widow,[12] wooed by a bourgeois, a pedlar – who gives a
list of his wares –, and an old soldier. In Act II, scene 1, Alizon's
three daughters fetch their work outside and converse in sisterly
fashion in the sun; a river picnic is planned, and duly takes
place in Act III; Alizon discusses the arrangements for her
marriage with the bourgeois; three young men discuss the amusements offered by Paris in Act III, scene 2; and at the end of
Act III, a *charivari* takes place in front of the window of Alizon
and her husband.[13]

*Le Pédant joué* (1645) of Cyrano de Bergerac – written in
prose and probably not performed – is set in the collège de
Beauvais, and the pedant of the title bears the name (Granger) of
a former principal of that college. In Mareschal's comedy, *Le
Railleur* (1635), there is a scene in which a poet reads his verses
and departs in dudgeon because they are condemned. One of the
characters is a courtezan, and there are some interesting descriptions of the *mœurs* of honest women, *femmes galantes*, and
courtezans, of dress, of literary life and fashions, of the occupations of a man of fashion, and of tax-farmers aping noblemen. Of
particular interest is Claude de l'Estoile's *Intrigue des Filous*
(1646), which introduces us to the Paris underworld, with a
number of thieves, a receiver, and a *revendeuse* who is also a
go-between:

> je revends et fais prêter sur gages;
> Je prédis l'avenir, et fais des mariages:
> Cherchez-vous un mari, je sais bien votre fait . . .
>
> (I, 5)

We see the *revendeuse* selling her wares to a client. Three thieves
and the receiver prepare to break into a house, collect their tools,
and discuss their probable fate:

> Je n'avais pas quinze ans que le vol d'un manteau
> Fit que l'on m'attacha le dos contre un poteau,
> Où, le col dans le fer et les pieds dans la boue,
> Aux passants malgré moi je fis longtemps la moue:
> Je fus marqué depuis à la marque du roi,
> Et si l'on me reprend n'est-ce pas fait de moi?
> . . . . . . .
> Il faudra qu'en charrette, et suivi du bourgeois,
> J'aille sans violons danser au bout d'un bois.
>
> (V, 2)

---

[12] Alizon was the stage-name of an actor who played the part of elderly
women.
[13] *Charivari*: a kind of serenade, consisting of shouts and whistles and
the beating of pots and pans, to express disapproval of elderly widows
who had remarried.

A fourth thief passes himself off as a man of fortune and woos the daughter of a *partisan*. Unfortunately, the proportion of these scenes to the rest of the play is not as high as one would wish. *La Belle Plaideuse* (1654) of Boisrobert, which, like *La Galerie du Palais*, contains a scene in a shop (Act II is set at the foire Saint-Germain), includes amongst its characters a *plaideuse*, and a miser who is also a usurer and whose meanness drives his son to extravagance and into the hands of the moneylenders. The action of the play is largely concerned – like that of *Le Pédant joué* – with the attempts of the son and his valet to obtain money. In one scene, the son is brought face to face with a moneylender who turns out to be no other than his father; later he hears the terms of another, who, instead of cash, expects him to accept a ship's cargo. Molière's *Avare* owes something to this play.

The main interest in most of the plays of the period is in the plot. Sometimes, as we have seen, there are contemporary references, some attempt to depict contemporary types or manners, but not always. There is no realism, for example, in Mairet's *Galanteries du duc d'Ossone* (1632), an amusing, but unedifying, comedy, set in Italy. The same is true of Rotrou's comedies, which – whether he adapts Plautus, as in *Les Ménechmes* (1630–1631), *Les Sosies* (1637 – a treatment of the Amphitryon theme to which Molière's *Amphitryon* is indebted), and *Les Captifs* (1638), or Italian plays, as in *Clarice* (1641) and *La Sœur* (1645) – frequently turn on exchanges of identity between characters. In *La Sœur*, Lélie, sent to bring back his sister, Aurélie, who was captured by pirates in infancy, falls in love with a slave, marries her and passes her off as his sister, Aurélie. When his father decides to marry his two children, Lélie is in a dilemma and looks to his wily valet, Ergaste, to extricate him from it. Géronte, a friend of Lélie's father, comes back from Turkey with his son, Horace, who speaks nothing but Turkish, and recognizes Aurélie as a servant-girl from Venice. In an amusing scene, the valet, Ergaste, pretends to speak Turkish with Horace and interprets his replies as meaning that Géronte was telling lies; in another, Géronte speaks Turkish with his son, and says that he could not understand what Ergaste was saying – Molière probably remembered these scenes when he was writing *Le Bourgeois gentilhomme*.[14] Lélie's mother returns from captivity and identifies Aurélie as her daughter and Lélie's

---

[14] *Anselme.* T'en a-t-il pu tant dire en si peu de propos?
  *Ergaste.* Oui, le langage turc dit beaucoup en deux mots.
Cf. *Le Bourgeois gentilhomme* (IV, 4):
  *M. Jourdain.* Tant de choses en deux mots?
  *Covielle.* Oui, la langue turque est comme cela, elle dit beaucoup en peu de paroles.

sister. Then, however, it is discovered that Aurélie and another girl were changed in infancy, and all ends happily. *La Sœur*, with its children changed in infancy and its long-lost relatives returning from captivity in time to provide a happy ending, is typical of a number of plays (Tristan's *Parasite*, 1653, is another): Molière uses, and makes fun of, these conventions.

On the whole, the playwrights of the 'forties and 'fifties made more use of Spanish than of Italian sources – Corneille in his *Menteur* (1643) and *Suite du Menteur* (1644–5), for example, which, however, are set in France and contain details of French life, but Scarron and Thomas Corneille above all. In these plays, confusion of identity takes a slightly different form: instead of boys or girls exchanged in infancy, someone in the play mistakenly believes one character to be another. In *Le Menteur*, Dorante is in love with Clarice, but thinks she is Lucrèce. In Thomas Corneille's *Engagements du Hasard* (1649), the hero is not sure whether he is in love with a mysterious beauty who has written to him and whom he has met, or Elvire; fortunately they turn out to be one and the same. In Boisrobert's *Belle Plaideuse* (though this is not a Spanish play), Amidor consents to his son's marriage with the comtesse de Grègue, not knowing that she is Corinne, of whom he disapproves. The situations of these plays are often paradoxical. In Thomas Corneille's *Charme de la Voix* (1656), the hero has fallen in love with a girl's voice, though he has never seen the girl. Another woman pretends to be the woman he thinks he loves. When he discovers that it was not she whom he heard singing, he does not know which of the two he ought to marry. In *Le Geôlier de soi-même* (1655), also by Thomas Corneille, Jodelet, taken for the prince of Sicily, whose discarded armour he has assumed, is arrested and placed in the custody of none other than the prince of Sicily who, his identity being unknown, has been made governor of the castle of the princess of Salerno whose brother he has just killed.

The comedies of the period are not always funny – the distinction between comedy and tragedy, after all, lay in the rank of the characters, rather than in the nature of the play. They are more often light-hearted in tone with an amusing plot, than comic in the manner of Molière – though occasionally we find traces of a comic technique which anticipates Molière. If Corneille's *Mélite*, Mareschal's *Railleur* (1635), Corneille's *Menteur*, Cyrano's *Pédant joué*, Boisrobert's *Belle Plaideuse*, and Rotrou's *Sœur* are predominantly amusing, there are many plays of which the same cannot be said. The *Vendanges de Suresne* of Du Ryer is not consistently comic in tone; nor are some of Corneille's other comedies. Thomas Corneille wrote a number of quite amusing plays – *Les Engagements du*

*Hasard* (1649), *Le Feint Astrologue* (1650), *Dom Bertrand de Cigarral* (1651), *L'Amour à la Mode* (1651), and *Le Berger extravagant*, a *pastorale burlesque* and a dramatization of Sorel's novel (1652) – followed by three comedies which are wholly or mainly serious in tone, *Les Illustres Ennemis* (1655), *Le Geôlier de soimême* (1655), and *Le Charme de la Voix* (1656). *Les Illustres Ennemis*, which is not funny at all, is more of a tragi-comedy than a comedy; the other two have comic valets.

The humour of the comedies of the period depends mainly on sprightly badinage, the inventiveness of the wily valet (Ergaste in *La Sœur*, Corbineli in *Le Pédant joué*, etc.), amusing intrigues and imbroglios, exaggerated stock characters such as the pedant, the braggadocio, and the parasite, and, associated particularly with these, an amazing verbal virtuosity – Corneille's Matamore in *L'Illusion comique* and Fripesauces in Tristan's *Parasite* are good examples of the kind. One of the most striking plays from this point of view is *Le Pédant joué*, which contains a pedant, a braggadocio, and a peasant speaking dialect. Occasional scenes reminiscent of Molière are found. In *Le Pédant joué*, a true (if at times coarse) comedy, there is a scene in which Granger, with the help of his servant, Paquier, is trying to climb up to Genevote's window, while his son's valet, Corbineli (Granger and his son are rivals), plays tricks on them in the dark. At one point, the stage direction tells us,

Corbineli transpose l'échelle d'un côté et d'autre avec tant d'adresse, que Paquier faisant aller sa main à droite et à gauche, frappe toujours un des côtés de l'échelle sans trouver d'échelons.

(IV, 1)

The same play contains two scenes (II, 4 and III, 2) which have passed into *Les Fourberies de Scapin*, those in which the valet gets money from the old man by telling him that his son is being held for ransom by pirates, and in which the son's young woman tells the whole story to the father, not knowing who he is.[15] One or two scenes in Thomas Corneille's *Amour à la mode* make one think a little of Molière – the self-satisfaction of Eraste (I, 2) and the identical letters sent by Dorotée to two lovers (I, 3) faintly recall the *scène des marquis* and the conduct of Célimène in *Le Misanthrope*; and the amusing scene (V, 8) in which Oronte, set upon by three ladies to whom he has made love and rejected by two of them, anticipates another scene in the same play. Similarly, in *Dom Bertrand de Cigarral*, two women summon Alvar to say which of them he really loves (III, 11).

A slightly different form of comedy is found in the burlesque

[15] It is à propos of this play that—according to Grimarest—Molière remarked: 'Je reprends mon bien où je le trouve.'

plays of Scarron and Thomas Corneille, associated with the comic actor, Jodelet, who also played the part of the valet in Corneille's *Menteur* and its *Suite*, and who, later entering Molière's company, appears in *Les Précieuses ridicules*. Like the plays in which pedants and braggadocios figure largely, the burlesque comedy represents a fusion of literary comedy and farce. The humour, in the burlesque plays, consists of showing a nobleman behaving like a vulgar commoner. In Scarron's *Jodelet ou le Maître valet* (1643) — as in Thomas Corneille's *Geôlier de soi-même* and Molière's *Précieuses ridicules* — Jodelet changes places with his master. He is rude and conceited, smells of garlic, picks his teeth, asks for a *cure-oreille* because his ear is itching, unbuttons his clothes, snores after a meal, shows himself to be an arrant coward, expresses an undue interest in his mistress's dowry, and pays her tasteless compliments:

> Dites-moi, ma maîtresse, avez-vous bien du liège?
> Si vous n'en avez point, vous êtes, sur ma foi!
> D'une fort belle taille, et digne d'être à moi.

(II, 2)

Don Japhet d'Arménie, in Scarron's play of that name (1647), is not a valet dressed up, but Charles V's buffoon. His absurd pretentions of nobility and his conceit contrast with his vulgarity, his cowardice, and the ludicrous situations in which a series of practical jokes places him.[16] Don Bertrand de Cigarral in Thomas Corneille's play is a similar character.

The burlesque characters give an absurd twist to the finer feelings. Don Japhet, for example, serenades his mistress in these terms:

> Amour nabot,
> Qui, du jabot,
> De don Japhet,
>    As fait
> Une ardente fournaise;
>    Hélas! hélas!
>   Je suis bien las
> D'être rempli de braise.
>
> Ton feu grégeois
> M'a fait pantois,
> Et dans mon pis
>    As mis
> Une essence de braise.
>   Bon Dieu! bon Dieu!
>   Le cœur en feu,
> Peut-on être à son aise?

(IV, 5)

---

[16] This play was first performed at the Hôtel de Bourgogne, so that the chief part was not played by Jodelet, who was at the Marais theatre.

They are given to fabricating comic words—Don Japhet coins *démétaphoriser, noblifié, tauricider, dulcifier,* and says:

> Je t'aurai dépaulé, décuissé, détêté . . .
> (V, 9)

The burlesque writers, too, like to pile up proper names with comic effect. Don Japhet is

> Le mari d'Azatèque,
> Le gendre d'Uriquis, de Chicuchiquizèque.
> (II, 5)

At the end of the play he is ordered to marry a Peruvian:

> L'héritier du soleil, le grand Manco-Capac,
> Souverain du pays d'où nous vient le tabac,
> Qui prit Caïa Mama, sa sœur, en mariage,
> Du pays du Pérou la fille la plus sage.
> Du valeureux Manco, de la belle Caïa
> Est sortie, en nos jours, l'infante Ahihua . . .[17]

Finally, in this period, comedy of character begins. The stock characters derived from Italian comedy which abound in the plays of this period are a form of character comedy—the braggadiocio (Fierabras in *La Comédie des Proverbes* (1633) attributed to the comte de Cramail, Matamore in Corneille's *Illusion comique* and Tristan's *Parasite,* Taillebras in Mareschal's *Railleur,* Artabaze in Desmarets de Saint-Sorlin's *Visionnaires,* Rhinocéronte in Rotrou's *Clarice,* Chateaufort in *Le Pédant joué*); the parasite (Fripesauces in Tristan's *Parasite*); the pedant (docteur Thesaurus in *La Comédie des Proverbes,* Fabrice in Le Vert's *Docteur amoureux,* 1638, Hippocrasse in Rotrou's *Clarice,* Granger in *Le Pédant joué*); the wily valet (Ergaste in *La Sœur,* Corbineli in *Le Pédant joué,* Filipin in *La Belle Plaideuse*); the buffoon (Jodelet), etc. In some plays, more realistic, contemporary types are portrayed—the miser who is also a usurer, and the *plaideuse,* in *La Belle Plaideuse,* for example. Charles Beys (c. 1610–1659), in *L'Hôpital de Fous* (1634), a tragi-comedy, which was revised and republished as a comedy in 1653, takes us into a lunatic asylum and shows us the inmates—a musician who thinks he is Orpheus, a philosopher who thinks he created the universe, an astrologer who thinks he is the sun, an alchemist, a *plaideur,* a

---

[17] Boisrobert similarly makes fun of Breton names in *La Belle Plaideuse*:
> Il est vers Lantriquet,
> Entre Kertronquedic et Kerlovidaquet.
> (II, 3)

> Ce baron si fameux d'Orgardec,
> De Kerybourdaguec et de Chertronquedec.
> (V, 2)

gamester, a poet, and an actor. In *Les Visionnaires* (1637), Desmarets de Saint-Sorlin (1595–1676) shows a similar selection of eccentric characters — a *capitan*, a disciple of Ronsard, a man who loves poetry but does not understand it and falls in love with a satirical description of a woman, a man who talks extravagantly of wealth he does not possess, and three sisters — one in love with Alexander the Great, one mad about the theatre, and a third who fancies all men in love with her and has been thought to have provided Molière with the idea of Bélise in *Les Femmes savantes*. These plays — and particularly the second, which has virtually no plot — are interesting — like Molière's *Fâcheux* later — above all for the characters they bring on to the stage.

The writer who comes nearest to true comedy of character, however — for, despite its title, Mareschal's *Railleur* is disappointing in this respect — is Corneille. Corneille, who, in *La Galerie du Palais*, substituted a psychological obstacle for the trick separating the lovers, went on, in *La Place Royale*, to create the character of Alidor, determined not to be enslaved by love. If *La Place Royale* is, in the main, serious in tone, *Le Menteur* is genuinely comic. Although it has been pointed out that Dorante's failing — his propensity to invent tall stories — is a foible rather than a vice, and although the plot of the play does not depend on this feature of his character, this highly amusing play, in which the main interest is the unfailing fertility of Dorante's imagination, can fairly be regarded as the first true comedy of character.

*Chapter 10*

# POETRY AND PROSE

## I. TRISTAN

TRISTAN L'HERMITE (1601?–55), a descendant of Peter the Hermit, besides a number of plays, some of which have been mentioned in an earlier chapter, published an autobiographical novel, *Le Page disgracié* (1642), and several volumes of verse between 1633 and 1648.

*Le Page disgracié*, which relates the author's adventures up to the age of nineteen and was, so he tells us at the end, to have been followed by two further volumes, is a delightful work, combining the two strains of the French novel in the first half of the century, the idealistic and the realistic. In narrating his life as a page at the French court and in the service of various noblemen, Tristan takes us straight into seventeenth-century France, into a world of unruly pages and swashbucklers, of alchemists and gamesters and cardsharpers, of pranks and practical jokes, of pitched battles between peasants and students, of duels and sieges. In the middle, however, is an episode of a very different character – his sojourn in England and an account of an idyllic love affair between the adolescent page and a young girl, the daughter of a noble family in whose house he resided to teach her French.

As a poet, Tristan writes charming verse of the kind favoured by the society of the first half of the seventeenth century, treating the themes of love, nature, praise of the great and the immortality conferred by poets. He also wrote *consolations*, and published a volume of religious verse.

In his love poems he praises the charms of his mistress in the conventional way, –

> Sa bouche est de rubis, ses dents de perles fines,
> Ses yeux de diamants.

> Le reste de son corps dont je suis idolâtre
> Est de vivant albâtre,
> Animé d'un esprit des cieux ...
> *(Le Triomphe d'Iris)*

– and usually ends with a *pointe*:

> La glace qui vous représente
> Est moins glace que votre cœur.
> *(Pour Mademoiselle Souscarrière qui se mirait)*

He laments the absence of his mistress, and sings of the sufferings love inflicts upon him. Sometimes, in more personal vein, he relates nightmares which foretell further suffering, or tells how he has seen and embraced his beloved in a blissful dream, or broods in a cemetery – Tristan reveals from time to time an almost romantic love of the macabre:

> Ainsi disait Tersandre en regardant les cieux,
> Mille tristes hiboux passaient devant ses yeux,
> Faisant autour de lui mille plaintes funèbres:
> Il tenait un poignard pour ouvrir son cercueil,
> Et la nuit déployant sa robe de ténèbres,
> N'attendait que sa mort pour en prendre le deuil.
> *(Le Désespoir)*

Into the conventional lover's attitudes, there creeps from time to time a note of sensuousness or of intensity. Watching his mistress arrange her hair in front of a mirror (Tristan is fond of reflections in mirrors or in water), he calls her tresses 'Doux flots où ma raison se noie' (*Le Miroir enchanté*). A kiss is thus described:

> Cette douceur où je me noie
> Force par un excès de joie
> Tous mes esprits à s'envoler:
> Mon cœur est palpitant d'une amoureuse fièvre,
> Et mon âme vient sur ma lèvre
> Alors que tes baisers l'y veulent appeler.
> *(Les Baisers de Dorinde)*

Tristan's love of nature is genuine. In the *Plainte à la belle Banquière*, praising the pleasures of relative poverty, he writes:

> Le bien de sentir des fleurs
> De qui l'âme et les couleurs
> Charment mes esprits malades,
> Et l'eau qui d'un haut rocher
> Se va jetant par cascades
> Sont mon trésor le plus cher.
>
> Le doux concert des oiseaux,
> Le mouvant cristal des eaux,
> Un bois, des prés agréables;
> Echo qui se plaint d'Amour,
> Sont des matières capables
> De m'arrêter tout un jour.

In his descriptions, in the manner of the age, he humanizes nature – in *La Mer*, for instance, the sun 'tâche à se mirer

dedans/Comme on ferait dans une glace –, peoples it with nymphs
and Tritons and the like, and describes it in terms of jewels and
precious metals; but at the same time he has considerable evocative
power. *La Mer* is a fine description of the sea, changing with the
time of day and the weather – calm, at dawn and at sunset, then
raging during a gale and a thunderstorm successively, then finally
calm after the storm. *La Maison d'Astrée* is a description of the
estate at Berny of the marquise de Puisieux, a distant relative of
Tristan's. In a different vein again, *Les Terreurs nocturnes* is a description of a ride through a forest by night. Night is a favourite
subject of Tristan, and not always associated with terror:

> Et vous, ô nuit, d'étoiles couronnée,
> Reine des feux qui font la destinée:
> Nuit qui placez une pâle blancheur
> Dans le silence et parmi la fraîcheur,
> Et vous montrant si sereine et si claire,
> Semblez prétendre à l'honneur de me plaire:
> Pour m'obliger, éteignez ces flambeaux
> De qui l'image errante dans ces eaux,
> Du vif éclat de sa flamme incertaine
> Nuit au repos des Nymphes de la Seine.
>
> *(L'Absence de Phillis)*

In some of Tristan's best poems, love and nature are associated. *Le Promenoir des deux amants* is a delightful description
of a meeting of two lovers in a grotto, where

> L'onde lutte avec les cailloux,
> Et la lumière avecque l'ombre.
>
> . . . . .
>
> L'ombre de cette fleur vermeille,
> Et celle de ces joncs pendants
> Paraissent être là-dedans
> Les songes de l'eau qui sommeille.

In *Les Plaintes d'Acanthe*, the shepherd, Acanthe, bewails his
unhappy love in a pastoral setting. *Les Forges d'Antoigné* is a
striking description of a forge, in which the poet sees the image
of his own situation:

> Le fer dont la masse allumée
> Rougit les objets d'alentour,
> C'est une image de l'amour
> Qui gêne mon âme enflammée.
> Cette enclume en sa dureté
> Représente ma fermeté.
> Cette rivière fond mes larmes,
> Ce brasier ardent, mes désirs,
> Ces marteaux, mes vives alarmes:
> Et ces soufflets ont moins de vent que mes soupirs.

The themes of love and nature by no means fill all Tristan's
work. There is grotesque realism in *La Gouvernante importune*;

his ode to Schomberg is a fine battle piece; and his long narrative
poem, *L'Orphée*, if love and nature play a considerable part in
it, shows other gifts. In other poems, he is more reflective, dwelling on the pleasures of country life in *A M. de Chaudebonne*,
meditating on the universality of death in *Les Misères humaines*
and the *Consolation à Idalie* –

> Alexandre n'est plus, lui dont Mars fut jaloux,
> César est dans la tombe aussi bien qu'un infâme:
> Et la noble Camille aimable comme vous,
> Est au fond du cercueil ainsi qu'une autre femme.

– and brooding on the futility of the life lived by those (such
as himself) dependent on the great (*Misère de l'homme du
monde, Prosopopée d'un courtisan, La servitude*). Perhaps the
best example of this side of Tristan is this valedictory sonnet:

> C'est fait de mes destins; je commence à sentir
> Les incommodités que la vieillesse apporte.
> Déjà la pâle mort pour me faire partir,
> D'un pied sec et tremblant vient frapper à ma porte.
>
> Ainsi que le soleil sur la fin de son cours
> Paraît plutôt tomber que descendre dans l'onde;
> Lorsque l'homme a passé les plus beaux de ses jours,
> D'une course rapide il passe en l'autre monde.
>
> Il faut éteindre en nous tous frivoles désirs,
> Il faut nous détacher des terrestres plaisirs
> Où sans discrétion notre appétit nous plonge.
>
> Sortons de ces erreurs par un sage conseil;
> Et cessant d'embrasser les images d'un songe,
> Pensons à nous coucher pour le dernier sommeil.

## II. SAINT-AMANT

Marc-Antoine de Gérard, known as Saint-Amant (1594–1661),
is master of a number of different styles. He is a nature poet in
the manner of Théophile or Tristan. *Le Soleil levant*, for example,
records the sights and sounds of the early morning; *La Solitude* –
which Théophile imitated in his poem with the same title – describes the countryside in which the poet loves to wander and to
meditate. The taste for the gloomy and sinister aspects of nature,
which we have already noted in Tristan, is more pronounced in
Saint-Amant.

> Que j'aime à voir la décadence
> De ces vieux châteaux ruinés,
> Contre qui les ans mutinés
> Ont déployé leur insolence!

Les sorciers y font leur sabbat;
Les démons follets s'y retirent,
Qui d'un malicieux ébat
Trompent nos sens et nous martirent;
Là se nichent en mille trous
Les couleuvres et les hiboux.

L'orfraie, avec ses cris funèbres,
Mortels augures des destins,
Fait rire et danser des lutins
Dans ces lieux remplis de ténèbres.
Sous un chevron de bois maudit
Y branle le squelette horrible
D'un pauvre amant qui se pendit
Pour une bergère insensible,
Qui d'un seul regard de pitié
Ne daigna voir son amitié.

*(La Solitude)*

Similarly, in *Le Contemplateur*, giving an account of his occupations at Belle-Isle, he tells us that,

Tantôt, saisi de quelque horreur
D'être seul parmi les ténèbres,
Abusé d'une vaine erreur,
Je me feins mille objets funèbres;
Mon esprit en est suspendu,
Mon cœur en demeure éperdu,
Le sein me bat, le poil me dresse,
Mon corps est privé de soutien,
Et, dans la frayeur qui m'oppresse,
Je crois voir tout, pour ne voir rien.

In the next stanza, it is true, these nocturnal imaginings are dissipated, and, looking up at the starry heavens,

J'écoute, à demi transporté,
Le bruit des ailes du Silence,
Qui vole dans l'obscurité.

—wonderfully suggestive lines. But *Le Contemplateur* ends with a description, suggested by the rising sun, of the resurrection of the dead and the final destruction of the cosmos. *Les Visions*, describing the poet's state of mind after the murder of his friend, François de Molière (1628), relates his nocturnal terrors and imaginations, and describes how the sights and sounds of day are rendered lugubrious by the melancholy fancy of the poet — an interesting treatment of the theme of illusion and reality, showing how the real world is transfigured by the mood of the perceiver. It would be wrong to leave Saint-Amant as a nature poet without referring to his four richly evocative sonnets on the four seasons, spring in the neighbourhood of Paris, summer in

Rome, autumn in the Canaries, and winter in the Alps. The
octave of this last is a remarkable description of a snow scene:

> Ces atomes de feu qui sur la neige brillent,
> Ces étincelles d'or, d'azur, de cristal
> Dont l'hiver, au soleil, d'un lustre oriental
> Pare ses cheveux blancs que les vents éparpillent;
>
> Ce beau coton du ciel de quoi les monts s'habillent,
> Ce pavé transparent fait du second métal,
> Et cet air net et sain, propre à l'esprit vital,
> Sont si doux à mes yeux que d'aise ils en pétillent.

Saint-Amant is also the poet of sensual joys, which he celebrates with great verve – there is something of Rabelais in him:
food and drink above all, but also the tavern, the pleasures of
love, tobacco, and sloth. One of his best-known poems is *Le
Melon*, a dithyrambic description of a melon:

> Non, le cocos, fruit délectable,
> Qui lui tout seul fournit la table
> De tous les mets que le désir
> Puisse imaginer et choisir,
> Ni les baisers d'une maîtresse,
> Quand elle-même nous caresse,
> Ni ce qu'on tire des roseaux
> Que Crète nourrit dans ses eaux,
> Ni le cher abricot, que j'aime,
> Ni la fraise avec la crème,
> Ni la manne qui vient du ciel,
> Ni le pur aliment du miel,
> Ni la poire de Tours sacrée,
> Ni la verte figue sucrée,
> Ni la prune au jus délicat,
> Ni même le raisin muscat
> (Parole pour moi bien étrange),
> Ne sont qu'amertume et que fange
> Au prix de ce MELON divin,
> Honneur du climat angevin.

This is followed by a burlesque account of a feast of the gods,
at which the ancestor of Saint-Amant's melon figured. In *Le
Palais de la Volupté*, he celebrates the country house of the duc
de Retz, as Tristan had celebrated Berny in *La Maison d'Astrée*,
but with the difference that Saint-Amant sings of the pleasures
offered by the duke to his visitors. The poem closes with a list
of people to be excluded, reminiscent of the inscription placed by
Rabelais over the gates of the abbey of Thélème.

There is a strong vein of humour in Saint-Amant. We see it
in his poems in praise of sensual pleasures. His *Imprécation* is
a string of curses, written with a verve that again reminds us of
Rabelais, on the town of Evreux:

> On y voit plus de trente églises,
> Et pas un pauvre cabaret.

*Les Caprices* is a humorous account of a naval expedition in which he took part. Humour is often closely associated with realism and satire in Saint-Amant, as frequently in the seventeenth century as a whole. In singing the praise of wine, he sometimes evokes his boon companions:

> Vous y voyez Bilot pâle, morne et transi,
> Vomir par les naseaux une vapeur errante;
> Vous y voyez Sallard chatouiller la servante,
> Qui rit du bout du nez en portrait raccourci.

*L'Enamouré* is a description of an amorous drunkard; *Cassation de Soudrilles* enumerates the various types of soldier who appear in war-time. In one of his sonnets ('Vos attraits n'ont plus rien que l'épée et la cape'), he portrays a seventeenth-century grotesque, and, in another, we see the poet himself composing:

> Fagoté plaisamment comme un vrai Simonnet,
> Pied chaussé, l'autre nu, main au nez, l'autre en poche,
> J'arpente un vieux grenier, portant sur ma caboche
> Un coffin de Hollande en guise de bonnet.

> Là, faisant quelquefois le saut du sansonnet,
> Et dandinant du cul comme un sonneur de cloche,
> Je m'égueule de rire, écrivant d'une broche
> En mots de Pathelin ce grotesque sonnet.

*Les Goinfres* depicts the destitution to which extravagance reduces its victims. Saint-Amant's realism, like Régnier's, does not always recoil before the unpleasant and the disgusting:

> Un étui de luth tout cassé,
> Qui traînait au coin d'une salle,
> Pour tout loyer du temps passé
> Lui sert de chevet et de malle;
> Les flegmes jaunes et séchés
> Qu'en sa vérole il a crachés
> Lui servent de tapisserie,
> Et semble que les limaçons
> Y rehaussent en broderie
> Des portraits de toutes façons.
> (*La Chambre du Débauché*)

In two longer poems, realism is accompanied by more extended satire. *Le Poète crotté*, a poet's farewell to Paris, contains at once an interesting evocation of seventeenth-century Paris and a satirical account of Parisian society. *L'Albion, caprice héroï-comique* is an account of Saint-Amant's experiences in England in 1643, at the time of the Civil War. The poet denounces the rebels and gives his impressions – interesting, if unflattering – of various aspects of English life: churches, inns, thieves who robbed Saint-Amant and his companions, the theatre and the drama, English women, the English climate, English manners, and English cooking are treated in turn.

Finally, as an epic poet in *Moïse sauvé*, Saint-Amant displays his rich narrative and descriptive gifts. The following description of fishing, a pastime in which the poet tells us that he had often indulged on the banks of the Seine, may illustrate his versatility:

> Mais dans l'onde déja cette guerre s'allume,
> Déjà le crin retors que le plomb et la plume
> Tire au fond et retient, à l'œil est dérobé,
> Et déjà sous l'appât le piège recourbé,
> Offre au poisson béant, mu d'une brusque envie,
> Sa véritable mort sous une ombre de vie;
> Déjà la canne ploye, et, déjà haut en l'air,
> Le nageur étant pris vole comme un éclair.
> Il s'y secoue en vain, de sa chute on s'approche,
> On y court, on le prend, du fer on le décroche;
> Il s'échappe des doigts, tombe, sautelle, fuit,
> Fait voir mille soleils en l'écaille qui luit,
> Bat l'herbe de sa queue, et, sur la plaine verte,
> D'une bouche sans cri, de temps en temps ouverte,
> Bâille sans respirer, comme né sans poumon,
> Et laisse à qui l'étreint un reste de limon.

### III. VOITURE

The letters of Vincent Voiture (1598–1648),[1] the life and soul of the Hôtel de Rambouillet, contrast sharply with those of his contemporary, Guez de Balzac. Whereas the latter was the master of the formal period, Voiture — it is significant that he published none of his works — is distinguished by his naturalness and his lightness of touch.

On peut dire que Voiture nous a appris cette manière d'écrire aisée et délicate qui règne présentement. Avant lui on pensait n'avoir de l'esprit que quand on parlait Balzac tout pur et qu'on exprimait de grandes pensées avec de grands mots,

wrote Bouhours, who much preferred the 'charmes secrets' and the 'grâces fines et cachées' of Voiture to the 'beautés régulières' of Balzac. There are, it is true, amongst the letters of Voiture, many written in the conventional polite or gallant style of the seventeenth century — love letters and letters to friends and patrons in which he praises the nobility of their character or their military or diplomatic prowess, protests his friendship, or expresses his solicitude for their safety; but it is not for these that

---

[1] Voiture was also a poet. His verses are witty, neatly turned, and graceful. He cultivated *rondeaux*, *ballades*, and *épîtres*.

he is still read, but for those in which he shows his ready wit by turning a neat compliment to accompany a poem or a gift, by writing a sprightly letter of thanks, by composing a suitable letter of congratulation or condolence, and above all those in which he converses entertainingly, pen in hand, with his absent friends.

Voiture knows how to vary his letters, how to surprise his correspondents by his unfailing novelty. Sometimes a letter will begin with a compliment which is not what it seems:

Je ne puis pas dire absolument que je sois arrivé à Turin. Car il n'y est arrivé que la moitié de moi-même. Vous croyez, que je veux dire, que l'autre est demeurée auprès de vous. Ce n'est pas cela. C'est, que de cent et quatre livres, que je pesais en partant de Paris, je n'en pèse plus que cinquante-deux.

Or he will begin with an apparently uncivil remark, which turns into a compliment later. One letter to Mlle de Rambouillet opens:

Si vous n'étiez la plus aimable personne du monde, vous seriez la plus haïssable: et vous avez une fierté qui serait insupportable en toute autre qu'en vous.

A reproach to Cardinal de la Valette on neglecting the classics introduces a compliment on his victories. Another letter to La Valette begins with the jesting remark that war is making him quarrelsome, which introduces a compliment on his exploits. A letter to Mlle de Rambouillet opens with the statement that he has been unable to think of her, because of his *fourgon* — which introduces an amusing account of the discomforts of his journey. A letter to Costar begins: 'Sans mentir, avec tout votre latin, vous êtes un grand niais.' But this remark is toned down later: 'Mais il faut avouer, que si vous manquez de jugement, en récompense vous avez bien de l'esprit.'

A letter may be filled with a humorous scolding of a friend — like that in which he reproaches a correspondent with having gone to a ball instead of writing to him. Or he deliberately exaggerates his compliments, as when he writes to Mlle de Rambouillet:

Tout de bon, je vous assure, que quand on ne vous voit pas, on se ferait pendre pour un double: et on se sent sur l'estomac une si grande pesanteur, qu'il vaudrait peut-être mieux être étranglé tout d'un coup. [ ... ] Le premier jour on est tout endormi, le second tout assoupi, le troisième tout étourdi: et puis quand on commence à se reconnaître, et que le sentiment est revenu, on soupire à dire D'où venez-vous? Et soupir deçà: et soupir delà: et vous en aurez.

During another journey, he describes to Mlle de Rambouillet how separation from her made him shed great tears and heave great sighs, adding: 'Car je vous jure, que les Nymphes des eaux

furent touchées de ma douleur et que le Dieu du fleuve en fut
ému' – in the style of the poets of the time. But he assures her
later that if the nymphs and the river-god are an exaggeration,
his grief is not. Or he will begin with a flowery compliment and
then confess his inability to continue in the same strain.

Humour is one of the salient characteristics of Voiture's
letters. The letter to La Valette just mentioned ends with the
statement that he cannot join La Valette who is besieging a
stronghold, because he has urgent business in Paris:

Ces affaires très importantes: c'est un siège que j'ai commencé d'une
place assez jolie, et fort bien située. J'en ai fait la circonvallation à la
mode de Hollande, et à la vôtre: et Piccolomini ne me saurait empêcher
de la prendre. Les choses étant si avancées, il me déplairait extrêmement de lever le siège. Car entre nous autres Conquérants, cela est
**fâcheux.**

He is given to teasing his correspondents.

Vous serez, s'il vous plaît, averti, Monseigneur, [he writes to Cardinal de la
Valette] que toutes les fois que je dirai 'nous trouvâmes, nous vîmes, nous
allâmes,' c'est en qualité de Cardinal que je parle.

He teases the hypochondriac Mme de Sablé about her fear of
disease; or he tells La Valette that, after his exploits, the siege
of Bapaume must seem a relaxation, and amusingly contrasts the
hard lot of the modern soldier with the comparatively easy
life of the knights of the old romances. In another letter, with
pedantic accuracy, he tells La Valette that his health was not
drunk at supper:

Souffrez, s'il vous plaît, Monseigneur, que je ne vous flatte point; et qu'en
fidèle historien, je raconte nûment les choses comme elles sont. Car je ne
voudrais pas, que la Postérité prît une chose pour l'autre: et que d'ici à
deux mille ans, on crût que l'on eût bu à vous, cela n'ayant point été.

The humorist's disparagement of himself is a feature of Voiture's
letters. He ends a gallant letter with a self-portrait:

Ma taille est deux ou trois doigts au-dessous de la médiocre. J'ai la tête
assez belle, avec beaucoup de cheveux gris; les yeux doux, mais un peu
égarés: et le visage assez niais. En récompense, une de vos amies vous
dira, que je suis le meilleur garçon du monde, et que pour aimer en cinq
ou six lieux à la fois, il n'y a personne qui le fasse si fidèlement que moi.

Or he sets out to write a description of the Castello del Valentino
near Turin for the marquise de Rambouillet – and cannot:

En arrivant, on trouve d'abord: je veux mourir, si je sais ce qu'on trouve
d'abord. Je crois que c'est un perron. Non, non, c'est un portique. Je me
trompe, c'est un perron. Par ma foi, je ne sais si c'est un portique, ou un
perron. Il n'y a pas une heure, que je savais tout cela admirablement: et
ma mémoire m'a manqué.

Humour in Voiture is closely allied with fancy. Being struck by the tomb of Marshal Strozzi and being in ill health, he tells Mme de Rambouillet, he thought of getting himself buried there: 'Mais on en fit quelque difficulté, pource que l'on trouva que j'avais encore trop de chaleur.' A good example is the famous letter describing how he was tossed up in a blanket and what he saw as he soared up into the heavens. He writes to Mlle Paulet (nicknamed 'la lionne') from Africa that he is about to send challenges to the Moors, undertaking to defend her qualities against all comers, and that he is about to ask her relatives, the African lions, for her hand in marriage. He writes a description of a journey, as if he and his companions were knights of old, surprised to find the world so changed:

et partout où nous avons hébergé, nos hôtes n'ont point fait difficulté de prendre de l'argent de nous. Messire Lac et moi, en avons beaucoup de regret.

In another letter, he tells Mlle de Rambouillet that his soul is with her —

Je crois que vous y aurez du plaisir, car elle fait un bruit de Diable, et se tourmente, et fait une tempête si étrange, qu'il vous semblera que le logis sera prêt à se renverser—

and that he had thought of sending his body by post:

Mais il est en un si pitoyable état, qu'il eût été en pièces, devant que d'être auprès de vous: et puis j'ai eu peur que par le chaud, il ne se gâtât.

In this connection, too should be mentioned the letter he wrote to Mlle de Rambouillet as coming from Gustavus Adolphus, and the famous letter from the carp (himself) to the pike (the duc d'Enghien, later the *grand* Condé) – in allusion to a game played at the Hôtel de Rambouillet, the *jeu des poissons*.

Sometimes fancy takes the form of humorous exaggeration, as when he describes his military exploits:

Je n'ai point encore enlevé de femme, ni de fille, pource que je me suis trouvé un peu las du voyage, et que je n'étais pas en trop bonne consistance: et tout ce que j'ai pu faire, a été de mettre le feu à trois ou quatre maisons.

He tells Chapelain that, at the thought of writing to such a distinguished man, 'les cheveux me dressent en la tête si fort, qu'il semble d'un hérisson', but that, at the thought of his indulgence, 'mes cheveux s'aplatissent tout à coup, plat comme d'une poule mouillée'. He describes M. de Chaudebonne's chagrin in these terms:

Outre qu'il s'est mis en fantaisie de se laisser croître une barbe qui lui
vient déjà jusques à la ceinture, il a pris un ton de voix beaucoup plus
sévère que jamais, et qui a à peu près le son du Cor d'Astolfe. A moins
que de traiter de l'immortalité de l'âme, ou du souverain bien, et d'agiter
quelqu'une des plus importantes questions de la morale, on ne lui saurait
plus faire ouvrir la bouche.

He affects horror that M. de Saint Mégrin should be in love with
seven ladies, 'car pour moi, je n'en ai aimé que six, lorsque j'en
ai aimé le plus: et il faut être bien infâme pour en aimer sept'.
    Voiture loves playing with words, too. He suggests that M. de
Montausier might like to become King of Madeira: 'Imaginez-
vous, je vous supplie, le plaisir d'avoir un Royaume de Sucre,
et si nous ne pourrions pas vivre là avec toute sorte de douceur.'
'Il ne pleut pla, ple, pli, plo, plus,' he tells M. d'Avaux. The most
elaborate example of Voiture in a punning mood is the letter
to Mme de Condé explaining that he could not visit her because
of a *clou* on his *derrière*:

A moins que d'etre cloué à Paris, rien n'eût pu m'empêcher d'aller
aujourd'hui à Poissy. [ ... ] Mais comme vous savez, Madame, qu'un
clou chasse l'autre: il a fallu que la passion que j'ai pour vous, ait
cédé à une nouvelle, qui m'est survenue, et qui, si elle n'est plus forte,
est pour le moins à cette heure plus pressante. [ ... ] Mais je vous
assure, que j'ai une raison fondamentale de ne bouger d'ici, sur laquelle
je n'ose appuyer, et qu'il n'est pas à propos de vous expliquer davantage.
J'ai délibéré longtemps en moi-même, si je devais aller: et il y a eu un
grand combat entre mon cœur, et une autre partie que je ne nomme pas.
Mais enfin, Madame, je vous avoue, que celle qui raisonnablement doit
être dessous, a eu le dessus: et que j'ai mis devant toutes choses, ce
qui naturellement doit être derrière.

Another letter draws an elaborate comparison between Mlle de
Rambouillet and the sea. Yet another has four beginnings to show
his embarrassment:

MADAME,
Le long temps ...

MADAME,
Si je ne savais jusqu'où s'étend votre bonté ...

MADAME,
Si l'extrême repentir que ...

MADAME,
En vérité, l'on est bien empêché, comme vous pouvez voir ici [ ... ]

Amusing, sprightly, fanciful conversations with his friends,
Voiture's letters bring us under the spell of the delightful personality which charmed the Hôtel de Rambouillet. But there is
a more serious side to his nature. Somewhat of a libertine and an

inveterate gambler, Voiture's character is redeemed by two ster-
ling qualities. One is his independence. The son of a wine-
merchant, he was neither ashamed of his humble origins – à
propos of some derogatory verses in which Voiture was made
to rhyme with *roture*, he wrote to Costar, 'je voudrais que tout
le monde sût qui je suis' – nor servile. He tells Mme de Sablé
roundly that she was right to apologize for the style of her letters,
'Car, sans mentir, ce jargon de Marfise, de Merlin, et d'Alexis,
me semble insupportable'. Excessive hesitation to ask him for a
favour draws on the same lady the reproach, 'sans mentir, il ne
se peut rien de plus offensant'. A dignified letter reproaches his
patron, the comte d'Avaux, with having too lightly formed a
grudge against him:

... quoique j'estime vos bienfaits, j'aime encore mieux vos caresses [ ... ]
Si vous ne faites cas de moi, Monseigneur, qu'à cause que l'on dit que
j'ai quelque sorte d'esprit, et que je sais faire quelquefois une belle lettre:
vous ne m'estimez que par la qualité que j'estime le moins.

The other is his genuine affection for his friends and the Hôtel de
Rambouillet. Time after time, when he is away from Paris,
he describes his destitute state, his low spirits, his longing for his
absent friends, and the comfort he derives from their letters in
accents of sincerity.

J'eus plus de plaisir [he writes from Rome to Mlle de Rambouillet], il y a
quelque temps, à voir avec vous deux ou trois allées de Rueil, que je n'en
ai eu, à voir toutes les vignes de Rome, et que je n'en aurais à voir le
Capitole, quand il serait en l'état où il a été autrefois, et que même
Jupiter Capitolin s'y trouverait en personne. Mais afin que vous sachiez,
que ce n'est pas raillerie, et que je suis tout de bon, aussi mal que je le
dis: il y a huit jours, que me promenant le matin avec le Chevalier de
Jars, je fusse tombé de mon haut, s'il ne m'eût reçu entre ses bras, et le
lendemain au soir, je m'évanouis encore une fois dans la chambre de
Madame la Maréchale d'Estrée. Les médecins disent, que ce sont des
vapeurs mélancoliques ...

If Voiture's letters are interesting first and foremost for their
wit and humour, for their easy and natural style, and for what
they reveal to us of the personality of their author, they are also
sometimes of value for the intrinsic interest of their subject
matter. The long letter on the recapture of Corbie and in praise of
Richelieu and his policy is exceptional, it is true; but news of
the Hôtel de Rambouillet and gossip about friends are more
common. The account in a letter to Cardinal de la Valette of
the visit to Mme du Vigean's[2] vividly recaptures for us a day in
the life of Mlle de Rambouillet and her companions; and the
famous letter on the word *Car* reminds us of the interest of the
Hôtel de Rambouillet in matters of language.

2 See above, p. 78n.

Voiture, on his travels, felt himself too much of an exile to devote much space to the description of the countries he was visiting, but from time to time there are some interesting accounts of what he has done and seen, particularly in Spain, and some interesting impressions of seventeenth-century travel. Before embarking, for example, he is compelled to buy

un lit, des matelas, des couvertures, un petit troupeau de moutons, vingt bêtes à corne, cinquante poules, et quelques *chats de volière*. Car le Capitaine ne veut pas nourrir les passagers.

And, for safety's sake, he travels through Piedmont in the company of brigands. He affords us a brief glimpse of the French court at Tours in 1638. One of the letters he wrote in 1642, when he accompanied the French court on its journey to the South of France, contains a vivid evocation of the arrival of Richelieu in Avignon, and another, a long one, is devoted to an account of the arrest of Cinq-Mars.

### IV. SCARRON AND 'LE ROMAN COMIQUE'

Assured of a niche in history as the first husband of Mme de Maintenon, Paul Scarron (1610–60) occupies a place in French literature in his own right. Like Tristan, he was a poet, a playwright, and a novelist, though of a rather different kind: a hopelessly deformed cripple, he nevertheless managed to maintain his good humour and to write in a comic vein. It was he who popularized the burlesque in France[3] – in poetry with his *Vers burlesques* (1643), his *Œuvres burlesques* (1646–51), and two narrative poems, *Le Typhon ou la Gigantomachie* (1644) and *Virgile travesti* (1648–52), the latter a retelling of the *Aeneid*, in which he makes the gods and heroes of antiquity speak and behave like ordinary, everyday, commonplace people; in the theatre with his *Jodelet ou le Maître valet* (1645) and subsequent plays.

His best known, and his best, work, *Le Roman comique*, of which only two parts (published in 1651 and 1657 respectively) were written,[4] is a burlesque novel. Scarron delights in parodying the epic style. The story, for example, opens thus:

Le soleil avait achevé plus de la moitié de sa course, et son char, ayant attrapé le penchant du monde, roulait plus vite qu'il ne voulait. Si ses chevaux eussent voulu profiter de la pente du chemin, ils eussent achevé

[3] His chief disciple in the burlesque style was the poet, d'Assoucy (1605–77), author of *L'Ovide en belle humeur* (1650), but chiefly read nowadays for his *Adventures*, an entertaining autobiography.
[4] Continuations by Jean Girault and Preschac were published in 1678 and 1679 respectively.

*ce qui restait du jour en moins d'un demi quart-d'heure; mais, au lieu de tirer de toute leur force, ils ne s'amusaient qu'à faire des courbettes, respirant un air marin qui les faisait hennir et les avertissait que la mer était proche, où l'on dit que leur maître se couche toutes les nuits. Pour parler plus humainement et plus intelligiblement, il était entre cinq et six . . .*

At other times, in the epic manner, he introduces 'la discorde aux crins de couleuvres' or uses an epic simile – 'Elle lui sauta aux yeux, furieuse comme une lionne à qui on a ravi ses petits', destroying the effect by adding, 'j'ai peur que la comparaison ne soit ici trop magnifique'. Breaking the illusion is a favourite trick of Scarron, who is fond of intervening personally in this way. Several times he suggests that he does not know what is coming next, reminding the reader that this is only a story: 'cependant que ses bêtes mangèrent, l'auteur se reposa quelque temps et se mit à songer à ce qu'il dirait dans le second chapitre'. Or he calls attention to his own artistry or efforts:

Il y a bien d'autres choses à dire sur ce sujet; mais il faut les ménager et les placer en divers endroits de mon livre pour diversifier.

. . . sur mon honneur, cette description m'a plus coûté que tout le reste du livre, et encore n'en suis-je pas trop bien satisfait.

Paradoxically, the same effect may be produced by suggestions that his book is true – by statements of the author's ignorance ('pour moi, je n'en doute point, quoique je n'en sache rien de particulier') or elaborate explanations how a detail has come to be known to him. Moreover, Scarron deliberately ridicules contemporary novels:

Je ne vous dirai point exactement s'il avait soupé et s'il se coucha sans manger, comme font quelques faiseurs de romans, qui règlent toutes les heures du jour de leurs héros . . .

. . . la salle était la plus magnifique du monde, et, si vous voulez, aussi bien meublée que quelques appartements de nos romans, comme le vaisseau de Zelmande dans le *Polexandre*, le palais d'Hibraim dans l'*illustre Bassa*, ou la chambre où le roi d'Assyrie reçut Mandane dans le *Cyrus*, qui est sans doute, aussi bien que les autres que j'ai nommés, le livre du monde le mieux meublé.

If the novel owes something to the burlesque, however, its chief attraction is its comic realism, in which Scarron is in the tradition of Saint-Amant and Régnier, Sorel and Rabelais. The novel deals with the adventures of a company of actors – hence the title[5] – in the provincial town of Le Mans, a town in which

---

[5] The word *comique* means both 'comic' and 'connected with the stage' (a *comédie* was any kind of play, and a *comédien* any kind of actor). Cf. the title of Corneille's comedy, *L'Illusion comique*.

Scarron had lived for seven years. It opens with an unforgettable picture of the actors entering Le Mans – one of them

portait sur ses épaules une basse de viole, et, parce qu'il se courbait un peu en marchant, on l'eût pris de loin pour une grosse tortue qui marchait sur les jambes de derrière.

We see them establishing themselves in a *tripot* (or *jeu de paume*), where three of them – the rest of the company not having yet arrived – manage to perform Tristan's *Mariane*. The complete company consists of three actors, Le Destin, L'Olive, and the disappointed, embittered, malicious La Rancune, together with their valets, three actresses, and the poet, Rocquebrune. The young men of the town crowd into the actresses' room, taking liberties with one of them – 'mais un coup de pied dans l'os des jambes, un soufflet ou un coup de dent, selon qu'il était à propos, la délivraient bientôt de ces galants à toute outrance'. The company is hired to give performances in private houses, and Scarron describes how they go thither, how the stage is set up, and how they are received. There are anecdotes of performances, and one of the characters, Ragotin, recalls a play about the battle of Pont-de-Cé staged at the Jesuit college of La Flèche. The company enjoys the patronage of a nobleman who gives them 200 pistoles to stay for an extra fortnight in Le Mans and entertain him and his friends. There are literary discussions between the actors and their patrons, and talk about plays, writers, and novels. We learn how one of the valets of the company was killed at the entrance to the theatre 'par des écoliers bretons, qui firent cette année-là beaucoup de désordre dans La Flèche, parce qu'ils y étaient en grand nombre et que le vin y fut à bon marché'; we learn, too, of the provincial preference for farce – 'La farce divertit encore plus que la comédie,[6] comme il arrive d'ordinaire partout ailleurs hors de Paris.'

Provincial society is equally vividly portrayed. We are introduced into several inns, and shown the household of the rapacious and thievish *lieutenant de prévost*, La Rappinière, who

mangeait d'ordinaire au cabaret aux dépens des sots, et sa femme et son train si réglé étaient réduits au potage aux choux, selon la coutume du pays.

We see Le Mans in the hunting season, packed with huntsmen and their wives, eager to see ladies from the court,

pour en parler le reste de leurs jours auprès de leur feu. Ce n'est pas une petite ambition aux provinciaux que de pouvoir dire quelquefois qu'ils ont

[6] Here used in the sense of 'the main play'. The *comédie* referred to was, in fact, Garnier's *Bradamante*.

vu en tel lieu et en tel temps des gens de la cour, dont ils prononcent toujours le nom tout sec, comme par exemple: 'Je perdis mon argent contre Roquelaure,—Créqui a tant gagné,—Coaquin court le cerf en Touraine.'

An *opérateur* or vendor of nostrums figures in the book, with his wife and his monkey, and there is a graphic account of the crowd of porters waiting at the landing stage in Orléans and seizing upon the luggage of the passengers as they disembark.

The humour of the book depends largely on the character of the crazy, conceited, dwarfish lawyer and poetaster, Ragotin, on nocturnal adventures at inns, on brawls and fisticuffs, on the repeated discomfiture of Ragotin, on pranks and practical jokes, and similar facetious episodes.

*Le Roman comique* has obvious weaknesses. It has little plot, and is little more than a succession of episodes. Moreover, from time to time, the story, such as it is, is interrupted, while one of the characters relates the history of his life or, more often, tells a story. Then again, unity of tone is lacking. The adventures of the main characters, the two pairs of lovers, Le Destin and L'Etoile, and Léandre and Angélique, and the intercalated stories (derived from Spanish sources and set in Spain) are romantic in character, whereas the other characters, actors and provincials, and their exploits are comic and earthy. The comic episodes are somewhat repetitive. Nevertheless, *Le Roman comique* is always readable and entertaining, and the vividness of its portrayal of some aspects of the life of seventeenth-century France more than compensates for its defects.

## V. CYRANO DE BERGERAC

The *Etats et Empires de la Lune* and the *Etats et Empires du Soleil* of Cyrano de Bergerac (1619–55), published posthumously in 1657 and 1662 respectively,[7] are amongst the earliest essays in science fiction. In them, the author relates how he visited the moon and the sun, displaying a great deal of ingenuity in the variety of machines he devises for the purpose of travel in space,[8] and describes what he saw there. On the moon, he lands in the terrestrial paradise, where he meets Elijah. Travelling on, he meets the inhabitants of the moon, who go on all fours, have long noses (like Cyrano himself), converse by music or movements, sleep on heaps of flowers, dine on the vapours exhaled by

[7] The published versions were considerably toned down, as two manuscripts of the *Etats et Empires de la Lune* show.

[8] He constructs two different machines to take him to the moon and another to take him to the sun. He also describes how a number of others travelled between the earth and the moon.

food, use glow-worms for illumination and poems as currency, live in movable houses, have gramophone records (or something similar) for books, cremate the dead, and insist that fathers should obey their sons. On the sun, he meets a race of people who can metamorphose themselves at will into any shape, visits a country of birds, encounters invisible talking trees, witnesses a fight between a salamander and a remora or *animal glaçon*, and is taken by Campanella[9] to the province of philosophers, where Descartes has just arrived.

The two journeys are more than pretexts for Cyrano's imagination to run riot; he uses them to satirize European customs and to ridicule current ideas. On the moon, for example, the mark of nobility is the wearing, not of a sword, but of a phallus, since to give life is noble, whereas to take it away is infamous. Quarrels between states on the moon are settled by battles between exactly equal armies or, better, by disputes between men of wit and learning – victories on earth merely representing the triumph of might or the power of fortune. On the sun, the birds elect their kings for six months only; a weekly assembly is held, at which the king is dethroned if three birds complain of him, and at which any bird may kill him if he deems him worthy of death. The weakest, the meekest, and the most peaceable are always chosen as kings:

... nous les prenons faibles, afin que le moindre à qui ils auraient fait quelque tort se pût venger de lui. Nous le choisissons doux, afin qu'il ne haïsse ni ne se fasse haïr de personne; et nous voulons qu'il soit d'une humeur pacifique pour éviter la guerre, le canal de toutes les injustices.

The views of the inhabitants of the celestial spheres are in many ways the reverse of those on earth. At the beginning of the *Etats et Empires de la Lune*, Cyrano's friends ridicule the notion that the moon may be a world: 'Ainsi peut-être, leur dis-je, se moque-t-on maintenant dans la Lune de quelque autre qui soutient que ce globe-ci est un monde.' In fact, he finds that the Selenites are convinced that they live on the earth and pour scorn on the notion that their moon (our earth) may be inhabited. Men on earth believe that they alone have the faculty of reason and immortal souls; the priests on the moon deny that a monster from another world walking on two legs can have either, and issue a decree stating that the apparent manifestations of reason in Cyrano are merely the operations of instinct. Similarly, the birds on the sun believe that they alone are endowed with reason and immortal souls, and deny both to men. Indeed, they place Cyrano on trial for the crime of being a man, and the prosecuting counsel, a bird who has suffered at the hands of men, pronounces a long

---

[9] An Italian philosopher (1568–1639), author of the *City of the Sun*.

indictment of the human race for its tyranny, its cruelty, and
its innate love of servitude.

The rationalist tendency of Cyrano's mind is apparent in his
book. The priests on the moon, who try to put Cyrano to death
for maintaining that the earth is not a moon, provide Cyrano
with an opportunity to put a plea for tolerance into the mouth
of his defending counsel: force, he argues, can make a man say
he believes a thing; it cannot make him believe it. On all occasions, Cyrano provides a rational explanation of apparently supernatural phenomena. The chariot of fire in which Elijah was
snatched up to heaven becomes, in the *Etats de la Lune*, a
machine operated by magnetism, which he constructed to carry
him up to the moon. The daemon of Socrates — whom Cyrano
meets on the moon — was an inhabitant of the sun, and the oracles,
nymphs, ghosts, and so forth of antiquity were his companions — not
spirits; everything, he assures us, in nature is material. In the *Etats
du Soleil*, Cyrano seems to be prepared to accept that the imagination of pregnant women may affect the children in their wombs,
that Pygmalion's statue could come to life, and that Campanella
can read his thoughts and even know what is happening three
leagues away — but for all these things he provides a natural, if
sometimes fantastic, explanation, one that is in accordance with
the laws of the universe as Cyrano understands them. The possibility of miracles and supernatural phenomena is, in fact, expressly
denied by a Selenite — miraculous cures, for example, are merely
illustrations of the power of the mind over the body.[10]

The *Etats et Empires de la Lune et du Soleil* contain a
thorough explanation of the universe, as Cyrano conceives it.
His universe is that of the new science, that of Copernicus,
Galileo, and Gassendi, whose pupil Cyrano had been — not that
of Aristotle, who, say the Selenites, 'accommodait des principes
à sa philosophie, au lieu d'accommoder sa philosophie aux
principes'. Cyrano, on his travels, observes the earth rotating
and the planets revolving round the sun, from which they derive
their light. The universe, he claims, has evolved according to
natural laws. Given the existence of atoms of different shapes, it
was inevitable that they should group themselves into stars and
planets, into the substances which compose the world and the
creatures that inhabit it. For there is no distinction between

---

[10] In one of his *Lettres diverses*, entitled *Contre les Sorciers*, Cyrano
attacks the belief in witchcraft and diabolic possession. 'Ni le nom d'Aristote plus savant que moi, ni celui de Platon, ni celui de Socrate ne me
persuadent point, si mon jugement n'est convaincu par raison de ce qu'ils
disent. La raison seule est ma reine, à qui je donne volontairement les
mains.' This profession of faith is followed by an exposition of his
reasons for scepticism.

matter and spirit: what we call spirit is merely a less gross form
of matter; the senses are operated by material particles emanated
by external objects. Thus man is not different in kind from any
other being: men, animals, birds, plants, are alike sentient; birds
and trees have a language to communicate their thoughts as well
as men. A philosopher on the moon asserts that 'il y a des
mondes infinis dans un monde infini'. There is an immense chain
of being from the infinitely great to the infinitely small. The universe is like an enormous animal, containing the stars; these contain
animals and men; and we in our turn contain other animals. Possibly, he surmises, the flesh, the blood, and the spirits are composed
of tiny animals.

   In this material universe, God has no place. The hypothesis of
a divine act of creation is superfluous: it is no easier to imagine
an eternal God than to believe that the universe has always
existed; and it is much easier to believe in the eternity of matter
than to believe that God suddenly created something out of
nothing. The existence of man can be explained as naturally
as that of anything else; and, on the sun, Cyrano witnesses the
birth of a man, spontaneously generated by the action of the sun
on mud. A Selenite expressly denies both the immortality of the
soul and the existence of God. The soul, he points out, has no
existence apart from the body, being entirely dependent on the
senses for perception; and he goes on to demonstrate the absurdity
of the doctrine of the resurrection of the body. As for God, had
belief in him been necessary, he would have revealed himself
more clearly. It is true that Cyrano describes himself as being
shocked by such impieties, and that in one version the devil
appears and carries the speaker off to Hell. Nevertheless, in the
sun, Campanella explains how, when any creature – plant, animal,
or man – dies, its soul ascends to the sun (philosophers alone preserve their identity):

Or toutes ces âmes unies qu'elles sont à la source du jour, et purgées
de la grosse matière qui les empêchait, elles exercent des fonctions bien
plus nobles que celles de croître, de sentir et de raisonner; car elles sont
employées à former le sang et les esprits vitaux du Soleil, ce grand et
parfait animal: Et c'est aussi pourquoi vous ne devez point douter que le
soleil n'opère de l'esprit bien plus parfaitement que vous, puisque c'est
par la chaleur d'un million de ces âmes rectifiées, dont la sienne est un
élixir, qu'il connaît le secret de la vie, qu'il influe à la matière de vos
mondes la puissance d'engendrer, qu'il rend des corps capables de se
sentir être, et enfin qu'il se fait voir et fait voir toutes choses.

On the sun, too, the birds attribute the belief in gods to the innate
love of servitude of the human race:

... ces pauvres serfs ont si peur de manquer de maîtres, que comme s'ils
appréhendaient que la liberté ne leur vînt de quelque endroit non attendu,

ils se forgent des Dieux de toutes parts, dans l'eau, dans l'air, dans le feu, sous la terre; ils en feront plutôt de bois, qu'ils n'en aient; et je crois même qu'ils se chatouillent des fausses espérances de l'immortalité, moins par l'horreur dont le non-être les effraye, que par la crainte qu'ils ont de n'avoir pas qui leur commande après la mort.

Cyrano also expresses the *libertin* doctrine that men should follow their natural instincts. One of the Selenites attacks celibacy and the asceticism of the Church on earth:[11]

En vérité, je m'étonne, vu combien la religion de votre pays est contre nature et jalouse de tous les contentements des hommes, que vos prêtres n'ont fait un crime de se gratter, à cause de l'agréable douleur qu'on y sent...

The *Etats et Empires de la Lune et du Soleil* is, of course, a work of imagination. The various opinions that Cyrano puts into the mouths of the philosophers, birds, trees, and men he encounters, are not always completely consistent with each other; some are fanciful, and they are not all to be taken equally seriously. Nevertheless, this work, interesting and enjoyable in its own right, provides a fascinating insight into the mind of a mid-seventeenth-century *libertin*; in Cyrano, 'one of the most daring speculative thinkers of his generation',[12] the modern rationalistic, scientific view of the universe is taking shape.

[11] In one of his *Lettres satiriques*, Cyrano attacks the institution of Lent (*Contre le Carême*).
[12] Professor J. S. Spink, *French Free-thought from Gassendi to Voltaire*, 1960, p. 48.

*Chapter 11*

# PASCAL

ON 14 January 1656, Antoine Arnauld was condemned by the Sorbonne on the *question de fait*.[1] Feeling that his Latin pamphlets appealed to too narrow a public, he drafted one in French and read it to the *solitaires* at Port-Royal des Champs. Their silence caused Arnauld to remark to a young man who was present: 'Mais vous qui êtes jeune, vous devriez faire quelque chose.' The young man was Blaise Pascal (1623–62), a distinguished scientist, mathematician, and inventor,[2] who, after a first conversion in 1646, had undergone a mystical experience in November 1654 and become a thorough-going ascetic. The seed fell on fertile ground. The first *Lettre écrite à un Provincial* appeared on 27 January 1656. This was the beginning of what Voltaire has called 'le premier livre de génie qu'on vit en prose'. Seventeen other letters followed between then and May 1657,[3] written by Pascal in concealment – Arnauld and Nicole helped to provide him with quotations – and published clandestinely.

In the first three letters, Pascal, in a light, clear, ironical style, deals with the theological questions at issue. After briefly showing the absurdity of the *question de fait*, –

Et si la curiosité me prenait de savoir si ces propositions sont dans Jansénius, son livre n'est pas si rare ni si gros que je ne le pusse lire tout entier pour m'en éclaircir sans en consulter la Sorbonne,

– he makes Arnauld's opponents look foolish (Letters I and II) by demonstrating that, while Jesuits and Dominicans are agreed about terminology, they attach very different meanings to the terms, the Dominicans in everything essential being in complete agreement with the Jansenists and in complete disagreement with the Jesuits. The third letter, which followed Arnauld's final condemnation, shows the bad faith of the Sorbonne. In saying

---

[1] See above, p. 101.

[2] He is known above all for his experiments on the Torricellian vacuum and for his work on the calculus of probability and on conic sections. He invented a calculating machine, which was placed on sale in 1652, and of which there is an example in the Musée des Arts et Métiers in Paris.

[3] A nineteenth letter was begun but abandoned.

that St. Peter was a just man who lacked grace, Arnauld said nothing which the Fathers of the Church had not said before him, and no reasons have been given for the censure: 'il leur est bien plus aisé de trouver des moines que des raisons'. In fact, 'ce ne sont pas les sentiments de M. Arnauld qui sont hérétiques; ce n'est que sa personne. C'est une hérésie personnelle'.

In the next seven letters, Pascal abandons the theological issues and delivers a scathing attack on the lax moral principles of the Jesuits. They have, it is true, a severe moral code for those who require it, but, to extend the influence of their Order, they are prepared to be all things to all men; and for this purpose, they have a much laxer moral code, one so lax, in fact, Pascal shows, that virtually no one can sin. Their main instruments for abolishing sin are the doctrine of *grâce actuelle*, probabilism, *direction de l'intention*, and *dévotion aisée*. According to the first of these, no action is a sin without *grâce actuelle*, i.e. full consciousness of the enormity of the action and deliberate intention to commit it – an action committed in ignorance, without reflexion, or involuntarily is not a sin:

Béni soyez-vous mon Père [says Pascal], qui justifiez ainsi les gens! Les autres apprennent à guérir les âmes par des austérités pénibles: mais vous montrez que celles qu'on aurait cru le plus désespérément malades se portent bien.

Probabilism is the contention that a moral doctrine advanced by even a single theologian is 'probable'; and Pascal shows by quotations from Jesuit theologians that by this means almost anything – even though it may have been condemned by Papal Bulls, the Bible, or Church Councils – is permissible: 'Si quelque Dieu nous presse, un autre nous délivre.' What may be a sin if performed from one motive, may be innocent if performed from another, and *direction de l'intention* consists in finding the blameless motive for all actions: duelling, for example is wrong, but 'quel mal', asks Pascal's Jesuit, 'y a-t-il d'aller dans un champ, de s'y promener en attendant un homme, et de se défendre si on l'y vient attaquer?' By this means, bribery and corruption, even murder itself, may cease to be sins. Finally, in order not to make religion seem difficult, the Jesuits teach that it is enough to wear an image of the Virgin to be saved; that a lie is not a lie if uttered with a mental restriction; that it is enough to attend mass even if one is present in body, not in spirit, and for a motive which is not devotional; that a confessor may absolve a man even though he is impenitent and has no intention of mending his ways; and that one may be saved by merely taking the sacraments, without loving God. The tenth letter closes with a passage in which Pascal drops his irony and gives vent to his indignation:

Etrange Théologie de nos jours! On ose lever l'anathème que S. Paul prononce *contre ceux qui n'aiment pas le Seigneur* JESUS; on ruine ce que dit S. Jean, que *qui n'aime point demeure en la mort,* et ce que dit Jésus-Christ même, *que qui ne l'aime point ne garde point ses préceptes.* Ainsi on rend dignes de jouir de Dieu dans l'éternité ceux qui n'ont jamais aimé Dieu en toute leur vie. Voilà le mystère d'iniquité accompli. Ouvrez enfin les yeux, mon Père, et, si vous n'avez point été touché par les autres égarements de vos Casuistes, que ces derniers vous en retirent par leurs excès. Je le souhaite de tout cœur pour vous et pour tous vos Pères, et prie Dieu qu'il daigne leur faire connaître combien est fausse la lumière qui les a conduits jusqu'à de tels précipices, et qu'il remplisse de son amour ceux qui en dispensent les hommes.

In these seven letters, Pascal produces telling quotations from Jesuit theologians and casuists to prove that the Jesuit doctrines are in themselves monstrous:

Un bénéficier peut sans aucun péché mortel désirer la mort de celui qui a une pension sur son bénéfice, et un fils celle de son père, et se réjouir quand elle arrive, pourvu que ce ne soit que pour le bien qui lui en revient, et non pas par une haine personnelle.

On peut tuer celui qui a donné un soufflet, quoiqu'il s'enfuie, pourvu qu'on évite de le faire par haine ou par vengeance . . .

He shows that the Jesuits are subverting not merely the laws of God, but also those of the land. He points out, further, that the Jesuit doctrines are all recent, and that, since all works by a Jesuit are published with the approval of the Order, the Jesuits as a body cannot escape responsibility for the pernicious doctrines of their theologians.[4]

These first ten letters are the best and the essential part of the *Lettres provinciales.* Pascal now, in answer to Jesuit replies to his attacks, drops the pretence that his letters are addressed to a friend in the provinces, and addresses the Jesuits directly; the tone is more serious; reasoning and indignation take the place of irony. He defends his *Provinciales,* written in a spirit of reverence and charity alien to the Jesuits (Letter XII), develops Jesuit doctrines about alms-giving, simony, usury, and murder (Letters XII–XIV), and shows that the Jesuits, so far from condemning calumny, regard it as a legitimate weapon against their opponents (Letter XV). By a natural transition, Pascal repudiates

---

[4] There is something to be said for the Jesuit point of view. It is arguable that religion should be adapted to ordinary humanity, and that circumstances alter cases. Social life would be impossible without the conventional 'white lie'; and the guilt of Hugo's Jean Valjean, who steals bread for his starving children, is clearly less than that of a bank robber or the promoter of a fraudulent company. But some of the Jesuits went too far.

the Jesuit calumnies against himself and Port-Royal, defending
his friends against the charge of Calvinism and asserting that the
only point at issue between the Jansenists and the Church is the
*question de fait.*

Of the effectiveness of the *Provinciales* there is no doubt:
discredited in the eyes of the public, the *morale relâchée* of the
Jesuits was condemned by the clergy of France, by the Sorbonne
(1658), and subsequently by several Popes. And it is, in part, at
least, because they are so effective a polemical work that they
are still read with delight today – by those who love a good fight,
take pleasure in the spectacle of David pounding Goliath, and
appreciate convincing or subtle pieces of reasoning: the *Provinciales* are a masterpiece of the genre.

The first ten letters, cast in the form of conversations, are
highly diverting: the writer, trying to find out what all the fuss
is about, is sent, like a shuttlecock, from one theologian to the
other. The rueful helplessness of the Dominican is comic; so,
above all, is the Jesuit, naïvely delighted by the subtle ingenuity
of the theologians of his Order, occasionally embarrassed or non-
plussed by an objection, unaware of the implications of the
doctrines he upholds, though a pious and well-meaning man himself, and oblivious to the ironical and double-edged comments of
the speaker. The dialogue is delicious:

—Qu'importe, dit le Père, *par où nous entrions dans le paradis, moyen-
nant que nous y entrions?* comme dit sur un semblable sujet notre célèbre
P. Binet [ . . . ]
—J'avoue, luis dis-je, que cela n'importe; mais la question est de savoir
si on y entrera.
—La Vierge, dit-il, en répond. Voyez-le dans les dernières lignes du
livre du P. Barry. [ . . . ]
—Mais, mon Père, qui voudrait pousser cela vous embarrasserait: car
enfin, qui nous a assuré que la Vierge en répond?
—Le P. Barry, dit-il, en répond pour elle, p. 465 [ . . . ]
—Mais, mon Père, qui répondra pour le P. Barry?
—Comment! dit le Père, il est de notre Compagnie!

In one passage, he shows himself a master of the burlesque
writers' trick of exploiting the comic possibilities of proper names.
Who, asks the writer, are the theologians who have ousted St.
Augustine, St. Ambrose, and the rest?

Ce sont des gens bien habiles et bien célèbres, me dit-il; c'est Villalobos,
Conink, Llamas, Achokier, Dealkozer, Dellacruz, Veracruz, Ugolin,
Tambourin, Fernandez, Martinez, Suarez, Henriquez, Vasquez, Lopez,
Gomez, Sanchez, De Vechis, De Grassis, De Grassalis, De Pitigianis, De
Graphaeis, Squilanti, Bizozeri, Barcola, De Bobadilla, Simancha, Perez de
Lara, Aldretta, Lorca, De Scarcia, Quaranta, Scophra, Pedrezza, Cabrezza,
Bisbe, Dias, De Clavasio, Villagut, Adam à Mandem, Iribarne, Binsfeld,

Volfgangi à Vorberg, Vosthery, Strevesdorf. 'O mon Père, lui dis-je tout effrayé, tous ces gens-là étaient-ils Chrétiens?'

The book is diversified. The parable in the second letter and the story of Jean d'Alba in the sixth vary the comedy of the first ten letters. The style is simple, clear, and witty, the sentences short and crisp; and Pascal has something of Voltaire's art of making things look ridiculous by reducing them to their bare essentials. But he can range from irony to serious reasoning and argument, indignation, invective, and sustained eloquence. These letters are, indeed, as the *Réponse du Provincial*, prefixed to the third letter, asserts, 'agréables aux gens du monde, et intelligibles aux femmes mêmes'. This had been Descartes's aim, too; how much nearer Pascal comes to achieving it is evident if, with the long, leisurely first sentence of the *Discours de la Méthode*, we compare the terse, arresting opening of the *Provinciales*: 'Nous étions bien abusés. Je ne suis détrompé que d'hier.'

But in addition to its interest as a polemical work, the *Provinciales* has a more fundamental appeal. It deals – like any other classical work – in an interesting way with problems of universal and perennial interest, in this case with the problem that constantly confronts us as we pass from childhood to old age, with the problem of *Le Misanthrope*, that of adapting our absolute standards to a world in which everything is relative, the conflict between compromise and intransigence. And the writer of this book, maintaining that standards of right and wrong are absolute, believed heart and soul in the cause for which he was fighting: Blaise Pascal, as we know from his sister's life of him, spared neither himself nor his relatives in the service of his Master.

The miracle of the Holy Thorn, which took place while Pascal was writing the *Provinciales*, set him thinking about miracles in general, and of his reflections on the truth of miracles and on miracles as proof of religion was born the idea of a work to combat atheism. In 1658, he held a conference at Port-Royal, at which he gave an outline of his projected work. At the end of the year, however, ill-health interrupted him, and though in the last year or two of his life he made some further jottings, the work was never written; he died in 1662, leaving a mass of notes. These are the *Pensées*, published first by Port-Royal in 1670 and subsequently by various editors in accordance with different principles. The best editions in which to read them are those based on the copy of Pascal's MSS. made by Port-Royal in 1663, which, as M. Lafuma has established, preserved Pascal's own arrangement; though, since Pascal might well have had second

thoughts about his arrangement, and since he did not classify
the *pensées* written after 1658, it does not, perhaps, matter very
much in what order the *Pensées* are read.

The *Pensées*, then, are mostly – not all[5] – notes for an apology
for the Christian religion. Like the rest of us when we are writing
something, Pascal did not always remember whether he had
already noted an idea down or not and could not always decide
where the best place for it was: hence the repetitions and the
reappearance of the same idea in several places. And, being notes,
while some could take their place in the finished work without
modification, others are cryptic or difficult to interpret. '*Misère* –
Job et Salomon' (174 *bis*),[6] for example, is not immediately
clear. Fortunately, if we read on, we find the explanation:

*Misère.*—Salomon et Job ont le mieux connu et le mieux parlé de la misère
de l'homme: l'un le plus heureux, et l'autre le plus malheureux; l'un
connaissant la vanité des plaisirs par expérience, l'autre les remèdes des
maux.                                                                       (174)

But we are not always so fortunate. Even when a *pensée* is
clear, it is not always easy to know what construction to place
upon it. A famous example is No. 206: 'Le silence éternel de ces
espaces infinis m'effraie.' Some critics, thinking that Pascal was
here speaking directly, have concluded that he was beset with
doubts; if – as seems more probable – the remark was to have
been placed in the mouth of a *libertin*, no such conclusion can
legitimately be drawn.

Pascal, who had given much thought to the art of persuasion
and the nature of belief, conceived his apology on novel principles. He believed, his sister, Mme Périer, tells us, that, in order
to persuade, one must be clear and give pleasure, put oneself in
the place of one's hearer and adapt one's arguments to his *cœur*
and *esprit*, and make him feel that what one is saying matters
to him. Pascal himself, in one of his *pensées*, says that it is useless to combat one's opponent's arguments, because from his
point of view he is right; one must make him see things from
another point of view:

Quand on veut reprendre avec utilité, et montrer à un autre qu'il se
trompe, il faut observer par quel côté il envisage la chose, car elle est
vraie ordinairement de ce côté-là, et lui avouer cette vérité, mais lui
découvrir le côté par où elle est fausse. Il se contente de cela, car il voit
qu'il ne se trompait pas, et qu'il manquait seulement à voir tous les côtés;
or on ne se fâche pas de ne pas tout voir, mais on ne veut pas s'être

---

[5] Some of the *pensées* give his views on style, literary standards, and
*honnêteté*, and make the famous distinction between the *esprit de géométrie* and the *esprit de finesse*.
[6] The numbering used here is that of the Brunschvicg edition, which
most editions give.

trompé; et peut-être que cela vient de ce que naturellement l'homme
ne peut tout voir, et de ce que naturellement il ne se peut tromper dans
le côté qu'il envisage; comme les appréhensions des sens sont toujours
vraies.                                                                    (9)

Belief, for Pascal, is not primarily or exclusively a matter of
reason. Reason has a part to play, but feeling and habit are at
least as important. What we believe only with our reason, we
scarcely believe at all; whereas what we believe with the *cœur*
(i.e. instinctively) is part of us. We may not be able to refute the
arguments of philosophers, but we *know* that we are awake and
not dreaming. We may not be able to prove the existence of
space, time, and so forth, but we *know* they exist: 'le cœur a ses
raisons que la raison ne connaît point' (277). Religious belief
should be of this kind. Christianity, in fact, is a religion not for
the reason but for the emotions:

Le Dieu des chrétiens ne consiste pas en un Dieu simplement auteur des
vérités géométriques et de l'ordre des éléments; c'est la part des
païens et des épicuriens. Il ne consiste pas seulement en un Dieu qui
exerce sa providence sur la vie et sur les biens des hommes, pour donner
une heureuse suite d'années à ceux qui l'adorent; c'est la portion des
Juifs. Mais le Dieu d'Abraham, le Dieu d'Isaac, le Dieu de Jacob, le Dieu
des chrétiens, est un Dieu d'amour et de consolation; c'est un Dieu qui
remplit l'âme et le cœur de ceux qu'il possède; c'est un Dieu qui leur fait
sentir intérieurement leur misère, et sa miséricorde infinie; qui s'unit au
fond de leur âme; qui la remplit d'humilité, de joie, de confiance, d'amour;
qui les rend incapables d'autre fin que de lui-même.              (556)

The memorial in which Pascal recorded his own mystical experience of 1654 testifies that this was precisely what Christianity
was for him.

Another important factor in belief is habit, which has a double
part to play. In the first place, habit determines what we believe
— we are Christians or Mahometans, for example, because our
parents are Christians or Mahometans, not because of our reason.
Similarly, we believe that the sun will rise tomorrow — simply
because it always has done. Secondly, when we do believe something, unless we believe it as a matter of habit, of instinct, we
shall not really believe it — we cannot always be recalling to mind
the rational proofs of our belief.

Il faut donc faire croire nos deux pièces: l'esprit, par les raisons, qu'il
suffit d'avoir vues une fois en sa vie; et l'automate, par la coutume, et en
ne lui permettant pas de s'incliner au contraire.                 (252)

All this helps to explain Pascal's purpose, which was to persuade *le cœur*, rather than to convince the reason. He specifically
rejects the attempt to prove the truth of religion by rational
arguments, not only because of the weakness of such arguments —

in the last resort, he did not believe that there were any conclu-
sive proofs of the truth of religion; God is a *Dieu caché*, the
evidence for whose existence is there, but only for those who
seek it — but also because such arguments do not get to the heart
of the matter.

Quand un homme serait persuadé que les proportions des nombres sont
des vérités immatérielles, éternelles et dépendantes d'une première vérité
en qui elles subsistent, et qu'on appelle Dieu, je ne le trouverais pas
beaucoup avancé pour son salut. (556)

He attempts, therefore, to shake the *libertin* out of his apathy, to
rouse him to the importance of the question, to make him really
want to know whether God exists or not. For, if he really wants
to know, he will find God — will, too, has an important part to
play in belief:

La volonté est un des principaux organes de la créance; non qu'elle forme
la créance, mais parce que les choses sont vraies ou fausses, selon la
face par où on les regarde. La volonté qui se plaît à l'une plus qu'à l'autre,
détourne l'esprit de considérer les qualités de celles qu'elle n'aime pas à
voir; et ainsi l'esprit, marchant d'une pièce avec la volonté, s'arrête à
regarder la face qu'elle aime; et ainsi il en juge par ce qu'il y voit. (99)

Reason has a part to play in conversion, but only a minor part.
It is not until the *libertin* has been shaken out of his torpor and
predisposed to seek the truth, that there is any point in attempting
to prove the truth of religion. When those two processes are
complete, faith may come — but faith is the gift of God: 'on ne
croira jamais d'une créance utile et de foi, si Dieu n'incline le
cœur; et on croira dès qu'il l'inclinera' (284).

Pascal's knowledge of his adversary, his psychological subtlety,
his insight into the nature of belief, make him a formidable
opponent. His apology was to have been addressed to *libertins*,
and — some of the *pensées* suggest — to have been cast in the form
of dialogues or letters, or both (the *Provinciales*, after all, are
letters reporting conversations). It was to have placed the *libertin*
in a favourable disposition to religion before attempting to prove
the truth of religion:

Ordre.—Les hommes ont mépris pour la religion; ils en ont haine et
peur qu'elle soit vraie. Pour guérir cela, il faut commencer par montrer
que la religion n'est point contraire à la raison; vénérable, en donner
respect; la rendre ensuite aimable, faire souhaiter aux bons qu'elle fût
vraie; et puis montrer qu'elle est vraie.

This approach reminds one very much of that of Chateaubriand
in the *Génie du Christianisme*, but the next sentence shows us
that they were poles apart:

Vénérable, parce qu'elle a bien connu l'homme; aimable, parce qu'elle
promet le vrai bien. (187)

The work, then, was to have been in two parts – one aiming at shaking the *libertin* or the lukewarm Christian out of his complacency or apathy, by making him acutely aware of the importance of the questions at issue, the other giving proofs of the truth of religion.[7]

In the first part, Pascal brings the *libertin* face to face with eternity and shows him that the question of the hereafter is of the utmost importance in this life:

> Il ne faut pas avoir l'âme fort élevée pour comprendre qu'il n'y a point ici de satisfaction véritable et solide, que tous nos plaisirs ne sont que vanité, que nos maux sont infinis, et qu'enfin la mort, qui nous menace à chaque instant, doit infailliblement nous mettre, dans peu d'années, dans l'horrible nécessité d'être éternellement ou anéantis ou malheureux. (194)

That anyone should be complacent in such a situation, or content to put up with doubt, is to Pascal so inconceivable as to constitute a proof of the corruption of human nature, to reveal 'un appesantissement de la main de Dieu'. He puts the position to the *libertin* in the form of a wager. Eternity is long and human life short; it is uncertain whether after death we are annihilated or not, but the chances are at least equal. Is it not, then, worth staking this life in order to have a chance of winning the prize of eternal bliss? Gamblers risk far more to win far less. Why not, then, spend this life in seeking God (not through reason, but by subduing one's passions and practising religion)? Not merely has one nothing to lose, but one has everything to gain: 'Vous serez fidèle, honnête, humble, reconnaissant, bienfaisant, ami sincère, véritable' (233).

But the main means which Pascal uses to arouse the *libertin* from his lethargy is the spectacle of the dual nature of man. Man, in fact, is at the centre of Pascal's apology in two ways – his approach is based on the study of the psychology of man, and it is human nature that he uses as his main argument. Man is characterized both by *grandeur* and by *misère*, and Pascal develops the paradox of man with a view to reducing the *libertin* to a state of utter perplexity:

> S'il se vante, je l'abaisse,
> S'il s'abaisse, je le vante;
> Et le contredis toujours,
> Jusqu'à ce qu'il comprenne
> Qu'il est un monstre incompréhensible.
>
> (420)

---

[7] Pascal's plan is known to us (1) from the *Pensées* themselves, and in particular the order in which they appear in the copy made by Port-Royal; and (2) from the conference he held at Port-Royal, as it is known to us from (a) the *Discours* of Filleau de la Chaise, and (b) the preface written by Pascal's nephew, Etienne Périer, for the Port-Royal edition of the *Pensées*.

The *libertin* should now be ready to seek the truth without passion. Pascal shows him that neither the philosophies nor the religions of the world can explain the contradictions of human nature, or serve as a reliable guide to life. Reason is no help, God and Nature being incomprehensible. None of the three basic philosophies – stoicism, epicureanism and Pyrrhonism – corresponds to the reality of human nature. Stoicism lays too much stress on the *grandeur* of man; epicureanism over-estimates his baser instincts;[8] Pyrrhonism is unsatisfying because, although we cannot prove anything, we instinctively believe that truth exists. The religions of the world are no more satisfying than the philosophies – none can explain the mystery of human nature, or teach us how to 'guérir l'orgueil et la concupiscence'.

At this point, however, Pascal draws the attention of the *libertin* to the Jews and the Bible. There, one learns that the world was the work of God, and that man, created by God in his own image, fell from Grace by the misuse of his free-will. There, in the doctrine of the Fall and original sin, is the key to the paradox of the *grandeur* and the *misère* of man. Moreover, Christianity teaches man not to despair: God and man are reconciled through Christ; it is through Christ that God is made known to man. Christianity is thus the only perfect and satisfactory religion. It alone explains and takes into account both the *grandeur* and the *misère* of man; it alone provides the remedy for our weakness humility and mortification); it alone teaches virtue and the love of God; it alone can give happiness.

La connaissance de Dieu sans celle de sa misère fait l'orgueil.
La connaissance de sa misère sans celle de Dieu fait le désespoir.
La connaissance de Jésus-Christ fait le milieu, parce que nous y trouvons et Dieu et notre misère. (556)

In the Second Part, Pascal goes on to show that Christianity is true. His arguments are that Christianity, although contrary to nature, has established itself; that the doctrine of the Fall and the hope of redemption have existed since the creation of the world; that the history of Moses, the Mosaic Law, and the Old Testament prefigure Christ; that the prophecies, the miracles, and the lives of saints and martyrs prove its truth. This part of the work has dated and is of little interest.

In placing man at the centre of his apology for Christianity, Pascal is very much of his age; and it is precisely because he did so that we read the *Pensées* today. The proofs of religion drawn from the Bible are now of little interest; his portrayal of the *condition humaine* is as valid and as powerful as it ever was.

[8] Cf. the *Entretien de Pascal avec M. de Sacy sur Epictète et Montaigne.*

Human nature, for Pascal, can be summed up in three words —
'inconstance, ennui, inquiétude' (127). Man is changeable and
inconstant, capable of laughing and crying at the same time,
fickle in every sense of the word. He is naturally bored, aware of
the vanity of human life — and this, indeed, is one reason for his
inconstancy: 'Le sentiment de la fausseté des plaisirs présents,
et l'ignorance de la vanité des plaisirs absents causent l'inconstance' (110). Hence we cannot live in the present, but are always
looking forward or backward. As for *inquiétude*,

> Nous sommes si malheureux que nous ne pouvons prendre plaisir à une
> chose qu'à condition de nous fâcher si elle réussit mal; ce que mille
> choses peuvent faire, et font, à toute heure. Qui aurait trouvé le secret de
> se réjouir du bien sans se fâcher du mal contraire aurait trouvé le point;
> c'est le mouvement perpétuel.                                          (181)

The pre-eminent quality of man is his reason; and yet reason
plays little part in our lives. Reason has nothing to do with the
great events of history. A fly can cause the loss of a battle;
Cromwell would have ravaged Christendom and established a
new dynasty but for the grain of sand which brought about his
death. Love can change the course of history, and its origin is an
inexplicable *je ne sais quoi*: 'Le nez de Cléopâtre: s'il eût été
plus court, toute la face de la terre aurait changé' (162). Reason
has nothing to do with the most important decisions in our own
lives: our choice of a trade or a religion are matters of chance,
decided by the examples of those around us. Habit is an important factor in our beliefs — in the following *pensée*, this is
illustrated by an interesting anticipation of the idea of a conditioned reflex:

> La coutume de voir les rois accompagnés de gardes, de tambours, d'offi-
> ciers, et de toutes les choses qui plient la machine vers le respect et la
> terreur, fait que leur visage, quand il est quelquefois seul et sans ces
> accompagnements, imprime dans leurs sujets le respect et la terreur,
> parce qu'on ne sépare point dans la pensée leurs personnes d'avec leurs
> suites, qu'on y voit d'ordinaire jointes. Et le monde, qui ne sait pas que
> cet effet vient de cette coutume, croit qu'il vient d'une force naturelle; et
> de là viennent ces mots: 'Le caractère de la Divinité est empreint sur
> son visage, etc.'                                                      (308)

Custom is to society what habit is to the individual. We take our
ideas of right and wrong from the society around us. These vary
from country to country — the Swiss set more store by commoners
than by noblemen; in France, it is the other way about. Prevalent ideas of morality are far from rational: murder is wrong,
and yet it is thought just to kill a foreigner in war.

Although men are creatures of reason, they do not behave
rationally. 'L'homme n'agit point par la raison, qui fait son

être' (439). We feel deeply about trifles ('Un bout de capuchon arme 25.000 moines', 955),[9] interest ourselves in futile things such as art ('Quelle vanité que la peinture, qui attire l'admiration par la ressemblance des choses dont on n'admire point les originaux', 134), devote our lives to the pursuit of vain objects, such as rank, or wealth and learning, neither of which we can possess securely:

Toutes les occupations des hommes sont à avoir du bien; et ils ne sauraient avoir de titre pour montrer qu'ils le possèdent par justice, car ils n'ont que la fantaisie des hommes, ni force pour le posséder sûrement. Il en est de même de la science, car la maladie l'ôte. Nous sommes incapables de vrai et de bien.                                                (436)

Learning, in any case, is useless:

La science des choses extérieures ne me consolera pas de l'ignorance de la morale, au temps d'affliction; mais la science des mœurs me consolera toujours de l'ignorance des sciences extérieures.        (67)

Our motive is less a genuine desire to do these things than a desire to show off: no one would travel without an opportunity to talk about his travels later. *Gloire* is such a potent motive that we prefer it to life itself.

Human judgment is fallible. Our tastes are not rational: we like or dislike a thing first, and find reasons to justify ourselves afterwards. Reason is easily swayed by extraneous circumstances:

Si on est trop jeune, on ne juge pas bien; trop vieil, de même. Si on n'y songe pas assez, si on y songe trop, on s'entête, et on s'en coiffe. Si on considère son ouvrage incontinent après l'avoir fait, on en est encore tout prévenu; si trop longtemps après, on n'y entre plus. Ainsi les tableaux, vus de trop loin et de trop près; et il n'y a qu'un point indivisible qui soit le véritable lieu; les autres sont trop près, trop loin, trop haut ou trop bas.
                                                                        (381)

The buzzing of a fly or the creaking of a weathercock or a pulley can throw us off our balance, and it is practically impossible not to be influenced, one way or the other, by the judgment of others. The senses may easily deceive us, and, in their turn, are often led astray by the passions. Other sources of error are sickness, self-interest, and imagination – it is difficult, for example, to listen seriously to a sermon if the preacher is funny-looking or has a disagreeable voice, or to keep one's head on a narrow plank over an abyss.[10]

[9] A reference to a lengthy dispute in the order of *cordeliers* over the breadth of their cowl.
[10] The power of the imagination was a favourite theme of seventeenth-century philosophers—see H. Busson, *La Pensée religieuse française de Charron à Pascal*, 1933, p. 322; see, too, Montaigne's essay on the subject (I, 22). The example of the philosopher on a plank had been used by others

There are many signs of the fallibility of the human reason.
We are never sure of our sanity. Philosophy has never achieved
any certainty about anything, not even about what constitutes
the *souverain bien*: according to Montaigne, there are 280
*souverains biens*. Reason must not be trusted too far. Like La
Rochefoucauld, Pascal thinks that at times it is better to be mad
than sane: 'Les hommes sont si nécessairement fous, que ce
serait fou, par un autre tour de folie, de n'être pas fou' (414).
Reason must not be rejected, but its limitations must be acknow-
ledged; we must recognize that many things surpass our understanding:

> La dernière démarche de la raison est de reconnaître qu'il y a une infi-
> nité de choses qui la surpassent; elle n'est que faible, si elle ne va jusqu'à
> connaître cela.
> Que si les choses naturelles la surpassent, que dira-t-on des surnatu-
> relles?                                                          (267)

Human nature is dispassionately analysed by Pascal. Men are
egoistical, full of self-love, full of faults which, however, they are
unwilling to acknowledge, so that they are continually playing a
part and being hypocritical. Society — here again Pascal is at one
with La Rochefoucauld — could not exist without this hypocrisy
(100). Human nature is naturally vicious, animated by *concupiscence*. Our seeming virtues are but vices — here again we recall
La Rochefoucauld; pity, for example, is a form of self-interest
(452). Sometimes virtue is merely the balance between two
contrary vices. We are selfish, naturally possessive, tyrannical:
'Le *moi* est haïssable [ ... ] chaque *moi* est l'ennemi et voudrait
être le tyran de tous les autres [ ... ]' (455).[11] And yet, Pascal
insists, this *moi*, to which each of us would willingly sacrifice
the whole world, has no reality:

> ... celui qui aime quelqu'un à cause de sa beauté, l'aime-t-il? Non: car
> la petite vérole, qui tuera la beauté sans tuer la personne, fera qu'il ne
> l'aimera plus.
> Et si on m'aime pour mon jugement, pour ma mémoire, m'aime-t-on
> *moi*? Non, car je puis perdre ces qualités sans me perdre moi-même. Où
> est donc ce moi, s'il n'est ni dans le corps, ni dans l'âme? et comment
> aimer le corps ou l'âme, sinon pour ces qualités, qui ne seront point ce
> qui fait le moi, puisqu'elles sont périssables? car aimerait-on la sub-
> stance de l'âme d'une personne, abstraitement, et quelques qualités qui

---

before Pascal—and is, indeed, to be found in Burton's *Anatomy of Melancholy* (Part I, Section 2, Member 3, Sub-section 2).

[11] This is often quoted as a literary principle, which it is not. Pascal is
pointing out the egoism of man, not objecting to the use of the first person
pronoun, which is common enough, not only in seventeenth-century literature in general, but in the *Provinciales* and the *Pensées* in particular. It is
true that Pascal, according to his sister, held that an *honnête homme*
should avoid the words *je* and *moi* as much as possible.

y fussent? Cela ne se peut, et serait injuste. On n'aime donc jamais personne, mais seulement des qualités.

Qu'on ne se moque donc plus de ceux qui se font honorer pour des
charges et des offices, car on n'aime personne que pour des qualités
empruntées. (323)

Man is not capable of extremes – he cannot understand if he
reads too fast or too slowly, cannot see if there is too much light
or too little, is thought mad if he has too much intelligence or if
he has too little: 'Rien que la médiocrité n'est bon. [...]
C'est sortir de l'humanité que de sortir du milieu' (378). Similarly,
in nature, he is a mediocre creature poised between the infinitely
great and the infinitely small – his life a brief space with an
eternity on either side of it, himself a petty creature incapable of
understanding the vastness of the universe but equally incapable
of entering into the world of the infinitely small. *Pensée* No. 72,
one of the most powerful and most terrifying expressions of
Pascal's view of the human state, is too long to quote in full, but
this is the climax of it:

Voilà notre état véritable. C'est ce qui nous rend incapables de savoir
certainement et d'ignorer absolument. Nous voguons sur un milieu vaste,
toujours incertains et flottants, poussés d'un bout vers l'autre. Quelque
terme où nous pensions nous attacher et nous affermir, il branle et nous
quitte et, si nous le suivons, il échappe à nos prises, nous glisse et fuit
d'une fuite éternelle. Rien ne s'arrête pour nous. C'est l'état qui nous
est naturel, et toutefois le plus contraire à notre inclination; nous brûlons
de désir de trouver une assiette ferme, et une dernière base constante
pour y édifier une tour qui s'élève à l'infini; mais tout notre fondement
craque, et la terre s'ouvre jusqu'aux abîmes.

Human society is a reflection of human nature, founded not
on reason, but on folly, custom, and force. The principle of
hereditary succession, for example, is absurd: 'On ne choisit pas
pour gouverner un vaisseau, celui des voyageurs qui est de
meilleure maison' (320). Society rests not on justice, but on
force – but this is, in fact, inevitable, since we have no means of
knowing what justice is, and conceptions of justice and laws
change from country to country: 'Plaisante justice qu'une rivière
borne! Vérité au deçà des Pyrénées, erreur au delà' (294). For
– like Joseph de Maistre in the nineteenth century – Pascal is fond
of developing the paradox that, however foolish, unjust, and
irrational society may be, it is better than if it were rationally
organized: the madness of society is, in fact, a kind of sanity. Approval or disapproval of social usages varies with the degree of intelligence of the observer: the common people accept what is,
though for the wrong reasons; the more intelligent denounce it; the
really intelligent understand that it is for the best. Thus extremes

meet; ignorance and the highest intelligence agree. In one *pensée*, Pascal establishes as many as five degrees of opinion:

Le peuple honore les personnes de grande naissance. Les demi-habiles les méprisent, disant que la naissance n'est pas un avantage de la personne, mais du hasard. Les habiles les honorent, non par la pensée du peuple, mais par la pensée de derrière. Les dévots qui ont plus de zèle que de science les méprisent, malgré cette considération qui les fait honorer par les habiles, parce qu'ils en jugent par une nouvelle lumière que la piété leur donne. Mais les chrétiens parfaits les honorent par une autre lumière supérieure. Ainsi se vont les opinions succédant du pour au contre, selon qu'on a de lumière.                    (337)

Various social usages are examined and, although at first sight irrational, shown to be useful. The principle of hereditary succession, though absurd, is a means of avoiding disputes and civil war.

Pascal, it is clear, is no revolutionary. Society is based on folly and injustice, but, given the nature of man, it must be. We do not know what justice is, and, if might and custom did not impose some sort of order, we should be fighting one another incessantly. Society must be accepted, both for practical reasons and because it is the will of God. Pascal's sister tells us that, during the Fronde, he steadfastly supported the government against the rebels.

The state of man, in short, is not a happy one. We instinctively desire happiness, but never achieve it:

Tous se plaignent: princes, sujets, nobles, roturiers, vieux, jeunes; forts, faibles; savants, ignorants; sains, malades; de tous pays, de tous les temps, de tous âges et de toutes conditions.
Une épreuve si longue, si continuelle et si uniforme devrait bien nous convaincre de notre impuissance d'arriver au bien par nos efforts; mais l'exemple nous instruit peu.                                      (425)

There is, however, another side to the picture. Man is also great; indeed, his very *misère* is a sign of his greatness. Inanimate objects and animals have no feelings; man alone is wretched, a sure sign that he is a 'roi dépossédé'.

La grandeur de l'homme est grande en ce qu'il se connaît misérable. Un arbre ne se connaît pas misérable.
C'est donc être misérable que de se connaître misérable; mais c'est être grand que de connaître qu'on est misérable.                    (397)

There are several signs of human greatness. The sense of deprivation and loss, the instinctive desire for happiness and certainty is one. Man is great because he *can* turn his vices into virtues, and because he has a soul – without something immaterial within us we should not feel pleasure or have the power of subduing our passions. The desire for glory is at once 'la plus grande bassesse de l'homme' and 'la plus grande marque de son excellence' (404), because the desire for the esteem of others shows how much we instinctively prize the human soul: animals do not admire one another.

Nous avons une si grande idée de l'âme de l'homme que nous ne pouvons souffrir d'en être méprisés et de n'être pas dans l'estime d'une âme; et toute la félicité des hommes consiste dans cette estime. (400)

Above all, man is great because he has the faculty of reason. Reason is our master, and if we disobey, we have to pay the penalty of being foolish. Thought is the characteristic quality, the distinctive mark of man: 'Pensée fait la grandeur de l'homme' (346).

L'homme n'est qu'un roseau, le plus faible de la nature; mais c'est un roseau pensant. Il ne faut pas que l'univers entier s'arme pour l'écraser: une vapeur, une goutte d'eau, suffit pour le tuer. Mais, quand l'univers l'écraserait, l'homme serait encore plus noble que ce qui le tue, puisqu'il sait qu'il meurt, et l'avantage que l'univers a sur lui; l'univers n'en sait rien. (347)

Man is thus a paradoxical creature, great and wretched, in whom the reason and the passions are ever at war, akin both to the angels and to the beasts, 'juge de toutes choses, imbécile ver de terre, dépositaire du vrai, cloaque d'incertitude et d'erreur: gloire et rebut de l'univers' (434). The best evidence of this paradox, of this fallen nature of man, is his need for *divertissement*, the subject of some of Pascal's most striking *pensées*. Man is great because he has the power of thought; but if, in his fallen state, he thinks, he is conscious of his wretchedness. He therefore turns to frivolous games and pursuits to stop himself from thinking. Without anything to occupy him, a man becomes bored, melancholy, depressed: 'tout le malheur des hommes vient d'une seule chose, qui est de ne savoir pas demeurer en repos, dans une chambre' (139).

Cet homme si affligé de la mort de sa femme et de son fils unique, qui a cette grande querelle qui le tourmente, d'où vient qu'à ce moment il n'est pas triste, et qu'on le voit si exempt de toutes ces pensées pénibles et inquiétantes? Il ne faut pas s'en étonner: on vient de lui servir une balle, et il faut qu'il la rejette à son compagnon; il est occupé à la prendre à la chute du toit, pour gagner une chasse; comment voulez-vous qu'il pense à ses affaires, ayant cette autre affaire à manier? Voilà un soin digne d'occuper cette grande âme, et de lui ôter toute autre pensée de l'esprit. Cet homme né pour connaître l'univers, pour juger de toutes choses, pour régir tout un Etat, le voilà occupé et tout rempli du soin de prendre un lièvre! Et s'il ne s'abaisse à cela et veuille toujours être tendu, il n'en sera que plus sot, parce qu'il voudra s'élever au-dessus de l'humanité, et il n'est qu'un homme, au bout du compte, c'est-à-dire capable de peu et de beaucoup, de tout et de rien: il n'est ni ange ni bête, mais homme. (140)

Like all great writers, Pascal transcends his period, but he is of it. He is of it in his views on *honnêteté* and on style and, more important, by the great part played by the study of human nature in his apology. He is of it in the stress he lays on the restlessness and inconstancy of human nature, and the fickleness of fortune:

J'ai vu tous les pays et hommes changeants; et ainsi, après bien des changements de jugement touchant la véritable justice, j'ai connu que notre nature n'était qu'un continuel changement, et je n'ai plus changé depuis; et si je changeais, je confirmerais mon opinion.                       (375)

Qui aurait eu l'amitié du roi d'Angleterre, du roi de Pologne et de la reine de Suède, aurait-il cru manquer de retraite et d'asile au monde? (177)

He is of it in the picture he paints of human hypocrisy, and in his preoccupation with the problem whether one can distinguish between a state of waking and one of dreaming – 'la vie est un songe un peu moins inconstant', he concludes (386). He is of it in his Pyrrhonism and his fideism, in his acute consciousness of the unreliability and the limitations of the human reason. He is of it, finally, in his love of paradox.

Paradox plays an important part in Pascal's *Pensées*. Not only does he delight in pointing out particular paradoxes of human nature and behaviour, but the paradox of human nature, the *grandeur* and the *misère* of man, is at the very heart of his apology. Moreover, the test of truth itself for Pascal is that it should be paradoxical, that it should reconcile apparently irreconcilable antinomies. Man is great; man is wretched: Christianity alone provides the solution which takes both these contradictory truths into account and shows that man is fallen from Grace. Pascal, indeed, states this as a principle:

Les deux raisons contraires. Il faut commencer par là: sans cela on n'entend rien, et tout est hérétique; et même, à la fin de chaque vérité, il faut ajouter qu'on se souvient de la vérité opposée.                    (567)[12]

For Pascal, as we have seen, all men are right from their point of view; error consists, not in being wrong, but in seeing only one aspect of truth. This sense of the complexity of truth is, perhaps, one of the most rewarding aspects of the *Pensées*.

In his insistence that truth lies in the reconciliation of antinomies, Pascal has been seen as the ancestor of Hegel (thesis – antithesis – synthesis) and the dialectical materialists. He is also – in his rejection of metaphysics in favour of the study of human existence, and in his sense of the impotence of the reason, of the irrationality of society, of the futility of life as it is usually lived, and of the imminence of death – a forerunner of existential-

---

[12] Cf. Nos. 684, 862.

ism. But it is not merely for his historical interest that Pascal is read, but for his stimulating and provocative ideas, his original investigation into the nature of belief and the art of persuasion, and his searching analysis of the human condition. Even if his picture of man is slightly overtinged with black, it is essentially true. The clarity of Pascal's vision strips reality of the protective veils in which our complacency swathes it, and sheds an unfamiliar and disturbing light upon it; sham and pretence disappear, and we see ourselves and our place in the universe as they are. Reading Pascal is a chastening but a salutary experience, which sets things in their true perspective.

Intensity is a word one cannot avoid in speaking of Pascal, and his greatness consists in his ability to communicate his vision effectively. To the intensity of his vision corresponds the emotional intensity of his style. Pascal is, perhaps, the best illustration of Mme de Staël's famous remark: 'Nos premiers poètes lyriques, en France, ce sont peut-être nos grands prosateurs.' Pascal has the imagery, the language charged with emotion, the evocative power of a great poet:

Le dernier acte est sanglant, quelque belle que soit la comédie en tout le reste: on jette enfin de la terre sur la tête, et en voilà pour jamais.          (210)

Qu'on s'imagine un nombre d'hommes dans les chaînes, et tous condamnés à la mort, dont les uns étant chaque jour égorgés à la vue des autres, ceux qui restent voient leur propre condition dans celle de leurs semblables, et, se regardant les uns et les autres avec douleur et sans espérance, attendent à leur tour. C'est l'image de la condition des hommes.          (199)

Such passages, in which unemotional statements only partially conceal emotion, have the unmistakable ring of Pascal, and strike home.

# Part III

## 1660–1685

*Chapter 12*

# INTRODUCTION

THE PERIOD from 1660 to 1685, a short span of twenty-five years prolific in masterpieces, is termed by the French the 'classical age'. It is the period in which were performed nearly all the plays of Molière and Racine, and many of Corneille's; in which were published the *Pensées* of Pascal, the *Maximes* of La Rochefoucauld, and *La Princesse de Clèves*; in which two great poets, La Fontaine and Boileau, wrote the best of their work; in which Bossuet preached sermons and delivered funeral orations; in which Mme de Sévigné corresponded with her daughter, and Cardinal de Retz prepared his memoirs.

Il peut y avoir eu en d'autres temps plus d'écrivains en France qu'il n'y en a [wrote Saint-Réal in 1691], mais il faudrait bien être de mauvais goût pour trouver qu'il y en ait jamais eu tant d'excellents à la fois, que nous en avons vus ensemble.

And Voltaire wrote, not without nostalgia, in the following century:

C'était un temps digne de l'attention des temps à venir que celui où les héros de Corneille et de Racine, les personnages de Molière, les symphonies de Lulli, toutes nouvelles pour la nation, et (puisqu'il ne s'agit ici que des arts) les voix des Bossuet et des Bourdaloue, se faisaient entendre à Louis XIV, à Madame si célèbre par son goût, à un Condé, à un Turenne, à un Colbert, et à cette foule d'hommes supérieurs qui parurent en tout genre. Ce temps ne se retrouvera plus, où un duc de La Rochefoucauld, l'auteur des *Maximes*, au sortir de la conversation d'un Pascal et d'un Arnauld, allait au théâtre de Corneille.

After the Fronde, the tendency towards absolutism and centralization was strengthened. Nobles and bourgeois alike accepted without question the authority of Louis XIV, who completed the work of Richelieu and Mazarin. It was not only that France needed a king, but Louis XIV seemed to be the king France needed. Young, handsome, and gallant, he was the centre of a brilliant court.

Après quelque séjour à Paris, Monsieur et Madame s'en allèrent à Fontainebleau. Madame y porta la joie, et les plaisirs. Le Roi [ ... ] s'attacha fort à elle, et lui témoigna une complaisance extrême. Elle disposait de toutes les parties de divertissement, elles se faisaient **toutes**

pour elle, et il paraissait que le Roi n'y avait de plaisir, que par celui qu'elle
en recevait. C'était dans le milieu de l'été, Madame s'allait baigner tous
les jours, elle partait en carrosse à cause de la chaleur, et revenait à
cheval, suivie de toutes les dames habillées galamment, avec mille plumes
sur leur tête, accompagnées du Roi, et de la jeunesse de la Cour; après
souper on montait dans des calèches, et au bruit des violons on s'allait
promener une partie de la nuit autour du Canal.          (Mme de Lafayette)

There we have a glimpse of the court at the outset of the reign.
The King, moreover, was avid for prestige, for glory. In 1661,
he secured for the French ambassador in London the right of
precedence over his Spanish counterpart; in 1662, he took
advantage of an alleged insult to the French envoy in Rome to
impose a humiliating treaty on the Pope; and, in 1667, he invaded
the Spanish Netherlands and Franche-Comté, to which he had
a dubious claim through his wife (the War of Devolution).

A strong hand was at the helm. After the death of Mazarin,
in 1661, Louis XIV showed himself determined to be master.
That same year, Foucquet, the *surintendant des finances*, whom
Louis XIV had inherited from Mazarin, was arrested, placed on
trial for peculation, and eventually imprisoned for the rest of his
days. On the fall of Foucquet, Colbert was appointed *intendant
des finances*, an office to which he added others subsequently, so
that he had power to carry out considerable reforms. He suppressed the worst abuses in the system of tax collection, re-
organized French finances, and by 1662 had achieved a surplus.
He encouraged existing industries with bounties, and introduced
new ones, directly or indirectly controlled by the state. He
founded factories for lace, glass, tapestry and textiles, opened
copper and lead mines in the South, and encouraged metal work.
He increased production by every means in his power – ordering
wine shops to be closed during working hours, persuading the
Church to abolish seventeen feast days, getting monasteries and
municipalities to manufacture goods, and forbidding workmen
to leave France. He believed in the strict regimentation of
industry, maintaining the guild system, imposing it on many
trades hitherto free, and issuing numerous regulations for every
industry.

Nor were other aspects of economic life neglected. He forbade
the export of corn, imported cattle to improve French stock,
rewarded the best stock raisers, developed forests, subsidized horse-
breeding establishments, and drained marshes. Communications
were improved. The number of internal tolls and customs levies
was reduced, roads were improved, and the great Languedoc
canal, joining the Mediterranean to the Atlantic, was dug
(1664–81). French ports were developed, the navy strengthened,
colonial ventures subsidized, overseas dominions extended, and

laws codified. Colbert was a convinced protectionist: to prevent
gold from leaving the country, in other words to maintain a
favourable balance of trade, he placed heavy duties on English
and Dutch goods, and these were to some extent responsible for
the Dutch War of 1672–8, which helped to undo the prosperity he
had laboured so hard to create.

The determination of the government to be absolute was felt
in many fields. The parlement of Paris dared not exercise its
right of remonstrance; the provincial *états* were either abolished
or deprived of their powers. A police force was organized in
Paris; in the provinces, the *intendants* came more and more to
supersede all the other local authorities. Literature, science, and
the arts were brought under the control of the government. A
number of academies were set up to cover all branches of intellectual life: the Académie des Inscriptions et Belles-Lettres (1663);
the Académie de Peinture et de Sculpture (founded 1648, recon-
stituted 1664); the Académie des Sciences (1666); the Académie de
France in Rome (1666); and the Académie d'Architecture (1671).
When, in 1672, Colbert became the vice-protector of the French
Academy, a number of innovations were made. Henceforth, the
reception of a new member took place in public; the Academy had
to meet more frequently and to work harder; and to encourage
members to attend meetings, those who clocked in by a certain
time were given a *jeton de présence* (worth thirty-two sous). Occasionally, the government intervened to influence the Academy's
choice. Racine was imposed on it. After the election of La Fontaine, Louis XIV would not allow the Academy to admit him
formally until a vacant seat had been given to Boileau (1684). In
1704, when Tréville was elected, Louis XIV ordered the Academy
to make another choice.

Literature was influenced by a policy of the stick and the
carrot. The stick was the censorship. Severe penalties were inflicted on those who criticized the government. In 1662, abbé
Marigny was imprisoned in the Bastille for a sonnet comparing
Louis XIV's government to those of Tiberius and Nero. Bussy-
Rabutin was imprisoned and then exiled from court for his
*Histoire amoureuse des Gaules*. Claude le Petit was burnt at the
stake in 1662 for having spoken disrespectfully of the authorities
and established religion in his poems. When, in 1667, the office of
*lieutenant-général de police* was created and an efficient police
system established, the censorship became stricter than ever. The
carrot was a pension list. It was decided to give pensions to men
of letters, and in 1663 a small committee (Chapelain, Bourzeis,
abbé Cassagnes, Charles Perrault, Charpentier) was formed to
dispense the King's bounty. Pensions varied between 600 and

3,000 livres a year, according to the genre in which the author concerned wrote. Racine, Molière, and Corneille, all received pensions, but the highest one went to Chapelain (an epic poet) as 'le plus grand poète qui ait jamais été, et du plus solide jugement'. The pensions were later paid irregularly, and the total amount distributed was reduced after the outbreak of the Dutch War in 1672. Louis XIV also patronized the arts in other ways. Many of the plays of Racine and Molière were written for the court, or first performed at court; one at least owed its success to the appreciation of the King — Les Plaideurs, which had originally met with a poor reception in Paris.

While Colbert was increasing the wealth, the prosperity, and the self-sufficiency of France, another secretary of state, Louvois, had been building up a strong army. In 1672, Louis, having bribed Charles II of England and several German states to support him, decided to invade Holland — partly out of annoyance with the Dutch for having thwarted him in the War of Devolution, partly as the result of the trade war to which Colbert's tariffs had given rise. This was the beginning of an aggressive policy which Louis pursued until his death. At first, all went well; then the Dutch organized a coalition (the Empire, Brandenburg, and Holland), public opinion in England compelled Charles II to make peace (1674), and Turenne was killed (1675). The war was brought to an end in 1678 by the Peace of Nymwegen: though Louis was compelled to remove the objectionable tariffs, France made considerable territorial gains. Louis XIV was at the height of his power:

Le roi [says Voltaire] fut en ce temps au comble de la grandeur. Victorieux depuis qu'il régnait, n'ayant assiégé aucune place qu'il n'eût prise, supérieur en tout genre à ses ennemis réunis, la terreur de l'Europe pendant six années de suite, enfin son arbitre et son pacificateur, ajoutant à ses états la Franche-Comté, Dunkerque, et la moitié de la Flandre; et ce qu'il devait compter pour le plus grand de ses avantages, roi d'une nation alors heureuse, et alors le modèle des autres nations. L'hôtel-de ville de Paris lui déféra quelque temps après le nom de *grand* avec solennité (1680), et ordonna que dorénavant ce titre seul serait employé dans tous les monuments publics.

Ten years of peace followed, during which, however, Louis pursued his policy of aggrandisement, and 'fit de la paix un temps de conquêtes' (Voltaire). The treaty of Westphalia had ceded to France the ill-defined authority of the House of Austria over Alsace. Louis set up *Chambres de Réunion* to interpret the treaty in a sense favourable to France. These Chambers, consisting of members of the parlements of Metz, Breisach, and Besançon, awarded Louis all that remained free in Alsace (except Strasbourg) and a good deal of Lorraine. In 1681, Louis seized Strasbourg and bought Casal (in Piedmont) from the Duke of Mantua. Spain protested, and a minor war followed, as a result of which France gained Luxembourg and Oudenarde by the truce of Ratisbon (1684).

Social life continued to flourish. The great days of the Hôtel de Rambouillet were over, but other salons had taken its place. There was for example, the salon of Mme du Plessis-Guénégaud in the Hôtel de Nevers[1] and at her country seat, the château de Fresnes. Among her guests were Mme de Lafayette, La Rochefoucauld, and Mme de Sévigné; and at the Hôtel de Nevers, Racine is said to have read three and a half acts of his *Alexandre*. M. du Plessis-Guénégaud was a secretary of state, and this salon, which sided with Foucquet against Colbert and was sympathetic to the Jansenists (the Arnaulds were amongst its habitués), was a centre of opposition. It ceased to exist in 1669, when M. du Plessis-Guénégaud was forced to resign his post. Another hostess was Mme de la Sablière, a financier's wife and a cultured woman, who knew Latin and Greek, and was interested in mathematics, science, and astronomy, as well as in poetry and music. Her salon was opposed to Cartesianism and stoicism and favoured the philosophy of Gassendi; and her visitors included the oriental traveller, Bernier, who wrote a summary of Gassendi's philosophy, many scientists, Mme de Sablé, Mme de Lafayette, and La Fontaine – who indeed lived in her house for about twenty years until her death in 1693. Mme de Lafayette was a hostess in her own right, receiving, at her house in the rue de Vaugirard, La Rochefoucauld, La Fontaine, Mme de Sévigné, Huet, Condé, Segrais, and Cardinal de Retz.

There were also 'academies' or societies of men. Ménage used to receive his friends on Wednesdays (his *mercuriales*): Chapelain, Furetière, Conrart, Sarrazin, and Pellisson were members of the group. And Guillaume de Lamoignon, *premier président* of the parlement of Paris, formed an academy in 1667, which met at his house every Monday from five to seven. Its members included Rapin, Boileau, Bouhours, Pellisson, Bourdaloue, Huet, Ménage, Guy Patin and his son, and Bossuet, besides many *gens de robe*. This group, Cartesian in sympathy, comprised both Jesuits and Jansenists.

If this is a period of absolutism and centralization, we must not overlook the other side of the picture. Although a sycophantic attitude towards Louis XIV is sometimes found, there is a good deal of individualism left. Some of the *salons* were opposed

---

[1] There were two Hôtels de Nevers. The other one, that of the duc de Nevers, played an important part in the intrigues against Racine's *Phèdre*.

to the policy of Louis XIV or his ministers. In 1665, a special
court, the Grands Jours, was sent to Auvergne to deal with the
nobles of that province who were particularly lawless, and it is
interesting to see that Louis XIV could not prevail upon the
magistrates of the Grands Jours to accept his nominee as their
chairman. In 1672, maréchal de Bellefonds was disgraced for
flatly refusing, in an interview with Louis XIV, to serve under
Turenne, and two other marshals followed his example.
In 1675, the parish priest of Versailles refused absolution to
Mme de Montespan, the King's mistress; Bossuet upheld the
priest, and — for a time — Louis XIV and Mme de Montespan
separated.

Nor must we overestimate the refinement of the time. The
absent-minded Ménalque in La Bruyère betrays his absent-
mindedness by spitting on the bed, instead of on the floor. Even
at court, manners and morals were far from exemplary. A contemporary observer, Primi Visconti, describes the men stepping
with muddy feet, and without apology, on the skirts of the
women. He notes that Mme Bossuet, Bossuet's niece, lived apart
from her husband, 'comme quasi presque toutes les dames de
Paris'. Gaming was fashionable, and gambling-dens were numerous. A scandal broke out in 1679, when the sorceress, Mme Voisin,
was arrested. In the course of the interrogation, she and her accom-
plices accused many of the greatest figures of French society of
resorting to them for the purchase of poisons, love philtres, and
black masses.

The work of religious reform had largely spent itself by 1660.
It was from 1662 onwards that Rancé undertook the reform of
Notre-Dame de la Trappe in Normandy. Mme de Miramion —
whom Bussy-Rabutin had once kidnapped with a view to
marriage — founded the Miramionnes in 1661 to keep schools and
tend the sick,[2] and in 1666, the Dames de Saint-Maur were
founded for the free education of poor girls. In 1684, Saint Jean-
Baptiste de la Salle founded the Frères des Ecoles chrétiennes
to set up elementary schools for boys and to train teachers. Otherwise there is little to relate.

The persecution of Port-Royal, postponed by the miracle of
the Holy Thorn, began in earnest in 1661. Louis XIV ordered
that the formulary should be signed by monks, priests, and schoolmasters. The two Port-Royals were obliged to send away their
boarders and novices, and the *solitaires* were dispersed once more.
Most of the nuns refused to sign. In 1664, the new Archbishop of

[2] They amalgamated in 1665 with the Filles de Sainte Geneviève, founded
in 1635 by Mlle Blosset.

Paris[3] made an attempt to persuade them to sign: sixteen of the most obstinate were forcibly carried off and placed in other houses, where pressure was brought to bear on them. In July, the nuns of both convents were shut up together at Port-Royal des Champs, deprived of the sacraments, and guarded by sentries so that they could have no communication with the outside world.

... le crime pour lequel il [the Archbishop of Paris] les traitait si rude-ment, était de n'avoir point la créance humaine que des propositions étaient dans un livre qu'elles n'avaient point lu, qu'elles n'étaient point capables de lire, et qu'il n'avait vraisemblablement jamais lu lui-même.

(Racine)

In 1664, Louis XIV resolved to make the signature of the formulary universal, and in 1665 the Pope issued a bull making it the law of the Church. Four French bishops issued pastoral letters allowing members of their diocese to sign with mental reservations. The Pope ordered them to withdraw their per-mission and have the formulary signed 'purement et simplement', and set up a commission of nine bishops to try them. With the death of Alexander VII and the election of a new Pope, Clement IX, however, the way was open for reconciliation. Negotiations between the four bishops and the Holy See were conducted by Arnauld and Mme de Longueville, and agreement was reached (the *Paix de l'Eglise*) in 1668 – or rather appeared to have been reached, for the bishops submitted with reservations, expressed in a letter which the negotiators withheld from the Pope. How-ever, Port-Royal submitted to the Archbishop of Paris, and the persecution ended.

Port-Royal was now left in peace for ten years, during which it was at the height of its influence, receiving visits from far and wide, and enjoying the protection of many great ladies, such as the princesse de Conti and the duchesse de Liancourt. Some resided within the precincts of Port-Royal – Mme de Longue-ville and Mlle de Vertus at Port-Royal des Champs, Mme de Sablé in Paris. Moreover, a member of the Arnauld family, Pomponne, was secretary of state for foreign affairs. Mme de Sévigné, whose uncle built the cloisters of Port-Royal, describes a visit to Port-Royal des Champs in 1674:

Ce Port-Royal est une Thébaïde; c'est le paradis; c'est un désert où toute la dévotion du christianisme s'est rangée; c'est une sainteté répandue dans tout ce pays à une lieue à la ronde. Il y cinq ou six soli-taires qu'on ne connaît point qui vivent comme les pénitents de saint Jean Climaque. Les religieuses sont des anges sur terre. Mlle de Vertus

[3] Port-Royal, a Cistercian convent, had at its own request been removed from the jurisdiction of its order and placed under that of the Archbishop of Paris.

y achève sa vie avec une résignation extrême et des douleurs inconce-
vables: elle ne sera pas en vie dans un mois. Tout ce qui les sert, jusqu'-
aux charretiers, aux bergers, aux ouvriers, tout est saint, tout est modeste.
Je vous avoue que j'ai été ravie de voir cette divine solitude, dont j'avais
tant ouï parler; c'est un vallon affreux, tout propre à faire son salut.

(26 Jan. 1674)

The progress of rationalism continues. In 1660, the parlement
of Paris refused to hear cases of witchcraft. Scholasticism,
Aristotelianism and Thomism were defunct, and theology and
science were free to go their own separate ways. Cartesianism
spread amongst the general public — Rohault's *Physique* (1671),
it has been said, is 'le livre qui a le plus efficacement popularisé
le système cartésien du monde';[4] with Malebranche, it spread
even into theology.

Stoicism, too, had had its day, and gave way to epicureanism.
Gassendi's philosophy was popularized by Bernier's *Abrégé* (1678);
the chief representative of the new hedonistic philosophy of life is
Saint-Evremond. A more pessimistic view of human nature — perhaps due in part to the influence of Jansenism — is evident in the
literature of the period — in La Rochefoucauld, in Mme de Lafayette,
in Racine, in La Fontaine, and in *Le Misanthrope* of Molière.

The *libertins* were silent in this period, but continued to exist.
Bossuet fulminated against them in his funeral oration on Anne
de Gonzague (1685):

Mais qu'ont-ils vu, ces rares génies, qu'ont-ils vu plus que les autres?
Quelle ignorance est la leur! et qu'il serait aisé de les confondre, si,
faibles et présomptueux, ils ne craignaient d'être instruits! Car pensent-
ils avoir mieux vu les difficultés à cause qu'ils y succombent, et que les
autres qui les ont vues, les ont méprisées? Ils n'ont rien vu, ils n'enten-
dent rien; ils n'ont pas même de quoi établir le néant auquel ils espèrent
après cette vie, et ce misérable partage ne leur est pas assuré.

But the nature of *libertinage* was changing:

... des milieux humanistes elle émigre vers les centres de culture scienti-
fique: désormais c'est chez les physiciens, médecins, qu'il faudra chercher ses représentants, et le conflit séculaire qui opposait la raison à la
foi va affronter la religion et la science.[5]

Two imaginary voyages were published, which show how
radically traditional beliefs were being undermined — Gabriel de
Foigny's *Terre Australe connue* (1676 — probably published at
Geneva), and the *Histoire des Sévarambes* of Denis Vairasse or
Veiras. Both these novels enjoyed considerable success — Foigny's
book was republished in Paris in 1692, 1693, and 1705, and at
Amsterdam in 1732 and 1787–9; Veiras's work, the first part

    [4] H. Busson, *La Religion des Classiques*, 1948, p. 70.
    [5] *Ibid.*, p. 393.

of which appeared in London in English in 1675, was reprinted at Brussels in 1682, and at Amsterdam in 1682, 1702, 1716, and 1787. Both must have contributed to the spread of rationalism. Gabriel de Foigny depicts a kind of Utopia, in which a race of hermaphrodites lead a life free of passion in a society based on liberty and equality – all have the same education, and all property is held in common. Revealed religion is ridiculed, the authority of the Old Testament denied, and the religious disputes of Europe criticized. The Australians are deists, but never speak of God, to avoid dissension, since he is incomprehensible. Denis Veiras similarly depicts a country in which all property belongs to the State, in which there is no hereditary nobility and all men are equal. The history of the impostor, Omigas, who passes himself off as the child of the Sun and works sham miracles, is a parody of the life of Christ; like the Australians, the Sévarambes are deists.

At the same time, serious Biblical criticism began in France with Richard Simon, the author of an *Histoire critique du Vieux Testament* (1678) and other similar works. Simon studies the text critically and without respect for preconceived notions. He shows the mistakes of scribes and the improbabilities of the narrative, concluding, for example, from the incoherence of the account of the creation that it was composed at different periods and clumsily touched up. There is no question of divine inspiration.

Ni la philosophie, ni le dogme, ne pesaient sur ses décisions; importaient seulement le manuscrit, l'encre, l'écriture, les caractères, les lettres, les virgules, les points, les accents. La science profane refusait de reconnaître l'autorité sacrée.[6]

Although the classical doctrine which held sway in this period remained unchanged, there are signs of a certain shift of emphasis, of an evolution of taste. There is a tendency to lay less stress on rules, and to attach more importance to the irrational, indefinable, inexplicable quality, the *je ne sais quoi*, which makes a work please the reader. 'Je voudrais bien savoir si la grande règle de toutes les règles n'est pas de plaire, et si une pièce de théâtre qui a attrapé son but n'a pas suivi un bon chemin,' says Dorante in Molière's *Critique de l'Ecole des Femmes*. 'La principale règle est de plaire et de toucher. Toutes les autres ne sont faites que pour parvenir à cette première,' says Racine in the preface to *Bérénice*. 'Mon principal but est toujours de plaire,' wrote La Fontaine in *Psyché*. Even the literary theorists are inclined to agree, albeit reluctantly sometimes. Bouhours

[6] P. Hazard, *La Crise de la conscience européenne*, [1935], p. 188.

devotes one of the *Entretiens d'Ariste et d'Eugène* to the *je ne sais quoi.* 'Ce qui réussit vaut mieux que les règles,' says Méré, a firm upholder of the overriding necessity for *agréments*, both in social life and in literature; for him, neither beauty nor conformity with the rules are sufficient without *agréments*.[7] In the preface to the second part of his *Contes*, La Fontaine excuses the negligence of his style on the grounds that the main thing is 'd'attacher le lecteur, de le réjouir, d'attirer malgré lui son attention, de lui plaire enfin.' He adds:

...le secret de plaire ne consiste pas toujours en l'ajustement, ni même en la régularité: il faut du piquant et de l'agréable, si l'on veut toucher. Combien voyons-nous de ces beautés régulières qui ne touchent point, et dont personne n'est amoureux?

He inserted into *Psyché* the allegory of Anaphrodite and Aphrodisée to illustrate this point.[8] Rapin, who says that a work can only please if it obeys the rules, nevertheless admits that 'l'avantage du génie est toujours préférable à celui de l'art,' and says:

Il y a encore dans la poésie, comme dans les autres arts, de certaines choses ineffables, et qu'on ne peut expliquer: ces choses en sont comme les mystères. Il n'y a point de préceptes, pour enseigner ces grâces secrètes, ces charmes imperceptibles, et tous ces agréments cachés de la poésie qui vont au cœur.

(He is inclined to attribute them to arrangement.) Boileau was deeply preoccupied with this very problem.

At the same time, there is a growing preference for simplicity, associated with good taste. Rapin and Bouhours, Méré and Boileau condemn the *pointes*, the elaborate and far-fetched metaphors, the bombast of some of the writers of the earlier seventeenth century; Balzac's reputation is on the wane. Bouhours formulates the ideal of the new generation:

...le beau langage ressemble à une eau pure et nette qui n'a point de goût, qui coule de source, qui va où sa pente naturelle la porte, et non pas à ces eaux artificielles qu'on fait venir avec violence dans les jardins des grands et qui y font mille différentes figures.

In another *Entretien*, he writes:

Car enfin on veut aujourd'hui dans le langage des qualités qu'il est assez difficile d'allier ensemble: une grande facilité et une grande exactitude; des paroles harmonieuses, mais pleines de sens; de la brièveté et de la clarté; une expression fort simple, et en même temps fort noble; une

[7] For Saint-Evremond's views, see below, p. 304.
[8] 'Il semble qu'un caprice de la nature fasse naître les agréments de l'irrégularité, et que les beautés achevées qui ont toujours de quoi se faire admirer, aient rarement le secret de savoir plaire.'
(Saint-Evremond, *Idée de la femme, qui ne se trouve point*)

extrême pureté, une naïveté admirable, et avec cela je ne sais quoi de fin et de piquant.

Méré denounces affectation and *éclat*: 'il faut que tout soit tempéré pour être agréable'. He prefers the *joli* and the *délicat* to beauty and magnificence, and he affirms that Caesar's greatness is revealed by the simplicity, not the pomposity, of his style – we are here close to Boileau's conception of the sublime. Rapin's views are similar: 'La simplicité soutenue d'un grand sens, et de quelque air de majesté, est à mon avis la souveraine perfection du discours,' he writes, speaking of oratory. Poetic style, he affirms, besides being correct and clear, should be natural, simple, and unaffected, and yet noble, elevated, and *nombreuse*. In addition, 'il faut surtout qu'il règne dans le discours un certain air de grâce et de délicatesse, qui en fasse le principal ornement, et la beauté la plus universelle'.

The writers of the period from 1660 to 1685 are more supple, have a lighter touch, than their predecessors. Their style tends to be more graceful, lighter, more varied in tone, wittier, less monumental: in this respect, the *Provinciales* already belong to the new age. The prose of Mme de Sévigné, of Mme de Lafayette, of La Fontaine, of *Le Comte de Gabalis*, the dialogue of Molière, the verse of Racine and La Fontaine illustrate the point. Form, too, tends to be more flexible. Méré insists that art and arrangement should be concealed, that negligence is better than studied regularity; and, indeed, it is not always easy to follow the sequence of his thought. Racine borrows Corneille's technique, but conceals the reversals of the situation and the surprises to such an extent that he has been thought to have no interest in plot; Molière's plots are slighter than those of his forerunners and have similarly been thought defective.

Strains that were separate in the previous period tend to merge in this. The ideal world of *L'Astrée* was sharply divided from the crude realism of the satires of Régnier or the burlesque of Scarron and Thomas Corneille, for example. Now, on the one hand, grotesque caricatures tend to disappear:

> Nous avons changé de méthode:
> Jodelet n'est plus à la mode,
> Et maintenant il ne faut pas
> Quitter la nature d'un pas,

wrote La Fontaine in 1661 after seeing Molière's *Fâcheux*. On the other, psychological truth and realism banished the romance: of Mlle de Scudéry's *Clélie*, Donneau de Visé wrote, in 1663,

Ce n'est que par là qu'on réussit présentement; décrire ce qui se dit et ce qui se fait tous les jours, et le bien représenter, c'est avoir trouvé l'unique et véritable moyen de plaire. Il n'y a maintenant que ces tableaux qui soient non seulement de vente, mais même de grand prix, l'on n'en achète point d'autres, et le peintre et le marchand les vendent ce qu'ils veulent; ce qui montre que les choses les plus fortes et les plus relevées ne sont plus en crédit, que l'on n'aime que les plus communes, bien exprimées, et que l'on ne veut plus rien que de naturel.

In Molière, in Boileau, in La Fontaine, humour and psychological truth, realism and fancy, high life and low life are united in a blend which respects decency.

All this is, perhaps, a way of saying that *honnêteté* and literature are more intimately associated than previously. On the whole, the writers of the preceding period were not *honnêtes hommes*; most of the writers of the classical period were. Corneille lived most of his life in Rouen, lacked the social graces, and kept himself to himself; Descartes spent most of his life outside France; Pascal was a savant, and, if we are to believe Méré, something of a pedant until his eyes were opened during a journey he made early in the 'fifties with the duc de Roannez and Méré. Racine, on the other hand, was a courtier; so was Boileau; so was Molière. All three lived on intimate terms with the great; so did La Fontaine, if he was not actually a courtier. La Rochefoucauld, Mme de Lafayette, and Mme de Sévigné were themselves of noble rank. The connection between *honnêteté* and literature is most evident in the writings of Méré, who, concerned as he is with defining the qualities of the *honnête homme*, is naturally led to discuss how the *honnête homme* should speak and write.

Classicism, however, was far from universal, even in the so-called classical period. Machine plays and operas enjoyed an enormous popularity, and some critics feared lest the vogue of opera might put an end to regular tragedy:

… la fantaisie des opéra de musique, dont le peuple et même la plupart des honnêtes gens se sont laissés entêter, sera peut-être capable dans la suite de décourager les esprits pour la tragédie, si l'on ne pense à les exciter par la gloire et par la récompense. C'est à ceux qui gouvernent à y penser.[9]　　　　　　　　　　　　　　　　　　　　　　　　　(Rapin)

Thomas Corneille and Donneau de Visé wrote a highly successful machine play, *La Devineresse,* in 1679, on the occasion of the arrest of Mme Voisin. It is about a sorceress, Mme Jobin. In Act III, parts of a body fall down the chimney; Mme Jobin makes a sign, and the stage direction reads:

Le tonnerre et les éclairs redoublent, et pendant ce temps les parties du corps s'approchent et se rejoignent. Le corps se lève, marche et vient jusqu'au milieu du théâtre. Le corps s'abîme dans le milieu du théâtre.

This play was appreciated by the same public as *Phèdre.*

　　[9] 'Ce qui me fâche le plus de l'entêtement où l'on est pour l'opéra, c'est qu'il va ruiner la tragédie' … 　　　　　(Saint-Evremond, *Sur les opéra*)

It was in this period, too, that there took place the first pre-liminary skirmishes of the battle between the ancients and the moderns. Controversy centred on three points: the Christian epic, the superiority of the French language to Latin, and the general superiority of the moderns.

The Christian epic was a manifestation of the spirit of the Counter-Reformation and of baroque. Tasso led the way with his *Gerusalemme Liberata*, and in seventeenth-century England Milton wrote *Paradise Lost* and *Paradise Regained*. A score of French epics were written, from Le Moyne's *Saint Louis* and Saint-Amant's *Moïse Sauvé* (both 1653) to the revised edition of Desmarets de Saint-Sorlin's *Clovis* and L'Abbé's *Eustachius* in 1673. Some—Boileau, for example, in the *Art poétique*—con-demned the theory of the Christian epic with the *merveilleux chrétien*, and regarded the *merveilleux païen* as more suitable for poetic effect. The principle of the Christian epic was upheld by Desmarets de Saint-Sorlin,[10] by abbé de Marolles in his *Traité du poème épique* (1662), by Louis le Laboureur in the preface to his epic, *Charlemagne* (1664), and rather later by Charles Perrault, who, in 1686, published a poem, *Saint-Paulin*, using the *merveilleux chrétien*, and attacked the *merveilleux païen*.

As regards the second point, Louis le Laboureur in 1669 published a book entitled *Avantages de la langue française sur la langue latine*, maintaining the superiority of contemporary French over Latin poetry. Bouhours in one of the *Entretiens d'Ariste et d'Eugène* asserted that the French language was superior to all others, including Greek and Latin, and that French literature was in most genres the equal of the literatures of antiquity. In 1676, the Académie des Inscriptions et Médailles discussed whether the inscription on a triumphal arch should be in French or Latin. The outcome of the controversy was two works by Charpentier, *Défense de la langue française* (1676) and *De l'Excellence de la langue française* (1683).

There was a growing feeling that seventeenth-century France was no wit inferior to the ancients. Furetière attacked humanism in his *Nouvelle allégorique* (1659). Both Marolles and Le Laboureur, in defending the Christian epic, rejected the authority of the ancients and the imitation of antiquity. Desmarets de Saint-Sor-lin attacked the ancients in his *Comparaison de la langue et de la poésie françaises avec la langue et la poésie grecques et latines* (1670), in his *Traité pour juger des poètes grecs, latins et français* (published with *Clovis*, 1673), and in his *Défense de la poésie et de*

[10] *Clovis* (1657); *Marie-Magdelaine* (with a preface; 1669); preface to the revised edition of *Clovis* (1673).

*la langue françaises* (1675). Charpentier asserted, in his *De l'Excellence de la langue française*, that French literature was as good as Latin literature, and that 'notre siècle est plus éclairé que le leur'. Pierre Perrault criticized the *Alcestis* of Euripides in his *Critique de l'Opéra* (1674), and attacked the ancients in the preface to his translation of Tassoni's *Secchia rapita* (1678). The ancient philosophers, especially Aristotle and the stoics, were somewhat roughly handled in Malebranche's *Recherche de la Vérité* (1675), and the ancients were depicted in an unfavourable light in Bayle's *Pensées diverses sur la comète* (1682), which dwells on their superstition and idolatry, on the absurdity of their religious beliefs. In one of Fontenelle's *Dialogues des Morts* (1683), Socrates declares that men are the same in all ages: 'Ce qui fait d'ordinaire qu'on est si prévenu pour l'antiquité, c'est qu'on a du chagrin contre son siècle, et l'antiquité en profite'; in another, in anticipation of the *Histoire des Oracles*, Montezuma criticizes the *sottises* – the superstitious credulity – of the Greeks and the Romans.

The defenders of the ancients partly compensated for their lack of numbers by their authority. Boileau came down on the side of the ancients in 1674, with his translation of Longinus and his *Art poétique*:

> Entre ces deux excès la route est difficile.
> Suivez, pour la trouver, Théocrite et Virgile:
> Que leurs tendres écrits, par les Grâces dictés,
> Ne quittent point vos mains, jour et nuit feuilletés.

Racine answered Pierre Perrault's strictures on Euripides in the preface to his *Iphigénie* (1675). But Boileau and Racine were in a minority in the Academy.[11]

If one of the bases of French classicism, respect for the ancients and the principle of imitation of antiquity, was being more and more undermined, a number of baroque features still survive in the works of the writers of this period. Indeed it has been said that French classicism is a 'classicisme de coloration baroque'.[12]

The stock theme of the inconstancy of fortune keeps recurring:

> ... d'autres la consolèrent sur l'inconstance de la fortune ...
> (Furetière, *Le Roman bourgeois*)

> Jusques ici la fortune ne m'avait pas montré son inconstance; mais elle me fit bientôt voir qu'elle ne se fixe pour personne.
> (Mme de Lafayette, *Zaïde*)

Fate produces paradoxical situations. In Molière's *Dépit amoureux*, Ascagne has married Valère without his knowing it – he thinks he has married someone different; in *L'Avare*, Harpagon and

[11] For Saint-Evremond's views, see below, pp. 334–5.
[12] J. Rousset, *La littérature de l'âge baroque en France*, 1954, p. 233.

Anselme are both rivals of their sons in love. Paradox is an important element in Racine. *Alexandre* and *Andromaque* both treat the theme of the captor-captive. *Britannicus* is full of paradox: '*Britannicus* sets in motion a chain of ironies; the unnatural mother expectant of natural devotion in her son, the poisoner dismayed at the poisoning of her protégé...'[13] The situation of *Bérénice — invitus invitam —* is essentially paradoxical; so is that of Phèdre, virtuous and incestuous. Human inconstancy is treated as well as the inconstancy of fate, e.g. by La Rochefoucauld and by Boileau (Satire VIII). Molière's *Dom Juan*, not only treats the theme of inconstancy in love, but introduces a supernatural dénouement and does not observe the unities.

The problem of illusion and reality remains a fundamental one; appearances frequently turn out to be false. In Molière's *Sganarelle*, Sganarelle and his wife each think the other unfaithful: they are misled by appearances. *Dom Garcie* is a more serious treatment of the same theme. The falseness of appearances is the central theme of La Rochefoucauld's *Maximes*; and La Fontaine treats it in some of his fables:[14] *Le Chameau et les bâtons flottants* (IV, 10) is indeed more of a discourse on this subject than a fable. Disguise is common enough in Molière, and not merely as a device to help on the plot. It is the basic theme of the *Précieuses ridicules*, in which the valets, Mascarille and Jodelet, masquerade as noblemen, and are not detected by the two *précieuses*. Here, not only have we a paradoxical situation, but we are close to the burlesque of Scarron and Thomas Corneille. Religious hypocrisy is the theme of *Tartuffe* (and recurs in *Dom Juan*), social hypocrisy that of *Le Misanthrope*. In *Amphitryon*, a play on a subject already treated by Rotrou, there is a real confusion of identities: Amphitryon and Sosie return from the wars to find their places taken by Jupiter and Mercury, who have assumed their outward appearance. Hermione, in *Andromaque*, is a hypocrite of another kind:

> Hermione, Seigneur, au moins en apparence,
> Semble de son amant dédaigner l'inconstance,
> Et croit que trop heureux de fléchir sa rigueur
> Il la viendra presser de reprendre son cœur.
> Mais je l'ai vue enfin me confier ses larmes.
> Elle pleure en secret le mépris de ses charmes.

Hypocrisy is important in *Britannicus*:

> dans cette cour
> Combien tout ce qu'on dit est loin de ce qu'on pense!

The stage on the stage is seen in Molière, notably of course in the *Impromptu de Versailles* (a play introducing a play), but

[13] J. C. Lapp, *Aspects of Racinian Tragedy*, 1955, p. 11.
[14] E.g. IV, 14; V, 21; VI, 5 and 17; VIII, 23; XI, 7.

elsewhere, too, in a different form. There are several allusions in Molière's plays to Molière or his characters: Philinte, for example, compares Alceste and himself to Sganarelle and Ariste in the *Ecole des Maris*. Similarly, La Fontaine sometimes gives us a fable within a fable (VIII, 4, 18; X, 9; XI, 5).

The uncertainty of human judgment and the irrationality of mankind is a theme of La Rochefoucauld, and of Boileau (Satires IV and VIII). One of La Fontaine's fables illustrates the fact that standards of beauty differ (V, 18).

Taken aback by a change in his friend's fortunes, the hermit in one of La Fontaine's fables wonders whether he is waking or dreaming:

> Veillé-je? et n'est-ce point un songe que je vois?
>
> (X, 9)

'Je doute si je veille', says Monime in *Mithridate*, and Achille in *Iphigénie* inquires: 'Veillé-je? ou n'est-ce point un songe?' Aricie in *Phèdre* asks similarly: 'Veillé-je? Puis-je croire un semblable dessein?', and Thésée says:

> Je ne sais où je vais, je ne sais où je suis.

As for stylistic features, Molière often uses double-entendre and characters talking at cross-purposes. Paradox is common enough in the classical writers:

La passion fait souvent un fou du plus habile homme, et rend souvent les plus sots habiles.                                  (La Rochefoucauld)

> Ne me trompent jamais, en me mentant toujours.
>
> (La Fontaine, VII, 17)

> Il peut, Seigneur, il peut dans ce désordre extrême,
> Epouser ce qu'il hait, et punir ce qu'il aime.
>
> (*Andromaque*)

> Je l'aime, je le fuis; Titus m'aime, il me quitte.
>
> (*Bérénice*)

> Mon unique espérance est dans mon désespoir.[15]
>
> (*Bajazet*)

Racine is fond of word echoes, too:

> Une femme mourante et qui cherche à mourir.[16]
>
> (*Phèdre*)

[15] Cf. *Le Cid*:
> Ma plus douce espérance est de perdre l'espoir.

[16] There are direct references to echoes in *Phèdre*:
> Les forêts de nos cris moins souvent retentissent.

> Mes seuls gémissements font retentir les bois ...

> De nos cris douloureux la plaine retentit ...

Affinities between Racine and the baroque artists have been noted. Baroque chiaroscuro occurs in some of his descriptions – e.g. the description of Pyrrhus entering the palace of Troy:

> Songe, songe, Céphise, à cette nuit cruelle
> Qui fut pour tout un peuple une nuit éternelle.
> Figure-toi Pyrrhus, les yeux étincelants,
> Entrant à la lueur de nos palais brûlants,
> Sur tous mes frères morts se faisant un passage . . .
> *(Andromaque)*

Here there is a double contrast: light is contrasted both with night and with the night of death. There are, too, the description of Junie, arriving by night in Nero's palace ('les ombres, les flambeaux'), and that of Titus in *Bérénice*:

> De cette nuit, Phénice, as-tu vu la splendeur?
> Tes yeux ne sont-ils pas tout pleins de sa grandeur?
> Ces flambeaux, ce bûcher, cette nuit enflammée . . .

Here, too, Racine gives Titus the same majesty, the same super-human greatness that baroque painters give their kings. Like the baroque painters, too, Racine likes to open up perspectives. *Britannicus* ends with a hint of the future evolution of Nero, and, in other plays, Racine is fond of suggesting the infinity of the sea behind the restricted setting. It has been remarked, too, that there is in Racine the equivalent of the mirror technique of baroque painters. In the first scene of *Phèdre*, Hippolyte recalls his father's early life, as related by Théramène:

> Tu me contais alors l'histoire de mon père.
> Tu sais combien mon âme, attentive à ta voix,
> S'échauffait au récit de ses nobles exploits,
> Quand tu me dépeignais ce héros intrépide . . .
> . . . . . .
> Mais quand tu me récitais des faits moins glorieux,
> . . . . . .
> Tu sais comme à regret écoutant ce discours,
> Je te pressais souvent d'en abréger le cours . . .

Here the facts of Thésée's life are blended with the spectacle of Théramène relating them, and with the attitude to them of Hippolyte, now seized with admiration, now shocked and disgusted.

*Chapter* 13

# MOLIÈRE

JEAN-BAPTISTE POQUELIN DE MOLIÈRE (1622–73), the son of a wealthy bourgeois, joined a company of actors (the Illustre Théâtre) which was formed in Paris in 1643, and when it came to grief the following year, he became a member of a provincial company. In 1658, now the director of his company, he returned to Paris, played before the King, was allowed to share a theatre with the Italians,[1] and established himself in the capital with the patronage of Monsieur frère du Roi and later of the King himself. There were thus, besides the Italians, three French companies now in the capital.[2] Many of Molière's plays were written for the court or first performed there. He died on the night of 17–18 February 1673, a few hours after playing the title rôle in *Le Malade imaginaire*. After his death, his company and that of the Marais theatre were amalgamated: the theatre in the Palais-Royal was given to Lully as an opera house, and the new company played in the rue Guénégaud.[3] The two remaining French companies combined in 1680 to form the Comédie-Française.

Molière's career as a dramatist falls roughly into three parts. The first, the period up to and including *Les Fâcheux*, is a period of trial and error, of experiment. Molière began by writing short one-act farces, two of which—*La Jalousie du Barbouillé* and *Le Médecin volant*—survive. His first biographer, Grimarest, tells us that these farces provided him with a store of subjects for later plays, and that is certainly true of the two extant. *La*

[1] It was in the Hôtel du Petit-Bourbon, near the Louvre. When it was demolished in 1660 to make way for extensions to the Louvre, Molière and the Italians moved to the Palais-Royal.

[2] The Italians enjoyed a royal pension of 15,000 livres; the Hôtel de Bourgogne one of 12,000; and the Marais theatre one of 6,000. Molière's company was, in 1665, granted a pension of 6,000 livres, which was later increased to 7,000.

Other companies appeared from time to time—e.g. the Comédiens de Mademoiselle played in Paris, in 1660 and 1661, and a Spanish company from 1660 to 1673. The Académie d'opéra was founded in 1669 for opera; it became the Académie royale de musique in 1672.

[3] In 1677, the Confrérie de la Passion was abolished and its property given to the Hôpital général, to which the Hôtel de Bourgogne's rent was now paid.

212

*Jalousie du Barbouillé* is a preliminary sketch of *George Dandin*, and the scene with the doctor resembles the Métaphraste scene in *Le Dépit amoureux*. *Le Médecin volant* resembles *Le Médecin malgré lui*, and one scene in it is reminiscent of the scene in *Le Malade imaginaire* in which Toinette appears both as herself and as a doctor. While Molière was still in the provinces, he wrote two five-act comedies in verse, based on Italian originals. *L'Etourdi* (1655), is an intrigue play, set in Messina, with no attempt at realism. It shows how the valet, Mascarille, devises eleven schemes to further his master's amorous designs, each one of which is frustrated by his master's *étourderie*. The play is thus a *comédie de caractère* of a kind; and its construction – an episode repeated over and over with variations – is one of which Molière remained fond. Moreover, the valet, Mascarille, played by Molière wearing a mask, figures again in *Le Dépit amoureux* – in other words, Molière, like Jodelet or the Italian actors, had some idea of creating a stage personality for himself. *Le Dépit amoureux* (1656), set in Paris, is interesting above all for the scenes to which it owes its name (those in which the lover and his mistress fall out and are reconciled); they show that Molière had already achieved a high degree of comic technique, and they recur in *Tartuffe* and *Le Bourgeois gentilhomme*.[4]

Back in Paris, Molière wrote two one-act farces, *Les Précieuses ridicules* and *Sganarelle*. *Les Précieuses* (1659) is the first really characteristic play of Molière, and a masterpiece. It is a topical comedy, and a lively satire on contemporary manners; it raises problems, and shows two opposing attitudes to them; and it is extremely funny. In *Sganarelle* (1660), another one-act play, this time in verse, Molière drops the part of Mascarille and resumes that of Sganarelle, who had already figured in *Le Médecin volant*. As Sganarelle, Molière wore no mask, but blackened his eyebrows and moustache. Sganarelle had a longer life than Mascarille, appearing in five further plays after *Sganarelle*.[5]

These two plays were followed by a *comédie héroïque*, *Dom Garcie de Navarre* (1661), in five acts and in verse. This work, which treats the same theme as *Sganarelle* – jealousy aroused by a series of false appearances –, is a serious comedy of the kind written by Thomas Corneille. It did not succeed, and was dropped after seven performances; and Molière did not repeat the experiment, though parts of *Dom Garcie* passed into subsequent plays, notably *Le Misanthrope*. Instead, he returned to comedy – his own kind of comedy – with two three-act plays in verse, *L'Ecole des*

[4] Act I, scene 3 anticipates the *scène des marquis* in *Le Misanthrope*.
[5] *L'Ecole des Maris, Le Mariage forcé, Dom Juan, L'Amour médecin*, and *Le Médecin malgré lui*.

*Maris* (1661) and *Les Fâcheux* (1661). The former, another play
raising a problem and showing opposing attitudes to it, is the first
play to contain a *raisonneur*, i.e. a character expressing a moderate, common-sense attitude (Ariste's balanced view is clearly right,
and Sganarelle's absurd; whereas in *Les Précieuses*, the earthy,
practical attitude of Gorgibus is no less comic than the romantic
notions of the two girls). *Les Fâcheux*, which was performed at
Vaux and aroused the enthusiasm of La Fontaine there, is a series
of character-sketches, and may also be regarded as the origin
of a new genre created by Molière – the *comédie-ballet*. The acts
of this play are separated by *ballets*, and, in the *Avertissement*,
Molière shows his awareness of the lack of unity due to divided
authorship:

> Le dessein était de donner un ballet aussi; et comme il n'y avait
> qu'un petit nombre choisi de danseurs excellents, on fut contraint de
> séparer les entrées de ce ballet, et l'avis fut de les jeter dans les entr'-
> actes de la comédie, afin que ces intervalles donnassent temps aux mêmes
> baladins de revenir sous d'autres habits: de sorte que, pour ne point
> rompre aussi le fil de la pièce par ces manières d'intermèdes, on s'avisa de
> les coudre au sujet du mieux que l'on put, et de ne faire qu'une seule
> chose du ballet et de la comédie; mais comme le temps était fort préci-
> pité, et que tout cela ne fut pas réglé entièrement par une même tête,
> on trouvera peut-être quelques endroits du ballet qui n'entrent pas dans
> la comédie aussi naturellement que d'autres. Quoi qu'il en soit, c'est un
> mélange qui est nouveau pour nos théâtres, et dont on pourrait chercher
> quelques autorités dans l'antiquité; et comme tout le monde l'a trouvé
> agréable, il peut servir d'idée à d'autres choses qui pourraient être médi-
> tées avec plus de loisir.

The second period opens with *L'Ecole des Femmes* (1662) and
closes with *Le Misanthrope* (1666). *L'Ecole des Femmes* is the
first great, full-length comedy of Molière's career. Besides being
in five acts and in verse, and discussing a problem, it contains
the first fully developed comic character, Arnolphe. Its success
provoked a number of attacks, to which Molière replied by his
brilliant *Critique de L'Ecole des Femmes* (1663) and his *Impromptu de Versailles* (1663). *L'Ecole des Femmes* was followed
by character comedies, *Tartuffe* (1664), *Dom Juan* (1665), and *Le
Misanthrope* (1666), interspersed with a one-act farce, *Le Mariage
forcé* (1664), and two *comédies-ballets*, *La Princess d'Elide* (1664)
and *L'Amour médecin* (1665). The three character comedies of
this period form a group apart in Molière's work, in that they are
the least comic of Molière's comedies and that they are all three
enigmatic and controversial, giving rise to different and conflicting
interpretations. Molière, says Brunetière, with exaggeration, but
not wholly without truth,

> a voulu faire 'autre chose' que dans *l'Ecole des Femmes*; il a voulu rap-
> procher la comédie de la réalité de la vie, la rendre 'sérieuse' en ne lui

ôtant rien de ce qu'elle comportait de 'plaisant'; il a voulu lui faire porter, en quelque sorte, plus de pensée qu'elle n'en avait soutenu jusqu'alors; il a voulu, conformément à l'ambition qu'il avait exprimée dans la *Critique de l'Ecole des Femmes*, l'égaler à la tragédie pour l'importance des intérêts qui s'y agitaient; et nous disons qu'étant Molière, s'il n'y a pas réussi, c'est que son génie s'est heurté aux bornes infranchissables du 'genre' [ . . . ] *Le Misanthrope* et *Tartuffe* sont déjà des tragédies bourgeoises que Molière a vainement essayé de faire entrer dans le cadre de la comédie.[6]

Let us, however, immediately dismiss the suggestion that these three plays are failures. It is, perhaps, precisely to the fact that they are enigmatic that they owe their suggestiveness and their appeal – like *Hamlet*.

After *Le Misanthrope*, Molière concentrated more on amusing his audience, and wrote the funniest, most extravagant works of his whole career. If we exclude a number of court entertainments of a somewhat special nature (*Mélicerte, pastorale héroïque*, 1666; *La Pastorale comique*, a ballet, 1667; *Les Amants magnifiques*, 1670; *Psyché, tragédie-ballet*, 1671), the bulk of Molière's work in this period consists of comedies or *comédies-ballets* in one act (*Le Sicilien*, 1667; *La Comtesse d'Escarbagnas*, 1671) or in three acts (*Le Médecin malgré lui*, 1666; *Amphitryon*, 1668; *George Dandin*, 1668; *Monsieur de Pourceaugnac*, 1669; *Les Fourberies de Scapin*, 1671; *Le Malade imaginaire*, 1673). There are only three five-act comedies in this period: *L'Avare* in prose (1668), *Le Bourgeois gentilhomme* (1670), which is a *comédie-ballet* in prose, and which rather looks as if it had been originally planned as a three-act play, and *Les Femmes savantes* (1671). The ballet element is considerable in the plays of this last period, the majority of which are in prose.

Two features strike one immediately in Molière's production. The first is its great variety – ranging as it does from farce, through *comédie-ballet*, comedy of manners, and character comedy, to *tragédie-ballet*. The second is the simplicity, or rather the tenuousness, of the structure. Broadly speaking, from this point of view, Molière's plays fall into two groups. In the first, one action is simply repeated over and over. *L'Etourdi*, as we have seen, is an early example of this kind of play; but the same kind of structure is found in *Dom Garcie, Les Fâcheux, L'Ecole des Maris, L'Ecole des Femmes, Le Misanthrope* (Alceste waiting to have an interview with Célimène is repeatedly interrupted, like the lover in *Les Fâcheux*), and *George Dandin*. In the second – which may overlap with the first – the framework is provided by a slender plot: a girl's father or mother wishes her to marry, not her lover, but a rival, the

[6] F. Brunetière, *Etudes critiques*, vol. 8, pp. 113–14 and 116–17.

two young lovers being united at the end as the result of a trick or the discovery of the lover's real identity. Such, with some variations, are *L'Ecole des Femmes, L'Amour médecin, Tartuffe, L'Avare, Le Bourgeois gentilhomme, Les Fourberies de Scapin, Les Femmes savantes,* and *Le Malade imaginaire.* Molière often makes it clear that he is using a theatrical convention which he does not intend to be taken seriously.

> Si j'ai plutôt qu'aucun un tel moyen trouvé,
> Pour les ressusciter sur ce qu'il a rêvé,
> C'est qu'en fait d'aventure il est très ordinaire
> De voir gens pris sur mer par quelque Turc corsaire,
> Puis être à leur famille à point nommé rendus,
> Après quinze ou vingt ans qu'on les a crus perdus.
> Pour moi, j'ai vu déjà cent contes de la sorte.
> Sans nous alambiquer, servons-nous-en ; qu'importe ?

says Mascarille in *L'Etourdi* (IV, 1). In *L'Ecole des Femmes,* the discovery of Agnès's real identity is announced in a series of couplets spoken by Chrysalde and Oronte alternately. Introducing the trick he intends to play on M. Jourdain, Covielle admits: 'Tout cela sent un peu sa comédie.' The discovery of the real identity of Valère and Marianne in *L'Avare* is too rapidly narrated for any importance to be attached to it. At the end of *La Comtesse d'Escarbagnas,* the vicomte receives news that he is to marry Julie and tells the comtesse, 'si vous m'en croyez, pour rendre la comédie complète de tout point, vous épouserez Monsieur Tibaudier, et donnerez Mademoiselle Andrée à son laquais, dont il fera son valet de chambre'.

Molière's main preoccupation is clearly not with the plot, but with other things, with four other things to be precise: with entertaining his audience, with studying his characters, with depicting reality, and with provoking thought. It is here that his originality lies.

Molière's plays are comic, as anyone who has ever seen one on the stage knows. This, on the whole, as we have seen, was something new in the seventeenth-century theatre; and it seems likely that Molière learned something, at least, of his comic technique from the Italian actors with whom he shared a theatre in Paris and whose speciality was the *commedia dell'arte* or improvised comedy, with its stock types and its mime. Molière is said to have attended their performances assiduously, and Le Boulanger de Chalussay in his *Elomire* [an anagram of Molière] *hypocondre* (1670) writes:

> Par exemple, Elomire
> Veut se rendre parfait dans l'art de faire rire,
> Que fait-il, le matois, dans ce hardi dessein ?
> Chez le grand Scaramouche il va soir et matin.

Là, le miroir en main et ce grand homme en face,
Il n'est contorsion, posture ni grimace
Que ce grand écolier du plus grand des bouffons
Ne fasse et ne refasse en cent et cent façons.

Be that as it may, Molière, with his puns and word play and his verbal virtuosity, exploiting the comic effects of dress and of physical peculiarities, revelling in the tricks and pranks of valets, arousing laughter by showing men behaving as automata or by a sudden anticlimax, is a master of almost every form of comic technique.

It has sometimes been observed that tragedy is latent in Molière's plays – some of them at least –, since the monomania of the main character threatens to destroy his family and ruin the lives of those dependent on him. Too much must not be made of this: the latent tragedy is not stressed; the main characters are comic and ineffectual, not monstrous; any scene that borders on the serious is followed by a comic one; and the happy dénouement is usually not in doubt – Dorine, in *Tartuffe* (II, 4), suggests to Mariane several ways of avoiding the marriage with Tartuffe; two means of bringing about a happy ending are suggested in *L'Avare*; and Eraste, in *Monsieur de Pourceaugnac*, tells Julie: 'déjà nous avons préparé un bon nombre de batteries pour renverser ce dessein ridicule'.

Molière developed the character comedy which had only occasionally and tentatively been attempted in the earlier seventeenth century. Such characters as Arnolphe in *L'Ecole des Femmes*, Orgon and Tartuffe in *Tartuffe*, Don Juan, Alceste in *Le Misanthrope*, Harpagon in *L'Avare*, M. Jourdain in *Le Bourgeois gentilhomme*, Philaminte in *Les Femmes savantes*, and Argan in *Le Malade imaginaire* are something quite new on the stage. Such characters – Tartuffe, Don Juan, and Alceste stand somewhat apart from the rest – are the victims of an obsession or a monomania, which prevents them from seeing the world as it is, from viewing life whole. Arnolphe's fear of cuckoldry, Orgon's religiosity and his gullibility, Harpagon's love of money, M. Jourdain's aspirations to be a nobleman, Philaminte's preoccupation with learning and belles-lettres, Argan's obsession with disease, prevent them from forming balanced judgments and living life to the full. Such characters verge on caricature, but they remain human. Sometimes they show human inconsistencies, as when Tartuffe, Alceste, or Harpagon fall in love, and yet retain their essential characteristics when they are in love – Tartuffe is still a religious hypocrite when he is in love, as Alceste is a misanthropist and Harpagon a miser. Sometimes, they show human or noble traits. Dorante in the *Critique de l'Ecole des*

*Femmes*, in answer to the criticism that Arnolphe was not wholly ridiculous, remarks: 'il n'est pas incompatible qu'une personne soit ridicule en de certaines choses et honnête homme en d'autres.' Arnolphe treats Horace with generosity, and some readers feel sympathy when he is compelled to acknowledge that he loves Agnès in defiance of his principles (III, 5). M. Jourdain has a childlike and naïve delight in his purchases and acquirements which makes him lovable for all his silliness. Philaminte nobly practises her stoicism at the end of the play, when she believes herself ruined. And, of course, two of Molière's characters are so complex that agreement will no doubt never be reached when and how far they are comic: Don Juan and Alceste. Alceste is ridiculous in some ways, but, even if his ideal of sincerity is shown to be impracticable, he certainly enjoys his creator's sympathy in his aspirations and his sufferings. Don Juan has many noble qualities (courage, intelligence, wit, generosity), and at many points of the play we laugh with him rather than at him.

Molière, too, in many of his plays, raises and discusses problems and provokes thought: this again is, on the whole, a new feature in French comedy. Moreover, an attitude to these problems, a philosophy of life, does seem to emerge from his plays. This has been denied, on the grounds that what appears to be Molière's philosophy does not square altogether with what we know of his own life, that the commonsense outlook and the doctrine of moderation which we find in some plays are banal and unworthy of Molière, and that Molière was a busy actor and producer with no time to think of anything but entertaining his audience. To which it may be replied, that to fail to practise what one preaches is human; that common sense, though unfashionable, perhaps, nowadays, was not mistrusted in the seventeenth century; that moderation was certainly a doctrine of which the exuberant and eccentric characters of the age were in need; that Molière, in common with his contemporaries, held that art should combine pleasure with instruction; and that — as Brunetière says — 'Molière ne serait pas Molière s'il n'avait pensé quelquefois'.[7]

To judge, then, by the butts of his humour, Molière is opposed to affectation and insincerity, and in favour — like La Rochefoucauld — of sincerity, genuineness, naturalness. He ridicules the affectation of the *marquis* and in *Les Femmes savantes* of the poems of Trissotin, and the hypocrisy of Tartuffe. He makes fun of those who cannot come to terms with life — of the *précieuses* in *Les Précieuses ridicules,* with their romantic notions derived from books, of monomaniacs like Harpagon, and so forth. He

[7] F. Brunetière, *Etudes critiques,* vol. 4, p. 179.

makes fun of pedants and of theorists whose theories do not fit
the facts. 'Vous êtes dévot, et vous vous emportez!' Dorine
mocks Orgon in *Tartuffe*. In *Le Bourgeois gentilhomme*, the
music master and the dancing master claim that the arts they
teach bring harmony and peace, and immediately afterwards
fight with the philosophy master, who claims that philosophy can
eradicate anger. Similarly, Nicole, who has had no lessons in
fencing, worsts M. Jourdain, who tries to apply the rules he has
just learnt.

Molière's hatred of shams explains his attitude towards the
education of women. There is no inconsistency between *L'Ecole
des Femmes* and *Les Femmes savantes*. The affectation of the
*précieuses* and the *femmes savantes*, and their contempt for
marriage and domestic cares, are ridiculed in precisely the same
way as the affectation or the pedantry of men. Molière is not
opposed to education or to learning, whether in men or women;
he is expressing – like so many others – the ideal of the *honnête
homme* and his feminine counterpart, who shall not be specialists,
who 'ne se piquent de rien'. Hence, too, his attitude to doctors
of medicine, ridiculed first in *Dom Juan*, and then later in
*L'Amour médecin*, *Le Médecin malgré lui*, and *Le Malade
imaginaire*. They are ridiculed, not merely because they kill their
patients, but because they reject new discoveries and facts that
conflict with their theories, because they grow rich by exploiting
human fears, because they attach more importance to observing
the forms than to saving the lives of their patients ('Il vaut mieux
mourir selon les règles que de réchapper contre les règles', says one
of the doctors in *L'Amour médecin*), and because they regard the
patient as existing for the doctor rather than the doctor for the
patient.

The *honnête homme* will conform with society. Contemporary
fashions may be absurd, but cannot be rejected:

> ... il vaut mieux souffrir d'être au nombre des fous,
> Que du sage parti se voir seul contre tous.
>                    (*L'Ecole des Maris*, I, 1)

Some degree of hypocrisy is necessary if social life is to be possible
at all (*Le Misanthrope*). One makes oneself ridiculous if one tries
to live above one's station – as *George Dandin* and *Le Bourgeois
gentilhomme* show clearly enough.

The tyranny of Sganarelle in *L'Ecole des Maris* and of
Arnolphe in *L'Ecole des Femmes*, who believe that women should
be immured and kept in subjection, contrasts unfavourably with
the tolerant attitude of Ariste in the first of these plays, who
believes that women should be allowed freedom and trusted.

Sganarelle and Arnolphe are suspiciously like *dévots*; and Orgon
and Mme Pernelle in *Tartuffe* certainly are. Which brings us to
the question of Molière's religion. He is opposed to tyranny and
austerity: is he also a *libertin*, expressing a doctrine of following
nature and instinct, in opposition to the austerity of Christianity?
Opinions on the point are divided. *Tartuffe* and *Dom Juan*
are the crucial plays in this connection, and it is relevant to recall
that the first was banned for five years as the result of the intervention of the Compagnie du Saint-Sacrement, and that the
second was taken off after fifteen performances and never played
again or published during Molière's lifetime.

*Tartuffe* is, of course, ostensibly a play about a hypocrite, but
it is not impossible that, just as the *Précieuses ridicules* is a
play about two *pecques provinciales* but makes fun of some of
the attributes of the genuine *précieuse* as well, so *Tartuffe*,
while attacking hypocrisy, may attack Christianity into the
bargain. Certainly Molière, both in his play and in the *placets*
prefixed to it, seems to confuse religious austerity or intolerance
with hypocrisy. When, in the *premier placet*, he says that 'les
originaux enfin ont fait supprimer la copie', one cannot forget
that the 'originaux', members of the Compagnie du Saint-
Sacrement, were *dévots*, but not hypocrites. In the play, Cléante
describes his ideal Christians:

> Jamais contre un pécheur ils n'ont d'acharnement;
> Ils attachent leur haine au péché seulement.
>
> (I, 5)

To punish offenders may be uncharitable, but is certainly not a
mark of hypocrisy. Moreover, the lessons that Orgon learns from
Tartuffe he might just as easily have learned from a sincere
Christian:

> Il m'enseigne à n'avoir affection pour rien;
> De toutes amitiés il détache mon âme;
> Et je verrais mourir frère, enfants, mère et femme,
> Que je m'en soucierais autant que de cela.
>
> (I, 5)

The doctrine that one should love all men equally and none with
particular affection, though it is here made to sound absurd, is
that of Pascal; and something very similar to it is found in the
Gospels.[8]

[8] 'Then one said unto him, Behold, thy mother and thy brethren stand
without, desiring to speak with thee.

'But he answered and said unto him that told him, Who is my mother?
and who are my brethren?

'And he stretched forth his hand toward his disciples, and said, Behold
my mother and my brethren!

'For whosoever shall do the will of my Father which is in heaven, the
same is my brother, and sister, and mother.'          (Matthew, 12, xlvii–l)

As for Don Juan, all one can say is that, while he is a villain, he has also many noble qualities, that he is certainly not ridiculous in everything, that when he attacks doctors and hypocrites he is undoubtedly expressing the views of Molière; so that we cannot be sure that when he is expressing scepticism about religion or about the hermit ('un homme qui prie le Ciel tout le jour, ne peut pas manquer d'être bien dans ses affaires', III, 2), Molière meant him to be absurd. Moreover, the defence of Christianity is chiefly entrusted to the fool, Sganarelle, who talks nonsense and is no more willing to pay his debts to M. Dimanche than his master. As the prince de Conti pointed out:

Après avoir fait dire toutes les impiétés les plus horribles à un athée qui a beaucoup d'esprit, l'auteur confie la cause de Dieu à un valet, à qui il fait dire, pour le soutenir, toutes les impertinences du monde.

While certainty is impossible, if we recall that Molière was the associate of *libertins*, it is difficult to disagree with the conclusion of Professor Spink:

The reading of his work gives one the moral conviction that the only spectator who can have sat through all the plays without being made to squirm at some time or another must have been a man who was passably sceptical without making a show of anticlericalism, but making no show of devotion either, confessing his sins rarely and making a Christian end only to avoid scandal. For such a man the word 'nature' must also have evoked many intellectual and moral associations, all of them pleasant and somehow connected with young love, mating and happiness.[9]

Molière also perfected the comedy of manners which we have seen growing up in the first part of the seventeenth century. Observation of the real world about him was the starting-point for his plays. Contemporaries called him 'le contemplateur' and 'le peintre' (because he represented reality). Donneau de Visé describes people providing him with information for his plays:

Notre auteur, ou pour ne pas répéter ce mot si souvent, le héros de ce petit récit, après avoir fait cette pièce [*Sganarelle*], reçut des gens de qualité plus de mémoires que jamais, dont l'on le pria de se servir dans celles qu'il devait faire ensuite, et je le vis bien embarrassé, un soir, après la comédie, qu'il cherchait partout des tablettes pour écrire ce que lui disaient plusieurs personnes de condition dont il était environné, tellement que l'on peut dire qu'il travaillait sous les gens de qualité pour leur apprendre après à vivre à leurs dépens et qu'il était en ce temps, et est encore présentement, leur écolier et leur maître tout ensemble.

According to the authors of the preface to the 1682 edition of his works, La Grange (who had been an actor in Molière's company) and Vivot,

il observait les manières et les mœurs de tout le monde; il trouvait moyen ensuite d'en faire des applications admirables dans les comédies,

[9] J. S. Spink, *French Free-thought from Gassendi to Voltaire*, 1960, p. 151.

où l'on peut dire qu'il a joué tout le monde, puisqu'il s'y est joué le
premier en plusieurs endroits sur des affaires de sa famille et qui regar-
daient ce qui se passait dans son domestique. C'est ce que ses plus
particuliers amis ont remarqué bien des fois.

Molière's biographer, Grimarest, says that 'Molière travaillait
d'après la nature, pour travailler plus sûrement'. Above all,
Molière himself confirms these statements. In the *Critique de
l'Ecole des Femmes*, comparing comedy and tragedy, Dorante
says:

Lorsque vous peignez des héros, vous faites ce que vous voulez. Ce sont
des portraits à plaisir, où l'on ne cherche point de ressemblance; et vous
n'avez qu'à suivre les traits d'une imagination qui se donne l'essor, et qui
souvent laisse le vrai pour attraper le merveilleux. Mais lorsque vous
peignez les hommes, il faut peindre d'après nature. On veut que ces portraits ressemblent; et vous n'avez rien fait, si vous n'y faites reconnaître
les gens de votre siècle.

And the *Impromptu de Versailles* contains a list of seventeenth-
century types suitable for treatment in a comedy – most of which
in fact occur in subsequent plays.

There is, then, realism of various kinds in the plays of Molière.
Although he claims in the *Impromptu de Versailles* that 'son
dessein est de peindre les mœurs sans vouloir toucher aux personnes et [...] tous les personnages qu'il représente sont des
personnages en l'air, et des fantômes proprement, qu'il habille à
sa fantaisie, pour réjouir les spectateurs,' this is not entirely
true. There are allusions in his plays to real people. The four
doctors in *L'Amour médecin* are based on four of the court
doctors, and the actors playing the parts are said to have worn
masks which resembled the faces of the originals; the huntsman
in *Les Fâcheux* was modelled on M. de Soyecourt; Trissotin
and Vadius in *Les Femmes savantes* represent Cotin and Ménage;
and Boileau claims that Alceste in the sonnet scene was taken
from him. Similarly, the episode in *L'Avare* in which the would-
be borrower finds, when brought face to face with the unscrupulous usurer, that it is his own father, and the episode in *Le
Bourgeois gentilhomme* in which Mme Jourdain returns home to
surprise her husband entertaining a lady to supper, both occurred
in real life.

More important, Molière's plays give a remarkably comprehensive picture of seventeenth-century France. We see salons of different kinds – an aristocratic one in *Le Misanthrope*, a bourgeois one
in *Les Femmes savantes*, two provincial girls aping Parisian ladies
in *Les Précieuses ridicules*, and a provincial hostess in *La Comtesse d'Escarbagnas*. We are taken into middle-class households in
*Tartuffe*, *L'Avare*, *Le Bourgeois gentilhomme*, *Les Femmes savantes*, and *Le Malade imaginaire*. M. de Pourceaugnac brings a

whiff of the Limousin to Paris with him; and Molière takes us into
the provinces in *George Dandin*, with its vivid portrayal of the
arrogance of provincial aristocrats, compelled by poverty to contract a marriage alliance with a wealthy peasant, and in *La Comtesse d'Escarbagnas*, the heroine of which is wooed by a *receveur des
tailles* and a *conseiller*. There is an impression of provincial life in
*Tartuffe*:

> Vous irez par le coche en sa petite ville,
> Qu'en oncles et cousins vous trouverez fertile,
> Et vous vous plairez fort à les entretenir.
> D'abord chez le beau monde on vous fera venir;
> Vous irez visiter, pour votre bienvenue,
> Madame la baillive et Madame l'élue,
> Qui d'un siège pliant vous feront honorer.
> Là, dans le carnaval, vous pourrez espérer
> Le bal et la grand'bande, à savoir, deux musettes,
> Et parfois Fagotin et les marionnettes,
> Si pourtant votre époux . . .
>
> (II, 3)

Peasants appear in *Dom Juan* and *George Dandin*. There are
descriptions of current fashions, and, in *Les Fâcheux*, a delightful account of a nobleman at the theatre noisily taking his seat
on the stage. Plenty of seventeenth-century types appear in
Molière's plays — a duellist, a *précieuse*, a gamester, a huntsman,
and so forth in *Les Fâcheux*, and a description of a provincial
*nouvelliste* in *La Comtesse d'Escarbagnas*, for example. Doctors
occur in several plays, and, however exaggerated it may appear,
Molière's account of French medicine in the period is sub-
stantially accurate — his summary of the available courses of
treatment in *Monsieur de Pourceaugnac*, for instance:

*Premier Médecin:* Quinze fois saigné?
*La Paysanne:* Oui.
*Premier Médecin:* Et il ne guérit point?
*La Paysanne:* Non, Monsieur.
*Premier Médecin:* C'est signe que la maladie n'est pas dans le sang.
Nous le ferons purger autant de fois, pour voir si elle n'est pas dans les
humeurs; et si rien ne nous réussit, nous l'enverrons aux bains.      (I, 6)

Characters like Mme Pernelle, or Mme Jourdain with her
common turns of phrase, or the henpecked Chrysale, or some of
the servants (Dorine, Nicole, Martine, Toinette) have the ring
of truth; and so many counterparts of Tartuffe and Harpagon
can be found in the real life of the age that we cannot doubt
their essential truth.

But the extent of Molière's realism should not be exaggerated.
If he depicts the real life of his own period in his comedies, he
also creates a world of fancy, of extravagance, of exuberant fun

and improbability. The proportions vary, of course – there is most realism and least improbability in *Tartuffe* and *Le Misanthrope*, and least realism in the *comédies-ballets* such as *Monsieur de Pourceaugnac* and *Le Bourgeois gentilhomme*. But both elements are almost always present, in a blend which is that of Molière and no one else.

Molière's world, then, is a world of fancy and improbability, in which valets pass themselves off as noblemen, a woodcutter finds himself compelled to be a doctor, lovers woo their ladies under the noses of hostile parents, and long-lost parents opportunely arrive and recognize their children at the end. It is a world in which M. de Pourceaugnac is pursued round the stage by an apothecary wanting to give him an enema, assailed by women accusing him of being the father of their children, and compelled to escape from Paris in female dress; in which, with comic ceremonial, M. Jourdain is made a *mamamouchi* and Argan a doctor. It is, above all, a comic world, abounding in humorous repartee, –

> —J'ai quatre pauvres petits enfants sur les bras.
> —Mets-les à terre.
>
> (*Le Médecin malgré lui*, I, 1)

– and in verbal virtuosity and exuberance[10] – one thinks of Scapin's diatribe against the law in *Les Fourberies* (II, 9), or the succession of different dialects in *Monsieur de Pourceaugnac* and *Les Fourberies*, or the pedantry of Pancrace in *Le Mariage forcé*, or the long-winded and faulty reasoning of Eraste in *Le Dépit amoureux* (IV, 2) or of Sganarelle in *Dom Juan*:

> Sachez, Monsieur, que tant va la cruche à l'eau, qu'enfin elle se brise; et comme dit fort bien cet auteur que je ne connais pas, l'homme est en ce monde ainsi que l'oiseau sur la branche; la branche est attachée à l'arbre; qui s'attache à l'arbre, suit de bons préceptes; les bons préceptes valent mieux que les belles paroles; les belles paroles se trouvent à la cour; à la cour sont les courtisans; les courtisans suivent la mode; la mode vient de la fantaisie; la fantaisie est une faculté de l'âme; l'âme est ce qui nous donne la vie; la vie finit par la mort; la mort nous fait penser au Ciel; le Ciel est au-dessus de la terre; la terre n'est point la mer; la mer est sujette aux orages; les orages tourmentent les vaisseaux; les vaisseaux ont besoin d'un bon pilote; un bon pilote a de la prudence; la prudence n'est pas dans les jeunes gens; les jeunes gens doivent obéissance aux vieux; les vieux aiment les richesses; les richesses font les riches; les riches ne sont pas pauvres; les pauvres ont de la nécessité; nécessité n'a point de loi; qui n'a point de loi vit en bête brute; et, par conséquent, vous serez damné à tous les diables.                    (V, 2)

– a fine example of a *coq-à-l'âne*. It is a world in which resourceful servants devise endless schemes and pranks, and their victims

[10] Molière occasionally invents words in the manner of the burlesque writers—*je me dessuisse* (*L'Etourdi*), *tartufiée*, *des-Sosie*, *des-Amphitryonne*, and so forth.

fall an easy prey. It is a world in which a character may persistently fail to see another who is on the stage and trying to speak to him, or in which people – inadvertently or deliberately – may make it impossible for others to speak by not letting them get a word in. It is a world in which people betray themselves as they would not in real life – in which, for example, an apothecary praises a doctor for killing his patients ('Au reste il n'est pas de ces médecins qui marchandent les maladies: c'est un homme expéditif, expéditif, qui aime à dépêcher ses malades; et quand on a à mourir, cela se fait avec lui le plus vite du monde'),[11] Harpagon tells Valère that he would have done better to let his daughter drown than to steal his *cassette*, M. de Pourceaugnac betrays his humble origins by his precise knowledge of the law, M. Jourdain threatens to make his daughter a duchess ('si vous me mettez en colère, je la ferai duchesse', III, 12), or Argan keeps forgetting that he is ill.

It is a world – as Bergson pointed out – in which men behave like automata. Agnès tells of her first meeting with Horace:

> ... je vis passer sous les arbres d'auprès
> Un jeune homme bien fait, qui rencontrant ma vue,
> D'une humble révérence aussitôt me salue:
> Moi, pour ne point manquer à la civilité,
> Je fis la révérence aussi de mon côté.
> Soudain il me refait une autre révérence:
> Moi, j'en refais de même une autre en diligence;
> Et lui d'une troisième aussitôt repartant,
> D'une troisième aussi j'y repars à l'instant.
> Il passe, vient, repasse, et toujours de plus belle,
> Me fait à chaque fois révérence nouvelle;
> Et moi, qui tous ces tours fixement regardais,
> Nouvelle révérence aussi je lui rendais ...
> (*L'Ecole des Femmes*, II, 6)

On the stage, we see Arnolphe removing Alain's hat thrice to teach him manners and Orgon, Harpagon, and Géronte betraying their obsessions by repeating 'Et Tartuffe?', 'Sans dot', and 'Que diable allait-il faire dans cette galère?' respectively over and over again. In *L'Amour médecin*, Lisette keeps insisting that her mistress needs a husband, while Sganarelle turns a deaf ear:

*Sg:* Une coquine, qui ne me veut pas dire ce qu'elle a.
*L:* C'est un mari qu'elle veut.
*Sg:* Je l'abandonne.
*L:* Un mari.
*Sg:* Je la déteste.
*L:* Un mari.
*Sg:* Et la renonce pour ma fille.

[11] *Monsieur de Pourceaugnac*, I, 5.

*L.* Un mari.
*Sg:* Non, ne m'en parlez point.
*L:* Un mari.
*Sg:* Ne m'en parlez point.
*L:* Un mari.
*Sg:* Ne m'en parlez point.
*L:* Un mari, un mari, un mari.                                    (I, 3)

Characters speak in turn, like Eraste and Valère in *Le Dépit
amoureux*:

*E:*                    Hé bien, seigneur Valère?
*V:* Hé bien, seigneur Eraste?
*E:*                    En quel état l'amour?
*V:* En quel état vos feux?

                                                          (I, 3)[12]

This is, perhaps, particularly amusing when a servant repeats
his master's remarks, transposing them into a different plane:

*Cléonte:* Après tant de sacrifices ardents, de soupirs, et de vœux que j'ai
faits à ses charmes!
*Covielle:* Après tant d'assidus hommages, de soins, et de services que je
lui ai rendus dans sa cuisine!
*Cléonte:* Tant de larmes que j'ai versées à ses genoux!
*Covielle:* Tant de seaux d'eau que j'ai tirés au puits pour elle!
*Cléonte:* Tant d'ardeur que j'ai fait paraître à la chérir plus que moi-
même!
*Covielle:* Tant de chaleur que j'ai soufferte à tourner la broche à sa place!
                                   (*Le Bourgeois gentilhomme*, III, 9)

It is a world, too, of sudden and complete reversals of behaviour or of situation. Vadius deplores the habit authors have
of reading their compositions in public, and then pulls out his own
verses (*Les Femmes savantes*, III, 3). Lovers, in *dépit amoureux*
scenes, fall out, quarrel, and come together again; Alain and
Georgette both refuse to open the door to Arnolphe, then quarrel
about which of them shall open it (*L'Ecole des Femmes*, I, 2);
Trissotin and Vadius greet each other with flattery, and then
fall out and abuse each other. Mascarille is beaten successively
for telling lies and for telling the truth (*Le Dépit amoureux*, I, 4);
Léandre beats Scapin and immediately afterwards is compelled
to implore his help (*Les Fourberies de Scapin*, II, 3–4). And
finally, it is a world of anti-climaxes — in which, for example, the
missing word in Agnès's sentence, 'Il m'a pris le ...', turns out
merely to be 'ruban', or Agnès, expecting to hear that she is to be
married to Horace, finds that Arnolphe intends to marry her
himself (*L'Ecole des Femmes*, II, 5). It is a stylized world, which
is anything but realistic.

Molière's plays, then, are profoundly comic and profoundly

[12] Cf. *Le Dépit amoureux*, III, 10, and *Le Misanthrope*, V. 2.

human. They portray — sympathetically and without spleen — characters in whom we recognize ourselves and those about us; they take us back into seventeenth-century France; and they transport us into a fantastic, comic, extravagant world in which our spirit finds release. One understands what Sainte-Beuve meant, when he wrote — with only slight exaggeration — 'Chaque homme de plus qui sait lire est un lecteur de plus pour Molière'.

*Chapter 14*

# RACINE

ALTHOUGH a considerable number of Racine's letters have survived and a good deal is known about his life, since that knowledge relates mainly to the period before and after he wrote his plays, it may well be irrelevant to the appreciation of his work. The main facts, however, are these: that Jean Racine (1639–99), left an orphan at an early age, was brought up and educated at Port-Royal; that he subsequently embarked on a career as a man of letters and a courtier, breaking with his friends and relatives at Port-Royal; that two actresses, Mlle Duparc and Mlle Champmeslé, were his mistresses successively;[1] that, after *Phèdre* (1677), in consequence of having been appointed historiographer to the King, he abandoned the theatre; that at about the same time he married and was reconciled with Port-Royal; that – either then (as his family believed) or later (as some modern critics think) – he turned devout; and that, at the behest of Mme de Maintenon, he wrote two plays for performance by the schoolgirls of Saint-Cyr (*Esther*, 1689, and *Athalie*, 1691).

Racine served a long apprenticeship to the theatre. His first three tragedies were rejected by the theatres of Paris, and have been lost. His next two, *La Thébaïde* (1664) and *Alexandre* (1665), though by no means devoid of interest for students of Racine, would probably have been forgotten by now if they had had only their intrinsic merits to preserve them from oblivion. *Andromaque* (1667), his sixth play, is the first to display his originality and his genius. Treating, like *La Thébaïde*, a subject taken from Greek drama, and depicting, in great poetry, the ravages of passion, *Andromaque* – as was later said of Baudelaire – brought a *frisson nouveau* into French seventeenth-century tragedy.

*Andromaque* was followed by a comedy, *Les Plaideurs* (1668), adapted from the *Wasps* of Aristophanes, and by a tragedy of a rather different kind, *Britannicus* (1669), dealing with a political and historical subject taken from Roman history. The influence of Corneille on Racine's work so far had been considerable. *La*

---

[1] Mlle Duparc may have been his wife.

*Thébaïde*, written after Corneille had treated an earlier episode in the history of the Theban royal house in his *Œdipe* (1659), had contained a number of Cornelian features. *Andromaque*, though vastly different from a play of Corneille's, has the same basic situation, the same chain of lovers, as Corneille's *Pertharite* (1651–2). *Britannicus* treats the kind of subject favoured by Corneille, and indeed one close historically to that of Corneille's *Othon* (1664); moreover, if Néron in Racine's play is a 'monstre naissant', Corneille had depicted a *monstre tout court* in his *Attila* (1667). But Racine's next play, *Bérénice*, there can be little doubt, was written in deliberate competition with Corneille: *Bérénice* was performed at the Hôtel de Bourgogne on 21 November 1670, and Corneille's *Tite et Bérénice* a week later by Molière's company. If we reject — as, since Gustave Michaut's study of the play, most modern scholars have rejected — the traditional story that Henriette d'Angleterre suggested the subject to both dramatists, the most likely explanation of the coincidence is that Racine had chosen a subject that he knew Corneille was treating. Racine's play was — deservedly — the more successful of the two.

After *Bérénice* came *Bajazet* (1672), a political play set in the seraglio of seventeenth-century Constantinople, embodying a similar conception of character and passion to that of *Andromaque*, — though the episode in which Atalide tells Bajazet to pay his addresses to Roxane, but cannot suppress her jealousy when he does, and in which Bajazet cannot make his hypocrisy convincing, was borrowed from *Othon*. *Mithridate*, which followed (1673), is Racine's most Cornelian play. It is reminiscent of *Nicomède*: both plays deal with a state bordering on the Roman Empire, split into two factions, one hostile to Rome and the other pro-Roman; and, in both, the political disagreement between two brothers is accentuated by rivalry in love. Moreover, the council scene (III, 1) is a type of scene in which Corneille excelled, and the figure of the elderly Mithridate in love with Monime resembles such a character as Martian in Corneille's *Pulchérie* (1672). On the other hand, there is much in *Mithridate* that is unlike Corneille. Love plays a more important part in it than in Corneille's play, in which there is no equivalent to the rivalry of Mithridate and his son, Xipharès, for the love of Monime; and the general outline of the play anticipates *Phèdre* — Mithridate, reported dead, returns unexpectedly to find that his son is in love with his father's betrothed, as Thésée in the later play, reported dead, returns unexpectedly to learn (but the accusation in this case is false) that his son is in love with his own stepmother.

For his next two tragedies, *Iphigénie* (1674) and *Phèdre* (1677), Racine adapted two plays of Euripides – his first return to a Greek source and a Greek setting since *Andromaque*: perhaps because, more confident of his own powers and less preoccupied with his rival (who, in any case, wrote no more after *Suréna*, 1674), he felt free to go his own way; perhaps, as Professor Knight suggests, in protest against the way Quinault had treated a Greek theme in his opera, *Alceste*. In both these plays there is a considerable supernatural element – in the first, a victim has to be sacrificed to appease the gods who have becalmed the Greek fleet, and in the second, Hippolyte is killed by a sea-monster sent by Neptune, in answer to Thésée's supplication. But, whereas *Iphigénie* has a happy ending, *Phèdre* has not and is a genuine tragedy in every sense of the word, and the first for five years.

Racine's last two plays, written long afterwards, are very different. Written to be performed by the girls of Saint-Cyr, they treat Biblical subjects, and are a cross between tragedy and opera.

> ... je m'aperçus qu'en travaillant sur le plan qu'on m'avait donné, j'exécutais en quelque sorte un dessein qui m'avait souvent passé dans l'esprit, qui était de lier, comme dans les anciennes tragédies grecques, le chœur et le chant avec l'action, et d'employer à chanter les louanges du vrai Dieu cette partie du chœur que les païens employaient à chanter les louanges de leurs fausses divinités.          (Preface to *Esther*)

The result is a new genre, and a delightful one, as those who had the good fortune to see *Esther* or *Athalie* performed a decade or so ago at the University of Bristol are unlikely to forget. *Esther* is a slight play in three acts, but *Athalie* ranks with the finest of Racine's tragedies. It contains no love element, but in other respects is not unlike *Phèdre* – the Jewish or Christian God having replaced the Greek mythological deities, and the Biblical setting and atmosphere being created with the same painstaking attention to detail as the mythological atmosphere in the earlier play.

Péguy once said, unkindly, that Racine wrote only one play. There is a sense in which this remark is not without truth – in most of his tragedies, one finds the same basic situation, a pair of lovers and a jealous rival (Hémon, Antigone, and Créon in *La Thébaïde*; Porus, Axiane, and Taxile in *Alexandre*; Titus, Bérénice, and Antiochus in *Bérénice*; Bajazet, Atalide, and Roxane in *Bajazet*; Xipharès, Monime, and Mithridate in *Mithridate*; Achille, Iphigénie, and Eriphile in *Iphigénie*; Hippolyte, Aricie, and Phèdre in *Phèdre*[2] – *Andromaque*, with its chain of lovers, and the two Biblical plays are exceptions). But if this same

---

[2] Cf. Cinna, Emilie, and Maxime in *Cinna*.

situation recurs frequently, it is of unequal importance, and very differently treated. The author of *Alexandre*, of *Britannicus*, of *Bérénice*, of *Bajazet*, of *Mithridate*, of *Iphigénie*, of *Phèdre*, and of the two Biblical tragedies cannot justly be accused of monotony.

Racine, as we have seen, and as was indeed inevitable, was strongly influenced by his great predecessor and contemporary, Corneille. In the main, he adopts the form created by Corneille, the reversals of the situation, the alternation of hope and fears, the suspense and surprise. Attenuated as they may be, these things are nearly always present in Racine, even in *Bérénice*. In the first act, Bérénice's confidence that Titus will marry her contrasts with the doubts of her confidante. In the next act, we learn that Titus is resolved to send Bérénice away, but he is quite unable, in her presence, to make his decision known to her. This act ends, like the first, with a scene between Bérénice and her confidante: this time, Bérénice is disturbed by Titus's embarrassment and retreat, but ends by reassuring herself. In the third act, Antiochus breaks the news to Bérénice on Titus's behalf, but she declares her intention of seeing Titus herself. This she does in the fourth act; he is inflexible, but in the following scenes it is clear that he has been shaken, and there is some doubt whether he will carry out his intention. In Scene 6, he says:

> Je ne souffrirai point que Bérénice expire.
> Allons, Rome en dira ce qu'elle en voudra dire.

In Scene 7, Antiochus asks Titus to see Bérénice, who is in a state of frenzy, and Titus replies:

> Hélas! quel mot puis-je lui dire?
> Moi-même en ce moment sais-je si je respire?

The act ends on the same ambiguous note. Titus is summoned to the Senate, and commands his confidant:

> Voyez la Reine. Allez. J'espère, à mon retour,
> Qu'elle ne pourra plus douter de mon amour.

It is not until the last act, therefore, that we know that Titus will not marry Bérénice; and then a new question arises: will Bérénice commit suicide or not? The ending is in doubt until the last scene of the play. The events of the play arouse suspense particularly if looked at from the point of view of Antiochus, who sees his chances of marrying Bérénice alternately increasing and diminishing throughout the play, and who indeed says:

> Qu'ai-je donc fait, grands Dieux? Quel cours infortuné
> A ma funeste vie aviez-vous destiné?
> Tous mes moments ne sont qu'un éternel passage
> De la crainte à l'espoir, de l'espoir à la rage.

> (V, 4)

But if Racine accepts Corneille's form, the spirit of his tragedies is rather different. For one thing, he lays more stress on simplicity. This is already evident in his second extant play, *Alexandre*, in the preface to which he writes:

Mais de quoi se plaignent-ils,[3] si toutes mes scènes sont bien remplies, [...] et si, *avec peu d'incidents et peu de matière*, j'ai été assez heureux pour faire une pièce qui les a peut-être attachés malgré eux, depuis le commencement jusqu'à la fin?

In the preface to *Britannicus*, he insists that a tragedy should have

une action simple, chargée de peu de matière, telle que doit être une action qui se passe en un seul jour, et qui s'avançant par degrés vers sa fin, n'est soutenue que par les intérêts, les sentiments et les passions des personnages . . .

And, in the preface to *Bérénice*, he emphasizes that simplicity is a consequence of the principle of *vraisemblance* and the unity of time:

Il n'y a que le vraisemblable qui touche dans la tragédie. Et quelle vraisemblance y a-t-il qu'il arrive en un jour une multitude de choses qui pourraient à peine arriver en plusieurs semaines?[4] Il y en a qui pensent que cette simplicité est une marque de peu d'invention. Ils ne songent pas qu'au contraire *toute l'invention consiste à faire quelque chose de rien*, et que tout ce grand nombre d'incidents a toujours été le refuge des poètes qui ne sentaient dans leur génie ni assez d'abondance, ni assez de force, pour attacher durant cinq actes leurs spectateurs par une action simple, soutenue de la violence des passions, de la beauté des sentiments et de l'élégance de l'expression.

Simplicity is carried to its extreme point in *Bérénice*. The subject is taken from Suetonius: 'Titus reginam Berenicen [ . . . ] statim ab urbe dimisit invitus invitam', and Victor Hugo once, wickedly but wittily, summarized the play thus: Act I: Titus; Act II, reginam Berenicen; Act III, invitus; Act IV, invitam; Act V, dimisit. If this is a slight distortion of the play, it scarcely exaggerates its simplicity. In Act I, we learn that Bérénice is expecting Titus to marry her; in Act II, we learn that Titus has decided not to; in Act III, the decision is made known to Bérénice; in Act IV, we see her distress and that of Titus; and in Act V, they separate. No other play, it is true, has quite such a paucity of action as *Bérénice*.

More important, tragedy is equated in Racine's mind with sadness

---

[3] His critics.
[4] In spite of this, Mithridate at least—like Rodrigue in *Le Cid*—has a busy day.

Ce n'est point une nécessité qu'il y ait du sang et des morts dans une tragédie;[5] il suffit que l'action en soit grande, que les acteurs en soient héroïques, que les passions y soient excitées, et que tout s'y ressente de cette tristesse majestueuse qui fait tout le plaisir de la tragédie.

(Preface to *Bérénice*)

Moreover, a much higher proportion of his plays than of Corneille's have an unhappy ending, and are tragic. This, it should be stressed, is a difference of degree, not an absolute difference. There is nothing tragic about *Alexandre*. Although *Bajazet* ends with the death of the main character, one hesitates to call the play tragic, since the unhappy ending is not inherent in the situation; chance plays a large part — had Atalide not fainted, so that Roxane's confidante could find Bajazet's letter in her bosom and apprise Roxane of the deception of which she had been a victim, or had Acomat and his troops arrived a moment or two earlier in the last act, disaster might have been averted. *Mithridate* has a happy ending. It is true that Mithridate, the character who gives the play its name, kills himself at the end; but, had he waited a little longer before doing so, his act would have been unnecessary, and, above all, our sympathies are with the young lovers, Xipharès and Monime, to whose union Mithridate is an obstacle — in much the same way as Œdipe, in Corneille's version of the play, forfeits our sympathy by opposing the union of Dircé and Thésée, so that his death, so far from appearing tragic, removes the obstacle to a happy ending. *Iphigénie* ends happily, the heroine's life being spared at the expense of that of another victim:

Quelle apparence que j'eusse souillé la scène par le meurtre horrible d'une personne aussi vertueuse et aussi aimable qu'il fallait représenter Iphigénie?

(Preface to *Iphigénie*)

The two Biblical tragedies end with the triumph of the chosen people over their oppressors. *Athalie*, like *Mithridate*, ends with the destruction of the character who gives the play its name; but Racine expressly states in his preface that this tragedy

a pour sujet Joas reconnu et mis sur le trône; et j'aurais dû dans les règles l'intituler *Joas*. Mais la plupart du monde n'en ayant entendu parler que sous le nom d'*Athalie*, je n'ai pas jugé à propos de la leur présenter sous un autre titre, puisque d'ailleurs Athalie y joue un personnage si considérable, et que c'est sa mort qui termine la pièce.

(Preface to *Athalie*)

But even so, tragedies that are genuinely tragic make up half Racine's work; this is a much higher proportion than in Corneille.

[5] Probably in opposition to Corneille, who contended that a play was not a tragedy unless the main character was in danger of losing his life or his kingdom, or of banishment, and who entitled his *Tite et Bérénice* a *comédie héroïque* because these perils were absent from it.

Racine accepts the opinion expressed by Aristotle, that the heroes of tragedies should be neither wholly good nor wholly bad, and concludes:

Il faut donc qu'ils aient une bonté médiocre, c'est-à-dire une vertu capable de faiblesse, et qu'ils tombent dans le malheur par quelque faute qui les fasse plaindre sans les faire détester.          (Preface to *Andromaque*)

Racine's characters bring about their own destruction: to take one example, had Hermione in *Andromaque* not listened to Andromaque's supplications with contemptuous insolence, Andromaque would not have been compelled to see Pyrrhus again, and Hermione would not have lost him. It is because Iphigénie has no tragic flaw that Racine saves her life; and he prides himself on having given Hippolyte a weakness that justifies his death:

J'appelle faiblesse la passion qu'il ressent malgré lui pour Aricie, qui est la fille et la sœur des ennemis mortels de son père.          (Preface to *Phèdre*)

Of Phèdre herself, Racine claims that she has all the qualities required to arouse pity and terror:

En effet, Phèdre n'est ni tout à fait coupable, ni tout à fait innocente. Elle est engagée par sa destinée, et par la colère des Dieux, dans une passion illégitime dont elle a horreur toute la première. Elle fait tous ses efforts pour la surmonter. Elle aime mieux se laisser mourir que de la déclarer à personne. Et lorsqu'elle est forcée de la découvrir, elle en parle avec une confusion qui fait bien voir que son crime est plutôt une punition des Dieux qu'un mouvement de sa volonté.

If the tragedy in Racine is due to human failings, it is frequently enhanced by the sensation that

> As Flies to wanton Boyes, are we to th'Gods,
> They kill us for their sport.

There are several references in *Andromaque* to fate (*le sort, le destin, la fortune*) and the gods who persecute Oreste:

> De quelque part sur moi que je tourne les yeux,
> Je ne vois que malheurs qui condamnent les Dieux.
> (III, 1)

The gods participate directly in the action of *Iphigénie* and of *Phèdre*, though it is interesting to see how the supernatural in these two plays is rationalized. In *Iphigénie*, it is the gods who have becalmed the Greek fleet, and when the victim is sacrificed, the winds begin to blow. Racine adds, however, not that Diana was seen descending from the heavens, but that

> *Le soldat étonné dit que* dans une nue
> Jusque sur le bûcher Diane est descendue . . .
> (V, 6)

Similarly, in *Phèdre*, Hippolyte falls a victim to a sea-monster
sent by Neptune; but Racine is at pains to explain that love has
made him neglect his horsemanship, and, once again, the presence
of a god is merely reported at second hand:

> *On dit qu'*on a vu même, en ce désordre affreux,
> Un Dieu qui d'aiguillons pressait leur flanc poudreux.
>
> (V, 6)

In *Esther* and *Athalie*, the arbitrary gods of Greek mythology
give way to the Jewish God, who punishes the wicked and
protects his chosen people: these two plays are in some ways
like a dramatization of Bossuet's *Discours sur l'histoire universelle*.
'Dieu des Juifs, tu l'emportes!' cries Athalie at the end:

> Impitoyable Dieu, toi seul as tout conduit.
> C'est toi qui me flattant d'une vengeance aisée,
> M'as vingt fois en un jour à moi-même opposée,
> Tantôt pour un enfant excitant mes remords,
> Tantôt m'éblouissant de tes riches trésors,
> Que j'ai craint de livrer aux flammes, au pillage.
>
> (V, 6)

Since it is the character and the passions of the tragic hero
which – aided and abetted by fate and the gods – are responsible
for his downfall, it is worth considering briefly what kind of
picture Racine paints of mankind.

In *Andromaque*, love is the tragic weakness in Hermione,
Oreste, and Pyrrhus. It deceives them, so that they do not know
themselves. Oreste had thought that he had overcome his love
for Hermione; he was mistaken: 'Je me trompais moi-même'
(I, 1). Trying to convince her confidante and herself that she no
longer loves Pyrrhus, Hermione confesses:

> Je crains de me connaître en l'état où je suis.
>
> (II, 1)

When Pyrrhus decides to marry her, she easily convinces herself
against all the evidence that he must love her:

> Il veut tout ce qu'il fait; et s'il m'épouse, il m'aime.
>
> (III, 4)

> Ah! ne puis-je savoir si j'aime, ou si je hais?

she asks (V, 1) – only to have her doubts cruelly resolved thereafter.

But if the characters of *Andromaque* are in doubt about their
real feelings, they betray them involuntarily. Hermione may feign

indifference, but she cannot bring herself to abandon hope and
tear herself away from Pyrrhus:

> Elle pleure en secret le mépris de ses charmes.
> Toujours prête à partir, et demeurant toujours . . .
>
> (I, 1)

She agrees to receive Oreste, but, finding that he is close at hand,
she cannot prevent herself from sighing,

> Ah! je ne croyais pas qu'il fût si près d'ici.
>
> (II, 1)

Similarly, Pyrrhus may resolve to marry Hermione, but his inability to stop talking and thinking of Andromaque betrays his
real feelings (II, 5).

> Tout nous trahit, la voix, le silence, les yeux;
> Et les feux mal couverts n'en éclatent que mieux,

Oreste tells Hermione (II, 2); and Racine's characters (not only
in *Andromaque*) are quick to note all such signs. 'Vous,' says
Hermione to Oreste,

> Vous que mille vertus me forçaient d'estimer;
> Vous que j'ai plaint, enfin que je voudrais aimer.

Oreste does not fail to see the implications of this last remark:

> Je vous entends. Tel est mon partage funeste:
> Le cœur est pour Pyrrhus, et les vœux pour Oreste.
>
> (II, 2)

Love and hatred are close together, and one turns easily into
the other.

> Songez-y bien: il faut désormais que mon cœur,
> S'il n'aime avec transport, haïsse avec fureur,

says Pyrrhus (I, 4), echoed by Hermione in the following scene:

> Ah! je l'ai trop aimé pour ne le point haïr.
>
> (II, 1)

Hence, the characters easily become violent, and try to hurt each
other, mentally or physically. Of Pyrrhus, we are told:

> Il peut, Seigneur, il peut, dans ce désordre extrême,
> Epouser ce qu'il hait, et punir ce qu'il aime.
>
> (I, 1)

One of the reasons for which he decides to marry Hermione is
the hope that it might make Andromaque jealous (II, 5); and he
is prepared, despite his promises, to use the threat of handing
Andromaque's son over to the Greeks to compel her to marry him.
It was Hermione who first drew the attention of the Greeks to

Astyanax, in order to make her rival suffer. Oreste is determined
to abduct Hermione in order that she may share his torments:

> J'irais loin d'elle encor tâcher de l'oublier?
> Non, non, à mes tourments je veux l'associer.
> C'est trop gémir tout seul. Je suis las qu'on me plaigne:
> Je prétends qu'à mon tour l'inhumaine me craigne,
> Et que ses yeux cruels, à pleurer condamnés,
> Me rendent tous les noms que je leur ai donnés.
>
> (III, 1)

Hermione in her fury incites Oreste to kill Pyrrhus, but, after
he has done so, disavows him with the famous question: 'Qui
te l'a dit?' (V, 3).

A similar view of human nature is found in later plays. In
*Britannicus*, Agrippine is ruthless in her ambition, and Néron,
the 'monstre naissant', is almost sadistic:

> J'aimais jusqu'à ses pleurs que je faisais couler,
>
> (II, 2)

— as Eriphile in *Iphigénie* comes near to masochism.[6] Titus loves
without thought of the future:

> Mon cœur se gardait bien d'aller dans l'avenir
> Chercher ce qui pouvait un jour nous désunir.
>
> (*Bérénice*, IV, 5)

Bérénice appears at the beginning of the fourth act in a state
of disorder:

> Mais voulez-vous paraître en ce désordre extrême?
> Remettez-vous, Madame, et rentrez en vous-même.
> Laissez-moi relever ces voiles détachés,
> Et ces cheveux épars dont vos yeux sont cachés.
> Souffrez que de vos pleurs je répare l'outrage.
>
> (IV, 2)

At the end of the act she is in a paroxysm of despair:

> Elle n'entend ni pleurs, ni conseil, ni raison;
> Elle implore à grands cris le fer et le poison.
>
> (IV, 7)

6

> Dans les cruelles mains par qui je fus ravie
> Je demeurai longtemps sans lumière et sans vie.
> Enfin mes tristes yeux cherchèrent la clarté;
> Et me voyant presser d'un bras ensanglanté,
> Je frémissais, Doris, et d'un vainqueur sauvage
> Craignais de rencontrer l'effroyable visage.
> J'entrai dans son vaisseau, détestant sa fureur,
> Et toujours détournant ma vue avec horreur.
> Je le vis: son aspect n'avait rien de farouche;
> Je sentis le reproche expirer dans ma bouche.
> Je sentis contre moi mon cœur se déclarer;
> J'oubliai ma colère, et ne sus que pleurer.
>
> (*Iphigénie*, II, 1)

The point is emphasized by Iphigénie in II, 5.

Mithridate in his jealousy surprises Monime's secret by a base
trick and thinks of killing his rival, his son, Xipharès.

But the two plays which have most in common with *Andromaque* are *Bajazet* and *Phèdre*. Atalide, though she bids Bajazet
feign to love Roxane, cannot control her jealousy when he does.
He betrays his real feelings by his frigid reception of Roxane's
offers ('Quel est ce sombre accueil, et ce discours glacé'... ?),
as Atalide gives herself away by her warm justification of Bajazet
(III, 5–6). Roxane is credulous:

> Tu ne remportais pas une grande victoire,
> Perfide, en abusant ce cœur préoccupé,
> Qui lui-même craignait de se voir détrompé.
>
> (IV, 5)

Vindictive and cruel, at the discovery of Bajazet's love for Atalide,
she is filled with a desire for vengeance –

> Libre des soins cruels où j'allais m'engager,
> Ma tranquille fureur n'a plus qu'à se venger.
>
> (IV, 5)

– which she, in fact, satisfies. In Phèdre, 'la fille de Minos et de
Pasiphaé', monstrous or unhappy love is a hereditary affliction:

> O haine de Vénus! O fatale colère!
> Dans quels égarements l'amour jeta ma mère!
> . . . . . . .
> Ariane, ma sœur! de quel amour blessée,
> Vous mourûtes aux bords où vous fûtes laissée![7]
>
> (I, 3)

Phèdre's own love for her stepson is both monstrous and unhappy;
it is also involuntary, and Phèdre struggles against it in vain, and
confesses it in spite of herself. Jealousy makes her cruel, as it does
Hermione and Roxane, and she allows Hippolyte to go to his death.

When we think of Racine, we think, perhaps, first and foremost of characters such as these – passionate, uncontrolled, un-
balanced, distraught, violent, vacillating; and it is the exploration
of these aspects of human nature, this study of the psychology of
the subconscious mind, that interests modern readers most. But
Hermione and Phèdre are not by any means the whole of human
nature, and they are not the whole of Racine, whose variety should
not be overlooked. The high-priest Joad, the Machiavellian
Acomat and Mathan, normal young men like Achille or Bajazet,
characters capable of subordinating their passions to the claims
of duty, such as Titus, or Xipharès and Monime, the tender love

---

[7] Pasiphae lusted for a bull; Ariadne was deserted by Theseus on
Naxos.

of Junie for Britannicus or of Atalide for Bajazet, the undemand-
ing love of Antiochus for Bérénice —

> Mais moi, toujours tremblant, moi, vous le savez bien,
> A qui votre repos est plus cher que le mien . . .
>
> (III, 3)

or of Bérénice for Titus —

> Elle passe ses jours, Paulin, sans rien prétendre
> Que quelque heure à me voir, et le reste à m'attendre,
>
> (II, 2)

— or the innocence of the child, Joas: all these things are part
of Racine, too.

If Racine interests us, appeals to us, moves us, it is, of course,
because he portrays the human condition, the plight of man
doomed by his own character and passions to unhappiness, if not
to destruction; but it is also, and above all, because he portrays it
poetically. Exactly how Racine achieves this poetry is not easy to
analyse. Partly, no doubt, it is by the suggestion in many of his
tragedies that man is the victim, not only of himself, but of some
hostile, supernatural force. Partly, too, it is by evoking the past
of his characters and their present environment, thus helping
to give his characters that *éloignement* of which he speaks
in the preface to *Bajazet* ('*major e longinquo reverentia*'). The
characters in *Andromaque* are the descendants of the heroes of
the Trojan war, if they did not participate in it themselves; and
we are never allowed to forget this, or the pathos of the fall of
Troy. Andromaque is not just a widow with a son; she is Hector's
widow, full of tragic memories:

> J'ai vu mon père mort, et nos murs embrasés;
> J'ai vu trancher les jours de ma famille entière,
> Et mon époux sanglant traîné sur la poussière,
> Son fils, seul avec moi, réservé pour les fers.

In *Bérénice*, we are conscious of the East, where Titus fought
and whence Bérénice comes. In *Bajazet*, the atmosphere of the
seraglio of an oriental despot is continually evoked. In *Phèdre*, we
are conscious not only of the close links between the characters
of the play and the gods, but of the forests which surround the
city, where Hippolyte hunts, and where Phèdre longs to be:

> Dieux! que ne suis-je assise à l'ombre des forêts!
> (*Phèdre*, I, 3)

*Athalie* takes place in the Jewish temple; Athalie is the daughter
of Jezebel, doomed to destruction at the hands of the God of

the Jews like her mother; and Joad, in a moment of prophecy, looks forward into the future and foretells the coming of Christianity.

Racine's plays are poetic, however, principally because of the poetry of his style – without which, indeed, the attempt to create atmosphere would be doomed to failure. Always elegant, but poor in vocabulary, Racine's verse, whether he is describing a scene or expressing an emotion, is rich in suggestive and evocative power, in lines which strike home and linger in the mind – so that Racine's plays, like Shakespeare's, are 'full of quotations', or of what have been called 'talismans poétiques'. To attempt to analyse how he achieves this result would require far more space than a single chapter, if indeed it were possible at all; but a few lines may help to illustrate the characteristic quality of Racine's verse. Antiochus is taking leave of Bérénice:

> Et c'est ce que je fuis. J'évite, mais trop tard,
> Ces cruels entretiens, où je n'ai point de part.
> Je fuis Titus. Je fuis ce nom qui m'inquiète,
> Ce nom qu'à tous moments votre bouche répète.
> Que vous dirai-je enfin? Je fuis des yeux distraits,
> Qui me voyant toujours, ne me voyaient jamais.
> Adieu: je vais, le cœur trop plein de votre image,
> Attendre, en vous aimant, la mort pour mon partage.
>
> (*Bérénice*, I, 4)

Why these lines haunt us, who can say? The subject-matter has something to do with it – the idea of a faithful lover who cannot bear to see his lady preoccupied with his rival, talking about him, *seeing* him ('des yeux distraits/Qui me voyant toujours, ne me voyaient jamais.').[8] So has the flexible rhythm – attenuated, not strongly marked, varying from line to line (it is difficult to sub-divide the first hemistich; the third line is a *vers ternaire*; the caesura of the seventh line is irregular). So have the repetitions – the word *fuis* is repeated four times, the expression *ce nom* used in the third line and repeated in the fourth, the verb *voir* used twice in different forms in the sixth line. So, too, have the asson-ances and alliterations – 'Je f*uis* Titus. Je f*uis*,' the frequency of the sounds *i*, *é*, or *è*, the repetition of consonants (*s*'s and *t*'s in line one; *p*'s in line two; *k*'s in line three; *d*'s in line five; *v*'s and

---

[8] Cf. Camille in *Horace*:

> je rencontrai Valère,
> Et contre sa coutume, il ne put me déplaire,
> Il me parla d'amour sans me donner d'ennui:
> Je ne m'aperçus pas que je parlais à lui;
> Je ne lui pus montrer de mépris ni de glace:
> Tout ce que je voyais me semblait Curiace;
> Tout ce qu'on me disait me parlait de ses feux;
> Tout ce que je disais l'assurait de mes vœux.
>
> (I, 2)

*j*'s in lines six and seven; *p*'s, *r*'s, and above all *m*'s in the last line; and so forth). These things, which contribute to the harmony of the verse, help, perhaps, to explain — but do not account for — the beauty and the emotional power of passages such as these.

## Chapter 15

# BOILEAU

THE FIFTEENTH child of a *commis au greffe* of the parlement of Paris, and trained as a barrister, Nicolas Boileau-Despréaux (1636–1711) inherited enough money from his father in 1657 to give up his profession and devote himself to literary pursuits. With his brother, Gilles, he frequented the circles of Chapelain and d'Aubignac, but gradually broke with them and joined their critics. In 1663, he was introduced to the cabaret de la Croix-blanche, a meeting-place for the irreverent, where he met poets, like Molière, Racine, and La Fontaine, and *libertins*, like La Mothe le Vayer and Des Barreaux. He began to attack established authority – Chapelain in his seventh satire, which he read at the Croix-blanche, and in *Chapelain décoiffé*, an amusing parody of some scenes of *Le Cid*, written by Boileau, together with Chapelle, Racine, Furetière, and Gilles Boileau (1665); and Colbert in *Colbert enragé*, written in conjunction with his brother, Gilles. He published his first collection of satires in 1666.

Hitherto an iconoclastic young man, he now began to sober down – partly, perhaps, because he was growing older, partly because his earlier audacity had made him enemies, and partly because he was moving in new circles. We find him reading his ninth satire in the house of M. de Brancas, in the presence of Mme de la Sablière and Mme Scarron (the future Mme de Maintenon), and, in 1667, he became a member of the academy of Lamoignon:[1]

... l'accès obligeant qu'il me donna dans son illustre maison fit avantageusement mon apologie contre ceux qui voulaient m'accuser alors de libertinage et de mauvaises mœurs.

(Preface to the 1683 edition of his works)

He ceased writing satires and turned to the verse epistle instead.

Boileau was now a respectable member of society, gaining in authority and influence. His intimacy with Racine seems to date from 1671, and he and Racine seem to have shared their patrons and protectors. Three of the *épîtres* are dedicated to the King, and

---

[1] See above, p. 199.

three others to people of influence (Guilleragues, Lamoignon, and Seignelay). In 1672, he dined at Ninon de l'Enclos's with La Rochefoucauld and Dangeau, and visited La Rochefoucauld and Mme de Lafayette. He read his poems at the houses of Gourville, Pomponne, and Mme de Montespan; he was presented to Condé, and read his first *épître* and part of *Le Lutrin* at court; he enjoyed the protection of Colbert. In 1674, he published an important volume of *Œuvres diverses*, containing the *Art poétique*, his translation of Longinus, the satires and epistles written by that date, and part of *Le Lutrin*. Louis XIV granted him a pension of 2,000 livres, and the following year he figured in the *chambre du Sublime*.[2]

Two years later, Boileau and Racine were appointed *historiographes du roi*. Henceforth, apart from the last two cantos of *Le Lutrin*, he wrote little.

Boileau's natural bent seems to have been towards satire. He began by writing satires;[3] he wrote satires at the end of his life; and there are plenty of satirical traits in his other works, the *Dialogue sur les Héros de Romans*, the *Art poétique*, the *Epîtres*, and *Le Lutrin*. He himself complains, humorously, that, try as he may, he cannot help being satirical:

> Je ne puis pour louer rencontrer une rime . . .
> . . . . . .
> Mais, quand il faut railler, j'ai ce que je souhaite.
> . . . . . .
> Je ne puis bien parler, et ne saurais me taire;
> Et, dès qu'un mot plaisant vient luire à mon esprit,
> Je n'ai point de repos qu'il ne soit en écrit.
> (Satire VII)

In Satire II, complaining of the difficulty he has in finding rhymes, he says:

> Si je pense exprimer un auteur sans défaut,
> La raison dit Virgile, et la rime Quinault.[4]

[2] This was a gift from Mme de Thianges, Mme de Montespan's sister, to the young duc du Maine, the illegitimate son of Louis XIV and Mme de Montespan. It was a model of a room in which, around the young prince, were grouped wax figures representing Mme Scarron, La Rochefoucauld, Bossuet, Mme de Thianges, Mme de Lafayette, Racine, La Fontaine, and Boileau—this last, armed with a pitchfork, holding at bay a number of poetasters who were trying to break in.

[3] According to M. Adam, Boileau's satires were composed in the following order: VII (1663), II (1663), IV (1664), V (August 1664), *Discours au Roi* (Sept. 1664), VI (1664—originally begun in 1656), I (1665—originally begun in 1657: satires VI and I were originally part of one long poem), III (1666—begun in 1664), IX (1667), VIII (1668).

[4] Cf.

> Le mal est qu'en rimant, ma muse un peu légère
> Nomme tout par son nom, et ne saurait rien taire.
> (*Discours au Roi*)

He defends satire and the right of the satirist to speak out in the *Discours sur la Satire* and in the ninth satire which it accompanied. Satire is beneficial, he argues, because it attacks vice and folly. Literary criticism, which Boileau had been attacked for introducing into satire, is the birthright of all:

> Un clerc, pour quinze sous, sans craindre le holà,
> Peut aller au parterre attaquer *Attila* . . .

His criticisms, he adds, are not personal: if he attacks Chapelain, for example, it is as a poet, not as a man:

> Ma muse en l'attaquant, charitable et discrète,
> Sait de l'homme d'honneur distinguer le poète.

Be that as it may, Boileau's satires are not timeless, but topical, often expressing the views and animosities of the circle to which he belonged at the moment, the objects of his attack varying from edition to edition as circumstances and his allegiance changed. The seventh satire, written after the first pension list, attacks Chapelain (who had been liberally rewarded) and his friends. Satire IV is an answer to *Macarise*, in which d'Aubignac had glorified reason (1664), and betrays the influence of the circle of the Croix-blanche. Satire V was written at a time when Condé was threatening to have the unworthy, legitimate son of Mme de Longueville, the comte de Dunois, disinherited in favour of his younger brother, Saint-Paul, her illegitimate child by La Rochefoucauld; at a time, too, when the government had ordered patents of nobility to be examined. The first satire in its earliest version (1661) was an attack on Foucquet. The third satire ridicules, in the person of the narrator, P, abbé de Broussin, a gourmet whom Boileau had met at the Croix-blanche. The ninth satire is a reply to the criticisms which the publication of Boileau's satires in 1666 had elicited. The eighth satire is a further reply: Cotin had objected to the anti-rationalism of Satire IV, and Boileau in answer develops the theme.

One of the main features of interest of Boileau's satires is the criticism they contain of the society of his day. The theme of the first satire is that merit and virtue pass unrecognized, whereas wealth, even if it has been acquired by unjust means, is respected. Such people as the *partisans* can live in Paris —

> Mais moi, vivre à Paris! Eh! qu'y voudrais-je faire?
> Je ne sais ni tromper, ni feindre, ni mentir . . .

The last line calls to mind *Le Misanthrope*, which Molière may already have begun when Boileau wrote this satire: this is not the only occasion on which the two poets treated similar themes.

Later in the poem there is a daring allusion to the Archbishop of
Paris and the persecution of Port-Royal:

> Où[5] le vice orgueilleux s'érige en souverain,
> Et va la mitre en tête et la crosse à la main;
> Où la science triste, affreuse, délaissée,
> Est partout des bons lieux comme infâme chassée ...

Boileau returns to the attack on the *partisans* in Satire VIII – it
is a theme which La Bruyère was to take up.

The fifth satire, on nobility, develops the idea – expressed at
the same period by Molière in his *Dom Juan* – that noble birth is
worthless without personal merit, and gives an interesting picture
of the aristocracy of the time. Primitive simplicity has gone;
nobles have become extravagant, got into debt, and are marrying
the daughters of the wealthy middle-classes – once again we are
reminded of Molière (*Le Bourgeois gentilhomme*) and La Bruyère.
In Satires VI and III, there is realism of a rather different kind.
Satire VI very amusingly describes the discomforts of life in Paris,
the noise and the traffic, and gives us a vivid impression of the
forms these inconveniences took in Paris three centuries ago. Satire
III describes a seventeenth-century dinner party, second-rate from
the point of view both of the food and of the conversation, and the
indignation of the gourmet who had been induced to attend it.

Two of the satires deal with more general questions. The fourth
satire is an attack on the human reason. Men are not rational
beings; their tastes and ambitions are mad. Reason is not a safe
guide to conduct:

> Comme on voit qu'en un bois que cent routes séparent
> Les voyageurs sans guide assez souvent s'égarent,
> L'un à droit, l'autre à gauche, et, courant vainement,
> La même erreur les fait errer diversement:
> Chacun suit dans le monde une route incertaine,
> Selon que son erreur la joue et le promène;
> Et tel y fait l'habile et nous traite de fous,
> Qui sous le nom de sage est le plus fou de tous.

Nor is it a source of contentment:

> Souvent de tous nos maux la raison est le pire.
> C'est elle qui, farouche au milieu des plaisirs,
> D'un remords importun vient brider nos désirs.

There is, here, a hint of *libertinage*, of epicureanism and the
doctrine of following nature. Satire VIII returns to the theme of
human nature. Men are foolish, and variable, governed by their
vices and passions; they respect nothing but money, and learning
goes unrewarded. Although men have reason, while animals have
only instinct, they are irrational and capricious, superstitious and

[5] I.e. in Paris.

idolatrous. In both these satires, Boileau is giving powerful expression to a view of man which we have already encountered.

Though different in tone from the satires, the *Epîtres*[6] contain the same ingredients, in different proportions. Even the satirical vein is still there: Boileau cannot refrain from hitting out at his *bêtes noires* (*Epîtres* VII and VIII), and the second *épître* (*Contre les procès*) might equally well have been called a satire. Flattery of the King, already seen in the *Discours au Roi* and in Satires I and V, occurs more frequently. The first *épître* (*Contre les conquêtes*) celebrates the work of Colbert and condemns conquest, a theme already treated in Satire VIII. But it was ill-timed, since, when it appeared, the Dutch War had begun; and Boileau wrote the second *épître* (*Le Passage du Rhin*) to celebrate Louis's military exploits, as he does also in the sixth and eighth *épîtres*, and in the *Art poétique*.

More interesting is the philosophy of the epistles, which is again a continuation of ideas already found in the satires. In the fifth *épître*, the theme is that the true aim of life is self-knowledge and peace of mind, not the false aims which men set themselves (cf. Satires IV and VIII); and in the sixth *épître*, Boileau praises the country in contrast to Paris (cf. Satire VI):

> Qu'heureux est le mortel, qui, du monde ignoré,
> Vit content de soi-même en un coin retiré;
> Que l'amour de ce rien qu'on nomme renommée
> N'a jamais enivré d'une vaine fumée;
> Qui de sa liberté forme tout son plaisir
> Et ne rend qu'à lui seul compte de son loisir!

In the ninth *épître*, he returns to the theme of self-knowledge: in contrast to the hypocrisy of the age, its desire to appear what it is not, one should be oneself, know oneself, not try to be anything but what one really is: 'rien n'est beau que le vrai'.

In the second satire, one catches a glimpse of Boileau at work, having difficulty in finding rhymes. But the vein of personal poetry is much richer in the *Epîtres*. In *Epître* V, he says something of his early life, and describes the change which has come over him since the days of the satires:

> Aujourd'hui vieux lion je suis doux et traitable;
> Je n'arme point contre eux [his enemies] mes ongles émoussés.
> Ainsi que mes beaux jours mes chagrins sont passés;
> Je ne sens plus l'aigreur de ma bile première,
> Et laisse aux froids rimeurs une libre carrière.

We see Boileau in the country and the town in *Epître* VI.

[6] According to M. Boudhors, the order of composition of the *Epîtres* is: III (1670–2), I (1669–72), IV (1672), II (1672 or 1673), V (1674), IX (1675), VII (February–April 1677, after the controversy about *Phèdre*), VI (July–August 1677, after Boileau's appointment as historiographer), VIII (1678).

*Le Lutrin,* together with Tassoni's *Secchia rapita* which preceded it and Pope's *Rape of the Lock* which followed, is one of
the classic mock-heroic epics.

C'est un burlesque nouveau, dont je me suis avisé dans notre langue:
car, au lieu que dans l'autre burlesque, Didon et Enée[7] parlaient comme
des harengères et des crocheteurs, dans celui-ci une horlogère et un
horloger parlent comme Didon et Enée.

The poem was also an attempt to illustrate Boileau's views on
the epic, namely, that 'un poème héroïque pour être excellent,
devait être chargé de peu de matière,' and that 'c'était à l'invention à la soutenir et à l'étendre'. *Le Lutrin,* which is in six
cantos, is in fact very simple. Its subject is a dispute (which
actually occurred) between the *trésorier* and the *chantre* of the
Sainte-Chapelle. The former erected a *lutrin* (lectern) to hide
the latter as he sat in his place; the latter had it removed;
and eventually the parties were reconciled by Boileau's friend,
Lamoignon.

The poem, which satirizes the Church, provides some amusing
scenes from the life of the clergy. The mixture of realism and
satire, similar to that of some of the satires, is delightful, as in the
description of the *trésorier*:

> Dans le réduit obscur d'une alcôve enfoncée
> S'élève un lit de plume à grands frais amassée:
> Quatre rideaux pompeux, par un double contour,
> En défendent l'entrée à la clarté du jour.
> Là, parmi les douceurs d'un tranquille silence,
> Règne sur le duvet une heureuse indolence.
> C'est là que le prélat, muni d'un déjeuner,
> Dormant d'un léger somme, attendait le dîner.
> La jeunesse en sa fleur brille sur son visage:
> Son menton sur son sein descend à double étage:
> Et son corps, ramassé dans sa courte grosseur,
> Fait gémir les coussins sous sa molle épaisseur.
>     La déesse [Discord] en entrant, qui voit la nappe mise,
> Admire un si bel ordre, et reconnaît l'Eglise.

The *Art poétique,* a vigorous and diversified poem, is a useful
starting-point for a survey of Boileau's criticism; but it should not
be read in isolation. It is divided into four cantos, the first containing general principles, the second dealing with the minor genres
(the idyll, the elegy, the ode, the sonnet, the epigram, the rondeau,
the ballade, the madrigal, the satire, and the vaudeville), the third
dealing with the major genres (tragedy, epic, and comedy), and the

---

[7] A reference to Scarron's *Virgile travesti.*

fourth giving general advice, such as seek criticism, be virtuous, do not write for money, and be an *honnête homme*:

> Que les vers ne soient pas votre éternel emploi.
> Cultivez vos amis, soyez homme de foi:
> C'est peu d'être agréable et charmant dans un livre,
> Il faut savoir encore et converser et vivre.

The *Art poétique* is, naturally, an expression of the classical doctrine. Not only should literature have a moral aim, but the writer must himself be virtuous:

> Le vers se sent toujours des bassesses du cœur.
> (Canto IV)

A work must have unity of tone, and obey the principles of *vraisemblance* and *bienséance*. Truth, reason, and good sense are the ideals to aim at. But here we must be on our guard. These three words, more or less synonymous in Boileau, are also synonymous, as the contexts show, with good taste: Boileau is not an exponent of rationalism in poetry.

> Au dépens du bon sens gardez de plaisanter:
> Jamais de la nature il ne faut s'écarter.
> (Canto III)

This couplet shows how closely *bon sens* and *nature* are associated; they are also associated with *raison* and taste:

> Le faux est toujours fade, ennuyeux, languissant;
> Mais la nature est vraie ...          (*Epître* IX)

> J'aime sur le théâtre un agréable auteur
> Qui, sans se diffamer aux yeux du spectateur,
> Plaît par la raison seule, et jamais ne la choque.
> Mais pour un faux plaisant, à grossière équivoque,
> Qui pour me divertir n'a que la saleté,
> Qu'il s'en aille ...
> (Canto III)

*Bon sens, nature, raison*, the essential qualities, are the antithesis of the boring, the crude, and the vulgar.[8]

[8] Cf.

> Evitons ces excès: laissons à l'Italie
> De tous ces faux brillants l'éclatante folie.
> Tout doit tendre au bon sens ...
> (Canto I)

> Au mépris du bon sens, le burlesque effronté ...
> (Canto I)

> La raison outragée enfin ouvrit les yeux,
> La [= la pointe] chassa pour jamais des discours sérieux ...
> (Canto II)

It is not only in Boileau, of course, that *bon sens* means good taste. To take only one example, Tristan, in *Le Page disgracié*, quoting a poem

In style, Boileau urges the need for clarity, concision, nobility,[9] variety, and purity:

> Soyez simple avec art,
> Sublime sans orgueil, agréable sans fard.
>
> (Canto I)

One must strike the happy mean between excessive detail and excessive brevity. Obscurity is the result, above all, of imprecision of thought: to be clear, one must learn to think clearly:

> Ce que l'on conçoit bien s'énonce clairement,
> Et les mots pour le dire arrivent aisément.
>
> (Canto I)

Correctness is the chief need:

> Surtout qu'en vos écrits la langue révérée
> Dans vos plus grands excès vous soit toujours sacrée.
> En vain vous me frappez d'un son mélodieux,
> Si le terme est malpropre, ou le tour vicieux:
> Mon esprit n'admet point un pompeux barbarisme,
> Ni d'un vers ampoulé l'orgueilleux solécisme.
>
> (Canto I)

Good style is the result of effort:

> Vingt fois sur le métier remettez votre ouvrage:
> Polissez-le sans cesse et le repolissez;
> Ajoutez quelquefois, et souvent effacez.
>
> (Canto I)

This is a point to which Boileau attached particular importance. 'Un ouvrage ne doit point paraître trop travaillé, mais il ne saurait être trop travaillé [...] Il y a bien de la différence entre des vers faciles et des vers facilement faits,' he wrote in the preface to the 1701 edition of his works; and he boasted to Louis Racine that he had taught the latter's father to 'faire difficilement des vers faciles'. This seems to have been his own method of composition:

> Ainsi recommençant un ouvrage vingt fois,
> Si j'écris quatre mots, j'en effacerai trois.
>
> (Satire II)

---

addressed to him, comments: 'Ces vers ne sont pas à la mode et polis comme on les fait aujourd'hui, mais avec ce qu'ils ont de bon sens, ils ont quelque chose de bien digne que je m'en souvienne'...
[9] Cf. *Epître XI*, in which he gives his poetic ideal as:
> un écrit
> Qui dît, sans s'avilir, les plus petites choses...

In a letter to Maucroix (1695), he says: 'Plus les choses sont sèches et malaisées à dire en vers, plus elles frappent quand elles sont dites noblement, et avec cette élégance qui fait proprement la poésie.'

Boileau has often been misrepresented. Mme de Staël, for example, complains:

> Boileau, tout en perfectionnant le goût et la langue, a donné à l'esprit français, l'on ne saurait le nier, une disposition très défavorable à la poésie. Il n'a parlé que de ce qu'il fallait éviter, il n'a insisté que sur des préceptes de raison et de sagesse qui ont introduit dans la littérature une sorte de pédanterie très nuisible au sublime élan des arts.

This is almost the antithesis of the real Boileau. Boileau, in fact, says very little about rules in the *Art poétique*: even the rule of the unities is dismissed in a couplet. He is much more concerned with characterizing the kind of poetry that will be interesting and effective. He was fully aware that correctness and discipline were not everything. The *Art poétique* opens with an explicit reminder that the poet is born, not made, and he adds later:

> Soyez plutôt maçon, si c'est votre talent,
> Ouvrier estimé dans un art nécessaire,
> Qu'écrivain du commun, et poète vulgaire.[10]
>
> (Canto IV)

The principle of truth, on which he insists, besides meaning truth to human nature, has two further implications. It means that one must be true to oneself, and be aware of one's own strength and limitations, since we all have different gifts:

> Mais souvent un esprit qui se flatte et qui s'aime
> Méconnaît son génie, et s'ignore soi-même . . .
>
> (Canto I)

It also means sincerity — the poet must feel what he is trying to express:

> C'est peu d'être poète, il faut être amoureux.
>
> (Canto II)

> Pour me tirer des pleurs, il faut que vous pleuriez.
>
> (Canto III)

Boileau recognizes, too, that genius is above rules:

> Quelquefois dans sa course un esprit vigoureux,
> Trop resserré par l'art, sort des règles prescrites,
> Et de l'art même apprend à franchir leurs limites.
>
> (Canto IV)

---

[10] Cf. Satire IX:

> Quelle verve indiscrète
> Sans l'aveu des neuf sœurs vous a rendu poète?
> Sentiez-vous, dites-moi, ces violents transports
> Qui d'un esprit divin font mouvoir les ressorts?
> Qui vous a pu souffler une si folle audace?
> Phébus a-t-il pour vous aplani le Parnasse?
> Et ne savez-vous pas que, sur ce mont sacré,
> Qui ne vole au sommet tombe au plus bas degré,
> Et qu'à moins d'être au rang d'Horace ou de Voiture,
> On rampe dans la fange avec l'abbé de Pure?

Finally, he was, like his contemporaries, conscious of the importance of the *je ne sais quoi,* which defies explanation and analysis. In the *Dissertation sur Joconde* (1664), he wrote:

Ces sortes de beautés sont de celles qu'il faut sentir, et qui ne se prouvent point. C'est je ne sais quoi qui nous charme, et sans lequel la beauté même n'aurait ni grâce ni beauté.

And in the 1701 preface, he returned to the problem:

Un ouvrage a beau être approuvé d'un petit nombre de connaisseurs: s'il n'est plein d'un certain agrément et d'un certain sel propre à piquer le goût général des hommes, il ne passera jamais pour un bon ouvrage, et il faudra à la fin que les connaisseurs eux-mêmes avouent qu'ils se sont trompés en lui donnant leur approbation.

Que si on me demande ce que c'est que cet agrément et ce sel, je répondrai que c'est un je ne sais quoi, qu'on peut beaucoup mieux sentir que dire. A mon avis néanmoins, il consiste principalement à ne jamais présenter au lecteur que des pensées vraies et des expressions justes.

In fact, so far was Boileau from being indifferent to what Mme de Staël calls the 'sublime élan des arts', that he devoted much time to precisely this problem. If there was one thing that Boileau hated, it was mediocrity, the absence of positive greatness; and throughout his life he was preoccupied with the problem of the 'sublime', the positive quality which makes for greatness. It was this preoccupation which led him to translate Longinus and to write the last three of his *Réflexions sur Longin.*

Boileau's translation of Longinus is more than a literary exercise. Begun at least as early as 1663 and far advanced, if not completed, by 1667, it was Boileau's 'first sustained literary interest'.[11] It was Boileau's translation, moreover, that first drew the attention of the literary public to Longinus,[12] and he remarks in his preface that he had a serious purpose: 'il ne s'agissait pas simplement ici de traduire Longin, mais de donner au public un *Traité du sublime* qui pût être utile'. The translation was clearly intended to be complementary to the *Art poétique*: Boileau, indeed, says in the preface to the 1674 volume:

J'ai fait originairement cette traduction pour m'instruire, plutôt que dans le dessein de la donner au public; mais j'ai cru qu'on ne serait pas fâché de la voir ici à la suite de la *Poétique*, avec laquelle ce traité a quelque rapport, et où j'ai même inséré plusieurs préceptes qui en sont tirés.

11 J. Brody, *Boileau and Longinus*, 1958, p. 35.
12 Brossette was not in error when he wrote to Boileau in 1708: 'Votre traduction mérite de grands éloges, non seulement par elle-même, mais parce qu'elle a donné lieu à quantité d'excellents ouvrages que plusieurs savants ont faits depuis ce temps sur Longin; et je ne craindrai point d'en dire trop en assurant que Longin est plus connu dans le monde par votre traduction, qu'il ne l'était auparavant par lui-même.'

With this in mind, it may be worth looking into Boileau's translation. The *Traité du sublime* is an enquiry into literary excellence. The sublime is 'ce qui forme l'excellence et la souveraine
perfection du discours', or, as Boileau puts it in his preface, 'cet
extraordinaire et ce merveilleux qui frappe dans le discours, et qui
fait qu'un ouvrage enlève, ravit, transporte'. 'Sublime' is in fact
synonymous with 'interesting', 'vivid', 'moving', 'vigorous', and
the antithesis of 'insipid' and 'dull';[13] and Longinus illustrates
this quality and the means of expression by which it may be
achieved. The sublime owes more to nature than to technique:
Longinus says that it has five sources, *élévation d'esprit, le
pathétique* (defined as 'cette véhémence naturelle qui touche et
qui émeut'), figures of speech, nobility of style, and arrangement
of words, and adds that the first and most important of these is
'plutôt un présent du ciel qu'une qualité qui se puisse acquérir'.
For Longinus, imperfect greatness is far better than perfect
mediocrity; and there is plenty of evidence that Boileau agreed:

Ce n'est pas, monsieur, que je veuille faire passer ici l'ouvrage de M. de
La Fontaine pour un ouvrage sans défauts [ ... ] Il suffit, pour moi, que
le bon y passe infiniment le mauvais et c'est assez pour faire un ouvrage.

*(Dissertation sur Joconde)*

He remarked of Balzac, that 'quoique ses beautés soient vicieuses,
ce sont néanmoins des beautés; au lieu que la plupart des auteurs
de ce temps pèchent moins par avoir des défauts que par n'avoir
rien de bon'. Conversely he says that M. de Bouillon's version of
*Joconde* is 'moins à blâmer pour les fautes qui y sont, que pour
l'esprit et le génie qui n'y est pas'; and he condemns Godeau for
his lack of positive qualities:

... il est toujours à jeun, et [ ... ] il n'a rien qui remue ni qui échauffe;
en un mot, [ ... ] il n'a point cette force de style et cette vivacité d'expression qu'on cherche dans les ouvrages, et qui les font durer.

He had no patience with mediocrity:

Il n'est point de degrés du médiocre au pire ...

*(Art poétique*, Canto IV)

For Longinus, who constantly attacks bombast and bad taste,
the sublime is associated with simplicity. Boileau discusses this
point in his preface and in the tenth *Réflexion sur Longin*, and
distinguishes sharply between the sublime and the *style sublime*,

[13] 'Le sublime est une certaine force de discours propre à élever et à
ravir l'âme, et qui provient ou de la grandeur de la pensée et de la noblesse du sentiment, ou de la magnificence des paroles, ou du tour harmo-
nieux, vif et animé de l'expression; c'est-à-dire d'une de ces choses re-
gardées séparément, ou, ce qui fait le parfait sublime, de ces trois choses
jointes ensemble.'                        *(XIIᵉ Réflexion sur Longin)*

between the genuinely striking and the affectation of dignity. 'God said, Let there be light' is sublime (this example is in Longinus, too), and yet it is simple, not in the *style sublime*. If the same idea were expressed in the style sublime – 'le souverain arbitre de la nature d'une seule parole forma la lumière'[14] – it would no longer be either simple or sublime. The true sublime, insists Boileau, is simple – another example is the 'Qu'il mourût' of Corneille's *Horace*; indeed, it is often sublime because it is simple. It, again, is a quality which cannot be analysed, only felt:

> le sublime n'est pas proprement une chose qui se prouve et qui se démontre; mais [ ... ] c'est un merveilleux qui saisit, qui frappe et qui se fait sentir.                                                                                     (*X<sup>e</sup> Réflexion sur Longin*)

Boileau, then, requires of a work of art that it should be clear, in good taste, and have positive qualities to commend it to the reader. As a critic, he has two criteria, neither of which is obedience to rules. The first is success, the judgment of the public. The poet whose style is varied, he says in the *Art poétique*, will be a success:

> Son livre, aimé du ciel, et chéri des lecteurs,
> Est souvent chez Barbin entouré d'acheteurs.
>                                 (Canto I)

And he ridicules the poet (Chapelain?) who has a high opinion of himself, but whose works do not sell. In the 1701 preface he formulates this doctrine explicitly:

> Puisqu'une pensée n'est belle qu'en ce qu'elle est vraie, et que l'effet infaillible du vrai, quand il est bien énoncé, c'est de frapper les hommes, il s'ensuit que ce qui ne frappe point les hommes n'est ni beau ni vrai, ou qu'il est mal énoncé, et que par conséquent un ouvrage qui n'est point goûté du public est un très méchant ouvrage. Le gros des hommes peut bien, durant quelque temps, prendre le faux pour le vrai, et admirer de méchantes choses; mais il n'est pas possible qu'à la longue une bonne chose ne lui plaise; et je défie tous les auteurs les plus mécontents du public de me citer un bon livre que le public ait jamais rebuté, à moins qu'ils ne mettent en ce rang leurs écrits, de la bonté desquels eux seuls sont persuadés.

Hence, posterity alone can judge a work (*VII<sup>e</sup> Réflexion sur Longin*). The second criterion is that of all good critics, feeling; for Boileau is not an objective critic, attempting to judge in the name of rules. He explicitly recognizes that the qualities that make a work good or great, taste, the *je ne sais quoi*, the sublime, are things that cannot be analysed and can only be felt.

Boileau dislikes bad taste and mediocrity. He attacks the excesses

---

[14] More than a century before Chateaubriand, Boileau uses the sublimity of the Bible as an argument in favour of its divine origin (*X<sup>e</sup> Réflexion sur Longin*).

of the baroque style, in particular *pointes* and word play, which he condemns in the *Art Poétique* and in the twelfth satire. In the preface to the 1701 edition of his works, he holds up to ridicule the famous couplet from Théophile's *Pyrame*:

> Ah! voici le poignard qui du sang de son maître
> S'est souillé lâchement. Il en rougit, le traître!

'Toutes les glaces du nord ensemble ne sont pas, à mon sens,' he comments, 'plus froides que cette pensée.' In the *Dialogue des Héros de Romans* he mocks the baroque *pointes* and word play of Chapelain's *Pucelle*:

> De flèches toutefois aucune ne l'atteint;
> Ou pourtant l'atteignant de son sang ne se teint.
>
> ... Consumons-nous d'une flamme si belle:
> Brûlons en holocauste aux yeux de la Pucelle.

He condemns Saint-Amant in the *Réflexions sur Longin* for the macabre elements in his ode on Solitude and, both there and in the *Art poétique*, criticizes the lack of grandeur of the style of his *Moïse sauvé*. He had a hearty dislike for the burlesque style, which he attacks in the *Art poétique*. He told Louis Racine, 'Votre père avait la faiblesse de lire quelquefois le *Virgile travesti*, et de rire; mais il se cachait bien de moi'; and he made a blunder one day at court, when he criticized Scarron in front of his widow (Mme de Maintenon) and her second husband (Louis XIV). He disliked, too, the eternal love interest of the novels and plays of the period. He makes one of the guests at the *repas ridicule* say of Quinault,

> Et jusqu'à *Je vous hais*, tout s'y dit tendrement.

He ridicules this tendency in the *Dialogue des Héros de Romans* and in the *Art poétique*.

The baroque style, the burlesque, the long romances — Boileau is in fact reacting against the taste of the older generation, of the first half of the century. And his admiration was accorded unerringly to the great writers of his own day, to La Fontaine (*Dissertation sur Joconde*), to Corneille and Racine, and to Molière. If, in the *Art poétique*, his admiration for Molière seems qualified, no doubt because of the exigencies of an *Art Poétique*, —

> Etudiez la cour et connaissez la ville;
> L'une et l'autre est toujours en modèles fertiles.
> C'est par là que Molière illustrant ses écrits,
> *Peut-être* de son art *eût* remporté le prix,
> *Si*, moins ami du peuple, en ses doctes peintures
> Il n'eût point fait souvent grimacer ses figures,
> Quitté pour le bouffon, l'agréable et le fin,

Et sans honte à Térence allié Tabarin.
Dans ce sac ridicule où Scapin s'enveloppe,
Je ne reconnais plus l'auteur du *Misanthrope*.[15]

(Canto III)

— it was genuine. One day, Louis XIV asked Boileau who was the
greatest writer of his reign: 'Sire, c'est Molière. — Je ne l'aurais pas
cru; mais vous vous y connaissez mieux que moi.'

Boileau formulates the essential part of the classical doctrine
(clarity, good taste, artistic conscience) in a striking and memorable
way. He shows himself keenly interested in the wider question,
what really makes literature great, a question fraught with consequences for the future. He helped to clear away the lumber of the
past and to express the taste of his own generation. He was not the
'legislateur du Parnasse', but something infinitely more exciting —
a fighter against mediocrity and a champion of great literature.

The last satires and epistles belong to Boileau's old age. Satire X
(*Les Femmes*), begun in 1677 but abandoned, and completed in
1692 and 1693 after the appearance of the third volume of Perrault's *Parallèles*, belongs to the *querelle des Anciens et des
Modernes*. It attacks women, who were strongly on the side of the
moderns. It is a dialogue between a man on the point of being
married and a friend who warns him of the dangers of matrimony
— a common theme in French literature, treated, notably, in the
*Quinze Joies du Mariage*, in the third book of Rabelais, and in
Molière's *Mariage forcé*. The main interest of the poem, in which
the influence of La Bruyère has been detected, is in the portraits of
different contemporary types — the faithless wife, the coquette
(this passage recalls Frosine's speech in *L'Avare*), the gamester, the
*avare*, the scold, the jealous wife, the hypochondriac, the *savante*,
the *précieuse*, the snob, the *dévote*, the *plaideuse*, and so forth.

*Epître X* (1694–5), an answer to critics of the tenth satire, and
*Epître XI* (1695–6), both very attractive, are personal in tone.
*Epître X* gives some account of Boileau's life, and contains a self-
portrait:

... un esprit doux, simple, ami de l'équité,
Qui, cherchant dans ses vers la seule vérité,
Fit sans être malin ses plus grandes malices,
Et qu'enfin sa candeur seule a fait tous ses vices.
Dites que, harcelé par les plus vils rimeurs,
Jamais, blessant leurs vers, il n'effleura leurs mœurs:
Libre dans ses discours, mais pourtant toujours sage,
Assez faible de corps, assez doux de visage,

[15] M. Adam has explained the meaning of this last line. Scapin used to
come on with the sack, which Géronte was later to be induced to enter,
draped round him like a cloak.

> Ni petit, ni trop grand, très peu voluptueux,
> Ami de la vertu plutôt que vertueux.

And in *Epître XI*, we see Boileau and his gardener in the garden of his house at Auteuil.

> Que dis-tu de m'y voir rêveur, capricieux,
> Tantôt baissant le front, tantôt levant les yeux,
> De paroles dans l'air par élans envolées
> Effrayer les oiseaux perchés dans mes allées?

*Epître XII* (1695–7) is more philosophical. It reflects the religious preoccupations and Jansenist sympathies of his last years, when he was more and more friendly with Bossuet, Mme de Maintenon, and the cardinal de Noailles, as well as with Racine and Arnauld. Boileau's *épître*, written after some Jesuits had asserted that a man could win salvation without loving God, had the approval of Bossuet, the Archbishop of Paris (Noailles), and Arnauld; like Pascal in the *Provinciales*, Boileau condemns the doctrine.

Satire XI (*Sur l'honneur*), written in 1698 and published in 1701, was composed on the occasion of a lawsuit brought against Gilles Boileau for having usurped titles of nobility – the Boileau family won its case. It returns to the themes of the fourth, fifth, and eighth satires, or at least to a kindred theme. It attacks the false conception of honour current in the world, the false sense of values which leads men to aim at money, conquest, and worldly success; true honour, it asserts, resides in justice.

Satire XII (*L'Equivoque*, 1705–6) takes up the theme of religion, already occurring in Satires X and XI. In a long digression in the tenth satire, Boileau had attacked – like Molière in *Tartuffe* and La Bruyère in *Les Caractères* – *directeurs de conscience*, attacking them, amongst other things, for their moral teaching, their *morale relâchée*, and siding with Pascal. In Satire XI, at a time when to be suspected of Jansenism was to incur Louis XIV's displeasure, he had praised Jansenism in a daring couplet:

> La vertu n'était point sujette à l'ostracisme,
> Ni ne s'appelait point alors un jansénisme.

(The word *jansénisme* was left blank, but the gap was not hard to fill up.) Now, in his last satire, on ambiguity – to which he attributes false values, legal jargon, heresy, and schism – he criticizes probabilism at length in a passage which is a verse summary of the *Provinciales*.[16] Louis XIV, in fact, influenced by his Jesuit con-

---

[16] Boileau was not a Jansenist and numbered both Jansenists (e.g. Arnauld) and Jesuits amongst his friends. But there is no doubt that on this question his sympathies were with the Jansenists. Mme de Sévigné

fessor, Père Le Tellier, forbade the publication of this satire, which first appeared posthumously.

Boileau gives some valuable and amusing glimpses of life in France three hundred years ago; he castigates society for defects which, in one form or another, are likely to be with us always; he expresses a sane and balanced philosophy of life. In all his work, his literary criticism as well as his other poetry, he is on the right side, fighting for sincerity, justice, and genuineness, tilting at cant and false idols. It is difficult to imagine that there could be an age in which it would not be salutary and stimulating to read Boileau. The last word may be left to the poet himself:

> Sais-tu pourquoi mes vers sont lus dans les provinces,
> Sont recherchés du peuple, et reçus chez les princes?
> Ce n'est pas que leurs sons, agréables, nombreux,
> Soient toujours à l'oreille également heureux;
> Qu'en plus d'un lieu le sens n'y gêne la mesure,
> Et qu'un mot quelquefois n'y brave la césure:
> Mais c'est qu'en eux le vrai, du mensonge vainqueur,
> Partout se montre aux yeux, et va saisir le cœur,
> Que le bien et le mal y sont prisés au juste;
> Que jamais un faquin n'y tient un rang auguste;
> Et que mon cœur, toujours conduisant mon esprit,
> Ne dit rien aux lecteurs, qu'à soi-même il n'ait dit.
> Ma pensée au grand jour partout s'offre et s'expose,
> Et mon vers, bien ou mal, dit toujours quelque chose.
> *(Epître IX)*

---

has a very amusing account of Boileau, pressed by some Jesuits to say who, in his opinion, was the greatest writer of the age, hedging and then bursting out, 'Pascal'.

*Chapter 16*

# LA FONTAINE

ALTHOUGH Jean de La Fontaine (1621–95) wrote much in various genres ('je suis volage en vers comme en amours'[1]), it is for his *Fables* that he is chiefly remembered and deserves to be remembered. However attractive such poems as *Adonis* or the *Songe de Vaux*, however sprightly his epistles in verse and prose, however delightful the ballet entitled *Les Rieurs du Beau-Richard*, they remain trifles.[2] The content is not equal to the form, and universality is lacking. Even the *Contes*, amusing as many of them are, are too much concerned with a single theme, and that an unedifying one, not to pall. Only in the *Fables* did La Fontaine really come into his own. Here alone could he make full use of his various gifts, find a content worthy of his technical virtuosity, and combine diversity of style with seriousness of purpose. Here alone could he express all the facets of his rich personality – his gaiety and his melancholy, his love of solitude and repose, his interest in politics and society, in philosophy and letters. Here alone could he draw freely upon his wide experience. For La Fontaine knew his country better than most of his contemporaries. As seminarist of the Oratory and friend of Port-Royal, as the associate of *libertins*, as the pensioner of Foucquet and the gentleman-servant of Mme d'Orléans, as *maître des eaux et forêts* and *capitaine des chasses* at Château-Thierry for some twenty years, as the intimate of the Bouillons and the Condés, of Mme de la Sablière and the Vendômes, he was acquainted with most aspects of seventeenth-century French life and in touch with the main intellectual movements of the age. The country and the town, the great and the small, literature and the arts, science, free-thought and religion – none of these was unknown to him. Probably Molière alone could boast of a similar breadth of experience.

Why La Fontaine should have chosen to write fables, devoting himself to what had hitherto been a non-literary genre, is not clear.

---

[1] *Discours à Mme de la Sablière.* (This is not the *Discours à Mme de la Sablière* contained in the *Fables*, but another one.)

[2] One or two poems, such as the *Discours à Mme de la Sablière* and the *Epître à Monseigneur l'évêque de Soissons*, must be excepted. *Psyché* is discussed below in Chapter 18.

It is not unreasonable to suppose that he felt himself above all to be a story-teller; and it may well be that the poet who acknowledges a weakness for folk-tales —

> Si Peau d'âne m'était conté,
> J'y prendrais un plaisir extrême
>
> (VIII, 4)

— was unusually sensitive to the spell of the fables of Aesop and of Phaedrus, with which he had undoubtedly become familiar in his schooldays. Moreover, the shortness of fables must have been an attraction for a poet who held that 'les ouvrages les plus courts/ Sont toujours les meilleurs' (X, 14), and who confessed that 'les longs Ouvrages me font peur' (VI, Epilogue). Be that as it may, the first six books of the Fables, dedicated to the dauphin and based mainly on Aesop and Phaedrus and their adaptors,[3] appeared in 1668. Books VII–XI, dedicated to Mme de Montespan, followed in 1678 and 1679; and the collection was completed in 1694 by the twelfth book, dedicated to the young duc de Bourgogne.

In the avertissement to the second collection, La Fontaine claims that most of the new fables have 'un air et un tour un peu différent' from those of the first six books, though his friend, Maucroix, admitted that he could not see the difference, which later critics have, perhaps, been inclined to exaggerate. La Fontaine does, however, mention two new features. The first is a new source, the Indian, Pilpay:[4] 'je dirai par reconnaissance que j'en dois la plus grande partie à Pilpay, sage indien'. This is not quite accurate: of just under ninety fables in the five books of the

---

[3] G. Corrozet, Fables du très ancien Esope phrygien (1542); G. Haudent, Trois cent soixante-six apologues d'Esope (1547); Nevelet, Mythologica Aesopica (1610, second edition 1660); Jean Meslier, Aesopi fabulae (in Latin and French, 1629, republished 1641 and 1650); Baudoin, Fables d'Esope phrygien (1631, republished 1649 and 1659); Jacques Régnier, Apologi Phaedrii (1643); Lemaître de Sacy's edition of Phaedrus with a French translation (1646); Pierre Millot's prose translation of Aesop (1646); Audin, Fables héroïques (1648); Roger Trichet, sieur du Fresne, Figures tirées des Fables d'Esope et autres (1659).
Since three of the above-mentioned works were published or reprinted in 1659 and 1660, since a new edition of Verdizotti's Cento Favole bellissime dei più illustri Antichi e Moderni graeci e latini (1570) appeared in 1661, and since Ménage and Lefebvre wrote Latin fables, and Patru and Furetière fables in French, about this time, it has been surmised that there was a certain quickening of interest in fables around 1660.
[4] Known to La Fontaine from the Livre des lumières ou la conduite des Rois composé par le sage Pilpay, Indien; traduit en français par David Sahid d'Ispahan (the Orientalist Gaulmin?; 1644), and Père Poussines, Specimen Sapientiae Indorum Veterum (1666). La Fontaine's attention may have been drawn to Pilpay by Huet, who discusses Père Poussines's book in the Lettre sur l'origine des romans, published together with Mme de Lafayette's Zaïde (1671). His interest in the East is even more likely to have been awakened by the oriental traveller, Bernier, who was one of the members of the circle of Mme de la Sablière.

second collection, it has been estimated that not more than twenty
come from Pilpay; but the greater variety of the later fables *is* due
to the fact that La Fontaine has drawn on a wider range of sources,
including the oriental fabulist. The second feature pointed out by
La Fontaine is that the fables of the second collection are more
developed: 'Il a [ . . . ] fallu que j'aie cherché d'autres enrichisse-
ments, et étendu davantage les circonstances de ces récits, qui
d'ailleurs me semblaient le demander de la sorte.' These fables,
in fact, tend to be longer, and the narratives more detailed; and
La Fontaine uses his originals with greater freedom. He tends,
too, to be bolder in introducing and developing his own reflections,
and the vein of personal poetry is more pronounced. After the
success of the first collection, La Fontaine seems to have been surer
of himself and to have had some confidence that his fables would
confer immortality on him:

> Protégez désormais le livre favori
> Par qui j'ose espérer une seconde vie.
> (*A Madame de Montespan*)

But it should, perhaps, be stressed that the differences between the
earlier and the later fables are differences of degree rather than of
kind.

La Fontaine, like so many of his contemporaries, had the dual
aim of giving pleasure and imparting instruction:

L'apparence en est puérile, je le confesse; mais ces puérilités servent
d'enveloppe à des vérités importantes.

Je ne doute point, MONSEIGNEUR, que vous ne regardiez favorablement
des inventions si utiles et tout ensemble si agréables . . .
> (*A Monseigneur le Dauphin*)

> Je me sers d'Animaux pour instruire les Hommes.
> (*A Monseigneur le Dauphin*, poem)

> En ces sortes de feinte il faut instruire et plaire
> Et conter pour conter me semble peu d'affaire.
> (VI, 1)

But wherein consists the usefulness of fables? In the first place,
obviously in the moral:

> Une Morale nue apporte de l'ennui;
> Le conte fait passer le précepte avec lui.
> (VI, 1)

But not only in the moral: La Fontaine claims that fables are also
a means of teaching natural history and of describing human
nature:

Elles ne sont pas seulement Morales, elles donnent encore d'autres connaissances. Les propriétés des Animaux et leurs divers caractères y sont

exprimés; par conséquent les nôtres aussi, puisque nous sommes l'abrégé
de ce qu'il y a de bon et de mauvais dans les créatures irraisonnables.
Quand Prométhée voulut former l'homme, il prit la qualité dominante de
chaque bête: de ces pièces si différentes il composa notre espèce; il fit cet
ouvrage qu'on appelle *le Petit Monde*. Ainsi ces fables sont un tableau où
chacun de nous se trouve dépeint.

(Preface to first collection)

In other words, the fables are not merely a means of sugaring the
pill: in them, La Fontaine is giving a picture of human nature in
general. He adds, later — and here he comes close to Molière —, that
he is trying to make vice ridiculous:

> Je tâche d'y tourner le vice en ridicule
> ......
> ..... faisant de cet ouvrage
> Une ample Comédie à cent actes divers,
>         Et dont la scène est l'Univers.

(V, 1)

> Les Bêtes, à qui mieux mieux
> Y font divers personnages;
> Les uns fous les autres sages,
> De telle sorte pourtant
> Que les fous vont l'emportant;
> La mesure en est plus pleine.
> Je mets aussi sur la Scène
> Des Trompeurs, des Scélérats,
> Des Tyrans et des Ingrats,
> Mainte imprudente pécore,
> Force Sots, force Flatteurs;
> Je pourrais y joindre encore
> Des légions de menteurs ...

(IX, 1)

La Fontaine's aim is not a narrowly didactic one: it is that of his
great contemporaries, that of depicting human nature.

Since one object of the fables is to inculcate a moral, it is worth
considering what message, if any, they contain. Here an immediate
difficulty presents itself: since La Fontaine is adapting fables from
previous writers, can we be sure what his own philosophy is? When,
for instance, he shows that might is right, counsels prudence and
wariness, warns us not to imitate others blindly, advises us to help
ourselves, reminds us that the best way to do a thing well is to do it
oneself, tells us that it does not pay to despise the small or that
honesty is the best policy, he is merely giving us the traditional
wisdom of writers of fables. This no doubt explains the co-existence
of contradictory principles: it is not easy, for example, to reconcile
the doctrine that we should help one another (VI, 16) with that of
mistrust (II, 7, VI, 13), the principle that honesty is the best policy
(IV, 11) with the recommendation of duplicity (II, 5), the praise

of foresight (I, 8) with its condemnation (VIII, 12), or the principle of prudence with that of 'nothing venture, nothing have' (X, 13); though La Fontaine would no doubt argue that 'toutes ces choses-là ont deux faces, aussi bien que la plupart de celles que nous louons ou que nous blâmons tous les jours'.[5]

At times, however, it is clear that La Fontaine is writing with his own age very much in mind. When he treats the themes of mistrust of flattery and of false appearances, he is treating themes very dear to his contemporaries. Sometimes he is at pains to make clear the relevance of his fable to seventeenth-century life:

> Le monde est plein de gens qui ne sont pas plus sages:
> Tout Bourgeois veut bâtir comme les grands Seigneurs,
> Tout petit Prince a des Ambassadeurs.
> Tout Marquis veut avoir des pages.
>
> (I, 3)

Similarly, the moral of *L'Ane vêtu de la peau du Lion* is:

> Force gens font du bruit en France...
> (V, 21)

Another begins:

> Se croire un personnage est fort commun en France.
> (VIII, 15)

One of his fables is a plea for more liberal rewards to poets (I, 14), and another substitutes praise of the *Maximes* of La Rochefoucauld for the traditional warning against vanity (I, 11).

More interesting is the fact that one can discern in the *Fables* a personal view of life, that of the man who had earlier written in an *épître* to Foucquet:

> Bon Dieu! que l'on est malheureux
> Quand on est si grand personnage!
> ......
> A jouir pourtant de vous-même
> Vous auriez un plaisir extrême...[6]

and who held that the secret of life was to 'jouir des vrais biens avec tranquillité'.[7] It is a philosophy of contentment and moderation. Know yourself and do not imitate others blindly:

> Ne forçons point notre talent;
> Nous ne ferions rien avec grâce...
> (IV, 5)

---

[5] *Comparaison d'Alexandre, de César et de Monsieur le Prince* (1684).
[6] Cf. the *Elégie* written after Foucquet's downfall and La Fontaine's praise of Condé for having in his old age found 'le secret de jouir de soi' (*Comparaison d'Alexandre, de César et de Monsieur le Prince*).
[7] *Discours à Mme de la Sablière*.

Limit your ambitions: greatness and success have their dangers;
modest competence is better than wealth which destroys peace of
mind:

> Ni l'or ni la grandeur ne nous rendent heureux...
>
> (XII, 25)

Whereas men make the mistake of being immoderate, particularly in their ambitions, it is wiser to be content with one's lot; if
one tries to change it, one is likely to be worse off; a bird in the
hand is worth two in the bush. La Fontaine attacks stoicism, because the stoics, in trying to extirpate all desire and passion from
the human heart,

> ... ôtent à nos cœurs le principal ressort;
> Ils font cesser de vivre avant que l'on soit mort.
>
> (XII, 20)

He holds nevertheless a modified form of stoicism, the belief that
one should accept without complaint what comes;[8] Providence
knows best.

Life, for La Fontaine, is something to be enjoyed. It is a mistake
to hoard one's goods:

> Jouis dès aujourd'hui...
>
> (VIII, 27)

> Le bien n'est bien qu'en tant que l'on s'en peut défaire.
>
> (X, 4)

The wise man is he who follows the substance, not the shadow. The
really important things in life are independence and seclusion:

> Elle offre à ses amants des biens sans embarras,
> Biens purs, présents du Ciel, qui naissent sous les pas.
>
> (XI, 4)

Seclusion, however, with friends:

> Il aimait les jardins, était Prêtre de Flore,
>     Il l'était de Pomone encore:
> Ces deux emplois sont beaux: Mais je voudrais parmi
>     Quelque doux et discret ami.[9]
>
> (VIII, 10)

In the last fable of all, the point is made that self-knowledge is the
highest duty of the sage, and that it is possible only in solitude:

> Apprendre à se connaître est le premier des soins
> Qu'impose à tous mortels la Majesté suprême.

[8] Cf.

> Les dieux nous ont jadis deux vertus députées,
> La constance aux douleurs, et la sobriété...
>
> (Poème du Quinquina)

[9] La Fontaine celebrates friendship in VIII, 11, and XII, 15.

Vous êtes-vous connus dans le monde habité?
L'on ne le peut qu'aux lieux pleins de tranquillité:
Chercher ailleurs ce bien est une erreur extrême.

The last lines of this fable suggest that La Fontaine regarded this
as his final message:

Cette leçon sera la fin de ces Ouvrages:
Puisse-t-elle être utile aux siècles à venir!
Je la présente aux Rois, je la propose aux Sages:
Par où saurais-je mieux finir?

(XII, 29)

That La Fontaine himself loved solitude is not in doubt. The
lines just quoted from *Le Songe d'un habitant du Mogol* (XI, 4)
introduce a passage in which La Fontaine expresses his own love
of a country life. Glimpses of the poet's own personality, such as
these lines afford, are one of the attractions of the fables, particularly of the last six books. In *La Laitière et le Pot au Lait*, he
replaces the traditional moral ('don't count your chickens before
they are hatched') by a confession of his own addiction to day-
dreaming. In *Les Deux Amis*, he gives us a delicious description of
true friendship; and, in a famous passage of *Les Deux Pigeons*, the
elderly poet nostalgically recalls the days when he, too, was in love.

In some of his fables, La Fontaine discusses more general
philosophical questions, particularly in the second collection.
Already in the second book, *L'Astrologue qui se laisse tomber dans
un puits* is a good example of a philosophical fable. The story is
contained in the first line and a half; the rest of the poem is a discussion, and condemnation, of astrology—a theme to which La
Fontaine returns in *L'Horoscope*, in which he expresses his own
belief in free will. In *Un Animal dans la lune*, he discusses the
fundamental question of the senses: are they reliable, or are they
always deceptive? He agrees with Descartes, that they can be
trusted, providing the reason is used as a check. A problem which
naturally interests him, as a writer of fables about animals, is the
problem of animal intelligence. Have animals the power of reasoning? have they souls? or are they mere machines, as Descartes had
asserted? La Fontaine rejects equally the oriental solution of the
problem, the doctrine of the transmigration of souls (IX, 7), and
that of Descartes, whose theory he discusses in detail in the
*Discours à Mme de la Sablière* in Book IX. There, and later in the
*Discours à Monsieur le duc de la Rochefoucauld*, *Les Souris et le
Chat-huant*, and *Le Renard anglais*, he gives examples of animal
intelligence and concludes that animals have

Non point une raison selon notre manière,
Mais beaucoup plus aussi qu'un aveugle ressort ...

Here he is in agreement with Montaigne, who, in the *Apologie de Raymond Sebond*, had also given examples of intelligent behaviour on the part of animals and had decided: 'Nous devons conclure de pareils effets pareilles facultés.' La Fontaine adopts a middle course: like Gassendi, he envisages the existence of two kinds of soul, a material kind of soul and a spiritual soul. The former he attributes to animals, though only man has the second:

> . . . la nature
> A mis dans chaque créature
> Quelque grain d'une masse où puisent les esprits:
> J'entends les esprits corps, et pétris de matière.
> (X, 14)

For La Fontaine in fact, there is little to choose between men and animals: both are equally unjust and rapacious. If the behaviour of the goshawk justifies the birdcatcher in *L'Oiseleur, l'Autour, et l'Alouette*, that of the shepherds justifies the wolf in *Le Loup et les Bergers*; Alexander and the lion are kindred spirits (IV, 12). This becomes a recurring theme in Book X. The first fable of that book (*L'Homme et la Couleuvre*) is a condemnation of man's injustice and ingratitude by various living creatures; incensed, the man in the fable kills the adder. The third fable leads to the conclusion:

> Qu'importe qui vous mange? homme ou loup; toute panse
> Me paraît une à cet égard . . .
> (X, 3)

The fifth is the fable of the wolf and the shepherds; and the fourteenth, the *Discours à Monsieur le duc de la Rochefoucauld*, begins:

> Je me suis souvent dit, voyant de quelle sorte
> L'homme agit et qu'il se comporte
> En mille occasions, comme les animaux:
> Le Roi de ces gens-là n'a pas moins de défauts
> Que ses sujets . . .
> (X, 14)

The examples given in this poem are not particularly flattering: men who have escaped from danger are as thoughtless as rabbits; and the village dogs who bark at strange dogs merely show the same egoism as men who want to prevent newcomers from sharing in the profits:

> Le moins de gens qu'on peut à l'entour du gâteau,
> C'est le droit du jeu, c'est l'affaire.
> (X, 14)

The *Compagnons d'Ulysse* (XII, 1) deals with the companions of Ulysses who, having been turned into animals, refuse to become men again, finding themselves better off as they are. If they are

condemned for servility to their passions, the wolf at least makes
some shrewd comments about human life:

> Si j'étais Homme, par ta foi,
> Aimerais-je moins le carnage?
> Pour un mot quelquefois vous vous étranglez tous:
> Ne vous êtes-vous pas l'un à l'autre des Loups?
> Tout bien considéré, je te soutiens en somme
> Que scélérat pour scélérat,
> Il vaut mieux être un Loup qu'un Homme . . .
>
> (XII, 1)

La Fontaine's avowed aim is to study human nature. Many
fables, in fact, instead of inculcating a maxim of conduct, illustrate
some aspect of human nature or behaviour:

> Nous nous pardonnons tout, et rien aux autres hommes.
>
> (I, 7)

> Il n'est, je le vois bien, si poltron sur la terre
> Qui ne puisse trouver un plus poltron que soi.
>
> (II, 14)

Similarly, *La Chatte métamorphosée en femme* and *L'Ivrogne
et sa Femme* illustrate the force of habit, *La Jeune Veuve* the
transience of grief, *Jupiter et le Passager* the fact that promises
made in the hour of need are forgotten when danger is past, and
*Le Loup et le Renard* human credulity. And the characters —
animals or men — created by La Fontaine are living and vividly
portrayed human types.

Moreover, the fables give an impression of seventeenth-century
society. This, too, was a conscious aim:

> Si j'ajoute du mien à son [Aesop's] invention,
> C'est pour peindre nos mœurs . . .
>
> (IV, 18)

The injustice, the insincerity, the ruthless egoism of court life,
the susceptibility of kings to flattery are the subject of several of
the best fables. In *Jupiter et les Tonnerres*, La Fontaine takes up
a favourite theme of Corneille, that the defects of monarchical
government are to be attributed, not to the King (Jupiter), but to
his subordinates. The nobles usually appear in an unfavourable
light: the man who kills the adder (X, 1) because its arguments
are just, we are told, is typical of 'les grands'; and their wealth is
by no means matched by real worth:

> Oh! que de grands seigneurs, au Léopard semblables,
> N'ont que l'habit pour tous talents!
>
> (IX, 3)

There is a vivid portrayal of a provincial nobleman in *Le Jardinier et son Seigneur*, and, in *La Chauve-souris, le Buisson, et le Canard*, a glimpse of the impecunious *grand seigneur* in debt,

> qui tous les jours se sauve
> Par un escalier dérobé.
>
> (XII, 7)

The Church appears in the *Fables*, too. We catch a glimpse of a rich, gouty prelate (III, 8) and of a comfortable, prosperous, selfish monk (VII, 3). Court prelates are satirized in *Le Songe d'un habitant du Mogol*, and, at the other end of the social scale, there is the *curé*, for whom a funeral is a profitable piece of business to be despatched as quickly as possible:

> Il fondait là-dessus l'achat d'une feuillette
> Du meilleur vin des environs:
> Certaine nièce assez propette
> Et sa chambrière Pâquette
> Devaient avoir des cotillons.
>
> (VII, 10)

Nor is the *tiers état* absent. The extravagance of tax-farmers is alluded to (XII, 3), as well as the greed of the *échevin*:

> Je crois voir en ceci l'image d'une ville,
> Où l'on met les deniers à la merci des gens
> Echevins, Prévôt des Marchands,
> Tout fait sa main: le plus habile
> Donne aux autres l'exemple . . .[10]
>
> (VIII, 7)

Descending the social hierarchy, we have the comfortably-off citizen ('demi Bourgeois, demi manant,') who owns the garden in *Le Jardinier et son Seigneur*, the shoemaker who complains of the number of saints' days (VIII, 2), a milkmaid (VII, 9), the wretched servant girls awakened at the crack of dawn by their mistress —

> L'une entr'ouvrait un œil, l'autre étendait un bras . . .
>
> (V, 6)

— and the poor woodcutter (I, 16).

[10] 'Dans la plupart des villes, un certain nombre de familles, fortes de leurs richesses, unies entre elles par des mariages, appuyées sur une nombreuse clientèle, détenaient, parfois de toute antiquité, les fonctions municipales. Elles se succédaient à la mairie ou à l'échevinage: les magistrats ne quittaient l'hôtel de ville que pour faire place à leurs fils, à leurs gendres, à leurs neveux. Malgré les injonctions de la Cour des comptes, ils ne donnaient aucune explication sur leur gestion financière, et une partie des fonds étaient employés pour leur usage privé ou pour acheter des partisans. En Provence, les municipalités avaient reçu du peuple le nom de *mange-communes*.' (A. Rambaud, *Histoire de la Civilisation française*, 1887, vol. II, pp. 119–20.) In 1668, Colbert issued an edict to prevent this abuse of public money. Magistrates were forbidden to appear at court without authorization, to charge their travelling expenses to the town, and to make the town incur debts on their behalf.

Within this general framework, a host of different seventeenth-century social types appear – the court spy (XII, 11), the busy-body (VII, 8), the *précieuse* whose history reminds one of that of Mademoiselle (VII, 4), fortune-tellers (VII, 14), a miser (IV, 20), doctors (V, 12), men of letters (V, 10 and 16, VIII, 19), a scold (VII, 2), schoolmasters (I, 19, IX, 5), and children (V, 11, IX, 5), for both of which last La Fontaine has a cordial dislike.

Some of the fables contain allusions to, or comments on, current events. *La Belette entrée dans un grenier* may refer to the government's attempts to strip tax-farmers of their ill-gotten gains; *Le Rat qui s'est retiré du monde* to the unwillingness of the religious orders to contribute to the Dutch War in 1675; *Le Savetier et le Financier* to Colbert's suppression of a number of church holidays. The weakness of coalitions in the face of a strong single command (such as France) is the theme of *Le Dragon à plusieurs têtes et le Dragon à plusieurs queues* and *Le Chat et le Rat*. *Les Voleurs et l'Ane* alludes to the fate of the province of Transylvania. *La tête et la queue du Serpent*, on the weakness of democratic states, is directed against Holland, with whom France was at war. *Un Animal dans la lune*, with its praise of peace and of Charles II of England, relates to a moment when there was hope that Charles might mediate between the French and the Dutch; and *Le Pouvoir des fables*, addressed to the French ambassador in England, was written when the English were on the point of forming an alliance with the Dutch. In *Le Lion*, the leopard probably represents Charles II of England and the lion Louis XIV, the fable admonishing the former to stand by the latter; just as *Le Bassa et le Marchand* admonishes the Dutch:

> mieux vaut en bonne foi
> S'abandonner à quelque puissant Roi,
> Que s'appuyer de plusieurs petits princes.

*Le Paysan du Danube*, on the other hand, is a protest against the French treatment of the occupied Dutch provinces. *L'Ecrevisse et sa fille* is possibly intended as a justification of Louis XIV's retreats.

La Fontaine has no illusions about human society. The strong prey upon the weak, in human society as in the world of beasts:

> Hélas! on voit que de tout temps
> Les petits ont pâti des sottises des grands.
>
> (II, 4)

The privileged are undeserving of their privileges; the under-privileged worthy of pity.

> Jupin pour chaque état mit deux tables au monde.
> L'adroit, le vigilant, et le fort sont assis

A la première; et les petits
Mangent leur reste à la seconde.

(X, 6)

La Fontaine is fully aware of the injustice of society. But he is neither a revolutionary nor a reformer. He observes without bitterness: this is how things are, and how they will always be. Constitutional change would not improve matters, for, if La Fontaine has a poor opinion of monarchies, he has an even poorer opinion of other forms of government. Popular government is topsy-turvy and inept (VII, 16), and the voice of the people is not that of God (VIII, 26).

La Fontaine, however, is primarily a story-teller. Whereas his predecessors 'ont fui l'ornement et le trop d'étendue' (VI, 1), he deliberately aims at filling out his fables – 'égayer' and 'étendre les circonstances' are the guiding principles he acknowledges in his prefaces. He individualizes his characters, so that they cease to be mere names and abstractions. He gives them titles (Maître Corbeau, Maître Renard, Maître Jean Lapin, Capitaine Renard) and names (Rodilardus, Raminagrobis, Bertrand, Raton, etc). He describes them, or rather conjures up an impression by a slight touch. The mule, cockahoop,

. . . marchait d'un pas relevé,
Et faisait sonner sa sonnette . . .

(I, 4)

The disappointed fox returns home 'serrant la queue, et portant bas l'oreille' (I, 18). There are many vivid, impressionistic descriptions of animals – 'Dame Belette au long corsage' (VIII, 22), 'Le Héron au long bec emmanché d'un long cou' (VII, 4), the vulture 'Au bec retors, à la tranchante serre' (VII, 7), the cat:

. . . velouté comme nous,
Marqueté, longue queue, une humble contenance,
Un modeste regard, et pourtant l'œil luisant . . .

(VI, 5)

La Fontaine invents lively dialogue:

Regardez bien, ma sœur;
Est-ce assez? dites-moi; n'y suis-je point encore?
—Nenni.—M'y voici donc?—Point du tout.—M'y voilà?
—Vous n'en approchez point.

(I, 3)

His men and animals talk in character, and he has the imagination to see the world through their eyes: the stream is an 'Océan' to

the ant who has fallen into it, and a blade of grass 'un promontoire'
(II, 12); and, when the rat leaves his hole,

> Que le monde, dit-il, est grand et spacieux!
> Voilà les Apennins, et voici le Caucase:
> La moindre taupinée était mont à ses yeux.
>
> (VIII, 9)

The setting is described, too, by a few touches:

> Un vieillard sur son Ane aperçut en passant
> Un Pré plein d'herbe et fleurissant.[11]
>
> (VI, 8)

The fables are modernized – the mule in *Les deux Mulets* is carrying 'l'argent de la Gabelle'; it is in Quimper-corentin that the
cart sticks in the mud (VI, 18).

La Fontaine enriches the standard poetical vocabulary of his
day with made-up words or familiar expressions:

> Tous les gens querelleurs, jusqu'aux simples mâtins,
> Au dire de chacun étaient *de petits saints*.
>
> (VII, 1)

He is fond, too, of archaisms: in one fable, using the word
*engeigner*, he confesses:

> J'ai regret que ce mot soit trop vieux aujourd'hui:
> Il m'a toujours semblé d'une énergie extrême.
>
> (IV, 11)

He has, thus, at his disposal a wide choice of vocabulary, and the
fables owe much to the use of the most telling – if not the most
usual – word:

> Tandis que coups de poing *trottaient* . . .
>
> (I, 13)

This line illustrates another favourite device of La Fontaine –
the suppression of inessential (though grammatically necessary)
words to achieve rapidity:

> Point de raison; fallut deviner et prédire . . .
>
> (VII, 14)

> Holà, Martin bâton!
> Martin bâton accourt; l'Ane change de ton.
>
> (IV, 5)

[11] Sometimes a more detailed description is found:

> A l'heure de l'affût, soit lorsque la lumière
> Précipite ses traits dans l'humide séjour,
> Soit lorsque le soleil rentre dans sa carrière,
> Et que n'étant plus nuit, il n'est pas encor jour,
> Au bord de quelque bois sur un arbre je grimpe . . .
>
> (X, 15)

La Fontaine excels at describing movement, by an accumulation of verbs:

> Qui les croque, qui les tue,
> Qui les gobe à son plaisir . . .
>
> (III, 4)

> Se vautrant, grattant, et frottant,
> Gambadant, chantant et broutant,
> Et faisant mainte place nette.
>
> (VI, 8)

He is an adept at noting the characteristic movements of each species of animal. The mice in *Le Chat et un vieux Rat*,

> Mettent le nez à l'air, montrent un peu la tête,
> Puis rentrent dans leurs nids à rats,
> Puis, ressortant, font quatre pas,
> Puis enfin se mettent en quête.

In *Le Chat, la Belette, et le petit Lapin*, it is the rabbit's turn:

> Après qu'il eut brouté, trotté, fait tous ses tours,
> Janot Lapin retourne aux souterrains séjours.

In *L'Ours et les deux Compagnons*, we can see and hear the bear snuffling at the body:

> Le tourne, le retourne, approche son museau,
> Flaire aux passages de l'haleine.

By the choice of words and rhythms, solemnity or speed are suggested. The hare, for example, allows the tortoise to

> Aller son train de Sénateur.
> Elle part, elle s'évertue;
> Elle se hâte avec lenteur.
>
> (VI, 10)

Similarly, the contrast between the mournful progress of the dead man and the cheerfulness of the *curé* is admirably brought out:

> Un mort s'en allait tristement
> S'emparer de son dernier gîte;
> Un Curé s'en allait gaiement
> Enterrer ce mort au plus vite.
>
> (VII, 10)

A humorous effect is achieved by the use of puns, archaisms, invented or familiar words. In the manner of Scarron, La Fontaine sometimes intervenes to tell us that he is omitting inessential detail:

> Quelqu'un vint au secours: qui ce fut, il n'importe . . . [12]
>
> (II, 10)

In the burlesque manner, too, he reduces his gods to human proportions He is particularly fond of passing from the sublime to

[12] Cf. VI, 10, and X, 15.

the ridiculous, from the heroic to the homely, or vice versa. The effect of this is always amusing, as when the *ânier* is compared to a Roman Emperor:

> Un Anier, son Sceptre à la main,
> Menait, en Empereur Romain,
> Deux Coursiers à longues oreilles.
> (II, 10)

Similarly, the grand style in which daybreak is announced contrasts amusingly with the homely realism with which the servant-girls and their tasks are described:

> Dès que Thétis chassait Phébus aux crins dorés,
> Tourets entraient en jeu, fuseaux étaient tirés . . .
> . . . . . .
> Dès que l'Aurore, dis-je, en son char remontait,
> Un misérable Coq à point nommé chantait.
> (V, 6)

More briefly, in *Le Mal Marié*, we hear of 'certaines Philis qui gardent les dindons'. In *Le Cierge*, after expressing the idea in elevated style, La Fontaine – like Scarron – puts it bluntly in everyday language:

> Quand on eut des palais de ces filles du Ciel
> Enlevé l'ambroisie en leurs chambres enclose,
> Ou, pour dire en Français la chose,
> Après que les ruches sans miel
> N'eurent plus que la Cire, on fit mainte bougie . . .
> (IX, 12)

Here the impact is all the greater for the suggestion that the poetical way of putting it is not French.

When the mock-heroic style is used for animals, the effect is more subtle. The ducks, urging the tortoise to travel, quote the example of Ulysses, and La Fontaine comments:

> . . . On ne s'attendait guère
> De voir Ulysse en cette affaire.
> (X, 2)

We forget, and are suddenly reminded, that this is a fable, not about men, but about animals. In *Le Chat et le vieux Rat*, the cat is compared to Alexander and Attila:

> J'ai lu chez un conteur de Fables,
> Qu'un second Rodilard, l'Alexandre des Chats,
> L'Attila, le fléau des Rats,
> Rendait ces derniers misérables:
> J'ai lu, dis-je, en certain Auteur,
> Que ce Chat exterminateur,
> Vrai Cerbère, était craint une lieue à la ronde . . .
> (III, 18)

One is struck first, perhaps, by the comic effect of the comparison: it is ludicrous to compare a cat to these great conquerors, and the absurdity is driven home by the fact that the cat was feared for but a league around. But the lines also suggest that the cat is equivalent for the mice to Alexander and Attila, and that, in the last resort, Alexander and Attila are no better than cats (except that they prey upon their own species). The general effect is a blurring of distinctions between men and the animal kingdom. There is a particularly good use of this device in Book XI. The fox breaks into the poultry shed and wreaks havoc:

> Tel, et d'un spectacle pareil,
> Apollon irrité contre le fier Atride
> Joncha son camp de morts: on vit presque détruit
> L'ost des Grecs, et ce fut l'ouvrage d'une nuit.
> Tel encore autour de sa tente
> Ajax, à l'âme impatiente,
> De moutons et de boucs fit un vaste débris,
> Croyant tuer en eux son concurrent Ulysse
> Et les auteurs de l'injustice
> Par qui l'autre emporta le prix.
> Le Renard autre Ajax aux volailles funeste . . .
> (XI, 3)

Here, the juxtaposition of the two similes brings home the point. Apollo kills men as the fox kills hens. Ajax, the man, kills animals, but in error only: men alone prey on each other. The distinction between men and animals is to a certain extent blurred here too; but, in so far as it is maintained, it is maintained to the disadvantage of men. A similar blurring of the difference between men and animals is achieved by the use of such expressions as 'la gent marécageuse' (III, 4), 'La gent Marcassine', 'la gent Aiglonne' (III, 6), 'la gent trotte-menu' (III, 18), 'le peuple Souriquois' (IV, 6), 'la gent qui porte crête' (VII, 12), 'la dindonnière gent' (XII, 18), etc. – where the word *gent* or *peuple* suggests the kinship with man and the qualification the difference. A more elaborate example of this kind of confusion is contained in the rat's meditations in *La Grenouille et le Rat*:

> Un jour il conterait à ses petits-enfants
> Les beautés de ces lieux, les mœurs des habitants,
> Et le gouvernement de la chose publique
> Aquatique.

The reader, lulled into forgetting that this is anything but a human traveller recalling his experiences, is pulled up with a start by the last word.[13]

---

[13] In XII, 21, he points out that great and small are alike in the eyes of God.

This last quotation reminds us how effective is La Fontaine's use of short and long lines together – for most of the fables are written in a mixture of alexandrines and shorter lines (usually octo-syllables). This combination not only facilitates transitions of mood and style, but enables La Fontaine to achieve various effects. Often, a short line coming after an alexandrine is emphatic in its terseness, as the word 'Aquatique' above or as in the following examples:

> A ces mots, il se fit une telle huée,
> Que le pauvre écourté ne put être entendu.
> Prétendre ôter la queue eût été temps perdu;
> La mode en fut continuée.
>
> (V, 5)

> C'est promettre beaucoup: mais qu'en sort-il souvent?
> Du vent.
>
> (V, 10)

Sometimes a short line preceding an alexandrine, by contrast, brings out the dignity and amplitude of the latter:

> Le vent redouble ses efforts,
> Et fait si bien qu'il déracine
> Celui de qui la tête au ciel était voisine,
> Et dont les pieds touchaient à l'Empire des Morts.
>
> (I, 22)

(The enjambment between the second and third lines fuses them almost into one very long line, rapid at first and then slowing down to prepare the slow, dignified, sonorous closing line.) Sometimes, it is the shorter line which gives an effect of dignity after an alexandrine:

> Le Pot de terre en souffre; il n'eut pas fait cent pas
> Que par son compagnon il fut mis en éclats,
> Sans qu'il eût lieu de se plaindre.
>
> (V, 2)

Here, the strongly marked caesura breaks the two alexandrines into four six-syllabled lines (continuing the tripping effect of the series of seven-syllabled lines which have preceded them), so that in contrast the octosyllable appears long and slow.

If, in its variety, La Fontaine's style has one pre-eminent quality, it is its easy grace, its naturalness, its flexibility – 'La force est un point/Dont je ne me pique point' (V, 1). This owes something to the mixture of short and long lines and to the variety of the caesura; it is due, too, to the free use of enjambment and the habit of beginning and ending sentences or clauses in the middle of a line, so that often the sense structure cuts across the verse structure.

> On cherche les Rieurs; et moi je les évite.
> Cet art veut sur tout autre un suprême mérite.

Dieu ne créa que pour les sots
Les méchants diseurs de bons mots.
J'en vais peut-être en une Fable
Introduire un ; peut-être aussi
Que quelqu'un trouvera que j'aurai réussi.
Un Rieur était à la table
D'un financier ; et n'avait en son coin
Que de petits poissons : tous les gros étaient loin.

(VIII, 8)

This is clearly, as the lay-out and the rhymes show, two alexandrines, followed by four octosyllables, an alexandrine, an octosyllable, a decasyllable, and an alexandrine. But if we read this
passage according to the sense, we find a different set of divisions.
The first alexandrine with its clearly marked caesura is really two
six-syllabled lines. On the other hand, the first two octosyllables
are so closely connected by sense that they form a group of
sixteen syllables. The third is prolonged by the enjambment into a
group of twelve syllables. The second half of the fourth is connected
by enjambment so closely with the following alexandrine that it
forms with it a group of sixteen syllables. The next three lines similarly are decomposed by the sense and grammatical structure into
groups of thirteen, twelve, and six syllables. A passage which thus in
one way may be scanned as $12+12+8+8+8+8+12+8+10+
12+12$ appears, if looked at in another way, as $6+6+12+16+12
+16+13+12+6$. The reader is conscious of both kinds of struc-
ture.

Perhaps the most striking quality of the fables is their variety.
When La Fontaine, in the *Contes*, wrote: 'Diversité, c'est ma
devise', he was not talking of literature ; but the line is equally
applicable to his literary compositions. A fable conveys a moral,
for example ; but there is great variety even in this aspect of La
Fontaine's *Fables*. Sometimes the moral is a precept, sometimes
an observation ; sometimes it comes at the beginning, sometimes
at the end, sometimes at the beginning and at the end (IV, 14).
Sometimes the moral is put into the mouth of one of the characters ;
sometimes it is given as a personal reflection of La Fontaine :

Je hais les pièces d'éloquence
Hors de leur place, et qui n'ont point de fin,
Et ne sais bête au monde pire
Que l'Ecolier, si ce n'est le Pédant.
Le meilleur de ces deux pour voisin, à vrai dire,
Ne me plairait aucunement.

(IX, 5)

VII, 11 begins with a long passage of twenty-one lines on the
theme, 'Qui ne court après la Fortune ?' Sometimes instead of a
reflection, La Fontaine, as we have seen, gives us a personal reminiscence or a confession. And sometimes there is no moral.

There is similar variety in the subjects and the tone of the *Fables*. Sometimes the fables deal with animals, sometimes with the gods, with the sun and the winds, with trees and plants, with inanimate objects, with men and women. Sometimes there is little or no story, or La Fontaine may relate something he has himself observed, and the fable becomes a discourse (II, 13, VII, 17, IX, 11, X, 14, XI, 9). Sometimes two fables are strung together to illustrate the same theme, and the fable becomes a kind of essay like some of Montaigne's (I, 20, IV, 10, VIII, 16). Sometimes there is a fable within a fable.[14] Sometimes the fable is more an allegory than a fable (VI, 20). If the fable deals with men and women, it may border on the pastoral (VIII, 13, XII, 4) or on the *conte* (VI, 21, VIII, 6):

*Les Deux Pigeons* sont une élégie, *Tircis et Amarante*, une pastorale, *Le mal marié*, une satire contre les femmes d'un emportement rabelaisien, *La Fille*, un conte narquois et attendri, *Le Berger et le roi*, un conte édifiant, *Les Souhaits*, un conte de fées, *Le Lion*, un essai politique, *La Souris et le Chat-huant*, une observation de naturaliste, *Le Songe d'un habitant du Mogol*, une méditation poétique, *le Paysan du Danube*, un tableau d'histoire.[15]

It is not surprising that the poet whom we see on two occasions deliberately writing a pastiche of different styles (in *Clymène* and in the fables, II, 1), should have been able to vary his style to suit his subjects. The heroic and the homely, rapid narrative and nostalgic reminiscence, comic, melancholy, and lyrical passages succeed one another, not only in different fables, but in the same one. *Le Rieur et les Poissons* is a comic anecdote, but it broadens out and ends on a serious note:

> . . . mais enfin, il les sut engager
> A lui servir d'un monstre assez vieux pour lui dire
> Tous les noms des chercheurs de mondes inconnus
> Qui n'en étaient pas revenus,
> Et que depuis cent ans sous l'abîme avaient vus
> Les anciens du vaste empire.
>
> (VIII, 8)

We have a vision of the vast ocean bed, littered with wrecked ships and the corpses of drowned men, and the silent fish swimming around and peering at them.

Because the fables are so varied and so numerous (there are close on 250 of them), the best way to appreciate La Fontaine's skill and originality is to look at particular fables and compare them with those of other writers who have treated the same subject. It so

---

[14] See above, p. 210.
[15] P. Clarac, *La Fontaine*, 1959, p. 120.

happens that Boileau – to take a great contemporary of La Fontaine – twice wrote fables on a subject treated by La Fontaine. After the publication of the first collection, Boileau pointed out to La Fontaine that in *Le Bûcheron et la Mort* he had departed from Aesop and missed out one of the best features of his original; Boileau wrote a version of Aesop, and La Fontaine a second fable on the same subject. Here is Boileau's version:

> Le dos chargé de bois, et le corps tout en eau,
> Un pauvre bûcheron, dans l'extrême vieillesse,
> Marchait en haletant de peine et de détresse.
> Enfin, las de souffrir, jetant là son fardeau,
> Plutôt que de s'en voir accablé de nouveau,
> Il souhaite la Mort, et cent fois il l'appelle.
> La Mort vint à la fin: 'Que veux-tu? cria-t-elle.
> —Qui? moi! dit-il alors prompt à se corriger:
> Que tu m'aides à me charger.'

And here is La Fontaine's.

> Un pauvre Bûcheron tout couvert de ramée,
> Sous le faix du fagot aussi bien que des ans
> Gémissant et courbé marchait à pas pesants,
> Et tâchait de gagner sa chaumine enfumée.

La Fontaine is at once fuller and more vivid. His woodcutter, laden with *ramée*, with a *fagot* (so much more precise than the vague *bois*), is not merely walking, he is bowed down under his load and plodding his homeward way – and his home is a *chaumine enfumée*. La Fontaine continues:

> Enfin, n'en pouvant plus d'effort et de douleur,
> Il met bas son fagot, il songe à son malheur.
> Quel plaisir a-t-il eu depuis qu'il est au monde?
> En est-il un plus pauvre en la machine ronde?
> Point de pain quelquefois, et jamais de repos.
> Sa femme, ses enfants, les soldats, les impôts,
>     Le créancier, et la corvée
> Lui font d'un malheureux la peinture achevée.

This passage is unique; there is nothing like it, not only in Boileau's fable, but in seventeenth-century literature. La Fontaine, in these few lines, by his use of the *style indirect libre*, takes us into the mind of a seventeenth-century woodcutter, and makes us see life through his eyes. La Bruyère has a famous passage about peasants[16] – but he depicts them from the outside. La Fontaine's sympathetic insight is in marked contrast with Boileau's fable, in which the woodcutter is merely tired. Having seen the wretched life of the woodcutter, having perhaps been reminded through it of 'der Menschheit ganze Jammer', one feels all the more the strength of

[16] See below, p. 371.

the woodcutter's attachment to life. Boileau's woodcutter, who calls
for death merely because he is weary, scarcely arouses our sympathy; in La Fontaine's we recognize ourselves.

> Il appelle la mort, elle vient sans tarder,
> Lui demande ce qu'il faut faire.
> C'est, dit-il, afin de m'aider
> A recharger ce bois; tu ne tarderas guère.
> Le trépas vient tout guérir;
> Mais ne bougeons d'où nous sommes.
> Plutôt souffrir que mourir,
> C'est la devise des hommes.

Boileau included a fable in his second epistle. This time it was
La Fontaine who competed with Boileau. He treated the same
subject in *L'Huître et les Plaideurs* (IX, 9). Boileau begins:

> Un jour, dit un auteur, n'importe en quel chapitre,
> Deux voyageurs à jeun rencontrèrent une huître.
> Tous deux la contestaient . . .

With this colourless statement of the bare facts, the opening of La
Fontaine's fable contrasts sharply:

> Un jour deux Pèlerins sur le sable rencontrent
> Une Huître que le flot y venait d'apporter . . .

We know who the travellers are and what they are doing there; we
know that the scene is the seashore and how the oyster came to be
there – Boileau tells us none of these things. Moreover, we see the
behaviour, the gestures of the pilgrims when they see the oyster:

> Ils l'avalent des yeux, du doigt ils se la montrent;
> A l'égard de la dent il fallut contester.

Whereas Boileau merely tells us that they 'contestaient', La Fontaine gives us the details of the quarrel, of the actions and words
of his characters:

> L'un se baissait déjà pour amasser la proie;
> L'autre le pousse, et dit: Il est bon de savoir
> Qui de nous en aura la joie.
> Celui qui le premier a pu l'apercevoir
> En sera le gobeur; l'autre le verra faire.
> —Si par là on juge l'affaire,
> Reprit son compagnon, j'ai l'œil bon, Dieu merci.
> —Je ne l'ai pas mauvais aussi,
> Dit l'autre, et je l'ai vue avant vous, sur ma vie.
> —Eh bien! vous l'avez vue, et moi je l'ai sentie.

An excellent piece of dialogue, all the more piquant for being put
into the mouth of two pilgrims.

So far, La Fontaine has developed two and a half lines of

Boileau's into fourteen. In the next half, the proportions are rather different, Boileau goes on:

> [Tous deux la contestaient,] lorsque dans leur chemin
> La justice passa, la balance à la main.
> Devant elle à grand bruit ils expliquent la chose.
> Tous deux avec dépens veulent gagner leur cause.
> La justice, pesant ce droit litigieux,
> Demande l'huître, l'ouvre, et l'avale à leurs yeux,
> Et par ce bel arrêt terminant la bataille:
> 'Tenez; voilà, dit-elle à chacun, une écaille;
> Des sottises d'autrui nous vivons au palais.
> Messieurs, l'huître était bonne. Adieu. Vivez en paix.'

To these nine lines and a half of Boileau correspond seven of La Fontaine's. Having elaborated the circumstances, having individualized the characters and made them talk and argue, he narrates the crisis more rapidly and concisely than Boileau:

> Pendant tout ce bel incident,
> Perrin Dandin arrive...

Instead of the abstract figure of justice, La Fontaine introduces a judge — moreover a judge we already know from Rabelais, so that the very name suggests a personality.

> ... ils le prennent pour juge.
> Perrin *fort gravement* ouvre l'Huître, et la gruge,
>      *Nos deux Messieurs le regardant,*
> Ce repas fait, il dit *d'un ton de Président:*
> Tenez, la cour vous donne à chacun une écaille
> Sans dépens, et qu'en paix chacun chez soi s'en aille.

The italicized words help to evoke the scene vividly — the gravity and solemn way of speaking of Perrin Dandin, the anxiety of the pilgrims as they look on. Perrin Dandin, by the way, says nothing so uncharacteristic or improbable as 'Des sottises d'autrui nous vivons au palais'. Finally, La Fontaine ends with a general reflection:

> Mettez ce qu'il en coûte à plaider aujourd'hui;
> Comptez ce qu'il en reste à beaucoup de familles;
> Vous verrez que Perrin tire l'argent à lui,
> Et ne laisse aux plaideurs que le sac et les quilles.

Comparisons such as these perhaps help us to understand La Fontaine's remark:

> Mon imitation n'est point un esclavage...
>                    (*A Monseigneur l'évêque de Soissons*)

## Chapter 17

# LA ROCHEFOUCAULD

FRANÇOIS DUC DE LA ROCHEFOUCAULD (1613–80), courtier and soldier, took part in intrigues against Richelieu and Mazarin, and, during the Fronde, fought against the government until he was severely wounded in 1652. In 1659, it appears from his correspondence, he began to distil his experience into maxims, with some idea of publishing a volume in collaboration with Mme de Sablé and Jacques Esprit. The *Maximes*, however, when they appeared at the end of 1664 (a pirated edition had been published in Holland earlier in the year), were the work of La Rochefoucauld alone, with the exception of one or two which were eliminated in subsequent editions. Four revised editions were brought out during La Rochefoucauld's lifetime, the last (1678) of which contained 504 maxims, as against the 317 of the first edition.[1]

The motto, first prefixed to the fourth edition, 'Nos vertus ne sont le plus souvent que des vices déguisés', sums up the leading idea of the book, which was written, so La Rochefoucauld wrote in a letter to Père Thomas Esprit, the brother of Jacques Esprit, to prove

> que la vertu des anciens philosophes païens dont ils ont fait tant de bruit a été établie sur de faux fondements, et que l'homme, tout persuadé qu'il est de son mérite, n'a en soi que des apparences trompeuses de vertu, dont il éblouit les autres, et dont souvent il se trompe lui-même lorsque la foi ne s'en mêle point.

The idea is not completely new — there are occasional passages in Montaigne, in Charron, and in *L'Astrée*, pointing out that human virtue owes much to human weakness and vice; but, in these writers, the point is made incidentally, and not worked out in detail, as it is by La Rochefoucauld.

Man is actuated by *intérêt* and *amour-propre*, two terms which

---

[1] Besides the *Maximes*, La Rochefoucauld wrote a volume of *Mémoires*, a pirated edition of which appeared in 1662, and a number of posthumously-published *Réflexions diverses*.

are synonymous,[2] and most of his virtues and apparently disinterested actions can be traced back to them:

Les vertus se perdent dans l'intérêt, comme les fleuves se perdent dans la mer.                                                                                     (171)

Les vices entrent dans la composition des vertus comme les poisons entrent dans la composition des remèdes.                                        (182)

Nous aurions souvent honte de nos plus belles actions si le monde voyait tous les motifs qui les produisent.                                                   (409)

It should, however, be borne in mind that the word *intérêt* is used in a wide sense, and does not necessarily imply a base or sordid motive, but may include enlightened self-interest: in a preface added to the book from the second edition onwards, we read: 'Par le mot d'Intérêt on n'entend pas toujours un intérêt de bien, mais le plus souvent un intérêt d'honneur ou de gloire [ . . . ]'

The idea that virtues and virtuous actions are vices in disguise is worked out in considerable detail. Clemency in princes is often merely a means of winning the affection of their subjects; it is the result of vanity, laziness, or fear, usually of all three together. Sincerity is a means of winning the confidence or respect of others. If we acknowledge our defects, it is to compensate for them by a show of sincerity, or to place them in a favourable light; 'on ne se blâme que pour être loué' (554). Curiosity springs either from a desire to know what may be of use to us, or from a desire to feel superior to others. If we love justice, it is because we are afraid of suffering injustice. Liberality is a form of vanity. As for politeness, 'la civilité est un désir d'en recevoir et d'être estimé poli' (260). All unselfishness is essentially selfish, a means of winning people over: 'c'est prêter à usure sous prétexte de donner' (236). Friendship is an association of interests, in which concern for our friends comes second to our own emotions: 'Nous nous consolons aisément des disgrâces de nos amis lorsqu'elles servent à signaler notre tendresse pour eux' (235). As for love,

Il n'y a point de passion où l'amour de soi-même règne si puissamment que dans l'amour; et on est toujours plus disposé à sacrifier le repos de ce qu'on aime qu'à perdre le sien.                                              (262)

Similarly, repentance is fear of the consequences of wrongdoing, trustworthiness a means of inspiring trust, compassion a mark of superiority. If we pity and succour the unfortunate, it is often in the hope of being pitied and helped in similar circumstances: 'La pitié est souvent un sentiment de nos propres maux dans les maux d'autrui [ . . . ]' (264). Modesty is a love of praise: 'Le

---

[2] La Rochefoucauld attempts to differentiate them in maxim No. 510, published posthumously.

refus des louanges est un désir d'être loué deux fois' (149). It is for the same reason that we praise others: 'On ne loue d'ordinaire que pour être loué' (146) – unless praise is a form of indirect criticism. Valour is due to several causes – 'l'amour de la gloire, la crainte de la honte, le dessein de faire fortune, le désir de rendre notre vie commode et agréable, et l'envie d'abaisser les autres' (213). Magnanimity, which 'méprise tout pour avoir tout' (248), is a form of ambition, a desire for praise. Humility is a means of making one's way in the world, of acquiring influence over others. Gratitude is due to a desire for further benefits; sensibility is a mask for self-interest. Weeping for the dead is hypocrisy – we weep for our own loss, or to acquire a reputation for sensibility:

... on pleure pour avoir la réputation d'être tendre; on pleure pour être plaint; on pleure pour être pleuré; enfin, on pleure pour éviter la honte de ne pleurer pas.                                                                                                                     (233)

All women are flirts, and feminine virtue is no less a form of self-interest than other virtues:

La sévérité des femmes est un ajustement et un fard qu'elles ajoutent à leur beauté.                                                                                                                                                            (204)

L'honnêteté des femmes est souvent l'amour de leur réputation et de leur repos.                                                                                                                                                            (205)[3]

And if we are unwilling to admit the truth of all this, says La Rochefoucauld in a posthumous maxim, it is because we are afraid of the truth about ourselves being known.

Man, as depicted by La Rochefoucauld, is weak, dominated by passions, dangerous guides, over which he has no control: 'La durée de nos passions ne dépend pas plus de nous que la durée de notre vie' (5). The will is weak and the slave of the humours of the body; 'nous n'avons pas assez de force pour suivre toute notre raison' (42). Human reason is equally impotent. Sentiment is stronger than reason; 'l'esprit est toujours la dupe du cœur' (102). The judgment is warped by self-interest or fashion. Intelligence is often ineffective in life and 'il arrive quelquefois des accidents dans la vie d'où il faut être un peu fou pour se bien tirer' (310). Deluded by vanity, we do not know ourselves as we are, over-estimate ourselves, and fall easy victims to flattery:

Quelque bien qu'on nous dise de nous, on ne nous apprend rien de nouveau.                                                                                                                                                            (303)

Il n'y a point d'homme qui se croie en chacune de ses qualités au-dessous de l'homme du monde qu'il estime le plus.                                                                                    (452)

[3] *La Princesse de Clèves* illustrates this.

Nor can we see things as they are:

Nous ne désirerions guère de choses avec ardeur si nous connaissions parfaitement ce que nous désirons.                (439)

Indeed, self-deception and delusions are necessary to our happiness:

On n'aurait guère de plaisir si on ne se flattait jamais.                (123)

L'espérance, toute trompeuse qu'elle est, sert au moins à nous mener à la fin de la vie par un chemin agréable.                (168)

Mutual deception is equally necessary:

Dans l'amitié, comme dans l'amour, on est souvent plus heureux par les choses qu'on ignore que par celles que l'on sait.                (441)

Les hommes ne vivraient pas longtemps en société s'ils n'étaient les dupes les uns des autres.                (87)

La Rochefoucauld does not paint a flattering portrait of mankind. Addicted to the pursuit of things that are not worth having (reputation and glory), men are ungrateful, lazy, envious, spiteful, vain, proud, inconsistent, capricious, hypocritical, full of contradictions, and all in some way ridiculous. They are selfish ('Nous avons tous assez de force pour supporter les maux d'autrui', 19), self-centred, and egotistical: 'Ce qui fait que les amants et les maîtresses ne s'ennuient point d'être ensemble, c'est qu'ils parlent toujours d'eux-mêmes' (312). La Rochefoucauld is conscious, above all, of man's limitations; like Pascal, he sees him as incapable of extremes:

Il semble que la nature ait prescrit à chaque homme, dès sa naissance, des bornes pour les vertus et les vices.                (189)

Il y a un excès de biens et de maux qui passe notre sensibilité.                (464)

There is nothing heroic in man as La Rochefoucauld sees him. Great actions are due to chance or the passions; the war between Augustus and Antony was, perhaps, due less to ambition than to jealousy. Heroes are no different from other men:

Lorsque les grands hommes se laissent abattre par la longueur de leurs infortunes, ils font voir qu'ils ne les soutenaient que par la force de leur ambition, et non par celle de leur âme, et qu'à une grande vanité près, les héros sont faits comme les autres hommes.                (24)

Valour is due to self-interest or temperament: 'La vanité, la honte, et surtout le tempérament, font souvent la valeur des hommes et la vertu des femmes' (220). Virtue is merely apparent; it may be due to self-interest, to vanity, the desire for reputation;

it may be a mark of absence of temptation, or of old age; it may be
the result of timidity or laziness; it may be a cloak for wrongdoing or a matter of calculation; it may even be due to vice —
several vices may cancel one another out, or a vice may even give
rise to its opposite. Wisdom similarly is merely apparent:

La folie nous suit dans tous les temps de la vie. Si quelqu'un paraît sage,
c'est seulement parce que ses folies sont proportionnées à son âge et à
sa fortune.                                                          (207)

In any case, wisdom is not a reliable guide:

Qui vit sans folie n'est pas si sage qu'il croit.                    (209)

C'est une grande folie de vouloir être sage tout seul.             (231)[4]

The stoical philosophy of the first half of the century is examined
and found wanting. Moderation, 'la langueur et la paresse de
l'âme' (293), is due, like other apparent virtues, to the absence of
passion or to amour-propre:

La modération est une crainte de tomber dans l'envie et dans le mépris
que méritent ceux qui s'enivrent de leur bonheur: c'est une vaine ostenta-
tion de la force de notre esprit; et enfin, la modération des hommes dans
leur plus haute élévation est un désir de paraître plus grands que leur
fortune.                                                             (18)

Fortitude is either impossible — 'La philosophie triomphe aisément des maux passés et des maux à venir; mais les maux présents
triomphent d'elle'[5] (22) — or a mere outward show: 'La constance
des sages n'est que l'art de renfermer leur agitation dans le cœur'
(20). Fear of death cannot be overcome: 'Le soleil ni la mort ne se
peuvent regarder fixement' (26). Detachment, again, is merely a
form of amour-propre; by despising wealth, the stoical philosophers
hoped to gain that respect of which lack of wealth might otherwise have deprived them.

There is, however, a more positive, constructive aspect to the
*Maximes*. Not only does La Rochefoucauld attempt to strip away
pretence, he urges his readers to be sincere, clear-sighted, genuine.
He attacks affectation repeatedly: 'On n'est jamais si ridicule par
les qualités que l'on a que par celles que l'on affecte d'avoir' (134).
Both in the *Maximes* and in the *Réflexions diverses*, he is pre-

[4] Cf. Molière:

      ... il vaut mieux souffrir d'être au nombre des fous,
      Que du sage parti se voir seul contre tous.
                                      (*L'Ecole des Maris*)
[5] Cf. Shakespeare: 'For there was never yet philosopher /That could
endure the tooth-ache patiently' (*Much Ado about Nothing*).

occupied with the question of *honnêteté*, which for him implies freedom from affectation:

Les faux honnêtes gens sont ceux qui déguisent leurs défauts aux autres et à eux-mêmes; les vrais honnêtes gens sont ceux qui les connaissent parfaitement et les confessent.                                        (202)

In the third of the *Réflexions diverses* (*De l'air et des manières*), he stresses the importance of being natural, of being oneself:

Il y a un air qui convient à la figure et aux talents de chaque personne: on perd toujours quand on le quitte pour en prendre un autre. Il faut essayer de connaître celui qui nous est naturel, n'en point sortir, et le perfectionner autant qu'il nous est possible.

In the thirteenth of the *Réflexions diverses* (*Du faux*), he recommends another kind of naturalness — sincerity in taste:

Les honnêtes gens doivent approuver sans prévention ce qui mérite d'être approuvé, suivre ce qui mérite d'être suivi, et ne se piquer de rien;[6] mais il y faut une grande proportion et une grande justesse; il faut savoir discerner ce qui est bon en général et ce qui nous est propre, et suivre alors avec raison la pente naturelle qui nous porte vers les choses qui nous plaisent. Si les hommes ne voulaient exceller que par leurs propres talents, et en suivant leurs devoirs, il n'y aurait rien de faux dans leur goût et dans leur conduite; ils se montreraient tels qu'ils sont ...

The *honnête homme*, in other words, must strive to rid himself of some of the weaknesses and foibles of man in general.

It would be misleading to give the impression that the *Maximes* are exclusively concerned with the elaboration of a system. With sureness and subtlety, La Rochefoucauld analyses the emotions, particularly love, jealousy, and friendship — his analysis of love owes something to *L'Astrée* and the novels of Mlle de Scudéry. Like Racine, he points out that love easily changes to hatred: 'Plus on aime une maîtresse, et plus on est prêt de la haïr' (111). He discusses old age, eloquence, *honnêteté* and the art of conversation, distinguishes different social types, and includes many penetrating observations of different facets of human nature. Here, for example, is a shrewd piece of advice: 'Ce n'est pas assez d'avoir de grandes qualités, il faut en avoir l'économie' (159). And here is an observation which perhaps shows its author in a new light: 'L'accent du pays où l'on est né demeure dans l'esprit et dans le cœur comme dans le langage' (342).

In these penetrating observations on man and society, to which their economy of language and their extreme concision give such

---

[6] Cf. 'Le vrai honnête homme est celui qui ne se pique de rien' (203). Méré says: 'Il serait à souhaiter pour être toujours agréable, d'exceller en tout ce qui sied bien aux honnêtes gens, sans néanmoins se piquer de rien: je veux dire sans rien faire qui ne s'offre de soi-même, et sans rien dire qui puisse témoigner qu'on se veut faire valoir' (*Des Agréments*).

force, it might be thought that one has the quintessence of classicism, a picture of universal man. In a sense, that is so; of the universal validity of La Rochefoucauld's *Maximes* there can be little doubt: yet they are also very much the expression of their age.

The habitués of the salons of the seventeenth century loved to analyse the passions, especially love and jealousy; and the writers of the period loved to embody the fruit of their observation in *sentences* and maxims, which abound, for example, in the plays and memoirs of the period. Moreover, the picture of human nature and human life that La Rochefoucauld gives us has much in common with that which we find in the literature of the first half of the century; many of the themes which occur so frequently in French writers from Montaigne onwards recur in La Rochefoucauld. He, too, is aware of the uncertainty of human judgment and sees man as an irrational creature. He, too, stresses the importance of chance, of fortune, in human destiny:[7]

La fortune et l'humeur gouvernent le monde.                    (435)

Toutes nos qualités sont incertaines et douteuses en bien comme en mal, et elles sont presque toutes à la merci des occasions.[8]                    (470)

Il semble que nos actions aient des étoiles heureuses ou malheureuses à qui elles doivent une grande partie de la louange et du blâme qu'on leur donne.                    (58)

La nature fait le mérite, et la fortune le met en œuvre.                    (153)

He, too, is conscious of the difficulty of distinguishing between appearance and reality: 'Il y a une infinité de conduites qui paraissent ridicules, et dont les raisons cachées sont très sages et très solides' (163). One of the central themes of the *Maximes* is that virtues are vices in disguise; La Rochefoucauld also points out that society sets more store by appearances than genuine merit, and that we are all more or less hypocrites acting a part:

Dans toutes les professions, chacun affecte une mine et un extérieur pour paraître ce qu'il veut qu'on le croie. Ainsi on peut dire que le monde n'est composé que de mines.                    (256)

La gravité est un mystère du corps inventé pour cacher les défauts de l'esprit.                    (257)

Like so many of the writers of the earlier seventeenth century, La Rochefoucauld sees man as ever-changing ('On est quelquefois

[7] Maxim No. 613, which expresses the conviction that the world is ordered by providence, was suppressed in later editions.
[8] But see No. 61: 'Le bonheur et le malheur des hommes ne dépend pas moins de leur humeur que de la fortune'—i.e. temperament and fortune must co-operate.

aussi différent de soi-même que des autres,' 135) and fickle–
paradoxically enough, even when he is constant:

La constance en amour est une inconstance perpétuelle qui fait que notre
cœur s'attache successivement à toutes les qualités de la personne que
nous aimons, donnant tantôt la préférence à l'une, tantôt à l'autre...
(175)

The love of paradox which this last maxim reveals is evident, not
only in La Rochefoucauld's thought (virtue is really vice, vice
engenders virtue, success is more often due to our faults than to our
good qualities),[9] but also in its expression: 'Il n'y a point de sots si
incommodes que ceux qui ont de l'esprit' (451).

La Rochefoucauld, then, imposes seventeenth-century categories
on the world of his observation. But we must not forget that the
world he observed was the seventeenth-century world, that the
*Maximes* condense the personal experience of the author. This is
clear from the *Mémoires* of La Rochefoucauld. If he speaks of
ingratitude in the *Maximes*, we know from the *Mémoires* that he
bitterly resented that of the Queen and of Mme de Chevreuse.
We see him noting the effects of vanity on Miossens:

...la vanité, qui était la plus forte de ses passions, l'empêchait souvent
de me dire vrai, et il feignait des espérances qu'il n'avait pas et que je
savais bien qu'il ne devait pas avoir.

In writing, 'Il faut de plus grandes vertus pour soutenir la bonne
fortune que la mauvaise' (25), it is more than likely that he was
thinking of Mazarin, who, La Rochefoucauld says in the *Mémoires*,
'parut si enflé de cette prospérité, qu'il renouvela dans tous les
esprits le dégoût et la crainte de sa domination'. It has been con-
jectured that in penning maxim No. 344 – 'La plupart des hommes
ont, comme les plantes, des propriétés cachées que le hasard fait
découvrir' – La Rochefoucauld had in mind his servant, Gourville,
who showed his talent for diplomacy during the Fronde and eventually rose to great heights.

The experiences of the Fronde are particularly important in the
*Maximes*. The *Mémoires* suggest that two of the maxims reflect
the negotiations between the Frondeurs and the government:

La réconciliation avec nos ennemis n'est qu'un désir de rendre notre condition meilleure, une lassitude de la guerre, et une crainte de quelque
mauvais événement.[10]
(82)

Ce qui fait que l'on est souvent mécontent de ceux qui négocient est
qu'ils abandonnent presque toujours l'intérêt de leurs amis pour l'intérêt

[9] In the seventeenth of the *Réflexions diverses* (*Des Evénements de ce
siècle*), he dwells on the paradoxes of contemporary history.
[10] Cf. 'M. le prince de Conti était porté à la paix, par l'ennui et par la
lassitude qu'il avait d'une guerre où il ne s'était engagé que pour plaire à
Madame sa sœur' ... (*Mémoires*)

du succès de la négociation, qui devient le leur par l'honneur d'avoir
réussi à ce qu'ils avaient entrepris.                               (278)

It was from the Fronde that La Rochefoucauld learned that men
are not always rational, and that success is attributable more to
chance than to prudence:

... les esprits étaient trop échauffés pour écouter la raison, et tous ont
éprouvé à la fin que personne n'a bien connu ses véritables intérêts. La
cour même, que la fortune a soutenue, a fait souvent des fautes considé-
rables; et l'on a vu, dans la suite, que chaque parti s'est plus maintenu par
les manquements de celui qui lui était opposé, que par sa bonne
conduite.[11]

Above all, the Fronde supplied La Rochefoucauld with plenty of
examples of the power of self-interest; he devotes several pages of
the *Mémoires* to the analysis of the selfish motives which actuated
the nobles during the Fronde – pages the gist of which is contained
in maxim No. 615 (suppressed in later editions). Victory, it says,
is the result of:

une infinité d'actions qui, au lieu de l'avoir pour but, regardent seulement
les intérêts particuliers de ceux qui les font, puisque tous ceux qui composent une armée, allant à leur propre gloire et à leur élévation, procurent
un bien si grand et si général.

[11] Cf. 'La fortune même sembla se réconcilier avec lui [Condé] en cette
rencontre, pour avoir part à un succès dont l'un et l'autre parti ont donné
la gloire à sa valeur et à sa conduite'... (*Mémoires*). Cf., too: 'Cependant
de si grands avantages lui [to Bouillon] furent souvent inutiles, par l'opiniâtreté de sa fortune, qui s'opposa presque toujours à sa prudence'...
(*Mémoires*).

## Chapter 18

# THE NOVEL

### I. MME DE LAFAYETTE

LONG episodic romances went out of fashion in the 1660's – the last to appear were Mlle de Scudéry's *Clélie* (1654–60) and *Almahide* (1660–3), La Calprenède's *Faramond* (1661–70); Boileau ridiculed them in 1665 in his *Dialogue sur les Héros de Romans*. They were superseded by a new genre, short stories or *nouvelles*, depicting in a more realistic way characters taken from a more recent period of history. An early example of this kind of fiction is the *Nouvelles françoises* of Segrais (1656), who makes one of his narrators say:

Au reste il me semble que c'est la différence qu'il y a entre le Roman et la Nouvelle, que le roman écrit ces choses comme la bienséance le veut, et à la manière du Poète; mais que la Nouvelle doit un peu davantage tenir de l'histoire et s'attacher plutôt à donner les images des choses comme d'ordinaire nous les voyons arriver, que comme notre imagination se les figure.

Segrais's example was followed by other writers, notably Mme de Villedieu (née Desjardins);[1] most important, it led to a masterpiece: Mme de Lafayette's *Princesse de Clèves*.

Marie-Madeleine de la Vergne, Mme de Lafayette (1634–93), the intimate friend of Mme de Sévigné and La Rochefoucauld, wrote four novels or stories, *La Princesse de Montpensier* (1662), *Zaïde* (1669–71), *La Princesse de Clèves* (1678), and *La Comtesse de Tende* (published posthumously in 1724). In writing her stories, she enlisted the help of her friends: *La Princesse de Montpensier* was corrected by Ménage, who may have helped, too, with the historical background; *Zaïde* was published under the name of Segrais,[2] who probably provided the plan and the historical details, and corrected by Huet and by La Rochefoucauld, who

---

[1] Saint-Réal's *Dom Carlos, nouvelle historique* (1672), dramatized by Campistron (*Andronic*) and Schiller (*Don Carlos*), deserves mention.

[2] *La Princesse de Montpensier* and *La Princesse de Clèves* were published anonymously.

289

contributed some passages; and *La Princesse de Clèves* was corrected by Segrais and La Rochefoucauld.[3]

Posterity has done Mme de Lafayette no great injustice in remembering her chiefly for one of her stories. Not only is *La Princesse de Clèves* the best of them, but it contains the essence of all the others. *La Princesse de Montpensier* and *Zaïde* are anticipations of it; *La Comtesse de Tende* is a prolongation of it. *La Princesse de Montpensier*, which is no more than a long short story, resembles its successor in having a sixteenth-century setting and in treating the subject of a woman who loves a man other than her husband. The parallel can be continued in more detail. Both Mme de Montpensier and Mme de Clèves have been thought to be based on Henriette d'Angleterre; it is jealousy that reveals to both that they are in love; Mme de Montpensier is abandoned by her lover, a fate which Mme de Clèves fears; and both stories depict passion as dangerous and inimical to peace of mind. The second part of the opening sentence of *La Princesse de Montpensier* might serve equally well for the *Princesse de Clèves*:

Pendant que la guerre civile déchirait la France sous le règne de Charles IX, l'Amour ne laissait pas de trouver sa place parmi tant de désordres et d'en causer beaucoup dans son Empire.

Nor would it be out of place in *Zaïde* – for *Zaïde*, though at first sight very different, treats essentially the same theme. Set in medieval Spain and loosely constructed, the novel is mainly of interest for the stories of four characters: Consalve, who leaves the Spanish court on discovering that his mistress has betrayed him; Alphonse, whose irrational and overwhelming jealousy causes Bélasire to refuse to marry him and to retire to a convent; the fickle Alamir, who ends by falling in love with Zaïde, who does not return his passion; and Félime, who secretly loves him and dies of grief after his death. 'On ne peut être heureux en aimant quelqu'un,' says Bélasire.

The *Comtesse de Tende*, the shortest of Mme de Lafayette's stories, carries the theme of marital infidelity a stage further than *La Princesse de Montpensier* and *La Princesse de Clèves*. Like them it has a sixteenth-century setting, and like them it relates the story of a married woman who loves another; but the love of Mme de Tende and M. de Navarre is a guilty one, and Mme de Tende, when M. de Navarre dies, leaving her pregnant, has no choice but to confess her shameful secret to her husband.

·                ·                ·

[3] Besides her novels, Mme de Lafayette wrote an *Histoire de Madame, Henriette d'Angleterre* and *Mémoires de la Cour de France pour les années 1688 et 1689*, both published posthumously.

*La Princesse de Clèves* treats, in a historical setting, a basic and eternal human situation – in much the same way, in fact, as the plays of Corneille and Racine. The action takes place at the French court at the close of the reign of Henry II, with Henry VIII and Anne Boleyn appearing in an episode, and the *reine dauphine* (our Mary Queen of Scots) playing a considerable part. But despite her careful documentation, Mme de Lafayette was not primarily interested in reconstructing the past; her characters belong to the seventeenth century, and, like the plays of Corneille and Racine, *La Princesse de Clèves* constantly reminds us of seventeenth-century France. 'Surtout ce que j'y trouve,' Madame de Lafayette wrote later, 'c'est une parfaite imitation du monde de la cour et de la manière dont on y vit.' In accordance with the principle of *bienséance*, the crudities of the sixteenth century are pruned away, and many details are àt least as applicable to the court of the seventeenth century as to that of the sixteenth.

L'ambition et la galanterie étaient l'âme de cette cour, et occupaient également les hommes et les femmes. Il y avait tant d'intérêts et tant de cabales différentes, et les dames y avaient tant de part que l'amour était toujours mêlé aux affaires et les affaires à l'amour. Personne n'était tranquille, ni indifférent; on songeait à s'élever, à plaire, à servir ou à nuire; on ne connaissait ni l'ennui, ni l'oisiveté, et on était toujours occupé des plaisirs ou des intrigues. Les dames avaient des attachements particuliers pour la reine, pour la reine dauphine, pour la reine de Navarre, pour Madame, sœur du roi, ou pour la duchesse de Valentinois [...] Celles qui avaient passé la première jeunesse et qui faisaient profession d'une vertu plus austère, étaient attachées à la reine. Celles qui étaient plus jeunes et qui cherchaient la joie et la galanterie, faisaient leur cour à la reine dauphine.

This may be an accurate picture of the court of Henry II; but to make it serve as a description of the court of Louis XIV, we have only to substitute for the name of the Queen, that of Anne of Austria, devout in her old age, – for that of the *reine dauphine*, that of Henriette d'Angleterre –, for that of the duchesse de Valentinois, that of Louise de la Vallière or of Mme de Montespan. The state of the court when the death of Henry II is imminent is admirably evoked in a single sentence:

Une cour, aussi partagée et aussi remplie d'intérêts opposés, n'était pas dans une médiocre agitation à la veille d'un si grand événement; néanmoins, tous les mouvements étaient cachés et l'on ne paraissait occupé que de l'unique inquiétude de la santé du roi.

As we read, the centuries blend together and we recall the year 1643, when Louis XIII lay dying and the court struggled and intrigued to bring about a new balance of power. The queen of Henry II, dismissing the *connétable* after his death and giving her confidence to cardinal de Lorraine, reminds us of Anne of Austria, after her husband's death, calling to power another cardinal. The letter episode recalls the occasion, during the regency of Anne of Austria, when a letter from a lady was picked up in Mme de Montbazon's house, written, Mme de Montbazon said, by Mme de Longueville to Coligny: she was compelled to apologize formally to the princesse de Condé for this slur on her daughter's good name. Finally, Mme de Lafayette's heroine, Mme de Clèves, the most brilliant lady of the court, married to a husband whom she does not love, attracting lovers in a corrupt court and in love with one of them, is in many ways reminiscent of the King's sister-in-law, the first Madame, Henriette d'Angleterre, duchesse d'Orléans, with whom Mme de Lafayette was well-acquainted, and whose life she had written.[4]

The form of *La Princesse de Clèves* is masterly. The historical and the invented elements are skilfully interwoven: the actions of the main characters are governed by the public events affecting the life of the court of which they form part, and their relationship stands out against the background of the amorous intrigues of the court as a whole, so that we see at once how much they have in common with their contemporaries and how different they are. Moreover, if we look at the original division into four volumes — which some modern editions preserve —, we see that the subject-matter is skilfully distributed into the four parts, as that of a play of Corneille or Racine is into its five acts. Each volume carries the story one stage forward:

*Vol. I. Exposition. Mme de Clèves and M. de Nemours meet and each falls in love with the other.* The court of France is described, and the events leading up to the marriage of M. de Clèves with Mlle de Chartres, a love match on his side only. Subsequently, Mme de Clèves and M. de Nemours meet and fall in love. This volume contains the story of Mme de Valentinois and ends with the narrative of the death of Mme de Chartres.

*Vol. II. The two lovers become aware that their love is mutual.* This volume also contains the history of Mme de Tournon, that of Anne Boleyn, and the first part of the story of the vidame de Chartres and Mme de Thémines.

*Vol. III. M. de Clèves learns of the love of his wife and of M. de Nemours.* This volume opens with the second part of the story of M. de Chartres and Mme de Thémines, contains Mme de Clèves's confession to her husband, and ends with the account of the death of Henry II.

---

[4] Ashton points out that Mme de Clèves's emotion on hearing that Nemours has been hurt is similar to that of Madame (in the *Histoire d'Henriette d'Angleterre*) on learning that Guiche is in danger.

*Vol. IV. Dénouement*: the jealousy and death of M. de Clèves, the interview of the two lovers, and their final separation.

The dénouement is very carefully prepared. Mme de Clèves is brought up by her mother to fear love and the insincerity and fickleness of men, and to prize the peace of mind and the distinction which are the rewards of virtue. Later, Mme de Chartres warns her daughter that Nemours is incapable of a serious attachment, and, on her deathbed, urges her not to give way to her inclination for M. de Nemours:

... ne craignez point de prendre des partis trop rudes et trop difficiles, quelque affreux qu'ils vous paraissent d'abord: ils seront plus doux dans les suites que les malheurs d'une galanterie.

Experience seconds the counsels of Mme de Chartres. On two occasions, Mme de Clèves knows the pangs of jealousy – the first time, on hearing from her mother that Nemours is suspected of being in love with the *reine dauphine,* and later, when she thinks that the love letter which was in fact lost by the vidame de Chartres fell out of Nemours's pocket. Indeed, in her final interview, she harks back to this episode: the jealousy that she then knew, she tells him, has left with her 'une idée qui me fait croire que c'est le plus grand de tous les maux'. This experience, moreover, causes her to reflect on the improbability of Nemours's being a constant lover. Her mistrust of him is deepened by his betrayal of her confession to her husband. It is only natural, therefore, that Mme de Clèves should decide after her husband's death not to marry her lover. This decision is due partly to the feeling that Nemours has been indirectly responsible for her husband's death, but chiefly to her conviction that she would not be happy if she did marry him. She is sure that he would not be faithful, and that his infidelities would cause her suffering and jealousy; and she refuses to marry him in the interest of her own peace of mind. 'Ce que je crois devoir à la mémoire de M. de Clèves serait faible,' she tells him, 's'il n'était soutenu par l'intérêt de mon repos; et les raisons de mon repos ont besoin d'être soutenues de celles de mon devoir.' But if *devoir* and *repos* are here placed on an equal footing, *repos* is in reality the stronger motive of the two, for we are told later:

Les raisons qu'elle avait de ne point épouser M. de Nemours lui paraissaient fortes du côté de son devoir et insurmontables du côté de son repos.

The novel has been criticized for its digressions, for the intercalated episodes. It was, of course, a convention of the time that a novel should be diversified by the introduction of episodes, of the adventures of incidental characters; but it is not difficult to defend the episodes of *La Princesse de Clèves.* They give an impression of the moral laxity of the court, and they all treat the theme of illicit passion and the sufferings caused by jealousy and infidelity. They have, in other words, a direct bearing on the main action and on the motivation of Mme de Clèves, since the spectacle of the world around her can only illustrate the wisdom of her mother's advice. Moreover, one of the episodes directly influences the main plot – that of Mme de Tournon, which causes M. de Clèves to remark:

> ... la sincérité me touche d'une telle sorte que je crois que si ma maîtresse, et même ma femme, m'avouait que quelqu'un lui plût, j'en serais affligé sans en être aigri. Je quitterais le personnage d'amant ou de mari, pour la conseiller et pour la plaindre.

This remark prepares his wife for her confession to him.

The action is purely psychological. The situation develops logically and ruthlessly: chance plays little or no part;[5] there is little or no external action. The interest is focused on the relations of the characters, on the development of their emotions, and on the analysis of their states of mind. Mme de Lafayette excels at disentangling complex emotions and at indicating different points of view. Mme de Clèves, for instance, having learnt that Nemours would be unhappy to know that his mistress was at a ball which he could not attend, stays away from one on the pretext of illness. Mme la dauphine suggests that Nemours's remark was the real reason for her absence; Mme de Clèves blushes; Mme de Chartres asserts that her daughter's illness was genuine. Mme de Lafayette goes on:

> Mme la dauphine crut ce que disait Mme de Chartres, M. de Nemours fut bien fâché d'y trouver de l'apparence; néanmoins la rougeur de Mme de Clèves lui fit soupçonner que ce que Mme la dauphine avait dit n'était pas entièrement éloigné de la vérité. Mme de Clèves avait d'abord été fâchée que M. de Nemours eût eu lieu de croire que c'était lui qui l'avait empêchée d'aller chez le maréchal de Saint-André; mais ensuite elle sentit quelque espèce de chagrin que sa mère lui en eût entièrement ôté l'opinion.

Here, the different attitudes of the different characters are admirably suggested: the dauphine uncritical; M. de Nemours undecided – on the one hand, hesitating to believe that Mme de Clèves loves him, on the other, attentive to the least details of her comportment and quick to interpret them; Mme de Clèves, torn between sorrow that her love has been betrayed and regret that her lover should have no inkling of her true feelings. Again:

> Mme de Clèves savait que Mme de Martigues aimait le vidame; mais Mme de Martigues ne savait pas que Mme de Clèves aimât M. de

[5] There are one or two minor coincidences—the lost letter; the presence of Nemours at the confession; and the fact that at Coulommiers Nemours should see Mme de Clèves at the precise moment at which she is occupied with souvenirs of her lover.

Nemours, ni qu'elle en fût aimée. La qualité de nièce du vidame rendait Mme de Clèves plus chère à Mme de Martigues; et Mme de Clèves l'aimait aussi comme une personne qui avait une passion aussi bien qu'elle et qui l'avait pour l'ami intime de son amant.

Sentences such as these, concisely and subtly analysing complex motives, are the flowering of seventeenth-century civilization, the culmination of decades of salons and court life.

*La Princesse de Clèves* treats a universal theme. At the same time, as we have seen, it has a topical interest, depicting seventeenth-century society in the guise of the preceding period. Nor can there be much doubt that it represents the sum of its authoress's experience. The seventeenth-century writers put much of themselves and their lives into their work, but transmuted, so that it is not easy to tell when and where the personal element appears; but the fact that all Mme de Lafayette's stories treat the theme of illegitimate love and the perniciousness of passion seems to show that it was one very dear to her heart. As early as 1653, in the first letter of hers which has been preserved, she wrote to Ménage: 'Je suis ravie que vous n'ayez pas de caprice. Je suis si persuadée que l'amour est une chose incommode, que j'ai de la joie que mes amis et moi en soyons exempts.' It has been suggested that her attitude may have originated in her observation of Mme de Sévigné's unhappy marriage; that it may owe something to the shock she herself sustained in 1650, when the chevalier Renaud de Sévigné, whom she had regarded as her suitor, married her mother instead;[6] and that it may have been strengthened by her knowledge of the career of Henriette d'Angleterre. None of this is certain; but that Mme de Lafayette had a deep-seated mistrust of passion and that this provides the theme of all her novels, there can be no doubt.

The names of Corneille and Racine have kept recurring in these pages. Mme de Lafayette's novel has, indeed, much in common with the tragedies of these dramatists. The combination of a historical setting with a basic human situation, of *bienséance* and dignity with psychological truth, of universality with topicality, of objective analysis with a more personal note – all these are found in Mme de Lafayette, as well as in Corneille and Racine. Moreover, she treats the same kind of subject as they: a husband

[6] The gazetteer, Loret, reporting the second marriage of Mme de Lafayette's mother, wrote:

> Mais cette charmante mignonne
> Qu'elle a de son premier époux
> En témoigne un peu de courroux,
> Ayant cru pour être belle
> Que la fête serait pour elle . . .

whose love for his wife is not returned, a wife who loves another man – this is the situation, not only of *La Princesse de Clèves*, but of *Polyeucte*[7] and of *Phèdre*. The conflict of inclination with duty, responsibility, or morality is common to all three. What is more, the subject is treated by Mme de Lafayette in much the same way as it is by Corneille and Racine, the situation developing logically, without external events, the interest being centred on the emotions of the characters.[8]

The question is sometimes asked, whether Mme de Lafayette's characters are 'Cornelian' or 'Racinian'. Unless these terms, which are usually used in an over-simplified way, are accurately defined – a difficult task –, the question is unanswerable. One can say, however, that Mme de Lafayette seems to regard humanity as weak and irrational. M. de Clèves says that, if his wife were to confess to him that she loved another, 'je quitterais le personnage d'amant ou de mari, pour la conseiller et pour la plaindre': in fact, when he has heard just such a confession from his wife, he cannot master his suspicions and his jealousy. We have no control over our passions: Mme de Clèves can make herself neither love her husband nor stop loving Nemours – the only thing which eventually weakens her passion is a prolonged illness which fixes her mind on death and the other world, and even then we are told specifically that 'lorsqu'elle revint de cet état, elle trouva néanmoins que M. de Nemours n'était pas effacé de son cœur'. But if one cannot control one's passions, one can conceal them; one can control one's actions. Mme de Clèves 'ne se flatta plus de l'espérance de ne le pas aimer; elle songea seulement à ne lui en donner jamais aucune marque'. Her virtuous conduct, however, does not bring her happiness. In the end, it is true, she renounces her lover; but her renunciation is in the interests of her peace of mind rather than of her duty, and Mme de Lafayette stresses that her heroine is exceptional. On the other hand, Mme de Lafayette's characters do not know the violent passion and despair, the deep distress of some of Racine's characters: Mme de Clèves is nearer to

---

[7] *La Princesse de Montpensier* is even more like *Polyeucte*. In it, Mlle de Mézières marries M. de Montpensier while loving Guise, as Pauline marries Polyeucte with love for Sévère in her heart.

[8] In *La Princesse de Clèves*, too, the love of Queen Elizabeth for Nemours is similar to that of the Infante for Rodrigue in *Le Cid*. One might add that when Mme de Montpensier, in *La Princesse de Montpensier*, tells Guise to talk to Madame but is jealous when he does, we are reminded of *Othon*, and that when he breaks off his marriage with Madame and arranges to marry the princesse de Portien and she is pleased, we think of several of Corneille's heroines. In the same story, Chabannes, concealing, but not mastering, his jealousy, resembles some of Corneille's characters; though, on the whole, the rôle of Chabannes, who serves his mistress's passion for another and is ill-treated by her, is more reminiscent of that of Antiochus in *Bérénice*.

Bérénice, Monime, or Iphigénie, than to Hermione, Roxane, or
Phèdre. If we are sometimes reminded of Corneille and Racine,
we are perhaps more often reminded of La Rochefoucauld: the
triumph of virtue in *La Princesse de Clèves* is above all a victory
of *amour-propre*.

*La Princesse de Clèves* is usually considered to be the first
French novel. This is not to say that it is completely new. There
is much that is traditional in it – the historical background and the
episodes, and the exceptional attractions of the hero and heroine.
M. de Nemours is 'un chef-d'œuvre de la nature', and Mme de
Clèves is surpassingly beautiful:

La blancheur de son teint et ses cheveux blonds lui donnaient un éclat
que l'on n'a jamais vu qu'à elle; tous ses traits étaient réguliers, et son
visage et sa personne étaient pleins de grâce et de charmes.

Short novels had been written before Mme de Lafayette, and
novels with some psychological interest and which treated the
theme of the married woman in love with another man, had not
been completely lacking. But the great superiority of Mme de
Lafayette is in the mastery with which she handles her subject.
With its universality of situation, the sense of timelessness that
comes from the fusion of a historical setting with seventeenth-
century references, the purely psychological interest, the subtle and
realistic analysis of emotions and relationships, and its simple,
clear, and logical structure, *La Princesse de Clèves* is the first
great French novel.

## II. FURETIÈRE, GUILLERAGUES, LA FONTAINE

If *La Princesse de Clèves* reminds us of Corneille and Racine,
*Le Roman bourgeois* (1666) of Furetière (1620–88)[9] calls to mind
Scarron and Molière and the Racine of *Les Plaideurs*.[10] It consists
of two parts, connected only by the character of Charroselles, the
second of which, though by no means without interest, is inferior
to the first. Not only are the grotesque characters of the *plaideuse*,
Collantine, and of the ignorant magistrate, Belâtre, the rather
tasteless satire of Charles Sorel in the person of Charroselles, and
the legal satire less appealing than the domestic interiors of the

---

[9] Furetière's chief work, besides *Le Roman bourgeois*, was his great
dictionary of the French language, the *Dictionaire universel* (1690), for
compiling which he was expelled from the Academy in 1685.
[10] E.g. Bedout in the first part is at once reminiscent of the illiberal husbands of *L'Ecole des Maris* and *L'Ecole des Femmes* and an anticipation
of Thomas Diafoirus of *Le Malade imaginaire*. Javotte owes something to
the Agnès of *L'Ecole des Femmes*. The second part, which is largely a
satire of the law and contains a *plaideuse*, resembles Racine's *Plaideurs*.

first part, but the second part is more formless: the negligible
plot is little more than a pretext for descriptions of the characters
and anecdotes about the law, and the Mythophilacte episode has
nothing to do with the rest.

In *Le Roman bourgeois*, the element of literary satire and parody
is strong. Furetière's novel opens with a parody of the epic style;
and he pokes fun at contemporary novels – at their length, the
coincidences with which they are filled, the frequency of shipwrecks
and *enlèvements* (with the concomitant conflicts of love and
honour), the monotony of the declarations of love, the unreality
of the temples and palaces which they describe, their habit of
ending with a whole series of marriages, and their exclusive preoccupation with love. The artlessness of his heroine, Javotte, allows
him to parody the conventional gallantry of the heroes and
heroines of novels:

... il n'y a personne qui, en vous donnant l'aumône, ne vous ait en même
temps donné son cœur. Je ne sais (repartit Javotte) ce que vous voulez
dire de cœurs; je n'en ai trouvé pas un seul dans ma tasse.

Furetière is concerned with everyday events in the lives of
ordinary, unheroic, unromantic characters:

... je vous raconterai sincèrement et avec fidélité plusieurs historiettes
ou galanteries arrivées entre des personnes qui ne seront ni héros ni héro-
ïnes, qui ne dresseront point d'armées, ni ne renverseront point de
royaumes, mais qui seront de ces bonnes gens de médiocre condition,
qui vont tout doucement leur grand chemin, dont les uns seront beaux et
les autres laids, les uns sages et les autres sots; et ceux-ci ont bien la
mine de composer le plus grand nombre.

Javotte, the heroine of the first part, is a simpleton; her father a
mean and grasping lawyer. Her rival, Lucrèce, belongs to a shady
family, and is seduced by a marquis. He gives her a false promise
of marriage and recovers it by a low trick; she accuses another
lover of being the father of her child. The second part deals with
the unsuccessful man of letters, Charroselles, the *plaideuse*,
Collantine, and the ignorant magistrate, Belâtre. In contrast to
the omniscience of other novelists, Furetière professes ignorance
of what his characters feel and of what they do or say in private.

*Le Roman bourgeois* is, perhaps, of interest above all for the
picture it gives of seventeenth-century life. There are descriptions,
complete with details of dress and physical appearance, of characteristic social types – the popular preacher, the lawyer with social
aspirations ('un homme amphibie qui était le matin avocat et le
soir courtisan'), the dishonest *procureur*, Vollichon (according to
Brossette, the Rolet mentioned in Boileau's satires), a marquis, a
*plaideuse*, an ignorant magistrate, and the *suisse* 'qui chasse les
chiens et loue les chaises dans l'église, et qui gagne plus à savoir

les intrigues des femmes du quartier qu'à ses deux autres métiers ensemble'. The story begins in the Carmelite church where there is much flirting among the members of the congregation and where the collection is taken by a pretty girl, tricked out for the occasion in borrowed finery. A marriage is arranged and (as, later, in *Le Malade imaginaire*) the first visit of the prospective husband to his bride-to-be is described. She, helped by her fiancé, winds wool, while her mother converses with his cousin:

Elle lui avait déjà fait des plaintes de l'embarras et des soins que donnent les enfants; de la difficulté d'avoir de bonnes servantes [ . . . ] Elle lui avait aussi fait plainte de la dépense de la maison et de la cherté des vivres . . .

The conversation is interrupted by one of the children who rides round on his hobby-horse, chased by his father on a broomstick — Furetière is very hard on 'la sottise des bourgeois, qui quittent l'entretien de la meilleure compagnie du monde pour jouer et badiner avec leurs enfants'. We see Javotte and her mother hemming her trousseau, and Mme Vollichon sleeping with the key of the door under her pillow and lamenting with her husband the good old days when children obeyed their parents and girls were modest. We are shown life in a convent and are taken into a gambling-den and a middle-class salon.

There are references to a multiplicity of aspects of contemporary life — bourgeoises aping the dress of their betters, the muddy streets of Paris, the frequent changes of fashion and the custom of judging people by the extravagance of their dress, the price of sedan chairs, the idleness of servants, the amusements of Paris:

L'après-dînée il allait aux conférences du bureau d'adresse,[11] aux harangues qui se faisaient par les professeurs dans les collèges, aux sermons, aux musiques des églises, à l'orviétan,[12] et à tous les autres jeux et divertissements publics qui ne coûtaient rien . . .

There are details of legal procedure, and anecdotes about the law. The *tarif des partis sortables* in the first part, with some exaggeration no doubt, gives an idea of the dowry needed to purchase different types of husband in the matrimonial market, and the Mythophilacte episode in the second part provides some interesting sidelights on literary life in the seventeenth century.

The realism of Furetière, like that of Scarron — but unlike that of, say, Balzac or Zola —, derives from the satirical purpose and is comic. The style in which the story is narrated is constantly humorous or ironical; the book is enlivened by comic anecdotes and farcical episodes — as when Javotte and Nicodème bump their

[11] Renaudot's establishment. See above, p. 7.
[12] The performances of the charlatans on the Pont-Neuf.

heads together and a whole chapter of accidents ensues; and some
of the characters are grotesque caricatures.

The *Lettres portugaises* (1669) are the antithesis, not only of the
*Roman bourgeois,* but also of the *Princesse de Clèves* – although
the Portuguese nun suffers the fate which Mme de Clèves fears.
Whereas, in Mme de Lafayette's novel, emotion is subdued and
hinted at rather than openly expressed, these five letters, purporting to be from a Portuguese nun to her faithless French lover, are
an uninhibited outpouring of emotion. The impact made on the
seventeenth-century public by this little book – it can be read with
ease in less than an hour – can be gauged by the large number of
editions and imitations to which it gave rise; it has often been
reprinted since.

The *Lettres portugaises* may properly be included in the present
chapter. It has been established that the letters are not genuine, as
was long believed, but fictitious, the work of Guilleragues (1628–
1685);[13] moreover, they tell a story. In the course of her letters,
Mariane recalls the story of her life – her early years in her convent; the day on which, from a balcony, she first noticed her lover
out riding and fell in love with him; how she succumbed to his
blandishments and her passion; their meetings; her emotions and
fears – fears lest her lover should prove fickle or lest he should be
discovered entering the convent and exposed to the wrath of her
family; her unhappiness when military duties called him away.
The five letters, written after his departure, trace her growing
realization, due to her lover's long silence and brief, cold letters,
of his infidelity and unworthiness, until she finally resolves to
renounce him for ever:

... je me suis laissé enchanter par des qualités très médiocres, qu'avez-
vous fait qui dût me plaire? quel sacrifice m'avez-vous fait? n'avez-vous
pas cherché mille autres plaisirs? avez-vous renoncé au jeu et à la
chasse? n'êtes-vous pas parti le premier pour aller à l'armée? n'en êtes-
vous pas revenu après tous les autres? [ ... ] n'avez-vous point cherché les
moyens de vous établir en Portugal, où vous étiez estimé; une lettre de
votre frère vous en a fait partir, sans hésiter un moment; et n'ai-je point su
que, durant le voyage, vous avez été de la plus belle humeur du monde?

The interest of the letters, however, resides less in the meagre
story than in the outpourings of the distracted woman. Here is
no lucid analysis, but a passionate woman confiding her love and
her wretchedness, torn between conflicting emotions. She wishes
that her lover could suffer; she is anxious to spare him suffering.

[13] It is not impossible that the letters were suggested by a genuine love
affair, the protagonists of which have long been identified as the comte de
Chamilly (who, in fact, fought in Portugal from 1663 to 1668) and Maria
Alcaforado of Beja.

She is jealous of the other woman who may have won his love; she feels that she would rather he were faithless than merely indifferent. 'Je suis jalouse avec fureur de tout ce qui vous donne de la joie, et qui touche votre cœur et votre goût en France,' she writes; and then: 'Il y a des moments où il me semble que j'aurais assez de soumission pour servir celle que vous aimez.' She feels remorse, and knows that it is not genuine. She wishes that she had never seen her lover, and immediately afterwards: 'j'aime bien mieux être malheureuse en vous aimant, que de ne vous avoir jamais vu'. She begins her last letter by saying that she will not write again; then she says that she will write again; she ends:

... il faut vous quitter et ne penser plus à vous, je crois même que je ne vous écrirai plus; suis-je obligée de vous rendre un compte exact de tous mes divers mouvements?

Very different again is La Fontaine's *Amours de Psyché et de Cupidon* (1669), a fanciful, delightful work, though more of a fairy-tale than a novel in the accepted sense.

Not the least of the attractions of the book is its setting. It opens with an account of four friends, Poliphile, Acaste, Ariste, and Gélaste,[14] who spend a day at Versailles, of which La Fontaine gives a charming description. In the course of the day, Poliphile reads *Psyché* to his companions. They interrupt from time to time with comments, and in the middle there is a lively debate between Ariste and Gélaste on the relative merits of tragedy and comedy. At the end of the book the friends admire the sun setting over Versailles and depart by moonlight.

Poliphile's composition is a highly original retelling of the story of Cupid and Psyche, told by Apuleius in Books IV, V, and VI of *The Golden Ass* — a good example of what the great seventeenth-century writers understood by imitation of the ancients. The story follows the original in its main outlines, though La Fontaine amplifies and expands it. He makes several changes, most of which he mentions in his preface. His Psyché, in the palace of Cupid, is not attended by invisible servants, but by nymphs with whom she disports herself; she wanders about the grounds and meets her husband in dark grottoes. She goes to seek her sisters *after* Mercury's proclamation requesting news of her, instead of *before*, which allows La Fontaine to describe Psyché coming upon her sister as she is gloating over the notice. Cupidon, in La Fontaine, is more of a lover and plays an active part in helping Psyché to fulfil the impossible tasks set her by Vénus. One of the tasks is changed, and the visit to Hades is told in much greater detail and

14 The identification of these friends with Molière, Racine, Boileau, and La Fontaine is now generally discredited.

much more amusingly. Proserpine's box, on being opened, instead
of sending Psyché to sleep, turns her black – again, La Fontaine's
version is more comic. The sojourn of Psyché with the old fisherman, and the delightful conversation of his daughters between
themselves and then with Psyché (who expresses an anti-stoical
philosophy) is an addition of La Fontaine's; so is the description of
the temple of Vénus and the allegory of Anaphrodite and Aphrodisée, expressing the superiority of charm over regular beauty.

La Fontaine's chief originality is his delicate humour.

> Mon principal but est toujours de plaire: pour en venir là, je considère
> le goût du siècle. Or, après plusieurs expériences, il m'a semblé que ce
> goût se porte au galant et à la plaisanterie [ . . . ] dans un conte comme
> celui-ci, qui est plein de merveilleux, à la vérité, mais d'un merveilleux
> accompagné de badineries, et propre à amuser des enfants, il a fallu
> badiner depuis le commencement jusqu'à la fin; il a fallu chercher du
> galant et de la plaisanterie.

The effect is produced by various means – the light, amusing,
occasionally ironical style; allusions to contemporary manners; the
author's interventions – to explain that he found such and such a
detail in a manuscript, or that he has forgotten or is ignorant of
another, or to give his own reflections.[15] The speeches and conversations, too, are amusing and convincing; the tone is that of mortal
men and women of the seventeenth century, not that of legendary
gods and heroes. Here, La Fontaine uses a technique akin to that
of the burlesque poets; but whereas Scarron and d'Assoucy debase
their gods and make them talk like fishwives, La Fontaine, with
more discretion, merely makes his contemporary and human. The
characters are humanized, not merely in their speech, but in their
motivation. In *The Golden Ass*, for example, Ceres and Juno are
sympathetic to Psyche, but unable to help; in La Fontaine, Psyché
offends Cérès, so it is suggested, by addressing her as 'nourrice des
hommes' and Junon by forgetting to praise her beauty. Similarly,
Junon and Cérès, trying to persuade Vénus to agree to the marriage of Cupidon and Psyché, offend her by suggesting that she
will soon be a grandmother: 'Je me suis regardée tout ce matin,'
she retorts, 'mais il ne m'a point semblé que j'eusse encore l'air
d'une aïeule.' We are told of Vénus:

> Quand Cythérée était lasse des embarras de sa Cour, elle se retirait en
> ce lieu avec cinq ou six de ses confidentes. Là, qui que ce soit ne l'allait
> voir. Des médisants disent toutefois que quelques amis particuliers
> avaient la clef du jardin.

[15] Like Furetière, La Fontaine occasionally satirizes the novels of the
day, e.g. 'Un amant que nos romanciers auraient fait serait demeuré deux
heures à considérer l'objet de sa passion sans l'oser toucher, ni seulement
interrompre son sommeil: l'Amour s'y prit d'une autre manière.'

The last sentence reduces Vénus to the level of any seventeenth-century *précieuse galante*. Cupidon describes the life of the gods in these terms:

... ne vivez-vous pas ici [he says to Jupiter] heureux et tranquille, dormant les trois quarts du temps, laissant aller les choses du monde comme elles peuvent, tonnant et grêlant lorsque la fantaisie vous en vient? Vous savez combien quelquefois nous nous ennuyons: jamais la compagnie n'est bonne s'il n'y a des femmes qui soient aimables. Cybèle est vieille, Junon, de mauvaise humeur; Cérès sent sa divinité de province, et n'a nullement l'air de la Cour; Minerve est toujours armée; Diane nous rompt la tête avec sa trompe: on pourrait faire quelque chose d'assez bon de ces deux dernières; mais elles sont si farouches qu'on ne leur oserait dire un mot de galanterie. Pomone est ennemie de l'oisiveté, et a toujours les mains rudes. Flore est agréable, je le confesse; mais son soin l'attache plus à la terre qu'à ces demeures. L'Aurore se lève de trop grand matin, on ne sait ce qu'elle devient tout le reste de la journée. Il n'y a que ma mère qui nous réjouisse ...

Above all, Psyché, in La Fontaine's version of the tale, becomes a girl endowed with ordinary human weaknesses. She is inquisitive, wily, and naïvely eager to show off her good fortune to her sisters; she knows how to coax and to dissemble:

Tous les artifices dont les femmes ont coutume de se servir quand elles veulent tromper leurs maris furent employés par la belle: ce n'étaient qu'embrassements et caresses, complaisances perpétuelles, protestations et serments de ne point aller contre le vouloir de son cher époux ...

She is vain: she wears a different dress each day, enjoys seeing her likeness everywhere in the palace of Cupidon, and, on meeting the fisherman's two daughters, 'ce qui fit principalement que Psyché crut trouver de l'esprit en elles, ce fut l'admiration qu'elles témoignèrent en la regardant'.

*Psyché* is essentially a fable of La Fontaine composed on a very large scale—a 'fable contée en prose,' La Fontaine calls it in his preface;[16] and it bears much the same relation to Apuleius as a fable of La Fontaine to the original of Aesop or of Phaedrus.

[16] Occasional touches remind us of specific fables. When Psyché determines to commit suicide, for example: 'Elle regarda encore le précipice; et en même temps *la mort se montra à elle sous sa forme la plus affreuse.*' The old man tells her that man has two conflicting impulses: 'il court incessamment vers la mort, il la fuit aussi incessamment.' Cf. *La Mort et le Malheureux*. He also says: 'La véritable grandeur à l'égard des philosophes est de régner sur soi-même, et le véritable plaisir, de jouir de soi. Cela se trouve en la solitude, et ne se trouve guère autre part.' Cf. *Le Juge arbitre, l'Hospitalier, et le Solitaire*.

## Chapter 19

# MME DE SÉVIGNÉ

'ON EST si aise de se transporter un peu en d'autres siècles!' wrote Mme de Sévigné to her daughter;[1] and it is precisely because her letters transport the reader so effectively into seventeenth-century France that we read them with such delight today. Between 1644 and 1696, Marie de Rabutin-Chantal, marquise de Sévigné (1626–96), the grand-daughter of Sainte Jeanne de Chantal, kept up a varied correspondence. Of the 1,154 letters of hers which have been preserved, the largest number, and on the whole the longest and the best, are those written to her daughter, Françoise-Marguerite, during the years of separation (1671–90) which followed the latter's marriage to the comte de Grignan, lieutenant-général of Provence.[2]

If Balzac is too formal and the intrinsic interest of Voiture slight, Mme de Sévigné has the qualities of the perfect letter-writer. She writes easily and naturally – writing as she would have talked, straying from one subject to another. 'Voilà bien de la conversation,' she says at the end of one of her letters (3 November 1688); 'car c'est ainsi qu'on peut appeler nos lettres; si celle-ci vous ennuie, j'en suis fâchée, car je l'ai écrite de bon cœur, et *currente calamo*.' She tells her daughter:

Quand je commence, je ne sais point du tout où cela ira, si ma lettre sera longue ou si elle sera courte; j'écris tant qu'il plaît à ma plume, c'est elle qui gouverne tout: je crois que cette règle est bonne, je m'en trouve bien, et je la continuerai. (30 July 1677)

Her letters to Mme de Grignan, indeed, were usually written over a period of several days: 'A tout moment je vous viens dire un mot; cela me fait un amusement qui m'est toujours meilleur que toute autre chose' (25 October 1679). She fills her letters with all kinds of news and gossip – 'vous savez comme j'aime à ramasser des rogatons pour vous divertir,' she writes to Mme de Grignan (14 October 1676), and again, 'je vous mande tout' (8 July 1680). Nor was she chary of talking about herself:

[1] 1 January 1690.
[2] His first wife had been Angélique-Clarisse d'Angennes, daughter of Mme de Rambouillet.

Quand on s'aime, et qu'on prend intérêt les uns aux autres, je pense qu'il n'y a rien de plus agréable que de parler de soi: il faut retrancher sur les autres pour faire cette dépense entre amis. (5 January 1676)

Mme de Sévigné, in fact, enjoyed writing to her daughter:

...me tenant à ce que vous m'en dites, je ne vous épargnerai aucune bagatelle, grande ou petite, qui vous puisse divertir. Pour moi, c'est ma vie et mon unique plaisir[3] que le commerce que j'ai avec vous; toutes choses sont ensuite bien loin après. (20 January 1672)

...c'est une douceur que d'écrire, mais on n'a ce sentiment que pour une personne au monde... (29 September 1679)

Consequently, she put the best of herself into her letters, as she herself was fully aware:

Je vous donne avec plaisir le dessus de tous les paniers, c'est-à-dire, la fleur de mon esprit, de ma tête, de mes yeux, de ma plume, de mon écritoire; et puis le reste va comme il peut. Je me divertis autant à causer avec vous, que je laboure avec les autres. (1 December 1675)

The result is a unique blend: almost everything, almost every aspect of the seventeenth century is there — court news, accounts of campaigns and battles, of public events and scandals; news of her friends, their love affairs, their illnesses and their deaths; gossip, descriptions of fashions or hair styles, comments on books; advice to her daughter about the education or upbringing of her children, or about the treatment of their ailments or those of Mme de Grignan; news of herself — her daily routine, her diet, her dress, her state of mind and body, her journeys, her move to the Hôtel Carnavalet; news of her son, and later of her grandson, and so on. And all intensely readable, because Mme de Sévigné, although she was not a professional writer and did not write for publication,[4] was a great writer.

The value and interest of Mme de Sévigné's letters as social and historical documents to anyone interested in the past is great. Living in Paris, well-connected, intimate with such people as La Rochefoucauld and Mme de Lafayette, Mme de Maintenon and the duc de Chaulnes, welcomed by the Grande Mademoiselle in her hours of anguish in 1671, favourably received by Louis XIV when she went to court, Mme de Sévigné was well-placed to know what was going on. And, being a highly intelligent, lively, vital

[3] Cf. 'Je n'écris point mes lettres tout d'une haleine; je les reprends; et bien loin de me donner de la peine, c'est mon unique plaisir' (23 June 1677).
[4] Her jesting remarks — 'Comme j'espère que vous ne ferez pas imprimer mes lettres' (14 July 1680) and 'Vous louez tellement mes lettres au-dessus de leur mérite, que [...] je craindrais tout d'un coup de me voir imprimée par la trahison d'un de mes amis' (15 February 1690) — are scarcely evidence to the contrary.

person, keenly interested in the world about her, she made good use of her opportunities. Moreover, as a letter-writer she had one advantage over the writer of memoirs or the historian: she did not know what was going to happen. Hence what we see in her pages is history unfolding itself day by day, history with the comments of an intelligent observer, history with the emotions, the anxiety, the uncertainty, the speculations of contemporaries. If she relates a victory, we catch her exultation, her grief for the friends or the relatives of friends who have fallen, her relief at the safety of her son or grandson. She describes the pitiable state of Mme de Longue-ville on receiving news of the death of her son in battle. When she writes of the death of Turenne, she conveys the grief and the con-sternation of his fellow-countrymen. We learn from her pages what it was like to be a member of Parisian society when the *affaire des poisons* was at its height:

Il y a deux jours que l'on est assez comme le jour de Mademoiselle et de M. de Lauzun: on est dans une agitation, on envoie aux nouvelles, on va dans les maisons pour en apprendre, on est curieux . . .
(26 January 1680)

*We* know that James II escaped from England in 1688 and arrived safely in France: Mme de Sévigné did not:

M. de Lamoignon a mandé à Monsieur le Chevalier que le roi d'Angleterre était arrivé à Boulogne; un autre dit à Brest; un autre dit qu'il est arrêté en Angleterre; un autre, qu'il est péri dans les horribles tempêtes qu'il y a eu sur la mer: voilà de quoi choisir.          (29 December 1688)

As we read Mme de Sévigné, we are present at the trial of Foucquet and visit Mademoiselle, who has just been forbidden to marry Lauzun; we are entertained with the court at Chantilly by Condé, on the lamentable occasion on which Vatel, Condé's *maître d'hôtel*, committed suicide; we are in Brittany on several occasions when the Etats are held, and follow closely the suppres-sion of the peasants' revolt in 1675; we have an interview with Colbert and find him a man of few words; we go to Saint-Germain and converse with the Queen, Monsieur, and Madame, or exchange a few words with Louis XIV at Saint-Cyr after a performance of *Esther*; we accompany Mademoiselle to the Carmelites to see Louise de la Vallière; we feel the shock of the death of Turenne, and shed tears with Mme de Pomponne after the fall from power of her husband; we sup at Gourville's together with La Rochefou-cauld, and we take the waters at Vichy. News of the court is, of course, always welcome; and Mme de Sévigné regales her daughter with anecdotes of courtiers flattering the King or gambling recklessly and with descriptions of current fashions, traces the declining fortunes of Mme de Montespan, notes the strained relations between her and Mme de Maintenon, and the growing favour of Mlle de Fontanges and Mme de Maintenon, and describes a visit to the newly-arrived dauphine or the reception of the Queen of England and James II.

In her pages, too, the men and women of the seventeenth century come alive — Brancas is absent-minded, and Montausier blunt; Mme de Montespan and the duc de Chaulnes travel in state; Mme de Brinvilliers jests in the torture chamber; the Archbishop of Reims drives furiously, knocks over a man, and overturns his carriage; Boileau's blood boils as he argues with a Jesuit and he rushes up and down the room in a passion; Corbinelli puts on a wig for the first time and looks twenty years younger; Charles de Sévigné laughs at his mother's stiff neck. A few moments of the vanished past are caught by Mme de Sévigné's pen and perpetuated. The Breton militia (in 1689, France was at war with England) drills awkwardly:

... c'est une chose étrange que de voir mettre le chapeau à des gens qui n'ont jamais eu que des bonnets bleus sur la tête; ils ne peuvent comprendre l'exercice, ni ce qu'on leur défend. Quand ils avaient leurs mousquets sur l'épaule et que M. de Chaulnes paraissait, ils voulaient le saluer, l'arme tombait d'un côté et le chapeau de l'autre: on leur a dit qu'il ne faut point saluer; et quand ils sont désarmés, ils voient passer M. de Chaulnes, ils enfoncent leurs chapeaux avec les deux mains, et se gardent bien de le saluer. On leur a dit qu'il ne faut pas branler ni aller et venir quand ils sont dans leurs rangs: ils se laissaient rouer l'autre jour par le carrosse de Mme de Chaulnes, sans vouloir se retirer d'un seul pas, quoi qu'on pût leur dire. (15 May 1689)

The procession of sainte Geneviève passes by:

Toutes les religions, toutes les paroisses, toutes les châsses, tous les prêtres des paroisses, tous les chanoines de Notre-Dame, et Monsieur l'Archevêque pontificalement, qui va à pied, bénissant à droite et à gauche, jusqu'à la Cathédrale; cependant il n'a que la main gauche; et à la droite, c'est l'abbé de Sainte-Geneviève, nu-pieds, précédé de cent cinquante religieux, nu-pieds aussi, avec sa crosse et sa mitre, comme l'Archevêque, et bénissant aussi, mais modestement et dévotement, et à jeun, avec un air de pénitence qui fait voir que c'est lui qui va dire la messe dans Notre-Dame. Le parlement en robes rouges et toutes les compagnies souveraines suivent cette châsse qui est brillante de pierreries, portée par vingt hommes habillés de blanc, nu-pieds. (19 July 1675)

A handsome young man of Rennes dances with his wife:

Il dansa ces belles chaconnes, les folies d'Espagne, mais surtout les passe-pieds avec sa femme, d'une perfection, d'un agrément qui ne se peut représenter: point de pas réglés, rien qu'une cadence juste, des fantaisies de figures, tantôt en branle comme les autres, et puis à deux seulement comme des menuets, tantôt en se reposant, tantôt ne mettant pas les pieds à terre. (24 July 1689)

M. de Pomponne remembers Mme de Grignan and her brother as children:

M. de Pomponne se souvient d'un jour que vous étiez petite fille chez mon oncle de Sévigné. Vous étiez derrière une vitre avec votre frère, plus belle, dit-il, qu'un ange; vous disiez que vous étiez prisonnière, que vous étiez une princesse chassée de chez son père. Votre frère était beau comme vous: vous aviez neuf ans. (15 January 1674)

Not the least attractive are the glimpses the letters afford of the writer herself. They contain accounts of her daily routine, even of what she ate—

... j'aime le beurre charmant de la Prévalaie, dont il nous vient toutes les semaines; je l'aime et je le mange comme si j'étais bretonne: nous faisons des beurrées infinies, quelquefois sur de la miche; nous pensons toujours à vous en les mangeant; mon fils y marque toujours toutes ses dents, et ce qui me fait plaisir, c'est que j'y marque aussi toutes les miennes ... (19 February 1690)

They contain details of her health and how she looked after herself:

Je ne laisse pas de me purger, et je le ferai toujours de temps en temps, parce que j'y suis accoutumée, et que mon fils se purge aussi assez souvent, et ma belle-fille par compagnie; et ils me pressent toujours de faire comme eux. C'est une débauche; nous n'avons que cela à faire ... (2 July 1690)

They show her talking to her friends or writing to her *fermier*, delighted with a dog that a friend has sent her or the company of a little girl on her estate, resolved to continue a journey, but at last dissuaded because of the state of the roads:

Ainsi coffres qu'on rapporte, mulets qu'on dételle, filles et laquais qui se sèchent pour avoir seulement traversé la cour, et messager que l'on vous envoie ... (20 December 1672)

They show her dining in Brittany with the princesse de Tarente—

Voici comme votre mère était habillée: une bonne robe de chambre bien chaude, que vous avez refusée, quoique fort jolie; et cette jupe violette, or et argent, que j'appelais sottement un jupon, avec une belle coiffure de toutes cornettes de chambre négligées ... (29 November 1684)

—or instructing Mme de Grignan, who was to stay at the Hôtel Carnavalet during her mother's absence, how to deal with a smoky fire:

Il [her uncle, the *bien bon*] vous mande que s'il y a de la fumée, vous ouvriez de deux doigts seulement la fenêtre près de la porte, comme il faisait; sans cela vous serez incommodés. (15 November 1684)

The letters take us further into the marquise's intimacy than that; they give us an insight into her character and her mentality. She was affectionate, a loyal friend, devoted to her uncle, *le bien bon*, an adoring grandmother, proud particularly of her grandson, though sorry that he had no taste for books, and a good mother – solicitous for her son's career and welfare and full of adoration for her daughter, delighted to meet anyone who had recently seen her in Provence, concerned about her health and well-being, and lavishing advice of all kinds on her; so excessively fond of her daughter, indeed, that 'mon cœur n'étant capable d'aucune autre pensée, on m'a défendu de faire mes dévotions à la Pentecôte' (5 June 1675). She loved reading and read widely: 'Je plains ceux qui n'aiment point à lire', she wrote (17 July 1689), and knew from experience that reading is a remedy for boredom and idleness, though not anxiety ('on relit vingt fois la même page', 1 February 1690). She often tells her daughter what she is reading and passes comments on it, so that we know her literary tastes quite well. She was fond of memoirs and history (including Church history), and we find her reading Josephus and Tacitus. She enjoyed Virgil and Tasso, Cervantes and Montaigne, La Fontaine and Boileau, Voiture and *La Princesse de Clèves* ('une des plus charmantes choses que j'aie jamais lues', 18 March 1678). She read, too, theological and religious works – Pascal's *Provinciales*, St. Augustine, Nicole, Bossuet, and so forth. For Mme de Sévigné was a pious woman, with Jansenist leanings and a firm belief in Providence, though she was not a *dévote* and regretted that her religion had not touched her heart – 'un cœur de glace, un esprit éclairé' (1 May 1680).

Although she was sociable and vivacious, she preferred tranquillity to social life. 'Ce sera,' she writes from Rennes, 'avec une joie sensible que je retrouverai le repos et le silence de mes bois' (10 August 1680). Her daily routine, at least when she was in the country, always included time for walking as well as reading.

Quand il fait beau [she writes from Brittany in November], comme il a fait depuis trois jours, je sors à deux heures, et je vais me promener *quanto va*; je ne m'arrête point, je passe et repasse devant des ouvriers qui coupent du bois, et représentent au naturel ces tableaux de l'hiver: je ne m'amuse point à les contempler; et quand j'ai pris toute la beauté du soleil en marchant toujours, je rentre dans ma chambre [ ... ] La chaise de Coulanges, des livres que mon fils lit en perfection, et quelque conversation, feront tout le partage de mon hiver ... (26 November 1684)

She enjoyed making improvements to her estate, Les Rochers, in Brittany and rambling in it, and her letters show a keen appreciation of nature, close observation, and a considerable gift of describing what she saw. The song of the birds, the silence of the woods, the countryside of Vichy or Normandy, all delighted her. The moonlight set her fancy playing freely:

L'autre jour on me vint dire: 'Madame, il fait chaud dans le mail, il n'y a pas un brin de vent; la lune y fait des effets les plus brillants du monde.'

Je ne pus résister à la tentation; je mets mon infanterie sur pied; je mets tous les bonnets, coiffes et casaques qui n'étaient point nécessaires; j'allai dans ce mail, dont l'air est comme celui de ma chambre; je trouvai mille coquecigrues, des moines blancs et noirs, plusieurs religieuses grises et blanches, du linge jeté par-ci, par-là, des hommes noirs, d'autres ensevelis tout droits contre des arbres, des petits hommes cachés, qui ne montraient que la tête, des prêtres qui n'osaient approcher. Après avoir ri de toutes ces figures, et nous être persuadés que voilà ce qui s'appelle des esprits, et que notre imagination en est le théâtre, nous nous en revînmes sans nous arrêter, et sans avoir senti la moindre humidité.

(12 June 1680)

Even mountains appeal to her: 'nous ne respirons que de la neige; nos montagnes sont charmantes dans leur excès d'horreur' (3 February 1695). She notes the shades of leaves and studies the colour of buds:

Que pensez-vous donc que ce soit que la couleur des arbres depuis huit jours? Répondez. Vous allez dire: 'Du vert.' Point du tout, c'est du rouge. Ce sont de petits boutons, tout prêts à partir, qui font un vrai rouge; et puis ils poussent tous une petite feuille; et comme c'est inégalement, cela fait un mélange trop joli de vert et de rouge. Nous couvons tout cela des yeux; nous parions de grosses sommes—mais c'est à ne jamais payer—que ce bout d'allée sera tout vert dans deux heures; on dit que non: on parie. Les charmes ont leur manière, les hêtres une autre.

(19 April 1690)

Intelligent and enlightened as she was, free from superstition and sceptical about ghosts and the influence of comets, she is nevertheless not completely modern in outlook. She speaks enthusiastically of the *dragonnades*:

En un mot, tout est missionnaire présentement; chacun croit avoir une mission, et surtout les magistrats et les gouverneurs de province, soutenus de quelques dragons: c'est la plus grande et la plus belle chose qui ait été imaginée et exécutée.                          (24 November 1685)

Her belief in Providence is at times a little naïve—her comments on the death of the Bishop of Evreux, for instance:

... je vois Dieu qui tourne les volontés de ce bonhomme d'une manière extraordinaire, pour le conduire à être massacré et déchiré, et tiré enfin à quatre chevaux: voyez par combien de circonstances on voit la destinée s'opiniâtrer à vouloir premièrement qu'il se remette en équipage à quatre-vingts ans; des chevaux neufs, point de postillon, les avertissements de tout le monde; point de nouvelles, il faut qu'il périsse, il faut qu'il soit déchiré, il faut que MM. de Grignan en profitent.[5]       (11 September 1680)

And the remedies in which she has faith seem sometimes to smack more of magic than of medicine. She went to the Capuchins to have a swollen leg treated:

... nos chers pères l'ont voulu traiter à loisir, sans me contraindre, et en me jouant, avec ces herbes, que l'on retire deux fois le jour toutes mouil-

[5] One succeeded M. d'Evreux as Bishop, and the other gained a pension.

lées: on les enterre, et à mesure qu'elles pourrissent, riez-en si vous
voulez, cet endroit sue et s'amollit... (13 June 1685)

Vipers and *poudre d'yeux d'écrevisse* are amongst the remedies in
which she has faith.

'One reads Mme de Sévigné first for herself',[6] writes her most
recent critic. This is a matter of opinion, and the appeal of Mme
de Sévigné's letters will be different for every reader. Nevertheless, her attractive and interesting personality is certainly one of the
reasons for the appeal of her letters. All in all, there is no other
seventeenth-century character whom one knows so well, so intimately, so much in the round as Mme de Sévigné.

She was a great stylist. Although she was not a professional
writer, she lived at a time when people were conscious of the
importance of writing well – and the compliments Mme de Sévigné
pays her correspondents on their style shows that she was of her
age in this. Her own style is easy and natural, can adapt itself to
all tones from the sprightly to the serious, and can make everything
interesting – even the weather:

Vous avez eu un temps bien charmant au milieu de votre hiver: temps
à faire que Monsieur le Comte ne peut s'empêcher d'aller à la chasse;
temps où vous quittez vos malades; temps où vous préférez le plaisir de
vous promener à celui d'écrire: ah! que vous faites bien! il ne faut point
perdre ces jours enchantés. Nous en avons eu d'horribles: c'était un
temps à garder le coin du feu; temps à ne pas mettre le nez dehors; temps
à ne voir goutte du brouillard, sans préjudice du verglas et de la gelée;
enfin temps tout contraire au vôtre, et où pourtant mon fils avait cinq ou
six de ses voisins, qui jouaient et faisaient du bruit dans cette chambre.
(1 January 1690)

Two qualities that strike the reader are her sense of humour and
her vividness. Her sense of humour is evident, for example, in the
description of the ceremony of the *chevaliers de l'ordre* in 1689,
at which maréchal de Bellefonds was

totalement ridicule, parce que par modestie et par mine indifférente, il
avait négligé de mettre des rubans au bas de ses chausses de page, de
sorte que c'était une véritable nudité.

– at which M. de Montchevreuil and M. de Villars

s'accrochèrent l'un à l'autre d'une telle furie, les épées, les rubans, les
dentelles, tous les clinquants, tout se trouva tellement mêlé, brouillé,
embarrassé, toutes les petites parties crochues étaient si parfaitement
entrelacées, que nulle main d'homme ne put les séparer: plus on y
tâchait, plus on brouillait, comme les anneaux des armes de Roger; enfin
toute la cérémonie, toutes les révérences, tout le manège demeurant
arrêté, il fallut les arracher de force, et le plus fort l'emporta.

[6] H. R. Allentuch, *Madame de Sévigné: a portrait in letters*, 1963, p. 29.

— and at which M. d'Hocquincourt was

tellement habillé comme les Provençaux et les Bretons, que, ses chausses
de page étant moins commodes que celles qu'il a d'ordinaire, sa chemise
ne voulut jamais y demeurer, quelque prière qu'il lui en fît; car sachant
son état, il tâchait incessamment d'y donner ordre, et ce fut toujours
inutilement; de sorte que Madame la Dauphine ne put tenir plus longtemps les éclats de rire: ce fut une grande pitié; la majesté du Roi en
pensa être ébranlée . . .                                    (3 January 1689)

To appreciate the interest and vividness of Mme de Sévigné's
descriptions and narratives, we have only to compare them with
those of others. Mme de Sévigné was not at Chantilly when Vatel
committed suicide; Gourville was, and indeed it was Gourville
who stepped into the breach after Vatel's death. But there is no
comparison between the colourless page of Gourville's *Mémoires*
and Mme de Sévigné's letter on the subject. She excels at conveying an impression of movement or bustle by an accumulation of
verbs or nouns:

J'ai été à cette noce de Mlle de Louvois: que vous dirai-je? Magnificence,
illustration, toute la France, habits rabattus et rebrochés d'or, pierreries,
brasiers de feu et de fleurs, embarras de carrosses, cris dans la rue, flambeaux allumés, reculements et gens roués; enfin le tourbillon, la dissipation, les demandes sans réponses, les compliments sans savoir ce que
l'on dit, les civilités sans savoir à qui l'on parle, les pieds entortillés dans
les queues . . .                                    (29 November 1679)

Dîner, souper en festin chez M. et Mme de Chaulnes, avoir fait mille
visites de devoirs et de couvents, aller, venir, complimenter, s'épuiser,
devenir toute aliénée, comme une dame d'honneur, c'est ce que nous
fîmes hier, ma bonne.                                    (6 August 1680)

On the birth of the duc de Bourgogne:

. . . quel bruit, quels feux de joie, quelle effusion de vin, quelle danse de
deux cents Suisses autour des portes, quels cris de *vive le Roi*, quelles
cloches sonnées à Paris, quels canons tirés, quel concours de compli-
ments et de harangues, et tout cela finira.                                    (7 August 1682)

Mme de Sévigné's way of writing by no means excluded artistry,
as the following passage shows:

M. de Langlée a donné à Mme de Montespan une robe d'or sur or,
rebrodé d'or, rebordé d'or, et par-dessus un or frisé, rebroché d'un or
mêlé avec un certain or, qui fait la plus divine étoffe qui ait jamais été
imaginée: ce sont les fées qui ont fait en secret cet ouvrage; âme
vivante n'en avait connaissance. On la voulut donner aussi mystérieuse-
ment qu'elle était fabriquée. Le tailleur de Mme de Montespan lui apporta
l'habit qu'elle avait ordonné; il en fit le corps sur des mesures ridicules:
voilà des cris et des gronderies, comme vous pouvez penser; le tailleur dit
en tremblant: 'Madame, comme le temps presse, voyez si cet autre habit
que voilà ne pourrait point vous accommoder, faute d'autre.' On découvre
l'habit: 'Ah! la belle chose! ah! quelle étoffe! vient-elle du ciel? Il n'y
en a point de pareille sur la terre.' On essaye le corps: il est à peindre.

Le Roi arrive; le tailleur dit: 'Madame, il est fait pour vous.' On com-
prend que c'est une galanterie; mais qui peut l'avoir faite?' C'est Langlée
dit le Roi.—C'est Langlée assurément, dit Mme de Montespan; personne
que lui ne peut avoir imaginé une telle magnificence.'—'C'est Langlée,
c'est Langlée;' tout le monde répète: 'C'est Langlée;' les échos en
demeurent d'accord, et disent: 'C'est Langlée;' et moi, ma fille, je vous dis
pour être à la mode: 'C'est Langlée.'                    (5 November 1676)

The tripartite composition of this paragraph (the dress, the
manner of its presentation, speculation about the mysterious
donor), the description of the dress with its repetition of the word
*or* and the carefully chosen synonyms which echo one another
(*rebrodé*, *rebordé*, *rebroché*), and the repetition of the name
Langlée at the end, reminiscent of the verbal echoes of the first
sentence and suggestive of echoes spreading outward from the King,
like ripples in a pool, and dying away in the remote distance, leave
little doubt of Mme de Sévigné's conscious artistry. She may not
have written a draft of this before composing her letter; but one
imagines her turning it over in her head.

By such means does Mme de Sévigné conjure up the society of
the seventeenth century. And because the people she describes are
so intensely individual and alive, the reader's interest is accompanied by a feeling of pathos, provoked by the reflection that this
brilliant court, this group of friends, this affectionate family circle
have long since ceased to exist, save in her pages.

*Chapter 20*

# FAITH AND REASON: BOSSUET, MALEBRANCHE, VILLARS, AND SAINT-EVREMOND

## I. BOSSUET

JACQUES-BÉNIGNE BOSSUET (1627–1704), Bishop first of Condom (1669) and later of Meaux (1681), appointed tutor to the dauphin (1670), was a prominent member of the French Church, a distinguished theologian, and a great preacher in an age of great preachers.[1] His *Oraisons funèbres*, his sermons, and his panegyrics testify to his gifts as an orator. As tutor to the dauphin, he took his duties seriously and composed a number of works for the edification of his pupil, notably a *Discours sur l'histoire universelle* (1681) and his *Politique tirée des propres paroles de l'Ecriture sainte*. As churchman and theologian, he waged ceaseless war on all whom he regarded as enemies of the Church — on Richard Simon, whose *Histoire critique du Vieux Testament* was suppressed through Bossuet's influence in 1678; on the Protestants (*Histoire des Variations des Eglises protestantes*, 1688); on Malebranche; and on the quietism of Mme Guyon and Fénelon (*Relation sur le Quiétisme*, 1698). His place in French literature is due chiefly to his *Oraisons funèbres*.

Ten funeral orations have been preserved — four early ones and the six great ones on prominent court figures, Henrietta, Queen of England (1669), her daughter, Henriette d'Angleterre, the sister-in-law of Louis XIV (1670), Maria Theresa, Queen of France (1683), Anne de Gonzague, princesse palatine (1685), the Chancellor, Le Tellier (1686), and the great Condé (1687). A funeral oration was a solemn harangue, delivered before a large and distinguished congregation; those of Henriette d'Angleterre and of the Queen of France in Saint-Denis, that of Condé in Notre-Dame. It was an occasion on which the life of the deceased had to be narrated and his virtues praised in an exalted style, an occasion for solemn, resounding periods.

[1] The most celebrated of the others were Bourdaloue (1632–1704), Fléchier (1632–1710), Mascaron (1634–1703), and Massillon (1663–1742).

314

In one of his early funeral orations, that on Père François Bourgoing, Bossuet acknowledges the difficulty of the undertaking:

Je vous avoue, Chrétiens, que j'ai coutume de plaindre les prédicateurs, lorsqu'ils font les panégyriques funèbres des princes et des grands de ce monde. Ce n'est pas que de tels sujets ne fournissent ordinairement de nobles idées [...] Mais la licence et l'ambition, compagnes presque inséparables des grandes fortunes; mais l'intérêt et l'injustice, toujours mêlés trop avant dans les grandes affaires du monde, font qu'on marche parmi des écueils; et il arrive ordinairement que Dieu a si peu de part dans de telles vies, qu'on a peine à y trouver quelques actions qui méritent d'être louées par ses ministres.

Bossuet avoided the difficulty, to some extent, at least, by conceiving of the funeral oration primarily as a sermon, in which the life of the deceased is used to illustrate a lesson. He chooses a Biblical text which makes clear the theme of his oration. In his exordium, in which he usually repeats the text, he explains his theme more fully. The life of Henrietta of France is a lesson to princes; that of Henriette d'Angleterre illustrates the vanity of human life; that of the Queen of France is a lesson in piety; that of Anne de Gonzague illustrates the power of the Grace of God; that of Le Tellier is an example of true wisdom; that of Condé shows that human greatness is nothing without piety. Then follows the life of the person he is celebrating, nearly always in two contrasting parts – Bourgoing as priest and Bourgoing as head of the Oratory; Nicolas Cornet a *trésor*, but a *trésor caché*; Henrietta in prosperity and in adversity; the greatness of Henriette d'Angleterre, of Marie-Thérèse, and of Condé, contrasted with their piety; the aberrations of Anne de Gonzague and her return to the fold. Finally, Bossuet closes with a peroration, in which he exhorts his hearers to profit by the lesson to be drawn from the life he has just related.

It is clear that we cannot expect Bossuet's funeral orations to be straightforward biography. He says himself that he is no historian:

Ce n'est pas un ouvrage humain que je médite. Je ne suis pas ici un historien qui doive vous développer le secret des cabinets, ni l'ordre des batailles, ni les intérêts des partis: il faut que je m'élève au-dessus de l'homme, pour faire trembler toute créature sous les jugements de Dieu.
(*Oraison funèbre d'Henriette-Marie de France*)

Taisons-nous; ce n'est pas des larmes que je veux tirer de vos yeux. Je pose les fondements des instructions que je veux graver dans vos cœurs ...
(*Oraison funèbre de Marie-Thérèse d'Autriche*)

Si, touchés des saints exemples que je vous propose, vous laissez attendrir vos cœurs, si Dieu a béni le travail par lequel je tâche de vous enfanter en Jésus-Christ, et que, trop indigne ministre de ses conseils, je

n'y aie pas été moi-même un obstacle, vous bénirez la bonté divine qui
vous aura conduits à la pompe funèbre de cette pieuse princesse, où vous
aurez peut-être trouvé le commencement de la véritable vie.

*(Oraison funèbre d'Anne de Gonzague de Clèves)*

The life of the deceased is of interest, not for itself, but as an
illustration of some point – it provides us with an example of what
to follow or what to avoid: Bossuet holds up Père Bourgoing as an
ideal priest, and Le Tellier as an ideal magistrate; he urges his
hearers to live Christian lives and to die Christian deaths like
Henrietta of France, Henriette d'Angleterre, Anne de Gonzague,
Condé, and so forth; he uses Anne de Gonzague as a warning
against *libertinage*. Hence he does not deal in detail with the lives
of the characters he is celebrating, but stresses those aspects which
are germane to his theme – usually their greatness, their virtues,
and their piety. He does not give his narrative the same proportions
as a historian or a biographer would; he does not always observe
the chronological order; he occasionally slurs over some of the less
worthy characteristics of his heroes; and in one case, at least, he
distorts the career of his hero by saying practically nothing of Le
Tellier's services as Secretary of State for War. Nevertheless, the
historical and biographical interest of Bossuet's *Oraisons funèbres*
is considerable. The lives of his heroes allow him to evoke the battle
of Rocroy and other victories of Condé, to draw a parallel between
Turenne and Condé as commanders, to recount the English civil
wars (*Henriette de France, Henriette d'Angleterre*) and the Fronde
(*Anne de Gonzague, Le Tellier, Condé*), to eulogize Le Tellier's
work as Chancellor and the revocation of the Edict of Nantes.
Moreover, Bossuet is speaking of people he knew, so that his
accounts of them have a documentary value: for example, he was
summoned to the deathbed of Henriette d'Angleterre, and his
description of her last moments is that of an eyewitness.

The main themes of Bossuet's *Oraisons funèbres* are death and
providence. The duty of priests charged with delivering a funeral
oration, says Bossuet in his earliest essay in the genre, is to make
their congregation

contempler [ ... ] la commune condition de tous les mortels, afin que la
pensée de la mort leur donne un saint dégoût de la vie présente, et que
la vanité humaine rougisse en regardant le terme fatal que la Providence
divine a donné à ses espérances trompeuses.

*(Oraison funèbre de Madame Yolande de Monterby)*

This duty he never omitted. The universality of death rendering
all men equal, the vanity of human greatness and glory, the
annihilation of all human achievement, are stressed time and time
again. But there is another side to this bleak description of the
human condition. Immortality can be achieved through God, and

no life is vain in so far as it is directed to this purpose. Moreover,
God is constantly watching over humanity, and in everything that
befalls, his providence is at work. It is God who sends conquerors,
who distributes talents, who ordains victories. It was God who
made Cromwell prosper as a warning to kings of the dangers of
heresy, God who made Maria Theresa Queen of France 'afin de
rendre la pureté et la perpétuelle régularité de sa vie plus
éclatante et plus exemplaire', God who sent the Fronde in order
to show 'qu'il donne la mort, et qu'il ressuscite, qu'il plonge
jusqu'aux enfers, et qu'il en retire, qu'il secoue la terre et la brise,
et qu'il guérit en un moment toutes ses brisures'. Providence is no
less concerned with the fate of individuals than with the destinies
of nations. It was God who made Anne de Gonzague see the errors
of her ways, who ensured that Le Tellier as *intendant de justice* in
Piedmont should be consulted by Mazarin as ambassador, thus
giving him training in statecraft; it was even God who caused the
English civil wars in order that Henriette d'Angleterre might become a Catholic.

Besides these main themes, Bossuet manages to touch upon a
variety of other topics. He attacks casuistry and avidity for
ecclesiastical preferment in the *oraison funèbre* on Nicolas Cornet;
he fulminates against the *libertins* in the *oraison funèbre* on Anne
de Gonzague;[2] and he protests against the diminution of ecclesiastical jurisdiction in the *oraison funèbre* on Michel Le Tellier. He
weighs up the comparative merits of the prodigal son and his
elder brother in the *oraison funèbre* on Anne de Gonzague, and
discusses the errors and duties of kings (*Henriette-Marie de
France*) and their sorrows (*Marie-Thérèse*).

Bossuet is one of the great masters of French prose. Narrative,
*portraits*, historical tableaux, indignation, exhortation, pathos – all
varieties of prose writing and of tone are there; and Bossuet is
equal to them all. If the mixture of short and long sentences makes
his style what it is, it is perhaps as the master of the solemn,
complex period that the reader remembers him afterwards. To take
an example at random:

I    1.   Quand Dieu laisse sortir du puits de l'abîme/ la fumée qui
          obscurcit le soleil,/ selon l'expression de l'Apocalypse,/ c'est-
          à-dire,
                 (i) l'erreur
                 (ii) et l'hérésie;/

     2.   quand,
                 (i) pour punir les scandales,/
                 (ii) ou pour réveiller

2 See above, p. 202.

$\left\{\begin{array}{l}\text{(a)  les peuples}\\\text{(b)  et les pasteurs,/}\end{array}\right.$

il permet à l'esprit de séduction/

$\left\{\begin{array}{l}\text{(i)  de tromper les âmes hautaines,/}\\\text{(ii) et de répandre partout/}\end{array}\right.$

$\left[\begin{array}{l}\text{(a)  un chagrin superbe,/}\\\text{(b)  une indocile curiosité,/}\\\text{(c)  et un esprit de révolte,/}\end{array}\right.$

II   il détermine, /dans sa sagesse profonde, /les limites qu'il veut donner/

$\left\{\begin{array}{l}\text{(i)  aux malheureux progrès de l'erreur/}\\\text{(ii) et aux souffrances de son Eglise./}\end{array}\right.$

*(Oraison funèbre d'Henriette-Marie de France)*

This is a masterly sentence. Two subordinate clauses, the second repeating and expanding the ideas contained in the first, balance the main clause, and the whole sentence is built up of rhythmic groups; the dignity of the whole being enhanced by the use of nouns and infinitives in pairs, three linked nouns occurring at the end of the second clause for the sake of variety and to mark the end of the first half of the sentence.

One of the best of the *Oraisons funèbres* is that on Henriette d'Angleterre, delivered in Saint-Denis on 21 August 1670. We should imagine the scene – the west door hung with black, and over it the arms of the princess, six feet high, with a skeleton on either side; the chancel equally draped in black, with a skeleton on each of its pillars; in the middle of the chancel, a dais on which stood a mausoleum and a tomb, above which was suspended the coffin; the church brightly lit with tapers and candles; a numerous and distinguished congregation – the parlement, the Chambre des Comptes, the Cour des Aides, the Cour des Monnaies, the Corps de Ville, the University, and the clergy were there; so was the princesse de Condé, the duchesse de Longueville, and, incognito, the Queen, the King of Poland, the English ambassador, and the Duke of Buckingham.

Au milieu de la messe [says the *Gazette de France*], le héraut de Bourgogne alla quérir l'abbé Bossuet, nommé à l'évêché de Condom, pour faire l'éloge funèbre, dont il s'acquitta d'une manière qui lui attira l'admiration de son illustre et nombreux auditoire.

Cut off suddenly in the flower of her age – she was just turned twenty-six – after successfully negotiating the Treaty of Dover with her brother, Charles II, Henriette's sudden death two months before had filled the court with consternation, all the more so as there was an unfounded suspicion that she had been poisoned by her husband or one of his minions. Bossuet does not hesitate to revive the emotions aroused by the princess's death. 'Vanitas vanitatum, dixit Ecclesiastes', he takes as his text, setting the tone for his discourse; 'vanitas vanitatum, et omnia vanitas'. Reminding his hearers that only ten months previously Henriette had been present at the obsequies of her mother, he takes her as the symbol of the vanity of human life and declares his intention:

Je veux dans un seul malheur déplorer toutes les calamités du genre humain, et dans une seule mort faire voir la mort et le néant de toutes les grandeurs humaines.

But human life is not altogether vain, since it is the gateway to eternity. Henriette is the symbol at once of man's *néant* and of his dignity; and he proposes to divide his discourse into two heads, what she has lost by death and what she has gained by death, with a view to teaching piety and detachment from worldly things.

Death, he begins his first part by saying, makes all men equal and he illustrates this point with an elaborate simile:

Leurs années se poussent successivement comme des flots; ils ne cessent de s'écouler; tant qu'enfin après avoir fait un peu plus de bruit, et traversé un peu plus de pays les uns que les autres, ils vont tous ensemble se confondre dans un abîme où l'on ne reconnaît plus ni princes, ni rois, ni toutes ces autres qualités superbes qui distinguent les hommes; de même que ces fleuves tant vantés demeurent sans nom et sans gloire, mêlés dans l'Océan avec les rivières les plus inconnues.

If any permanent distinctions could exist, no one could have been more distinguished than Henriette, and Bossuet dwells, with occasional reminders of her premature death, on her greatness, on her rank, and on her intellectual qualities, with a neat compliment to Louis XIV:

Mais pourquoi m'étendre sur une matière où je puis tout dire en un mot? Le Roi, dont le jugement est une règle toujours sûre, a estimé la capacité de cette princesse, et l'a mise par son estime au-dessus de tous nos éloges.

A reference to the Treaty of Dover leads Bossuet to deplore the death of Henriette 'pendant que la confiance de deux si grands rois l'élevait au comble de la grandeur et de la gloire'. These two words, *grandeur* and *gloire*, provide the transition to the other half of the first part, to a consideration of man's *néant*. All distinctions — rank, intellectual qualities, great conceptions — are ephemeral. From general considerations, Bossuet passes to the death of Henriette —

O nuit désastreuse! ô nuit effroyable! où retentit tout à coup, comme un éclat de tonnerre, cette étonnante nouvelle: Madame se meurt! Madame est morte!

— a sentence which, with its rhythmic groups, its alliterations and its assonances, is poetry in every sense of the word. A long passage on the death of Henriette now follows – but if, in dwelling on her greatness, he introduced reminders of her death, now, in dwelling on her death, he harks back from time to time to her greatness. He describes the courage and fortitude displayed by Henriette on her deathbed and, in a passage of astonishing realism, evokes the fate of her body in the tomb:

Elle va descendre à ces sombres lieux, à ces demeures souterraines, pour y dormir dans la poussière avec les grands de la terre, comme parle Job, avec ces rois et ces princes anéantis, parmi lesquels à peine peut-on la placer, tant les rangs y sont pressés, tant la mort est prompte à remplir ces places! Mais ici notre imagination nous abuse encore. La mort ne nous laisse pas assez de corps pour occuper quelque place, et on ne voit là que les tombeaux qui fassent quelque figure. Notre chair change bientôt de nature. Notre corps prend un autre nom; même celui de cadavre, dit Tertullien, parce qu'il nous montre encore quelque forme humaine, ne lui demeure pas longtemps: il devient un je ne sais quoi, qui n'a plus de nom dans aucune langue; tant il est vrai que tout meurt en lui, jusqu'à ces termes funèbres par lesquels on exprimait ses malheureux restes!

From *grandeur* and *gloire* Bossuet has brought us down into the abyss. He now takes us back to the heights. Is there no hope, then, for man, he asks? Yes; Madame is no longer in the tomb; death is the gateway to eternal life.

The second part opens with a general consideration of the human condition. The body is mortal, but the soul is divine; when the one returns to the earth from which it came, the other is united with God and achieves true *grandeur* and *gloire*. Hence, true wisdom consists of preparing for eternity, of fearing God:

Voulez-vous sauver quelque chose de ce débris si universel, si inévitable? Donnez à Dieu vos affections: nulle force ne vous ravira ce que vous aurez déposé en ses mains divines. Vous pourrez hardiment mépriser la mort, à l'exemple de notre héroïne chrétienne.

From the general, Bossuet thus returns to the particular, to the consideration of the grace of God as shown in the life of Henriette – shown first in the fact that God sent the English civil wars in order to make her a Catholic, and, second, in her death. There follows a second account of the death of Henriette – this time showing how she died a Christian death. Although death came to her in its bitterest form – she was young, her death was sudden, and it was painful –, she was ready and encountered it with fortitude and piety. He ends by saying that death has saved Henriette from temptations – particularly that of *gloire*, of taking delight in being idolized. The shortness of her life was no fault:

C'est l'effet d'un art consommé, de réduire en petit tout un grand ouvrage; et la grâce, cette excellente ouvrière, se plaît quelquefois à renfermer en un jour la perfection d'une longue vie.

In his peroration, Bossuet urges his hearers to think of themselves, exhorts them to be converted. The death of the princess is
a warning that human *grandeur* and *gloire* must perish. His closing
sentence takes up all the themes of the discourse:

Commencez aujourd'hui à mépriser les faveurs du monde; et, toutes les
fois que vous serez dans ces lieux augustes, dans ces superbes palais à
qui Madame donnait un éclat que vos yeux recherchent encore; toutes les
fois que, regardant cette grande place qu'elle remplissait si bien, vous
sentirez qu'elle y manque; songez que cette gloire que vous admiriez faisait
son péril en cette vie, et que dans l'autre elle est devenue le sujet d'un
examen rigoureux, où rien n'a été capable de la rassurer que cette sincère
résignation qu'elle a eue aux ordres de Dieu, et les saintes humiliations
de la pénitence.

Here we have the exhortation to the congregation, the evocation
of the greatness of Madame (*lieux augustes, superbes palais*), the
melancholy evocation of her sudden death (*recherchent encore,
y manque*), the moral lesson that greatness is a peril and only
piety salvation, the use of the word *gloire*: this sentence skilfully
knits together all the strands which have run through the discourse.
It is clear from the foregoing that this is not really biography.
The death of Henriette is described at inordinate length and in
two halves. It is not until the second part of the discourse that
Bossuet says anything of Henriette's early life. Moreover, if we
look at Mme de Lafayette's life of Madame, we notice some omis-
sions. Anne of Austria, says Bossuet, loved Henriette 'tendrement'. Possibly, but Mme de Lafayette makes it clear that the
relations between mother-in-law and daughter-in-law were not
always so idyllic. 'L'aigreur s'augmentait tous les jours entre
la reine-mère et elle,' she says, for example; Bossuet says nothing
of this. Nor does he allude to the rumours that Henriette had
been poisoned. More important: in Mme de Lafayette's account
of the life of Henriette, a good deal of space is taken up with her
amorous intrigues with Vardes and Guiche; Bossuet says nothing
of all this. The funeral oration on Henriette d'Angleterre, then,
is not a biography — though what Bossuet has to say of her life and
death is of interest — but a forceful and vigorous meditation on the
human condition. Skilfully composed, moving from the general to
the particular and the particular to the general, interweaving
skilfully the themes of human greatness and human nothingness
but always harking back from one to the other, closely knit by the
recurrent use throughout of the words *grandeur* and *gloire* in
different senses to unify the themes, written in some of the noblest
and most moving prose in all French literature, in prose that
reminds us that Mme de Staël classed Bossuet with Pascal as one
of the greatest of French poets, the *Oraison funèbre d'Henriette*

*d'Angleterre* is a fine example of the ability of the *grand siècle* to express eternal truths with burning conviction and with consummate art.

The *Discours sur l'histoire universelle* is as much a theological and polemical work as a study of history. Bossuet's avowed aims are to show the perpetuity of religion and the transience of empires; and, after a rapid summary of the history of the world up to the time of Charlemagne, he devotes a section of his book to each of these, leading to his closing paragraph:

Pendant que vous les[3] verrez tomber presque tous d'eux-mêmes, et que vous verrez la religion se soutenir par sa propre force, vous connaîtrez aisément quelle est la solide grandeur, et où un homme sensé doit mettre son espérance.

The work is intended as an answer to the *libertins* and the Biblical critics. A good deal of space is devoted to attempting to demonstrate the authenticity of the Scriptures and to reconcile the chronology of the Bible (Bossuet accepts the date 4004 B.C. as the date of the Creation) with that of the ancient historians. In the face of Biblical criticism – brushed aside as 'des chicanes sur des nombres, sur des lieux, ou sur des noms' – , Bossuet asserts the divine inspiration of the Scriptures. Moses, he says,

parle en maître: on remarque dans ses écrits un caractère tout particulier, et je ne sais quoi d'original qu'on ne trouve en nul autre écrit: il a dans sa simplicité un sublime si majestueux, que rien ne le peut égaler; et si, en entendant les autres prophètes, on croit entendre des hommes inspirés de Dieu, c'est pour ainsi dire Dieu même en personne qu'on croit entendre dans la voix et dans les écrits de Moïse.

The whole history of the Church is miraculous. The prophets of the Old Testament foretold accurately the coming of Christ, the destruction of the Jewish kingdom, and the conversion of the Gentiles, and their lives prefigured that of Christ:

Si on ne découvre pas ici un dessein toujours soutenu et toujours suivi; si on n'y voit pas un même ordre des conseils de Dieu, qui prépare dès l'origine du monde ce qu'il achève à la fin des temps, et qui, sous divers états, mais avec une succession toujours constante, perpétue aux yeux de tout l'univers la sainte société où il veut être servi, on mérite de ne rien voir, et d'être livré à son propre endurcissement, comme au plus juste et au plus rigoureux de tous les supplices.

The miracles of Christ are authentic, because neither the Jews nor the Gentiles cast doubts on them, and the sincerity of the apostles is 'justifiée par la plus forte épreuve qu'on puisse imaginer, qui est

[3] *Vous:* the dauphin. *Les:* the empires.

celle des tourments et de la mort même'. The triumph of Christianity is miraculous:

Les apôtres et leurs disciples, le rebut du monde, et le néant même, à les regarder par les yeux humains, ont prévalu à tous les empereurs et à tout l'empire.

The Church itself, 'toujours attaquée, et jamais vaincue,' is 'un miracle perpétuel, et un témoignage éclatant de l'immutabilité des conseils de Dieu'. Man himself, with his different faculties and his union of body and soul, is proof of the Trinity and the Incarnation. The *libertins* are attacked, and the view that the universe was the result of chance or evolved naturally is dismissed:

Ce n'est pas ici l'univers tel que l'ont conçu les philosophes; formé, selon quelques-uns, par un concours fortuit des premiers corps; ou qui, selon les plus sages, a fourni sa matière à son auteur; qui, par conséquent, n'en dépend, ni dans le fond de son être, ni dans son premier état, et qui l'astreint à certaines lois que lui-même ne peut violer.

Moïse et nos anciens pères, dont Moïse a recueilli les traditions, nous donnent d'autres pensées. Le Dieu qu'il nous a montré a bien une autre puissance: il peut faire et défaire ainsi qu'il lui plaît; il donne des lois à la nature et les renverse quand il veut.

Providence — and this is the main theme of Bossuet's book — rules the universe. It is seen not only in the history of the Jews and the Church, in the prophecies and their fulfilment, but in the rise and fall of all other states (several of which were the subject of Old Testament prophecies). Conquerors are mostly but instruments of divine vengeance. If, in the third part of his discourse, Bossuet analyses at length the human causes of the rise and fall of empires — the wisdom or the dissensions of the Romans, for example —, he emphasizes in his conclusion that these human causes are not independent of Providence:

Dieu tient du plus haut des cieux les rênes de tous les royaumes; il a à tous les cœurs en sa main: tantôt il retient les passions, tantôt il leur lâche la bride; et par là il remue tout le genre humain. Veut-il faire des conquérants; il fait marcher l'épouvante devant eux, et il inspire à eux et à leurs soldats une hardiesse invincible. Veut-il faire des législateurs; il leur envoie son esprit de sagesse et de prévoyance; il leur fait prévenir les maux qui menacent les Etats, et poser les fondements de la tranquillité publique. Il connaît la sagesse humaine, toujours courte par quelque endroit; il l'éclaire, il étend ses vues, et puis il l'abandonne à ses ignorances: il l'aveugle, il la précipite, il la confond par elle-même: elle s'enveloppe, elle s'embarrasse dans ses propres subtilités, et ses précautions lui sont un piège. Dieu exerce par ce moyen ses redoutables jugements, selon les règles de sa justice toujours infaillible. C'est lui qui prépare les effets dans les causes les plus éloignées, et qui frappe ces grands coups dont le contre-coup porte si loin.

How does Bossuet, with his strong belief in Providence, conceive of the state? What is his political theory? The posthumous

*Politique tirée des propres paroles de l'Ecriture sainte,* originally composed for the dauphin, gives us the answer. The best form of government, he states unequivocally, is a hereditary monarchy in which women are excluded from the succession:

Ainsi la France, où la succession est réglée selon ces maximes, peut se glorifier d'avoir la meilleure constitution d'état qui soit possible, et la plus conforme à celle que Dieu même a établie. Ce qui montre tout ensemble, et la sagesse de nos ancêtres, et la protection particulière de Dieu sur ce royaume.

One must, nevertheless, accept whatever form of government is established in one's own country. Kings are sacred, and images of God. They are absolute, and even bad kings must be respected. On the other hand, they must govern for the good of their subjects. Their authority is paternal – they should be beneficent (caring for the poor, avoiding violence and cruelty, and being sparing of bloodshed), but firm and resolute. Their authority, too, is subject to reason – they must govern wisely according to the laws of God and those of the kingdom. They must support the true religion and destroy false creeds (Bossuet, as we have seen, approved of the revocation of the Edict of Nantes), and respect the authority of the priesthood. They must be just; they must eschew wars of conquest; they must be virtuous and avoid illicit unions; they must be majestic –

Les dépenses de magnificence et de dignité ne sont pas moins nécessaires, à leurs manières, pour le soutien de la majesté, aux yeux des peuples et des étrangers.

If Bossuet is thus the theorist of the absolute monarchy of Louis XIV, some of the maxims of the *Politique* are an implicit condemnation of some of the aspects of Louis's reign.


## II. MALEBRANCHE

Nicolas Malebranche (1638–1715) was an Oratorian when he was first introduced to the philosophy of Descartes:

Un jour [writes Fontenelle], comme il passait par la rue Saint-Jacques, un libraire lui présenta le *Traité de l'Homme* de Descartes, qui venait de paraître. [ ... ] Il se mit à feuilleter le livre, et fut frappé comme d'une lumière qui en sortit toute nouvelle à ses yeux. [ ... ] Il acheta le livre, le lut avec empressement, et, ce qu'on aura peut-être peine à croire, avec un tel transport, qu'il lui en prenait des battements de cœur qui l'obligeaient quelquefois d'interrompre sa lecture. [ ... ]

Il abandonna donc absolument toute autre étude pour la philosophie de Descartes.

The result of his meditations was his first and main work, *De la Recherche de la Vérité* (1674–5), in which – priest and Cartesian

— he attempts a synthesis of the philosophy of Descartes and Christianity.

The first five books of *La Recherche de la Vérité* are an analysis of the sources of human error, and hence of perception and thought. They are devoted to errors arising from the senses, the imagination, the intellect, the inclinations, and the passions; after which the concluding book expounds, with examples, the correct method — essentially that of Descartes — of reaching the truth. More interesting than the study of method is the study of error. The senses and the instincts, insists Malebranche, were given us for the preservation of our body, not for the pursuit of truth, and, whereas they fulfil the first purpose admirably, they are unreliable for the latter. The main errors into which we fall are: attributing our sensations to objects (colours, flavours, and scents are not qualities of objects, but modifications of our minds); attributing our own sensations and passions to others; being misled by our passions, our inclinations, the influence of others, or by habit and prejudice; believing that what we cannot understand is impossible; and allowing our natural restlessness or the impressions of our senses to distract us from sustained effort or abstract thought.

If Malebranche insists that Descartes must not be accepted uncritically and disagrees with him on some points, he greatly admires him and agrees with much of his philosophy. He trounces Aristotle mercilessly, and he adopts not only Descartes's principles and method, but also many of his tenets — the rejection of authority in all but matters of faith; his proofs of the existence of God; the complete separation between mind (the property of which is thought) and matter (the property of which is extension); the denial that animals, having no souls, can feel pleasure and pain; and the vortices or *tourbillons* which Descartes invented to account for the movement of the heavenly bodies.

God, however, plays a much more important part in the philosophy of Malebranche than in that of Descartes. The purpose of human life is union with God, which may be achieved in two ways, by virtue, and by the search for truth; so that the whole book is religious in its aim.

Qu'ils condamnent au feu des poètes et les philosophes païens, les rabbins, quelques historiens, et un grand nombre d'auteurs qui font la gloire et l'érudition de quelques savants, on ne s'en mettra guères en peine. Mais qu'ils ne condamnent pas la connaissance de la nature comme contraire à la religion; puisque la nature étant réglée par la volonté de Dieu, la véritable connaissance de la nature nous fait connaître et admirer la puissance, la grandeur, et la sagesse de Dieu. Car enfin il semble que Dieu ait formé l'univers afin que les esprits l'étudient, et que par cette étude ils soient portés à connaître et à révérer son auteur. De sorte que

ceux qui condamnent l'étude de la nature, semblent s'opposer à la volonté
de Dieu . . .

Moreover, from Descartes's distinction between mind and matter,
Malebranche proceeds to draw some further conclusions of his
own. All ideas, including all sensations, are spiritual, not physical;
they are therefore modifications of the soul. When we think we
see an object, the mind does not leave the body, and material
objects cannot influence the mind or send out immaterial images
of themselves. Clearly, therefore, we do not see the object; we
have a mental picture of it, which cannot come either from the
object or from our minds, and must therefore come from God, who
contains ideas of all created objects and is present in our minds. We
thus see everything in God. Similarly, if we eat a fruit or prick
our finger, the sweet taste or the feeling of pain comes from God.
We are thus completely dependent on God:

Ainsi nos âmes dépendent de Dieu en toutes façons. Car de même que
c'est lui qui leur fait sentir la douleur, le plaisir, et toutes les autres sensations, par l'union naturelle qu'il a mise entre elles et nos corps, qui n'est
autre que son décret et sa volonté générale: ainsi c'est lui qui par l'union
naturelle qu'il a mise aussi entre la volonté de l'homme, et la représentation des idées que renferme l'immensité de l'être divin, leur fait connaître tout ce qu'elles connaissent, et cette union naturelle n'est aussi que
sa volonté générale. De sorte qu'il n'y a que lui qui nous puisse éclairer,
en nous représentant toutes choses; de même qu'il n'y a que lui qui nous
puisse rendre heureux, en nous faisant goûter toutes sortes de plaisirs.
    Demeurons donc dans ce sentiment, que Dieu est le monde intelligible,
ou le lieu des esprits, de même que le monde matériel est le lieu des
corps. Que c'est de sa puissance qu'ils reçoivent toutes leurs modifications: que c'est dans sa sagesse qu'ils trouvent toutes leurs idées: et
que c'est par son amour qu'ils sont agités de tous leurs mouvements
réglés; et parce que sa puissance et son amour ne sont que lui, croyons
avec saint Paul, qu'il n'est pas loin de chacun de nous, et que c'est en lui
que nous avons la vie, le mouvement, et l'être.

Similarly, a moving object cannot move itself; it cannot therefore communicate its movement to another object, nor can finite
minds move matter. If a ball strikes another and seems to set it
in motion, it does not do so in reality – it is only the natural or
occasional cause of the movement of the second ball; the real cause
is God.

Une cause naturelle n'est donc point une cause réelle et véritable, mais
seulement une cause occasionnelle, et qui détermine l'auteur de la nature
à agir de telle et telle manière, en telle et telle rencontre.

But all forces of nature are essentially movement:

Toutes les forces de la nature ne sont donc que la volonté de Dieu toujours efficace. Dieu a créé le monde parce qu'il l'a voulu [ . . . ]: et il
remue toutes choses, et produit ainsi tous les effets que nous voyons

arriver, parce qu'il a voulu aussi certaines lois selon lesquelles les mouvements se communiquent à la rencontre des corps: et parce que ces lois
sont efficaces, elles agissent, et les corps ne peuvent agir. Il n'y a donc
point de forces, de puissances, de causes véritables dans le monde
matériel et sensible . . .

In the same way, our minds can know or feel or will only because
God modifies them. Nor can we control our bodies: there can be
no interaction between mind and body; and in any case most of
us do not even know that we have nerves and animal spirits, and
we obviously cannot control something of which we have no
knowledge. Once again, our will is merely the occasional cause of
our movements: the real cause is God. In other words, according
to Malebranche, if I see a ball coming towards me, if I move my
arm, and if, by striking the ball with a racket in my hand, I send
it back, the ball is merely the occasional cause of the image of the
ball in my mind, my will is only the occasional cause of the movement of my arm, and the movement of the racket is only the
occasional cause of the movement of the ball; in all these cases, the
real cause is the intervention of God. And Malebranche stresses
that, whereas the Aristotelian philosophy, which attributed qualities
and powers to material objects, was idolatrous in tendency, his
philosophy is in complete conformity with the Christian religion:

Car, si la religion nous apprend qu'il n'y a qu'un vrai Dieu; cette philosophie nous fait connaître qu'il n'y a qu'une véritable cause. Si la religion
nous apprend que toutes les divinités du paganisme ne sont que des pierres
et des métaux sans vie et sans mouvement, cette philosophie nous découvre
aussi que toutes les causes secondes, ou toutes les divinités de la philosophie,
ne sont que de la matière et des volontés inefficaces. Enfin si la religion
nous apprend qu'il ne faut point fléchir le genou devant des Dieux qui ne
sont point Dieu; cette philosophie nous apprend aussi que notre imagination et notre esprit ne doivent point s'abattre devant la grandeur et la
puissance imaginaire des causes qui ne sont point causes: qu'il ne faut ni
les aimer ni les craindre: qu'il ne faut point s'en occuper: qu'il ne faut penser qu'à Dieu seul, voir Dieu en toutes choses, craindre et aimer Dieu en
toutes choses.

Malebranche's ethical system is widely different from that of
Descartes. He does not accept Descartes's account of the mechanism
of the passions: for Descartes, an impression of the senses causes a
movement of the animal spirits which, through the pineal gland,
induces a passion in the soul; for Malebranche,

Les passions de l'âme sont des impressions de l'auteur de la nature,
lesquelles nous inclinent à aimer notre corps et tout ce qui peut être utile
à sa conservation . . .

Since mind and matter cannot interact, animal spirits cannot
possibly be the cause of a passion. The passions are aroused in the
soul by God; the sense impressions are merely the occasional

cause. Moreover, Malebranche, who attacks the stoics on several
occasions, can clearly not accept the stoicism of Descartes. Since
external objects are not the cause of pleasure or pain, they are
neither agreeable nor disagreeable; we must love and fear God,
from whom alone come pleasure and pain.

Nous ne pouvons être heureux que par une foi vive et par une forte
espérance, qui nous fasse jouir par avance des biens futurs; et nous ne
pouvons vivre selon les règles de la vertu, et vaincre la nature, si nous
ne sommes soutenus par la grâce que Jésus-Christ nous a méritée.

The passions and the senses, as obstacles to the union of our minds
with God, must be held in check. Thus reason and the Scriptures
teach the same lesson,

parce que c'est la même sagesse qui parle immédiatement par elle-même
à ceux qui découvrent la vérité dans l'évidence des raisonnements, et
qui parle par les saintes Ecritures à ceux qui en prennent bien le sens.

The *Recherche de la Vérité*, however unacceptable Malebranche's occasionalism may be, is interesting — not only for the
light it sheds on the outlook of the seventeenth century (Malebranche was widely read, and Mme de Sévigné admired his
*Conversations chrétiennes*), but for its intrinsic value. Malebranche
has much to say that is pertinent and acute on the subject of
human perception and judgment, indeed about human nature in
general — for Malebranche covers a great deal of ground and,
like his contemporaries, believed in combining instruction with
pleasure:

Je me fais un ordre pour me conduire, mais je prétends qu'il m'est permis
de tourner la tête lorsque je marche, si je trouve quelque chose qui mérite
d'être considéré. Je prétends même qu'il m'est permis de me reposer en
quelques lieux à l'écart, pourvu que je ne perde point de vue le chemin
que je dois suivre. Ceux qui ne veulent point se délasser avec moi peuvent
passer outre; il leur est permis; ils n'ont qu'à tourner la page: mais s'ils
se fâchent, qu'ils sachent qu'il y a bien des gens, qui trouvent que ces
lieux que je choisis pour me reposer, leur font trouver le chemin plus
doux et plus agréable.

### III. VILLARS

*Le Comte de Gabalis ou Entretiens sur les sciences secrètes*
(1670) of abbé Montfaucon de Villars (1635–73)[4] consists of five
dialogues between a German cabalist, the comte de Gabalis, and
a Frenchman whom he is trying to convert. It has been compared
to the *Provinciales*; and, though Gabalis never attains the comic

[4] He was murdered, so it was said, by the sylphs and gnomes, outraged
by the revelation of their secrets. He is remembered also for his *Critique
de Bérénice* (1671), on Racine's *Bérénice* and Corneille's *Tite et Bérénice*.

individuality of Pascal's Jesuit, and though Villars's style lacks
the range of Pascal's, the naïve credulity of the cabalist recalls
that of Pascal's hero, and the light, easy style reminds us of Pascal.
Gabalis's list of cabalists resembles the list of casuists quoted as
authorities by the Jesuit:[5]

En croirez-vous toujours plus à votre nourrice, me dit-il, qu'à la raison
naturelle, qu'à Platon, Pythagore, Celse, Psellus, Procle, Porphyre, Jam-
blique, Plotin, Trismégiste, Nollius, Dornée, Fludd, qu'au grand Philippe-
Auréole-Théophraste-Bombast Paracelse de Honeinheim et qu'à tous nos
compagnons?

The light irony of the retort is not unworthy of Pascal:

Je vous en croirais, monsieur, répondis-je, autant et plus que tous ces
gens-là: mais mon cher monsieur, ne pourriez-vous pas ménager avec vos
compagnons que je ne serai pas obligé de me fondre en tendresse avec
ces demoiselles élémentaires.[6]

However light and entertaining, the book seems not to be without seriousness of purpose: after its publication, Villars was
forbidden to preach. It clearly mocks the doctrines of the Rosi-
crucians, those who believed that the elements were peopled by
sylphs, gnomes, undines, and salamanders, with whom it was
possible to converse, and through whom it was possible to dominate
nature. Gabalis's credulity and his beliefs are easily made ridiculous; his ideal is a fairy-tale world:

Ces hommes héroïques, ces amours des Nymphes, ces voyages au
paradis terrestre, ces palais et ces bois enchantés, et tout ce qu'on y voit
de charmantes aventures, ce n'est qu'une petite idée de la vie que mènent
les Sages et de ce que le monde sera quand ils y feront régner la Sagesse.

Villars's scepticism, however, is not restricted to sylphs; other
forms of superstition are attacked. The Frenchman maintains
that oracles were but 'une supercherie de l'avarice des prêtres
gentils ou [...] un artifice de la politique des souverains', and
the count's strongest proof of their genuineness, that they still exist
in the form of clairvoyance, is received with scepticism:

Ne consulte-t-on pas tous les jours les oracles aquatiques dans des verres
d'eau ou dans des bassins, et les oracles aériens dans des miroirs et sur la
main des vierges? Ne recouvre-t-on pas ainsi des chapelets perdus et des
montres dérobées? N'apprend-on pas ainsi des nouvelles des pays lointains et
ne voit-on pas les absents?
—Hé, monsieur, que me contez-vous là? lui dis-je.

At the mention of witches' sabbaths, the Frenchman declares
without hesitation: 'Ah! pour les contes du Sabbat, je vous assure

[5] See above, pp. 177–8.
[6] I.e. make love to the elemental spirits (sylphs, etc.).

que je n'en crois pas un.' Even religion is not spared. When the Frenchman asks if Gabalis is not a Jansenist, he replies:

Nous ne savons ce que c'est, mon enfant, et nous dédaignons de nous informer en quoi consistent les sectes différentes et les diverses religions dont les ignorants s'infatuent.

Gabalis denies that the devil has any power; and, to justify the ambiguity of oracles, he cites the Scriptures:

... les ténèbres ne sont-elles pas l'habit ordinaire de la vérité? Dieu ne se plaît-il pas à se cacher de leur voile sombre, et l'oracle continuel qu'il a laissé à ses enfants, la divine Ecriture n'est-elle pas enveloppée d'une adorable obscurité qui confond et fait égarer les superbes autant que sa lumière guide les humbles?

Montfaucon de Villars, it has been said with truth, expounds 'une vision du monde qui, toute fausse qu'elle fût, ne manquait pas de charme pour l'imagination et permettait de lancer quelques vérités hardies.'[7]

## IV. SAINT-EVREMOND

Although the period covered by the writings of Saint-Evremond (1616?–1703) extends from the early 1640's to the first years of the eighteenth century, his main works belong to this period. Forced to go into exile for a letter criticizing the Treaty of the Pyrenees discovered among Foucquet's papers, this most characteristic Frenchman of the *grand siècle* spent most of the last forty years of his life in England and was buried in Westminster Abbey. Although he was not a professional writer, his collected works fill several volumes and offer considerable variety. Letters, poems of a light social kind, and essays, at once graceful and sensible, pithy and witty, make up the bulk of them, diversified by one or two comedies – his earliest work is an amusing satire on the Academy, *Les Académistes*.

It is customary to call Saint-Evremond a *libertin*; but, as with so many seventeenth-century sceptics, it is difficult to define with precision how far his rationalism extended. He dismisses the fabulous elements in the early history of Rome and denies that there is anything providential about it. He relates the story of a bogus Irish prophet to illustrate human gullibility – 'n'y ayant rien que l'esprit humain reçoive avec tant de plaisir que l'opinion des choses merveilleuses, ni qu'il laisse avec plus de peine et de regret' (*Le Prophète irlandais*). He expresses the Pyrrhonian point of view – we can know nothing with certainty; reason cannot

---

[7] Max Milner, *Le Diable dans la littérature française*, 1960, t. I, p. 71, note 2. Villars's book influenced Pope's *Rape of the Lock*, Cazotte's delicious *Diable amoureux* (1772), and Anatole France's *Rôtisserie de la Reine Pédauque*.

prove the immortality of the soul or the truth of religion;[8] Descartes's attempts are no less unconvincing than any others.[9]

Le plus dévot ne peut venir à bout de croire toujours, ni le plus impie de ne croire jamais; et c'est un des malheurs de notre vie de ne pouvoir naturellement nous assurer s'il y en a une autre, ou s'il n'y en a point.
(*L'Homme qui veut connaître toutes choses, ne se connaît pas lui-même*)

He adds, however, the fideist argument that, in the lack of certainty, we must rely on faith, and he continually expresses his religious convictions. But, even if we accept his perfect sincerity, we cannot feel that his religion goes very deep.

There are, indeed, few signs in Saint-Evremond of any deep religious convictions. He likes to point out the folly and the futility of theological controversies, and he makes a Jesuit say of the controversy between the Jansenists and the Jesuits: 'Ce n'est ni la Grâce, ni les cinq propositions qui nous ont mis mal ensemble: la jalousie de gouverner les consciences a tout fait' (*Conversation du maréchal d'Hocquincourt avec le P. Canaye*). One scene of his comedy, *Les Opéra*, impugns the faith and the sincerity of the priesthood; and he bitterly attacks monastic life – 'Pour les Couvents, on y est malheureux, à moins que de devenir imbécile' (Letter to Mme Mazarin). If he is Christian, it is because of the superiority of its moral code; and if he prefers Catholicism, it is because it lays more stress on good works than Protestantism. 'La foi est obscure', he writes; 'la loi est nettement exprimée' (*A Monsieur le maréchal de Créquy*); and again:

Comme nous ne recevons point notre créance par la raison, aussi la raison ne nous en fait-elle pas changer [ . . . ]
La Doctrine est contestée partout: elle servira éternellement de matière à la dispute dans toutes les religions; mais on peut convenir de ce qui regarde les mœurs. (*Discours sur la religion*)

Convinced that doctrinal differences are without importance and that what matters is good works and morals, Saint-Evremond is close to the deism of the eighteenth century. At the end of his life, he summed up his attitude thus:

Au lieu de disputer toujours sur la créance
Par trop d'attachement à son opinion;

[8] In a letter dissuading Mme Mazarin from entering a convent, he does, it is true, say: 'C'est au milieu de l'univers que la contemplation des merveilles de la nature vous fera connaître celui dont elle dépend. La vue du soleil vous fera connaître la grandeur et la magnificence de celui qui l'a formé. Cet ordre si merveilleux et si juste, qui lie et entretient toutes choses, vous donnera la connaissance de sa sagesse.' But this is less a demonstration of the existence of God from the wonders of nature than a contrast between the richness of life outside the walls of a convent and the pettiness of life within.
[9] See above, p. 113.

Regardons comme on vit, sans chercher comme on pense,
Et dans le bien qu'on fait trouvons notre union.

(Letter to Des Maiseaux)

Logically, he is opposed to persecution and upholds toleration:

Selon mon sentiment, chacun doit être libre dans sa créance, pourvu
qu'elle n'aille pas à exciter des factions qui puissent troubler la tranquillité publique.                        (*A Monsieur le maréchal de Créquy*)

His ideas of conduct owe little to religion. Austerity of all
kinds repels him; he himself has never, he says, known a conflict
between reason and pleasure. He can advise Ninon de l'Enclos to
be fickle —

Il faut brûler d'une flamme légère,
Vive, brillante, et toujours passagère;
Etre inconstante aussi longtemps qu'on peut,
Car un temps vient que ne l'est pas qui veut.

— and he assures Mlle de Quérouaille, then on the verge of becoming mistress to Charles II, that it is enough to 'n'aimer qu'une
personne à la fois'. Not for Saint-Evremond the striving after
glory —

Comte, nous nous devons l'usage de nos jours:
On a peu d'intérêt à servir sa mémoire,
Puisque c'est pour autrui qu'elle dure toujours.
(*A mon héros, le comte de Grammont*)

or the austerity of the stoics —

Toute considérable qu'est la sagesse, on la trouve d'un faible usage parmi
les douleurs et dans les approches de la mort.         (*Sur les plaisirs*)

If he himself seems to bear his misfortunes with fortitude, like
Théophile he claims that it is less from constancy than from in-
sensibility. Not for him, either, the pursuit of science: 'nous avons
plus d'intérêt à jouir du monde, qu'à le connaître' (*Jugement sur
les sciences*). His philosophy is frankly epicurean — 'J'ai toujours
admiré la morale d'Epicure' . . . (*Sur l'amitié*).

. . . la seule jouissance du plaisir; la volupté, pour tout dire, est la véritable fin où toutes nos actions se rapportent.   (*Sur la morale d'Epicure*)

And his receipt for a happy life is:

faire peu de réflexions sur la vie; mais sortir souvent comme hors de soi,
et parmi les plaisirs que fournissent les choses étrangères, se dérober la
connaissance de ses propres maux.              (*Sur les plaisirs*)

It should be understood that the pleasures recommended by
Saint-Evremond, always an *honnête homme*, are not crude or
vulgar; they are the pleasures of the discriminating, and are a
matter of careful preparation and proportionment. Life is a work

of art, to be composed with care: 'Aussi la sagesse nous a été donnée principalement pour ménager nos plaisirs' (*Sur les plaisirs*). They should be enjoyed with moderation. Love and friendship should not be violent passions, but based on *l'esprit* rather than on the heart.

> Ayons autant d'amour qu'il en faut pour nous animer; pas assez pour troubler notre repos. Le cœur nous a été donné pour aimer, ce qui est un mouvement agréable; non pas pour souffrir, ce qui est un sentiment douloureux.                (*Pensées, sentiments, maximes*)

The pleasures of the table are not to be despised – Saint-Evremond is a gourmet, capable of discussing food and wine; but they should be characterized by *délicatesse* and enjoyed with sobriety.

Amongst the pleasures of life is literature – for, if Saint-Evremond has no use for science, he considers politics, ethics, and letters suitable occupations for the *honnête homme*. Many of his essays are devoted to literature, and he is probably the most interesting literary critic of the seventeenth century. In an age when literary criticism was usually a bitter and by no means disinterested attack, in the name of rules and principles, on a work which had won the public favour (Scudéry's attack on *Le Cid* and d'Aubignac's on *Sophonisbe*, for example), urbane judgments and subtle appraisals like those of Saint-Evremond are rare. According to his biographer, Des Maiseaux, Saint-Evremond, reading the ancient historians with the duc d'Enghien (later the *grand* Condé),

> laissait aux grammairiens l'explication scrupuleuse des mots et des phrases, et s'attachait à développer le sens des auteurs, à faire des observations sur la justesse et la beauté de leurs pensées, à remarquer l'habileté avec laquelle ils dépeignent les grands hommes, et les différences délicates qu'ils marquent dans leurs caractères.

He himself, in a discourse addressed from exile to maréchal de Créquy, criticizes commentators for their preoccupation with grammar and chronology, and adds: 'Il est vrai que j'estime infiniment une *Critique du Sens*, si on peut parler de la sorte.' We are not far from the later conception of criticism as the criticism of beauties, not faults.

Saint-Evremond's tastes are those of an enlightened man of the seventeenth century. He cares more about human nature than nature:

> Un discours où l'on ne parle que de bois, de rivières, de prés, de campagnes, de jardins, fait sur nous une impression bien languissante, à moins qu'il n'ait des agréments tout nouveaux: mais ce qui est de l'humanité, les penchants, les tendresses, les affections, trouvent naturellement au fond de notre âme à se faire sentir: la même nature les produit et les reçoit; ils passent aisément des hommes qu'on représente en des hommes qui voient représenter.                (*A Monsieur le maréchal de Créquy*)

He is not an intransigent supporter of rules: he held that the
severity of the rules governing versification was excessive, and he
insisted that rules could never produce a good work:

On n'a jamais vu tant de règles pour faire de belles tragédies; et on en
fait si peu, qu'on est obligé de représenter toutes les vieilles ...
(*De la tragédie ancienne et moderne*)

He recalled that abbé d'Aubignac had composed a perfectly regular
tragedy which was a miserable failure.

Il faut aimer la règle pour éviter la confusion; il faut aimer le bon sens
qui modère l'ardeur d'une imagination allumée; mais il faut ôter à la
règle toute contrainte qui gêne, et bannir une raison scrupuleuse, qui par
un trop grand attachement à la justesse, ne laisse rien de libre et de
naturel.                                (*De la comédie anglaise*)

He is equally independent in his attitude towards the ancients:
he considers antiquity overrated,[10] and he does not hesitate to
find fault with the writers of antiquity — with Virgil's Æneas and
with Greek tragedy; with their use of the supernatural. The
authority of Aristotle does not intimidate him:

Il faut convenir que la *Poétique* d'Aristote est un excellent ouvrage:
cependant il n'y a rien d'assez parfait pour régler toutes les nations
et tous les siècles. Descartes et Gassendi ont découvert des vérités
qu'Aristote ne connaissait pas: Corneille a trouvé des beautés pour le
théâtre qui ne lui étaient pas connues: nos philosophes ont remarqué
des erreurs dans sa *Physique*: nos poètes ont vu des défauts dans sa
*Poétique*, pour le moins à notre égard, toutes choses étant aussi
changées qu'elles le sont.              (*De la tragédie ancienne et moderne*)

The emotions of pity and terror he condemns as unworthy, the
principle of catharsis as ridiculous. Aristotle, he says, 'a mis quelquefois la perfection en ce qu'on croyait de mieux à Athènes, et non
pas en ce qui est véritablement le plus parfait' (*Sur nos comédies*).
The ancients should not be imitated.

Je veux que l'esprit des anciens nous en inspire, mais je ne veux pas que
nous prenions le leur même. Je veux qu'ils nous apprennent à bien penser;
mais je n'aime pas à me servir de leurs pensées.     (Letter to Mme Mazarin)

Greek tragedies no doubt pleased the Athenians, but they are alien
to modern taste: nothing, for example, could be 'plus barbare,
plus funeste, plus opposé aux vrais sentiments qu'on doit avoir'
than that 'chef-d'œuvre des Anciens', *Œdipus Rex*. Times have
changed:

On nous apporte une infinité de règles qui sont faites il y a trois mille ans,
pour régler tout ce qui se fait aujourd'hui; et on ne considère point que ce

[10] 'Ceux qui ont eu à se plaindre de leur siècle, ont donné mille louanges à l'antiquité, dont ils n'avaient rien à souffrir; et ceux dont le
chagrin trouve à redire à tout ce qu'on voit, ont fait valoir par fantaisie, ce
qu'on ne voyait plus' (*Réflexions sur les divers génies du peuple romain*).
Cf. Fontenelle, p. 208 above.

ne sont point les mêmes sujets qu'il faut traiter, ni le même génie qu'il faut
conduire.                                          (Letter to Mme Mazarin)

Tout est changé; les Dieux, la nature, la politique, les mœurs, le goût, les
manières. Tant de changements n'en produiront-ils point dans nos ouvrages?
   Si Homère vivait présentement, il ferait des poèmes admirables, accom-
modés au siècle où il écrirait. Nos poètes en font de mauvais, ajustés à
ceux des anciens, et conduits par des règles, qui sont tombées, avec des
choses que le temps a fait tomber.
   Je sais qu'il y a de certaines règles éternelles, pour être fondées sur un
bon sens, sur une raison ferme et solide, qui subsistera toujours: mais il
en est peu qui portent le caractère de cette raison incorruptible.
                                        (*Sur les poèmes des Anciens*)

As Ogier's preface to *Tyr et Sidon* makes us think of Hugo and the
*Préface de Cromwell*, so these lines make us think of Stendhal and
*Racine et Shakespeare*. Although Saint-Evremond was well-versed
in the classics, no writer before him went so far in his insistence
on independence. Not merely should the *merveilleux païen* be
discarded, he insisted; the ancients should not be imitated even to
the extent of the *merveilleux chrétien* being substituted.
   Even before Perrault's poem opened the *querelle des Anciens et
des Modernes*, Saint-Evremond upheld the superiority of the
moderns (except in historiography). Tragedy arousing pity and
terror is inferior to modern tragedy which arouses admiration
and admits of a love interest. 'Je ne croirai point flatter Corneille,
quand je donnerai l'avantage à beaucoup de ses tragédies sur
celles de l'antiquité' (*Sur les tragédies*). During the *querelle des
Anciens et des Modernes*, he gave his opinion in favour of the latter
in a poem, *Sur la dispute touchant les Anciens et les Modernes*.
   Saint-Evremond's independent, undogmatic attitude, his shrewd
and subtle mind, and his catholic tastes – besides the classics and
the works of his own century, he was fond of Rabelais, Montaigne,
and *Don Quixote* – make his criticism well worth reading. His
remarks are always judicious and penetrating, and he is always a
pleasure to read. It has been said of him that he was 'the first to
bring *l'art de plaire* into literary criticism'.[11] Some of his most
interesting pages are those devoted to Corneille, whom he always
preferred to Racine.
   Saint-Evremond has his limitations. He shows little acquaintance
with human passion and no concern with social justice; whether or
not he was a sincere Catholic, it is clear that religion meant little
to him, and that he was never animated by enthusiasm; it is
doubtful whether he was ever really tormented by doubts or fears.
His world is that of the salon. But his tolerant good-humour, his

   [11] Q. M. Hope, *Saint-Evremond. The Honnête Homme as critic*, 1962,
p. 3.

balanced outlook, his independent good sense, his philosophy of graceful acceptance of the vicissitudes of life, his wit and elegance, will no doubt always win him readers and friends. Saint-Evremond is the quintessence of seventeenth-century *mondanité*. He sent a self-portrait (c. 1685) to Ninon de l'Enclos:

> Passer quelques heures à lire,
> Est mon plus doux amusement;
> Je me fais un plaisir d'écrire,
> Et non pas un attachement.
>
> Je perds le goût de la satire;
> L'art de louer malignement,
> Cède au secret de pouvoir dire
> Des vérités obligeamment.
>
> Je vis éloigné de la France
> Sans besoin et sans abondance,
> Content d'un vulgaire destin;
>
> J'aime la vertu sans rudesse,
> J'aime le plaisir sans mollesse;
> J'aime la vie, et n'en crains pas la fin.

# Part IV

1685–1715

## Chapter 21

# INTRODUCTION

T HE LAST thirty years of the reign of Louis XIV lack the splendour of the previous period. The King had grown old and religious; Mme de Maintenon had succeeded Louise de la Vallière in a more respectable capacity. 'Hors de la piété, point de salut à la cour, aussi bien que dans l'autre monde,' comments Mme de Lafayette; and Louis's sister-in-law, the second Madame, princesse palatine, complains:

La cour de France est restée fort agréable jusqu'à ce que le roi a eu le malheur d'épouser la vieille sorcière;[1] elle l'a séquestré de tout le monde et lui a inspiré de ridicules scrupules au sujet des spectacles, lui représentant que, puisque les comédiens étaient excommuniés, il ne devait pas les voir ...

Court life seems to have grown stale. 'Il y a un certain train qui ne change point,' writes Mme de Lafayette: 'toujours les mêmes plaisirs, toujours aux mêmes heures, et toujours avec les mêmes gens'. So dreary were the court balls in 1689, she tells us, that they did not begin till nearly midnight and were always over by two o'clock.[2] Spanheim, about the same time, noted the constraint and dissimulation of the French court, and observed that 'la joie même et les plaisirs ne s'y goûtent plus avec cet épanchement visible qu'on a vu sous d'autres règnes, et même autrefois sous celui-ci'. 'Excepté le roi et Monsieur, personne ne sait plus ce que c'est que la politesse: les jeunes gens ne songent qu'à d'horribles débauches,' wrote Madame en 1702; and in 1707: 'Il n'y a plus à la cour que tristesse, ennui et méfiance.' Tired of the ceremony of the court, established since 1682 at Versailles, Louis XIV, who, according to Mme de Lafayette, disliked ceremony, would take refuge every fortnight in the informality of Marly.

A Marly, le roi n'avait pas la moindre cérémonie. Il n'était permis ni aux ambassadeurs, ni aux envoyés d'y venir; il ne s'y donnait pas d'audience;

---

[1] Mme de Maintenon.

[2] 'Le carnaval ne prend pas le train d'être bien gaillard,' wrote Mme de Sévigné (31 December 1688); and a week later: 'Je ne pense pas qu'on danse beaucoup cet hiver à Versailles.' Already, twelve years earlier, she had noted that gaiety was out of fashion at court, 'où chacun a ses tribulations, et où l'on ne rit plus depuis plusieurs années' (18 June 1676).

il n'y avait pas d'étiquette et tout courait pêle-mêle. A la promenade, le roi faisait mettre le chapeau aux hommes, et, dans le salon, il etait permis à tout le monde, jusqu'aux capitaines et sous-lieutenants de la garde à pied, de s'asseoir. Cela m'a donné tant de dégoût pour le salon que je n'ai jamais voulu y rester.                                                    (Madame)

Above all, the last part of the reign was made sombre by long, fruitless wars—the War of the League of Augsburg (1688–97) and the War of the Spanish Succession (1701–13). Already, at the death of Colbert in 1683, there was a deficit of 16 million livres, and in 1689, on the outbreak of war, the government was unable to pay pensions, a fact which caused consternation,

car il paraissait certain que, puisque, après dix ans de paix, ou peu s'en fallait, et le roi jouissant d'un aussi grand revenu, on ne trouvait pas un sou dans les coffres, deux ans de guerre mettraient un tel désordre dans les finances que l'on serait obligé de prendre le bien de tout le monde.

(Mme de Lafayette)

In 1697, expenditure was running at nearly 219 millions, only eighty-one millions of which were covered by receipts, so that the government was driven to all sorts of expedients to raise money— loans, the creation and sale of offices, the sale of patents of nobility, the issue of notes, lotteries, reduction of *rentes*, depreciation of the currency, and the creation of new taxes (the *capitation*, 1695, and the *dizième*, 1710). Twice, in 1689 and in 1709, the government ordered everybody to surrender his gold and silver; and in 1708, Louis XIV had to sweeten the banker, Samuel Bernard, by showing him over the gardens of Marly, to the consternation of his courtiers.

The War of the Spanish Succession brought unemployment, desperate poverty, and famine. Revolts broke out in several parts of France, and there were bread riots in Paris itself. In 1709, Boileau, writing to Brossette, spoke of 'la félicité publique, morte en France depuis plus de quatre ans', and added, 'il n'y a point de jour de marché où la cherté du pain n'y excite quelque sédition'. In 1713, the intendant of Limoges wrote a description of the state of that district:

L'on a trouvé quelques paysans morts dans leurs vignes; je puis vous assurer aussi qu'il est mort une vingtaine de personnes dans cette ville, qui dans l'espérance d'y trouver quelque charité, ont fait effort pour s'y rendre, et sont morts en arrivant dans des granges que M. l'évêque de Limoges a fait louer pour les retirer. Des personnes dignes de foi m'ont assuré aussi qu'il y a quelques paroisses où les paysans broutent l'herbe dans les prés, comme les bestiaux; d'autres, où ils font de la bouillie de cendre; d'autres où ils se nourrissent de racine de fougère; et, en général, la misère est fort grande.

Nor was this misery redeemed by military glory: Marlborough inflicted a series of crushing defeats on Louis's armies, at Blenheim

(1704), Ramillies (1706), Oudenarde (1708), and Malplaquet (1709).

In this last period of his reign, too, Louis XIV pursued a policy of intolerance in religious matters. Several years of attempts to induce or coerce Huguenots to become Catholics culminated in the revocation of the Edict of Nantes (October 1685). Protestant ministers were expelled from France, Protestant churches demolished, and Protestant services forbidden; the children of Huguenots were henceforth to be brought up as Catholics. This unfortunate measure led to widespread unrest in the Protestant districts, culminating in the revolt of the Camisards in the Cévennes (1702–5). Some 200,000 Huguenots illegally left France, and settled in the Protestant states, Holland, Brandenburg, and England; and, since the exiles included a high proportion of merchants, sailors, manufacturers, and skilled workmen, France was seriously weakened, militarily and economically. The persecution of the Huguenots intensified opposition to Louis XIV in the Protestant countries, and, in France itself, encouraged criticism of the régime and of the Church. Moreover, the exiled Huguenots helped to diffuse in their native country the philosophical and scientific ideas of their adopted countries. The revocation of the Edict of Nantes thus helped in several ways to undermine the *ancien régime*.

Port-Royal was left in peace from 1668 onwards, out of respect for Mme de Longueville, a princess of the blood, who resided there; but her death in 1679 was the signal for a new persecution. The nuns were forbidden to admit new members, and postulants, novices, and *pensionnaires* were dismissed; the *solitaires* were dispersed, and Arnauld went into exile. The number of nuns in Port-Royal des Champs gradually dwindled in consequence until, by 1705, only twenty-five remained.[3] In 1701, the attention of the authorities was drawn to the persistence of Jansenism, by a *cas de conscience* proposed by a Jansenist to the Sorbonne: could the sacraments be administered to a man who had signed the formulary, while believing in his heart that the Pope and the Church could err in matters of fact? Forty doctors answered in the affirmative, and a controversy broke out. Louis XIV, alarmed by the discovery, on the arrest of an exiled Jansenist, Quesnel, in Brussels (1703), that the exiled Jansenists were involved in plots against him, suggested to the Pope that action should be taken against the Jansenists. The Pope issued a Bull insisting that in signing the formulary one must believe Jansenius's book to be heretical. The Archbishop of Paris incorporated this doctrine in a pastoral letter:

[3] Port-Royal de Paris, which, during the previous persecution had had an abbess imposed on it by the Archbishop of Paris, had ceased to be suspect.

thirty-nine of the forty doctors retracted, and the nuns of Port-Royal accepted the Papal Bull, but with a restrictive clause which emphasized their refractoriness. In 1707, their domestics were reduced to ten; they were deprived of the sacraments and excommunicated; and three-quarters of their income was transferred to Port-Royal de Paris. The following year, a Papal Bull was issued, extinguishing the convent and transferring its property to Port-Royal de Paris; the remaining nuns were expelled in 1709; and two years later the convent was pulled down, and its graves (including that of Racine) desecrated. So ends the story of Port-Royal, if not of Jansenism.

Dissatisfaction with the policies of Louis XIV and his government led, not unnaturally, to criticism. This, of course, had never completely disappeared, even after the Fronde. In 1662, Marigny, suspected of having written a poem against the King, and various other persons found in possession of documents hostile to the government were sent to the Bastille; and Fléchier relates that, during the Grands Jours d'Auvergne,

on jugea [...] un bon curé de village qui, par un zèle extraordinaire, s'était emporté dans ses prônes contre le roi et ses ministres. Il avait dit fort sérieusement à ses paroissiens que la France était mal gouvernée; que c'était un royaume tyrannique; qu'il avait lu de si belles choses dans un vieux livre qui parlait de la république romaine, qu'il trouverait à propos de vivre sans dépendance et sans souffrir aucune imposition de tailles; que le peuple n'avait jamais été plus tourmenté, et plusieurs autres choses de fort grande édification, qui lui semblaient, aussi bien qu'à ses auditeurs grossiers, plus agréables que l'Evangile.

But such criticisms were oral, and – Fléchier's tone suggests – not general. In the last period of the reign, criticism became more widespread and more serious.

Much criticism came from Holland. Several periodicals, political and literary, were published there by Protestant exiles – La Font's *Nouvelles extraordinaires de divers endroits* (known as the *Gazette de Leyde*, 1680–1714), Bayle's *Nouvelles de la République des Lettres* (1684–7) and its successor, Basnage de Beauval's *Histoire des Ouvrages des savants* (1687–1709), Leclerc's *Bibliothèque universelle et historique* (1686–93), amongst others.[4] Violent attacks on Louis's religious policy emanated from Holland and were clandestinely distributed in France.[5] The *Voyages* of Baron

[4] In opposition, the Jesuits started the *Journal de Trévoux* in 1701.
[5] Bayle, *Ce qu'est la France toute catholique sous le règne de Louis le grand* (1686) and *Commentaire philosophique sur ces paroles de J.-Christ: Contrains-les d'entrer* (1686); pasteur Claude, *Les Plaintes des protestants cruellement opprimés* (1686); Jurieu, *Lettres pastorales aux fidèles qui gémissent sous la captivité de Babylone* (1686–9); *Les Soupirs de la France esclave qui aspire à la liberté* (1689–90); *Avis aux réfugiés* (1690). Jurieu, defending the English revolution, put forward the notion of

Lahontan (1666–1715) in North America, published at The Hague in 1703, together with some *Dialogues curieux entre l'Auteur et un Sauvage de bon sens qui a voyagé*,[6] may serve as a specimen of the kind of ideas that could be discussed on the other side of the French frontier. Lahontan contrasts civilized society in general, based as it is on property and self-interest, unfavourably with the equality, the freedom, and the peace of mind of the Indians; he points out, moreover, that the French, in particular, are slaves 'd'un seul homme qui peut tout, et qui n'a d'autre loi que sa volonté'.

But it was not only outside France that criticism was voiced. Fénelon, in 1694 or thereabouts, penned a long *Lettre de remontrance à ce prince sur divers points*, attacking Louis XIV's aggressive policy which had ruined France. 'La France entière n'est plus qu'un grand hôpital désolé et sans provision,' he wrote.

Vous n'aimez point Dieu; vous ne le craignez même que d'une crainte d'esclave; c'est l'enfer, et non pas Dieu que vous craignez [..] Vous n'aimez que votre gloire et votre commodité. Vous rapportez tout à vous comme si vous étiez le Dieu de la terre, et que tout le reste n'eût été créé que pour vous être sacrifié.

He called attention, too, to the disaffection of France:

Le peuple même (il faut tout dire) qui vous a tant aimé, qui a eu tant de confiance en vous, commence à perdre l'amitié, la confiance, et même le respect [ . . . ] il est plein d'aigreur et de désespoir.

Boisguillebert, in his *Détail de la France sous le règne présent* (1695) and his *Factum de la France* (1707), criticized the French fiscal system: both works were suppressed by the censorship. The great military engineer, Vauban, put forward similar ideas in his *Projet d'une dîme royale* (1707), proposing a single and universal tax on produce and profits. Once again the vested interests were too strong, and Vauban's book was condemned. Another critic was Saint-Simon, who, in 1712, sent a long, anonymous letter to the King, remonstrating with him. Such constructive criticisms could be suppressed or ignored; but it was not so easy to deal with the disrespectful songs which were circulated, or with the placards which, in 1709, were posted all over Paris.

Apart from Louis XIV's persecution of the Huguenots and the Jansenists, and the controversy between Bossuet and Fénelon over Mme Guyon and quietism (which ended with the condemnation of Fénelon's *Maximes des Saints* by the Pope in 1699), there is little in the religious history of the period to attract attention.

---

an implicit contract between King and people, and asserted the right of the latter to rebel if the former broke the contract.

[6] An English edition was published the same year.

Bossuet was zealously defending orthodox Catholicism against the forces which threatened it – not only the mysticism of Mme Guyon and Fénelon, but also Protestantism, Spinoza, Biblical criticism, and scepticism; but he was fighting a losing battle. 'Rien n'est plus rare en France que la foi chrétienne,' wrote Madame in 1699.

There were still *libertins* of the kind we have seen throughout the century, convinced that no part of a man survived death and that in consequence it was wise to follow one's instincts, to indulge one's passions, to enjoy life – the poetess, Mme Deshoulières (1637–94), the poets, Chaulieu (1639–1720) and La Fare (1644–1712), and the circle of the duc de Vendôme in the Temple, for instance. But the last thirty years of the reign of Louis XIV are characterized by a more serious kind of scepticism, based no longer on the mistrust of reason, but on faith in reason, the determination to accept nothing unless it was clearly true: the influence of Cartesianism and of the new science had broken through. Of this scepticism Bayle and Fontenelle are the main representatives.

A growing interest in foreign lands assisted the separation of morality and religion, and the progress of deism. Many accounts of travels in the East were published – notably, from 1702 onwards, a collection of *Lettres édifiantes et curieuses* by Jesuit missionaries; and Galland translated the *Thousand and One Nights* (1704–1711). In 1700 – the *querelle des cérémonies chinoises* – , the Sorbonne condemned a Jesuit, Père Louis le Comte, who, in his *Mémoires sur l'état présent de la Chine* (1696), had praised the virtues of the Chinese: 'La Chine a conservé plus de 2.000 ans la connaissance du vrai Dieu et pratiqué les maximes les plus pures de la morale, tandis que l'Europe et presque tout le reste du monde était dans l'erreur et la corruption.'[7] Both the Jesuit's praise and the Sorbonne's condemnation of him (since the virtue of the Chinese was not called in question by either side) were an implicit admission that morality and religion were not inseparable. The book was condemned as 'téméraire, injurieux à la sainte religion chrétienne; doctrine impie, contraire à la parole de Dieu; qui renverse la Foi et la religion chrétienne et rend inutile la Passion et la mort de Jésus-Christ'.

Lahontan's *Voyages* have already been mentioned. This work, as its modern editor, M. Chinard, says, supplies valuable evidence about the spread of 'les idées dites philosophiques' at the beginning of the early eighteenth century. The Indians believe in a supreme Deity and the immortality of the soul. The other dogmas of Christianity are shown to be absurd in themselves and to rest on insecure foundations:

---

[7] Quoted by H. Busson, *La Pensée religieuse française de Charron à Pascal*, 1933, p. 417.

Si je disais qu'il est plus probable que ce sont des fables que des vérités, tu me payerais des raisons de ta Bible, or l'invention de l'Ecriture n'a été trouvée, à ce que tu me dis un jour, que depuis trois mille ans, l'Imprimerie depuis quatre ou cinq siècles, comment donc s'assurer de tant d'événements divers pendant plusieurs siècles? Il faut assurément être bien crédule pour ajouter foi à tant de rêveries contenues dans ce grand Livre que les Chrétiens veulent que nous croyions. J'ai ouï lire des livres que les Jésuites ont faits de notre pays [...] j'y ai reconnu vingt menteries les unes sur les autres. Or si nous voyons de nos propres yeux des faussetés imprimées et des choses différentes de ce qu'elles sont sur le papier: comment veux-tu que je croie la sincérité de ces Bibles écrites depuis tant de siècles, traduites de plusieurs langues par des ignorants qui n'en auront pas conçu le véritable sens, ou par des menteurs qui auront changé, augmenté et diminué les paroles qui s'y trouvent aujourd'hui.

The Scriptures, moreover, are far from clear, since Protestants and Catholics do not agree about their meaning, and are full of contradictions and absurdities, which are pointed out at length. Finally, neither Christians nor their priests live in accordance with the precepts of the Scriptures. The Christians, instead of attempting to proselytize the Indians, should learn from them:

L'innocence de notre vie, l'amour que nous avons pour nos frères, la tranquillité d'âme dont nous jouissons par le mépris de l'intérêt sont trois choses que le Grand Esprit exige de tous les hommes en général.

The celibacy of the clergy and the marriage laws of the Christians are singled out for attack as contrary to nature; so is the practice of disposing of daughters and younger sons by compelling them to become nuns or monks. Lahontan's book, constituting an attack on European religion, European society, and the institution of marriage and property, has far-reaching implications.

The feeling was growing that what mattered was what was common to all religions, the belief in God, not the dogmas about which they differed. In the *Caractères*, La Bruyère laments the noxious effects of travels on religious faith:

Quelques-uns achèvent de se corrompre par de longs voyages, et perdent le peu de religion qui leur restait. Ils voient de jour à autre un nouveau culte, diverses mœurs, diverses cérémonies; ils ressemblent à ceux qui entrent dans les magasins, indéterminés sur le choix des étoffes qu'ils veulent acheter: le grand nombre de celles qu'on leur montre les rend plus indifférents; elles ont chacune leur agrément et leur bienséance: ils ne se fixent point, ils sortent sans emplette.

Further imaginary journeys continued to attack orthodox religion and describe deist societies – the *Histoire de Caléjava* of Claude Gilbert (1700), all copies of which, save one, were destroyed by the author, and the *Voyages et aventures de Jacques Massé* (1710) of Tyssot de Patot. Gilbert's Avaïtes are deists, whose moral code is based on enlightened self-interest, and who hold their property in common. Tyssot de Patot points out the absurdities and the inaccurate chronology of the Old Testament, ridicules the doctrine of the resurrection and the story of the incarnation, and attacks the wiles and greed of the priesthood.

All these tendencies were encouraged by the diffusion in France of the works of English and Dutch philosophers, often translated by exiled Huguenots – the *Tractatus theologico-politicus* (1670) and the *Ethics* (1677) of Spinoza, the works of Bacon, Newton and Locke, and of the English deist, Shaftesbury. But the chief representatives of the new critical spirit, Bayle and Fontenelle, owed a good deal, too, to their French predecessors, the *libertins érudits* of the first half of the century.

... redevable pour une large part aux maîtres du libertinage érudit [writes Pintard of Bayle] de son éloignement des 'sentiments populaires', il a aussi partagé leur résignation aux 'périlleuses conséquences' des doctrines dont ils lui avaient fourni parfois les linéaments, et parfois tout le cadre. Il est devenu semblable à eux par les sinuosités de l'argumentation comme par les idées directrices et par la science; et c'est presque exactement leur esprit qui a fini par passer en lui.[8]

If religion and the political system of the *ancien régime* were under attack, classicism was threatened by the *querelle des Anciens et des Modernes* and by the emergence of a new sentimentality.

At a special meeting of the Academy, held on 27 January 1687 to celebrate Louis XIV's recovery from an operation, Charles Perrault read a poem of some five hundred lines entitled *Le Siècle de Louis le Grand*. His theme was that the ancients were but men like his own contemporaries and that the age of Louis XIV could stand comparison with the age of Augustus:

> La belle antiquité fut toujours vénérable,
> Mais je ne crus jamais qu'elle fût adorable.
> Je vois les anciens sans ployer les genoux:
> Ils sont grands, il est vrai, mais hommes comme nous;
> Et l'on peut comparer, sans crainte d'être injuste,
> Le Siècle de Louis au beau Siècle d'Auguste.

Louis was greater than any conqueror of antiquity; the philosophy of Aristotle and Plato was out of date; and the ancient writers were overrated – Homer, for instance, lacked refinement. He praised the great writers of the seventeenth century, Corneille, above all (omitting from his list the names of Boileau, Racine, and La Fontaine, who were amongst his hearers), and claimed that the age of Louis XIV was no less superior in the plastic arts, in landscape gardening, and in music.

This started a controversy. La Fontaine answered Perrault in his *Epître à Huet*. In August, a further poem of Perrault on the

[8] *Le Libertinage érudit*, 1943, vol. I, p. 575.

same theme, *Epître au Roi*, was read in the Academy by abbé de Lavau. The following year, Fontenelle published his *Digression sur les Anciens et les Modernes*, and Perrault read an *Epître sur le génie*, attacking Homer, in the Academy, and published the first volume of his *Parallèles des Anciens et des Modernes*;[9] whilst La Bruyère, in his *Caractères*, struck a blow in defence of the ancients.[10] The Academy being strongly in favour of the moderns, La Bruyère, who was a candidate for election to it, was rejected in favour first of Fontenelle and then of a poet, Pavillon. When he was eventually elected, in 1693, he praised only the partisans of the ancients in his *discours de réception* and spoke slightingly of Corneille in the presence of Thomas Corneille and Fontenelle (the nephew of the Corneille brothers). In June, the *Mercure galant*, of which Thomas Corneille was co-editor, attacked La Bruyère, who retaliated in the preface to the published edition of his speech.

At this point, Boileau, who had hitherto contented himself with some epigrams, entered the arena. He defended Pindar and attacked Perrault in the discourse prefixed to his *Ode sur la prise de Namur* (in the manner of Pindar), and the last stanza of the ode itself contains a slighting reference to Perrault's poem, *Saint Paulin* (1693).[11] In his tenth satire he attacked the *précieuses* who found fault with the ancients:

> Au mauvais goût public la belle y fait la guerre;
> Plaint Pradon opprimé des sifflets du parterre;
> Rit des vains amateurs du grec et du latin;
> Dans la balance met Aristote et Cotin;
> Puis, d'une main encor plus fine et plus habile,
> Pèse sans passion Chapelain et Virgile;
> Remarque en ce dernier beaucoup de pauvretés,
> Mais pourtant confessant qu'il a quelques beautés...

Above all, in his nine *Réflexions sur Longin* (1694),[12] he attacked the Perrault family in general, and in particular denounced the blunders of scholarship Perrault had made in his attacks on Homer, his ignorance, his presumption, and his taste, defended Homer and Pindar against Perrault's strictures, and claimed that time alone is the test of literary greatness:

L'antiquité d'un écrivain n'est pas un titre certain de son mérite: mais l'antique et constante admiration qu'on a toujours eue pour ses ouvrages, est une preuve sûre et infaillible qu'on les doit admirer.

Before the *Réflexions* (to which Perrault replied by a *Réponse aux Réflexions critiques de Mr. D\*\*\* sur Longin*), Perrault

[9] Four volumes (1688, 1690, 1692, 1697).

[10] Other supporters of the ancients were Longepierre (*Discours sur les Anciens*, 1687) and Callières (*Histoire poétique de la guerre des anciens et des modernes*, 1688).

[11] Perrault replied in a *Lettre à M. D\*\*\* touchant la préface de son ode*.

[12] *Réflexions X–XII* were written later and for a different purpose.

had written an *Apologie des Femmes* (1694), a copy of which he sent to Arnauld, then in exile. Arnauld came out strongly in support of Boileau (in his reply dated 5 May 1694); but Bossuet, chosen as arbiter, condemned Boileau's poem as incompatible with religion, and Boileau and Perrault were formally reconciled in the Academy on 30 August 1694. Henceforth, both made concessions. The fourth volume of Perrault's *Parallèles* (1697) was less intransigent than the preceding ones, and Boileau, in his *Lettre à Perrault* (1700), included in the 1701 edition of his works, was conciliatory. The excellence of Corneille, Molière, and Racine, he claimed, was largely due to their imitation of the ancients, but he agreed that the age of Louis XIV was superior to any single period of antiquity, even the age of Augustus, and admitted the superiority of the moderns over the Romans of the age of Augustus in many fields (comedy, the novel, philosophy, science, architecture, sculpture and painting).

Some years later, in 1713, a controversy broke out between Mme Dacier and Houdar de la Motte regarding the merits or demerits of Homer; it ended amicably in a dinner party (1716).[13] 'On but à la santé d'Homère et tout se passa bien', according to Mme de Staal-Delaunay. The main contribution to this debate was Fénelon's *Lettre sur les occupations de l'Académie*, in which he shows a marked preference for the ancients: 'Si jamais il vous arrive de vaincre les anciens, c'est à eux-mêmes que vous devrez la gloire de les avoir vaincus.' The quarrel lasted, however, until Mme de Staël's *De la Littérature* and Chateaubriand's *Génie du Christianisme*, each of which makes use of a different seventeenth-century argument, the former the inevitability of progress, the latter the superiority of Christianity.

The importance of the quarrel, which reflects the influence of Descartes, the great progress in science of the seventeenth century, its consciousness of achievement, and its modernism, was considerable. It helped to establish the principle of freedom of criticism, and it undermined one of the bases of French classicism – admiration for the ancients and the principle of imitation of the ancients. For Fontenelle, for example, the men of one age are just the same as the men of any other:

Toute la question de la prééminence entre les anciens et les modernes étant une fois bien entendue, se réduit à savoir si les arbres qui étaient autrefois dans nos campagnes étaient plus grands que ceux d'aujourd'hui.

[13] Mme Dacier's translation of Homer (1711); La Motte's version of Homer adapted to contemporary taste, published with a *Discours sur Homère*, pointing out Homer's defects (1714); Mme Dacier's *Causes de la corruption du goût* (1714); abbé de Pons's *Lettre sur l'Iliade de la Motte* (in support of La Motte, 1714); La Motte's *Réflexions sur la critique* (1714); abbé Terrasson's *Dissertation critique sur l'Iliade* (1715), etc.

En cas qu'ils l'aient été, Homère, Platon, Démosthène ne peuvent être égalés dans ces derniers siècles, mais si nos arbres sont aussi grands que ceux d'autrefois, nous pouvons égaler Homère, Platon et Démosthène [ . . . ]

La nature a entre les mains une certaine pâte qui est toujours la même, qu'elle tourne et retourne sans cesse en mille façons, et dont elle forme les hommes, les animaux, les plantes; et certainement elle n'a pas formé Platon, Démosthène ni Homère d'une argile plus fine ni mieux préparée que nos philosophes, nos orateurs et nos poètes d'aujourd'hui.

The only advantage of the ancients is that they came first and invented everything. In many spheres they have been surpassed, and in all can be equalled. Worship of the ancients is not only unreasonable, but may even impede progress. Moreover, in attacking Homer for his crudeness and his primitiveness – for not, in fact, having written in seventeenth-century France –, the moderns showed that taste was not absolute and unchanging, but relative. Taste, in fact, was becoming dissociated from reason – the ancients were attacked in the name of reason and defended in the name of taste.

Two important ideas emerged in the course of the debate. One was that technique evolved and the moderns were superior in this respect; hence, the ancients could not serve as models, and a wedge was driven in between the classical doctrine on the one hand, and the ancients on whom it was supposedly based, on the other. The moderns laid considerable stress on technique, and their decrying of the ancients led to the substitution of moderns as models – to pseudo-classicism. The second was the idea of progress, that progress is a law of history. 'Les hommes ne dégénéreront jamais,' says Fontenelle, 'et [ . . . ] les vues saines de tous les bons esprits qui se succéderont, s'ajoutent toujours les unes aux autres.' If, for Fontenelle, eloquence and poetry, depending on the imagination, not on ideas, do not progress like the sciences and the arts, Perrault insists that there is progress even in these fields – the moderns, for instance, have more insight into the human heart.

It is in this period, too, that the first symptoms can be detected of that sensibility which eventually culminated in the Romantic revolt. The seventeenth century, an age of robust individuality, had always been one of strong passions; people prided themselves on their tender-heartedness and tears flowed freely, but not without reason. Louis XIV wept when Mlle Mancini left him, and she 'lui reprocha, en lui voyant répandre des larmes lorsqu'elle monta en carrosse, "qu'il pleurait et qu'il était le maître"' (Mme de Lafayette). Similarly, once when Louise de la Vallière had run away from him after a quarrel, Mme de Lafayette tells us that Louis XIV

entra par un petit degré aux Tuileries et alla dans un petit cabinet où il fit venir Madame, ne voulant pas se laisser voir, parce qu'il avait pleuré.

Mademoiselle wept copiously when she was not allowed to marry
Lauzun. She went and besought Louis XIV to relent, in an interview which she thus describes:

Je me jetai une seconde fois à ses pieds, il se mit à genoux pour m'embrasser, nous demeurâmes trois quarts d'heure les joues l'une contre l'autre
sans nous rien dire, il pleurait d'un côté, et moi je fondais en larmes de
l'autre.[14]

Mme de Sévigné sobbed for five hours after the departure of her
daughter in 1671. On 28 August 1675, nearly a month after the
news of Turenne's death had reached Paris, she tells Mme de
Grignan how she and Mme de Lafayette had been invited to
dinner by Turenne's niece and nephew to talk of their loss:

Nous fîmes bien précisément ce que nous avions résolu: les yeux ne nous
séchèrent pas. Elle avait un portrait divinement bien fait de ce héros, et
tout son train était arrivé à onze heures: tous ces pauvres gens étaient
fondus en larmes, et déjà tous habillés de deuil. Il vint trois gentils-
hommes qui pensèrent mourir de voir ce portrait: c'étaient des cris qui
faisaient fendre le cœur; ils ne pouvaient prononcer une parole; ses valets
de chambre, ses laquais, ses pages, ses trompettes, tout était fondu en
larmes et faisait fondre les autres.[15]

In these instances, tears flow more freely than they would
nowadays; but they are an indication of strength of feeling. Later,
however, we begin to find them flowing without an adequate
reason, and rather as an indication of the tender-heartedness of the
person. Describing the performance of Racine's *Iphigénie* (1675),
the gazetteer, Robinet, wrote:

> L'on vit maints des plus beaux yeux
> Voire des plus impérieux
> Pleurer sans aucun artifice.

'Nul doute,' remarks M. Picard, 'que son succès n'annonce celui
des drames larmoyants du XVIII$^e$ siècle.'[16] Bossuet delivered
his funeral oration on Anne de Gonzague in 1685, and a contemporary noted: 'Il fut touchant jusqu'aux larmes; les princes et les
princesses en pleurèrent, comme je fis et tant d'autres.'[17] Ten years
later again, and Boyer's *Judith* was performed (1695). According
to Lesage, many women sat on the stage, 'tenant des mouchoirs
étalés sur les genoux, pour essuyer leurs yeux dans les endroits
touchants'.[18] One scene was known as the *scène des mouchoirs*:
the well-bred part of the audience burst into tears and made use of
its handkerchiefs, while the pit laughed. The wave of mysticism

---

[14] 'Naturellement [Louis XIV] pleurait aisément' (Saint-Simon).
[15] Cf. her letters of 16 and 30 August.
[16] *La Carrière de Racine*, 1956, p. 230.
[17] Abbé F. Ledieu, *Mémoires et Journal sur la vie et les ouvrages de
Bossuet*, quoted by H. Peyre, *Le Classicisme français*, 1942, p. 75.
[18] *La Valise trouvée*, letter XX.

which swept over Europe in the second half of the seventeenth
century – the Spaniard, Molinos, Mme Guyon in France, Quakers
in England, Pietists in Germany – has been seen as a kindred
phenomenon. Hounded by Louis XIV's dragoons, the Camisards
in the Cévennes acted on inspiration, and – like the English
Quakers – quaked when the spirit of God came upon them. Be that
as it may, it is in this period that the *âme sensible* appears in life
and in literature.

Various aspects of pre-romanticism can be traced back to this
period. The cult of primitive simplicity and the idealization of the
noble savage occur in Lahontan. Human nature, says Lahontan, is
corrupted by society; the Indians are a proof that it is not naturally
corrupt.

Nous [says Adario] vivons simplement sous les lois de l'instinct, et de
la conduite innocente que la Nature sage nous a imprimée dès le berceau.
Nous sommes tous d'accord, et conformes en volontés, opinions et sentiments. Ainsi, nous passons la vie dans une si parfaite intelligence, qu'on
ne voit parmi nous ni procès, ni dispute, ni chicane.

The vogue of fairy stories, begun by the publication of Perrault's
*Contes de ma mère Loye* (1697), shows a recrudescence of fancy
and imagination; and there are indications of a growing interest
in external nature. Travellers show an increasing awareness of the
visual aspects of the countries they visit. The description of moonlight in Fontenelle's *Entretiens sur la pluralité des mondes* (1686)
has been called 'le premier clair de lune préromantique':[19]

Il faisait un frais délicieux [ ... ] La lune était levée il y avait peut-être
une heure, et ses rayons, qui ne venaient à nous qu'entre les branches des
arbres, faisaient un agréable mélange d'un blanc fort vif avec tout ce vert
qui paraissait noir. Il n'y avait pas un nuage qui dérobât ou qui ob-
scurcît la moindre étoile; elles étaient toutes d'un or pur et éclatant, et
qui était encore relevé par le fond bleu où elles sont attachées. Ce spectacle me fit rêver ...

This last phrase is not the only one which betrays a pre-romantic
sensibility. 'Ne trouvez-vous pas,' the author asks the marquise,
'que le jour même n'est pas si beau qu'une belle nuit?' The marquise agrees: both day and night are beautiful, she says, 'mais la
beauté de la nuit est une beauté qui est plus *touchante*'. She adds:

Ce n'est rien que la beauté *si elle ne touche*. Avouez que le jour ne vous
eût jamais jeté dans une rêverie aussi douce que celle où je vous ai vu
près de tomber tout à l'heure, à la vue de cette belle nuit.

She asks in her turn why lovers praise night rather than day, and
the author answers:

C'est apparemment qu'il n'inspire point *je ne sais quoi de triste et de
passionné*. Il semble pendant la nuit que tout soit en repos. On s'imagine

[19] A. Monglond, *Le Préromantisme français*, 1930, vol. I, p. 154.

que les étoiles marchent avec plus de silence que le soleil; les objets que le ciel présente sont plus doux; la vue s'y arrête plus aisément; enfin, on rêve mieux, parce qu'*on se flatte d'être alors dans toute la nature la seule personne occupée à rêver.* Peut-être aussi que le spectacle du jour est *trop uniforme*; ce n'est qu'un soleil et une voûte bleue; mais il se peut que la vue de toutes ces étoiles *semées confusément, et disposées au hasard* en mille figures différentes, *favorise la rêverie et un certain désordre de pensées où l'on ne tombe point sans plaisir.*

The love of reverie, the insistence that beauty must be *touchante*, the preference for night over day, the love of solitude, the idea that beauty should not be uniform but varied and characterized by disorder, all these things are pre-romantic.

Rationalism, on the one hand, then: sensibility, fancy, and a growing interest in the exotic, on the other. Perrault's *Contes* and Galland's *Mille et une Nuits* rub shoulders with Bayle's Dictionary.

Spinoza, Malebranche, Leibniz! mais aussi Alexandre Bras de Fer et Schéhérazade. Les grands systèmes métaphysiques, fondés en raison; mais aussi, l'imagination qui vagabonde de contes en féeries, l'œil qui rêve en regardant avec quelque effroi le rhinocéros ou la vache marine. Tant d'efforts pour expliquer le monde, en profondeur; et à la surface, ces miroitements et ces jeux.[20]

So Hazard sums up the period. The seventeenth-century ideal of the *honnête homme* was disintegrating into the *homme d'esprit* and the *homme sensible*. French classical literature, which depended on a balance between reason and religion, between independence and acceptance of the social order, between imagination and the discipline imposed by common sense and the authority of the classics, was a temporary phenomenon. Already, in the last years of the reign of Louis XIV, the balance was being disturbed, and a new kind of literature was coming into being.

[20] *La Crise de la conscience européenne*, pp. 381–2.

## Chapter 22

# BAYLE AND FONTENELLE

## 1. BAYLE (1647–1706)

PIERRE BAYLE, a Protestant, left France when the Protestant Academy of Sedan at which he was teaching was closed down in 1681, and settled in Holland. It was there that all his works were published – his *Pensées diverses sur la Comète* (1682);[1] his attack on Louis XIV's persecution of the Protestants, *Ce qu'est la France toute catholique sous le règne de Louis le grand* (1686); his plea for toleration, *Commentaire philosophique sur ces paroles de Jésus-Christ: Contrains-les d'entrer* (1686); his literary gazette, the *Nouvelles de la République des Lettres* (1684–87); and his great *Dictionnaire historique et critique* (1697).[2]

The comet of 1680 and 1681 provided the occasion for the *Pensées sur la Comète*, for which, amongst other reasons, Bayle was deprived, in 1693, of his chair and of the right to teach. It is a rambling work, ill-proportioned, ill-arranged, full of digressions, written in a style which, if usually clear and sometimes eloquent, is also sometimes clumsy. Bayle compares it to a town, built piecemeal:

Voilà comment cet amas de pensées diverses a été formé; je suis revenu souvent sur mes pas, afin de faire des additions tantôt en un lieu, tantôt en un autre.

The framework is provided by eight arguments: – (1) There is no conceivable way in which comets could influence terrestrial events. (2) There are no grounds for thinking that their influence, if they have any, is bad rather than good. (3) The basis of the fear of comets is astrology, which is false. (4) If comets are followed by misfortunes, that is no proof that they are the cause of them – a Parisian who looks out of his window will see passers-by, but it is not because he looks out that they are there. (5) In fact, the appearance of comets is not a sign of misfortunes, since there are 'des

---

[1] The first edition was entitled *Lettre à M. L. A. D. C., Docteur de Sorbonne, où il est prouvé* [ ... ] *que les comètes ne sont point le présage d'aucun malheur.*

[2] In fact it appeared at the end of 1696.

malheurs sans comètes et des comètes sans malheurs'. (6) The fact
that the belief in comets is ancient and widely held is no argument
in favour of its truth. (7) If comets were portents, since most of the
world, even in modern times, is idolatrous, we should have to conclude that they were sent by God to confirm men in their idolatrous
ways, which is inconceivable. In the course of these last two arguments, Bayle adds some further reasons why comets cannot be
portents – they are too frequent; they are often invisible to all but
astronomers; and they appear indiscriminately to the whole world.
(8) The belief that comets are portents is a pagan superstition, due
to human curiosity about the future and love of the miraculous,
and exploited by dishonest priests, and by politicians and their
panegyrists. This brief summary, however, does no justice to the
closeness of Bayle's reasoning, to his serried arguments, and to the
wealth of facts and illustrations with which he supports them.

The book is more than an attempt to prove that comets are not
baneful; it is an attack on superstition in general. Astrology,
oracles, the belief that certain days or names are propitious and
others unpropitious, the conviction that the moon influences the
weather and that August is a hot month, the fear of the consequences of spilling salt or sitting thirteen at table or meeting a
weasel, the dread of eclipses, the faith in portents and omens are
all examined and found to be groundless – though Bayle recognizes that a superstition may have a moral effect and thus to some
extent bring about its own fulfilment. In examining the superstitious world of miracles and portents, Bayle makes three points.
First, the facts must be established before we attempt to explain
them. Second, the universe is governed by natural laws which are
not set aside for petty events on earth:

Plus on étudie l'homme, plus on connaît que l'orgueil est sa passion
dominante, et qu'il affecte la grandeur jusque dans la plus triste misère.
Chétive et caduque créature qu'il est, il a bien pu se persuader qu'il ne
saurait mourir, sans troubler toute la Nature, et sans obliger le Ciel à se
mettre en nouveaux frais, pour éclairer la pompe de ses funérailles. Sotte
et ridicule vanité! Si nous avions une juste idée de l'Univers, nous com-
prendrions bientôt, que la mort ou la naissance d'un Prince, est une si
petite affaire, eu égard à toute la Nature des choses, que ce n'est pas la
peine qu'on s'en remue dans le Ciel.

Third, the fact that a belief is ancient and widespread is no
guarantee of its truth. Men have a predilection for the miraculous
and the supernatural; they are naturally lazy, uncritical, and
prone to accept the beliefs of others without scrutiny; and they
tend to overlook facts contrary to their beliefs in favour of those
which support them. Hence, it is easy for error to take root.

Bayle's rationalism seems at times to extend beyond super-

stition to religion itself. For him, morality is much more important than doctrine, and he shows the triviality of theological
questions and criticizes the excessive importance which the Church
attaches to them: 'jamais on n'eût inquiété Galilée, si au lieu
de faire le Copernicien, il se fût attaché à entretenir plusieurs
concubines.' This curious scale of values seems to be that of God
himself,

qui témoigne plus d'indignation contre son peuple, lorsqu'il sacrifie sur
les montagnes et sous le feuillage des arbres, et qu'il honore les Divinités
des Gentils, que lorsqu'il tombe dans le larcin, dans le meurtre, et dans
l'adultère . . .

Moreover, for Bayle, the influence of religion on morality is
slight. In the part of the book which he devotes to showing that
atheism is preferable to idolatry, Christianity is inextricably linked
with the latter. Religion — except for the few Christians who have
received the Grace of God — is no bulwark against the vices and
passions of men.

. . . si les lois humaines n'y mettaient ordre, toutes les sociétés des
chrétiens seraient ruinées bientôt. Et je suis sûr qu'à moins d'un miracle
continuel, une ville comme Paris, serait réduite dans quinze jours au plus
triste état du monde, si on n'employait point d'autre remède contre le
vice, que les remontrances des prédicateurs et des confesseurs.

Example after example is quoted of the brutality of Christian
soldiers, of the ruthlessness and debauchery of Christian rulers, of
the unchastity of Christians in general. Moreover, religion is not
merely useless as a curb on human misdeeds, it is often positively
harmful:

. . . généralement parlant, (car j'excepte toujours ceux qui sont conduits
par l'esprit de Dieu) la foi que l'on a pour une religion, n'est pas la règle
de la conduite de l'homme, si ce n'est qu'elle est souvent fort propre à
exciter dans son âme, de la colère contre ceux qui sont de différent sentiment, de la crainte quand on se croit menacé de quelque péril, et quelques
autres passions semblables; et surtout un je ne sais quel zèle pour la
pratique des cérémonies extérieures, dans la pensée que ces actes ex-
térieurs, et la profession publique de la vraie foi, serviront de rempart à
tous les désordres où l'on s'abandonne, et en procureront un jour le
pardon.

Morality is not a matter of religion but of upbringing, temperament, fear of punishment, and the desire for esteem. This last, says
Bayle, is the essential human motive, as active in atheists as in
other men. Many atheists have led virtuous lives, and atheism has
even had its martyrs. Hence, a society of atheists could perfectly
well subsist, providing its laws punished crimes severely.

In the *Pensées diverses*, then, religion is associated with fanaticism, with crafty priests encouraging ignorance and superstition,

with quibbling theologians; it has no relevance to the only thing that matters, human behaviour. It is but a short step from Bayle to the deism of the eighteenth-century *philosophes*, whose ideas Bayle anticipates, too, in his dislike of wars of conquest and his attack on the aggression and religious intolerance of Louis XIV.

Bayle's Dictionary, which remained a standard work of reference for over a century, is a monumental piece of scholarship. Bayle had the characteristics of the great scholar – wide reading, painstaking accuracy, and thoroughness. There is an interesting passage in his article on Epicurus, in which he maintains that writers who bring together quotations are not inferior to others:

Il y a d'autres citateurs, qui ne se fient qu'à eux-mêmes; ils veulent tout vérifier, ils vont toujours à la source, ils examinent quel a été le but de l'auteur, ils ne s'arrêtent pas au passage dont ils ont besoin, ils considèrent avec attention ce qui le précède, ce qui le suit. Ils tâchent de faire de belles applications, et de bien lier leurs autorités; ils les comparent entre elles, ils les concilient, ou bien ils montrent qu'elles se combattent. D'ailleurs ce peuvent être des gens qui se font une religion, dans les matières de fait, de n'avancer rien sans preuve. S'ils disent qu'un tel philosophe grec croyait ceci ou cela, qu'un tel sénateur ou capitaine romain suivait certaines maximes, ils en produisent les preuves tout aussitôt; et parce qu'en certaines occasions la singularité de la chose demande plusieurs témoignages, ils en ramassent plusieurs. Je ne crains point de dire de cette méthode de composer, qu'elle est cent fois plus pénible que celle de notre Epicure et qu'on ferait un livre de mille pages en moins de temps selon la dernière méthode, qu'un livre de quatre cents pages selon la première.                                                    (EPICURE (*E*))

There, surely, is an account of Bayle's own method. In the article on Luther, we find him scrupulously examining the criticisms of Luther's adversaries, attempting to establish the facts, and concluding impartially that, if some accusations are unfounded, Luther cannot be exonerated from others.

Plus on examine ces choses [writes Bayle], plus on sent que c'est un travail d'Hercule que d'entreprendre de démêler la vérité au milieu de tant de déguisements, et de tant de supercheries.                    (LUTHER (*O*))

In the article MARCIONITES, examining whether they were persecuted or not, he assembles all the evidence – what he calls the *pièces du procès* – with the object of setting an example for others to follow, for he concludes:

Il serait à souhaiter qu'un bon critique prît la peine de ramasser toutes les pièces des procès semblables à celui-ci, et de les placer l'une après l'autre, comme je viens de le faire, à l'égard de la dispute sur les martyrs marcionites. J'ai voulu donner ici un échantillon de ce travail pour encourager à l'entreprise de cet ouvrage ceux qui en seront capables.

(MARCIONITES (*E*))

The Dictionary consists of articles in large print, the text of which is quite short, with several, usually lengthy, footnotes in small type and double columns, in which Bayle brings together his documents, weighs up the evidence, and discusses religious and philosophical problems. It is, on the whole, the footnotes that contain the interesting and controversial part of the work. Here we find Bayle expressing his dislike of war ('Bel avantage que d'entendre beaucoup mieux qu'eux l'art de tuer, de bombarder, et d'exterminer le genre humain!' – (MAHOMET (P)), attacking astrology, fanaticism, and intolerance (in Protestants no less than in their adversaries), and taking up a sceptical attitude towards miracles.

Bayle is not very respectful towards religion. Religion for most men is a matter of upbringing and prejudice, not of reason: we believe what we are brought up to believe, and we are much more accessible to arguments in its favour than against it. He dwells – in the interests of truth – on the debaucheries of St. Augustine's youth. He relates that when St. Bernard's prophecies about the Crusades were not fulfilled, he blamed the sins of the Crusaders: 'Il n'y a point d'imposteur, qui ne se puisse cacher derrière ce retranchement', comments Bayle. And, of St. Bernard's persecution of Abelard, he says, 'Ce sont les artifices ordinaires des cabalistes', adding cautiously, 'je ne dis pas que d'autres ne s'en soient jamais servis.' He compares the stoics to *dévots*:

Ils intéressaient la Religion dans leur querelle, ils faisaient craindre que la jeunesse ne fût pervertie, ils alarmaient tous les gens de bien, on ajoutait foi à leurs délations: le peuple se persuade aisément que le vrai zèle, et l'austérité des maximes, vont toujours ensemble.          (EPICURE (N))

He compares the Japanese bonzes to monks:

... le célibat mal observé, les tromperies cachées sous les apparences d'une morale rigide, le profit des enterrements, le secours envoyé aux âmes séparées du corps, fourniraient beaucoup de comparaisons.

(JAPON (A))

He points out that Descartes was wrong in assuming that God would not deceive men, since the Old Testament provides evidence to the contrary (RIMINI (B)).

Bayle stresses time and time again that the Christian dogmas – the Trinity, the Incarnation, transubstantiation – are contrary to reason, and that the everlasting torments of the damned are incompatible with the conception of a good God. His scepticism about miracles is far-reaching. In the article JONAS, he compares the story of Jonah and the whale with a similar episode in the life of Hercules, with the implication that there is nothing to choose between them, that both must be accepted, or both rejected; he points

out, moreover, that members of all religions and sects accept the
miracles of their own side without question, but critically scrutin-
ize those of their adversaries; and he quotes St. Augustine as saying that the resurrections of Lazarus and Christ himself are no
easier to believe than the story of Jonah.

He casts doubt on the divine inspiration of the scriptures by
showing the immorality of the Old Testament heroes, and by
critically examining the text. Abraham was not only incestuous in
marrying his half-sister, but deceitful in passing his wife off as his
sister, and an arrant coward in thus risking her virtue to save his
own life. By ordinary moral standards, David was a thoroughly
cruel, dishonest, treacherous usurper, polygamous, lecherous, and
a bad father. 'On ne me prouvera jamais que les lois exactes de
l'équité, et de la morale sévère d'un bon serviteur de Dieu,
puissent approuver cette conduite' (DAVID (H)). Since David could
be saved, there is, Bayle suggests, hope for all kings. Bayle also
uses the methods of Biblical criticism. He dwells on the improbability of Sarah's having been beautiful at the age of ninety,
but dismisses with – ironical? – horror the suggestion that the
chronology of Moses may have been confused:

> N'écoutons point la pensée de Hugues de Saint-Victor: les consé-
> quences en sont dangereuses, n'ouvrons point de brèche dans l'Histoire
> sainte, les profanes y entreraient par là comme des loups dans la bergerie,
> afin d'y faire mille ravages.                                (SARA (E))

In the article on David, he suggests that the two accounts of
David's sparing Saul's life (I Samuel 24 and 26) are two versions
of the same episode. He points out that there is no way of explaining satisfactorily why Saul, after the death of Goliath, should ask
who David was, when he knew him well (I Samuel 16 and 17), and
comments:

> Si une narration comme celle-ci se trouvait dans Thucydide ou dans
> Tite-Live, tous les critiques concluraient unanimement que les copistes
> auraient transposé les pages, oublié quelque chose en un lieu, répété quelque
> chose dans un autre, ou inséré des morceaux postiches dans l'ouvrage
> de l'auteur.

Typically, Bayle adds:

> Mais il faut bien se garder de pareils soupçons lorsqu'il s'agit de la Bible.

Equally typically, he adds again:

> Il y a eu néanmoins des personnes assez hardies, pour prétendre que tous
> les chapitres ou tous les versets du I Livre de Samuel n'ont point la place
> qu'ils ont eue dans leur origine.                              (DAVID (C))

Bayle was fully aware of the implications of all this: in the article
on SOCIN (FAUSTE), he states clearly enough: 'en ruinant la divinité

de l'Ecriture, on renverse toute la révélation, en suite de quoi tout n'est que dispute de philosophes'.

In the *Dictionnaire*, as in the *Pensées diverses*, Bayle shows his contempt for theological quibbles. The Catholic Church has made itself ridiculous by upholding St. Augustine and condemning Jansenius, though their doctrines are the same. And, discussing the accusation of atheism brought against Hobbes, he comments:

Une infinité de petits esprits, ou de gens malins, l'intentent à tous ceux qui bornent leurs affirmations aux grandes et aux sublimes vérités d'une solide métaphysique, et aux doctrines générales de l'Ecriture. On veut de plus les obliger à l'adoption de tous les articles particuliers, que l'on a coutume de proposer mille et mille fois au peuple.          (HOBBES (*M*))

As in the *Pensées diverses*, too, he is fond of pointing out that morality and religion are two separate things. Epicurus and his followers were disinterestedly virtuous, whereas Christians are actuated by fear of Hell and hope of Heaven. Knuzen, a German atheist, is proof that

les idées de la religion naturelle, les idées de l'honnêteté, les impressions de la raison, en un mot les lumières de la conscience, peuvent subsister dans l'esprit de l'homme, après même que les idées de l'existence de Dieu, et la foi d'une vie à venir, en ont été effacées.          (KNUZEN (*B*))

Spinoza was another virtuous atheist. Similarly, the harmonious life together of Epicurus and his disciples shows that religion is not a necessary bond in society.

Qu'on nous vienne dire après cela que des gens qui nient la Providence, et qui établissent pour leur dernière fin leur propre satisfaction ne sont nullement capables de vivre en société, que ce sont nécessairement des traîtres, des fourbes, des empoisonneurs, des voleurs, etc. [...] Voici la secte d'Epicure dont la morale pratique sur les devoirs de l'amitié ne s'est nullement démentie pendant quelques siècles: et nous allons voir qu'au lieu que les sectes les plus dévotes étaient remplies de querelles et de partialités, celle d'Epicure jouissait d'une paix profonde.          (EPICURE (*D*))

Men do not live according to their principles: despite their principles, the Mahometans are tolerant to other religions; despite *theirs*, Christians are intolerant (MAHOMET (*AA*)). In the article JAPON, Bayle paints a melancholy picture of Christianity – at least of sixteenth-century Christianity:

c'était une religion sanguinaire, meurtrière, accoutumée au carnage depuis cinq ou six cents ans. Elle avait contracté une très longue habitude de se maintenir et de s'agrandir, en faisant passer au fil de l'épée tout ce qui lui résistait. Les bûchers, les bourreaux, le tribunal effroyable de l'Inquisition, les Croisades, les bulles qui excitaient les sujets à se rebeller, les prédicateurs séditieux, les conspirations, les assassinats des princes étaient les moyens ordinaires qu'elle employait contre ceux qui ne se soumettaient pas à ses ordres.          (JAPON (*E*))

The morals of the Christians are in no wise superior to those of
the Mahometans:

... il semble [ ... ] que s'il y a quelque différence entre leurs mauvaises
mœurs c'est plutôt la diversité de climat qui en est la cause, que la diversité de religion.                                              (MAHOMET (P))

What holds society together is not religion, but the law ('il faut
être fou à lier, pour croire que le genre humain puisse subsister sans
les magistrats'; KNUZEN (B)) and self-interest ('Chacun est plus
capable d'être offensé que d'offenser; car entre vingt personnes
égales, il est manifeste que chacune a moins de force contre dix-
neuf que contre une' (SOCIN (FAUSTE)(I)).

Some of the stock arguments in favour of the divine origin of
Christianity are demolished in the Dictionary. Fortitude in face
of persecution and the appearance of saintliness, for example, are
no proof of divine protection – if they were, they could be used
not only by Protestants against Catholics, but by Anabaptists
against Protestants. Nor does the miraculous spread of Christianity
(an argument used by Bossuet, for example) prove anything.

... cette preuve n'aura plus de force dès que l'on pourra marquer une
fausse Eglise, qui ait acquis une semblable étendue par des moyens tout
semblables; et il est certain que l'on ruinerait cet argument, si l'on pouvait
faire voir que la religion mahométane ne doit point à la violence des
armes la promptitude de ses grands progrès.                    (MAHOMET (O))

But after this guarded statement, Bayle goes on to show, first, that
if Christianity was not established by force during its first three
centuries of existence, it has certainly not eschewed force since,
and, second, that Mahometanism has spread far more than
Christianity:

La religion de Mahomet a beaucoup plus d'étendue que n'en a le christianisme, cela n'est pas contestable: ses victoires, ses conquêtes, ses triomphes
ont incomparablement plus d'éclat que tout ce de quoi les chrétiens se
peuvent glorifier, en ce genre de prospérités.                 (MAHOMET (P))

Bayle discusses at length two problems of great consequence in
theology. The first is that of the souls of animals. The theory of
Descartes, Bayle says firmly – that animals are soulless machines –,
is the most compatible with faith; unfortunately, it is highly unlikely. Animals can reason, remember, and compare, and it is
impossible to show that there is any difference in kind between
them and men:

Je demande à ces messieurs s'ils trouveraient bon qu'on dît que l'âme
d'un homme est d'une autre espèce à l'âge de trente-cinq ans, qu'à l'âge
d'un mois; ou que l'âme d'un frénétique, d'un hébété, d'un vieillard qui
tombe en enfance, n'est pas substantiellement aussi parfaite que l'âme
d'un habile homme. Ils rejetteraient sans doute cette pensée comme une
erreur très grossière, et ils feraient bien; car il est sûr que la même âme,

qui dans les enfants ne fait que sentir, médite et raisonne d'une manière solide dans un homme fait; et que la même âme, qui fait admirer sa raison et son esprit dans un grand homme, ne ferait que radoter dans un vieillard, qu'extravaguer dans un fou, que sentir dans un enfant.

(RORARIUS (*E*))

He proceeds to assert that the soul of a dog in the body of Aristotle or Cicero 'n'eût pas manqué d'acquérir toutes les lumières de ces deux grands hommes'. The greatest objection to the theory of the Cartesians is not, he adds, the fact that animals can move, but that they appear to have the same emotions as men. If, says Bayle, a material soul is enough to explain the behaviour of animals, it is enough to account for human behaviour as well.

In discussing Descartes's theory about animals, Bayle makes a further point. If animals have no souls and yet suffer pain, the argument that suffering is a punishment for sin falls to the ground. And this brings us to the other great problem which Bayle considers at length, the problem of the existence of evil in a universe created by an omnipotent and beneficent Creator. The doctrine of the epicureans, who held that God did not create the universe and does not intervene in it, is consistent, says Bayle. If God found matter to hand, as it were, and created the universe, either he foresaw the evil it would contain, or he did not.[3] If he did, we cannot speak of his goodness. If he did not, he must have been a bad workman, ignorant of the nature of his materials; in any case, having realized what he had done, he would surely have destroyed his work again afterwards.

Il avait voulu construire un magnifique palais pour y loger commodément les créatures animées, qui devaient sortir du sein informe de la matière, et pour les y combler de bienfaits, et il se trouve que ces créatures ne firent que s'entremanger, incapables qu'elles étaient de continuer à vivre, si la chair des unes ne servait d'aliment aux autres. Il se trouva que le plus parfait de ces animaux n'épargna pas même la chair de son semblable; il y eut des anthropophages, et ceux qui ne se portèrent pas à cette brutalité, ne laissèrent pas de se persécuter les uns les autres, et d'être en proie à l'envie, à la jalousie, à la fraude, à l'avarice, à la cruauté, aux maladies, au froid, au chaud, à la faim, etc. Leur Auteur luttant continuellement avec la malignité de la matière productrice de ces désordres, et obligé d'avoir toujours la foudre à la main, et de verser sur la terre la peste, la guerre, et la famine, qui, avec les roues et les gibets dont les grands chemins abondent, n'empêchent pas que le mal ne se maintienne, peut-il être regardé comme un Etre heureux? Peut-on être heureux, quand au bout de quatre mille ans de travail on n'est pas plus avancé qu'au premier jour dans l'ouvrage qu'on a entrepris, et que l'on souhaite passionnément d'achever? Cette image d'infortune n'est-elle pas aussi parlante que la roue d'Ixion, que la pierre de Sisyphe, que le tonneau des Danaïdes?

(EPICURE (*S*))

[3] Elsewhere Bayle points out the difficulty of believing either that matter is eternal and different from God or that matter could be created out of nothing (SPINOZA (*O*)).

In the article XENOPHANES, Bayle concludes that the evil in the world predominates over the good, and that history records far more victories of the Devil than triumphs of Christ. At the time of the flood, God could find but eight people worthy of being preserved. As for the Christian world:

Les hérésies, les superstitions, les violences, les fraudes, les extorsions, les impuretés, qui ont paru dans tout le monde chrétien pendant plusieurs siècles, sont des choses que je ne saurais décrire qu'imparfaitement, quand même j'aurais plus d'éloquence que Cicéron.          (XENOPHANES (E))

He approaches the same problem from a slightly different angle in the articles on Manicheism. The chief argument against the universe's being governed by a single beneficent power is man:

Les voyages font des leçons perpétuelles là-dessus; ils font voir partout les monuments du malheur et de la méchanceté de l'homme; partout des prisons, et des hôpitaux; partout des gibets, et des mendiants. Vous voyez ici les débris d'une ville florissante; ailleurs vous n'en pouvez pas même trouver les ruines. [ . . . ] L'histoire n'est à proprement parler qu'un recueil des crimes et des infortunes du genre human . . .

                                                      (MANICHEENS (D))

On the other hand, virtue and happiness do exist. This mixture of good and evil points to the existence of two principles governing the world, to Manicheism.

Qui n'admirera et qui ne déplorera la destinée de notre raison? Voilà les manichéens qui, avec une hypothèse tout à fait absurde et contradictoire, expliquent les expériences cent fois mieux que ne font les orthodoxes, avec la supposition si juste, si nécessaire, si uniquement véritable d'un premier principe infiniment bon et tout-puissant.          (PAULICIENS (E))

It is quite impossible to reconcile the existence of evil with a good and omnipotent God. The best explanation is that human free will is the origin of moral evil, and physical evil the punishment for sin; but, Bayle shows in detail, this argument will not withstand examination. God must have foreseen the Fall, or at the very least, the danger of it. What should we think of a mother who allowed her daughter to go to a dance, knowing that she would be debauched, or who watched her daughter succumbing to the blandishments of a young man without intervening? And yet that is precisely how theologians would have us believe God behaved. God could easily have intervened by sending his Grace to Adam and Eve – for theologians hold that Grace is not incompatible with free will. It is true that Christians believe in the Devil: but they believe that the Devil, not being eternal, is the creation of God.[4] In Christian theology, the best solution to the difficulty is

---

[4] Bayle points out elsewhere that to say that God created an evil sp'rit who caused evil is tantamount to saying that God created evil—*quod est causae est causa causati* (ZOROASTRE (F)).

the doctrine of predestination – i.e. of a tyrannical God, the author of evil, 'un législateur qui défend le crime à l'homme, et qui néanmoins pousse l'homme dans le crime, et puis l'en punit éternellement' (PAULICIENS (*I*)).

There is a curious passage in the article on Rufin, in which Bayle says:

> Il ne faut pas que je finisse cette remarque sans observer l'injustice de certaines gens, qui croient que lorsqu'on rejette les raisons qu'ils donnent d'un dogme, on rejette le dogme même. Il y a une différence capitale entre ces deux choses... (RUFIN (*C*))

He adds, however, that there are, of course, abuses – the Pyrrhonians, on the pretext of combating their opponents' arguments in favour of the existence of God, did aim at destroying the belief in God. Bayle, this ambiguous remark suggests, does not want us to know his views too clearly. His most audacious remarks are in the small print of footnotes; they are often expressed in the form of quotations or put into the mouths of others – Bayle sometimes invents imaginary dialogues between philosophers of opposing views –, and opinions sympathetically expounded at length are summarily condemned. Moreover, time and time again, he falls back on Pyrrhonism and fideism – the powerlessness of human reason to resolve difficulties, the need to accept the Scriptures without question.

> Qu'on nous vienne dire avec un grand appareil de raisonnements, qu'il n'est pas possible que le mal moral s'introduise dans le monde, par l'ouvrage d'un principe infiniment bon et saint, nous répondrons que cela s'est pourtant fait, et par conséquent que cela est très possible. (MANICHEENS (*D*))

Is Bayle's fideism genuine, or is it a mask for scepticism? After the eloquent description of the misery of the world in EPICURE (*S*; quoted above), one finds Bayle in the following note (*T*) saying that Scripture reveals God's providence to us: God did create matter, and everything that happens in the world happens according to his plan:

> Il s'ensuit de là que la conduite du monde n'est pas une affaire qui puisse ou fatiguer ou chagriner Dieu, et qu'il n'y a point d'événements, quels qu'ils puissent être, qui puissent troubler sa béatitude. S'il arrive des choses qu'il a défendues, et qu'il punit, elles n'arrivent pas néanmoins contre ses décrets, et elles servent aux fins adorables qu'il s'est proposées de toute éternité, et qui font les plus grands mystères de l'Evangile.

After what has gone before, this Panglossian statement (with its facile *béatitude, fins adorables, mystères de l'Evangile*) is in danger of appearing ironical, especially as the rest of the note illustrates the value of revelation by showing that reason unaided would reach diametrically opposed conclusions. In the article on the

Paulicians, Bayle gives strong expression to the fideist point of view:

Il faut humblement reconnaître que toute la philosophie est ici à bout, et que sa faiblesse nous doit conduire aux lumières de la révélation, où nous trouverons l'ancre sûre et ferme.                    (PAULICIENS (H))

A little later, however, we come to note (M).[5] This opens with another expression of fideism. There is no point arguing, because reason cannot overcome two overriding objections against the Christian point of view, which Bayle states at length. They are briefly: (1) that God gave free will to make men miserable – a good God would have taken his gift away again, just as a human father would not allow his son to throw himself out of a window, merely to avoid interfering with his liberty of action; and (2) that God could have prevented the Fall, without encroaching on human free will, by giving Adam Grace. A fideist conclusion is tacked on, so that we have two insuperable arguments against Christianity sandwiched between two statements of fideism. Whatever Bayle's own views, what remains with the reader is an impression of the strength of the arguments against the existence of an omnipotent and beneficent God.

Bayle warns us against hasty conclusions:

Avons-nous droit de décider de ce qui se passe dans le cœur d'autrui? Connaissons-nous assez l'âme de l'homme, pour prononcer que telles ou telles combinaisons de sentiments n'y peuvent trouver de fond?

(SPINOZA (M))

Nevertheless, the Dictionary is a repertory of arguments against religion; Bayle was a highly intelligent man, with a quick eye for the inconsistencies of others and the implications of doctrines, and it is probable that he knew what he was doing. If he did not intend it to be what it is, he would be open to the criticism that – as we have seen – he brings against God, that of having been a bad workman, ignorant of the nature of his materials. In any case, exactly what Bayle's own views were does not much matter: it is the impression they made on his readers that counts.

## II. FONTENELLE

Bernard le Bovier de Fontenelle (1657–1757[6]), the nephew of Corneille, began his career as a dramatist, but quickly turned his attention to other things. A critic and man of letters, he was above all interested in philosophy and science – he became perpetual secretary to the Académie des Sciences (1697). More readable and

---

[5] This was added to the second edition.
[6] He died shortly before his hundredth birthday.

entertaining than Bayle, though a less profound scholar and a less original mind, his outlook is similar to Bayle's. The two works for which he is chiefly remembered and which display his qualities best are his *Entretiens sur la pluralité des mondes* and his *Histoire des Oracles*, both published in 1686.

The *Entretiens sur la pluralité des mondes* is an attempt to satisfy the growing interest in science and to bring astronomy within the reach of the *honnête homme* and the *honnête femme*.

J'ai voulu traiter la philosophie d'une manière qui ne fût point philosophique; j'ai tâché de l'amener à un point où elle ne fût ni trop sèche pour les gens du monde, ni trop badine pour les savants. (*Préface*)

Selon moi, il n'y a pas jusqu'aux vérités à qui l'agrément ne soit nécessaire. (*1er Soir*)

Here once again is the seventeenth-century insistence on combining instruction with pleasure; and Fontenelle claims that his book requires no more effort to read than *La Princesse de Clèves*.

In fact, the *Entretiens* is a delightful work. It consists of six dialogues between the author and a *marquise* (probably Mme de la Mésangère, the daughter of Mme de la Sablière), two *honnêtes gens* who are anything but pedantic, who take nothing too seriously, and jest readily. Their conversation, always sprightly and witty, is diversified by ingenious comparisons (of nature with the opera, for example), anecdotes, parallels drawn from history (the account of the arrival of Columbus in the New World) or natural history (the description of the life of the bees), fanciful speculations (about what one would see if one could watch the world rotate from outside, about life on the moon and the planets, and the different forms it might take), and accounts of mythological explanations of the universe.

The universe described by Fontenelle is that of Copernicus, with the earth and the other planets moving round the sun, which is one of the fixed stars; it is essentially that of modern astronomy, except that the distances between the heavenly bodies are smaller[7] and that Fontenelle adopts Descartes's vortices to explain their revolutions. It is a mechanistic universe:

On veut que l'univers ne soit en grand que ce qu'une montre est en petit, et que tout s'y conduise par des mouvements réglés qui dépendent de l'arrangement des parties. (*1er Soir*)

[7] Fontenelle did not, in fact, base his figures on the best authorities. His chief sources were not the works of reliable astronomers but two books by John Wilkins, Bishop of Chester, *Discovery of a New World* (1638) and *Discourse tending to prove that 'tis probable our Earth is one of the Planets* (1640; both translated into French in 1656), and Pierre Borel's *Discours nouveau prouvant la pluralité des mondes* (1657).

In its majestic simplicity, however, it is far more admirable than
the mysterious, inexplicable universe it has replaced:

Elle [la nature] est d'une épargne extraordinaire; tout ce qu'elle pourra
faire d'une manière qui lui coûtera un peu moins, quand ce moins ne
serait presque rien, soyez sûre qu'elle ne le fera que de cette manière-là.
Cette épargne néanmoins s'accorde avec une magnificence surprenante,
qui brille dans tout ce qu'elle a fait: c'est que la magnificence est dans le
dessein, et l'épargne dans l'exécution. Il n'y a rien de plus beau qu'un
grand dessein que l'on exécute à peu de frais.                    (1er Soir)

Nothing is permanent; old stars are continually dying, new stars
continually coming into existence; 'tout est dans un branle perpétuel' (5e Soir), though change is gradual. Since eclipses and
comets are natural phenomena, superstitious fears of them are ludicrous. Comets are merely planets. 'Ils ne font peur qu'aux enfants
[...] à cause de leur équipage extraordinaire; mais les enfants
sont en grand nombre' (5e Soir).

Fontenelle — like Cyrano de Bergerac and Bayle — mocks the
anthropocentrism responsible for the Ptolemaic view of the universe. We like to think that we are the centre of everything and
that all things were created for us:

Notre folie, à nous autres, est de croire aussi que toute la nature, sans
exception, est destinée à nos usages; et quand on demande, à nos philosophes, à quoi sert ce nombre prodigieux d'étoiles fixes, dont une partie
suffirait pour faire ce qu'elles font toutes, ils vous répondent froidement
qu'elles servent à leur réjouir la vue.                            (1er Soir)

Not merely is man not the centre of the universe for Fontenelle,
but he devotes a good deal of space to arguing — hence the title of
the work — that all the planets may be inhabited and that all the
stars may have inhabited planets.

... toutes les preuves qu'on peut souhaiter d'une pareille chose, vous les
avez; la ressemblance entière des planètes avec la terre qui est habitée,
l'impossibilité d'imaginer aucun autre usage pour lequel elles eussent
été faites, la fécondité et la magnificence de la nature, de certains égards
qu'elle paraît avoir eus pour les besoins de leurs habitants, comme d'avoir
donné des lunes aux planètes éloignées du soleil, et plus de lunes aux
plus éloignées; et ce qui est très important, tout est de ce côté-là, et rien
du tout de l'autre; et vous ne sauriez imaginer le moindre sujet de doute,
si vous ne reprenez les yeux et l'esprit du peuple.               (6e Soir)

This view is not without theological implications, which Fontenelle
mentions in his preface:

La postérité d'Adam n'a pas pu s'étendre jusques dans la lune, ni envoyer des colonies en ce pays-là. Les hommes qui sont dans la lune ne
sont donc pas fils d'Adam. Or, il serait embarrassant, dans la théologie,
qu'il y eût des hommes qui ne descendissent pas de lui.

He covers himself, however, by denying that he thinks that the inhabitants of the moon are men: the diversity of nature is such that they are certainly not like us.

In the *Histoire des Oracles*, Fontenelle is again a vulgarizer – this time of the Latin *Oracles of the Pagans* of the Dutch scholar, Van Dale, which he presents in a more palatable form: 'j'ai pris sa science, et j'ai hasardé de me servir de mon esprit tel qu'il est [...] je me suis imaginé que j'entretenais mon lecteur' (Preface). The work consists of two dissertations, the first showing that the oracles of antiquity were not the work of demons, and the second that they did not – as Bossuet, for example, held – disappear at the birth of Christ, but that they survived as long as paganism and that their decline was due to natural causes.

Scepticism about the supernatural is Fontenelle's main theme. A natural explanation is to be preferred to a supernatural one, but, above all, the facts must be carefully examined before a super-natural phenomenon is accepted: 'Assurons-nous bien du fait, avant que de nous inquiéter de la cause.' Mankind is only too prone to believe in the supernatural: 'si l'on a un peu étudié l'esprit humain, on sait quelle force le merveilleux a sur lui'. True to his principles, Fontenelle examines the evidence for oracles, shows that accounts of them are often untrustworthy and full of improbabilities and inconsistencies, and concludes that, far from being supernatural in origin, they were the work of unscrupulous priests exploiting human credulity:

... je voudrais bien qu'on me dît pourquoi les démons ne pouvaient pré-dire l'avenir que dans des trous, dans des cavernes et dans des lieux obscurs, et pourquoi ils ne s'avisaient jamais d'animer une statue, ou de faire parler une prêtresse dans un carrefour, exposée de toutes parts aux yeux de tout le monde.

The implications of Fontenelle's work are not quite so innocuous as this outline might suggest. In distinguishing between revelation and reason – like the fideists and Descartes –, he comes close to identifying revelation with what is unreasonable.

Car je conçois que Dieu n'a parlé aux hommes que pour suppléer à la faiblesse de leurs connaissances, qui ne suffisaient pas à leurs besoins, et que tout ce qu'il ne leur a pas dit est de telle nature qu'ils le peuvent apprendre d'eux-mêmes, ou qu'il n'est pas nécessaire qu'ils le sachent.

As an example, he quotes the existence of angels and demons, known to us by revelation, 'mais il n'est point permis à la raison humaine de nous en assurer'; he emphasizes this last point by showing that the belief in angels and demons is in fact not reason-able. For Fontenelle, it can be taken for granted that a widely held notion is false ('Il faut des forces pour résister au torrent, mais il n'en faut point pour le suivre'), and he argues that far more weight is to be attached to the opinion of the small number of ancients who were sceptical about oracles than to the credulous multitude. The application of this principle to contemporary life is not difficult. Further, Fontenelle attributes oracles to the trickery of priests taking advantage of human credulity. Since Fontenelle has no doubt that men are still gullible –

Donnez-moi une demi-douzaine de personnes à qui je puisse persuader que ce n'est pas le soleil qui fait le jour, je ne désespérerai pas que des nations entières n'embrassent cette opinion. Quelque ridicule que soit une pensée, il ne faut que trouver moyen de la maintenir pendant quelque temps; la voilà qui devient ancienne, et elle est suffisamment prouvée.

– it may have occurred to some of Fontenelle's readers to wonder whether modern religion is essentially different from that of antiquity.[8]

The real importance of the *Histoire des Oracles*, however, as of Bayle's *Pensées sur la comète*, is in its method. The critical scrutiny of evidence, the close reasoning with which they demolish unsound views, the formidable marshalling of facts in support of their own hypothesis – these things show how Cartesian rationalism has joined forces with *libertinage* to produce a devastating rational scepticism. Fontenelle and Bayle are completely modern in their outlook.

[8] Mention should also be made of the posthumous essay, *De l'Origine des Fables*, in which Fontenelle shows how fables were the first attempts of primitive man to explain the world about him. 'Ne cherchons donc autre chose dans les fables, que l'histoire des erreurs de l'esprit humain.'

## Chapter 23

# LA BRUYÈRE

THE *CARACTÈRES* of Jean de La Bruyère (1645–96), published in 1688, are interesting, amongst other things, as a critical account of French society in the last years of the seventeenth century. La Bruyère was admirably placed for such a survey. A bourgeois of independent means, he accepted, at the age of thirty-nine, a post as tutor to the grandson of the *grand* Condé, the duc de Bourbon, and spent the rest of his life in one capacity or another in the family, in Paris or Versailles. As a member of the household of a prince of the blood royal, he was excellently placed to observe the great; and there is little doubt that his own consciousness of superior merit, coupled with his position as an underling, gave trenchancy to his criticisms of social injustice.

La Bruyère's work appeared in 1688 in the form of a translation of the Greek writer, Theophrastus, with La Bruyère's observations tacked on as an appendix. Since his translation of Theophrastus is careless and inaccurate and based on the Latin commentaries of earlier scholars, chiefly Casaubon, it has been surmised that it was made hastily at the last minute to guard against accusations of imitating Pascal and La Rochefoucauld. The work won immediate success; two further editions appeared in the same year; five more followed in the author's lifetime; and a ninth, incorporating his corrections, appeared posthumously in 1696. These editions, from the fourth onwards, contained amendments and additions: whereas the first edition contained 420 observations, the eighth contained 1,120, nearly three times as many.

La Bruyère accords the courtiers one virtue: some of them are prepared to accept a man for his innate qualities. Apart from this, La Bruyère's picture of life at court is unflattering. Not only is merit unrewarded there, but it is an abode of vice of all kinds, where to be virtuous is to be ruined, and where the motive force is self-interest: 'L'on se couche à la cour et l'on se lève sur l'intérêt [ . . . ]' (*De la Cour*, 22). Selfishness is the universal motive force, and hypocrisy the means:

Un homme qui sait la cour est maître de son geste, de ses yeux et de son visage; il est profond, impénétrable; il dissimule les mauvais offices, sourit à ses ennemis, contraint son humeur, déguise ses passions, dément son cœur, parle, agit contre ses sentiments. Tout ce grand raffinement n'est qu'un vice, que l'on appelle fausseté, quelquefois aussi inutile au courtisan pour sa fortune, que la franchise, la sincérité et la vertu.

*(De la Cour, 2)*

The courtier fawns on the great and the influential, only to desert them if they fall from favour. He simulates religion, if that can further his interests: 'Un dévot est celui qui sous un roi athée serait athée' *(De la Mode, 21)*. The true courtier seizes all he can with avidity and, in prosperity, is arrogant and hard-hearted. Court life, a life of intrigue, of shameless demands for favours, of waiting for the King's smile, of dancing attendance on the great, is empty and fundamentally unsatisfying: 'La cour ne rend pas content; elle empêche qu'on ne le soit ailleurs' *(De la Cour, 8)*.[1]

Equally unflattering is the account of the great nobles, who lack discernment, surround themselves with inferior, untrustworthy men, and are blind to true worth. Ignorant and idle, neglectful even of their own affairs and occupied with trivialities, they have no real merit, though they are given to mockery of others. Their pretensions correspond to no reality:

... ce qu'il y a jamais eu de mieux pensé, de mieux dit, de mieux écrit, et peut-être d'une conduite plus délicate, ne nous est pas toujours venu de leur fonds. Ils ont de grands domaines et une longue suite d'ancêtres: cela ne leur peut être contesté.  *(Des Grands, 19)*

There is no essential difference between a nobleman and a commoner; indeed, in a famous paragraph, La Bruyère compares the two classes to the advantage of the latter:

Là se montrent ingénument la grossièreté et la franchise; ici se cache une sève maligne et corrompue sous l'écorce de la politesse. Le peuple n'a guère d'esprit, et les grands n'ont point d'âme: celui-là a un bon fond, et n'a point de dehors; ceux-ci n'ont que des dehors et qu'une simple superficie. Faut-il opter? Je ne balance pas; je veux être peuple.  *(Des Grands, 25)*

There are, not only in the *Caractères* themselves, but in the *Discours sur Théophraste* prefixed to them, some vivid glimpses of the capital – its public promenades and its traffic, its amusements and its way of life, the theatre, and the salons with their cliquishness, their puerile dissection of love, and their false refinement. The Parisians are condemned for their gaming, their *dévotion*, their marital infidelities, and the futility of their social life. La Bruyère protests – reminding us of *Le Bourgeois gentilhomme* – against the wealthy merchants who abandon their trade, ape the nobility,

[1] Mention should be made of the general description of the court *(De la Cour,* 74), the description of the courtiers following military campaigns *(Des Jugements,* 99), and the long portrait of a courtier *(De la Cour,* 62), which are too long to quote.

and ruin themselves, and lists the various dishonest practices of shopkeepers; otherwise, with the exception of the lawyers and the *partisans*, he says little about the middle classes. Of law and lawyers, however, he has a good deal to say – of the jealousy between the various classes of lawyers (*grande robe, petite robe,* and *avocats*), of their extravagance and pretensions to nobility, of the slowness of legal procedure, of the excessive importance attached to formalities, and of sundry legal abuses, such as the practice of soliciting judges, the use of torture, and the lack of provision for training magistrates. But it is above all the spectacle of the tax farmers, the *partisans*, that arouses his ire. Ex-valets for the most part, enriching themselves by unscrupulous means and squandering their wealth once it is amassed, La Bruyère pillories them above all for their inhumanity. 'Un bon financier ne pleure ni ses amis, ni sa femme, ni ses enfants' (*Des Biens de Fortune,* 34).

Si l'on partage la vie des P.T.S. en deux portions égales, la première, vive et agissante, est toute occupée à vouloir affliger le peuple, et la seconde, voisine de la mort, à se déceler et à se ruiner les uns les autres.
(*Des Biens de Fortune,* 32)

*Champagne,* au sortir d'un long dîner qui lui enfle l'estomac, et dans les douces fumées d'un vin d'Avenay ou de Sillery, signe un ordre qu'on lui présente, qui ôterait le pain à toute une province si l'on n'y remédiait. Il est excusable: quel moyen de comprendre, dans la première heure de la digestion, qu'on puisse quelque part mourir de faim? (*Des Biens de Fortune,* 18)

Though La Bruyère criticizes the Parisians for their lack of knowledge of the country, and though he regards a country life as preferable to, and healthier than, a city life, the provinces do not bulk large in the *Caractères.* He is scathing on the subject of provincial towns with their feuds and petty jealousies. His comments on the provincial nobility are pungent:

Le noble de province, inutile à sa patrie, à sa famille et à lui-même, souvent sans toit, sans habits et sans aucun mérite, répète dix fois le jour qu'il est gentilhomme, traite les fourrures et les mortiers de bourgeoisie, occupé toute sa vie de ses parchemins et de ses titres, qu'il ne changerait pas contre les masses d'un chancelier.      (*De l'Homme,* 130)

The peasants make one of their rare appearances in seventeenth-century literature in the pages of La Bruyère.

L'on voit certains animaux farouches, des mâles et des femelles, répandus par la campagne, noirs, livides et tout brûlés du soleil, attachés à la terre qu'ils fouillent et qu'ils remuent avec une opiniâtreté invincible; ils ont comme une voix articulée, et quand ils se lèvent sur leurs pieds, ils montrent une face humaine, et en effet ils sont des hommes. Ils se retirent la nuit dans des tanières, où ils vivent de pain noir, d'eau et de racines; ils épargnent aux autres hommes la peine de semer, de labourer

et de recueillir pour vivre, et méritent ainsi de ne pas manquer de ce pain
qu'ils ont semé.[2]                              (*De l'Homme*, 128)

Considerable space, on the other hand, is devoted to the Church
and the religious life of the period. He attacks the worldliness of
the Church – the foppish *abbé*, the wealthy *curé* who hires a
monk to take his services for him, the cathedral dignitaries who
draw their pay but do not bother to attend services, the convent
that will allow only the rich girl, as he puts it, to take the vow of
poverty, the practice of trying to tempt people to church by turning sacred edifices into places of entertainment, the fine, beauti-
fully-composed, dramatically-delivered sermons from which
edification is absent. He condemns some abuses – the common
practice of daughters being compelled to enter convents by self-
interested parents, and the fashionable custom of having a
*directeur* (often a layman) in addition to a *confesseur*.

La Bruyère's picture of French society is not only vivid, but
highly critical. All men, for him, are essentially equal:

> Les grands ne doivent point aimer les premiers temps: ils ne leur sont
> point favorables; il est triste pour eux d'y voir que nous sortions tous du
> frère et de la sœur. Les hommes composent ensemble une même famille:
> il n'y a que le plus ou le moins dans le degré de parenté.    (*Des Grands*, 47)

Society, on the other hand, is based on inequality. Some inequality is necessary and is ordained by God, but too much, too
great a disproportion between wealth and poverty, is bad and man-
made. La Bruyère's sympathies are with the poor:

> Ce garçon si frais, si fleuri et d'une si belle santé est seigneur d'une
> abbaye et de dix autres bénéfices: tous ensemble lui rapportent six vingt
> mille livres de revenu, dont il n'est payé qu'en médailles d'or. Il y a ail-
> leurs six vingt familles indigentes qui ne se chauffent point pendant l'hiver,
> qui n'ont point d'habits pour se couvrir, et qui souvent manquent
> de pain; leur pauvreté est extrême et honteuse. Quel partage! Et cela ne
> prouve-t-il pas clairement un avenir?[3]    (*Des Biens de Fortune*, 26)

The last sentence should be noted: the conclusion that La Bruyère
draws from the unequal distribution of worldly goods is not that
something must be done, but that the balance must surely be re-
dressed in another life.

   [2] This passage, which first appeared in the fourth edition (1689), has
been variously interpreted as an accurate description of the seventeenth-
century peasant and as a piece of literary exaggeration. The condition of
the peasant varied, not only with the social group to which he belonged,
but from place to place and from time to time (there were years of plenty
and years of famine). That there was another side to the picture, La
Bruyère himself admits when he speaks of the 'laboureur, qui jouit du ciel,
qui cultive la terre, qui sème à propos, et qui fait de riches moissons'...
(*De la Ville*, 21). But that La Bruyère is here giving an accurate picture of
some seventeenth-century peasants, I have little doubt.
   [3] Cf. *Des Biens de Fortune*, 47 and 83.

La Bruyère criticizes not merely the inequality of society but its values. It does not prize the things that really matter; it does not reward literature or learning: 'Le comédien, couché dans son carrosse, jette de la boue au visage de CORNEILLE, qui est à pied' (Des Jugements, 17). Merit usually goes unrecognized and unhonoured; people are respected in proportion to their wealth, and the wealthy are assumed to have merit.

Si le financier manque son coup, les courtisans disent de lui: 'C'est un bourgeois, un homme de rien, un malotru'; s'il réussit, ils lui demandent sa fille.                    (Des Biens de Fortune, 7)

The more arrogant and unapproachable they are, the more they are likely to be respected. The age is materialistic — avid for riches, but ostentatious and extravagant, and its wealth is soon squandered. La Bruyère is far from sharing the worship of riches of the society about him and despises the rich — they are usually contemptible, without ability, vicious, and dishonest, though arrogant and prone to consider the acquisition of wealth as a proof of ability.

The age of La Bruyère was an age of transition, in which the old class distinctions were beginning to disappear and wealth was becoming more and more important. La Bruyère observes this with regret. He disapproves of the new upstart nobility, of those who illegitimately pass themselves off as noble, and of genuine nobles who marry their daughters to wealthy partisans; and he sighs nostalgically for the good old days when the bourgeois lived frugally and went on foot, and the classes were distinguished by their dress, each remaining in its proper place.

Si certains morts revenaient au monde, et s'ils voyaient leurs grands noms portés, et leurs terres les mieux titrées avec leurs châteaux et leurs maisons antiques, possédées par des gens dont les pères étaient peut-être leurs métayers, quelle opinion pourraient-ils avoir de notre siècle?                    (Des Biens de Fortune, 23)

But if La Bruyère regards social injustice with the eyes of one seeking a proof of immortality rather than as a reformer, and if his social ideal is that of the past rather than that of the future, nevertheless he does suggest some reforms. He is opposed to the use of torture, would like magistrates to receive some training, dislikes public executions, and suggests that posts should be filled by qualified men who apply for them:

L'on se présente encore pour les charges de ville, l'on postule une place dans l'Académie française, l'on demandait le consulat: quelle moindre raison y aurait-il de travailler les premières années de sa vie à se rendre capable d'un grand emploi, et de demander ensuite, sans nul mystère et sans nulle intrigue, mais ouvertement et avec confiance, d'y servir sa patrie, son prince, la république?                    (De la Cour, 44)

In his political views, there is a similar mixture of conservatism and advanced thinking. Since no form of government is in itself better than any other, one should accept without question that established in one's own country. The French constitution is monarchical, but monarchy should not be allowed to degenerate into despotism or tyranny. A good king is not a tyrant: he has not only rights to enjoy, but duties to fulfil. In fact, there is an implicit contract between king and subject:

> Il y a un commerce ou un retour de devoirs du souverain à ses sujets, et de ceux-ci au souverain: quels sont les plus assujettissants et les plus pénibles, je ne le déciderai pas. Il s'agit de juger, d'un côté, entre les étroits engagements du respect, des secours, des services, de l'obéissance, de la dépendance; et d'un autre, les obligations indispensables de bonté, de justice, de soins, de défense, de protection. Dire qu'un prince est arbitre de la vie des hommes, c'est dire seulement que les hommes par leurs crimes deviennent naturellement soumis aux lois et à la justice, dont le prince est le dépositaire: ajouter qu'il est maître absolu de tous les biens de ses sujets, sans égards, sans compte ni discussion, c'est le langage de la flatterie, c'est l'opinion d'un favori qui se dédira à l'agonie.
> (*Du Souverain*, 28)

The good king is the father of his people, the shepherd of his flock; he avoids war, and encourages trade and commerce and the arts. Moreover, he chooses ministers who are popular:

> C'est un extrême bonheur pour les peuples quand le prince admet dans sa confiance et choisit pour le ministère ceux mêmes qu'ils auraient voulu lui donner, s'ils en avaient été les maîtres.        (*Du Souverain*, 23)

From this reflection, it is not a far step to the idea of a constitutional monarchy.

There is, then, much in La Bruyère that anticipates the future — his idea of a social contract, his criticisms of the inequality and injustice of society, for example. He would certainly have welcomed *la carrière ouverte aux talents*, and, if he does not express the ideal of liberty, it is clear that he would have liked more equality, and that he would not have been opposed to fraternity: discussing the embarrassment that arises from the social hierarchy, he remarks:

> ... ne reviendrait-il pas au même de renoncer à toute hauteur et à toute fierté, qui convient si peu aux faibles hommes, et de composer ensemble, de se traiter tous avec une mutuelle bonté, qui, avec l'avantage de n'être jamais mortifiés, nous procurerait un aussi grand bien que celui de ne mortifier personne?        (*De l'Homme*, 131)

His humanitarianism, his pity for the poor, his dislike of war, his disapproval of the use of torture and of public executions, his antipathy even for just punishments—

> Il faut des saisies de terre et des enlèvements de meubles, des prisons et des supplices, je l'avoue; mais justice, lois et besoins à part, ce m'est une chose toujours nouvelle de contempler avec quelle férocité les hommes traitent d'autres hommes.        (*De l'Homme*, 127)

– also anticipate the future. There are, indeed, moments in reading
La Bruyère when one seems to hear the rumble of the distant
tumbrils. And yet, in many ways he belongs to the past. He is not
only, unlike the *philosophes*, religious; he is intolerant, and approves
of the revocation of the Edict of Nantes. He sees kings as the
image of God, and he mistrusts reform.

*Les Caractères* are a study of seventeenth-century France; but
they are much more besides, and contain La Bruyère's reflections
on many subjects. He has, for instance, a good deal to say about
literature, particularly in his first chapter. In the main, his views
are the prevalent views of the seventeenth century – literature
should aim at instructing, as well as at giving pleasure; its field is
*le vrai*, and 'tout l'esprit d'un auteur consiste à bien définir et à
bien peindre' (*Des Ouvrages de l'Esprit*, 14), though not all subjects
that are true or natural are fit subjects for literature; imagination
should be held in check by judgment and taste; clarity and the use
of the one right word or expression are the mark of good style;
an author should welcome and seek criticism. In the *Caractères*,
published during the *querelle des Anciens et des Modernes*, La
Bruyère supports the ancients. He praises the writers of antiquity,
insists that one cannot 'rencontrer le parfait, et s'il se peut, surpasser les anciens que par leur imitation' (*Des Ouvrages*, 15), and
attacks the supporters of the moderns – Fontenelle, Perrault, and
the *Mercure Galant*. On the other hand, his classicism is not
narrow. Like Boileau, he considers that a work may be good despite its faults (*Le Cid*, for example); great geniuses, he asserts, are
not to be bound by rules, and works of literature should be judged
not by rules, but by their beauties, the feelings they arouse:

> Quand une lecture vous élève l'esprit, et qu'elle vous inspire des senti-
> ments nobles et courageux, ne cherchez pas une autre règle pour juger
> l'ouvrage; il est bon, et fait de main d'ouvrier. (*Des Ouvrages*, 31)

Like Boileau, too, La Bruyère is interested in the sublime, the
indefinable quality that makes a work great, and finds that it is
associated with simplicity. And like La Fontaine, La Bruyère
protests against usage which has deprived the French language of
so many expressive old words.

La Bruyère is not only a theorist, he is a critic, too, whose
judgments are always of interest. He is typical of his age in his
preference for Malherbe over Théophile and in his condemnation
of Ronsard. On the other hand, if he cannot accept the whole of
Rabelais, he appreciates some aspects of his genius. Particularly
interesting are his views on the great seventeenth-century writers,
Molière, Corneille, and Racine, though his famous parallel between

Corneille and Racine is not, it should be said, altogether fair to the former – as a supporter of the ancients and the adversary of Thomas Corneille and Fontenelle, La Bruyère could not be altogether just to the relative of two of his adversaries and one of the strongest arguments they could advance in favour of the superiority of the moderns. *Des Ouvrages de l'Esprit*, it is interesting to note, contains an analysis of the various reasons which prevent impartiality in judging works of literature – factiousness and *esprit de coterie* are there, along with jealousy and the fear of being in a minority.

La Bruyère, too, formulates his ideas on *honnêteté*, on conversation and behaviour in society. The *honnête homme* will adapt himself to the persons with whom he is speaking, will suit his remarks to his company, and will never be importunate:

...un homme habile sent s'il convient ou s'il ennuie; il sait disparaître le moment qui précède celui où il serait de trop quelque part.

(*De la Société*, 2)

He will not dogmatize or be pedantic, will draw others out rather than talk himself, will avoid boasting and buffoonery, and will not bear the stamp of a particular profession. He will eschew affectation – here, as in everything else, La Bruyère is the enemy of all sham –, speaking simply, straightforwardly, and sincerely. He will, however, unlike Alceste, combine sincerity with politeness, which 'fait paraître l'homme au dehors comme il devrait être intérieurement' (*De la Société*, 31). As for ladies, they, too, will be natural and unaffected in complexion as in character, and will avoid the hypocrisy of being *dévotes* or *prudes*.

More important, the *Caractères* are a study of man, seventeenth-century and universal. Many reflections are concerned with the study of human character, the analysis of the human heart, and the nature of human life. Less systematic than Pascal and La Rochefoucauld, La Bruyère treats a great variety of topics – giving and conferring benefits, stepmothers and mothers-in-law ('Un beau-père aime son gendre, aime sa bru. Une belle-mère aime son gendre, n'aime point sa bru. Tout est réciproque.' *De la Société*, 45), children, women, old age and death, for example. Some of his best reflexions are on love and friendship:

Etre avec des gens qu'on aime, cela suffit; rêver, leur parler, ne leur parler point, penser à eux, penser à des choses plus indifférentes, mais auprès d'eux, tout est égal. (*Du Cœur*, 23)

Il y a du plaisir à rencontrer les yeux de celui à qui l'on vient de donner.

(*Du Cœur*, 45)

Un beau visage est le plus beau de tous les spectacles; et l'harmonie la plus douce est le son de voix de celle que l'on aime. (*Des Femmes*, 10)

La Bruyère excels, in the seventeenth-century manner, at subtle distinctions, between love and friendship, hatred and antipathy, jealousy and emulation and envy, and so forth. He observes accurately, delicately:

Le commencement et le déclin de l'amour se font sentir par l'embarras où l'on est de se trouver seuls. *(Du Cœur*, 33)

Il est pénible à un homme fier de pardonner à celui qui le surprend en faute, et qui se plaint de lui avec raison: sa fierté ne s'adoucit que lorsqu'il reprend ses avantages et qu'il met l'autre dans son tort. *(Du Cœur*, 67)

And just as reflections like those make us feel that human emotions have not changed essentially in three hundred years, others show that men in society are not so different either — servants of the great looking down on those of lower rank than their masters, civilians in war time more eager for exciting news than for the avoidance of bloodshed, men and women disagreeing in their judgments on a woman, for example, are still recognizable types. So are the many characters who appear in the *portraits* which occupy so large a part of the *Caractères*.

La Bruyère's book contains a general picture of man, not on the whole an optimistic one, not far removed from the views of Pascal and La Rochefoucauld and indeed in some particulars directly influenced by them. Men are motivated by self-interest, self-seeking, avid for wealth, naturally quarrelsome, and addicted to war. They are inconstant, full of contradictions, constantly changing, and incapable of sustaining an emotion or a passion for long. Our judgment and our sense of values are affected by fashion; we value what is rare and fashionable, not what is intrinsically valuable — like the *fleuriste*, who

ne va pas plus loin que l'oignon de sa tulipe, qu'il ne livrerait pas pour mille écus, et qu'il donnera pour rien quand les tulipes seront négligées et que les œillets auront prévalu. *(De la Mode*, 2)

Our way of life is a matter of custom, not of reason; we devote ourselves to the idle social round.

Life itself is unhappy. We look forward, instead of living in the present; we are born for 'l'infortune, la douleur et la pauvreté' *(De l'Homme*, 23):

Les choses les plus souhaitées n'arrivent point; ou si elles arrivent, ce n'est ni dans le temps ni dans les circonstances où elles auraient fait un extrême plaisir. *(Du Cœur*, 62)

Il faut rire avant que d'être heureux, de peur de mourir sans avoir ri. *(Du Cœur*, 63)

Il n'y a pour l'homme que trois événements: naître, vivre et mourir. Il
ne se sent pas naître, il souffre à mourir, et il oublie de vivre.
                                                (*De l'Homme*, 48)

A certain melancholy disillusionment, alleviated by a sense of the
consolation to be derived from human relationships, is, perhaps,
the distinguishing mark of La Bruyère.

La Bruyère's own personal philosophy is the antithesis of human
life as it is generally lived. What matters are virtue and real worth,
not rank, or outward show, or wealth, or *gloire*; sham and affectation are to be avoided. Life is transient; it behoves us to bear in
mind how short it is, how soon we shall be gone, and, instead of
wasting time, to employ it well.

Chaque heure en soi comme à notre égard est unique; est-elle écoulée
une fois, elle a péri entièrement, les millions de siècles ne la ramèneront
pas. Les jours, les mois, les années s'enfoncent et se perdent sans retour
dans l'abîme des temps; le temps même sera détruit: ce n'est qu'un point
dans les espaces immenses de l'éternité, et il sera effacé. Il y a de lé-
gères et frivoles circonstances du temps qui ne sont point stables, qui
passent, et que j'appelle des modes, la grandeur, la faveur, les richesses,
la puissance, l'autorité, l'indépendance, le plaisir, les joies, la superfluité.
Que deviendront ces modes quand le temps même aura disparu? La vertu
seule, si peu à la mode, va au delà des temps.      (*De la Mode*, 31)

Il n'y a pour l'homme qu'un vrai malheur, qui est de se trouver en faute,
et d'avoir quelque chose à se reprocher.          (*De l'Homme*, 136)

The primary aim, then, is virtue; and for La Bruyère an *homme
de bien* is much more than a hero or a great man. La Bruyère is
no stoic – he specifically attacks the stoic doctrine –, but he urges
the practice of philosophy, detachment, tolerance, moderation,
being contented with little. His ideal is that of a secluded, tranquil
life, spent in reading and meditation – preferably in the country:

Le monde est pour ceux qui suivent les cours ou qui peuplent les villes;
la nature n'est que pour ceux qui habitent la campagne: eux seuls vivent,
eux seuls du moins connaissent qu'ils vivent.    (*Des Jugements*, 110)

Seclusion for La Bruyère, however, as for La Fontaine, does not
exclude friendship: indeed, in the interests of one's friends, the
philosopher will forgo his tranquillity.

La Bruyère was a pious, religious man, and the last chapter of
his book, *Des Esprits forts*, is an attack on free-thought and a
defence of religion. Faith, for La Bruyère, is a matter of feeling
rather than of reason, but he does attempt to advance some arguments to prove the truth of religion. In answer to the objections of
the *libertins*, he argues that the world is not unjust; and he adapts
Descartes – I think; therefore I am spirit, not matter; therefore
God exists. He also advances the argument of the wonders of
nature and the order of the universe (43) and that of the success of

Christian missionaries abroad (29). This chapter is, perhaps, the least interesting to the modern reader.

If the subject-matter of *Les Caractères* is full of variety, so is the manner in which La Bruyère presents his observations and reflexions, as he himself points out:

Quelques-unes de ces remarques sont [courtes et concises], quelques autres sont plus étendues: on pense les choses d'une manière différente, et on les explique par un tour aussi tout différent, par une sentence, par un raisonnement, par une métaphore ou quelque autre figure, par un parallèle, par une simple comparaison, par un fait tout entier, par un seul trait, par une description, par une peinture: de là procède la longueur ou la brièveté de mes réflexions. *(Préface)*

*Des Biens de Fortune*, 25, for example, is a double comparison. La Bruyère takes us first into a kitchen, then behind the scenes of a theatre, and contrasts the disorder in both with the admirable results produced; then comes the climax, the point to which he is leading up: 'De même n'approfondissez pas la fortune des partisans.' *Du Souverain*, 29 is a leisurely description of a flock of sheep with their shepherd; then he draws the analogy: 'Image naïve des peuples et du prince qui les gouverne, s'il est bon prince.' *Des Ouvrages de l'Esprit*, 19 begins with an anecdote related by Ariste, which La Bruyère then broadens into a general truth. *Des Ouvrages de l'Esprit*, 23 is a brief, rapid conversation, followed by a comment. *Des Femmes*, 81 opens with a brief maxim or general statement, which is then illustrated by a long story – this is almost a fable of La Fontaine in prose. *De l'Homme*, 35 is another story or fable.

If La Bruyère can be pithy ('Le plaisir de la critique nous ôte celui d'être vivement touchés de très belles choses', *Des Ouvrages*, 20), he is also a master of the long sentence (*Du Mérite personnel*, 11 is a good example, unfortunately too long to quote). He is fond of antithesis:

Le rebut de la cour est reçu à la ville dans une ruelle, où il défait le magistrat, même en cravate et en habit gris, ainsi que le bourgeois en baudrier, les écarte et devient maître de la place: il est écouté, il est aimé; on ne tient guère plus d'un moment contre une écharpe d'or et une plume blanche, contre un homme qui *parle au Roi et voit les ministres*. Il fait des jaloux et des jalouses: on l'admire, il fait envie: à quatre lieues de là, il fait pitié. *(Des Femmes, 29)*

This reflexion is based on the antithesis between the courtier who is despised at Versailles and lionized in Paris. It also illustrates two other features of La Bruyère's style. The first is his habit of working back to his starting-point: the 'rebut de la cour' is fawned upon in Paris, but the last phrase, 'à quatre lieues de là, il fait pitié', harks back to the beginning, and reminds us that this is the 'rebut de la cour'. The other is the visual form in which La Bruyère casts his reflexions: this is not an abstract generalization, like La Rochefoucauld's maxims; it is an animated scene. La Bruyère excels, too, in his careful preparation of a rapid climax.

J'approche d'une petite ville, et je suis déjà sur une hauteur d'où je la découvre. Elle est située à mi-côte; une rivière baigne ses murs, et coule ensuite dans une belle prairie; elle a une forêt épaisse qui la couvre des vents froids et de l'aquilon. Je la vois dans un jour si favorable, que je compte ses tours et ses clochers; elle me paraît peinte sur le penchant de la colline. Je me récrie, et je dis: 'Quel plaisir de vivre sous un si beau ciel et dans ce séjour si délicieux!' Je descends dans la ville, où je n'ai pas couché deux nuits, que je ressemble à ceux qui l'habitent: j'en veux sortir.                                  (*De la Société*, 49)

The lengthy description of the town – again we notice the visual appeal of La Bruyère's reflexions – leads up to the devastating climax, contained in four words: 'j'en veux sortir'. This rapid climax is, perhaps, a development of the *pointe* affected by the poets of the seventeenth century.

*Portraits* constitute a considerable part of the *Caractères* and of their appeal. Popularized in France by the Grande Mademoiselle (who published a collection of portraits in 1659), the portrait was a description of the physical appearance and an analysis of the character of a particular person. La Bruyère's portraits are different. He makes us see his characters in action.

N** arrive avec grand bruit; il écarte le monde, se fait faire place; il gratte, il heurte presque; il se nomme: on respire, et il n'entre qu'avec la foule.                                  (*De la Cour*, 15)

Is this a portrait or a scene from a comedy? La Bruyère picks out the significant details. A good example is the contrasting portraits of Giton, the rich man, and Phédon, the poor man, in *Des Biens de Fortune*, 83: the contrast is expressed entirely in terms of appearance, movement, action. Giton, for example, 'déploie un ample mouchoir, et se mouche avec grand bruit; il crache fort loin, et il éternue fort haut', whereas Phédon 'tousse, il se mouche sous son chapeau, il crache presque sur soi, et il attend qu'il soit seul pour éternuer, ou, si cela lui arrive, c'est à l'insu de la compagnie'.

One further example:

J'entends *Théodecte* de l'antichambre; il grossit sa voix à mesure qu'il s'approche; le voilà entré: il rit, il crie, il éclate; on bouche ses oreilles, c'est un tonnerre. Il n'est pas moins redoutable par les choses qu'il dit que par le ton dont il parle. Il ne s'apaise, et il ne revient de ce grand fracas que pour bredouiller des vanités et des sottises. Il a si peu d'égard au temps, aux personnes, aux bienséances, que chacun a son fait sans qu'il ait eu l'intention de le lui donner; il n'est pas encore assis qu'il a, à

son insu, désobligé toute l'assemblée. A-t-on servi, il se met le premier
à table et dans la première place; les femmes sont à sa droite et à sa
gauche. Il mange, il boit, il conte, il plaisante, il interrompt tout à la fois.
Il n'a nul discernement des personnes, ni du maître, ni des conviés; il
abuse de la folle déférence qu'on a pour lui. Est-ce lui, est-ce *Euthydème*
qui donne le repas? Il rappelle à soi toute l'autorité de la table; et il y a un
moindre inconvénient à la lui laisser entière qu'à la lui disputer. Le vin
et les viandes n'ajoutent rien à son caractère. Si l'on joue, il gagne au jeu;
il veut railler celui qui perd, et il l'offense; les rieurs sont pour lui: il n'y a
sorte de fatuités qu'on ne lui passe. Je cède enfin et je disparais, incapable
de souffrir plus longtemps Théodecte, et ceux qui le souffrent.

                                                      (*De la Société*, 12)

This might have been expressed as a precept about *honnêteté* –
the *honnête homme* will avoid the various faults of Théodecte.
Yet La Bruyère does not choose to give a direct lesson in *honnêteté*,
but a portrait. Eighteenth-century *clefs* to the *Caractères* identify
Théodecte with the comte d'Aubigné, the brother of Mme de
Maintenon; but whether La Bruyère has a particular character in
mind or not, and, if so, whether that character is d'Aubigné or
another, are immaterial. The important thing is that the character
struck contemporaries by its truth, and that, since the modern
reader similarly feels that he knows such people, the truth of the
portrait is universal. The structure of the passage is one which we
have seen before in La Bruyère: a long preparation, leading up to
a rapid antithetical climax. Théodecte, with his conceit, his self-
assurance, and his complacency, is described at length; we are
told that there are people who take him at his face value. Then the
bubble is pricked: La Bruyère's own disgust is expressed: 'Je cède
enfin et je disparais, incapable de souffrir plus longtemps Théodecte, et ceux qui le souffrent.' Until this last sentence, La Bruyère
describes Théodecte without comment; and even his final comment
is expressed half as an action – 'je disparais'. The portrait of
Théodecte is almost entirely painted from the outside: we know
Théodecte's character from the sound of his voice, his actions: he
is seen primarily in movement: 'J'entends Théodecte... il rit,
il crie, il éclate... Il mange, il boit, il conte, il plaisante, il interrompt tout à la fois.' Finally – it is almost unnecessary to add –
this portrait is comic. Such beatific self-assurance and complacency
are in themselves comic, but the comedy is enhanced by slight
exaggeration: 'on bouche ses oreilles, c'est un tonnerre. [...] Si
l'on joue, il gagne au jeu'.

La Bruyère's work reflects the age of transition in which he
lived. In his literary doctrines and tastes, his interest in man, his
pessimistic conception of human nature and human life, his
religion, his theory of *honnêteté*, he clearly has much in common

with the great classical writers. On the other hand, there are one or two new features. His portraits, as we have seen, are made up of external details; we see the man from outside. His social criticism and some of his political ideas anticipate those of the eighteenth-century *philosophes*. And there are occasional traces of *sensibilité*. The love of primitive simplicity is there, in the idyllic description of the shepherd with his flock (*Du Souverain*, 29), and in the *Discours sur Théophraste*, where La Bruyère evokes the simplicity of the life of the early Athenians:

> La nature se montrait en eux dans toute sa pureté et sa dignité, et n'était point encore souillée par la vanité, par le luxe, et par la sotte ambition. Un homme n'était honoré sur la terre qu'à cause de sa force ou de sa vertu; il n'était point riche par des charges ou des pensions, mais par son champ, par ses troupeaux, par ses enfants, et ses serviteurs; sa nourriture était saine et naturelle, les fruits de la terre, le lait de ses animaux et de ses brebis; ses vêtements simples et uniformes, leurs laines, leurs toisons; ses plaisirs innocents, une grande récolte, le mariage de ses enfants, l'union avec ses voisins, la paix dans la famille. Rien n'est plus opposé à nos mœurs que toutes ces choses...

M. Garapon, in his edition, points out the sensibility which animates *Des Biens de Fortune*, 12: 'Quelle interruption heureuse pour moi que celle qui vous est utile!' *Des Ouvrages de l'Esprit*, 50 is a plea for overt weeping in the theatre:

> ...l'extrême violence que chacun se fait à contraindre ses larmes, et le mauvais ris dont on veut les couvrir prouvent clairement que l'effet naturel du grand tragique serait de pleurer tous franchement et de concert à la vue l'un de l'autre, et sans autre embarras que d'essuyer ses larmes...

Penetrating reflections on life, human nature, and society, shrewd advice, a sane philosophy, amusing portraits which are fundamentally as true today as they were three hundred years ago, an impression of seventeenth-century French life and a critical judgment on it, an impeccable and vivid style, great variety and liveliness of presentation, these are some of the things that have kept La Bruyère's book alive. He realizes his own ideal: 'bien définir et bien peindre [...] il faut exprimer le vrai pour écrire naturellement, fortement, délicatement' (*Des Ouvrages de l'Esprit*, 14). The ultimate secret is, perhaps, that he put himself into his work — the impersonality of classical art is seldom more than apparent — so that, in reading La Bruyère, we recognize a kindred spirit across the centuries.

## Chapter 24

# DRAMA AND PROSE FICTION

### I. DRAMA

Sur le Racine mort le Campistron pullule!

HUGO'S line may not be entirely fair; but tragedy, to retain its interest, requires more than competence, and too often the tragic poets of this period – La Grange-Chancel (1677–1758), Longepierre (1659–1721), Campistron (1656–1723), and Crébillon (1674–1762) – have little more to offer. The tragedies of the period, however, are not entirely devoid of interest.[1] Campistron's *Andronic* (1685), a dramatization of Saint-Réal's *Dom Carlos*, transposed into an oriental setting, is a simple, moving play. In *Tiridate* (1691), going one better than Racine in *Phèdre*, he portrays a hero who, in spite of himself, has conceived an incestuous passion for his sister. These two plays, says Carrington Lancaster, 'are, among the tragedies of the century, surpassed only by those of Corneille and Racine'.[2] Crébillon, in his most sombre and powerful plays, harks back to the violent and unnatural passions found in Racine's *Thébaïde*, Corneille's *Rodogune*, and some of the plays of Hardy. Atrée, in *Atrée et Thyeste* (1707), wreaks vengeance on his brother, Thyeste, by serving up to him in a goblet, on pretext of a reconciliation, the blood of Thyeste's son, whom Atrée has murdered. In *Rhadamisthe et Zénobie* (1711), Pharasmane and his two sons, Rhadamisthe and Arsame, are all three rivals for the same woman and for the throne of Armenia. Rhadamisthe, violent and jealous, but not devoid of nobility, is an interesting character. Having compelled his cousin, Zénobie, to marry him by threatening to kill her father, he has not only killed her father, but, in a fit of jealousy, his wife as well. His subsequent remorse makes him a somewhat Byronic figure:

furieux, incertain,
Criminel sans penchant, vertueux sans dessein,

---

[1] Nor should it be forgotten that *Esther* and *Athalie* belong to this period.

[2] *A History of French Dramatic Literature in the Seventeenth Century*, Part IV, vol. I, 1940, p. 277.

> Jouet infortuné de ma douleur extrême,
> Dans l'état où je suis, me connais-je moi-même?
> Mon cœur, de soins divers sans cesse combattu,
> Ennemi du forfait sans aimer la vertu,
> D'un amour malheureux déplorable victime,
> S'abandonne aux remords sans renoncer au crime.
> Je cède au repentir, mais sans en profiter;
> Et je ne me connais que pour me détester.
> Dans ce cruel séjour sais-je ce qui m'entraîne,
> Si c'est le désespoir, ou l'amour, ou la haine?
> J'ai perdu Zénobie: après ce coup affreux,
> Peux-tu me demander encor ce que je veux?
> Désespéré, proscrit, abhorrant la lumière,
> Je voudrais me venger de la nature entière.
> Je ne sais quel poison se répand dans mon cœur;
> Mais, jusqu'à mes remords, tout y devient fureur.

At the end of the play, he dies at his father's hands. Pharasmane, the enemy of Rome, whose harshness has alienated his children's affection, and Zénobie, who loves her husband, even though he has killed her father, are worthy to stand beside him.

Far more comedies were written than tragedies in this period. The main comic dramatists were Jean-François Regnard (1655–1709) and Florent Carton, sieur Dancourt (1661–1725); but beside them were many others – Hauteroche (1630?–1707), Boursault (1638–1701), Baron (1653–1729), Brueys (1640–1723), and Dufresny (c. 1654–1724). Nor should it be forgotten that Lesage (1668–1747), although his main work, *Gil Blas*, belongs to the eighteenth century proper, wrote his earlier works in this period – comedies, notably *Crispin rival de son maître* (1707) and *Turcaret* (1709), and the novel, *Le Diable boiteux*.

The comedies of the period, mostly written in prose – Regnard's major plays are in verse –, deal, like those of Molière, with young lovers crossed in love, who, with the help of their wily servants, overcome the obstacles to their union (usually the opposition of their parents); and they have a family resemblance. The interest of most of them lies in the plot; but the level of comic technique is high, and they are lively, amusing, and readable. The influence of Molière is evident. Moreover, French writers were beginning to write for the Italians – Regnard's masterpieces, for example, were preceded by eleven plays composed (some in collaboration with Dufresny) for the Italian actors.[3] Two comedies of intrigue that, perhaps, deserve to be singled out for separate mention are *L'Avocat Patelin* of Brueys (1706), a version of the medieval farce, and Regnard's *Légataire universel* (1708).

In imitation of Molière, his successors frequently try their hand

---

[3] The Italians, who, since 1680, had occupied the Hôtel de Bourgogne, were expelled in 1697 for putting on a play entitled *La Fausse Prude*, taken as a slight on Mme de Maintenon.

at *comédies de caractère* – Baron, for example, in *L'Homme à bonne fortune* (1686), in which the main character, a kind of Don Juan, is an adventurer who carries on affairs with several ladies at once, and *La Coquette et la fausse prude* (1686), the title of which describes the main characters. Dancourt, too, has a play about a professional ladies' man, *Le Chevalier à la mode* (1687), and Dufresny one about a coquette, *La Coquette du village* (1715). Other types depicted are the bad-tempered man (*Le Grondeur*, 1691, of Brueys and Palaprat), the gamester (notably in *Le Joueur* of Regnard, 1696), the absent-minded man (Regnard, *Le Distrait*, 1697), and the masterful but froward woman (Dufresny, *L'Esprit de contradiction*, 1700). These attempts at character comedy are amusing, but not particularly memorable.

The most interesting comedies are those which afford us a glimpse of the manners of the age; and, on the whole, they confirm La Bruyère. The rage for gaming is described, not only in Regnard's *Joueur*, but also in Dancourt's *Désolation des Joueuses* (1687). The middle classes are seen imitating the style of life of the nobles in Dancourt's plays, *Le Chevalier à la mode* and *Les Bourgeoises à la mode* (1692). *Partisans*, usurers, and go-betweens occur in some plays. Several are set in the country, and contain various country types – millers, factors, farmers, *hobereaux*, and the like – though the characterization seems conventional. A particularly amusing play is *La Maison de campagne* of Dancourt (1688), in which the owner of a house in the country is so exasperated by the large number of friends, relatives, and neighbours who expect free hospitality, that he turns it into an inn. One is, perhaps, struck, above all, by the prevalence in the comedies of the period of pseudo-nobles, adventurers, and shady characters who earn a precarious living at the card table and by battening on women. The valets and soubrettes tend to be more selfish, more openly grasping and ambitious, than those of Molière. Husbands and wives are often on bad terms and unfaithful to each other (in spirit, at least), as in Dancourt's *Bourgeoises* and Dufresny's *Double Veuvage* (1702). Even the young lovers are sometimes affected by the prevailing corruption – the man, wanting to marry a wealthy wife, and prepared to resort to dishonest tricks to raise money (Valère in Lesage's *Crispin rival de son maître*, for example), the woman flighty and flirtatious (Angélique in Dancourt's *Parisienne*, 1691). Eraste in Regnard's *Légataire universel*, believing his uncle dead, removes the money from the corpse and allows his valet, Crispin, to impersonate his uncle and dictate a false will; when the uncle revives, he does not get his money back until he promises to maintain the will.

Boursault's plays stand somewhat apart. *La Comédie sans titre*, later renamed *Le Mercure galant* (1683), shows us the callers who beset the editor of the *Mercure*, wanting him to publish their work, write articles about them, or give them publicity. The two Aesop plays – *Les Fables d'Esope ou Esope à la Ville* (1690), and *Esope à la cour* (a *comédie héroïque;* 1701) – provide a framework for a large number of fables, a measure of La Fontaine's popularity. All three plays contain a certain amount of social criticism, attacking the corruption of the age, the hypocrisy and ruthless ambition of the court, the uselessness and injustice of country gentry, the dishonesty of tax officials, tax farmers, and lawyers, bourgeois usurping nobility, and the like; and the two Aesop plays show a strong moralizing tendency.

The most interesting, if not the most amusing, of the plays of this period is Lesage's *Turcaret*, which, indeed, contains the essence of the rest. It portrays a type, Turcaret, the unscrupulous tax-farmer, and Lesage's portrait agrees with those of La Bruyère. Turcaret, who began life as a valet, has enriched himself by unscrupulous means, and ruins himself by his extravagance. He lives apart from his wife, and passes himself off as a widower – as she passes herself off as a widow – to further his amorous designs. He is as heartless a brother as he is a husband. Around him are grouped a number of characters, equally grasping and dishonest. Turcaret loves a baroness, who mulcts him, while herself loving a chevalier, a gamester and adventurer, who battens on her:

J'admire le train de la vie humaine! Nous plumons une coquette, la coquette mange un homme d'affaires: l'homme d'affaires en pille d'autres: cela fait un ricochet de fourberies le plus plaisant du monde.

There are, too, Turcaret's wife; his sister, a vendor of toilet requisites and a marriage-broker; his agent, M. Rafle; a thriftless marquis; and the servants. The two valets are particularly interesting; they are clearly depicted as being at the beginning of a career similar to that of Turcaret himself, and the play ends with Frontin's words: 'Voilà le règne de M. Turcaret fini; le mien va commencer.'

## II. PROSE FICTION

Not one novel in the usual sense of the word has survived from the last period of the reign of Louis XIV, though one or two works of prose fiction deserve to be mentioned.

Courtilz de Sandras (c. 1644–1712) was a writer of pseudo-memoirs, roughly comparable to his English contemporary, Daniel Defoe. He published anonymously memoirs purporting to be genuine, as Defoe published the *Journal of the Plague Year*, with the difference that Courtilz de Sandras attributed his works to well-known characters who had really existed – the *Mémoires de M. L. C. D. R.* (M. le comte de Rochefort; 1686), the *Mémoires de M. d'Artagnan* (1700), and the *Mémoires de la Marquise de Fresne* (1701). The best-known of these are the *Mémoires de d'Artagnan*, known to all readers of Dumas's *Trois Mousquetaires*, because Dumas mentions them in the preface to his novel – he borrowed the names of his three musketeers and one or two other details from Courtilz de Sandras's book. The *Mémoires de d'Artagnan* are in no sense a novel: there is no plot, and the book reads very much like any volume of genuine memoirs. D'Artagnan entertainingly relates the history of the age with occasional peeps behind the scenes, and gives details of his own career, his campaigns, his private adventures, and his love affairs, devoting rather more space to these last than is usual in genuine memoirs. Courtilz de Sandras's works represent a transitional stage between memoirs and the memoir-novel of the following century.

It was in 1697 that Charles Perrault published his *Contes de ma mère Loye*, containing stories which have delighted children on both sides of the Channel ever since – Little Red Riding-hood, Bluebeard, Puss-in-Boots, Cinderella, Riquet à la Houppe, Hop o' my Thumb, and Sleeping Beauty.[4] Another writer of fairy-stories was Mme d'Aulnoy, whose *Contes nouveaux ou les Fées à la mode* appeared the year after Perrault's collection.

Although Lesage will properly be treated in the next volume of this *History*, a survey of this period would be incomplete without some mention of him. *Le Diable boiteux*, indebted to La Bruyère's *Caractères*, appeared in 1707. A young Spanish gentleman rescues the devil, Asmodée, from a phial in which a magician has imprisoned him; out of gratitude, the devil shows him what is going on in Madrid and tells him about the people he sees. Such is the framework of this collection of sketches, anecdotes, and stories. It should not be forgotten, either, that the first part of Lesage's main work, *Gil Blas*, appeared in 1715, at the very end of the period under consideration.

[4] My daughter, Anne, contributes the following note:

'For me, these tales of Perrault have always stood out from the mass of fairy stories by many authors which one reads as a child. It is not so much the actual content of his stories (the same events with slight variations are found throughout Grimm, Lang, Andersen and the rest) as the spontaneity of the telling and in particular the individuality of the characters, that makes what he gives us all his own. Who else but Perrault would have mentioned, in *La Belle au Bois Dormant*, the steward's difficulty in finding an animal to kill that was "aussi dure" as the Princess "qui avait vingt ans passés"? Who else but Perrault would have made the distinction between Cinderella's traditional ugly sisters, that one was more polite than the other and called her 'Cendrillon' instead of 'Cucendron'? These details, and many more like them, show how these fairy tales bear the stamp of Charles Perrault's own individual style.'

One of the most interesting works of fiction of the period is *Les Illustres Françoises* (1713) of Robert Chasles (1659–c.1721). Here again, we are on the borderline of fiction and truth, since Chasles tells us in his preface that his stories relate true happenings, though he has changed the names of his characters and moved the action from the provinces to Paris. The characters belong to the upper middle class or to the minor aristocracy, and the first six of the seven stories which compose the work deal with their marriages in the face of parental opposition. These six stories are arranged in pairs in ascending order of dramatic quality. In the first two, the *Histoire de Monsieur Des Ronais et de Mademoiselle Dupuis* and the *Histoire de Monsieur de Contamine et d'Angélique*, parental opposition is overcome – M. Dupuis dies, and Mme Contamine gives her consent. In the next two, the *Histoire de Monsieur de Terny et de Mademoiselle de Bernay* and the *Histoire de Monsieur de Jussy et de Mademoiselle Fenouil*, the lovers marry despite parental opposition, and achieve happiness. In the last two, the *Histoire de Monsieur Des Prez et de Mademoiselle de l'Epine* and the *Histoire de Monsieur Des Frans et de Silvie*, the lovers marry in opposition to their parents' wishes, but with disastrous consequences: Mlle de l'Epine dies of the brutal treatment she receives at the hands of her father-in-law and her own mother; Silvie, whose marriage with Des Frans has been kept secret, falls a victim to the wiles of a lover, and dies of the callous treatment of her jealous husband. The seventh story, which is of a somewhat different nature, relates the various love affairs of the libertine, Dupuis, until he is reformed by the love of the virtuous Mme de Londé. One of his mistresses, a widow, claims for women the same freedom to indulge their passions as men; she attributes female virtue to fear of the consequences; and she carries her love of freedom to the extent of refusing to marry her lover even when she is with child by him. Chasles's widow is clearly the daughter of one of abbé de Pure's *précieuses*.

Chasles prides himself on the realism of his stories: 'On ne verra point ici de brave à toute épreuve, ni d'incidents surprenants; et cela parce que tout, en étant vrai, ne peut être que naturel.' The characters are for the most part a human mixture of good and bad qualities, neither wholly virtuous nor wholly vicious. M. Dupuis is an excellent example. For somewhat egoistical reasons, he refuses to allow his daughter to marry Des Ronais; but he likes Des Ronais and gives him money, and he is portrayed as an upright, sensible man. Des Ronais himself says:

> Quoique sa morale me fît enrager, je ne laissais pas de la trouver de fort bon sens; et si tout le monde en agissait comme lui, les enfants auraient pour leurs parents plus d'égards et de vénération.

Similarly, Mme Des Frans refuses to acknowledge Silvie publicly as her daughter-in-law; but her son's advocate, we are told, 'ne put désapprouver sa résolution ni ses raisons'. On the other hand, the young lovers are not depicted in a wholly favourable light. Des Ronais's love for Mlle Dupuis does not prevent him from having an illegitimate child by another woman. Des Frans treats Silvie heartlessly. Dupuis is an unscrupulous profligate until Mme de Londé reforms him. Mlle Fenouil becomes M. de Jussy's mistress. M. de Contamine would not have married Angélique if he could have seduced her; and if Angélique resists, it is less from disinterested love of virtue than from policy:

Elle connaissait qu'il était trop bien pris pour pouvoir se dégager, et qu'avec le temps, elle l'amènerait au point de dire les grands mots: ainsi elle résolut de paraître avec toute la vertu et la fierté qu'une fille peut avoir, sans pourtant le dégoûter par aucune incivilité; et jamais fille ne s'est mieux tirée d'un pas si difficile.

The structure of the book is also of interest. Des Frans returns to Paris after a long absence, and meets some old friends; they tell one another the story of their lives and of those of other friends. A consequence of this framework is that the stories are connected and the same characters recur in them. Mlle Dupuis, the heroine of the story of Des Ronais and herself, recurs in the story of M. de Contamine (Angélique was brought up in the household of M. Dupuis) and in that of M. de Terny and Mlle Bernay. Since, indeed, a letter from M. de Terny addressed to Mlle Dupuis aroused Des Ronais's jealousy, the story of M. de Terny has a bearing on that of Mlle Dupuis, and the story of Mlle Dupuis is not complete until we have heard the explanation of the letter given in the story of M. de Terny. Similarly, the *Histoire de Monsieur Des Frans et de Silvie* is not complete until we have read the *Histoire de Monsieur Dupuis et de Madame de Londé*. In the former, we learn that M. Des Frans surprised Silvie with a lover, Gallouin, the brother of Mme de Londé; until we have read the latter, we are ignorant – despite one or two hints – of Silvie's innocence. The *personnages reparaissants* and the interrelation of some of the stories of Balzac's *Comédie humaine* spring to mind.

### III. FÉNELON'S 'TÉLÉMAQUE'

It is legitimate to include *Les Aventures de Télémaque* (1699), the work by which François de Salignac de la Mothe-Fénelon, Archbishop of Cambrai (1651–1715), is chiefly remembered,[5]

---

[5] Fénelon became involved in a controversy with Bossuet over Mme Guyon and quietism; Bossuet triumphed, and Fénelon's defence of quietism (*Maximes des Saints*) was condemned by the Pope (1699). Of Fénelon's other works, the treatise *De l'Education des Filles* and the *Lettre sur les occupations de l'Académie* (1714) deserve separate mention.

in this chapter, on the grounds that, in the seventeenth century, the novel was considered to be a branch of the epic – Huet, in his letter, *De l'Origine des romans*, for instance, defines 'romans réguliers' as 'ceux qui sont dans les règles du poème héroïque'. For *Télémaque*, which recounts the wanderings of the hero in his search for his father, Ulysse, is not a novel, but a prose epic. It is composed like an epic: it plunges *in medias res*, and is divided into books. The gods intervene in the action: in particular, Télémaque's guide and companion, Mentor – whose name provided both the French and the English languages with a new noun – is none other than the goddess, Minerva. The stock features of the classical epic are present – descriptions of battles and shipwrecks, of Télémaque's armour and his visit to the underworld. And *Télémaque* is written in a poetical prose, interspersed with epic similes:

Tel qu'un beau lys au milieu des champs coupé dans sa racine par le tranchant de la charrue, languit et ne se soutient plus: il n'a point encore perdu cette vive blancheur et cet éclat qui charme les yeux; mais la terre ne le nourrit plus, et sa vie est éteinte. Ainsi le fils d'Idoménée, comme une jeune et tendre fleur, est cruellement moissonné dès son premier âge.

Long a favourite book for children, *Télémaque* no doubt appealed to them by its very considerable charm, and to their parents and preceptors by its didacticism. Fénelon, tutor to the young duc de Bourgogne, the son of the dauphin and a successor to the throne,[6] aimed at instructing his pupil, at making him a virtuous man and a good king. *Télèmaque*, in fact, is primarily a work of political theory, the equivalent in Fénelon's work of Bossuet's *Politique tirée de l'Ecriture sainte*. Fénelon, who earlier had violently condemned the policies of Louis XIV in his *Lettre de remontrance*, and who later collaborated with the duc de Chevreuse in drawing up a project of reform for the duc de Bourgogne,[7] was much preoccupied with the state of France under Louis XIV and with the problem of good and bad government.

The subject of *Télémaque* is the education of the hero by Minerva – or Mentor – until he is ready to stand on his own feet. Fénelon's views are clearly expressed in the advice of Mentor (the goddess of wisdom in person), in the speeches and actions of Télémaque (except when they are the subject of rebuke by Mentor), and by the examples of the good and bad kings whom Télémaque sees in the world about him or in the course of his journey through the underworld.

[6] In fact, Louis XIV outlived both the dauphin and the duc de Bourgogne, who died in 1712.
[7] For whom he also composed an *Examen de conscience sur les devoirs de la royauté*.

It is no easy matter to be a king, and good kings are rare. It is the duty of a king to devote himself to the welfare of his subjects:

Il peut tout sur les peuples; mais les lois peuvent tout sur lui. Il a une puissance absolue pour faire le bien, et les mains liées dès qu'il veut faire le mal. Les lois lui confient les peuples comme le plus précieux de tous les dépôts, à condition qu'il sera le père de ses sujets.

He must learn to be a judge of men, select good ministers, beware of flatterers, and seek friends who will point out his mistakes. He must not act as judge in his own cause, or intervene in religious matters. He must concern himself with the broad lines of policy, and leave the details to his ministers.

The prosperity of the nation is based on free trade and, above all, on agriculture. Luxury and voluptuousness are condemned as sapping courage, spreading disease, and causing men to esteem nothing but wealth. In reforming the states of Idoménée, Mentor insists on simplicity in dress, dwellings, furniture, and food, the example being set by the King. He prohibits luxury goods, and sends the artisans engaged in their manufacture back to the land. Idoménée's subjects are educated to be frugal, industrious, pious, virtuous, and law-abiding. No one is to possess more land than he needs, and taxation is to fall more heavily on the inefficient than on the industrious. Sculpture and painting are to commemorate great men and great actions, and music to be reserved for temples.

War is to be avoided: 'Jamais aucun peuple n'a eu un Roi conquérant, sans avoir beaucoup à souffrir de son ambition.' A good king must, however, be prepared for war. A good general must be vigilant and foresighted, unite valour with prudence, share the hardships of his men, give clear and precise orders, and care for the wounded. Both in war and in peace, the maxims of state-craft are those of ordinary morality. Télémaque refuses to tell a lie to save his life or to overthrow his enemy, Adraste, by fraud. Upright dealing, says Mentor, is the best bulwark of a state, since it ensures allies against an aggressor. Télémaque treats the van-quished with the same kind of generosity as Rabelais's Grandgosier and Gargantua, and they respond to it.

In his rejection of Machiavellianism and of wars of conquest, Fénelon is in the tradition of a long line of French political theorists, going back as far as Rabelais. Not unnaturally, his book was taken to be an attack on Louis XIV, and banned.

If *Télémaque* is of its period in its critical outlook, it also shows signs of sensibility. The cult of primitive simplicity appears in the idyllic description of the life of the farmer, whose evenings are spent singing with his family round the fire, and in the account of the ideal country of Betica, favoured by nature and inhabited by a race of philosophical and patriarchal nomads, who dwell in tents and live on fruit and milk. The inhabitants are mostly shepherds and ploughmen; and, while the men engage in these activities, their womenfolk make clothes and shoes for the family. The few artisans are carpenters, or ironworkers, engaged in the manufacture of ploughshares; the inhabitants of Betica do not exploit their gold and silver mines. All are equal, and all property is held in common. Moreover, Télémaque is a 'jeune homme sensible'. As he listens to the recital of Diomède's misfortunes, for example, his face betrays his emotions:

Quand Diomède commença à parler de ses longs malheurs, il espéra que cet homme majestueux serait son père. Aussitôt qu'il eut déclaré qu'il était Diomède, le visage de Télémaque se flétrit comme une belle fleur que les noirs aquilons viennent de ternir de leur souffle cruel. Ensuite les paroles de Diomède [ ... ] l'attendrirent par le souvenir des mêmes disgrâces souffertes par son père et par lui. Des larmes mêlées et de douceur et de joie, coulèrent sur ses joues, et il se jeta tout à coup sur Diomède pour l'embrasser.

*Chapter 25*

# SAINT-SIMON

ONE of the main glories of the seventeenth century is its wealth of memoirs. For those interested in seventeenth-century France, there are the *Œconomies royales* of Sully, the memoirs of Bassompierre, of Mlle de Montpensier (the Grande Mademoiselle), of Mme de Motteville, of Bussy-Rabutin (Mme de Sévigné's cousin), of La Rochefoucauld, and of Cardinal de Retz. Two volumes of memoirs of a slightly different kind – written not by their subject, but by a friend – deserve to be mentioned: the *Mémoires* of Pontis, written by Thomas du Fossé, and those of the comte de Grammont, written by his brother-in-law, the Irishman, Anthony Hamilton. Nor should Mme de Lafayette's life of Henriette d'Angleterre be overlooked, or Racine's history of Port-Royal, or the *Historiettes* of Tallemant des Réaux (1619–90) – a French equivalent of Aubrey's *Brief Lives*, and an excellent introduction to seventeenth-century France.

The greatest work of this kind, however, is the *Mémoires* of Louis de Rouvroy, duc de Saint-Simon (1675–1755). These were the work of a lifetime. Begun in 1694, after a reading of Bassompierre, when the author was nineteen, they were cast in their final form between the years 1739 and 1749, and first published in full in the nineteenth century. The convention which assigns Saint-Simon to the seventeenth century, though somewhat arbitrary, can be justified on the grounds that he began to write over twenty years before the death of Louis XIV and that, in style and outlook, he has little in common with the eighteenth century.

Saint-Simon relates in his *Mémoires* how his ambition was fired by his early reading of history and memoirs, which

me firent naître l'envie d'écrire aussi ceux de ce que je verrais, dans le désir et dans l'espérance d'être de quelque chose, et de savoir le mieux que je pourrais les affaires de mon temps.

He states his two aims in his *avant-propos*. The first was to lay bare the causes of the events which he was relating:

les intérêts, les vices, les vertus, les passions, les haines, les amitiés, et tous les autres ressorts, tant principaux qu'incidents, des intrigues, des

393

cabales et des actions publiques et particulières qui ont part aux événements qu'on écrit, et toutes les divisions, les branches, les cascades qui
deviennent les sources et les causes d'autres intrigues et qui forment
d'autres événements.

The second was to make the reader feel more like a participant
or a spectator than a reader of memoirs:

mettre son lecteur au milieu des acteurs de tout ce qu'il raconte, en sorte
qu'il croie moins lire une histoire ou des mémoires, qu'être lui-même dans
le secret de tout ce qui lui est représenté, et spectateur de tout ce qui est
raconté.

With this object, he deliberately includes – incurring the gratitude
of the reader – trivial details of the kind that most memorialists
suppress, but which convey the atmosphere of the age and make us
feel that we are better able to imagine life – some of its aspects at
least – in France in the last years of the reign of Louis XIV and
the first years of Louis XV than at almost any other period. Saint-
Simon was conscious of the shortcomings of his forerunners in this
respect.

On voudrait y voir les princes, avec leurs maîtresses et leurs ministres,
dans leur vie journalière. Outre une curiosité si raisonnable, on en con-
naîtrait bien mieux les mœurs du temps et le génie des monarques, celui
de leurs maîtresses et de leurs ministres, de leurs favoris, de ceux qui les
ont le plus approchés, et les adresses qui ont été employées pour les
gouverner ou pour arriver aux divers buts qu'on s'est proposés.

This passage, in fact, introduces an account of the way Mme de
Maintenon was treated at court, which ends with the further
reflection:

Ces bagatelles échappent presque toujours aux Mémoires; elles donnent
cependant plus que tout l'idée juste de ce que l'on y recherche, qui est le
caractère de ce qui a été, qui se présente ainsi naturellement par les faits.

Both these aims Saint-Simon achieves.

    The *Mémoires* of Saint-Simon are a chronicle of French history
from 1691 to 1723. Since, in recording the death of a character,
Saint-Simon surveys his life, the *Mémoires*, in an unsystematic
way, cover in fact a much longer period. The death of Louis XIV,
for example, introduces a general survey of his reign, and that of
Saint-Simon's own father leads to information about the reign of
Louis XIII. The work – as indeed, given Saint-Simon's aims, it
was bound to be – is immensely detailed and enormously long: in
the recent Pléiade edition the text occupies nearly 7,500 pages.
Besides relating events, Saint-Simon surveys the life of his characters, describes their appearance, and analyses their character, so
that he is a Retz, a Tallemant, and a La Bruyère rolled into one.

    Saint-Simon did not disdain to use written sources in order to
gain information – the memoirs of Dangeau, for example, which he

read and annotated in 1730 – but he also relied on his own sources and observation. He was, indeed, admirably qualified to write such a work. Officer and courtier, a friend of the duc de Beauvilliers (the only nobleman whom Louis XIV appointed minister), intimate with Philip of Orléans and a member of the Council of Regency after the death of Louis XIV, he had plenty of opportunities to see and hear what was going on, and was at times an active participant. The list of friends in high places whom he himself mentions as sources of information is a long one, including, amongst others, the duc de Chevreuse, Chamillart, Pontchartrain, Villeroy, Torcy, Boufflers, Père Le Tellier, and the princesse des Ursins. Moreover, it is clear from the *Mémoires* that he did not hesitate to ply them with questions. He tells us, for instance, that, on the way from Fontainebleau to Paris, he asked Louville so many questions that 'il arriva sans voix et ne pouvant plus parler'.

A close observer, Saint-Simon was also a critical one. Although he was a courtier, he was under no illusions about court life – 'un pays où le crédit et la considération faisaient plus que tout le reste', where success was more often due to bribery or a talent for cards than for anything else, where hypocrisy, malice, and baseness were universal. Saint-Simon has the ability to seize significant scenes and make them permanent. When Mlle de Roquelaure ran away with her lover, for example,

Cela se répandit incontinent dans la chambre, où la bonté de la cour brilla incontinent dans tout son lustre: à peine eut-on plaint un moment Mme de Roquelaure, que les uns par aversion des grands airs impérieux de cette pauvre mère, la plupart saisis du ridicule de l'enlèvement d'une créature que l'on savait très laide et bossue par un si vilain galant, s'en mirent à rire, et promptement aux grands éclats, et jusqu'aux larmes, avec un bruit tout à fait scandaleux. Mme de Maintenon s'y abandonna comme les autres, et corrigea tout le mal, sur la fin, en disant que cela n'était guère charitable, d'un ton qui n'était pas monté pour imposer.

After the first instinctive reaction, however, notes Saint-Simon, self-interest caused many fathers and mothers to sympathize with Mme de Roquelaure.

Saint-Simon is, above all, critical of Louis XIV, both as a man and as a king. As a man, he was – according to Saint-Simon – majestic, but ignorant and utterly selfish: 'Tant d'occupations étrangères et domestiques n'empêchèrent pas le Roi de s'amuser à des bals à Marly.' His disapproval of him as a king is even more pronounced. Louis, who liked to think of himself as governing France, surrounded himself with mediocre ministers and inexperienced young men, succumbing to 'les grâces de l'obscurité et du néant'. Of Montrevel, Saint-Simon remarks:

Sa sorte de fatuité, qui pourtant était extrême, était toute faite pour le Roi. Les dames, les modes, un gros jeu, un langage qu'il s'était fait de

phrases comme en musique, mais tout à fait vides de sens et fort ordinairement de raison, les grands airs, tout cela imposait aux sots, et plaisait
merveilleusement au Roi . . .

A bad judge of men, the King chose his servants and his generals
badly; and their jealousies often frustrated his plans. His insistence
on controlling campaigns from Versailles was disastrous – Saint-
Simon, of course, is concerned with the last twenty years or so of
his reign. Moreover, he was controlled by his ministers and Mme de
Maintenon, who effectively kept the true state of affairs from him.
His blunders are criticized mercilessly – his failure to maintain
the dignity of the aristocracy and the privileges of dukes, his
exclusion of the nobles from posts of importance, his over-fondness
for his bastards, his preference for the middle-classes ('le règne de
la robe pour tout'), his introduction into the army of a system of
promotion by seniority regardless of merit, his persecution of the
Jansenists and Huguenots, his military and diplomatic errors (e.g.
the recognition of the Prince of Wales as King of England in 1701).
Saint-Simon, in fact, felt so strongly about Louis XIV's misgovern-
ment that, in 1712, he wrote a long *Lettre anonyme au Roi*.
   It goes without saying that so vehement a critic could not be
completely impartial. 'Je ne me pique donc pas d'impartialité;
je le ferais vainement.' His *Mémoires*, considered as a historical
work, have other defects. They are more of a chronicle than a
history. He occasionally repeats himself. Moreover, he is interested
above all in military affairs, in details of court life and intrigues,
in the filling of *charges* – who is appointed lady-in-waiting to this
or that *princesse du sang*, against what rivals, and by what means.
Economic affairs and the French people outside the circle of the
court are neglected. An inordinate amount of space is devoted to
matters of little significance – thirty pages to the intrigues (in
which Saint-Simon played a considerable part) leading up to the
marriage of the daughter of the duc d'Orléans to the duc de Berry
in 1710. Questions of etiquette, disputes over the right of precedence and petty privileges (such as the right of having the word
'pour' in front of one's name on the door of the room allotted to
one when the court was travelling), and genealogical matters loom
large. Sixty pages are devoted to a dispute of Saint-Simon and
others with maréchal de Luxembourg over a question of precedence. There is a long disquisition of ninety pages on the Spanish
grandees.
   And yet some of Saint-Simon's apparent defects turn out to be
in fact strong points. The lack of proportion, the concentration on
the court and the army, correspond to the preoccupations of the
author and his contemporaries: this is history as they saw it. The
details of disputes over precedence and the like give us the flavour

of the period, as Saint-Simon was well aware. Apologizing, for example, for having devoted several pages to the *affaire de la quête* (a dispute concerning the ladies who were to collect for the poor in church on certain feast-days), he writes:

Je me suis peut-être trop étendu sur une affaire qui se pouvait beaucoup plus resserrer; mais, outre qu'elle est mienne, il me semble que c'est plus par des récits détaillés de ces choses de cour particulières qu'on la fait bien connaître...

He adds that the character of the King in particular can be much better portrayed by such means than in any other way —

... tout cela[1] se touche au doigt par les récits mieux que par toutes les autres paroles, et c'est ce qui se voit bien naturellement dans celui-ci, et dans ce que j'ai raconté en son temps de l'affaire de Mme de Saint-Simon et de Mme d'Armagnac, et de la princesse d'Harcourt avec la duchesse de Rohan.

To this justification, one may add that, precisely because Saint-Simon felt deeply about such matters, such accounts of trivial bickerings are amongst the most fascinating and illuminating parts of the work.

For, of course, Saint-Simon's lack of objectivity, if in one sense it is a defect, is what gives his book its peculiar quality, animating it, drawing the reader into it; 'La vérité', wrote Saint-Simon to Rancé about his book, 's'y rencontre tout entière et [ ... ] la passion n'a fait qu'animer le style [ ... ]' Whether or not the first part of the statement is true, there can be no doubt about the second. Saint-Simon, the son of an elderly father who belonged to the reign of Louis XIII rather than to that of Louis XIV, a passionate upholder of the rights and responsibilities of the nobles in a world which no longer shared his views, in which the nobility, deprived of power, was misallying itself, and upstart families were usurping privileges, uses his history as a means of expressing his dissatisfaction and taking his revenge on reality — 'songeant à satisfaire mes inclinations et passions en tout ce que la vérité m'a permis de dire', as he wrote to Rancé. Or, as he puts it more explicitly at the end of the *Mémoires*:

... comme, au temps où j'ai écrit, surtout vers la fin, tout tournait à la décadence, à la confusion, au chaos, qui depuis n'a fait que croître, et que ces *Mémoires* ne respirent qu'ordre, règle, vérité, principes certains, et montrant à découvert tout ce qui y est contraire, qui règne de plus en plus avec le plus ignorant, mais le plus entier empire, la convulsion doit donc être générale contre ce miroir de vérité.

[1] I.e. the peculiar characteristics of the King, with whom, in the course of the dispute, Saint-Simon, whose wife was involved, had had a long interview.

He was a man who felt deeply – he says himself at one point: 'Il n'en fallait pas tant pour exciter puissamment un homme fort sensible, et qui savait si bien aimer et haïr que je ne l'ai que trop su toute ma vie.'

The *Mémoires* of Saint-Simon, then, are a comprehensive and complex work, full of variety. Saint-Simon relates the events of the time – the intrigues at the court of Spain preceding the death of Charles II, the battles of Blenheim and Oudenarde and the campaigns of the duc d'Orléans, the dispute between Bossuet and Fénelon over quietism, the deaths of everyone connected with the court, and so forth –, but he does not neglect less important matters. He relates in detail all the intrigues of the court, and narrates such lesser matters as Mademoiselle's entrails exploding in their urn or the mysterious theft of the golden fringes from Versailles; he tells us of the daily routine of the court, and gives details of court ceremonies and entertainments; he includes significant anecdotes.

A vast number of characters appear in his book, and he tells us not only what they are like in character, but also what they looked like. Moreover, not only their moments of dignity, but also more unfavourable aspects of their character are shown. At the centre of the work, of course, is Louis XIV – majestic, but self-centred. We see him treating Mme de Maintenon with unbecoming deference and witness the stupefaction of an officer who saw Louis bending over her sedan chair at the manoeuvres of Compiègne: 'il demeura court à regarder, la bouche ouverte, les yeux fixes et un visage sur lequel le plus grand étonnement était peint'. We hear Louis's amazing outburst when the duchesse de Bourgogne had a miscarriage:

Dieu merci! elle est blessée, puisqu'elle avait à l'être, et je ne serai plus contrarié dans mes voyages et dans tout ce que j'ai envie de faire par les représentations des médecins et les raisonnements des matrones. J'irai et viendrai à ma fantaisie, et on me laissera en repos.

Around Louis are grouped literally hundreds of other characters – the members of the royal family, valets and secretaries, generals, courtiers of all degrees of importance, all vividly evoked: M. d'Harlay, a ladies' man despite his 'figure de squelette et de spectre'; Mme de Castries, 'un quart de femme, une espèce de biscuit manqué'; Pussort, 'un fagot d'épines'; le duc de Brissac, 'avec une figure de plat apothicaire, grosset, basset, et fort enluminé'; la duchesse de Chaulnes, 'un soldat aux gardes, et même un peu suisse, habillé en femme'; Mme de Luxembourg, who 'ressemblait d'air, de visage et de maintien à ces grosses vilaines harengères qui sont dans un tonneau avec leurs chaufferettes sous

elles'; the duc de la Feuillade, with a 'physionomie si spirituelle,
qu'elle réparait sa laideur et le jaune et les bourgeons dégoûtants
de son visage'; Bélébat, 'une manière d'éléphant pour la figure,
une espèce de bœuf pour l'esprit'; Brissac, a 'manière de sanglier';
the maréchale de Villeroy, with a face 'exactement comme un gros
perroquet'; Vendôme on his *chaise percée*, receiving his officers
and visitors. . . . Who else gives us details such as these? – and who
else could find such striking phrases to convey them? Saint-Simon
notes the gestures and attitudes of his characters. At the *Conseil
d'Etat* which preceded the *lit de justice* of 1718, for instance:

Je vis en M. le duc d'Orléans un air d'autorité et d'attention, qui me fut
si nouveau, que j'en demeurai frappé. Monsieur le Duc, gai et brillant,
paraissait ne douter de rien. Le prince de Conti, étonné, distrait, con-
centré, ne semblait rien voir ni prendre part à rien. Le Garde des sceaux,
grave et pensif, paraissait avoir trop de choses dans la tête; aussi en
avait-il beaucoup à faire et pour un coup d'essai. Néanmoins, il se dé-
ploya avec son sac en homme bien net, bien décidé, bien ferme. Le duc de
La Force, les yeux en dessous, examinait les visages . . .

He disentangles the different emotions or motives of those he is
observing – on the death of the King's brother, Monsieur, for
example:

Monseigneur [the dauphin] semblait aimer Monsieur, qui lui donnait des
bals et des amusements avec toute sorte d'attention et de complaisance:
dès le lendemain de sa mort il alla courre le loup, et, au retour, trouva le
salon plein de joueurs, tellement qu'il ne se contraignit pas plus que les
autres. Mgr le duc de Bourgogne et M. le duc de Berry ne voyaient Monsieur qu'en représentation, et ne pouvaient être fort sensibles à sa perte.
Mme la duchesse de Bourgogne le fut extrêmement: c'était son grand-
père, elle aimait tendrement Madame sa mère, qui aimait fort Monsieur,
et Monsieur marquait toutes sortes de soins, d'amitié et d'attentions
à Mme la duchesse de Bourgogne, et l'amusait de toutes sortes de divertissements. Quoiqu'elle n'aimât pas grand chose, elle aimait Monsieur,
et elle souffrit fort de contraindre sa douleur, qui dura assez longtemps
dans son particulier.

Saint-Simon is himself a character in his book – these are, after
all, his *Mémoires*. He was not a disinterested observer, but one
whose emotions were constantly stirred by the people he watched
or the events he witnessed; and he was also a participant. He tells
us of his marriage, how he abandoned his military career, and how
he nearly withdrew from court life. He relates the intrigues in
which he took part, his interviews with the King, his conversations
with the duc d'Orléans and others, his journey to Spain, and his
final withdrawal from the court in 1723. He does not conceal his
emotions, and we see him jubilant when he has won a victory –
when the duc d'Orléans's daughter married the duc de Berry, for
instance. At the *Conseil d'Etat* which preceded the *lit de justice*

of 1718, we see him watching, looking away, composing his face, exulting:

Contenu de la sorte, attentif à dévorer l'air de tous, présent à tout et à moi-même, immobile, collé sur mon siège, compassé de tout mon corps, pénétré de tout ce que la joie peut imprimer de plus sensible et de plus vif, du trouble le plus charmant, d'une jouissance la plus démesurément et la plus persévéramment souhaitée, je suais d'angoisse de la captivité de mon transport, et cette angoisse même était d'une volupté que je n'ai jamais ressentie ni devant ni depuis ce beau jour.

Bouhours's remark that style should be like clear water is inapplicable to Saint-Simon, whose style is highly individual. He is in no sense a correct writer, but a vigorous, vehement, violent one, carried along by his emotions: in his style – as in his complex world – he anticipates Balzac and Proust. His long sentences are sometimes difficult to disentangle, sometimes downright obscure. His agreements are sometimes faulty:

Sa conduite impérieuse, le peu d'accès qu'il donnait auprès de lui, sa hauteur avec les officiers, même généraux, et ses propos durs, avec l'audace d'un étourdi qui compte éblouir par sa valeur, et tout permis au gendre du tout-puissant ministre, le *firent* détester de toute son armée, et *mit* les officiers généraux et particuliers en humeur et en usage de s'en tenir exactement et avec précision à leur fait et à leur devoir, sans se soucier de la besogne, ni daigner remédier ni rien faire, sur quoi que ce fût, à rien, quelque nécessité qu'ils y vissent, par pique, par dégoût, et par la crainte aussi qu'on leur demandât de quoi ils se mêlaient.

In his desire to explain, the phrases come tumbling forth, and in his haste he forgets that the plural subject requires a plural verb. His syntax is often unusual – 'raisonner si librement sur parler à Mme de Maintenon'; 'M. de Richelieu, très vivement offensé, fit sur-le-champ une réponse, et tout de suite imprimer et distribuer, par laquelle'...; 'elle passe pour très riche, mais aussi pour ne pas retenir ses vents, dont on fit force plaisanteries.' He is fond of ellipsis and loose grammatical relationships – to the *tout permis au gendre du tout-puissant ministre* in the sentence just quoted about La Feuillade, one or two other examples may be added:

Mme du Maine venait de faire l'étrange mariage d'une créature de rien, qui s'était fourrée à Sceaux je ne sais par où, qui était assez jolie, mais de l'esprit, de la flatterie et de l'intrigue au dernier point.

On verra dans les pièces, et dans les suites, que cette délicatesse ne fut que pour Monseigneur, et pour tâcher de se faire valoir: le Renard des mûres si on ne songeait point à lui, se faire prier si on y pensait.

He also sometimes coins words – often in the manner of the burlesque writers – *seigneurifié, se comtifia, une égueulée, se partalisèrent.*

The result of these features is a vigorous, bold, impressionistic style, full of striking phrases which might not have satisfied Boileau — 'Monseigneur, tout noyé [ . . . ] dans la graisse et dans l'apathie', 'après avoir rougi de la sorte' (i.e. become a Cardinal), 'l'odeur de la Ligue leur sortait par les pores'. He is excellent at conveying impressions, particularly impressions of sights and movements. Charost is overcome by a retort of Saint-Simon:

A ce mot, voilà Charost qui chancelle (nous étions debout), qui veut répondre, et qui balbutie: la gorge s'enfle, les yeux lui sortent de la tête, et la langue de la bouche; Mme de Nogaret s'écrie; Mme du Châtelet saute à sa cravate qu'elle lui défait, et le col de sa chemise; Mme de Saint-Simon court à un pot d'eau, lui en jette, et tâche de l'asseoir et de lui en faire avaler.

Saint-Simon visits the house of Chamillart after his dismissal:

Quel spectacle! une foule de gens oisifs et curieux, et prompts aux compliments, un domestique éperdu, une famille désolée, des femmes en pleurs, dont les sanglots étaient les paroles; nulle contrainte en une si amère douleur. A cet aspect, qui n'eût cherché la chambre de parade et le goupillon pour rendre ce devoir au mort? On avait besoin d'effort pour se souvenir qu'il n'y en avait point, et pour ne trouver pas à redire qu'il n'y eût point de tenture et d'appareil funèbre, et on était effrayé de voir ce mort,[2] sur qui on venait pleurer, marcher et parler d'un air doux, tranquille, le front serein, sans rien de contraint ni d'affecté, attentif à chacun, point ou très peu différent de ce qu'il avait coutume d'être.

Saint-Simon's *portraits* — abundant in number and in length — always give a graphic description of the appearance of the person, as well as an analysis of his character; the following description of M. de Chaulnes, although uncharacteristic in its brevity, is not a bad example:

C'était, sous la corpulence, l'épaisseur, la pesanteur, la physionomie d'un bœuf, l'esprit le plus délié, le plus délicat, le plus souple, le plus adroit à prendre et à pousser ses avantages, avec tout l'agrément et la finesse possible, jointe à une grande capacité et à une continuelle expérience de toutes sortes d'affaires, et la réputation de la plus exacte probité, décorée à l'extérieur d'une libéralité et d'une magnificence également splendide, placée et bien entendue, et de beaucoup de dignité avec beaucoup de politesse.

The style of Pascal and that of Saint-Simon are very different. Pascal had thought about style, and might serve as a model; Saint-Simon ends his *Mémoires* with an apology for his, and an admission that he does not know what good style is: 'Pour bien corriger ce qu'on a écrit, il faut savoir bien écrire; on verra aisément ici que je n'ai pas dû m'en piquer. Je n'ai songé qu'à l'exactitude et à la vérité.' Nevertheless, they have one quality in common — intensity. Both wrote because their feelings were

[2] Chamillart.

stirred; like Pascal, Saint-Simon grips the reader and makes him
see with his vision. As Chateaubriand admirably expressed it,
Saint-Simon 'a écrit à la diable pour l'immortalité'. Because of
this, because of the intensity of his vision and of his emotions,
Saint-Simon's world lives on in his book. Louis XIV and his courtiers move in his pages and disappear one by one from the scene. We
share Saint-Simon's aims and his ambitions; we are filled with the
same indignation, admire the virtue of one and loathe the turpi-
tude of another, feel that it is of the utmost importance who takes
precedence or sits on a *tabouret*, view with dismay the declining
greatness of France, and read with a pang the sentence which
brings to a close his account of the year 1701: 'Ainsi finit cette
année, et tout le bonheur du Roi avec elle.'

# Bibliography

# BIBLIOGRAPHY

Full bibliographies are contained in:

Cioranescu, A., *Bibliographie de la littérature française du dix-septième siècle*, vol. I, 1965.

Edelman, N. (ed.), *A Critical Bibliography of French Literature*. Vol. III, *The Seventeenth Century*, 1961.

Klapp, O., *Bibliographie der französischen Literaturwissenschaft*, vols. I–IV, 1960–5.

Rancœur, R., *Bibliographie de la littérature française moderne* (*XVI<sup>e</sup>–XX<sup>e</sup> siècles*). Published annually since 1963.

## PART I. GENERAL

### 1. *Political and Social History*

Ashton, H., *A Preface to Molière*, 1927.

Boulenger, J., *Le Grand Siècle*, revised edition, 1924.

Bray, R., *La Préciosité et les précieux de Thibaut de Champagne à Jean Giraudoux*, 1948.

Feillet, A., *La Misère au temps de la Fronde et Saint Vincent de Paul*, 1886.

Fidao-Justiniani, J.-E., *Qu'est-ce qu'un classique? Essai d'histoire et de critique positive. Le Héros ou du Génie*, 1930.
*Discours sur la raison classique*, 1937.

Gaiffe, F., *L'Envers du grand siècle* [1924].

Gaxotte, P., *La France de Louis XIV*, 1946.

Green, F. C., *The Ancien Régime. French Institutions and Social Classes*, 1958.

Lewis, W. H., *The Splendid Century*, 1953.

Lough, J., *An Introduction to Seventeenth-Century France*, 1954.

Magendie, M., *La Politesse mondaine et les théories de l'honnê-teté en France au XVII<sup>e</sup> siècle, de 1600 à 1660*, 1925.

Magne, E., *La Vie quotidienne au temps de Louis XIII*, 1942.

Mongrédien, G., *La Vie littéraire au XVII<sup>e</sup> siècle*, 1947.

*La Vie quotidienne sous Louis XIV*, 1948.

*La Vie de société aux XVII^e et XVIII^e siècles*, 1950.

Pagès, G., *La Monarchie d'ancien régime en France*, 1928.

Pure, abbé Michel de, *La Prétieuse ou le mystère des ruelles*, ed. E. Magne, 2 vols., 1938.

Somaize, *Le Dictionnaire des Précieuses*, ed. C.-L. Livet, 2 vols., 1856.

Tallemant des Réaux, G., *Historiettes*, ed. G. Mongrédien, 8 vols., 1932–4.

Tapié, V.-L., *La France de Louis XIII et de Richelieu*, 1952.

Voltaire, *Le Siècle de Louis XIV*, 1756.


2. *Religion and the Church*

Allier, R., *La Cabale des Dévots, 1627–1666*, 1902.

Argenson, comte René de Voyer d', *Annales de la Compagnie du Saint Sacrement*, ed. H. Beauchet-Filleau, 1900.

Bessières, A., *Deux grands méconnus précurseurs de l'action catholique et sociale, Gaston de Renty et Henry Buch*, 1931.

Bremond, H., *Histoire littéraire du sentiment religieux en France*, 11 vols., 1924–33.

Poinsenet, M. D., *France religieuse du XVII^e siècle*, n.d.

Prunel, L., *La Renaissance catholique en France au XVII^e siècle*, 1921.

Sainte-Beuve, *Port-Royal*, 1840–59.

Souriau, M., *Le Mysticisme en Normandie au XVII^e siècle*, 1923.


3. *Intellectual Movements*

*Philosophy and Free-Thought*

Adam, A., *Les Libertins au XVII^e siècle. Textes choisis*, 1964.

Atkinson, G., *The Extraordinary Voyage in French Literature before 1700*, 1920.

*The Extraordinary Voyage in French Literature from 1700 to 1720*, 1922.

Busson, H., *La Pensée religieuse française de Charron à Pascal*, 1933.

*La Religion des classiques (1660–1685)*, 1948.

Charron, D. J., *The 'Wisdom' of Pierre Charron*, 1961.

Copleston, F., *A History of Philosophy*. Vol IV, *Descartes to Leibniz*, 1958.

Hazard, P., *La Crise de la conscience européenne, 1680–1715*, 1935.

Lahontan, baron de, *Dialogues curieux entre l'auteur et un sauvage de bon sens qui a voyagé et Mémoires de l'Amérique septentrionale*, ed. G. Chinard, 1931.

Perrens, F.-T., *Les Libertins en France au XVII^e siècle*, 1899.

Pintard, R., *Le Libertinage érudit dans la première moitié du XVII^e siècle*, 1943.

Popkin, R. H., *The History of Scepticism from Erasmus to Descartes*, 1960.

Spink, J. S., *French Free-Thought from Gassendi to Voltaire*, 1960.

*Science*

Bell, A. E., *Christian Huygens and the Development of Science in the Seventeenth Century*, 1947.

Boas, M., *The Scientific Renaissance, 1450–1630*, 1962.

Butterfield, H., *The Origins of Modern Science 1300–1800*, 1949.

Hall, A. Rupert, *From Galileo to Newton, 1630–1720*, 1963.

*4. Literary trends*

*Baroque*

Buffum, I., *Studies in the Baroque from Montaigne to Rotrou*, 1957.

Mourgues, O. de, *Metaphysical, Baroque and Précieux Poetry*, 1953.

Raymond, M., *Baroque et renaissance poétique*, 1955.

Reynold, G. de, *Synthèse du XVII^e siècle*, 1962.

Rousset, J., *La Littérature de l'âge baroque en France. Circé et le paon*, 1953.

Tapié, V.-L., *Baroque et classicisme* [1957].

*Classicism*

Bénac, H., *Le Classicisme. La Doctrine par les textes*, 1949.

Bray, R., *La Formation de la doctrine classique en France*, 1927.

Chapelain, J., *Opuscules critiques*, ed. A. C. Hunter, 1936.

Peyre, H., *Le Classicisme français*, 1942.

Van Tieghem, Ph., *Petite histoire des grandes doctrines littéraires*, 1946.

Vial, F. and Denise, L., *Idées et doctrines littéraires du XVII^e siècle*, 1925.

*Querelle des Anciens et des Modernes*

Gillot, H., *La Querelle des Anciens et des Modernes en France*, 1914.

Rigault, H., *Histoire de la querelle des Anciens et des Modernes*, 1856.

## 5. Literary History

### General Works

Adam A., *Histoire de la littérature française au XVII<sup>e</sup> siècle*, 5 vols., 1948–56.

Bénichou, P., *Morales du grand siècle*, 1948.

Borgerhoff, E. B., *The Freedom of French Classicism*, 1950.

Calvet, J., *La Littérature religieuse de François de Sales à Fénelon*, 1956.

Faguet, E., *Dix-Septième Siècle. Etudes littéraires*, 1890.

Gaillard de Champris, H., *Les Ecrivains classiques*, 1960.

Grente, Cardinal G. (ed.), *Dictionnaire des lettres françaises. Le Dix-Septième Siècle*, 1954.

Howarth, W. D., *Life and Letters in France in the Seventeenth Century*, 1965.

Krailsheimer, A. J., *Studies in Self-Interest from Descartes to La Bruyère*, 1962.

Moore, W. G., *French Classical Literature. An Essay*, 1961.

Mornet, D., *Histoire de la clarté française*, 1929.

*Histoire de la litterature française classique, 1660–1700*, 1947.

Tortel, J., *Le Préclassicisme français*, 1952.

Vier, J., *Histoire de la littérature française*, vols 1 and 2, 1959–65.

### The Theatre

Attinger, G., *L'Esprit de la commedia dell'arte dans le théâtre français*, 1950

Aubignac, abbé d', *La Pratique du Théâtre*, ed. P. Martino, 1927.

Auerbach, E., *Das französische Publikum des 17. Jahrhunderts*, 1933.

Chappuzeau, S., *Le Théâtre françois*, ed. G. Monval, 1876.

Corneille, P., *Writings on the Theatre*, ed. H. T. Barnwell, 1965.

Deierkauf-Holsboer, S. W., *Le Théâtre du Marais*, 2 vols., 1954–8.

*L'Histoire de la mise en scène dans le théâtre français de 1600 à 1673*, 1960.

Dabney, L. E., *French Dramatic Literature in the Reign of Henri IV*, 1952.

Descotes, M., *Le Public de théâtre et son histoire*, 1964.

Despois, E., *Le Théâtre français sous Louis XIV*, 1874.

Fournel, V., *Le Théâtre au XVII<sup>e</sup> siècle. La Comédie*, 1892.

Gaiffe, F., *Le Rire et la scène française*, 1931.

Garapon, R., *La Fantaisie verbale et le comique dans le théâtre français du moyen âge à la fin du XVII<sup>e</sup> siècle*, 1957.

Gasté, A., *La Querelle du Cid. Pièces et Pamphlets*, 1898.

Granet, F., *Recueil de dissertations sur plusieurs tragédies de Corneille et de Racine*, 2 vols., 1739.

Lancaster, H. Carrington, *A History of French Dramatic Literature in the Seventeenth Century*, 9 vols., 1929–42.

Lanson, G., *Esquisse d'une histoire de la tragédie française*, 1920.

Lawrenson, T. E., *The French Stage in the XVII*$^{th}$ *century*, 1957.

Lintilhac, E., *Histoire générale du théâtre en France*. T. III. *La Comédie. Dix-septième siècle*, 1908.

Lough, J., *Paris Theatre Audiences in the Seventeenth and Eighteenth Centuries*, 1957.

Mélèse, P., *Le Théâtre et le public à Paris sous Louis XIV, 1659–1715*, 1934.
*Répertoire analytique des documents contemporains d'information et de critique concernant le théâtre à Paris sous Louis XIV, 1659–1715*, 1934.

Rigal, E., *Le Théâtre français avant la période classique*, 1901.

Perman, R. C. D., 'The Influence of the Commedia dell'Arte on the French Theatre before 1640', *French Studies*, 1955, vol. IX, pp. 293–303.

Scherer, J., *La Dramaturgie classique en France* [1950].

Schwartz, I. A., *The Commedia dell'arte and its influence on French comedy in the seventeenth century*, 1933.

Védier, G., *Origine et évolution de la dramaturgie néo-classique*, 1955.

Wiley, W. L., *The Early Public Theatre in France*, 1960.

*Poetry*

The poets discussed in the text are but a few of those who wrote in the seventeenth century. An impression of the richness of the period may be obtained from the following recently-published anthologies:

Allem, M., *Anthologie poétique française. XVII*$^e$ *siècle*, 2 vols., 1966.

Mourgues, O. de, *French Seventeenth-Century Lyric Poetry*, 1966.

Picard, R., *La Poésie française de 1640 à 1680*, 1964.

Rousset, J., *Anthologie de la poésie baroque française*, 2 vols., 1961.

Steele, A. J., *Three Centuries of French Verse, 1511–1819*, 1956.

*The Novel*

Dallas, D. F., *Le Roman français de 1660 à 1680*, 1932.

Green, F. C., *French Novelists, Manners and Ideas from the Renaissance to the Revolution*, 1928.

Le Breton, A., *Le Roman au XVII^e siècle*, 3rd edition, 1924.

Magendie, M., *Le Roman français au XVII^e siècle de l'*Astrée *au Grand Cyrus*, 1932.

Morillot, P., *Le Roman en France depuis 1610 à nos jours. Lectures et esquisses*, 1892.

Reynier, G., *Le Roman réaliste au XVII^e siècle*, 1914.
*Le Roman sentimental avant l'Astrée*, 1908.

## PART II. BIBLIOGRAPHIES TO PARTICULAR CHAPTERS

*Chapters 2–3*

*Malherbe*

Brunot, F., *La Doctrine de Malherbe d'après son commentaire sur Desportes*, 1891.

Lebègue, R., *La Poésie française de 1560 à 1620*, 2 vols., 1951.

Fromilhague, R., *La Vie de Malherbe. Apprentissages et luttes (1555–1610)*, 1954.
*Malherbe. Technique et création poétique*, 1954.

Winegarten, R., *French Lyric Poetry in the Age of Malherbe*, 1954.

*Régnier*

Vianey, J., *Mathurin Régnier*, 1896.

*Théophile*

Adam, A., *Théophile de Viau et la libre pensée française en 1620*, 1935.

*La Ceppède*

Ruchon, F., *Essai sur la vie et l'œuvre de Jean de la Ceppède*, 1953.

*Chapter 4*

*D'Urfé*

Magendie, M., *Du Nouveau sur l'Astrée*, 1927.
*L'Astrée. Analyse et extraits*, 1928.

*Sorel*

Sutcliffe, F. E., *Le Réalisme de Charles Sorel*, 1965.

*Saint François de Sales*

Lajeunie, E.-M., *Saint François de Sales et l'esprit salésien*, 1962.

Mor, A., *San Francesco di Sales scrittore*, 1960.

*Balzac*

Guillaumie, G., *J. L. Guez de Balzac et la prose française*, 1927.

Sutcliffe, F. E., *Guez de Balzac et son temps. Littérature et politique*, 1959.


*Chapter 5*

Deierkauf-Holsboer, S. W., 'Vie d'Alexandre Hardy, Poète du Roi', *Proceedings of the American Philosophical Society*, vol. 91, No. 4, 1947, pp. 328–401.

Faguet, E., *La Tragédie française au XVI<sup>e</sup> siècle*, 1912, (includes a chapter on Montchrestien).

Marsan, J., *La Pastorale dramatique en France à la fin du XVI<sup>e</sup> et au commencement du XVII<sup>e</sup> siècle*, 1905.

Rigal, E., *Alexandre Hardy et le théâtre français à la fin du XVI<sup>e</sup> et au commencement du XVII<sup>e</sup> siècle*, 1889.


*Chapter 7*

Alquié, F., *Descartes l'homme et l'œuvre*, 1956.

Kemp Smith, N., *New Studies in the Philosophy of Descartes*, 1952.


*Chapter 9*

*Corneille*

Couton, G., *Corneille*, 1958.
  *La Vieillesse de Corneille*, 1949.

Nelson, R. J., *Corneille. His Heroes and their Worlds*, 1963.

Vedel, V., *Deux Classiques français vus par un critique étranger*, 1935.

Yarrow, P. J., *Corneille*, 1963.

*Du Ryer*

Lancaster, H. C., *Pierre du Ryer dramatist*, 1912.

*Rotrou*

Orlando, F., *Rotrou. Dalla tragicommedia alla tragedia*, 1963.

*Tristan*

Valle, D. dalla, *Il Teatro di Tristan l'Hermite*, 1964.

*Thomas Corneille*

Reynier, G., *Thomas Corneille. Sa vie et son théâtre*, 1892.


*Chapter 10*

*Tristan*

Bernardin, N.-M., *Un Précurseur de Racine. Tristan l'Hermite*, 1895.

*Saint-Amant*

Gourier, F., *Etude sur les Œuvres poétiques de Saint-Amant*, 1961.
Lagny, J., *Le Poète Saint-Amant (1594–1661). Essai sur sa Vie et ses Œuvres*, 1964.

*Voiture*

Magne, E., *Voiture et l'Hôtel de Rambouillet*, 2 vols., 1911–12.

*Scarron*

Alméras, H. d', *Le Roman comique de Scarron*, 1931.

*Cyrano de Bergerac*

Mongrédien, G., *Cyrano de Bergerac*, 1964.


*Chapter 11*

Béguin, A., *Pascal par lui-même*, 1957.
Broome, J. H., *Pascal*, 1965.
Goldmann, L., *Le Dieu caché. Etude sur la vision tragique dans les Pensées de Pascal et dans le Théâtre de Racine*, 1955.
Mesnard, J., *Pascal l'homme et l'œuvre*, 1951.
Mortimer, E., *Blaise Pascal. The Life and Work of a Realist*, 1959.
Strowski, F., *Pascal et son temps*, 3 vols., 1907.


*Chapter 13*

Bergson, H., *Le Rire*, 1900.
Bray, R., *Molière homme de théâtre*, 1954.
Grimarest, *La Vie de M. Molière*, ed. G. Mongrédien, 1955.
Mongrédien, G., *La Vie privée de Molière*, 1950.

Moore, W. G., *Molière. A new criticism,* 1949.
Mornet, D., *Molière,* 1943.
Romano, D., *Essai sur le comique de Molière,* 1950.
Simon, A., *Molière par lui-même,* 1957.
Vedel, V., *Deux Classiques français vus par un critique étranger,* 1935.


Chapter *14*

France, P., *Racine's Rhetoric,* 1965.
Knight, R. C., *Racine et la Grèce,* 1950.
Lapp, J. C., *Aspects of Racinian tragedy,* 1956.
Lemaitre, J., *Jean Racine,* 1908.
Moreau, P., *Racine l'homme et l'œuvre,* 1943.
Picard, R., *La Carrière de Jean Racine,* 1956.
Pommier, J., *Aspects de Racine,* 1954.
Vinaver, E., *Racine et la poésie tragique,* 1951.


Chapter *15*

Adam, A., *Les Premières Satires de Boileau. Edition critique et commentaire,* 1949.
Bonfantini, M., *L' 'Art poétique' di Boileau e i suoi problemi,* 1957.
Bray, R., *Boileau l'homme et l'œuvre,* 1942.
Brody, J., *Boileau and Longinus,* 1958.
Fidao-Justiniani, J.-E., *Qu'est-ce qu'un classique? Essai d'Histoire et de critique positive. Le Héros ou du Génie,* 1930.
Mornet, D., *Nicolas Boileau,* 1941.


Chapter *16*

Bray, R., *Les Fables de la Fontaine,* 1929.
Clarac, P., *La Fontaine l'homme et l'œuvre,* 2nd edition, 1959.
*La Fontaine par lui-même,* 1961.
Couton, G., *La Poétique de La Fontaine,* 1957.
*La Politique de La Fontaine,* 1959.
Gohin, F., *L'Art de La Fontaine dans ses Fables,* 1929.
Guitton, M., *La Fontaine Poet and Counterpoet,* 1961.
Mourgues, O. de, *La Fontaine: Fables,* 1960.
*O Muse, fuyante proie ... Essai sur la poésie de La Fontaine,* 1962.
Taine, H., *La Fontaine et ses fables,* 1860.
Wadsworth, P. A., *Young La Fontaine,* 1962.

*Chapter 17*

Bourdeau, J., *La Rochefoucauld*, 1895.

Grandsaignes d'Hauterive, R., *Le Pessimisme de La Rochefoucauld*, 1914.

Grubbs, H. A., 'La Genèse des "Maximes" de La Rochefoucauld', *Revue d'Histoire littéraire*, vol. 39, 1932, pp. 481–99.

'The Originality of La Rochefoucauld's Maxims', *Revue d'Histoire littéraire*, vol. 36, 1929, pp. 18–59.

Kruse, M., *Die Maxime in der französischen Literatur. Studien zum Werk La Rochefoucaulds und seiner Nachfolger*, 1960.

Moore, W. G., 'La Rochefoucauld: une nouvelle anthropologie', *Revue des Sciences Humaines*, 1953, pp. 299–310.

'Le Premier Etat des Maximes', *Revue d'Histoire littéraire*, vol. 52, 1952, pp. 417–24.

'The World of La Rochefoucauld's *Maximes*', *French Studies*, vol. VII, 1953, pp. 335–45.

Zeller, Sister M. F., *New Aspects of Style in the Maxims of La Rochefoucauld*, 1954.


*Chapter 18*

*Mme de Lafayette*

Ashton, H., *Madame de La Fayette, sa vie et ses œuvres*, 1922.

Dédéyan, C., *Madame de Lafayette*, 1955.

DeJongh, W. F. J., 'La Rochefoucauld and *La Princesse de Clèves*', *Symposium*, vol. XIII, No. 2, Fall, 1959.

Durry, M.-J., *Madame de La Fayette*, 1962.

Pingaud, B., *Madame de La Fayette par elle-même*, 1959.

Scott, J. W., 'The "Digressions" of the *Princesse de Clèves*', *French Studies*, vol. XI, 1957, pp. 315–21.

*Guilleragues*

Guilleragues, *Lettres portugaises, Valentins et autres œuvres*. Introduction, notes, glossaire et tables d'après de nouveaux documents par F. Deloffre et J. Rougeot, 1962.


*Chapter 19*

Allentuch, H. R., *Madame de Sévigné: a portrait in letters*, 1963.

Kaufmann, L., *Die Briefe der Madame de Sévigné*, 1954.

Tilley, A. A., *Madame de Sévigné. Some Aspects of her Life and Character*, 1936.

*Chapter 21*

*Bossuet*

Calvet, J., *Bossuet l'homme et l'œuvre*, 1941.
Goyet, T., *L'Humanisme de Bossuet*, 2 vols., 1965.

*Malebranche*

Rodis-Lewis, G., *Nicolas Malebranche*, 1963.

*Saint-Evremond*

Barnwell, H. T., *Les Idées morales et critiques de Saint-Evremond* 1957.
Hope, Q. M., *Saint-Evremond. The* Honnête Homme *as critic*, 1962.

*Chapter 22*

*Bayle*

Beller, E. A. and Lee, M. du P., Jr, *Selections from Bayle's Dictionary*, 1952.
Labrousse, E., *Pierre Bayle*, 2 vols., 1963–4.
*Pierre Bayle et l'Instrument critique. Présentation, choix de textes, bibliographie*, 1965.
Mason, H. T., 'Pierre Bayle's Religious Views', *French Studies*, vol. XVII, 1963, pp. 205–17.
Raymond, M., *Pierre Bayle. Choix de Textes et Introduction*, 1948.
Robinson, H., *Bayle the Sceptic*, 1931.

*Fontenelle*

Carré, J.-R., *La Philosophie de Fontenelle ou le sourire de la raison*, 1932.
Bouchard, M., *L'Histoire des Oracles de Fontenelle*, 1947.
Fayol, A., *Fontenelle*, 1961.

*Chapter 23*

Lange, M., *La Bruyère critique des conditions et des institutions sociales*, 1909.
Michaut, G., *La Bruyère*, 1936.
Richard, P., *La Bruyère et ses 'Caractères'*, 1946.

*Chapter* 24

*Regnard*

Calame, A., *Regnard, sa vie et son œuvre*, 1961.

*Dancourt*

Lemaitre, J., *La Comédie après Molière et le théâtre de Dancourt*, 1882.

*Robert Chasles*

Deloffre, F., 'Un Mode préstendhalien de la sensibilité à la fin du XVIIᵉ siècle', *Cahiers de l'Association Internationale des Etudes françaises*, No. 11, mai 1959, pp. 9–32.
Chasles, R., *Les Illustres Françoises*, ed. F. Deloffre, 2 vols., 1959.

*Fénelon*

Goré, L.-D., *L'Itinéraire de Fénelon: Humanisme et spiritualité*, 1957.


*Chapter* 25

Astier d', E., *Sur Saint-Simon*, 1962.
Bastide, F.-R., *Saint-Simon par lui-même*, 1953.
La Varende, J. de, *M. le duc de Saint-Simon et sa comédie humaine*, 1955.

# *Index*

# INDEX

419

Printed in Great Britain by Western Printing Services Ltd, Bristol